STORIES OF THE GREAT HYMNS OF THE CHURCH

Stories of the Great Hymns of the Church

BY

SILAS H. PAINE

Introduction by

LUTHER D. WISHARD

FLEXO PRINTING COMPANY
461 Eighth Avenue, New York, N. Y.

Printed in the United States of America

Dedicated to

MARY S. PAINE

Whose constant collaboration with her husband made this book possible

Stanza of a

Favorite Hymn of

Lincoln

"If you are too weak to journey
Up the mountain steep and high,
You can stand within the valley,
As the multitude goes by;
You can chant in happy measure,
As they slowly pass along;
Tho' they may forget the singer,
They will not forget the song."

INTRODUCTION

By Luther D. Wishard

This monumental research in hymnology is not the author's only memorial. Neither is it his chief service. His varied activities are deserving of much fuller treatment than this brief foreword. Such treatment will be given them in the near future in a fitting biographical monograph. His aptitude for research led him into a number of other fields, covering the fauna and flora, the revolutionary and aboriginal history of the Lake George region and the pictorial teachings of the Bible. Such work was done after office hours throughout his working year and during his periodic vacations.

Hymnology was one of his chief diversions. A busy official of a corporation of world-wide note, he took time throughout a period of forty years to assemble a large and rare collection of hymn books and also to compile a mass of incidents concerning hymns, their authorship, the causes which gave them birth, and their influence upon lives. These incidents have now been published under the title "Stories of the Great Hymns of the Church." The most widely known man in the industrial world, his daily business associate for many years, was wont to say, "If Silas H. Paine says 'it is true,' it is." The accuracy of this rare work on hymnology can have no higher endorsement. I believe it can justly be said of Mr. Paine, as one of our former statesmen said of himself, "I would rather be right than be President." Mr. Paine had no patience with the legendary and apocryphal. "The truth, the whole truth, and nothing but the truth," was his motto in research. He once remarked to the writer, in questioning the authenticity of the birth story of a well known hymn, "I would rather not know so many things, than know so many things that are not so." In quoting our greatest American humorist he unconsciously let me into one of the great secrets of his successful life.

His interest in hymnology was undoubtedly awakened and deepened by reason of his many years' service as a Sunday School superintendent. This interest found first expression in the collection of five thousand hymn books without a duplicate, whose publication spanned eighteen centuries. Anyone passing through Hartford, with a few hours at his disposal, will be richly rewarded by visiting a library alcove of the Congregational Theological Seminary. He will there live over again his childhood as the writer did one winter day, by renewing his acquaintance with this collection of old time Church and Sunday School hymn books which he never expected to see again: "The Golden Chain," "Musical Leaves," "The Singing Pilgrim," "The Oriole," "Winnowed Hymns." How these familiar titles recall walks through clover fields to the village church in the good old summer time,—yes, and through snowdrifts in the good old winter time,—the ringing voices of singing children, the recital of Scripture verses, the wholesome admonitions of "our teachers dear," as they were characterized in song, the stroll through the village graveyard after Sunday School, as a reward for good behavior during the preceding week. As one recalls the words and melodies which come floating down the flood of years, is it because of the magic spell which time has woven around our memories that the old songs seem so superior to much of the semi-jazz jargon which marks the measure of too much of the juvenile singing of nowadays? If there be a larger, rarer collection of church hymnology on this continent or any continent we have yet to hear of it.

It was about 1883 when Mr. Paine first became so interested in hymnology. His interests were perennial. They ran on forever. When in 1900 I renewed with him my acquaintance first made in 1879, he was serving as host in his new hotel at Silver Bay. The event of the week was not the fishing excursion to Jabe's Pond, the ascent of Black Mountain, the steam yacht trip to Paradise Bay, the ride to Fort Ticonderoga, or even the Saturday night dance, as far removed from present day dancing as the span of a continent.

The chief event of the week during the early summers of our outings there was Mr. Paine's Sunday evening service of song in the auditorium. He furnished the prelude to every hymn with stories apt, fascinating, and inspiring, stories in quest of which he had ransacked libraries of music in America and Great Britain. Never until then had I heard an audience really "sing with the spirit and with the understanding also," and it was then that I first realized that one cannot sing with the spirit until he understands why, when, where, and by whom the hymn came into being, and what service the hymn has rendered in making and remolding men. I had joined in the singing of Reginald Heber's majestic missionary hymn in audiences which I had addressed almost all the way "From Greenland's Icy Mountains to India's Coral Strand," but never with the sensations with which I have heard the inspired and inspiring words sung after the thrilling account by Mr. Paine of the occasion of its composition. We have sung "I Love to Steal Awhile Away" since childhood without knowing that Phoebe Brown, who lived a century ago, "had so many children she didn't know what to do"; so, after putting them to bed (without spanking, I trow) she sought rest in prayer as she walked under the elms at "the hour of setting day," and wrote "I love to steal awhile away from little ones and care." What a hymn for tired mothers!

The time would fail me to thus allude to dozens, yes scores of hymns of whose birth and fruitful life I have heard Mr. Paine speak in the song service on the shore of Silver Bay at twilight, when his vibrant voice was accompanied by

> "Low stir of leaves and dip of oars,
> And lapsing waves on quiet shores."

It was then that I began urging him to give the entire church the inspiration of his many years of world-wide search for the ancestry of our greatest and most loved hymns. It is well that he did not then accede to my appeal, for his task of collection was far from completed. Now that it is finished, the churches need wait no longer for this rare ministry of song at the hands of one of its most loyal sons.

Even Silas Paine would have been unequal to this arduous labor of love had he toiled alone. His wife, Mary, collaborated with him in this, as in all of his varied researches, with unwearied devotion and fine discrimination. Her name deserves the place given it on the dedicatory page. It is owing to her loyalty and abounding generosity that this rare volume, a veritable De Luxe, containing eight hundred and five stories of hymns, is offered to the Christian world at a cost far below its commercial value.

The writer of the above is indeed honored in being accorded the opportunity to furnish this tribute to his old comrade-in-arms who, although "being dead, yet speaketh" through these glowing pages as with a tongue of fire. No—he is not dead, but alive forevermore.

"SINGING WITH THE SPIRIT AND WITH THE UNDERSTANDING ALSO."

A Lay Sermon by

SILAS H. PAINE.

A hymn book lies beside the Bible on every pulpit desk. One was given by inspiration of God. The other has been said to contain: "The holiest thoughts of holiest men in their holiest moments." One is "profitable for doctrine, for reproof, for correction, for instruction in righteousness," and the other is helpful in all departments of Christian work and worship. It has been quaintly said of hymns, that "they make Bible truths portable in men's memories"; and it is no disparagement of Scripture to assert that oftentimes a Bible truth, clothed in the language of a hymn, finds lodgment in the heart when in the plainer words of Scripture it had failed to do so.

One of the Secretaries of The American Board recently told me of an incident in his own career which illustrates the truth of this assertion. When, a young man, he was settled as colleague of a pastor, whose advancing years demanded help, one day his younger colleague was called to visit one of the aged members of the church, who was dying. He found her downcast and discouraged; and, in his effort to comfort and cheer her, he repeated all the Scripture verses he could think of that were adapted to that end, but entirely without success, and he left her discouraged over his failure. Going to the old pastor he told him of the case, and the latter at once responded: "Let us go back and see her again; I will go along." As they entered the room, where the dying woman lay, the old pastor gave her a cheerful greeting and then said: "I've just been thinking about the old hymn we've sung together so many times:

"How firm a foundation, ye saints of the Lord,
Is laid for your faith in His excellent word!
What more can he say than to you He hath said,—
To you, who for refuge to Jesus have fled?"

As if touched by magic fingers the clouds were dissipated, and now the same Scripture words, that had failed before, brought comfort and hope. This incident suggests the thought that a familiarity with hymns will be useful to you in your work as pastors.

A fire occurred over two hundred years ago in the rectory of a little church in Epworth, England. Two things escaped the flames: one was a bit of paper that was carried up into the air and fell singed and smoked upon the grass; the other was a puny child, who was with difficulty rescued from an upper window. Never fire yielded richer salvage, for the paper contained the words of a hymn just written by the rector, which has found a permanent place in Methodist hymnology:

"Behold the Saviour of Mankind
Nailed to the shameful tree!
How vast the love, that him inclined
To bleed and die for thee!"

The puny child became the leader of that mighty evangelical movement which swept over England in the eighteenth century, and which he developed and crystallized into that wonderful organization we know as the Methodist Church. The incident was prophetic, for John Wesley could never have succeeded in building that great organization had it not been for the hymns of his brother, Charles.

A singing church is almost sure to be a working and a spiritual church. If, when you become pastors, you find your churches cold and dead, get them to singing, and you will sing them into warmth and life and power.

The purpose of this lecture is to suggest some of the practical methods by which hymns can be made helpful in your work and worship.

The first method consists in giving information about the hymns themselves. Hymns have a history. Some of them were born out of rich and deep experience. The story of their birth has been told and is available. If you can tell these stories to your people, the hymns of which you tell them will always thereafter have greater value to them and will be more heartily sung. Take for example the familiar hymns:

"Rock of Ages."
"I Love to Steal Awhile Away."
"Abide with Me, Fast Falls the Eventide."
"Hear my Prayer, O Heavenly Father."
"Stand Up! Stand Up for Jesus!"
"Jesus, These Eyes Have Never Seen."
"Lead, Kindly Light! Amid the Encircling Gloom."
"Blest Be the Tie that Binds."
"My Days Are Gliding Swiftly By."
"My Country! 'Tis of Thee."

There, I have given you the titles of ten hymns, all of them familiar ones, and with them a very enjoyable evening, and one that will be profitable as well, can be arranged. A good name for such a song service would be, "HYMNS WITH A HISTORY."

But, information about the authors of hymns is of more value than the story of the hymns themselves. Among hymn writers are some of the choicest spirits that ever lived; and it is worth while to bring your people into touch with such characters as John Newton, Ann Steele, Ray Palmer, and Fanny Crosby. Such information has also the additional value that it gives to you in the preparation of services of song a far wider range; for example: if you can tell the story of Isaac Watts, you can in connection with the story use any one of his hymns. "AN HOUR WITH HYMN

Writers" is a good title to give to a song service of this sort.

Another class of facts about hymns partakes a little of the character of both classes already named, and yet is not just like either. I do not know that I can better define it than by giving you an example. Turn to:

"Art Thou Weary, Heavy Laden?"
"There's a Wideness in God's Mercy."
"Oh Sacred Head, Now Wounded."
"There Were Ninety and Nine."
"Shine, Mighty God!"

Next comes the story of what these hymns have done. In this connection the field is unlimited in scope, and full of rare adventure. Oh! how these old hymns have travelled through the whole earth in their mission of comfort and help! One sang its song of cheer to Livingstone in the heart of Africa; another uttered its cry of warning to a gambler in China; one soothed a maniac into calm in a New York asylum; another broke from the lips of a dying girl in a New York tenement house; one line, caught by an actress' ear as she walked the streets of London, changed her to a gospel singer; and another line, whispered by a lady over a suicide's shoulder, saved him from the fatal step.

These stories—simple little stories, most of them—are of value to you; for what these hymns have done they can do again; and it is possible for you to so use them that they shall become a veritable gospel and be endued with "The power of God unto salvation." Now come with me to the battlefield of Shiloh. All day the battle has raged, and night has drawn her curtain now, and the stars look down upon strange scenes. Here and there squads of soldiers are burying the dead, and surgeons and nurses are caring for the wounded, and chaplains are whispering to the dying. Stop here with me and listen where an agent of the Christian Commission kneels by the side of a dying boy. Already the chill of coming death is on his hands and brow, "Take off that ring from my finger, chaplain, and give it to my sister at home, and tell her to keep it to remember me by. Tell her that I spoke of her when I was dying and sent her my love. Reach into my pocket, chaplain, and get my wallet; there's a little money in it and a few keepsakes; give them to my mother, and tell her that I have lived in the army as I promised her I would, and that I did no dishonor to her or to my father's name on the battlefield. Say good-bye to them, chaplain, for me, and tell them that I died contented and happy. And now, chaplain, sing to me." And the chaplain began to sing:

"There is a fountain filled with blood,
Drawn from Immanuel's veins;
And sinners, plunged beneath that flood,
Lose all their guilty stains."

And the boy exclaimed: "Oh, yes, I know that hymn; I can sing that, too." And then as the chaplain sang the boy joined in, and every few words he broke into the song with some comment of his own.

"In that day there shall be a fountain opened in the house of David and to the inhabitants of Jerusalem for sin and for uncleanness."—Zech. 13: 1.

But tunes have stories to tell as well as hymns. I do not refer to the statelier music of the oratorio or that for the organ only, but the "Hymn-tunes," as we call them, such as are ordinarily used in the worship of the church. In the days of Watts and Wesley hymns were numbered by thousands, and tunes, suitable to sing them to, by dozens. It was Wesley's practice to seize upon any song of the theater or the street, the moment it became popular, and make it carry some newly written hymn into the homes of the people. The practice has outlived him, and many of the church tunes of the day began their career in secular connections. Greenville, which we use with the words: "Lord dismiss us with thy blessing," first appeared in a very short-lived opera in France, and later as a love song in England with the title, "Rosseau's Dream." Kirk White's hymn, "When Marshalled on the Nightly Plain," we sing to the tune of the Scotch song "Bonnie Doon." One of Fanny Crosby's sweetest hymns is sung to the love sick music of "Robin Adair." But there are others written for sacred use which also have their history; and interest in the singing of hymns will be greatly increased by "An Evening Among the Tunes."

Many of our hymns are paraphrases or imitations of the Psalms, and "An Evening with the Psalms" can be made instructive and profitable. I wish I were able to adequately describe the book from which such a service would be taken. It is the oldest hymn book in the world. Back of Wesley and Watts, back of Milton and Marot, back of the Bernards of Cluny and Clairvaux, back of St. Stephen of Mount Saba, and St. Clement of Alexandria, five hundred years before the time when Mary sang "Magnificat," its latest hymn was written. And a thousand years still farther back its earliest song was sung. What voices have sung these Psalms! David, the king, sang them to the music of his harp; Solomon, the wise, sang them; Nehemiah, the great prototype of our own Seth Low, in the mighty task of rebuilding a nearly ruined city—he sang these songs and a score of other old prophets and heroes whose names are writ large in Bible history, and the Master himself sang them as he met with his disciples in that upper chamber.

STORIES OF THE GREAT HYMNS OF THE CHURCH

No. 1.

"HOLY BIBLE—BOOK DIVINE!"—1805.

JOHN BURTON, 1773—1822.

When the Rev. Dr. Thomas Stockton, one of the celebrated preachers of the Protestant Methodist Church, was an old man, he visited Pittsburgh, Pennsylvania, and preached one Sunday morning in the pulpit of his friend and former colleague, Rev. Alexander Clark. The church was crowded to its utmost capacity. Dr. Stockton was so weak that a high arm chair was placed for him behind the pulpit, and he preached sitting. His subject was the value of the Bible to the world, and after some introductory remarks he asked Mr. Clark, who sat behind him, to remove the Bible from the desk, and then drew a vivid word picture of what the world would be were there no Bible in it. Then turning suddenly he exclaimed, "Brother Clark, give us back the Bible!" and as it was placed upon the pulpit desk, he grasped it in both hands, and sprang from his chair, and clasped it in his arms, and exclaimed:

"Holy Bible! Book Divine
Precious treasure, thou art mine!"

It was a dramatic act, and its effect upon the audience was thrilling. And then he closed with another picture, as vivid, but more beautiful than the first, of what the Bible has done for the world.

The author's son relates that his father taught this hymn to him before he was able to read.

No. 2.

"STAND UP, AND BLESS THE LORD"—1825.

JAMES MONTGOMERY, 1771—1854.

An old man lay seriously ill in England fifty years ago, and a friend often came in to talk and read to him. In earlier years this old man had written many a hymn, and one day he placed in the hands of his friend a manuscript copy of his hymns and asked to have him read from them. As he read, the poet became greatly affected, and the reader was about to stop, when he spoke up, "Read on, I am glad to hear you. The words recall the feelings which first suggested them. All my hymns embody some portion of the history of the joys or sorrows, the hopes and fears of this poor heart."

Here is one of the hymns which evidently was written in some time of joy.

No. 3.

"O FOR THE DEATH OF THOSE"—1804.

JAMES MONTGOMERY, 1771—1854.

It is not often the case that one is permitted to read his own obituaries, and to know what the world intends to say of him when he has left it. The author of this hymn was an exception, however, to this statement. By an error, the report of his death reached this country while he was yet living, and notices of his life and career were published in many of the religious papers. These papers crossed the Atlantic, and he had the privilege of reading them. His hymns, which nearly every hymnal in the country contained specimens of, had endeared him to the Christian people here, and the notices of his death brought tears to his eyes when he found what a place he held in the affection of the religious world. When his death took place, it was one of those translations of which it can be said, "He was not, for God took him," for he died in his sleep.

No. 4.

"WHEN JORDAN HUSHED HIS WATERS STILL"—1820.

THOMAS CAMPBELL, 1777—1844.

Lovers of American history and romance have probably all read "Gertrude of Wyoming, A Pennsylvania Tale," first published in 1809. Its author was Thomas Campbell, who won great distinction as a poet, but is only known in hymnology by this piece and one other, not often used, beginning "The rainbow shines! no fabling dreams."

No. 5.

"HAIL TO THE LORD'S ANOINTED"—1821.

JAMES MONTGOMERY, 1771—1854.

James Montgomery was greatly interested in the work of foreign missions and was in great demand as a speaker at the meetings of the missionary societies. At one such meeting held in the Wesleyan Chapel at Liverpool, April 14, 1822, he delivered an address, and closed it by repeating this hymn taken from a Christmas ode he had written the year before. It aroused the enthusiasm of the great audience to a very high pitch as we can easily imagine it would, coming fresh from the lips of its author. It is a rendering of the Seventy-second Psalm. Dr. Adam Clark was then writing his Commentary on the Bible, and he was presiding at this meeting. At its close he begged of Mr. Montgomery a copy of the hymn, and inserted it in his commentary on this Psalm.

No. 6.

"PRAYER IS THE SOUL'S SINCERE DESIRE"—1819.

James Montgomery, 1771—1854.

Rev. Edward Bickersteth had written a "Treatise on Prayer," and asked Mr. James Montgomery to write a hymn on the subject of prayer suitable for publication in this book. This hymn was written in accordance with that request.

The first five stanzas are simply a poetic definition of prayer, with no claim whatever to be called a hymn, and yet nearly every hymn book contains them and the piece is very popular.

No. 7.

"LORD OF HOSTS! TO THEE WE RAISE"—1821.

James Montgomery, 1771—1854.

On July 9, 1821, the cornerstone of a new Church to be called St. George's Church was laid at Sheffield, England. This was the home of James Montgomery, the poet, and he was asked to write a hymn to be sung at the ceremony. This is the hymn he wrote, and it was first sung then.

No. 8.

"HOW SWEET, HOW HEAVENLY IS THE SIGHT"—1792.

REV. JOSEPH SWAIN, 1761—1796.

Did you ever hear a workman singing at his work and did you ever listen to hear what kind of a song he was singing? An orphan boy in Birmingham, England, was apprenticed to a London engraver, and there he was exposed to all the moral dangers that surround the young when they are strangers in a great city. But he became a Christian soon, and then to give utterance to his happiness he began to write hymns, and to comfort himself by singing them. An acquaintance overheard the singing, and took the boy to Church, something he had not known anything about till then. He became a Baptist, and soon began to preach himself, and then became the pastor of a little church. He had great success, so that the little building had to be enlarged, and his church members increased from 27 to 200. And then at thirty-five, when apparently just beginning a useful life, he died.

No. 9.

"LATE, LATE, SO LATE! AND DARK THE NIGHT AND CHILL."

SIR ALFRED TENNYSON, 1809—1892.

Some of our hymns come from curious sources. One of Alfred Tennyson's most popular works was the series of poems called "Idyls of the King." Among these poems is one entitled "Guinevere," who was King Arthur's Queen, but who at last fled from the court, and sought refuge in a convent. Here she was waited upon by a little maid. Now listen to the story as Tennyson relates it:

"So the stately Queen abode
For many weeks unknown, among the nuns;
Nor with them mingled, nor told her name, nor sought,
Wrapt in her grief, for housel, or for shrift,
But communed only with the little maid,
Who pleased her with a babbling heedlessness,
Which often lured her from herself: but now,
This night, a rumor widely blown about
Came, that Sir Modred had usurped the realm,
And leagued him with the heathen, while the King
Was waging war on Lancelot! Then she thought
'With what a hate the people and the King
Must hate me,' and bowed upon her hands,
Silent, until the little maid, who brooked
No silence, brake it, uttering, 'Late! so late!
What hour, I wonder, now?' and when she drew
No answer, by and by began to hum
An air the nuns had taught her, 'Late, so late!'
Which, when she heard, the Queen looked up and said,
'O maiden, if indeed ye list to sing,
Sing, and unbind my heart that I may weep.'
Whereat, full willingly, sang the little maid."

No. 10.

"O FOR A CLOSER WALK WITH GOD"—1779.

WILLIAM COWPER, 1731—1800.

If we can know some of the little peculiarities of an author, as well as the more prominent traits of his character, we are more interested often, in what he has written. The author of this hymn was one of the most bashful of men. He held at one time the appointment of clerk to the Committees of the House of Lords, but gave it up because it necessitated his appearing now and then in the room where they were assembled. And at his home in the little village of Olney it was a long time before he could overcome his diffidence enough to offer prayer in their little weekly prayer meetings, although those who heard him pray testify that he was as gifted in that as in the writing of hymns. This hymn was quoted by Southey, who wrote a biography of Cowper as an evidence of his insanity.

No. 11.

"ON THE MOUNTAIN'S TOP APPEARING."

Rev. Thomas Kelly, 1769—1855.

Thomas Kelly was an Irish boy, the son of a judge. He studied law, but becoming a Christian he became a clergyman of the Established Church; but his preaching was too evangelical to suit the condition of that Church in Ireland at that time, and the pulpits of the Church were closed against him. Mr. Kelly was rich, and so, driven out of the Church, he built churches for himself. He was greatly interested in the work of foreign missions and wrote many hymns on this subject. Possibly we can get a glimpse of his character by this little conversation: An old schoolmate met him when he was well along in years and said to him, "You will live to a great age, Mr. Kelly." "Yes," was the reply, "I am confident I shall, for I expect never to die." But they were both right, for he lived to be eighty-six even in this world.

No. 12.

"JESUS WHERE'ER THY PEOPLE MEET"—1769.

William Cowper, 1731—1800.

"O LORD OUR LANGUID SOULS INSPIRE"—1769.

Rev. John Newton, 1725—1807.

In the little village of Olney more than a hundred years ago there lived in adjoining houses two intimate friends.

One was William Cowper, a despondent invalid; the other Rev. John Newton, curate of the parish. There was in the village an unoccupied residence, which because of its size as compared with the other cottages, was called "The Great House." John Newton and William Cowper carried on a little social weekly prayer meeting in the village, and in 1769 this was removed to "The Great House," and Newton decided to celebrate the event by a new hymn which should be first sung on that occasion. So he and his friend Cowper, each composed one and these are the hymns they wrote. Newton's hymn is often found with a different beginning. "Dear Shepherd of Thy people hear."

No. 13.

"MY LORD, HOW FULL OF SWEET CONTENT"—1702.

MADAME JEANNE B. DE LA MOTTE GUION, 1648—1717.

Madam Guion was a French woman, who suffered a great deal through the unkindness of friends, the death of a child, and her own sickness which at the age of twenty-two left her disfigured for life. She belonged to the sect called "Quietists," whose name explains quite well their peculiar views. She wrote a book in which was given an account of what was called the "Prayer of Silence," in which not only is there no utterance by the voice, but even the mind, instead of turning from one request to another, simply concentrates itself upon the thought "Thy will be done." This work was greatly feared by the Romanists, who collected it by hundreds and burnt all they could collect. She was imprisoned twice for her religious views, and then banished. Some of her hymns were written from behind prison walls, and this one in the first year of her banishment, so that its language is that of her own experience. It was written in French and translated by William Cowper.

No. 14.

(See No. 169.)

"SHOW PITY, LORD, O LORD, FORGIVE"—1719.

REV. ISAAC WATTS, 1674—1748.

A young man once complained of the hardening effect upon himself of a severe sermon on sin to which he had listened, and he was asked to read this Psalm. He attempted to do so, but his feelings as he read nearly overcame him, and at last when he reached the words "I am condemned but Thou art clear," he burst into tears and rushed from the room. From that day his life was that of a converted man.

No. 15.

"NOT ALL THE BLOOD OF BEASTS"—1709.

REV. ISAAC WATTS, 1674—1748.

A London City Missionary relates the story that a Jewess found this hymn printed on a piece of paper that came into the house as a wrapper for a piece of butter. Its reference to the sacrificial rites of her own church fixed it in her mind, and she could not shake off the impression it produced. She was led by it to a reading of the Bible and to an acceptance of Christ as her Savior. In consequence of her religious change her husband forsook her, and she lived in poverty, but remained faithful to Christ to the end of life. Do you know, I dislike to burn up even a scrap of paper that has anything good printed or written on it? Who knows if I spare it what eye may see it, or what heart may be comforted by it?

No. 16.

"THE GOD OF ABRAHAM PRAISE"—1770.

REV. THOMAS OLIVERS, 1725—1799.

In 1729, in a little village in England, a little boy four years old lost both his parents. He was taken by a farmer until he was eighteen, and then bound out as an apprentice to a shoemaker. By this time he had become about as bad as a fellow could be, so bad indeed, that he soon had to leave that neighborhood. After wandering from town to town, he went to Bristol, and there he heard Whitefield preach. The text was "Is not this a brand plucked out of the fire?" That sermon resulted in his conversion. I don't know as I can give you any better evidence that his conversion was genuine than by saying that as he had wandered about before his conversion he had left small debts owing to many people; and as soon as he was converted he retraced his steps from town to town, and with money he made at his trade repaid the sums he owed. In the year 1772, Mr. Olivers was visiting a friend in Westminster and one day strolled into a Jewish synagogue when he heard a celebrated Hebrew air sung by the priest, Signieur Leoni. Mr. Olivers was so captivated by the singing and by the melody that he resolved at once to write a Christian hymn to suit it, and the hymn was written before the visit ended. Although Mr. Olivers had had but little education, this hymn has been called one of the finest pieces in the English language. The Jewish priest gave him the melody, and it received his name "Leoni." In a note published with the original tract in which this hymn appeared are references to *sixty* passages of scripture used or illustrated by the hymn.

No. 17.

"GOD CALLING YET! SHALL I NOT HEAR?"—1730.

GERHARD TERSTEEGEN, 1697—1769.

Translated by Miss Jane Borthwick, 1825.

A German boy was on a journey, and while walking through a forest alone he was seized by violent spasms that threatened his life. He prayed earnestly that he might be spared in order that he might better prepare himself for eternity. His prayer was answered, and he at once dedicated himself entirely to Christ.

His father was dead, and his mother was poor, and to support her and himself he had already, when only fifteen years old, gone into a little business. There are one or two remarkable things about him. One is that finding the business he had entered upon to be one that interfered with his religious life, he left that business and chose another not open to that objection. Later on, to give himself still more time for religious work, he divided his business with a partner, and still later, to have all his time for evangelistic work, of which he did a great deal, visiting from house to house among the poor and the sick, he gave up his business entirely. His house became known as "The Pilgrims' Cottage," and it became the resort of multitudes of the poor and sick. They came for medicine and food, and clothing and comfort, and never were disappointed. And so he filled up his life with useful deeds, and they were all done in honor of and in imitation of the Christ to whose service he had dedicated his life. Coming from such a man as this, does not this hymn have a new and deeper interest for us?

He wrote a form of dedication of himself to Jesus in his own blood when twenty-seven.

He wrote more than one hundred hymns.

No. 18.

"BEHOLD THE SAVIOUR OF MANKIND"—1709.

REV. SAMUEL WESLEY, 1662—1735.

On February 9, 1709, the rectory of the little town of Epworth in Lincolnshire, England, was burned to the ground. Not much was saved from the fire. Not much, did I say? Two things were saved; almost by a miracle a six-year-old boy was rescued from the burning building; and by the saving of that life the moral history of the world was changed; for that boy was John Wesley, the founder of that great and valiant wing of the Christian army we know as Methodists. The other thing that was saved was a piece of paper somewhat singed by the flames, but legible yet, containing a piece of music and the words of a hymn, written by the rector whose house had been burned, who was none other than Samuel Wesley, the father of John and Charles Wesley, and of seventeen other Wesleys as well. This is the hymn that was saved. There never was a house burned from which so much was saved from the flames.

In 1803, a boy of fifteen named Samuel Rollerson was a baker's apprentice at Hilton, England. At this time a number of French prisoners were located near by, and young Rollerson's business frequently led him to the barracks. Methodism in those days had found its way into the army, and religious services were often held in an out-building belonging to the barracks. Samuel, whose mind had for some time been exercised on religious subjects, was admitted into these meetings and at one of them, while the hymn beginning "Behold the Saviour of mankind!" was being sung, he found his way to the Cross, the sin burden fell off, and the rough stable became to him the gate of heaven.

No. 19.

"RISE, CROWNED WITH LIGHT, IMPERIAL SALEM, RISE!"—1712.

ALEXANDER POPE, 1688—1744.

It was John Dryden, the poet, who translated from the Latin the hymn beginning:

"Creator, Spirit, by Whose aid."

One day he was sitting in a coffee house in London; the door opened and a friend of Dryden's brought in a delicate little boy twelve years old, who was eager to see the celebrated poet and had persuaded the gentleman to take him into the coffee house. The boy became a greater poet than the man he had been so curious to see, for he was Alexander Pope. He was a Roman Catholic, and that is no doubt the reason why he wrote no poems intended, when he wrote them, for hymns, for written in English at the time when he lived, his Church would have refused to use them. In the *Spectator*, a daily paper published in London, for Wednesday, May 14, 1712, Joseph Addison, one of the editors, said: "I will make no apology for entertaining the reader with the following poem, which is written by a great genius, a friend of mine in the country who is not ashamed to employ his wit in the praise of his Maker." Then follows a poem entitled "Messiah," and beginning:

"Ye nymphs of Solyma! begin the song!"

From this poem no less than five hymns have been taken for use in our hymn book, and this is one of them.

No. 20.

"VITAL SPARK OF HEAVENLY FLAME"—1712.

ALEXANDER POPE, 1688—1744.

This hymn, if indeed it is to be called by that name, is not only an imitation but a growth. There is a love poem by Sappho 600 years before Christ, and later a poem by the Roman Emperor Adrian (A. D. 138) written when he was dying. Pope says that he had both of these in his mind when he wrote. Then just before the time of Pope, Thomas Flatman made a translation of Adrian's poem and improved upon the sentiment, and last of all Pope improved upon his own version at the request of Mr. Steele, editor of the *Spectator*. Adrian only spoke of death in dim and timid uncertainty. Thomas Flatman rose a little higher and wrote of a life beyond, that might be better and could not be worse than this; but Pope, the Christian, concludes his poem with the Scripture words:

"O grave, where is thy victory!
O death, where is thy sting!"

No. 21.

(See No. 164.)

"ALL PRAISE TO THEE, ETERNAL LORD"—1524.

REV. MARTIN LUTHER, 1483—1546.

Four hundred years ago, a little boy fourteen years of age was sent away from home to school, at Magdeburg. His father was too poor to support him, and he earned his bread by singing ballads in the streets:

"Foxes to their holes have gone,
Every bird into its nest;
But I wander here alone,
And for me there is no rest."

A year later he was sent to another town where he had relatives who it was hoped would assist him, but they neglected him. As he was singing his plaintive little song one day before a house, the wife of the man who lived in it saw him and took him in. Her house became his home and she his benefactress, and he to please her learned to play on the flute and the lute. This was Martin Luther, and his own experience of the power of song in boyhood, led him to give it a very high place of importance in after years. When he was deep in the contest with the Church of Rome, he gathered a band of men at his own house who were skilled in music, and they arranged the hymns he had written to the favorite tunes of the German people, and then he had the hymns and the tunes printed on slips and circulated all over the land, until Luther's hymns and Luther's tunes were in the mouths of all the people. And the priests said, "Luther has done us more harm by his hymns than by his sermons."

No. 22.

"NOW THANK WE ALL OUR GOD"—1644.

Rev. Martin Rinkart, 1586—1649.

Martin Rinkart was a cooper's boy, and because his father was too poor to educate him, he supported himself by his musical skill while he studied theology. It is not always the case that a prophet has no honor among his own people, and Rinkart came back to the town of his birth and boyhood to be the pastor of their Church. He lived among them through a terrible pestilence which raged

in 1637, and then through a famine which followed it. The Thirty Years' War was also raging, and he was in full sympathy with his people in all these troubles. The Swedish army besieged their town and demanded thirty thousand thalers of the people. It was a sum far beyond their ability to pay, and Rinkart went out to the enemy's camp to intercede for his townsmen. Failing in this, when he returned he called on the people to gather for prayer, and God answered their request; and the Swedish commander consented to terms they were able to meet. Awhile after, in 1644, as Rinkart was sitting at his study window, he heard the sound of a trumpet, coming nearer and nearer. His heart sank within him, for he thought the soldiers of one side or the other were about to be quartered again upon the town. Just then his wife came in and told him that the people in the street were all gathering about a horseman who had just come in and had surely brought some great news, for the people were shouting at the top of their voices. Rinkart hurried out, and as he went his people gathered about him to tell him that the horseman brought the news that a treaty of peace had been signed and the long war was over. Rinkart went back to his study and offered up a prayer of thankfulness, and then seated himself at his desk, and continued his thanksgiving by writing this hymn. As he finished it, a melody seemed to strike his ear, and, taking up his pen, again he wrote music for his hymn. The tune to which the hymn is usually sung, however, is one that was composed for it by Johann Krüger, who lived at the same time as the author of the hymn. This tune is usually called "Nun Danket," these being the first German words of the hymn, but in some books it is known as "Wittenberg." This is said to be the best known tune in the world. In Germany, at midnight, on New Year's eve, it is the custom of every orthodox household to sing this hymn to this tune. It has also become a very popular tune in England. It has been often used in Germany on occasions of note. In Stuttgart in 1816-

1817 there was a great famine, and on July 28, 1817, the first load of wheat from the new crop, which gave promise that the famine was over, entered the town. It was decorated with flowers, and the people made the day one of festival and thanskgiving, and in the service this song was sung. The hymn is based on the Apocryphal book of Ecclesiasticus. The first two stanzas are a paraphrase of Eccles, 50:22-24, which was the text of the Swedish chaplain on New Year's day, 1649, when thanksgiving services were held upon the reestablishment of peace.

No. 23.

"TEACH ME, MY GOD AND KING."

REV. GEORGE HERBERT, 1593—1633.

George Herbert, born three hundred years ago (1593), has been called the prince and model of all country parsons. When fifteen, he went to Trinity College at Cambridge, and soon after he sent home to his mother (his father was dead) a little poem, as a testimony, as he told her, that his "poor abilities in poetry should be all and ever consecrated to God's glory." That was a good beginning, and he kept his vow as long as he lived. His whole life, as we look at it through the vista of three centuries, was a continuous poem, and it was all a song of praise to God; until at last, just the Sunday before he died, he arose from his bed and took his lute on which he had loved to play for nearly his whole life, and as he took it he said:

"My God, my God,
My music shall find Thee,
And every string
Shall have his attribute to sing."

It was he who wrote that hymn so much admired, beginning:

"Sweet day, so cool, so calm, so bright,
Bridal of earth and sky."

No. 24.

"COME, HOLY GHOST, IN LOVE. SHED ON US."

HERMANNUS CONTRACTUS, 1013—1054.

Veni Sancte Spiritus.

In the year 1013 there was born a boy to whom they gave the name of Herman. When he was seven years old, he stood but a poor chance in the world. He was "bowed, before and behind, and crippled and lame." That is to say, he was humpbacked, with a bent chest, otherwise deformed, and withal a paralytic. He was the son of a count, and counts in those days were expected to do hard riding and hard fighting. Little Herman could do neither, so he was carried off to a convent called the Convent of St. Gall, to be made into a monk. If you search for his name in history under the family name, you will not find it, for everywhere he is spoken of under a nickname which his crippled body suggested — Hermannus Contractus, which means Herman the cripple. He grew to be a master of verse, and is said to have written "many thousands" of songs, but they are now unknown. It is now supposed that he wrote this hymn which is now so celebrated.

This translation of it is by Rev. Ray Palmer.

No. 25.

"O MORNING-STAR, HOW FAIR AND BRIGHT." "WAKE, AWAKE, FOR NIGHT IS FLYING"—1598.

Rev. Philip Nicolai, 1556—1608.

In the town of Unna, Westphalia, in 1597, there raged a dreadful pestilence which carried off more than fourteen hundred persons. Dr. Philip Nicolai was the Lutheran pastor in this town and from his window saw the almost constant burial processions, and quite naturally his thoughts were much about death and the future world. He wrote his thoughts and published them for the good of others and added to them these two hymns. For the last of the two the tune is said also to have been composed by Nicolai, and harmonized by Jacob Pretorius, the organist of his Church.

The translations are by Miss Catherine Winkworth.

No. 26.

"THE LORD DESCENDED FROM ABOVE."

Thomas Sternhold, 1500—1549.

In a little town named Awre, in Gloucestershire, England, there is to be seen recorded in the parish register this statement: "Let it be remembered for the honour of this parish of Awre, that from it first sounded out the 'Psalms of David in English Metre, by Thomas Sternhold and John Hopkins.' "

Thomas Sternhold held the office of "Groom of the Robes," to Henry VIII and Edward VI of England. He was himself a pure man, and was so greatly scandalized by the obscene and wicked songs that were in common use in the court that he undertook to provide a higher and purer material by turning into English metre some of the Psalms of David. This explains the peculiar language in the title which he gave to his collection. "Very mete to be used of all sorts of people privately for their godly solace and comfort; laying apart all ungodly songes and ballads which tend only to the nourishing of vice and corrupting of youth." The courtiers, however, preferred their old songs, and would not sing Sternhold's Psalms. But the poetry and music were both better than any that had been composed at that time, uncouth as they seem now, and so they were adopted to be sung in parish churches. Among all the pieces in that old collection, but two or three have been thought worthy to live, and then usually in greatly altered form, but one stanza of this Psalm is just as Sternhold wrote it, and it is so nearly a perfect gem that it will probably live to the end of time. It is what is here used as the two first stanzas of the hymn.

No. 27.

"LET US WITH A GLADSOME MIND"—1624.

JOHN MILTON, 1608—1674.

It has been said of Milton that "his youth and his old age he devoted to himself and his fame; his middle life to his country." This rendering of the One Hundred Thirty-sixth Psalm was one of the products of his youth, having been written when he was a boy at school and fifteen years of age. As every one knows he wrote "Paradise Lost." Just as it was finished a Quaker friend, Thomas Ellwood, was visiting him, and read the poem. Then he said to Milton, "Thou hast said much here of Paradise Lost; what hast thou to say of Paradise Found?" Later, Ellwood visited Milton again, and had placed in his hand a copy of "Paradise Regained," of which Milton said to him, "This is owing to you, for you put it into my head by the question you asked me, which before I had not thought of."

No. 28.

"SHEPHERD OF TENDER YOUTH."

Clement of Alexandria, 150—220.

This hymn takes us farther back in point of time than any other hymn known. It is usually ascribed to Clement who died about the year 217, although he himself speaks of it as if he had quoted it from an author earlier still. He is supposed to have been born at Athens so he may have heard his grandfather tell of hearing Paul preach on Mars Hill. He was a heathen, however, but an earnest student. He found his way to Alexandria in Egypt, where was then the greatest library in the world, and here he fell under the teaching of a Christian teacher, and became a convert himself. His hymn as he wrote it was a catalogue of names applied to Christ; and the translation of it, as you will see, only follows that idea in a very general way. Something of the circumstances under which Clement lived and wrote can be gathered from the following, "Daily, martyrs are burned, beheaded, and crucified before our eyes."

The translation is by Rev. Henry M. Dexter, who says, "I first translated it literally into prose and then transfused as much of its language and spirit as I could into the hymn."

No. 29.

"THE ROYAL BANNERS FORWARD GO"—575.

Vexilla Regis prodeunt.

Venantius Fortunatus, 530—609.

In addition to their value for purposes of worship some of our hymns have an interest attaching to them because of their connection with important events in history. This is one of that sort. In 1670, messengers were sent out among all the Indian tribes of the Northwestern territory, inviting them to meet a representative of the King of France at the Sault St. Marie, which is the narrow stream connecting Lake Superior with Lake Huron. At the appointed time in the spring of 1671, the chiefs of fourteen tribes with their warriors and families were camping on the little stream awaiting the arrival of the great Frenchman of whom they had heard. On his arrival, one fine day in June of that year, he led his soldiers fully armed to the top of a little hill which overlooked the camp. The Jesuit priests accompanied in their robes of office, and all about them were gathered the wondering Indians. They had brought with them a cross, and after one of the priests had pronounced upon it a blessing, it was planted on the hill top, while all the priests and soldiers who could join them sang in the Latin tongue the words of this hymn:

"The Royal banners forward go,
The Cross shines forth with mystic glow!"

and then in the name of the King of France, St. Lusson, who led the expedition, took possession of the land to the ocean beyond them, and the gulf to the south.

The translation is by Rev. John Mason Neale.

No. 30.

"MY GOD, I LOVE THEE! NOT BECAUSE."

FRANCIS XAVIER, 1506—1552.

Written by a Jesuit priest and missionary. He went to India where he labored with extraordinary zeal and self-devotion, both among the natives and the vicious Europeans whom he found there. His enthusiasm rose above all fear, and Cross in hand singing hymns as he went, he used to venture amongst the worst of the heathen confident of success.

No. 31.

"SWEET THE TIME, EXCEEDING SWEET"—1779.

REV. GEORGE BURDER, 1752—1832.

George Burder was one of the active, industrious, useful ministers of a hundred years ago. The profession chosen for him was that of an artist, but after preaching awhile as a lay preacher, he gave up his artistic pursuits and was ordained. He originated the London "Religious Tract Society," which has for a century almost, occupied the same field in Great Britain as the American Tract Society has in this country. He saw a need among the smaller villages of volumes of sermons, written in a manner and upon subjects of interest to them, and he prepared, one after another, eight volumes of such sermons, which had an enormous sale, reaching nearly a million copies before his death. This hymn was first published in the London *Evangelical Magazine,* April, 1779, and its original purpose can be gathered from its title, "An Hymn for Christian Company."

No. 32.

"O JESUS CHRIST, GROW THOU IN ME"—1780.

REV. JOHANN CASPAR LAVATER, 1741—1801.

Some one has said that every one ought to have a hobby. Now here is a man who had a hobby. He lived 150 years ago in Switzerland, and was curate of a church in Zurich. He began to study the faces of his friends to see if he could tell their characters from their countenances. Then he extended his study to people whom he met and gathered pictures of people of whom he had heard; and at last he published a book, on "Physiognomy," in which he tried to prove by these faces which he had gathered and classified that character conformed to the outline of the face.

But he did better work than this, for he preached good sermons, set a good example of Christian living and wrote many good hymns, of which this is one.

No. 33.

"I KNOW THAT MY REDEEMER LIVES"—1789.

REV. SAMUEL MEDLEY, 1738—1799.

This hymn is a good illustration of a peculiarity of Medley's hymns. He delighted in repetition or alliteration. Here are sixteen lines and fourteen of them begin with the same two words. Dozens of his hymns exhibit the same peculiarity. His hymns illustrate the different conditions under which people lived and worked then. Books and printed matter were not so plentiful, and Medley, whenever he composed a hymn, printed it on a "broadside," as it was then called, for distribution among the people. After a while these broadsides were gathered together into a little book, and published.

No. 34.

"AM I A SOLDIER OF THE CROSS?"—1720.

REV. ISAAC WATTS, 1674—1748.

In the time of Doddridge and Watts it was a very common practice for the minister to write a hymn appropriate to the subject upon which he preached, and to give it out at the close of the sermon. The method then in vogue of lining out, two lines at a time, made this feasible. The minister could read the hymn he had prepared as the closing of the sermon, and the clerk could then line it out for the singers. Nearly all of Doddridge's hymns were written to be so used, and it was no unusual thing for Watts. This hymn was in this way read at the close of a sermon preached in 1727 entitled "Holy Fortitude or Remedies against Fear"; and the text was "Stand fast, quit you like men, be strong." Its appropriateness to the subject is apparent, and its effect upon an audience must have been great, when read for the first time at the close of such a sermon, by the author himself. The hymns named below were all written for such occasions by Rev. Isaac Watts.

"Blest Redeemer, how divine!"

Text: "All things whatsoever you would that men should do to you, do ye even so to them." (Matthew, 8:12.)

"Awake my zeal, awake my love."

Text: "Whether life or death . . . all are yours." (I Corinthians, 3:22.)

Watts wrote three sermons and three hymns on this text:

"What shall the dying sinner do?"

Text: "I am not ashamed of the Gospel of Christ, for it is the power of God unto salvation to every one that believeth." (Romans, 1:16.)

"And is this life prolonged to me?"

Text: "Whether life or death, . . . all are yours." (I Corinthians, 3:22.)

Watts wrote three sermons and three hymns on this text.

"Questions and doubts be heard no more."

Text: "He that believeth on the Son of God hath the witness in himself."(I John, 5:10.)

"How is our nature spoiled by sin."

Text: "Whom God hath set forth to be a propitiation." (Romans, 3:25.)

"Do I believe what Jesus saith?"

Text: "Finally, brethren, whatsoever things are true, whatsoever things are honest, whatsoever things are just, whatsoever things are pure, whatsoever things are lovely, whatsoever things are of good report, if there be any virtue and if there be any praise, think on these things." (Phillipians, 4:8.)

"Jesus! Thy blessings are not few."

Text: "I am not ashamed of the Gospel of Christ; for it is the power of God unto Salvation to every one that believeth." (Romans, 1:16.) Preached in 1723.

"Father of Glory! to Thy name."

Text: "For through Him we both have access by one Spirit unto the Father." (Ephesians, 2:18.) Preached in 1727.

"O that I knew the secret place!"

Text: "Oh that I knew where I might find Him! that I might come even to His seat! I would order my cause before Him, and fill my mouth with arguments." (Job, 23:3-4.) Preached in 1721.

"O happy soul that lives on high!"

Text: "For ye are dead, and your life is hid with Christ in God." (Colossians, 3:3.) Preached in 1721.

"Do flesh and nature dread to die?"

Text: "Followers of them who through faith and patience inherit the promises." (Hebrews, 6:12.)

"Must friends and kindred droop and die?"

Text: "Whether life or death, ... all are yours." (I Corinthians 3:22.) Watts wrote three sermons and three hymns on this text.

The hymns named below were all written for such occasions by Rev. Philip Doddridge (1702—1751).

"Great God of heaven and earth arise."

Written for a Fast Day, January 9, 1739.

"Hark the glad sound, the Saviour comes!"

Luke, 4:18-19. It is the passage beginning, "The Spirit of the Lord is upon me, because He hath anointed me to preach the gospel to the poor," etc.; and the sermon was a Christmas sermon preached December 28, 1735.

"Shepherd of Israel, bend Thine ear."

This hymn was composed "at a meeting of ministers at Bedworth, during their long vacancy." (April 10, 1735).

"Arise, my tenderest thoughts, arise."

Text: "I beheld the transgressors and was grieved: because they kept not Thy word." (Psalm 119:158.) Preached June 10, 1739.

"Lord of the Sabbath! hear our vows."

Text: "There remaineth therefore a rest to the people of God." (Hebrews, 4:9.) Preached January 2, 1736.

"O God of Bethel by whose hand."

Text: "And Jacob vowed a vow," etc. (Genesis, 28:20-22.) Preached January 16, 1736.

"Grace! 'tis a charming sound."

Text: "By grace ye are saved." (Ephesians 2:5.) Doddridge is not much more than the translator of this hymn. A Moravian woman, Esther Grünbeck, born at Gotha in 1717 and dying in 1796, wrote a hymn beginning "Grace! grace! Oh that's a joyful sound," and her hymn is probably the foundation for this one by Doddridge.

"Sovereign of all the worlds on high."

Text: "And because ye are sons, God hath sent forth the Spirit of his Son into your hearts, crying, Abba, Father." (Galatians, 4:6.)

"How gentle God's commands."

Text: "Casting all your care upon Him, for He careth for you." (I Peter, 5:7.) The last two lines contain an especially beautiful thought—exchanging a burden for a song.

"O happy day that fixed my choice."

Text: "And all Judah rejoiced at the oath: for they had sworn with all their heart, and sought him with their whole desire: and he was found of them and the Lord gave them rest round about." (II Chronicles 15:15.)

"Awake, my soul, stretch every nerve."

Text: "Not as though I had already attained, either were already made perfect; but I follow after, if that I may apprehend that for which also I am apprehended of Christ Jesus.

"Brethren, I count not myself to have apprehended: but this one thing I do, forgetting those things which are behind, and reaching forth unto those things which are before, I press toward the mark for the prize of the high calling of God in Christ Jesus." (Philippians, 3:12-14.)

"My gracious Lord, I own Thy right."

Text: "But if I live in the flesh, this is the fruit of my labor: yet what I shall choose I wot not." (Philippians, 1:22.)

"God of my life, through all my days."

Text: "While I live will I praise the Lord: I will sing praises unto my God while I have any being." (Psalm 146:2.)

"Great Source of being and of love!"

Text: Ezekiel, 47:1-12. It is the parable of healing the waters of the Dead Sea, by the waters of the Sanctuary.

"The Saviour when to heaven He rose."

Text: "And He gave some, apostles; and some, prophets; and some, evangelists; and some, pastors and teachers: For the perfecting of the saints, for the work of the ministry, for the edifying of the body of Christ." (Ephesians, 4:11-12.) The occasion was the ordination of the Rev. Abraham Tozer, June 20, 1745.

"Let Zion's watchmen all awake."

Text: "Obey them that have the rule over you," etc. (Hebrews 13:17.) The special occasion being the ordination of a minister at Floore, in Northamptonshire, England, October 21, 1736.

"See, Israel's gentle Shepherd stands."

Text: "But when Jesus saw it, He was much displeased, and said unto them, Suffer the little children to come unto me, and forbid them not; for of such is the kingdom of God." (Mark, 10:14.)

"The King of Heaven His table spreads."

Text: "And the servant said, Lord, it is done as thou hast commanded, and yet there is room." (Luke, 14:22.)

"And will the great eternal God."

Text: "And of Zion it shall be said, This and that man was born in her; and the Highest himself shall establish her." (Psalm, 87:5.) The special occasion was the opening of a new meeting house at Oakham, England.

"Jesus, my Lord, how rich Thy grace."

Text: "Inasmuch as ye have done it unto one of the least of these my brethren, ye have done it unto me." (Matthew, 25:40.)

"Father of mercies, send Thy grace."

Text: the Parable of the Good Samaritan. (Luke, 10:30-37.)

"These mortal joys how soon they fade."

"Rich are the joys which cannot die."

These are alterations of the same hymn. Text: "Provide yourselves bags which wax not old, a treasure in the heavens which faileth not." (Luke, 12:33.)

"Awake ye saints and raise your eyes."

Text: "Now is our salvation nearer than when we believed." (Romans, 13:11.)

"How swift the torrent rolls!"

Text: "Your fathers, where are they?" (Zechariah, 1:5.)

"Ye golden lamps of heaven farewell."

Text: "The sun shall be no more thy light by day; neither for brightness shall the moon give light unto thee: but the Lord shall be unto thee an everlasting light, and thy God thy glory.

"Thy sun shall no more go down; neither shall thy moon withdraw itself: for the Lord shall be thine everlasting light, and the days of thy mourning shall be ended." (Isaiah, 60:19-20.)

"Eternal Source of every joy."

Text: "Thou crownest the year with thy goodness." (Psalm, 65:11.)

"Now let the feeble all be strong."

Text: "There hath no temptation overtaken you but such as is common to all men: but God is faithful who will not suffer you to be tempted above that you are able, but will with the temptation also make a way to escape, that ye may be able to bear it." (I Corinthians, 10:13.) Preached June 24, 1739.

"Now let our mourning hearts revive."

Text: "Moses, thy servant is dead," etc. (Joshua, 1:2, 4, 5.) Preached August 22, 1736, on the death of a minister at Kettering.

"Thrice happy souls, born from heaven."

Text: "Let not thine heart envy sinners: but be thou in the fear of the Lord, all the day long." (Proverbs, 23:17.) Preached March 27, 1737.

"Jesus! I love Thy charming Name."

Text: "Unto you that believe He is precious." (I Peter, 2:7.) Preached May 8, 1737.

"Now let our cheerful eyes survey."

Text: "And Aaron shall bear the names of the children of Israel in the breast-plate of judgment upon his heart." (Exodus, 28:29.) His subject being, "Christ bearing the names of his people on his heart."

"Behold the amazing sight."

Text: "And I, if I be lifted up will draw all men to me." (John, 12:32.) Preached May 8, 1737.

No. 35.

"FATHER, WHATE'ER OF EARTHLY BLISS."

Miss Anne Steele, 1716—1778.

Miss Anne Steele was engaged to be married. The preparations were all made for the wedding. Some of the guests had already arrived and she was momentarily expecting the arrival of her lover, when a messenger came with the intelligence that he had just been drowned. Her reason almost fled at the sudden shock. It has been said that this hymn was the result of this early experience, but this is doubtful as her whole life was a succession of trials to any of which the hymn might have applied with equal appropriateness. The truth probably is that her trials led to a spirit of resignation and contentment which pervaded all her hymns.

No. 36.

"SINCE ALL THE VARYING SCENES OF TIME"—1746.

Rev. James Hervey, 1714—1758.

In the year 1729, a few students at Oxford banded themselves together under the leadership of John Wesley, and agreed that they would attend regularly every week the Sacrament of the Church, and observe the method of study prescribed by the University. It is safe for us to surmise from the fact that this band numbered only a few students, that to be faithful to the Church and the school was the exception and not the rule; and this is all the more certain from the fact that this little band brought down upon themselves the sneers of the other students who gave to them what they thought was the ridiculous nickname of "Methodists." And in this little band we have the germ of the great religious denomination which now bears this name. James Hervey, the author of this hymn, was a member of this band.

No. 37.

"LOVE DIVINE ALL LOVE EXCELLING"—1749.

Rev. Charles Wesley, 1708—1788.

We are apt to think of a poet doing his work in some quiet room, with books, and pictures, and statuary, and flowers perhaps, about him, and this hymn seems just one of the sort to be composed amid such surroundings; but there is no probability that it was written under any such circumstances. Charles Wesley was for a great part of his life a traveling preacher, going from village to village, now preaching in some Methodist home to the family and neighbors, and again in some churchyard, with a tombstone for his platform. His traveling was done on horseback, and he carried little cards in his pocket, on which he used to write hymns in shorthand as he jogged along the road, he and his horse. Then, when on his journey he would reach an inn, he would rush in and ask for pen and ink, and would write out the hymn he had composed, and mounting his horse, ride on again. Once he wrote in his journal, "Near Ripley my horse threw and fell upon me. My companion thought I had broken my neck; but my leg only was bruised, my hand sprained, and head stunned, which spoiled my making hymns till the next day."

No. 38.

"COME LET US WHO IN CHRIST BELIEVE"—1741.

REV. CHARLES WESLEY, 1708—1788.

The two Wesleys were in their day the great champions of what was called the Arminian doctrine, which has ever since been the distinguishing doctrine of the Methodist Church, and a theological warfare was hotly waged between them and the followers of Calvin, such as Whitefield, Toplady, and others. One of the weapons used with great effect by the Wesleys was a series of hymns, each bearing upon the question at issue, and which, under the title of "Hymns of God's Everlasting Love," they spread broadcast among the people in the form of tracts. This is one of these theological swords with which its author sought to slay the Calvinists.

No. 39.

"HOLY AS THOU, O LORD, IS NONE"—1762.

REV. CHARLES WESLEY, 1708—1788.

Did it ever occur to you how the Scriptures have been duplicated in our hymns? Not only their doctrines, but their historical facts have been restated in verse. The Psalms have been paraphrased in whole or in part by scores of poets, and selected passages from every book of the Bible have been made the subject of similar paraphrases. Rev. Samuel Wesley, the father of John and Charles, put the whole New Testament into verse, and Charles Wesley in addition to versifying most of the Psalms and writing many hymns based on Scripture passages, wrote nearly thirty-five hundred (3,491) short hymns which were practically paraphrases of verses selected from Genesis to Revelation. This hymn is one of these on I Samuel, 2:2.

No. 40.

"LET EARTH AND HEAVEN AGREE"—1741.

REV. CHARLES WESLEY, 1708—1788.

In the time of the Wesleys the theological warfare between Calvinism and Arminianism was hotly waged. The Wesleys were the champions of the Arminian faith and lost no opportunity for setting forth their views. One of their weapons in the contest was the hymn. They wrote quite a number for this special purpose, each setting forth some tenet of the Arminian creed, and these they distributed widely in the form of tracts, and afterward in collected form with the title of "Hymns on God's Everlasting Love." (1741). This was one of these hymns written to fight the Calvinists with. The doctrine of the last two lines:

"For all my Lord was crucified;
For all, for all, my Saviour died."

was a favorite one with Charles Wesley. In another of his hymns on the same subject, he uses the extravagant phrase:

"Take back my interest in Thy Blood
Unless it streamed for all the race."

No. 41.

"COME, SINNERS, TO THE GOSPEL FEAST"—1747.

REV. CHARLES WESLEY, 1708—1788.

One day more than a century ago (it was in 1790) a man stood under the old elm on Boston Common and began to sing. It was his method of calling together a congregation, for he was a preacher who had just come to the city from Connecticut, and his preaching had attracted great attention wherever he had been. This hymn was the song he sung: "Come, sinners, to the Gospel feast," and the event is a notable one because the sermon preached then and there was the first Methodist sermon ever preached in Boston, and it marked the beginning of Methodism in that region. The singer was a notable man in his time, Jesse Lee, who won for himself the title of the "Apostle of Methodism in New England."

No. 42.

"THERE IS NO FLOCK HOWEVER WATCHED AND TENDED."

HENRY W. LONGFELLOW, 1807—1882.

If you should ever see the journal of Henry W. Longfellow, you would find away back in 1847, the record of the birth of a little daughter who was named Fannie for her mother. And a little over a year later you would find an entry, "Little Fannie is quite ill and lies patient and mournful. All thoughts center on the little sufferer—which way will the balance of life and death turn?" Then he comforts himself by putting in a stanza of the old German hymn of Paul Gerhardt:

"Give to the winds thy fears,
Hope and be undismayed.
God hears thy sighs and counts thy tears,
God shall lift up thy head."

And a few days later you would find this, "A day of agony. The physicians have no longer any hope. I cannot yet abandon it. Motionless she lies—only a little moan now and then . . . lower and lower. Through the silent desolate rooms the clocks tick loud, and they all seem laboring on, to the fatal hour." And then he writes of her death. And while in this sorrow the father wrote a poem called "Resignation," which is often used as a funeral hymn when children are dead:

"There is no flock however watched and tended
But one dead lamb is there.
There is no fireside howsoe'er defended
But has one vacant chair."

No. 43.

"I KNOW NOT THE HOUR WHEN MY LORD WILL COME"—1876.

PHILIP BLISS, 1838—1876.

At the great Moody and Sankey revival services in Boston in the winter of 1876, there was one singer whose voice next to that of Mr. Sankey himself the great audiences most delighted to hear. His songs were written by himself and sung to music of his own composing, and were full of Christian experience. One evening he rose to sing and he prefaced his singing by saying, "I don't know as I shall ever sing here again, but I want to sing this as the language of my heart"; and then he sang his own song just written:

"I know not the hour when my Lord will come
To take me away to His own dear home:
But I know that His presence will lighten the gloom,
And that will be glory for me."

A few days later, while riding to his home in Chicago, the train crashed through a rotten bridge at Ashtabula, Ohio, and Mr. Bliss and his wife were burned to death.

The hymn was suggested by reading the well-known book, "The Gates Ajar."

No. 44.

"JESUS CHRIST OUR TRUE SALVATION."

REV. JOHN HUSS, 1369—1415.

We have many hymns that were written by people who were at some time imprisoned for their fidelity to their convictions, and some that were actually written behind prison bars, but this is the only one I remember that was written by a martyr. John Huss was a Bohemian reformer. He was excommunicated by the Romish Church; then his writings were collected and burned; then he was imprisoned, and finally on July 6, 1415, his own birthday, he was burnt at the stake.

The translation is by REV. R. F. LITTLEDALE.

No. 45.

"BEHOLD THE MOUNTAIN OF THE LORD."

MICHAEL BRUCE, 1746-1767.

Michael Bruce was the son of a Scotch weaver. He was a bright boy and as pious as bright. When only a child he sometimes led in the family devotions at home. His parents were poor, and in order to maintain himself at school during the summer he taught a school himself in the winter. He belonged to a singing class in the village where they lived, and at the teacher's request he wrote some songs to be used in place of some which the teacher thought unsuitable. One of these was an "Ode to the Cuckoo," and twelve were hymns, and many members of the class learned them by heart. But the poor boy worked and starved himself to death, and when twenty years old he returned to his father's home to die. The next spring he was too weak to longer sit up and walk about, but he wrote an "Elegy on Spring." Just listen to one stanza of it:

> "Now Spring returns, but not to me returns
> The vernal joy my better years have known;
> Dim in my breast life's dying taper burns,
> And all the joys of life with health are flown."

He had intended to publish his poems while yet he lived, but his strength waned; and so he spent his last days in selecting and transcribing such as he thought worthy of preservation. This he did in bed, and he died in that year only twenty-one years old. The manuscript he left was given by his parents to a friend of their dead boy, Rev. John Logan, to be published for their benefit. Awhile after he published a book which he claimed contained them, but it was found only to have a few, and these the poorest; but a number of years later Logan published a book of poems as of his own composition, and lo and behold! here were the songs of Michael Bruce, stolen by his friend and published as his own. This hymn was one of these.

No. 46.

"O MOTHER DEAR, JERUSALEM."

D. Dickson, 1583—1663.

This hymn and the one beginning "Jerusalem my happy home" have a common origin and are slightly different forms of the old hymn of Bernard of Cluny, and possibly all are of still earlier origin in a hymn of Gregory's. Many years ago a young Scotchman lay on his deathbed in New Orleans. He was visited by a Presbyterian minister, but for some time he seemed to shut himself up from all the minister's attempts to reach his heart. Discouraged, the visitor turned away, and scarcely knowing what he did began to sing to himself, "Jerusalem, my happy home, name ever dear to me." Unconsciously he had touched a tender chord in the sick man's heart, for he exclaimed, "My mother used to sing that hymn"; and through the gateway of this song the minister found entrance to his heart for the Gospel message.

No. 47.

"THERE IS A LAND OF PURE DELIGHT."

REV. ISAAC WATTS, 1674—1748.

Dr. Watts was born at Southampton on the south coast of England. The city stands, as those of you know who have landed there from any of the steamers from this country, between two bodies of water, and looks out toward the open sea, of which the Isle of Wight intercepts the view. Across the stream was the "New Forest" as it was called, with its green meadows. It was this view which as a boy Watts often saw, that tradition says, suggested the imagery of this hymn, only part of which is given here, for it begins with the well-known lines, "When I can read my title clear."

No. 48.

"WHEN RISING FROM THE BED OF DEATH"—1712.

JOSEPH ADDISON, 1672—1719.

For account of Addison and the *Spectator,* see No. 49.

This hymn appeared in the *Spectator,* Saturday, October 18, 1712, at the end of a prose article, in which occur these words: "Among all the reflections which usually arise in the mind of a sick man, who has time and inclination to consider his approaching end, there is none more natural than that of his going to appear naked and unbodied before Him Who made him." And this is the key-note of the hymn.

No. 49.

"WHEN ALL THY MERCIES, O MY GOD"—1712.

JOSEPH ADDISON, 1672—1719.

There is a famous old school in London known as the Charterhouse. Two hundred years ago, two boys were schoolmates and playmates there. One was very much of a romp, never well out of one scrape before he was in another, while the other was a studious, well-behaved boy, who took all sorts of prizes in school for progress and deportment. Yet the two boys were chums, and always together. They kept up the friendship until manhood and through life. The newspapers of that day were pretty poor from every point of view and poorest of all from a literary standpoint. They had little indeed to attract anyone. These two boys, now grown to manhood, whose names by the way were Richard Steele and Joseph Addison, started a daily paper of a new and better kind than anything before known. They called it *The Spectator*. The "Spectator" was an imaginary character supposed to be a gentleman of high culture, who had traveled abroad, and was now living in London. Here he walked of a morning among the banks and business houses, and later to the theaters and concerts and clubs. He knew all the fine ladies and gentlemen, and wherever he went he was always observing, always commenting, always criticizing. But he was a bashful man and only talked to a few intimate friends. One of these has ever since been a celebrated man because of the talks the "Spectator" had with him, and we have often heard of him under the name of Sir Roger De Coverley. The new paper lived only about a year, but while it lived it was all the go in London. Gentlemen read it over their breakfasts, and ladies in their parlors; and, "Have you read *The Spectator?*" became the common question when acquaintances met.

Steele and Addison furnished most if not all the matter, and it differed from any other paper then published in that its tone was moral and pure. Every Saturday Addison published in it an essay distinctively religious, and at the end of most of them he placed a religious poem. This hymn, containing thirteen stanzas, was appended to an article entitled "Praise to God," which appeared in *The Spectator,* August 9, 1712.

No. 50.

"THE SPACIOUS FIRMAMENT ON HIGH"—1712.

JOSEPH ADDISON, 1672—1719.

(See No. 49 for notice of the author and *The Spectator.*)

This hymn appeared in *The Spectator,* August 23, 1712, at the close of an essay on "The Right Means to Strengthen Faith."

No. 51.

"THE LORD MY PASTURE SHALL PREPARE"—1712.

JOSEPH ADDISON, 1672—1719.

(For notes on author see No. 49.)

This hymn appeared in *The Spectator* for July 26, 1712, at the end of an essay on "Trust in God." In the essay there is this beautiful sentence, "The person who has a firm trust in the Supreme Being, is powerful in His power, wise by His wisdom, happy in His happiness. He reaps the benefit of every Divine attribute, and loses his own insufficiency in the fullness of Infinite perfection."

No. 52.

"O, SOMETIMES THE SHADOWS ARE DEEP."

ERASTUS JOHNSON, 1826—

A poor hymn, with little poetic merit, and no particularly important religious sentiment, is often brought into great popularity because of its fortunate setting to a tune that strikes the popular fancy. Some of the so-called "Gospel hymns" and many of the Sunday school hymns are of this character; and on the other hand it is equally true that many a hymn that touches closely human experience and does it with poetic grace remains unused because it is wedded to a poor tune. I have in mind such a hymn. I know its author. I have worked with him, and slept with him. A man with true poetic genius, and deep piety. His whole life has been a struggle with poverty and disappointment, and sorrow, but he has always been true to his convictions and true to his God. He was born in Maine, and with the Yankee restlessness he has swapped farms from Maine to California and back again; and now, an old man, still struggling, still hoping, he is waiting for one more swap, by which he will exchange a little, barren, worn-out farm in Maine for a home in the fair fields of heaven.

This hymn is like the attar of roses, every stanza is the expressed fragrance of a thousand of life's roses crushed. Listen:

"Oh! sometimes the shadows are deep,
And rough seems the path to the goal:
And sorrows, sometimes how they sweep,
Like tempests down over the soul.
Oh! then to the Rock let me fly
To the Rock that is higher than I.

"Oh sometimes how long seems the day,
And sometimes how weary my feet!

But toiling in life's dusty way
    The Rock's blessed shadow, how sweet!
Oh! then to the Rock let me fly,
    To the Rock that is higher than I.

"Oh! near to the Rock let me keep,
    If blessings, or sorrows prevail:
Or climbing the mountain way steep,
    Or walking the shadowy vale.
Then quick to the Rock I can fly,
To the Rock that is higher than I.

There is the hymn, beautiful and true, but it has been set to an unsingable tune, and the tune has sunk the hymn.

No. 53.

"JESUS SHALL REIGN WHERE'ER THE SUN."

Rev. Isaac Watts, 1674—1748.

On Whitsunday, 1862, on one of the Samoan Islands in the South Pacific, there was gathered a wonderful assemblage. More than five thousand of the natives of the different islands were gathered there under the spreading branches of the banyan trees. Foremost among them sat the King of all the islands, King George the Sable. All around him were seated his old chiefs and warriors, who had shared with him the dangers and fortunes of many a battle, and were now assembled about him to join in the ceremony by which he and all the islands under his authority formally abandoned heathen chiefdom, and adopted a Christian form of government. Most of those present had been born as heathen and many of them had been cannibals: now they were, nominally at least, a Christian people, and the King himself was a preacher of the gospel. What would Isaac

Watts have thought, if he could have listened, while that great audience began their solemn service by singing the hymn he had written a century and a half before, when no missionary society had begun its work?

No. 54.

"GOD IS THE REFUGE OF HIS SAINTS."

REV. ISAAC WATTS, 1674—1748.

The Rev. Luke Scott was a Methodist missionary to Trincomalee, Ceylon. In 1863, soon after he landed, he was conducting a service in the chapel and had almost reached the end of the first hymn. The people were singing:

"Zion enjoys her Monarch's love,
Secure against the threatening hour."

when all at once the shock of an earthquake was felt, accompanied by a noise resembling that produced by a heavy train going over a wooden bridge. The congregation was thrown into alarm, but the preacher calmly gave out the next lines:

"Nor can her firm foundations move
Built on His faithfulness and power."

Then came the second shock very much louder than the first and accompanied by an awful shaking: the noise, too, was very strange, too complex for description. The alarm of the people increased as the building seemed to reel as though it would fall to the ground. Notwithstanding this, the service was proceeded with, Mr. Scott preaching from "I sought the Lord, and He heard me, and delivered me from all my fears."

REV. JOHN B. SIMON, in *Wesleyan Methodist Magazine*, September, 1880.

No. 55.

"FROM GREENLAND'S ICY MOUNTAINS"—1819.

REV. REGINALD HEBER, 1783—1826.

A general collection had been called for in all the Churches of England, to be taken up on Whitsunday, 1819. A young rector was visiting Dr. Shipley, his father-in-law, just at that time, and on Saturday Dr. Shipley said to the young minister, "Write something for them to sing in the morning."

So the young man went over to another part of the room, and soon the doctor shouted, "What have you written?" and the three stanzas which had already been completed were read to him.

"There, there, that will do very well."

"No! no! the sense is not complete yet." And so he added a fourth stanza, and the Dean stopped him, and would not let him write any more.

"Let me add one more stanza," said the young man, but the Dean was inexorable. And so our Missionary Hymn has but four stanzas, when its author wanted to give us five. It was printed on slips that evening and sung by the people next morning, but two or three years later the words found their way to this country, and fell into the hands of a lady in Savannah, Georgia, who liked them so much that she was anxious to find a tune to suit them. She ransacked her books in vain, and then happened to remember that down the street there was a young bank clerk who was thought to have considerable musical talent. So to him she went with the hymn and asked if he could write a tune to fit it. He complied, and in a half hour handed her the tune that with the words is sung all over the world as the "Missionary Hymn." The Savannah bank clerk was Lowell Mason.

No. 56.

"ROCK OF AGES, CLEFT FOR ME"—1776.

REV. AUGUSTUS MONTAGUE TOPLADY, 1740—1778.

An English widow and her boy sixteen years old were visiting in a country place in Ireland. The mother was a member of the Church of England, and the boy was accustomed to its service. One night he wandered past a barn in which an uneducated but earnest layman was preaching. The text was Ephesians 2:13: "But now in Christ Jesus ye who sometimes were far off, are made nigh by the Blood of Christ." Speaking of that text long after he said, "It was from that passage Mr. Morris preached on that memorable evening. Strange, that I who had so long sat under the means of grace in England, should be brought nigh unto God in an obscure part of Ireland, amidst a handful of God's people met together in a barn, and under the ministry of one who could hardly spell his name." This boy was Augustus Montague Toplady, author of this hymn.

If any of us could have gone into a little parish Church in a quiet village in the eastern part of Devonshire, about the time our national Declaration of Independence was issued, we should have found a vicar leading the devotions of the people, who was thus described: "He had an ethereal countenance and light, immortal form. His voice was music. His vivacity would have caught the listener's eye, and his soul-filled looks and movements would have interpreted his language, had there not been such commanding solemnity in his tones as made apathy impossible, and such simplicity in his words that to hear was to understand. From easy explanations he advanced to rapid and conclusive arguments, and warmed into importunate exhortations, till conscience began to burn, and feelings to take fire from his awe-kindled spirit, and himself and his hearers were together drowned in sympathetic tears." This is a word picture of Augustus Montague Toplady and his preaching.

In the *Gospel Magazine* for March, 1776, there appeared an article on the National Debt of England. Its enormous amount was given, how much was the annual interest; and the article ended with these questions and answers: "How doth the Government raise this interest annually? By taxing those who lent the principal and others. When will the Government be able to pay the principal? When there is more money in England's treasury alone than there is at present in all Europe. And when will that be? Never." Following this article the editor, Mr. Toplady, proceeded to write what he called "A Spiritual Improvement of the Foregoing," in which he tried to estimate how many sins each of the human race had committed, supposing he broke some law of God once a day, twice a day, once an hour, and so on, and then he asks the same questions concerning these debts we owe to God, that had been asked as to the debt owed by the Government of England. "When shall we be able to pay off this debt we owe to God? Never. But will not God accept of us less than we owe, and so enable us to pay? Impossible!" And then he turns to Christ as the only hope. "Christ hath redeemed us from the curse of the law, and then he gives this hymn."

Gladstone has translated this hymn into both Latin and Greek, but it has been also translated into a great many of the living languages of the world, as well as into the dead ones. Rev. Dr. Pomeroy, during a tour through Eastern countries, found his way into an Armenian Church in Constantinople, while the congregation were singing. The words he could not understand, but it was evident that the singers were singing "with the understanding", and were in earnest in their song. All sang with closed eyes, as if in prayer, and as the melody proceeded, he saw that tears were starting here and there and trickling down the singers' cheeks. He was interested to know what words could awaken such emotions, and found that it was a translation into their language of our English hymn "Rock of Ages."

No. 57

"I ASK NOT NOW FOR GOLD TO GILD."

JOHN GREENLEAF WHITTIER, 1807—1892.

In the town of Haverhill, Massachusetts, there lived a Quaker farmer, with an industrious, hard-working boy. He had few advantages of school or books, but he improved such as he had, and now and then wrote a bit of poetry. While he was still a farmer's boy, he sent, with great timidity, one of these little poems to the editor of a little paper published in the neighbouring town of Newburyport. The editor going to his office one day found the poem tucked under the door. It was written on coarse paper in blue ink, and thinking it was mere worthless rhyme, he was about to throw it into the waste basket, when he suddenly changed his mind, and read it through. He thought he discerned in it the genius of true poetry, and published it. Soon other poems came from the same source, and at last the editor, who was none other than William Lloyd Garrison, afterward the great apostle of anti-slavery, inquired of the postman where these letters came from, and got the reply that he believed they were sent by a farmer's boy over in East Haverhill. "I will ride over and see that farmer's boy," said Mr. Garrison, and when he went he found the young poet at work with his father on the farm. This was the introduction to the world of literature of John Greenleaf Whittier, "the Quaker Poet," who wrote this hymn, and whose poetry has been probably more widely read than that of any other American poet unless it be H. W. Longfellow.

No. 58.

"LEAD, KINDLY LIGHT! AMID THE ENCIRCLING GLOOM"—1833.

REV. JOHN HENRY NEWMAN, 1801—1890.

John Henry Newman was a clergyman of the Church of England, and one of the leaders in what was called the "High Church Party." At the time this hymn was written he was on a voyage in the Mediterranean Sea. He was sick in body and depressed in spirits. A great discussion was going on in the Church at home, in which he had borne a leading part, and in which he took an intense interest. He was wavering in his own views, not of personal faith, but as to whether he should remain in the Church of England or go over to the Roman Catholic Church. He was honestly and earnestly seeking for light, and this hymn, written there on shipboard in the Mediterranean Sea, was his prayer for guidance. To him the answer came that led him some years later to join the Romish Church, and he became one of its Cardinals, and one of its ablest men. But seekers for light and guidance of all religious faiths are using his hymn, and finding it helpful.

No. 59.

"WHAT OUR FATHER DOES IS WELL."

REV. BENJAMIN SCHMOLKE, 1672—1737.

Benjamin Schmolke, a Silesian, wrote this hymn in German. It was a hymn for farmers to be sung when the harvests were bad, but by the translation into English has been made one of our best hymns of submission to the Will of God, in all the events of life. Schmolke wrote more than a thousand hymns.

No. 60.

"WALK IN THE LIGHT! SO SHALT THOU KNOW."

BERNARD BARTON, 1784—1849.

Bernard Barton was a Quaker, and in England bore the title of the "Quaker Poet," as Whittier has borne it in America. At twenty-six, he became clerk in a bank in England, and stayed there forty years until he died. After he had been there thirty years and more, he said in a letter dated the eleventh month, sixteenth day of 1843, "I took my seat on the identical stool I now occupy at the desk to the wood of which I have now well-nigh grown, in the third month of the year 1810, and there I have sat for three and thirty years beside the odd eight months without one month's respite in all that time. I often wonder that my health has stood this sedentary probation as it has and that my mental faculties have survived three and thirty years of putting down figures in three rows, casting them up and carrying them forward, *ad infinitum.*"

No. 61.

"JESUS! I LOVE THY CHARMING NAME."

REV. PHILIP DODDRIDGE, 1702—1751.

In 1702, almost two hundred years ago, in London, there was born a boy, the twentieth child of his mother, and at his birth he seemed too feeble to live; but live he did, and when a child his mother used to show him the pictures on the Dutch tiles with which their fireplace was adorned and tell him the story about them. They represented Bible scenes, and so his mind was stored with Bible stories, and with them Bible truths, before he could read them himself.

Later he became a minister, a teacher, and an author. He it was who wrote the book called "The Rise and Progress of Religion in the Soul," which had a circulation unequalled perhaps by any other book in that century. As was the custom with many preachers in those times he usually ended his sermons with a hymn written to enforce the truth he had been preaching upon. One Sunday he preached a sermon from the text "Unto you that believe He is precious." (I Peter, 2:7.) and he wrote this hymn to be sung at the close of that sermon.

No. 62.

"O THOU, FROM WHOM ALL GOODNESS FLOWS."

REV. THOMAS HAWEIS, 1732—1820.

What the author of this hymn thought about the way church singing should be conducted may be gathered from what he said in the preface to a hymn book he compiled and in which this hymn appeared in 1792. He wrote: "Even in our public worship the voice of joy and gladness is too commonly silent, unless in that shameful mode of psalmody, now almost confined to the wretched solo of a parish clerk, or to a few persons huddled together in one corner of the church, who sing to the praise and glory of themselves, for the entertainment, or oftener for the weariness of the congregation; an absurdity too glaring to be overlooked, and too shocking to be ridiculous."

No. 63.

"JESUS, THY BLOOD AND RIGHTEOUSNESS."

This hymn has required the work of three people to prepare it for our use. Paul Eber was a German Lutheran who was born in 1511, and died in 1569. He was one of Luther's friends and Melanchthon's, too. The first stanza of this hymn, which then began, "Jesus, Thy robe of righteousness," he wrote. Count Zinzendorf (1700-1760) was a Bohemian Nobleman, and a noble man. He wrote two thousand hymns, and later improvised them on the occasions when they were used. He was a preacher as well as a poet, and was the protector and patron of the Moravians, when they were driven out of their home in Austria. He visited their missionaries in the West Indies, and on the Island of St. Eustatius he took this stanza of Paul Eber's and added thirty-two more of his own. Then came John Wesley, the founder of Methodism, and translated the whole into English in 1740.

There is a sweet little story told how Queen Christiana of Prussia saw one day a very beautiful little girl, a daughter of the palace gardener, playing among the flowers, and had the child brought to her in the palace and placed in a chair near her at dinner time. She was enjoying in anticipation the delight and surprise she thought the child would show at the beautiful things about her, but instead of looking about at these things the little girl quietly bowed her head, and before all the guests at the dinner of the Queen, she softly repeated a translation of the first stanza of this hymn:

"Christ's dear Blood and righteousness
Be to me as jewels given.
Crowning me when I shall press
Onward through the gates of heaven."

No. 64.

"THE LORD MY SHEPHERD IS."

REV. ISAAC WATTS, 1674—1748.

It may not be amiss now and then for us to do a little "looking backward," and to compare our hymns with those our ancestors sang. When the Pilgrims landed on Plymouth Rock in 1620, they brought with them "Ainsworth's Psalms." This had a prose translation of each Psalm and a paraphrase in so-called verse. Here is his version of this Psalm.

"1. Jehovah feedeth me, I shall not lack.
2. In grassy folds, he down dooth make me lye:
he gently-leads me, quiet waters by.
3. He dooth return my soul: for his name sake,
in paths of justice leads-me-quietly.
4. Yea, though I walk, in dale of deadly-shade,
ile fear none yll; for with me thou wilt be:
thy rod thy staff eke, they shall comfort me.
5. Fore me, a table thou hast ready-made;
in their presence that my distressers be:
Thou makest fat mine head with ointing-oil;
6. my cup abounds. Doubtless good and mercie
shal all the dayes of my life folow me:
also within Jehovah's howse, I shal
to length of days, repose-me-quietlie."

This Twenty-third Psalm is one of the easiest of the whole 150 to versify, and you can easily imagine what some of the more difficult ones would be under the spell of Ainsworth's muse. A few years later the worthy Pilgrims became discontented with these Psalms, and clamored for something better; so certain of their own ministers set to work on an improvement, and soon produced what is known as "The Bay Psalm Book." For a hundred years and more this was the New England hymn book; and here is the same Psalm as they sang it:

"1. The Lord to me a shepherd is,
Want therefore shall not I,
2. He in the folds of tender grass
Doth make me down to lie;
He leads me to the waters still.
3. Restore my soul doth he;
In paths of righteousness he will
For his name sake lead me.

4. In valley of death's shade although
I walk, I'll fear none ill:
For thou me with thy rod, also
Thy staff me comfort will.

5. Thou hast fore me a table spread
In presence of my foes:
Thou dost anoint with oil my head,
My cup it overflows.

6. Goodness and mercy my days all
Shall surely follow me:
And in the Lord's house dwell I shall
So long as days shall be."

Perhaps we can by comparison with these two paraphrases of this familiar Psalm as our ancestors sang it, appreciate the beauty of the one we now use, by Isaac Watts. It contains only four more words than the English translation of the Psalm as we have it in the Bible, and a pleasant way to sing it is to repeat the Bible verse as we remember it and then sing the corresponding verse of the hymn, to the tune of "Dennis."

During the civil war a soldier from a New England home was marching upon the enemy with fixed bayonet and at a double quick time. While thus running to meet what he felt might be sudden death, these lines flashed through his mind:

"The Lord my Shepherd is,
I shall be well supplied;
Since He is mine, and I am His,
What can I want beside?"

The thought came, "Oh, how I wish I could say, 'The Lord *my* Shepherd is!'" Then, suddenly, while rushing on, he turned the wish into a resolve, and said, "The Lord my Shepherd shall be!" Relating his experience months afterwards to a company of Christian Commission Delegates, he said, "and, dear friends, He has been ever since."

H. PORTER SMITH, of Cambridge, Massachusetts,
in *Congregationalist,* November 1, 1888.

No. 65.

MISS ALICE CAREY, 1820—1871.
MISS PHOEBE CAREY, 1824—1871.

In a family of nine children in a little settlement in Ohio sixty years ago, there were two sisters whose names have more frequently been spoken together than separately. Their parents were poor; so poor that one of the sisters said that "the first fourteen years of my life it seemed as if there was nothing in existence but work. The whole family struggle was just for the right to live free from the curse of debt." Worn out with the care of so great a family, the mother died when they were young, and a step-mother soon took her place. The girls wanted to read at night when their work was done, but she would not give them candles; but the girls got saucers of lard, and a rag, and by that light they read and wrote. They had one secret which they kept from each other, and that was that each wrote poetry. And so they went along side by side, together, each guarding her secret from the other until, when she was fourteen, Phoebe wrote a poem that was accepted and published in a paper. Alice, her sister, was four years older, but it was three years later before she got a poem into print. This was the childhood of Alice and Phoebe Carey.

No. 66.

"JESUS, STILL LEAD ON"—1721.

Count Nicholas Louis Zinzendorf, 1700—1760.

The author was Nicholas Louis Zinzendorf, a Bohemian Count, and one of the most remarkable men of the eighteenth century. When a child he used to gather children together to pray, and wrote letters to the Saviour. From eleven to sixteen he was at school at Halle, and formed himself and his companions into a religious order named the "Order of the Mustard Seed," with its mottoes and insignia; so that the Y. M. C. A. and the Y. P. S. of C. E., cannot claim to have been first in banding young Christians together in organized form. He began hymn writing when only a boy, and continued it all his life long, and some of his hymns were improvised. He used to preach, too, and said that "after the discourse I generally announce another hymn appropriate to the subject. When I cannot find one I compose one." He wrote in all about two thousand hymns. He was also a great believer in singing as a means of religious improvement, and organized meetings for practice. He had a wonderful memory and would often sing stanzas from various hymns and intersperse them with stanzas of his own composed at the moment.

This hymn was translated by Jane Borthwick, an English lady.

No. 67.

"LORD, IT BELONGS NOT TO MY CARE."

REV. RICHARD BAXTER, 1615—1691.

The present age is none the better that it has set aside so many of the books that proved helpful to past generations. The older people of today will remember that when libraries were smaller, and books in laymen's houses fewer, "Baxter's Call," and "Baxter's Saints' Rest," were two of the "old stand-bys," depended upon to bring the children into the kingdom, and to comfort those already in. Nothing worth mentioning distinguished the boyhood of Baxter. He was chaplain of one of Cromwell's regiments and after the Restoration was chaplain to Charles Second. He was imprisoned once for the character of his preaching. Later he was fined for a paraphrase of the New Testament, and being unable to pay the fine was again imprisoned. This hymn was written in the latter part of his life, and is the experience of a persecuted, sick man, tired of life, yet willing to live, and leaving the whole affair to God. He entitled it "The Covenant and Confidence of Faith," and at the end of it he wrote this note, "This covenant my dear wife in her former sickness subscribed with a cheerful will." She was already dead, but she had been a great comfort to him, having shared some of his prison life with him.

No. 68.

"HOW BRIGHT APPEARS THE MORNING STAR."

REV. PHILIP NICOLAI, 1556—1608.

In the town of Unna, in Westphalia, in 1597, there raged a dreadful pestilence which carried off above fourteen hundred persons. Dr. Philip Nicolai was the Lutheran pastor there and saw from his window the almost constant burial processions. Naturally his thoughts were much about death and the future world, and for the benefit of others he published his thoughts in a book, to which he added two hymns written at this time, this being one of the number. The music for it he arranged himself from a popular secular song. It was translated by two brothers-in-law, Philip Pusey and Algernon Herbert.

No. 69.

"IN THE CROSS OF CHRIST I GLORY."

John Bowring, 1792—1872.

It is a singular fact that one of the favorite hymns of Trinitarians was written by a Unitarian. John Bowring was an English Knight, and can claim to have been almost a universal genius, or at least to have distinguished himself in many and quite different departments of life. He was a prominent writer in defense of the principles of Unitarianism. He sat in the English Parliament for ten years, and was the consul of that government at Canton, and later the Governor of Hongkong, and went on a special political mission to Siam. He wrote a biography of Jeremy Bentham, the Unitarian theologian, books of travel in the Philippine Islands and in Siam, a book of morals for young people, books on commercial affairs: studied the Russian language and published a book of Russian poetry translated into English; did the same with Spanish, the Dutch, the Polish, the Hungarian, and the Bohemian. And even this list only partly tells the story of his life work. The first line of this hymn is inscribed on its author's tombstone.

No. 70.

"COME, HOLY SPIRIT, HEAVENLY DOVE."

REV. ISAAC WATTS, 1674—1748.

A young man, who had been a leader of gay companions, was induced one evening to attend a religious meeting, and the Word of God to which he listened went like an arrow to his heart. To stifle his convictions he went to a public house near by where he and his companions often spent the nights in revelry. His talent for singing made him a welcome comer always, and he was called on for a song. He began some rollicking piece, but in the very midst of it the words all seemed to vanish from his memory, and he tried in vain to recall them. But in their place there came rushing into his mind, the words, probably learned in boyhood, at church, or home:

"Come, Holy Spirit, heavenly Dove,
With all Thy quickening powers.
Come shed abroad a Saviour's love,
And that shall kindle ours."

As he had before left the house of prayer, he now left the house of revelry, with humbled pride, and shortly after he began a Christian life.

No. 71.

"THERE WERE NINETY AND NINE THAT SAFELY LAY."

MISS ELIZABETH C. CLEPHANE, 1830—1869.

A lady in Scotland, reading the parable of the Good Shepherd, was much impressed with the thought of Christ leaving the glories of heaven, and becoming a seeker of men who had gone astray, and she put her thoughts into verse. The little poem was published in a religious magazine in Scotland, and so drifted into newspapers in various places. This was in 1868. Six years later Moody and Sankey, after a series of wonderful revival meetings through Scotland, were on the way from Edinburgh to Glasgow to hold a farewell meeting there. Glasgow had been the scene of perhaps their most successful work, and this meeting promised to be one of great interest. Mr. Sankey wished to introduce some new hymn which would represent Christ as a compassionate and all-sufficient Saviour. Before getting on the train he gathered up at a newsstand several papers to read on the cars, and in one of them he found these verses. "There," said he; "that's just the hymn I have been wanting for the Glasgow meeting."

Next day, as he tells it, "This little tune or chant that it is set to came to me," and before he had written the tune down upon paper, he put the little newspaper scrap before him on the organ, and sang it to the people. And now a very strange thing occurred: away in the gallery there sat a lady who was at first startled and then greatly affected at the song; and she sent a little note to Mr. Sankey saying, "I thank you for having sung my dead sister's hymn."

No. 72.

"NOW IS THE ACCEPTED TIME."

John Dobell, 1757—1840.

A hundred years ago, if we had visited a Baptist Church in Skinner Street, Poole, in Dorsetshire, England, we should have noticed conspicuous among the worshipers a very tall man; and if we had asked who it was, we should have been told it was "Old Doble." "Old Doble's" real name was John Dobell, a somewhat remarkable and eccentric man whose occupation was that of port gauger of liquors. His wife was a member of the church, but his name does not appear upon its records. He had considerable leisure, which he used mostly in the writing of religious books. One day he visited a lady who was sick, and she said to him, "I wish I could see before I die a hymn book full of Christ and His Gospel, and without any mixture of freewill or merit." Such a hymn book he set himself to compile. He contributed to it about twenty of his own compositions, this hymn among the number.

No. 73.

"COME YE DISCONSOLATE, WHERE'ER YE LANGUISH."

THOMAS MOORE, 1799—1852.

Tom Moore was an Irish boy, the son of a Dublin grocer. He was a youthful prodigy, and when only a child excited admiration by his recitations. When fourteen years of age his verses were so well written as to appear in the *Dublin Magazine*. While a young man, he became an actor in a theatre at Kilkenny, and fell in love with one of the actresses and married her. There is nothing to indicate that he was in any sense a Christian man or even lived with any very high moral purpose, and yet he wrote and published thirty-three "Sacred Songs," some of which find place in nearly all our collections. If it may be said of Sir John Bowring's hymn, "In the Cross of Christ I glory," that it indicates a theology in his heart different from and better than that in his head, it may be said of Tom Moore's hymns, that they prove that there may be a religion of the head which never appears in the life.

No. 74.

"GLORY TO THEE, MY GOD, THIS NIGHT."

Bishop Thomas Ken, 1637—1711.

Old Izaak Walton, the patron saint of all the fishermen, married a girl named Ann Ken. She had a little brother whose care fell upon her when his mother died, as she died when the little boy was five years old. When thirteen years of age the boy went to Winchester School, and although that was two hundred and fifty years ago (1650), his name scratched upon one of the posts is still shown to visitors. He became a clergyman of the Church of England, and later one of its bishops. He had the courage of his convictions and was a prisoner at one time in the Tower of London because of his refusal to do what he deemed a wrong. He was chaplain to King Charles Second at one time, and after a night of revelry King Charles would often say, "Now I must go and hear good Bishop Ken tell me my faults." He never forgot his school, and composed for the boys who attended it a "Manual of Prayers," which became very popular. In this book he inserted three quite long hymns, which he entitled, respectively, "A Morning Hymn," "An Evening Hymn," and "A Midnight Hymn." In his advice to the students he says, "Be sure not to omit the morning, evening, and midnight hymn." Each one of these hymns ended with the stanza now universally sung by Christians, "Praise God from Whom all blessings flow," and this hymn is a part of his "Evening Hymn."

The tune now called "Evening Hymn," but which was at first called "Canon," is older than the hymn, and it is reasonably certain that it was the first one used with it, so that hymn and tune have kept together for two hundred and fifty years. Thomas Tallis, the composer, was an organist in Waltham Abbey and served in connection with the Royal Chapel under four sovereigns, King Henry

Eighth, King Edward, and Queens Mary and Elizabeth. Organists who get good salaries nowadays may be better contented by comparing theirs with his, which was seven pence a day.

A drunken printer of London was Roger Miller, but he became a missionary working among the poor and the outcast of the same city where he had once caroused. In 1847 his mother died, and he started by railroad from London to Manchester to attend the funeral. It was late at night, and Miller had suggested singing Ken's evening hymn, that day might end with a devotional song. Among the stanzas were these:

"Teach me to live that I may dread
The grave as little as my bed.
Teach me to die, that so I may
Rise glorious at the judgment day."

Never did the singing of earth come nearer to blending with the song of heaven, for scarcely had they ended their evening hymn when there came the crash of colliding cars and Roger Miller was dead.

No. 75.

"ABIDE WITH ME! FAST FALLS THE EVENTIDE."

Rev. Henry F. Lyte, 1793—1847.

The circumstances under which this hymn was written are peculiarly sad. The author was curate of "a sea-faring folk" at Brixham, Devonshire, England. Here he "made hymns for his little ones, and hymns for his hardy fishermen, and hymns for sufferers like himself." He had been in poor health, and it had been decided that he must make a trip to some more southern climate. Of this trip he said,

"While I talk of flying, I am just able to crawl, and ask myself whether I shall be able to leave England at all." Before leaving he met his people once more in a Communion Service, and spoke some parting words. At its close, he dragged himself to his room and remained there a long time. That evening he gave to a relative this hymn, written undoubtedly during the twilight of that Sabbath day. It recorded his own feelings; "the darkness" was "deepening," "life's little day" was "ebbing swiftly to its close," and not long afterward on this very journey, at Nice, France, he died. An English magazine in 1887 invited its readers to send in lists of what they considered to be the hundred best hymns. About thirty-five hundred lists were received, and this hymn stood second in favor among the hymns, "Rock of Ages" only receiving more votes.

Rev. George D. Baker of Philadelphia, when once at Nice, went to see the poet's grave and found there a young man in tears who had been led to Christ through this hymn.

No. 76.

"GUIDE ME, O THOU GREAT JEHOVAH."

REV. WILLIAM WILLIAMS, 1717—1791.

The author began studying medicine, but a sermon he listened to one day preached in a churchyard, turned him to Christ and to the work of the ministry. Opposed to the Established Church, he became an itinerant Methodist preacher, and spent fifty years in hurrying from place to place all over Wales, to preach the Gospel. His sermons were eloquent and they came hot from his heart and greatly stirred the audiences who heard them. At a meeting of ministers, Howell Harris, who, by the way, was the preacher whose sermon in the churchyard was the means of Williams' conversion, challenged his brother ministers to try their hands at composing a few stanzas to be read at their next meeting. Williams had never tried his pen at poetry, but now he tried it and with such success that he went on writing in both Welsh and English until his reputation as a hymn writer was as great as it was as an orator, and he was called the "Watts of Wales." This hymn is one of those written first in Welsh, and afterward translated into English.

No. 77.

"THERE IS A BOOK THAT ALL MAY READ."

Rev. John Keble, 1792—1866.

A clergyman of the Church of England who added to native talent, a fine education, and poetic taste, became the leader of a new movement in that Church intended to bring more into prominence and honor, its sacred days, its ritual and service. From it perhaps has grown what we now know as High Churchism. As leisure gave him opportunity, he wrote short poems intended to celebrate the Church days and festivals of the year. It was not his plan to publish these, but "to go on improving the series all his life and leave it to come out, if judged useful, only when he should be fairly out of the way." For the sake of getting the benefit of their suggestions and criticisms he read some of these poems to intimate friends, and so their existence became known, and their publication was insisted upon. This is the history of a volume of poems known as "The Christian Year: Thoughts in verse for the Sundays and Holidays throughout the year," published in 1827, when John Keble was but thirty-five, which has had such a sale both in England and America as to make it one of the wonders in the history of publishing. He clung to his original idea of improving the poems, and embodied his improvements in successive editions as they appeared, until a few days before he died he gave the final revision to the ninety-sixth edition. Scarcely a hymn book has been issued for many years either in England or America, that has not contained some of the hymns of John Keble, taken from "The Christian Year." This is one of them.

No. 78.

"FAR FROM THE WORLD, O LORD, I FLEE."

William Cowper, 1731—1800.

Cowper was easily depressed by his surroundings. At one time he became quite insane and was placed under the charge of a physician. Upon his cure he went to reside at Huntingdon, and on the way he enjoyed one of the seasons of religious ecstacy which often came to him between his periods of depression. Upon reaching his destination he found himself among strangers, and at once felt a depression coming over him. He withdrew from the room, and prayed for encouragement. God cheered him, and the next day at church the devotion of a stranger sitting near him greatly delighted him. Now full of joy, he went from the House of God, to that same place, where he had found happiness the night before and wrote this hymn as an expression of his feelings and gave it the name "Retirement."

No. 79.

"ALL HAIL THE POWER OF JESUS' NAME"—1779.

Rev. Edward Perronet, 1726—1792

In the diary of Charles Wesley, about the year 1750, there may be found references to a man with whom he had become so intimate that he often writes of him as "Ned." This was Rev. Edward Perronet, a preacher of the Methodist connection. The treatment received in those days by the Methodist preachers may be imagined from one quotation from Wesley's diary dated 1749 as follows: "From Rochdale went to Bolton, and soon found that the Rochdale lions were lambs in comparison with these at Bolton. Edward Perronet was thrown down and rolled in mud and mire. Stones were hurled and windows broken," etc. This is the man who wrote the hymn "All hail the power of Jesus' name." A tune for the hymn was composed by a friend of the author, William Shrubsole, who was a music teacher, and the tune with one stanza of the hymn was published together in *The Gospel Magazine,* November, 1779. The tune was called "Miles Lane." It is seldom used now, but Dr. Robinson gives it in his "Spiritual Songs." Perhaps it may serve to fix the author and the composer in our minds if I quote the last clause of Mr. Perronet's will, as follows: "Lastly, I do here give and bequeath all and every property I am at this time or may be at the time of my decease possest of, both real and personal, to the afore mentioned Mr. William Shrubsole, and to his heirs, to be by them enjoyed and disposed of as they shall see meet for ever, in consideration of his respect for me, his services to me, and that pure and disinterested affection he has ever shown me from our first acquaintance even when a proverb of reproach, cast off by all my relations, disinherited unjustly and left to sink or swim as afflictions and God's providence should appoint."

"An interesting incident is told in connection with 'Miles Lane,' and the late Henry Smart. It was formerly the custom for the organist to play a short interlude between every verse of the hymn. In Smart's early days there were some grumblers (the race is not yet quite extinct) who adversely criticised his manner of playing the organ in the service. Smart said nothing, but waited his opportunity.

It came when 'Mile's Lane' was to be sung. He started it in the original key, C. All went well at the first verse, and a 'hearty sing' was in prospect. In the interlude between verses one and two Smart modulated, almost imperceptibly, into D flat, a semitone higher. Between verses two and three he modulated into D, when it was found the high notes on 'Crown Him' did not come quite so easily. Between verses three and four, a semitone higher still, until the high notes of these and the remaining verses must have made the acquaintance of the 'Lost Chord.' Needless to say that the young organist effectually silenced his critics by this clever display of skill."

F. G. Edwards in *Nonconformist Musical Journal*, September, 1890.

"Some months ago the Fourth Massachusetts regiment was marching to battle. They had become quite wearied, and some of the men were even falling out by the way, when a soldier struck up that noble tune 'Coronation' to the well known words, 'All hail the power of Jesus name.' The effect was electric. The fine old tune rose as upon wings from the lips of the soldiers, and flew along the columns with such vigor and zest, that the troop sprang along with invigorated spirits, proving this grand old song to be as inspiring in the army as in the prayer meeting."

Ladies' Repository, March, 1865.

No. 80.

"OH! SING TO ME OF HEAVEN."

Mrs. Mary S. B. Shindler, 1810.

On one occasion when a little Irish boy was sitting on the doorstep, and singing, "There'll be no sorrow there," a doubting and downcast stranger who was passing said,

"What place can that be, my boy, in which there is no sorrow?"

The boy at once replied:

"In Heaven above, where all is love."

The words were simple, but they were used to calm his troubled heart and give him peace.

Rev. I. O. Sloan, relates an incident which occurred in one of the hospitals after the battle of Antietam. A young Massachusetts soldier, Charles Warren, had been led by unremitting care and faithful admonition to give himself up to Jesus. His leg, it was found, must be amputated to save his life. Mr. Sloan, unwilling to witness the scene, turned away as they carried the soldier to the operating table. He had not walked far, before he heard Warren's cheerful voice, singing:

"There'll be no sorrow there;
In Heaven above, where all is love,
There'll be no sorrow there."

He turned back and found the soldier drowsy from the chloroform administered. Thus he remained, for the operation proved useless, until he passed away.

The following incident occurred during the war between the United States and Mexico:

"While stopping at the town of Matamoros, a number of our soldiers, as was their custom, met together to spend their time in rude and noisy revelry. Amid these social gatherings, the sound of vocal and instrumental music was always heard. Indeed the majority of our men were excellent singers; and, as they came from various parts of the Union, the favorite airs of each section were soon made familiar. Although they generally preferred such as were of light and trifling nature, still they often sang the tunes most popular with the different churches. The persons to whom we have alluded had been assembled for some time; the wine was flowing freely, and their hilarity steadily increased; everything seemed to promise them enjoyment. At this time a soldier belonging to a Southern regiment entered the room, and taking a seat in the midst of the company, began singing very deliberately, a hymn commencing:

'O, sing to me of Heaven.'

"The tune was solemn and affecting; the language was moving and impressive. The strangeness of the circumstance at once secured the attention of all present, and, as the singer proceeded, the effect was striking; the liquor ceased to flow, the rude oaths were hushed, and the sound of merriment died away. When the last verse was concluded, a perfect stillness reigned; the spell of revelry had been broken, and the anticipated gayeties were doomed thus singularly to disappointment."

No. 81.

"BRIGHTLY BEAMS OUR FATHER'S MERCY."

PHILIP BLISS, 1838—1876.

This hymn was suggested by the following incident, told by Mr. D. L. Moody:

"On a dark and stormy night, when the waves rolled like mountains, and not a star was to be seen, a boat, rocking and plunging, neared the Cleveland harbor.

" 'Are you sure this is Cleveland?' " asked the captain, seeing only one light from the lighthouse.

" 'Quite sure, sir,' replied the pilot.

" 'Where are the lower lights?'

" 'Gone out, sir.'

"'Can you make the harbor?'

"'We must or perish sir.'" And with a strong hand and a brave heart, the old pilot turned the wheel. But alas! In the darkness he missed the channel, and with a crash upon the rocks the boat was shivered, and many a life lost in a watery grave. Brethren, the Master will take care of the great lighthouse: let us keep the lower lights burning."

No. 82.

"SAILOR, THOUGH THE DARKNESS GATHERS."

PHILIP BLISS, 1838—1876.

The following passage in a sermon by Rev. E. P. Goodwin, D.D., preached in the First Congregational church, Chicago, suggested this hymn. "Some ships cross the ocean with clear skies, smooth seas and fair winds, and come into port with streamers flying and bands of music making jubilee. Others come in storms, with the skies black as night, the wind like a hurricane, and the sea like mountains—and they come in all battered, yards gone, masts splintered, hardly enough left to hang together. But the difference amounts to nothing. The only important thing from first to last is, not what the log says about storm or calm, but that they all steer close to the compass, and do their best to make the harbor. So they only get there safely; what happened to them by the way is of no account. So as to God's children. There may, there will be vast variety of experience: to some, prosperity, success, joy—to others, adversity, defeat, grief. But what may be your lot or mine, is of no consequence. The only thing of moment is, that we stick close to our chart and push for shore with all our might. So we gain that, the pleasures or perils of the way do not matter."

No. 83.

"THERE'S A LIGHT IN THE WINDOW FOR THEE, BROTHER."

PHILIP BLISS, 1838—1876.

This hymn was suggested by the following incident: A boy of twelve years worked out by the day to support a widowed mother, carrying home his earnings at night. "One night," he says, "it being very dark and muddy, and having three miles to travel, and a heavy bundle to carry, I did not reach home until late. My mother, feeble and weary, had retired, but she quickly aroused when she heard my voice, and soon met me at the door with a warm kiss, and warmer tears and a 'God bless you, my dear boy.' As she received my bundle, she exclaimed, 'After this, my son, I'll set a light in the window for you,' and true to her word, the bright light in the window appeared, and Oh! how it cheered my heart ever for years. Health failing me, I left home, leaving brothers to help mother, and went to sea. When I had been three years from home and was on the Pacific Ocean, mother died: but just before she expired, she said to those around her, 'Give Edward my dying blessing, for he has been a good boy, and tell him I have gone to heaven, and I will set a light in the window for him.' "

No. 84

"HAVE YOU ON THE LORD BELIEVED?"

PHILIP BLISS, 1838—1876.

A vast fortune was left in the hands of a minister for one of his poor parishioners. Fearing that it might be squandered if suddenly bestowed upon him, the wise minister sent him a little at a time, with a note saying: "This is thine; use it wisely; there is more to follow." "Brethren, that's just the way the Lord deals with us."

The above incident, told by Mr. D. L. Moody, suggested this hymn.

No. 85.

"MY SOUL REPEAT HIS PRAISE."

REV. ISAAC WATTS, 1674—1748.

This is Dr. Watts' version of the One Hundred and Third Psalm. It is related concerning the family life of Rev. John Angell James, that it was his custom to read the One Hundred and Third Psalm always at prayers on Saturday night, but his wife died; and the Sabbath drew nigh while she lay dead in the house. The members of the stricken family gathered in the twilight; some of them wondered whether this old song of the temple, fairly ringing and vibrant with thanksgiving would be given out now while the shadows were hanging so deeply overhead. But the faithful servant of God simply turned to the familiar place, and said gently: "No reason do I see, why we should change our custom tonight; let us read our usual Psalm."

REV. C. S. ROBINSON, D.D.

No. 86.

"OF ALL THAT DECKS THE FIELD OR BOWER."

ABDUL MESSEEH.

Abdul Messeeh was a native of Delhi, one of the fruits of the ministry of Rev. Henry Martin. He himself engaged in missionary work with great zeal and efficiency. In 1825 he was admitted into the ministry of the Established Church by Bishop Heber, who said of him, "He is a very fine old man, with a magnificent gray beard, and of much more gentlemanly manners than any Christian native whom I have seen. He is in every way fit for holy orders, and is a most sincere Christian, quite free, so far as I could observe, from all conceit and enthusiasm. His long eastern dress, his long gray beard, and his calm, resigned countenance, give him already almost the air of an apostle." During his last sickness, in 1827, his own hymn afforded him much consolation. A part of India is inhabited by a race called "Khonds." They are very superstitious and have long offered human sacrifices, usually children whom they have kidnapped or bought. These children are tied to stakes on the day of sacrifice and their flesh cut away piece by piece, till they die. Some years ago some of these kidnapped children were rescued by English officers and sent to mission stations to be cared for and educated. One of these boys, to whom the missionaries had given the name of David, at first seemed very dull, but at last his mind opened, and he was converted. He made rapid progress after this and was soon put at work in a printing office. About this time a number of white spots appeared upon his body, and it was soon apparent that he had been seized by leprosy. He was sent to the hospital and placed in a tent by himself. Here he used to lie alone for hours: but when the time for worship came, he would crawl to the door of his tent, and get as near as he could to the company, that he might hear the missionary's voice, and join in the worship of God. One day, the missionary and his wife went into his tent to see him, and found him lying on his back, seemingly in deep thought. His Testament was close to his side, and his hymn book open in his hand. They feared to disturb him, so at once they went away. In a little while the missionary returned. Everything was just as before, the tent door open, the Testament, the hymnbook, all as they were. But his bright spirit had taken its flight to heaven. No human hand was there to smooth his pillow, or give the slightest help. Alone and in silence, the young leper died. The missionary was greatly affected by the sight, and looking down upon the open hymn book, his eye caught these words.

"Of all that decks the field or bower,
Thou art the fairest, sweetest flower;
Thou, blessed Jesus, let not me
In Thy kind heart forgotten be.

"Day after day, youth's joys decay,
Death waits to seize his trembling prey;
Then, blessed Jesus, let not me
In Thy kind heart forgotten be."

The lad had seemed to die with this prayer trembling on his lips.

No. 87.

"HOW HAPPY IS THE PILGRIM'S LOT."

REV. JOHN WESLEY, 1703—1791.

A Methodist preacher traveling in Indiana was, with his family suffering deep poverty. A settler who loved him, being a large landholder, presented him with a title deed of many acres. He went home, glad at heart, in freedom, as he thought, from his difficulties. Three months after this he came to his friend, the kind-hearted settler. He was welcomed; but he soon drew out the parchment.

"Here, sir," said he, "I want to give you back your title deed."

"What's the matter?" said the other, "any flaw in it?"

"No."

"Isn't it good land?"

"Good as any in the state."

"Do you think I repent the gift?"

"I have not the slightest reason to doubt your generosity."

"Why don't you keep it then?"

"Well sir," said the preacher, "you know I am very fond of singing, and there is one hymn in my book, the singing of which is one of the greatest comforts of my life. I have not been able to sing it with my whole heart since I have been here. A part of it runs this way:

> "'No foot of land do I possess,
> No cottage in this wilderness,
> A poor wayfaring man,
> I lodge awhile in tents below,
> Or gladly wander to and fro,
> Till I my Canaan gain.'

"Take your title deed," he added, "I would rather sing that hymn than own America."

He went on his way, and sang his hymn, fulfilling his ministry, and confiding in Him to Whose service he had sacrificed himself. Nor did he or his family ever lack bread. He is gone now to his "abiding home."

REV. S. W. CHRISTOPHERS.

No. 88.

"NOT ALL THE BLOOD OF BEASTS."

REV. ISAAC WATTS, 1674-1748.

Some time ago a Christian lady was looking out of her parlor window in the city of London, when she saw a poor blind beggar in front of her house. He had a violin in a bag hanging from his neck. In his right hand he had a cane or staff to lean on, while his left hand held a string that was fastened to the collar on the neck of his dog—his only guide, as he groped his way in darkness through the crowded streets of that busy city. The poor man looked cold, hungry, and sad. The lady pitied him, and sent her servant to ask him to come into the house, to get warmed, and rested, and have something to eat. The servant led the blind man and his dog up the steps into the dining room, and gave him a nice warm place by the fireside. As he sat there, with his dog lying beside him, the blind beggar showed his thankfulness by the smile that brightened his face, while the poor dog tried to say, "Thank you! thank you!" as well as he could by wagging his tail. While he was eating his dinner, the good lady sat by and talked with the poor man.

"How long have you been blind, my friend?"

"Fifteen years, ma'am. I had an attack of smallpox, and it took away my eyesight."

"And have you been begging all that time?"

"No ma'am; only a few years. I had two brothers who kindly took care of me; but they both died three years ago, and now I have no one to do anything for me; so I have to go out and beg."

"Can you play any hymns, or psalms, or sacred pieces?"

"No, ma'am, I only know two pieces, and they are both songs, or ballads. An old sailor taught me both of them."

"But there are many beautiful hymns and sweet psalm tunes that would sound well in the streets. People would like to hear them, and you would get more pennies in your little basket for singing them."

"I do not know any hymns, ma'am; I wish I did."

"Well, while you are getting your dinner, I will repeat one of my favorite hymns to you, and then I'll sing it; and when you have done, you must see if you can play it and sing it: will you?"

"Yes, ma'am, I will, and thank you for it."

Then the lady recited this hymn of Dr. Watts's. She repeated the hymn slowly and deliberately several times. Then she sang it to a very sweet tune. She had a fine full voice. The blind man stopped eating to listen. With his face uplifted to the ceiling, he rolled his sightless eyeballs in evident delight. Even the dog seemed to forget his crumbs and his bones, and wagged his tail vigorously.

"Would you please sing it for me again, ma'am?" said the blind man.

She sang it again and again. He seemed to take in every word of the hymn, and every note of the music. When he had finished his dinner, he took his violin, and standing in the middle of the room, he struck up the tune the lady had been singing and went through the whole hymn. The lady was delighted, and so was the poor blind fiddler. Then he repeated it, so as to be sure he had it right, and thanking the lady for her kindness, he went on his way.

About two months after this, the blind beggar with his dog called again at that lady's house. She shook hands with him and said, "Well, my friend, I'm glad to see you; how does the new music answer?"

"Wonderfully well, ma'am. I've just called to tell you about it; but I don't know how. The day I called here—oh! that blessed day! and several days after I sang pretty well; but one day I couldn't sing at all."

"Why, had you taken cold?"

"No, ma'am, but I had a guilty conscience. I was, as that hymn says, all stained with sin. The oftener I sang those lines, the worse I felt. The verses described my case exactly. I was indeed a penitent. I remained in the house all day in great sorrow. My dog knows when I'm in trouble, and he would come and put his paws on my knee, saying, as plain as he could, 'What's the matter, master?' I thought about the verses, though I could not play them nor sing them; but the last verse led me to trust in Jesus, and now, indeed, I can sing:

"'We bless the Lamb with cheerful voice,
And sing His bleeding love.'

Before that, my soul was blind as well as my body; but now I have new eyes. Jesus has opened the eyes of my soul. I see Him as my Saviour, my Lord, and my God. I thank you for calling me in that day, and teaching me that precious hymn. That was a blessed day to me."

REV. RICHARD NEWTON, D.D.

Rev. J. D. Reardon, speaking of himself, said, heavily laden with guilt and fear, and groping for a long while in darkness, he was in a moment brought into the light and liberty of God's people by the quoting of the third verse of this hymn. His pastor had been unfolding the way of salvation to him and other inquirers, when to impress the truth of the Bible contained in this verse, he reached out his hands just as the ancient priest was supposed to do when placing the sins of the people upon the scapegoat, and said, "Sinner, it is just this, only this, for you to do, and say:

"'My faith would lay her hand
On that dear head of thine,
While like a penitent I stand,
And there confess my sin.'

"My eyes opened at once to see it. I burst out with laughter; I couldn't help it. My heart in a moment was filled with joy and has been ever since."

No. 89.

"AWAY WITH OUR SORROW AND FEAR"—1744.

REV. CHARLES WESLEY, 1708—1788.

A minister once lost his way, while traveling in Nebraska. Late at night and in the midst of a pelting storm, he sought shelter in the cabin of a lonely Irish settler. He was warmly welcomed, and they spent the evening pleasantly in conversation. At the close of the evening his Irish host said to him, "Now, sir, will you please sing something before we go to rest? Can you sing John White's hymn?"

"John White's hymn? No, I never heard of it. What is it?"

"It's this, sir:

"'Away with our sorrow and fear,
We soon shall recover our home;
The city of saints shall appear,
The day of eternity come.'

"O yes! I've sung that good old hymn many a time. But why do you call it 'John White's hymn?'"

"I'll tell you, sir. When we were young people in old Ireland, my wife and I, we attended a meeting, where we learned to love Jesus. The minister was a young man named John White. He spent all his time among the people, telling them of the love of Jesus, and trying to persuade them to love and serve Him. He was often persecuted on account of his religion, but he never answered those who troubled him, except by singing some of the verses of this blessed hymn. My wife and I learned to sing it together, and it has been the greatest comfort to us. We have had many sorrows to bear, but when we sing this sweet hymn, and think of the dear, loving Saviour, it always lightens our burdens and makes us happy. A few years after we settled here, our little boy, our only child, lay dying. That was a heavy blow. The mother stood on one side of the cradle, and I on the other. We watched the death-drops gather on that patient little face. Then my wife looked up to me and said, 'O, Pat, sing John White's hymn.' So softly, and with a choking voice, I sang:

'Away with our sorrow and fear,
We soon shall recover our home.'

And we closed the little eyes that were never more to look into ours, until that glad day of eternity comes. A few months after this, sir, came the greatest trial of my life. My dear wife, who had always been such a comfort to me, was taken very ill. The doctor said she could not live. As I sat by her bedside, overwhelmed with sorrow, she put her arm around my neck, and drawing my face down close to hers, she gently whispered, 'Good-by Pat, dear, I'm going home. Sing John White's hymn for me, once more before I go.' So, with her cold hand clasped in mine, I tried to sing:

'Away with our sorrow and fear,
We soon shall recover our home.'

And the Lord took away my sorrow and fear. My dear patient wife was quite happy till she fell asleep in Jesus." Then the Irish settler wiped away the tears from his eyes, and while the storm was howling without, he and the minister, as they sat by the blazing fire sang once more John White's hymn:

"Away with our sorrow and fear."

REV. RICHARD NEWTON, D.D.

Some years ago, Mr. Brewster, a Methodist missionary, when traveling in Newfoundland, turned aside to visit an old settler whom he had heard of. He found him living with his daughters; and soon the talk turned upon the old country.

"And have you ever seen the Shannon?" said the old man; "and do ye know the river?"

"No," was the reply, "I don't know it."

The old man then told the story, how he had left the banks of the Shannon, and how, when all were sad and sighing as they parted from their friends, his little wife sang:

'Away with our sorrow and fear,
We soon shall recover our home.'

and then, how they started on their journey; how, when they came to the shore and were ready to embark and to leave the old country behind, the tears came, but his little wife again sang:

"Away with our sorrow and fear!"

They dried their tears, and were soon on board. By and by a storm came, and all was terror. The captain and sailors gave up all for lost. But the little wife, she was happy, and began to sing:

"Away with our sorrow and fear!"

The captain plucked up courage; the sailors went to the pumps; the storm passed, and all was well. They landed at length; and when they found themselves left in the wilderness, their hearts were sad and heavy; but the little wife, she sang again:

"Away with our sorrow and fear!"

and then they bestirred themselves; built their hut, and soon got over their difficulties. "But," said the old man, "and have you never seen the Shannon?" The family grew up; and then "the little wife" sickened; and while they were around her dying bed, the hymn she loved so well was on her lips, and she died singing:

"Away with our sorrow and fear!
We soon shall recover our home."

Rev. S. W. Christophers.

No. 90.

"THERE IS A FOUNTAIN FILLED WITH BLOOD."

WILLIAM COWPER, 1731—1800.

There was once a man who had been a very great sinner. He had long been in the way of committing all sorts of wickedness. But at last he grew weary of his evil ways, and wanted to become a Christian. But he thought his sins were too great to be forgiven. A Christian man talked and prayed with him. To encourage him he repeated the first verse of this hymn. But the poor man shook his head, and said, "There's nothing in that for me. My sins are too great to be washed away." Then his friend repeated the second verse:

"The dying thief rejoiced to see
That fountain in his day;
And there may I though vile as he,
Wash all my sins away."

"That means me," said the penitent sinner.

While Mr. Ralph Wells was once hurrying to meet a train, a Sunday school teacher hailed him, saying: "I have just come from the hospital, where I found on one of the beds, one of my scholars, a lad who sent for me. I found that he had met with a terrible accident, and had nearly severed both his limbs from his body.

"O teacher!" he said, "I have sent for you. I am glad you have come before I die. I have something to ask of you. I want you to tell me a little more about Jesus."

"Well, my dear boy, have you a hope in Him?"

"Yes, teacher, thank God, I have had it for six months."

"Why, you never said anything to me about it."

"No, I did not, teacher, but I have had it, and I find it

sustains me in this hour. I have only a few minutes to live, and I would like you to sing to me."

"What shall I sing?"

"O, sing:

'There is a fountain filled with blood,
Drawn from Immanuel's veins,
And sinners plunged beneath that flood,
Lose all their guilty stains.' "

The teacher began to sing. The dying lad joined in the song with a sweet smile on his countenance.

"It was that hymn," said he, "among other things, on which my heart rose to Christ."

He then put his arms up and said, "Teacher, bend your head." He bent it down. The dying boy kissed him.

"That is all I have to give you," said he. "Good-by," and he was gone.

Dr. Prime relates that in the Fulton Street prayer meeting, in New York, a man once rose to speak and said, "I bless God for the fountain hymn. Fourteen months ago I was a poor sinner, a very profane man, and a miserable prodigal. I was invited into a meeting where God's people were praying for poor outcasts like me. As I entered, I heard them singing of the "fountain filled with blood," and that song went to my heart. I felt that if ever a man needed cleansing I did, and so I sought the prayers of Christians in my behalf, and I was soon rejoicing in Christ."

Lieutenant G——, an officer in the U. S. Army, having received his death wound in a gallant charge at the head of his regiment, was visited in the hospital by the chaplain, who inquired how he felt. He said he had always been cheerful, and was now ready to meet God in peace. He thus proceeded, "Chaplain, I was once passing through the streets of New York on a Sunday, and heard singing. I went in and saw a company of poor people. They were singing:

'There is a fountain filled with blood.'

I was overpowered with the impression the hymn made upon me, and I gave my heart to God. Since then I have loved Jesus, and I love Him now."

That was his last speech. As the chaplain listened, the voice faltered, and the minister said, "Trust Jesus."

The officer whispered, "I do trust Jesus," and then expired.

During a great revival in Ireland, Belfast had a large share in its blessing. Soon after it began, the curate of the parish visited one of the factories in which two hundred girls were employed. On his entering the building with the manager, a young woman near the door, seeing her minister, began to sing with a very sweet voice:

"There is a fountain filled with blood."

The girl next to her took it up, and so onward it ran down the mill, till all the girls joined with deep and heartfelt fervency. Great as was the noise of the looms, the tender and subduing voice of praise rose above the din and clatter of machinery. They wanted no books to sing through that hymn, it was well known to nearly all there. The manager, a Manchester man, and an infidel, and ever on the watch to make ridicule of religion, was so completely overcome by that outburst of psalmody that he ran out of the mill. Meeting the curate afterwards, he said, "I never was so hard put to it as this morning; it nearly broke me down."

Some time later, singers brought this song to America, and today the message of Silent Night is sung in nearly every language of the world.

The words of this song came to Mr. Moore as he read from his Bible the Christmas story as recorded by Luke. "For unto you is born this day in the city of David, a Saviour, which is Christ the Lord. The words began to swell up into his soul as the full meaning of the birth of Christ came to him clearly and vividly.

written by Audrey H.

[illegible]

[illegible] Christmas [illegible]
[illegible] other [illegible] Joseph Howard [illegible]
[illegible]
[illegible]
[illegible]

[illegible]

THE BIRTH OF SILENT NIGHT

Two friends were talking together one day discussing the fact that a perfect Christmas song had never been written. One of these men was Hans Gruber.

A few days later on Christmas eve in the year 1818 the other man, Joseph Moore, wrote a poem. He showed it to Mr. Gruber, who said, GOD BE PRAISED you have found it - the right song. Immediately Mr. Gruber composed the music for the song now known as SILENT NIGHT.

Aut all did not run as smoothly as it may sound, for on Christmas day Mr. Gruber learned that the church organ would not play. What would Christmas be without music?! To him, music and Christmas went hand-in- hand.

The people began to gather in the church. There was a man present who could pick out some of the tu tunes on the guitar, and he was asked to accompany the congregation in the singing of the new carol.

No. 91.

"OH! WHY SHOULD THE SPIRIT OF MORTAL BE PROUD?"

William Knox, 1789—1825.

This poem was scarcely known until President Lincoln called attention to it. Said President Lincoln, "There is a poem that has been a great favorite with me for years, to which my attention was first called, when a young man, by a friend, and which I afterwards saw, and cut from a newspaper, and carried it in my pocket till by frequent reading I had it by heart." He then repeated eleven verses of this poem.

No. 92.

"JOY TO THE WORLD; THE LORD IS COME!"

Rev. Isaac Watts, 1674—1748.

A hymn book for skeptics was published in England in 1838, entitled "Social Hymns for the use of Friends of the Rational System of Society," sometimes called "Hymns for the New Moral World." It contains no recognition of God; but Nature, Light, and Moral Nature, take His place. The first hymn in that book is a perversion of this hymn. Here is the first stanza:

"Joy to the world! the light is come!
The only lawful King:
Let every heart prepare it room,
And moral nature sing!"

No. 93.

"OH! SAY CAN YOU SEE, BY THE DAWN'S EARLY LIGHT."

FRANCIS SCOTT KEY, 1779—1843.

When Fort McHenry was bombarded by the British fleet in 1814, Mr. Key was, by authority of President Madison, sent to the British fleet under a flag of truce to secure the release of his friend, Dr. Beanes, who had been captured by the enemy and was detained on board the flagship, on the charge of violating his parole. He met General Ross and Admirals Cockburn and Cochrane, and with difficulty secured from them a promise of the gentleman's release, but was at the same time informed that they would not be permitted to leave the fleet until after the proposed attack on Fort McHenry, which the admiral boasted he would carry in a few hours. The ship on which himself, his friend and the commissioner who accompanied the flag of truce were detained, came up the bay and was anchored at the mouth of the Patapsco, within full view of Fort McHenry. They watched the flag of the fort through the entire day with an intense anxiety, until night prevented them from seeing it. During the night they remained on deck, noting every shell from the time it was fired until it fell. While the bombardment continued it was evidence that the fort had not surrendered, but it suddenly ceased some time before day, and, as they had no communication with any of the enemy's ships, they did not know whether the fort had surrendered or the attack had been abandoned. They paced the deck for the rest of the night in painful suspense, watching with intense anxiety for the return of the day. As soon as it dawned, their glasses were turned to the fort, and, with a thrill of delight, they saw that "our flag was still there!" The song was begun on the deck of the vessel, in the fervor of the moment when he saw the enemy hastily retreating to their ships, and looked upon the proud flag he had watched for so anxiously as the morning opened. He had written on the back of a letter some lines, or brief notes, that would aid him in recalling them, and for some of the lines as he proceeded he had to rely on his memory. He finished it in the boat on his way to the shore, and wrote it out as it now stands immediately upon reaching Baltimore. In an hour after it was placed in the hands of the printer, it was on the streets hailed with enthusiasm, and at once took its place as a national song.

No. 94.

"JUST AS I AM WITHOUT ONE PLEA."

MISS CHARLOTTE ELLIOTT, 1799—1871.

After the revolution of 1868 in Spain, when Queen Isabella had fled, one of the first acts of the Central Junta at Madrid, was the proclamation of a bill of rights including religious liberty. Before, it had been unlawful to hold Protestant religious services or to have or read the Bible. But both had been secretly done by the few faithful ones who "obeyed God rather than man." Within a few Sabbaths after the flight of Isabella, the first Protestant service was held in Madrid. The room, an upper chamber, was crowded. The service was an adaptation from the Episcopal prayer book. The singing was congregational. For the solemn musical service of the Roman Catholic Mass was substituted that simple and beautiful hymn:

"Just as I am, without one plea,
But that Thy blood was shed for me,
And that Thou bid'st me come to Thee,
O Lamb of God! I come, I come!"

The melody, one of Luther's grand old tunes, was caught up by many voices. It welled out through the open windows, stopped many a passer-by, and invited him to enter. "Come," it seemed to say, "for all things are now ready." One might imagine it the voice of new Spain proclaiming its allegiance to Him who in all this wonderful revolution is the emancipator of them that were bound.

REV. LYMAN ABBOTT.

Mr. Thomas Atkinson, a delegate of the Christian Commission, tells the following: "The morning after Mr. Moody and I reached Nashville, we stood upon the hotel steps debating whither we should go. Thinking there was no time to be lost, we separated and went in different directions, he going to Hospital No. 3, and I to No. 8. It was my first venture into army work. I scarcely knew what to say or do. Entering the first floor of the large ward, I stood irresolute. Surgeons and nurses were moving hither and thither. A half doubt came to me whether I could do this work which the Lord had put upon me. Suddenly I noticed a man observing me attentively from a distant cot; I turned my eyes away from his, and letting them wander about the room awhile, looked at him again. He was watching me still. Putting up a silent prayer to God, I went to him. His name was John Hays. He had a wife and five children.

"'You seem to be very low, John,' I said.

"'Yes, sir, I am.'

"'Are you a Christian?'

"'No, sir, I'm not, but my wife is. And I was just asking the Lord this morning, to send me some one to tell me how I could get to be like her. When I saw you standing over there, I thought, "Maybe the Lord has heard me. Maybe this is the man he has sent to help me.'"

"The soldier's earnestness, my former indecision, the blessed opening evident, made me strong in faith: 'Yes, John, I am the Lord's messenger; and, moreover, I have come to tell you that you are to become a child of God.'

"'Do you think so, sir? Then thank God for it!'

"I told him of the only way by which he could come to

the cross. He waited as if I were going to say more, but I only asked him if he would accept the offered Atonement.

"'Why, sir,' said he, 'I didn't think that was the way. I thought I had to be sorry a long time—and—and—' and here he stopped because he hardly knew what more to say.

"'Listen,' said I; then I repeated:

"'Just as I am without one plea,
But that Thy blood was shed for me,
And that Thou bid'st me come to Thee,
O Lamb of God, I come, I come'"

"'And will He save me just for nothing at all?'

"'Yes,'" I went on:

"'Nothing in my hand I bring;
Simply to Thy cross I cling;
Naked, come to Thee for dress;
Helpless, look to Thee for grace;
Foul I to the Fountain fly;
Wash me Saviour, or I die!'

"'I never knew it before, sir. I never knew it was so easy. Thank God! Thank God!' There was a nurse standing by. The soldier turned to him and said, 'Nurse, when this gentleman goes away, I want you to write to my wife and tell her that I have found out how to trust Jesus. Thank God! Thank God.' He never faltered for a moment, during the five days that intervened before his death, in his simple, childlike attachment to Christ. At last the morning came when his cot was empty. I asked the nurse about him. Arrangements had been made by the dying man for the prompt transmission of his remains to his home. They were already upon the road. Then I discovered that the nurse had neglected the soldier's request to send a letter. The first intimation to the wife, of her husband's decease, would be the arrival of the casket which contained the body.

It was a sad mistake, but could not be remedied. I wrote her a letter, giving full particulars of her husband's triumphant departure. The answer was one of very precious interest:

" 'O, sir, I didn't think there were any earthly words which could comfort me as did those in your letter. I am afraid I sinned against God yesterday as I stood by my husband's grave. I know I had hard rebellious thoughts. No one knew about them but myself and God. As the minister said, "Earth to earth, ashes to ashes, dust to dust," I almost thought I could stand it no longer. It was hard to be separated from him thus, and to know so little—nothing about how he died. When I got back to the house, your letter was lying on the table. In it I learned that John had found Jesus, and I cried for joy. Children, I said, "dry up your tears. Your father is not dead. He is above in Heaven." Thank God! At the grave the war had seemed to me very cruel and wicked. It is all changed now. I shall meet John again; that is enough. Thank God Who saved my husband.' "

Rev. W. T. Eva, relates that while ministering to the wounded, after the battle of Gettysburg, away in the corner of a shed crowded with wounded, he found a dying man. His limbs were already cold and the death damp was upon his brow. Fellow sufferers were thick enough about him, yet he was dying alone. "He was still conscious when I came to him, not only conscious, but happy in the love of God. I can truly say that nowhere have I witnessed a more triumphant peace than his. We prayed by his side, and then sang:

"Just as I am, without one plea,"

with the chorus:

"Happy day! happy day!
When Jesus washed my sins away."

As we prayed and sang, the Holy Spirit seemed to come down not only upon the dying man, but on all in that dolorous place; and here and there, from among the wounded braves as they lay upon the floor, was uttered aloud the earnest cry, 'God have mercy on my soul!'"

While a pastor in St. Louis, Rev. Dr. McCook was sent for, to see a young lady who was dying of consumption. He soon found that she had imbibed infidelity through the influence of a school teacher, and with her keen intellect was enabled to ward off all the claims of the Gospel. After exhausting all the arguments he could think of during his visits, he was extremely puzzled to know what more to do, as she seemed unshaken in her doubts. She at length seemed so averse to the subject of religion that when he called one day, she turned her face to the wall and seemed to take no notice of him.

Dr. McCook said, "Lucy, I have not called to argue with you another word, but before leaving you to meet the issues of eternity, I wish to recite a hymn." He then repeated with much emphasis the hymn, "Just as I am without one plea," and then bade her adieu. She made no response. He was debating for some time whether, after so much repugnance on her part he should call again. But realizing her nearness to the eternal world he concluded to make one more visit. As he took his seat by her bedside she slowly turned around in bed. Her sunken eyes shone with unwonted luster, as she placed her thin, emaciated hands in his and said slowly, and with much emotion:

"'Just as I am, without one plea,
But that Thy blood was shed for me,
And that Thou bid'st me come to Thee,
O Lamb of God, I come! I come!'

"O sir, I've come. I've come." That hymn told the story. It had decided her eternal destiny. It had done what all the arguments had failed to do. In a few days she crossed the river.

Far out on the western prairies dwelt a father who had not been to Church for fifteen years. After death laid some of his family in the grave, God's still small voice came to him. "All alone," said he, "out there on the prairie, with no Christian teacher or friend, God spoke to me. I then gladly went to hear a missionary preach in a schoolhouse. Was this salvation for me? Could I, so long a wanderer, come and be forgiven? While agitated with these thoughts, they sang:

'Just as I am, without one plea,
But that Thy blood was shed for me.'

and before it was ended I could say: 'O Lamb of God, I come.'"

"The Fulton Street Prayer Meeting has a hymn book of its own. It is not a large volume, and its hymns are among the oldest of our sacred songs. While the voices blend, the hearts blend too, and many a man has been brought to his feet to tell some story of the Lord's goodness and mercy, which the strains of a hymn have recalled. We had been singing the words one day, 'Just as I am, without one plea,' when a stranger arose and said, 'That was the hymn that brought me to Christ. I long felt that I was a sinner, but I thought myself too bad for Jesus, so I endeavored to improve myself a little; the more I tried to make myself better, the worse I seemed to grow. Then I gave up all my attempts in despair. But I heard that hymn sung one day, and it shed light into my heart, and I saw that I was to come to Jesus just as I was. I came—came just as I was—and found pardon. That was a glad day for me.'"

Dr. Prime.

In one of the refuges for poor fallen women, one was admitted who had been brought up a Roman Catholic, but she was most anxious to conceal that fact lest it might lead to her exclusion, for she had neither home nor friends. Her conscience was callous and her prejudices intense; but through the influence of this hymn, she became a humble and penitent believer in the Lord Jesus Christ. It was brought about in this way. There was a short service every week in the chapel of the institution for the inmates; a hymn was sung and prayer offered. On one occasion the minister gave out that touching hymn:

"Just as I am, without one plea,
But that Thy blood was shed for me,"

and, contrary to his custom, read it through, each verse ending,

"O Lamb of God, I come! I come!"

These last words reached her heart, the stone was taken away, the unspeakable love of Jesus, which she had long resisted, softened her into tenderness and deep contrition, and the language of her soul was, "May I, so vile a sinner, come? Does Jesus bid me come? Will He wash my every sin away in His blood?" She doubted no more, but believed.

No. 95.

"WHILE ON THE VERGE OF LIFE I STAND."

Rev. Philip Doddridge, 1702—1751.

This hymn was suggested to the author by a remarkable dream which he had after a conversation with his early friend and patron, Dr. Samuel Clark, on the state of the soul after death. He dreamed that he died, and his spirit soared away into the regions beyond the stars. As he approached the borders of heaven, an angel met him, who conducted him to a beautiful palace which was assigned for his abode. There, in an inner apartment, he saw a golden cup with a large grape vine embossed upon it, which he learned signified the living union of Christ with His people. While he was still talking with the angel, a gentle knock was heard, and before him, through the opening door, he saw the Redeemer. The enraptured disciple fell at the feet of his glorified Lord, but was lifted up with sweet assurance of His favor. Then taking the cup, and first drinking of it Himself, the Savior put it into the hands of His disciple, who declined the honor, but was told, "If thou drink it not, thou hast no part with Me." Then the Savior left him for a time; and looking about him, lo! on the walls were picture illustrations of scenes in his earthly life—scenes of trial, and deliverance, of conflict and victory. A burst of joy broke the enchantment of his celestial dream; and amidst a flood of tears he woke to the consciousness that he was still in the body.

REV. R. T. ROBINSON.

No. 96.

"HOW SAD OUR STATE BY NATURE IS!"

REV. ISAAC WATTS, 1674—1748.

"The way of salvation is perfectly plain to me now," remarked a lady once to her pastor. "The darkness is all gone. Everything is clear to me now. I do not know how or why it is so. But you read a hymn the other night with these words:

'A guilty weak and helpless worm,
On Thy kind arms I fall;
Be Thou my strength and righteousness,
My Jesus and my all!'

I saw then at once that I had nothing to do but to trust in Jesus. I sat all the evening just thinking of those lines. I did not hear your prayer, nor your text, nor a word of your sermon. I thought of nothing but those lines then and ever since. I am so contented and happy. Why, sir, don't you think that the reason why we do not get out of our darkness sooner is that we don't believe?" From that evening on that lady had no difficulty with the way of salvation.

No. 97.

"THOU SON OF GOD, WHOSE FLAMING EYES"—1767.

Rev. Charles Wesley, 1708—1788.

Many years ago a revival was in progress in a little village called Pendeen, near Land's End, England. It happened that at that time there was a little band of men who were great chums, and in a good position in society, in fact they were regarded as influential men in the parish. One evening they were all together at an hotel in the neighboring town of Penzance, and, as men do on such occasions, they were drinking, and talking all kinds of nonsense, and not unfrequently all kinds of profanity. One happened to say, "I wonder what the people are doing just now over at Pendeen?"

Another replied, "I suppose they are all getting converted as fast as possible."

"Well," said one to a third, "I say, Captain B., I will tell you what it is. When I see you converted, I will begin to think there is something in it," and there was a roar of laughter from the whole company at the thought of Captain B's conversion.

The man thus referred to was a mine agent, occupying a very influential position, and a large employer of labor. As the laughter died away, he arose from his seat. His companions did not notice how pale was his cheek. One thought only had flashed across his mind, when he heard his friend's remark, and the roar of laughter which it provoked. It was this, "Is my salvation so utterly hopeless that these worldly men can afford to regard me as they do? Do my companions think me altogether lost—for time and eternity?"

He started up and darted out of the room. The company thought they had offended him. Another moment, and he was in the hotel yard, and crying to the hostler, "Saddle my horse!" He rode to his home as fast as he could ride. His wife could not understand what was wrong with him; he was so agitated. He took no food but immediately set out for the place at which the meetings were being held. He was the last man expected to be seen there. He came boldly forward and took his seat in the front of the congregation, in full view of many whom he was employing. He had overcome his moral cowardice. The preacher gave out the third stanza of this hymn:

"Is there a soul that knows Thee not,
Nor feels his need of Thee,
A stranger to the blood which bought
His pardon on the tree?
Convince him now of unbelief;
His desperate state explain";

As he uttered these last words, "His desperate state explain!" a cry was heard. The Captain was prostrate on his knees, and was sending up the thrilling prayer, before the eyes and ears of all, "God be merciful to me a sinner." It need hardly be told that he went home rejoicing. His conversion moved the whole neighborhood, and was the commencement of the most remarkable work of grace that ever occurred in those parts.

No. 98.

"HOW FIRM A FOUNDATION YE SAINTS OF THE LORD."

At the Fulton Street prayer meeting in New York, a city missionary one day said that he brought with him one day an unconverted man and his wife. They had come to New York on a pitiful errand—to identify the body of a murdered son. As they were without the consolation of the Gospel in this hour of their need and trial, the missionary friend felt deeply for them and induced them to attend the prayer meeting with him. Among the hymns sung was the one commencing with the above lines, and it was sung to the old familiar tune, "Portuguese Hymn." The sorrowing father's heart was touched. He had not heard these words sung for well nigh fifty years, when his mother used to sing them and to the same old tune. He was deeply touched and the missionary hoped not without good results.

Rev. S. I. Prime, D.D.

No. 99.

"AND MUST I BE TO JUDGMENT BROUGHT"—1763.

Rev. Charles Wesley, 1708—1788.

One of the habitual attendants at the Fulton Street prayer meeting, New York, relates that while passing through a down-town street in that city one day, he caught sight of the office of an old employer, and determined to make a call. He found there two young men, who entered the office when they were boys and were only boys when he left. When they saw him, they greeted him as "the old Methodist Captain." He was not a Methodist, he told them, but they persisted that he knew a number of Methodist hymns and must sing them one with a chorus. He did not feel prepared to sing just then, but who could say that this might not be an opportunity to sing home the Gospel to their hearts? So with this thought in his mind he prayed God to direct him, and commenced singing these solemn lines:

"And must I be to judgment brought,
And answer in that day
For every vain and idle thought,
And every word I say?"

At the end of each verse, he sang as a chorus, "The judgment day is rolling round," etc. When he had finished the first verse, he noticed that the young men were very still; at the second the tears were in their eyes; and when the third was sung both seemed deeply moved, and at least one besought him to pray for him.

REV. S. I. PRIME, D.D.

No. 100.

" 'MID PLEASURES AND PALACES THOUGH WE MAY ROAM"—1823.

JOHN HOWARD PAYNE, 1792—1852.

In 1864, a number of Union prisoners of war, who had been paroled, passed over a railroad in Maine on their way to their homes. Among their number, was a blue-eyed, pale-faced boy of not more than seventeen years, whose shoulders seemed scarcely equal to the task of carrying a forty-pound knapsack. For some time he had been looking intently out of the window, and suddenly, as the train was approaching Biddeford, he jumped up and with his face all aglow and eyes sparkling with delight, exclaimed, "Boys, there's my father's chimney." As if by a simultaneous inspiration the soldiers all sprang from their seats and sang, "Home, Sweet Home," and more than one bearded man looked out of the windows as an excuse to hide his tears.

A gentleman, now a Christian minister, relates how the music of a hymn proved the means of his salvation. Having run away as a prodigal from his father's home in Virginia, when a young man, he had had little regard for the broken-hearted parents that he had forsaken, until one Christmas night, when in the fourth story of a Philadelphia hotel, he was awakened by the chiming bells of an Episcopal Church near by. The tune of "Home, Sweet Home," was being played. As in the quiet of the midnight hour the sound of this hymn floated over the city, thoughts of his forsaken home began to echo through the chambers of his soul. A father's plaintive voice, and a mother's streaming eyes seemed to beckon him home again. His pillow soon became wet with tears of penitence. At the repetition of the tune he could no longer remain in bed. His own heart was now yearning for "Home, sweet, sweet home," and soon his hands were packing up to start for home, and not long after his feet were hastening down the flights of stairs, up Chestnut street, down Broad street, and at the Baltimore depot he took the first train of cars for home.

Rev. E. M. Long.

One who had recently returned from a sea voyage relates the following: "On one of the delicious afternoons in February, peculiar to the West Indies, as the sun was declining below the western horizon, the ship lay in a calm near the Island of Cuba. The sea was uncommonly smooth, and the sails lay listless against the masts. The sun was setting, and the whole ocean seemed of liquid gold. At this hour a few of the officers assembled on the forecastle to contemplate the scene; and recalling the joys of other days, to hold that converse which in a small degree alleviates the privations of a seaman's life. The father dwelt in tenderness on his distant family; the brother recalled the unbidden assiduities of a sister's love; and the son felt his heart softened by the recollections of a mother's care. Such was the state of feeling when a clear melodious voice slowly poured forth the first line of that exquisite song, 'Home, Sweet Home!' We had often heard that song, but never had it come so thrillingly as then. The singer continued. As the song drew to a close, his emotion increased with that of every one who listened. At length, as the line, 'There's no place like home,' rose on the stillness of the hour for the last time, a rush of feeling was evident and in many showed itself in tears. Oh! it was good to look on men whom I had considered hardened in iniquity, thus throwing open the flood gates of long pent affections, that they might once more gladden and purify the soul! No one spoke; and after a few moments in which all else was banished by the one dear thought of the distant home we had exchanged for our home on the deep, each one sought his pillow, I doubt not a better and purer man."

No. 101.

"ROCK OF AGES, CLEFT FOR ME."

REV. AUGUSTUS MONTAGUE TOPLADY, 1740—1778.

In how many instances was the precious Gospel brought to the soldiers, in the strains of music set to Psalms and hymns. In camp and hospital, on march and field, the sweet songs of Zion wooed many a prodigal back to the Father's loving embrace. None possibly was more effectual than that familiar hymn, "Rock of Ages." We first heard it sung in the army on the beach at Fortress Monroe, by some delegates of the Christian Commission, just beneath the "Lincoln Gun." Its grateful truth, borne on the winds, fell upon the ears of a soldier on the parapet; not only so, but touched his heart, and in time led him to build on the "Rock of Ages."

Again we heard the same hymn at Yorktown, sung by some of the same delegates. After its singing, as we were returning to our quarters, one of the delegates was overtaken by a soldier, who belonged to the "Lost Children." He asked, "Won't you please tell me how I may build on the 'Rock' you sang about? I was thinking of it while on guard the other day." He told his story in brief: He was from New York City, and received his mother's dying blessing. Before she breathed her last, she sang this hymn, and said, "George, my son, I would not feel so badly about your enlisting, if you were only built upon that 'Rock.'"

These sacred memories were revived by the singing of the hymn; and as the delegate and soldier knelt on the dusty roadside, beneath the stars, the wanderer lost his weariness and thirst for sin, in the shadow of the "Rock of Ages." Eighteen months after this incident, the same delegate, going to Fortress Monroe, on a boat which had as part of her passengers a gay and happy company of the Signal Corps, conversed, sang and prayed with them. He related to them the foregoing incidents, sang "Rock of Ages" and retired to his stateroom. Soon after, a gentle tap called him to the door, where he found a tall, graceful lieutenant, who, with tears streaming down his face, said, "O sir! I could not let you go to bed tonight until I had told you what you have done. As I sat, with my head leaning against a spar, and listened to your words and to that hymn, you brought back my dead mother with all her prayers and love. I have been a wanderer until this night, and now by God's grace I want to hide myself in that 'Rock of Ages.'"

REV. GEORGE BRINGHURST.

Rev. George Bringhurst says, "Passing through the woolen factory at Fredericksburg after the battle, my immense parish of wounded, dying men, I heard a low, mournful voice singing:

> 'While I draw this fleeting breath,
> When mine eyelids close in death,
> When I rise to worlds unknown,
> And behold Thee on Thy throne,—
> Rock of Ages, cleft for me,
> Let me hide myself in Thee.'

There were some pauses in the verse, as if strength were failing the singer. A look, as I passed on my errand, told me that the soldier was dying. Next morning, the last 'fleeting breath' had been drawn, the eyelids were 'closed in death,' and the life that had gone was hid with Christ in God."

After one of the battles of the war of the Rebellion, a chaplain relates, "Afar off, under the machinery of a mill, I heard the voice of singing. It reminded me of Paul and Silas singing their praises in the guarded dungeon. I walked over and leaned upon the ponderous wheel. Near me there rose a voice, sweet and clear, and the holy strains were:

> 'While I draw this fleeting breath.'

But soon the earth receded from the eyes of the soldier-boy, and the lips that gave forth so sweet a strain were still; while the spirit of the man walked in the light of the angels over the crystal pavement of the New Jerusalem."

It was a sultry day in June. The scorching beams of the noonday sun came slanting through the broad, uncurtained windows, falling directly on the operators and sewing girls ranged along the room, making their heads throb and ache almost to bursting. Wearily the machines turned, and the tired eyes of the girls glanced now and then at the clock noting the moments as they dragged heavily by. The calls on the ice cooler had been frequent that morning, and now at one o'clock the water was spent. One after another had gone to it, expecting to get a cooling drink, but had turned away disappointed. The merry song was hushed, the laughing jests were dropped, and tired hands toiled on, longing for the close of the day, that they might find rest and water. Suddenly, in the deep hush, came the sweet low voice of an operator, singing:

"Rock of Ages, cleft for me,
Let me hide myself in Thee."

One after another joined in forgetting their burning thirst, until the whole fifty girls were singing. Grandly the closing stanza rang out:

"Whilst I draw this fleeting breath,
When my eye-strings break in death,
When I soar through tracts unknown,
See Thee on Thy Judgment throne,
Rock of Ages, cleft for me,
Let me hide myself in Thee."

No more sadness, no more weary looks or anxious glances at the clock. Hymn after hymn was sung, and almost too soon came the six o'clock bell."

American Messenger.

A minister in Wales gave the following account of his conversion after the battle of Alma, during the Crimean war, in which he was engaged as a soldier.

"I had," said he, "gone down a hill to get some water. In consequence of the number of men lying dead on the field, the water there was not fit to drink, so I had to go a long way to get some. After getting all I required I retraced my steps to the camp. As I stepped over the bodies now stiff and cold in death, my thoughts wandered to those families in England who were deprived of a father, husband or brother, when all at once the sound of singing floated in the air. I drew near to the place and found a company of soldiers singing in the Welsh language. In the midst of them was a Welsh soldier whose sands of life were nearly gone, and he had requested his comrades to sing:

'Rock of Ages, cleft for me.'

When they sang the last verse:

'Whilst I draw this fleeting breath,
When my eye-strings break in death,'

he lifted his eyes to heaven and faintly exclaimed, 'Sing it again.' They did so. But before they had finished it his soul left the tenement of clay for the home above. The solemn scene had such an effect upon me that I began to see the way of salvation, and am now a minister of the gospel."

During revival services at Calvary Church, Cleveland, Ohio, in 1870, the subject one evening was "The Prodigal Son," and a prodigal had been drawn in from the street. The number of inquirers was great, and crowded the seats set apart for their use so full that this one could not find room and so he fell upon his knees in the aisle. An evening or two later, as he arose to testify how he had been plucked as a brand from the burning, he remarked that he found great difficulty in drowning the echo of the rowdy songs he had been accustomed to sing. "But," said he, "I have succeeded by singing, 'Rock of Ages,' and today I have been kept busy singing it from morning till night."

It was at the death bed, not long ago, of a man who had for many years been living a life of profligacy. For years his friends knew nothing of him, but at last he was taken sick and then he sought his home. His friends received him, attended him with all kindness, and as he lay in that sick bed Jesus came knocking at his heart and he received Him. A few days before his death, I asked him on what his hope was resting. He stretched forth his hand for a hymn book, and with his long, pale, wasted fingers, turned over its leaves, and then handing it to me pointed to one of the hymns, and said, "That is my hope." It was "Rock of Ages, cleft for me."

Rev. E. M. Long.

One Sabbath a poor drunken man walked into a church with a fashionable congregation, and seated himself near the pulpit, at the close of the first hymn. His shabby appearance attracted general observation. The minister had scarcely commenced preaching when the stranger had sunk into a deep sleep and snored aloud, when one of the officers of the church approached to lead him out. "Let him remain," said the minister; "he does not disturb me. Try and bear with him. I hope he may hear some word before he leaves which will persuade him to lead a new life. The man is not in his senses; there is some influence which we do not perceive which has led him here. I believe the Lord sent him."

He continued to sleep on, but more quietly. The pealing of the organ and the singing of the choir at last aroused him. He started in bewilderment and gazed around. It was the old hymn "Rock of Ages," which they were singing. He sat down, buried his face in his hands, and listened to the prayer which followed. The next Sabbath, he was again in church, and soon afterwards, in a prayer meeting, he arose and said he hoped he had become a Christian. On the Sabbath when he first entered the church he had heard the singing, and a voice seemed to bid him enter. He thought it might be the voice of God speaking to him for the last time. Half overcome with drink, and almost in rags, he entered the church. He heard part of the hymn,

"Rock of Ages," the hymn sung by his mother upon her death bed. The prayer which followed seemed meant for him. He resolved to leave off his old habit, and by the grace of God he had kept his resolution. He became a member of the church, and subsequently a deacon. "I do not know," said his pastor, "a man more earnest, or more successful in doing good than he."

G. J. STEVENSON.

No. 102.

"WE'RE TRAVELING HOME TO HEAVEN ABOVE."

One morning, toward the close of July, 1862, Chaplain Henries, passing through the rooms of the hospital at the Navy Yard at Annapolis, placed on the vacant bed of a soldier a single-paged tract entitled, "Will you go?" It was a copy of the hymn bearing that name. Its first lines read:

"We're traveling home to heaven above;
Will you go?
To sing the Savior's dying love;
Will you go?"

Other lines of it read:

"The way to heaven is straight and plain;
Will you go?
Repent, believe, be born again:
Will you go?"

Soon after the soldier came and sat down on his bed. He picked up the hymn, looked at the title, read a few lines of the invitation, and threw it down. Again he picked it up and read a little, then threw it upon the floor. But the invitation he was so unwilling to hear had reached him, through this silent messenger of the Lord. Playing with the tract for awhile with his foot, the soldier picked it up for the third time, and now read it carefully through. It was thrown down no more. The soldier read and reread it, and then holding it thoughtfully awhile in his hand, as if listening to the solemn voice speaking to him, "Will you go?" he drew a pencil from his pocket, and deliberately traced round the margin of the tract these words: "By the grace of God, I will try to go. John Waugh, Company G, 10th Regt. P.R.V.C."

A soldiers' prayer meeting was held that night in the hospital. Waugh came, and when opportunity was given—with his wounded arm in a sling, and the little tract in his other hand—he told his comrades of his conflict with that bit of paper. He read the promise which he had written on the margin, and asked all to pray that he might keep it and never be ashamed of his Savior, adding, "I'm not ashamed of Christ now, but I am ashamed of myself for having been so long ashamed of Him." Some months later he was killed in a skirmish in Virginia.

Rev. R. J. Parvin.

No. 103.

"NEARER MY GOD TO THEE"—1841.

Mrs. Sarah Flower Adams, 1805—1849.

At the siege of Fort Donelson, in 1862, a young soldier was wounded, and left by his comrades, who pressed on in the battle. When they returned, they found him resting against a tree, dead, with a hymn book open in his hand at this hymn:

"Nearer my God to Thee, nearer to Thee."

The story is told of a girl who had been very sick and whose disease had affected her eyes, so that she had to be kept in a dark room and it was feared she might lose her sight. She could not believe it possible that so dread a calamity could overtake her. While alone, one Sabbath day, she said to herself, "The Bible says we are not tried above that we are able to bear, and I could not endure that. Oh! no, I shall not be blind."

While musing thus a low sweet voice near her said: "Sister, may I come in?"

"Why, yes, if you want to."

"I want to recite my hymn to you; it is some new verses to 'Nearer my God, to Thee,' and I like them so much."

"Well, dear, say them; I don't mind."

"If where they led my Lord,
I, too be borne,
Planting my steps in His,
Weary and worn—
May the path carry me
Nearer my God, to Thee,
Nearer to Thee!"

"That's not for me," thought the sick girl, "it means the old-time martyrs." She tried to shake off the feeling. How could the dark path bring her nearer to God? But the childish voice continued:

"If Thou the cup of pain
Givest to drink,
Let not my trembling lips
From the draught shrink;
So by my woes to be
Nearer my God to Thee,
Nearer to Thee!"

"Never mind finishing it, sister, my head aches, and I want to be alone."

Once the thin, white hand was raised as if to dash the "cup of pain" from her lips. Days passed. As her strength came back the inflammation in her eyes decreased. She no longer spoke of her hopes and fears. She looked more and more calmly at her cross. The path, though dark, had one ray of light, which, if followed, must bring her to her Savior, for it came from Him. One day she cried, "O mamma! I cannot wait; let the light in now," but her mother said, "Have patience, darling; the noonday is too bright; I will promise you to let the morning sun into your room."

All day long she waited, her lips moving in prayer. The morning dawned. "Open the blinds wide, mamma; let in all the light you can before you take off the bandage."

She turned toward the window; on her bare arms she felt the warm sun and morning breeze, but no light came to her eyes.

"Mamma, mamma, why are you so silent? Is the room light?"

Her mother's low pained voice answered, "My darling, the sun shines in your face." She sank upon her knees; the clasped hands were uplifted, as if reaching for something unattainable; the face quivered with inward anguish; but the expression of her sightless eyes was more beautiful than in their days of vision they had ever been. As her mother bent over her she heard the pale lips whisper:

> "So by my woes to be
> Nearer my God, to Thee,
> Nearer to Thee."

A writer in the Nashville *Christian Advocate*, January, 1878, relates the following reminiscence of Bishop Marvin: "The bishop, at a prayer meeting he had conducted, stated that he had recently been traveling in the wilds of Arkansas, his mind oppressed, and his heart sad. He had been driven from his family and home by the invading foe, and could not hear of their welfare, and it seemed to him that clouds and darkness had completely enveloped him. In this state of heart he approached an old log cabin in a very dilapidated condition. As he drew nearer he distinguished the sound of some female singing:

'Nearer my God to Thee.'

He at once alighted and went in, for the sound seemed to enter his very soul. He there found the singer, a poor old widow woman, in the midst of poverty, but who was happy in spite of her loneliness and want. He felt and said that if an old widow in such want could sing such a song, that certainly he could. He gave to the wind his fears, his full confidence in an overruling Providence was brought into lively exercise, and from that day he went on singing:

'Nearer my God, to Thee.'

This simple personal narrative made a deeper impression on my mind, than even the rich sermons he preached, and with which I was delighted."

No. 104.

"WHEN I CAN READ MY TITLE CLEAR."

REV. ISAAC WATTS, 1674—1748.

At the battle of Shiloh a Christian Captain was shot through both thighs with a rifle bullet, a wound from which he could not recover. While lying on the field, he suffered intense agony from thirst. He supported his head upon his hand, while the rain was falling around him. In a little time, quite a pool of water collected in the hole made by his elbow. If he could only get to that puddle he could quench his thirst. He tried to get into a position to suck up a mouthful of muddy water, but was unable to quite reach it. Said he, "I never felt such disappointment before —so needy, so near, and yet so helpless. By-and-by night fell, and the stars shone out clear and beautiful above the dark field; and I began to think of the great God, Who had given His Son to die a death of agony for me, and that He was up there—up above the scene of suffering, and above those glorious stars; and I felt that I was going home to meet Him, and praise Him there; and that I ought to praise Him, here in my wounds and in the rain, and I began to sing with my parched lips:

'When I can read my title clear
To mansions in the skies,
I'll bid farewell to every fear,
And wipe my weeping eyes.'

There was a Christian brother in the brush near me. I could not see him, but I could hear him. He took up the strain; and beyond him another and another caught it up, all over the battlefield of Shiloh; and long into the night the echo was resounding, as we made the field of battle ring with hymns of praise to God." A writer in one of the magazines thus threw the story into song:

"Through the terror of the stillness,
Through the anguish of the moans,
Come the words, half sung, half whispered,
In exultant, hopeful tones,
'When I can read my title clear
To mansions in the skies.'
Heads are lifted, groans are stifled,
Wounded men forget their pain,
E'en the dying wait to listen
To that sweet and holy strain:
'I'll bid farewell to every fear,
And wipe my weeping eyes.'

Dying men smile as they sing it
With their last drawn earthly breath,
And their souls go out in music
To the shadow land of death,"
'Let cares like a wild deluge come,
And storms of sorrow fall,
May I but safely reach my home,
My God, my heaven, my all!' "

No. 105.

"HOW SWEET THE NAME OF JESUS SOUNDS."

REV. JOHN NEWTON, 1725—1807.

Major Whittlesey, of Gen. Howard's staff, tells of a chaplain who had been very attentive to a wounded soldier for several days, trying, if possible, to save his limb. It was decided that the leg must be taken off. The soldier was anxious that his chaplain should be present during the operation, but he felt as if he could not bear the sight. So, when the suffering man was put upon a stretcher and borne to the amputating table, the chaplain remained behind. How surprised and electrified was he, as he waited sadly for the result, to hear the voice of his friend sounding forth from the room of pain, singing those precious lines:

"How sweet the name of Jesus sounds
In a believer's ear!
It soothes his sorrows, heals his wounds
And drives away his fear."

No. 106.

"JESUS, LOVER OF MY SOUL."

REV. CHARLES WESLEY, 1708—1788.

Rev. Norman Fox, chaplain of the Seventy-seventh New York regiment tells the following story of the evening after the battle of Rappahannock Station: "I found a young man of the Tenth Massachusetts Regiment with his leg crushed and mangled by a piece of shell. The shock had been so severe that amputation was useless, and he was sinking rapidly. I inquired concerning his religious history. It was the old story—a bright hope, active church membership, army life and irregularities, and the abandonment of his profession. 'And now,' said he, 'if there can be forgiveness for such a wanderer, pray for me.'

"I confess I felt more backwardness than was right. There stood a circle of rough soldiers surveying the solemn scene with mere morbid curiosity. There stood another group, more educated and refined—a knot of surgeons, some of whom, I knew, had no belief in God or eternity, and considered my interview with the dying man as at best but amiable uselessness. But there lay the sinking sufferer, and I wore the uniform of a minister of Christ. Bending over the table where he lay, I asked the Good Shepherd to pardon the returning wanderer. Murmured responses throughout the prayer disclosed his own earnestness in the petition; the smothered hope revived again; and faint at first but growing brighter and brighter, there finally beamed on him the full radiance of that faith which supports in the stern hour. Meanwhile there stood by the table a noble looking soldier, a little older than the dying man, moistening the lips of the latter, affectionately smoothing his hair, but so perfectly calm and collected that I supposed he was only a hospital attendant. A casual remark startled my suspicion, and I asked him, 'Is he a friend of yours?'

"He answered, 'It is my younger brother.'

"Stooping over him, the brother said, 'What shall I tell mother for you?'

" 'Tell her I died for my country,' was the prompt cheery reply.

" 'Give me a kiss for her,' said the other; and the bronzed face bowed down to the pale lips as tenderly as if they had been an infant's. More than one turned aside to hide his tears; the brothers seemed least moved of all. The dying boy sank rapidly, but all clouds vanished, and faith grew bright and strong. I repeated, 'I know that my Redeemer liveth,' 'The Lord is my Shepherd,' 'In my Father's house are many mansions,' the hymn 'Rock of Ages, cleft for me,' and those lines, especially dear when the couch of dissolution was a rough board table in a dark, cold tent, with only a knapsack to rest the head upon:

> "Jesus can make a dying bed
> Feel soft as downy pillows are.'

He tried to repeat:

> 'Jesus, lover of my soul;'

I finished it for him. This hymn seemed to strengthen him even more than the others. But his voice was already beginning to fail. Said he, 'There's a—silver—pencil—in—my pocket—' It was with the deepest regret that we saw that he could not speak friendship's last message. There was but one Friend of Whom he could speak now. We watched him silently, while he lay for some minutes motionless; I thought all was over; but rousing suddenly, he said, 'Jesus, Lover of my soul;'—Oh! repeat that again!' My voice choked up so that I could hardly speak. I know not if he heard me, for before I reached the last verse, 'the storm of life' was over, 'the haven' was reached, and 'the billows' had died away in the eternal peace."

A minister in America, who was a stranger to the church, was on a certain occasion, called to officiate in a cold and dreary church. When he entered it, the wind howled, and loose clapboards and window shutters clattered. The pulpit stood high above the first floor; there was no stove, but a few persons in the church, and they beating their hands and feet to keep them from freezing. He asked himself: "Can I preach? Of what use can it be? What shall I do? If I read a hymn, can these two or three in the gallery sing?" He concluded to make the trial, and read:

"Jesus lover of my soul."

"They commenced," said the preacher, "and the sound of a single female voice has followed me with an indescribably pleasing sensation ever since, and probably will while I live. The voice intonation, articulation, and expression seemed to be perfect. I was warmed inside and out, and for the time was lost in rapture." The minister preached with unusual freedom and success, and learned never to be discouraged by unfavorable appearances.

A chaplain in the United States Army, one morning found Tom, the drummer boy, a great favorite with all the men, and whom, because of his sobriety and religious example, they called "The young deacon," sitting under a tree. At first he thought him asleep, but as he drew near, the boy lifted up his head, and he saw tears in his eyes.

"Well, Tom, my boy, what is it; for I see your thoughts are sad? What is it?"

"Why, sir, I had a dream last night, which I can't get out of my mind."

"What was it?"

"You know that my little sister Mary is dead—died when ten years old. My mother was a widow, poor but good. She never seemed like herself afterward. In a year or so she died too; and then I having no home and no mother, came to the war. But last night I dreamed the war was over, and I went back to my old home, and just before I got to the house, my mother and little sister came out to meet me. I didn't seem to remember they were dead. How glad they were! and how my mother, in her joy, pressed me to her heart! Oh! sir, it was just as real as you are real now!"

"Thank God, Tom, that you have such a mother, not really dead, but in heaven, and that you are hoping, through Christ, to meet her again."

The boy wiped his eyes and was comforted. The next day there was terrible fighting, Tom's drum was heard all day long here and there. Four times, the ground was swept and occupied by the contending armies. But as the night came on both paused, and neither dared to go on the field, lest the foe be there. Tom, "the young deacon," it was known, was wounded and left on the battlefield. His company encamped near by. In the evening, when the noise of the battle was over, and all was still, they heard a voice singing, away off on the field. They felt sure it was Tom's voice. Softly and beautifully the words floated on the wings of the night air:

"Jesus, lover of my soul,
Let me to Thy bosom fly,
While the nearer waters roll,
While the tempest still is high!
Hide me, O, my Savior, hide,
Till the storm of life is past;
Safe into the haven guide,
O receive my soul at last!

"Other refuge have I none;
Hangs my helpless soul on Thee:
Leave, O, leave me not alone,
Still support and comfort me;"

The voice stopped here, and there was silence. In the morning the soldiers went out, and found Tom sitting on the ground, and leaning against a stump—dead!

Sunday School Times.

About twenty years ago, on a winter's night, a heavy gale set in upon the precipitous, rock-bound coast near the British Channel. A little coasting vessel struggled bravely, but in vain, with the tempest. One dark, fearful headland could not be weathered—the bark must go ashore. Then came the last desperate effort of the captain and his ship's crew. Their toiling at the oars was soon over, their boat was soon swamped. They were supposed to have all sunk together; for, in the morning, they were all found lying side by side upon a reedy rock. On visiting the wreck, and going below to the cabin, there was found lying on the table the captain's hymn book, opened at the page containing the hymn:

> "Jesus, lover of my soul,
> Let me to Thy bosom fly,
> While the nearer waters roll,
> While the tempest still is high."

A fine, intelligent Virginia young man, while residing in the west, became an infidel and a blasphemer of the name of God. From this state he was delivered by reading the work of Soame Jenyns; but while he acquiesced in the truth of revelation, he did not yet feel its power. He was attacked by a lingering and fatal disease, which led him to reflection and prayer, but often made it difficult for him to converse. Three Christian friends sometimes visited him, to beguile the tedious hours by singing. They one day entered the room, and, almost without any previous remarks, began the hymn:

> "There is a fountain filled with blood."

He then said to them, "There is nothing I so delight to hear as the first hymn you ever sung to me:

'Jesus, lover of my soul!' "

They began to sing it to the tune of "Martin," and soon the solemnity which had reigned in the little circle while singing the former hymns began to be changed to weeping. They struck the touching strains of the second stanza, and the weeping became loud; the heart of him who had reviled Christ broke, and they feared that to sing the remaining stanzas, would be more than he could bear. When singing in his room a few days after, he said, "I don't think I shall ever hear 'Jesus, lover of my soul' sung again; it so excites me that my poor body cannot bear it."

G. J. Stevenson.

A party of Sunday school teachers and scholars went out one summer's day for a trip on Lake Winnepesaukee. Quite suddenly there broke over them the most terrific storm of wind, rain, lightning, and thunder ever known by the captain of the boat in an experience of twenty-five years. Terror now took possession of nearly all, as well it might. In a confusion amounting almost to a panic, all rushed for the ship's hold. Happening to be among the last to leave the deck, and standing about midway on the stairs, we witnessed a scene such as we had never beheld before, and never wish to experience again. Women were crying and fainting, children were frantic with fright, and strong men stood pale and trembling. We tried to inspire calmness and composure, but to very little purpose. Then we sang:

"Jesus, lover of my soul,
Let me to Thy bosom fly."

The lightning's flash seemed almost to envelop us in a sheet of flame, and the thunders seemed to shake the earth and the sea. And then we sang:

"Other refuge have I none;
Hangs my helpless soul on Thee!"

The gallant boat, in whose palpitating bosom we had taken refuge, met the storm bravely, but the gale was too mighty; she was beaten back by the buffeting waves and winds, and imperilled by hidden rocks; and then we sang:

"Thou, O Christ, art all I want;
More than all in Thee I find."

But the heart of the hurricane began to be touched, and the winds to relent; the lightning had a softer glare, and the thunder fell more tenderly on our ears; and then there was a calm. The hurricane had sped on with its accompaniment of flood and terror, and left us out in the clear sunshine. The singing saved us from a panic, and, saved from that, we were saved from consequences we dared not contemplate. The twilight found us all safe at our homes.

G. J. Stevenson.

No. 107.

"SWEET WAS THE TIME WHEN FIRST I FELT."

Rev. John Newton, 1725—1807.

A delegate of the Christian Commission relates that during the gloomy time of the siege of Chattanooga, he was riding down Waldorn's Ridge, on his way to Bridgeport. "The day was cold and wet, everything disheartening. It seemed probable that we were about to abandon Chattanooga, and that this would be my last trip over the mountains. Depressed with these thoughts and chilled with the rain, I jogged along alone, until I overtook a cavalry man riding solitarily, and seemingly as low in spirits as myself. As I came abreast of him, so as to look into his face, I saw his eyes were full of tears. In our conversation I let fall a word of Christian experience, when he turned to me in an earnest way, and said, 'Then you are a Christian. Perhaps you can help me out of my difficulty?' I expressed my readiness to do anything I could.

"'I was just trying to repeat the first verse of a blessed old hymn which I have been singing for years, but somehow that fourth line I can't get hold of this morning:

"Sweet was the time when first I felt
The Savior's pardoning Blood
Applied to cleanse my soul from guilt,—"

Now there's where I'm stopped; what's the next line?'

"I finished it up for him:

'And bring me home to God.'"

"'That's it; thank you,' said he; 'that's it. I wonder I could have forgotten it.'

"'You looked troubled,' said I, 'when I first saw you; your tears couldn't have been over the loss of that fourth line?' 'Oh, no,' he replied; 'it was the other three lines that brought the tears. I was thinking of the time of my conversion, and of the many times when I have "felt the pardoning Blood" since that day.'"

No. 108.

"IN THE CHRISTIAN'S HOME IN GLORY."

REV. SAMUEL YOUNG HARMER, 1809—.

Rev. Horace C. Hovey, relates the following incident which occurred after the battle of Fredericksburg: "A brave cavalry officer was dying of his wounds. He was delirious when I approached him. He imagined himself on the field at the head of his gallant men, and fancied that a heavy gun was just in front of them ready to be fired.

His distress was great. At length he thought the gun had been discharged, and his men, badly cut up, were retreating. Here I interposed, saying, 'There is no gun there; you are safe among friends here in Fredericksburg.'

'Let me alone,' he sternly replied; 'I must recover my command and renew the attack.'

'No,' said I, ' let us not talk of battle-scenes. You are soon to die. Let us talk of Jesus. The mention of that Name seemed to exert the powerful influence I had often heard ascribed to it. His agitation ceased at once; his delirium passed away; a smile lit up his pallid features. After a moment's silence he said, in a low sweet voice, 'Jesus! Jesus! It is He Who said, "Come unto Me, all ye that labor and are heavy laden, and I will give you rest." I am weary; can you sing:

"There is rest for the weary?" '

"I complied with his wishes, and with failing, faltering tongue, he tried to join in the song:

"In the Christian's home in glory
There remains a land of rest."

We sang the hymn entirely through, and when we closed there was not a dry eye in all that ward. He died soon after this, saying for his last words, 'I have no father here but my Heavenly Father.' "

No. 109.

"MINE EYES HAVE SEEN THE GLORY OF THE COMING OF THE LORD."

Mrs. Julia Ward Howe, 1819—1910.

Chaplain McCabe was confined in Libby Prison when the news of the battle of Gettysburg was received there.

He tells how the prisoners received it: "I had a relative in Richmond, a staunch rebel. The day they received the first tidings from Gettysburg he came to see me, his face wreathed in smiles, saying: 'Have you heard the news?'

"'What news?'

"'Forty thousand Yankee prisoners on their way to Richmond!'

"I was astounded. In dumb amazement I listened to the Rebel officers speculating where the new prisoners should be stowed away and how they were to be fed. I went up stairs and told the news. Despondency settled down into every heart. That night, as we assembled for 'family prayers' and sang, as was always our wont, the long metre Doxology, it trembled out from quivering lips up to Him Who has said, 'Glorify ye Me in the fires.' We felt we were so doing that night, if never before.

"I slept none that night, listening wearily to the watch calling the hours and singing out as he did so, 'All's well.' When the day broke I waited for the footsteps of 'Old Ben,' a character well known to every inmate of Libby. He was the prison news agent and sold papers at twenty-five cents apiece. At last his footfall came. He pushed the door ajar, looked round for a moment upon the sleepers, and then raising up his arms, shouted, 'Great news in de paper!'

"Did you ever see a resurrection? I never did but once. Oh, how those men sprang to their feet; and what was the news? The telegraph operator at Martinsburg, when putting those cyphers to the four, had clicked his instrument once too often. There was a mistake of only thirty-six thousand! More yet! Lee was driven back; the Potomac was swollen; the pontoons were washed away! I have stood by when friends long parted meet again with raining tears and fond embrace, but never did I witness such joy as swept into those strong men's faces, where the deepest sorrow sat but a moment before. Well, what did we do? Why, we sang as saved men do; sang till Captains Flynn and Sawyer, immured in the lowest dungeon below and doomed to die within ten days, heard us and wondered; sang till the very walls of Libby quivered with the melody as five hundred of us joined in the chorus of Mrs. Julia Ward Howe's 'Battle Hymn of the Republic':

'Mine eyes have seen the Glory of the coming
of the Lord;
He is trampling out the vintage where the
grapes of wrath are stored;
He hath loosed the fateful lightning of His
terrible, swift sword;
His truth is marching on.' "

No. 110.

"O, FOR A CLOSER WALK WITH GOD."

WILLIAM COWPER, 1731—1800.

A gay and thoughtless young lady left her home on a pleasure-seeking tour to a fashionable watering place. She arrived safely, but found amid the ceaseless hilarity, "an aching void within." Being seated near an open window, she heard the soft, smooth voice of a servant girl as it warbled forth the words of the hymn:

"O, for a closer walk with God
A calm and heavenly frame;
A light to shine upon the road
That leads me to the Lamb!"

As she listened her soul was drawn out in prayer with the words she heard:

"The dearest idol I have known,
Whate'er that idol be,
Help me to tear it from Thy throne,
And worship only Thee."

She wept tears of penitence, trusted in Christ, and rejoiced in peace.

No. 111.

"ONE SWEETLY SOLEMN THOUGHT"—1852.

Miss Phoebe Cary, 1824—1871.

In Macao, China, near Hong Kong, the principal occupation of the inhabitants is gambling. Here, on a certain occasion, a traveler found a company of gamblers in a back room on the upper floor of a hotel. At the table nearest him, there was an American, about twenty-five years old, playing with an old man. They had been betting and drinking. While the gray-haired man was shuffling the cards for a new deal, the young man, in a swaggering careless way, sang, to a very pathetic tune, the words of the hymn:

"One sweetly solemn thought
Comes to me o'er and o'er,
I'm nearer my home today
Than I've ever been before;"

Hearing the singing, several gamblers looked up in surprise. The old man, who was dealing the cards, putting on a look of melancholy, stopped for a moment, gazed steadfastly at his partner in the game, and then dashed the whole pack of cards on the floor under the table. Then said he, "Where did you learn that tune?"

The young man pretended that he did not know that he had been singing.

"Well, no matter," said the old man, "I've played my last game, and that's the end of it. The cards may lie till doomsday, and I will never pick them up." The old man, having won money from the young man, about one hundred dollars, took it out of his pocket, and handing it to the young man said: "Here, Harry, is your money; take it and do good with it. I shall with mine." As the traveler followed them down stairs, he saw them conversing by the doorway, and overheard enough to know that the old man was saying something about the song which the young man had sung.

No. 112.

"AND AM I ONLY BORN TO DIE?"

REV. CHARLES WESLEY, 1708—1788.

A nobleman of great wealth, whose pleasure was drawn from his riches, his honors and friends, had a daughter, who was the idol of his heart. She was highly accomplished, amiable in her disposition, and winning in her manners. At length she attended a Methodist meeting in London, was awakened, and soon happily converted. Afterward, to her the charms of Christianity were overpowering. The change was marked by her fond father with great solicitude, and was to him occasion of deep grief. He took her on long and frequent journeys, and attended her in the most engaging manner, in order to divert her mind from religion; but she still maintained her integrity as a Christian. After failing in all his projects, he introduced her into company under such circumstances that she must either join in the recreation of the party or give high offense. It had been arranged among his friends that several young ladies should, on the approaching festive occasion, give a song, accompanied by the piano. The hour arrived, the party assembled. Several pieces had been performed to the great delight of the company, who were now in high spirits. At last she was herself called on for a song, and many hearts beat high in hope of victory. Should she decline, she was disgraced. Should she comply, their triumph was complete. This was the moment to seal her fate. With perfect self-possession, she took her seat, ran her fingers over the keys and commenced playing and singing, in a sweet air, the following verses of the above hymn:

"No room for mirth or trifling here,
For worldly hope or worldly fear,
If life so soon is gone;
If now the Judge is at the door,
And all mankind must stand before
The inexorable throne!

"No matter which my thoughts employ,
A moment's misery or joy;
But O! when both shall end,
Where shall I find my destined place?
Shall I my everlasting days
With fiends or angels spend?"

She arose from her seat. The whole party was subdued. Not a word was spoken. Her father wept aloud. One by one the company left the house. The father never rested till he became a Christian. He lived an example of Christian benevolence, having given to various enterprises, up to the time of his death, nearly half a million dollars.

No. 113.

"ALMOST PERSUADED NOW TO BELIEVE."

PHILIP BLISS, 1838—1876.

During the winter of 1873-1874 Mr. P. P. Bliss was urged by Mr. D. L. Moody and other friends to give up his business and devote his life to singing the Gospel. There was much prayer and much hesitation on his part about taking such a step. He doubted his ability to be useful in the work.

At the same time Major D. W. Whittle was being urged to do the same thing. He says concerning it, "A solemn providence that occurred at this time and very deeply impressed both of us, is linked in the chain that drew us into the work. A friend received a telegram announcing the drowning of his four children in the loss of the *Ville de Havre.* His wife, who was with the children, had been saved, and sent the dispatch. He left at once for Europe to bring home his wife, and upon his return, he urged the matter upon us so as to lead us both to regard it as probable that we should respond to the call. Shortly after our friend's return, and while we were still undecided, we were invited to hold some meetings at Waukegan, Illinois, and agreed to go there for three or four evenings as an experiment. If the Lord blessed us and souls were converted, we would take it as indicating His will, and that He called us into the work. The first evening meeting was not an encouraging one, as to attendance, and had no marked result, except the very powerful impression upon our minds that the Lord was with us. The next day it rained, and we looked for a still smaller audience, but it was twice as large. Before the meeting closed, there were blessed indications of the work of the Holy Spirit, upon the people. The place became very solemn, and as Bliss sang 'Almost Persuaded,' every word seemed filled with power. In different parts of the house, sinners arose as he sang, presenting themselves for prayer, and souls that night rejoiced in Christ. Our hearts were very full, and a great responsibility was upon us. The next afternoon we met and spent some hours in prayer. Bliss made a formal surrender of everything to the Lord; gave up his musical conventions; gave up his writing of secular music; gave up everything, and placed himself, with any talent he might have at the disposal of the Lord." And this hymn marks the turning point in its author's own life as well as in that of many others.

No. 114.

"HO! MY COMRADES SEE THE SIGNAL."

PHILIP BLISS, 1838—1876.

During October, 1864, just before Sherman began his famous march to the sea, while his army lay camped in the neighborhood of Atlanta, the army of Hood in carefully prepared movement passed the right flank of Sherman's army, and gaining his rear, commenced the destruction of the railroad leading north, burning block houses, and capturing the small garrisons along the line. Sherman's army was put in rapid motion, following Hood, to save the supplies and larger posts, the principal of which was located at Altoona Pass, a defile in the Altoona range of mountains, through which ran the railroad. General Corse, of Illinois, was stationed here with a brigade of troops, in all about fifteen hundred men. A million and a half of rations were stored here, and it was highly important that the earthworks commanding the Pass and protecting the supplies should be held. Six thousand men were detailed by Hood to take the position. The works were completely surrounded and summoned to surrender, General Corse refused, and sharp fighting commenced. The defenders were slowly driven into a small fort upon the crest of the hill. Many had fallen, and the result seemed to render a prolongation of the fight hopeless. At this moment, an officer caught sight of a white signal flag, far away across the valley, twenty miles distant upon the top of Kenesaw Mountain. The signal was answered, and soon the message was waved across from mountain to mountain: "Hold the Fort; I am coming. W. T. Sherman." Cheers went up; every man was nerved to the full appreciation of the position; and, under a murderous fire, which killed or wounded more than half the men in the fort, they held the position for three hours, until the advance guard of Sherman's army came up, and the enemy were obliged to retreat. Mr. Bliss heard this incident related as an illustration of the inspiration derived by the Christian from the thought of Christ as our Commander, and of His coming to our relief. The song was at once suggested to his mind and soon written.

No. 115.

"I HAVE A SAVIOR, HE'S PLEADING IN GLORY."

PHILIP BLISS, 1838—1876.

In 187-, Mr. Bliss, in company with Mr. Whittle, held a series of revival meetings in Jackson, Michigan. At the closing meeting, after the sermon, Mr. Bliss sang this hymn, with its sweet refrain, "For you I am praying, I'm praying for you." As was his habit in singing this hymn, he made it his own prayer, and while he sang, more than a hundred arose asking for prayer. Sometimes in singing this hymn, Mr Bliss added a verse not given in the collections.

"And Jesus is calling, how can you reject Him?
He says He loves sinners so then He loves you.
O, friend, do believe it, arise and accept Him,
Give Jesus your heart while I'm praying for you."

No. 116.

"'TIS THE PROMISE OF GOD FULL SALVATION TO GIVE."

PHILIP BLISS, 1838—1876.

While holding meetings at Peoria, Illinois, a little German boy of eight years was converted and interested Mr. Bliss greatly. After Mr. Bliss' death the following letter was received by Major Whittle:

Peoria, Illinois,
January 27.

Dear Brother Whittle:

I saw a piece in the *Standard* of you and Mr. Bliss. I saw that you and the Rev. Mr. Morgan, of London, were getting up a book of the life of Mr. and Mrs. Bliss, and wanted to have letters from those who have been blessed or converted by his songs. I can say that I was converted when they were singing the second hymn, "Hallelujah, 'tis done." In singing the chorus of it, I thought, "Do I believe on the Son?" and so, as you gave the first invitation for all that were not Christians and wanted to be prayed for to rise, and then asked how many wanted to settle it now to rise, I was among that lot that rose as there were forty or fifty, you said. I saw five or six that rose that were right behind me. I attended all of Mr. Bliss' children's meetings, as also I attended all of yours. It was Thanksgiving night, at the Centennial Hall, in which I was converted I expect you to know me. I am eight years old. I remain, as ever, your friend.

William B. Herschberger.

This hymn has a curious origin. In compiling "Gospel Songs" in 1874, Mr. Bliss desired to use in it the well-known hymn, "Hallelujah! Thine the glory," then much used in religious services, but the owners of the copyright declined to give their consent, and "Hallelujah; 'tis done" was written to supply the want. Hundreds of souls have been led by this hymn to decide for Christ, and the church has reason to rejoice at that refusal.

No. 117.

"I AM SO GLAD THAT OUR FATHER IN HEAVEN."

PHILIP BLISS, 1838—1876.

At one of the revival meetings held by Moody and Sankey at Edinburgh, Scotland, a gay giddy girl attended. She went late and was unable to get a seat, so she wandered about in the hall outside. Inside the church they were singing, led by Mr. Sankey:

"I am so glad that Jesus loves me
Jesus loves me, Jesus loves me."

The words went to her heart and her conscience, and she said, "I cannot sing that." When that meeting broke up, she went to the meeting for anxious inquirers, and is now a rejoicing Christian.

A missionary of the American Sunday School Union in Missouri, after he had organized a Sunday School, sang to them this hymn, with the chorus:

"I am so glad that Jesus loves me,"

and followed it with the question, "Are you glad? If not, why?" He had hardly finished when a young man arose, and rushing up to him, threw his arms around his neck, sobbing, "Oh, sir, you must not leave here till I'm a Christian!" Prayer was offered for him, and he was saved. Then he exclaimed, "Oh, that song! I could not get away from it, and it has saved me."

D. W. WHITTLE.

A young woman in England went to a meeting where she heard Mr. Sankey sing this hymn, with the chorus:

"I am so glad that Jesus loves me,"

and while the hymn was being sung, began for the first time in her life to feel that she was a sinner. All her sins came up in array before her; and so numerous and aggravated did her sins appear, that she imagined she could never be saved. She said in her heart, "Jesus cannot love me. He could not love such a sinner as I." She went home in a state of extreme mental anguish, and did not sleep that night. Every opportunity of obtaining more light was eagerly seized. She took her place in the inquiry room. There she found to her astonishment and joy that Jesus could, did, does love sinners. She saw in God's opened Word that it was for sinners Jesus died, and for none others. When she realized this, she too began to sing:

"I am so glad that Jesus loves me,
Jesus loves even me."

Mr. Sankey relates that soon after he began teaching some children's singing classes in Chicago, a lady called on him one day and said, "There is a little singing girl belonging to one of your classes who is dying. She wants you to go and see her." Mr. Sankey says, "I went to her home—a little frame cottage—and there I found a little maid dying—one whom I had known so well in the Thursday evening meetings. I said, 'My dear child, how is it with you?'

" 'Will you pray for my father and mother as you pray for us?' was the reply.

" 'But how is it with yourself?' I again asked.

" 'Oh, sir,' she answered, 'they tell me I am about to die, but I have found the Lord Jesus Christ.'

" 'When did you become a Christian?" I inquired.

" 'Don't you remember one Thursday when you were teaching me to sing:

"I am so glad that Jesus loves me,
Jesus loves me, Jesus loves me";

and don't you remember how you told us that if we only gave our hearts to Him, He would love us?—and I gave mine to Him.'"

No. 118.

"I GAVE MY LIFE FOR THEE, MY PRECIOUS BLOOD I SHED."

FRANCIS R. HAVERGAL, 1838—1876.

During a Western Sunday School convention, there arose a cry of dissatisfaction, "A ring! A ring!" The strange and false charge was made that the managers were conducting the convention according to some arranged scheme. Quite a discordant excitement ensued, during which a distinguished singer who was present was called on to sing. He sang:

"I gave My life for thee,
My precious blood I shed
That thou might'st ransomed be,
And quickened from the dead;
All this I did for thee—
What hast thou done for Me?"

Through the song Christ seemed to whisper to the discordant convention, "Peace, be still," and when the song had ceased, a calm, Christ-like spirit had filled the convention and continued with it to the end.

No. 119.

"I'M BUT A STRANGER HERE."

REV. THOMAS RAWSON TAYLOR, 1807—1835.

In an almshouse there was an old colored woman who had no relatives in the world and no money but what visitors sometimes gave her. But she was a true Christian. She had known sorrows, but Jesus had blessed her by giving her comfort and strength to bear them. They called her "Aunty." She was too feeble to leave her room, and so she used to hold services by herself on Sundays; and once a month she was in the habit of taking the communion all alone. A Christian lady, who sometimes visited that almshouse, went there one Sunday morning. She generally visited "Aunty" in her room. On hearing that this was the day on which she took the communion by herself, she asked the matron to let her stand outside the open door, that she might see the good old Christian go through this service, without knowing that anyone was near. This is the account given by the lady of what she saw and heard: "What I saw was a picture for a painter. The door, which was partly open, was opposite a raised window. A vine had climbed up the wire grating of the window, and was filled with blossoms. The fragrance came in on the Sabbath air with the bright sunshine. There on a bench sat the old woman, not knowing that anyone was near. Her dress was clean and neatly ironed, and the cap upon her head was as white as snow. Before her was a little pine table, covered with a clean white cotton cloth. There was nothing on the table but a white earthen plate, on which were a few small pieces of bread, and an earthen tea cup filled with water, while at her side lay a Bible and a small hymn book. She began the service by singing a few verses from memory, of an old communion hymn. Then she opened the Bible and read the story of the Crucifixion as given by Matthew. At the close of the reading she reverently repeated the words: "The Lord Jesus, the same night He was betrayed took bread and blessed it;' then holding the plate of bread in her hands, upon the table, she bowed her head in silent prayer. Then she went on with the Bible words, 'Take, eat; this is My body, given for you. Do this in remembrance of Me.' As she spoke these words, she took a piece of bread from the plate, and with closed eyes, in silence and in tears she ate the bread. Again she sang a verse, 'Nearer my God, to thee.' Then she went on with the Bible words, 'After the same manner also He took the cup, and gave thanks"; and with the tea cup of water in her hand, she again offered prayer; but this time, though her voice was low, almost a whisper, I was able to catch her words. As I listened I lost sight of the almshouse, and felt almost as if I were in heaven. When her prayer and thanksgiving were over she solemnly took the cup, and as she lifted it to her lips, repeated the words of Jesus, 'Drink ye all of it; this cup is the new testament of my blood, shed for the remission of sins: do this in remembrance of Me.' Then she drank from the cup, and setting it down on the table, again bowed her head in silent prayer. Then suddenly raising her head she exclaimed, 'Hallelujah! Glory to God!' —a sweet smile like that of an angel lighting up her dark face. 'I sees de gates,' she said, looking up to the ceiling of the room. 'I sees de door ob Heben open! I hears de angels singing! Yes, I's on de road! I's almost home! Hallelujah!' Then she sang:

'I'm but a stranger here,
  Heaven is my home;
Earth is a desert drear,
  Heaven is my home:
Danger and sorrow stand
Round me on every hand;
Heaven is my fatherland—
  Heaven is my home.'

At the close of the service she turned and saw me standing at the door. 'Why, chile,' she said, 'I didn't know you was dere. I thought there was no one near ole "Aunty" but de blessed Lord and de angels."

No. 120.

"FREE FROM THE LAW, OH, HAPPY CONDITION."

PHILIP BLISS, 1838—1876.

A gentleman in Edinburgh was in great distress of soul, and happened to linger in a pew after the noon meeting. The choir had remained to practice, and began:

"Free from the law, oh happy condition!
Jesus hath bled, and there is remission";

Quickly the Spirit of God carried that truth home to the awakened conscience, and he was at rest in the finished work of Jesus.

No. 121.

"THROUGH THE VALLEY OF THE SHADOW I MUST GO."

PHILIP BLISS, 1838—1876.

When Moody and Sankey were holding meetings in Boston, a young lady came into the inquiry room one evening in great distress, saying she had been seeking for years for forgiveness of her sins, but had kept the matter very secret and never intended to confess Christ till He had given her abundant light and assurance. She would not promise to make known her seeking to her companions, and went away as dark as she came, carrying with her, however, the verse, "He that believeth not God maketh him a liar." She returned in a few nights, and while Mr. Sankey was singing:

"There's a light in the valley,
There's a light in the valley for me,
And no evil will I fear,
While my Shepherd is so near;
There's a light in the valley for me,"

she said, "I will do anything for such a Savior," and peace came to her at once. In the inquiry room she arose and said, "I will take Jesus."

No. 122.

"SOWING THE SEED BY THE DAYLIGHT FAIR."

MRS. EMILY S. OAKEY, 1828—1883.

The following letter was written to Major Whittle after the death of Mr. Bliss.

Chicago, March 8, 1877.

At the breaking out of the war in 1861, I hastened to take service in the army, and soon after was appointed a First Lieutenant in the regular army. At that time I was not yet eighteen years of age, and never had been away from home influences. I had never tasted any kind of intoxicating liquor, and did not know one card from another. The regiment to which I was assigned was principally officered by young men, many of whom were old in dissipation. The new life was an attractive one, and I entered upon it with avidity. In a very few months I became a steady drinker and a constant card player. I do not remember to have made any attempt to resist the encroachments of vice; on the contrary I took a mad delight in all forms of dissipation. I laughed at the caution of older heads, and asserted with all the egotism of a boy, that I could abandon my bad habits at any time. But the time speedily came when I recognized the fact that my evil desires had obtained the complete mastery of my will, and that I was no longer able to exercise any control over myself. From that hour I knew no peace. The years that followed were a succession of struggles against the dominion of my appetite, and a repetition of failures. With each failure, I lost something of my power of resistance and gained something of evil. In

1870, I resigned my commission and returned to civil life, determined to make one last stand against my passions by breaking away from my old associations and beginning a new life. The result was attained in my condition a few months ago. I do not like to recall the past six years. They are as a frightful dream, from which, thank God! I was awakened; but the recollection of which will always bring sorrow and remorse. When the Tabernacle was opened, last fall, I was in Chicago, presumably on my way to Minnesota. Only a few weeks before, I had left my family, promising with my last words that I would stop drinking, and try once more to be a sober man. I did not keep the promise five minutes; I could not. I stopped here actuated by a desire to indulge, unrestrained, my appetite for liquor and cards, and in those few weeks I had taken a fearful plunge downward. At last I had made up my mind that there was absolutely no hope for me, and I wanted the end to come quickly. I gave myself up to the wildest debauchery, and speculated with a reckless indifference on how much longer my body could endure the fearful strain. In anticipation of sudden death, I carefully destroyed all evidences of my identity, so that my friends might never know the dog's death I had died. It was while in this condition that I one day wandered into the Tabernacle and found a seat in the gallery. I looked at the happy faces about me, and I hated them. I had all the vindictive feeling of a wild animal hunted to his last covert and waiting in impotent rage the final blow that is to end his miserable life. I did not pay much attention to the service. I was drowsy and stupefied with liquor. But after a while there was a perfect stillness, out of which presently rose the voice of Mr. Sankey in the song, "What shall the harvest be?" The words and music attracted my attention, and I straightened up to listen. They stirred me with a strange sensation, and when presently he sang:

"Sowing the seed of a lingering pain,
Sowing the seed of a maddened brain,
Sowing the seed of a tarnished name,
Sowing the seed of eternal shame,
Oh, what shall the harvest be?"

The words pierced me like an arrow. My deadened conscience was aroused, and with one swift glance memory recalled my bright boyhood, my wasted manhood, and showed me my lost opportunities. Every word of the song was true of my own case, and in bitter agony I was reaping the harvest my misdeeds had brought me. I thought of my old mother, my loving, faithful wife and children, and of how they, too, were compelled to reap of my harvest of dishonor. My awakened conscience lashed me as with a whip of scorpions, and I rushed from the Tabernacle and sought to drown its voice in more whiskey. But it was of no use. Wherever I went, whether to the bar of the saloon, or to the gaming table, or to the solitude of my own room, before my eyes in letters of fire were always the words, "What shall the harvest be?" For two weeks I endured this torture, having no rest, until at last on my knees I cried to God for mercy, and He heard my prayer. Broken, weak, and vile and helpless, I came to Him, trusting that His love and compassion would regard even me. And I have not trusted in vain.

No. 123.

"SHALL WE GATHER AT THE RIVER?"

REV. ROBERT LOWRY, 1826—.

The following incident is given by an American lady writing from Cairo, Egypt. "The three hours we could stay were full of work for heart and hand. One boy from a Highland regiment especially excited my interest. He had lost a limb, and could not, the surgeon said, live through the night. I stopped at his side to see if there was anything I could do for him. He lay with closed eyes, murmuring 'Mother,—mother!' I dipped my handkerchief in a basin of ice-water, and bathed his forehead where the fever flushes burned. 'Oh, that is good!' he said opening his eyes. Seeing me bending over him, he caught my hand and kissed it. 'Thank you, lady,' he said, and smiled. 'It minds me o' my mother.' 'Could I write to your mother?' I asked.

" 'No,' he said, 'the surgeon promised to do that; but could you, would you sing to me?'

"I hesitated a moment and looked around. The gleam of the sun on the yellow water of the Nile, as the western rays slanted down, caught my eye, and suggested the river whose streams make glad the City of God. I began to sing in a low voice the hymn, 'Shall we gather at the river?' Eager hands were raised around us to listen more intently, while bass and tenor voices, weak and tremulous, came in on the chorus:

'Yes, we'll gather at the river,
The beautiful, the beautiful river—
Gather with the saints at the river
That flows by the throne of God.'

When the song was ended, I looked into the face of the boy—he was not over twenty—and said: 'Shall you be there?'

" 'Yes,' he answered, with his blue eyes shining, while the light, that never was on land or sea, irradiated his face, 'I'll gather with the saints at the river.'

"The tears gathered in my eyes as I thought of the mother, in her far off Scottish home, watching and waiting for tidings of her soldier boy who was breathing away his life in an Egyptian hosptial; and I sang:

'In the sweet by-and-by,
We shall meet on that beautiful shore."

then stooped and kissed his white forehead.

"'Come again, lady, come again,' I heard on all sides, as we left the barracks. I shall go, but I shall not find my Scottish laddie, for by tomorrow's reveille he will have crossed the river."

No. 124.

"BEGIN, MY TONGUE, SOME HEAVENLY THEME."

REV. ISAAC WATTS, 1674—1748.

On one occasion when William Dawson, the Yorkshire preacher, was giving out a hymn, he suddenly stopped, and said, "I was coming once through the town of Leeds, and saw a poor little half-witted lad rubbing at a brass plate, trying to rub out the name; but the poor lad did not know that the harder he rubbed, the brighter it shone. Now, friends, let us sing:

"Engraved as in eternal brass
The mighty promise shines;
Nor can the powers of darkness raze
Those everlasting lines."

Then, as though he saw the devil rubbing, he said, "Satan cannot rub it off"—

"His Hand hath writ the Sacred Word
With an immortal pen."

No. 125.

"HOW SWEET AND AWFUL IS THE PLACE."

REV. ISAAC WATTS, 1674—1748.

Rev. Robert Moffat many years ago sent home an account of a visit he paid to Borigelong, one of his out-stations. On the Sabbath that he was there, one hundred and fifteen native converts joined with him in partaking of the Lord's Supper. It happened that at the very same time, certain heathen ceremonies were being observed by the heathen at Borigelong. Outside the little chapel, there were shouting and dancing, and croaking, and grunting, and all kinds of wild noises. Inside, a band of Christians were quietly and solemnly seated around the table, on which stood the bread and wine, showing forth the broken Body and poured out Blood of their Savior; the sweet hymn rose upon their blended voices:

"Why was I made to hear Thy voice,
And enter while there's room;
When thousands make a wretched choice,
And rather starve than come?"

Here and there tears were seen rolling down the dark cheeks; and here and there the sigh of gratitude and love, or of pity, was heard, as they, who sat within that happy Christian fold, listened to the uproar of the wicked idolaters without and thought to themselves "And such were we! but we are washed, but we are sanctified, but we are justified."

No. 126.

"I WAS A WANDERING SHEEP."

REV. HORATIUS BONAR, 1808.

During a revival in a female seminary in Massachusetts, many of the pupils had shown the natural "enmity" of the "carnal mind" to spiritual things. Helen B—— was among those who noticed the Spirit's work only by a curling lip and a scornful laugh. It seemed in vain to talk with her, or seek to induce her to attend a prayer meeting. Christians could do nothing more than to pray for her. One evening, however, as a praying band had gathered, the door opened, and she entered. Her eyes were downcast and her face was calm and very pale. There was something in her look that told of an inward struggle. She took her seat silently, and the exercises of the meeting proceeded. A few lines were sung, two or three prayers offered, and then as was their custom, each repeated a few verses of some favorite hymn. One followed another in succession until it came to the turn of the newcomer. There was a pause, and a perfect silence, and then, without lifting her eyes from the floor, she commenced:

"I was a wandering sheep,
I did not love the fold."

Her voice was low, but distinct, and every word, as she uttered it, thrilled the hearts of the listeners. She repeated one stanza after another of that beautiful hymn and not an eye save her own was dry, as, with sweet emphasis, she pronounced the last lines:

"No more a wayward child,
I seek no more to roam;
I love my heavenly Father's voice,
I love, I love His home."

That single hymn told all. The wandering sheep, the proud and wayward child had returned.

No. 127.

"DEPTH OF MERCY, CAN THERE BE?"

REV. CHARLES WESLEY, 1708—1788.

During the Moody and Sankey meetings in Edinburgh, Scotland, in 1874, some ladies began to occupy the time between the morning and afternoon Sabbath services, in singing to a very destitute class, in a public institution, which is a sort of cross between a poorhouse and a prison. All the inmates are sufferers, some from poverty and sickness only, and some from something worse. The ladies have received a welcome that has filled them with delight. The poor creatures literally weep for joy on their entrance. One woman who has been stricken by a paralysis partly physical and partly mental, and has not spoken a word for three years, was observed by the matron to be saying something after the ladies retired. She was repeating over and over again to herself:

> "Depth of mercy, can there be
> Mercy still reserved for me?"

No. 128.

"A MIGHTY FORTRESS IS OUR GOD."

REV. MARTIN LUTHER, 1483—1546.

About four miles north of the village of Herkimer, New York, there lay in the days of the Revolutionary war, and remains to this day, a wealthy little German settlement called Shell's Bush. Its principal proprietor was John Christian Shell. This pious and fearless patriot, had a wife who equalled him in courage and nobility, and six children, the youngest two of whom were twins but eight years old.

Shell built a blockhouse for his defence against Indians, a large, substantial structure, two stories high. The first had no windows, only a strong door and small loopholes through which the inmates could thrust their rifles. The second story was well lighted and was built out two or three feet over the first with loopholes and trap doors in the projecting floor, so that shots could be fired or heavy missiles dropped upon any close assailants. On the afternoon of August 6, 1781, a large band of Indians under Donald McDonald, a savage Scotch refugee, made a sudden descent on the village of Shell's Bush. Most of the inhabitants, alarmed by rumors, had fled for refuge to Fort Dayton, now Herkimer. But Shell himself would not move a foot in flight. He said every man's house was his castle, and he should defend his to the last. He was at work with his sons in the field when the Indians sprang from the woods with fierce yells. The two little boys were so far from the house that the enemy seized them ere they could reach it, but the father and his remaining sons got inside the door, and had it firmly barricaded when the Indians rushed up. It was two o'clock when the battle began, and it raged fiercely till nightfall. The Indians hurled themselves furiously against the blockhouse, but were driven back by a volley, every shot of which laid a warrior low. Astonished at their reception, the enemy drew off to consider; but knowing there could be only a handful within, they charged again, and again were repulsed with heavy loss. They had not reckoned on the whole of their host, for the German's wife, whom they had not thought of was equal to several men. She loaded the rifles while her men folks fired, and she was so expert that they were never empty handed. Maddened by their losses the savages made desperate onslaughts once and again through the long summer afternoon, the German's rifles doing fearful work among them as they battered and shrieked against the house. At length they charged in a new form, led by McDonald with a crowbar in his hand. They sprang against the door, and while the Scotchman plied his bar vigorously, the Indians covered him with their bodies. The door began to grow weak, but none of the defendants could leave to defend it. Their place was aloft, whence they poured down the shot on the infuriated mass below. So deadly was their fire that the Indians wavered and broke. Shell drew a bead on McDonald thus exposed, and shattered his leg. The assailants fled, and rushing down to the door, the patriots drew the wounded leader in before he could escape. Weakened, and confused, the Indians drew off for a space to consult. It was a welcome respite for the little garrison, which sorely needed rest. But Shell had his own ideas as to how the time should be occupied. He was a Godly German, a lover of Luther, and like Cromwell's "Ironsides," he was a hymn-singer in hours of conflict. His first thought now was of gratitude to God. So calling his family to bless the Lord, their strength, who taught their hands to war and their fingers to fight, he mounted to the upper story and began, with a deep, powerful voice, to sing the noble hymn of Luther, that song of castles, that battle song, the song of trust and triumph. Suddenly on the calm summer air, which had so lately rung with noise of war and battle shriek, rose the strong words from the depths of the beleaguered blockhouse:

"A mighty fortress is our God,
A bulwark never failing;
Our helper, He, amid the flood
Of mortal ills prevailing.
For still our ancient foe
Doth seek to work us woe;
His craft and power are great,
And armed with cruel hate,
On earth is not his equal."

Again the contest was renewed and assault after assault was met and repulsed, until at last the savage foe fled to the woods carrying with them the two little prisoners. But as they went the brave, God-trusting German, lifted his voice once more in the closing burst of the mighty hymn:

"Let goods and kindred go,
This mortal life also:
The body they may kill:
God's truth abideth still,
His kingdom is forever."

Among the German dwellers in Herkimer, Shell's memory is green to this day. There, too, may be heard a rude ballad of his exploits, composed at the time, and which closes with these quaint words:

"Come all you Tryon country men,
And never be dismayed;
But trust in the Lord,
And He will be your aid.

"Trust in the Lord with all your might,
And call upon His Name;
And He will help you as He did Shell,
To His immortal fame."

—*Christian Weekly.*

No. 129.

"MAXWELTON'S BRAES ARE BONNIE."

MR. DOUGLAS.

Just at evening on the night before the attack on the Great Redan, the Scottish soldiers in the Crimea joined in the familiar ballad-song of "Annie Laurie." A few began it outside the tents, but in a very little while hundreds came forth through the whole camp, and, with the manliest of voices and tenderest of hearts, struck in, hardy old veterans as they were, unused to the melting mood, yet subdued at times even to tears as they sang. The voices on the earlier lines of the verses were gentle and plaintive; but when they reached the closing chorus it seemed as if they could hardly sing strongly enough. Great waves of sound rolled across the plain, over the trenches, and up against the walls of the moonlit citadel. The enthusiasm was intense; there seemed but the throbbing of one mighty heart, the beating of one pulse through all the battalions.

No. 130.

"SINGING FOR JESUS, SINGING FOR JESUS."

MRS. FANNY J. VAN ALSTYNE, 1823.

The singing of this hymn by its author, on one occasion in the Effingham Theater, Whitechapel, London, caught the ear of a poor, despairing man who was on his way to the docks to drown himself. It reminded him of a mother's prayers in boyhood's days, and brought him a penitent to the Savior.

No. 131.

"LORD, I AM THINE, ENTIRELY THINE."

REV. SAMUEL DAVIES, 1723—1761.

A Christian captain, who had a Christian crew, was caught near a rocky shore, in a driving storm. They were being driven rapidly toward the rocks, when he ordered them to cast anchor. They did so but it broke. He ordered them to cast the second. They did so but it dragged. He then ordered them to cast the third and last. They cast it while the captain went down to his room to pray. He fell on his knees and said, "O Lord, this vessel is Thine, these noble men on deck are Thine. If it be more for Thy glory that our vessel be wrecked on the rocks, and we go down in the sea, Thy will be done. But if it be more for Thy glory that we live to work for Thee, then hold the anchor." Calmly he arose to return to the deck, and as he went, he heard a chorus of voices singing:

"Lord, I am Thine, entirely Thine,
Purchased and saved by blood divine;
With full consent Thine would I be,
And own Thy sovereign right in me."

It seemed like an angel song. Reaching the deck, he found his brave men standing with their hands on the cable, that they might feel the first giving of the anchor, on which hung their lives, and looking calmly on the raging of the elements, as they sang the hymn. The anchor held till the storm was past, and they anchored safe within the bay.

"Trophies of Song."

No. 132.

"SHOW PITY LORD, O LORD FORGIVE."

Rev. Isaac Watts, 1674—1748.

At an inquiry meeting, an old gentleman once said, "Over forty years ago, during a revival in Virginia, a young prodigal felt it was time for him to start home. He had never been accustomed to pray and felt afraid to venture near the Majestic Ruler of the universe. He was then attending an academy, a mile distant from his father's home. Taking a short cut through the fields to his home, he thought he could possibly find some suitable place to unburden his heavily laden heart in prayer. As he saw a retired place in a fence corner, he concluded to open his lips there. But his courage failed him, and he said to himself, 'In the distance is a big oak tree; that will shield me.' But when under the tree his stubborn will would still not yield. A fork in the road, and nearly a dozen other places he tried, but when he drew near to them, the tempter also drew near, and caused postponement, until at length he got to the gate at the head of the lane leading to the house. This was the last resort where he could pray unseen. It seemed to him as the turning point. As he sank at Jesus' feet, a hymn came to his lips as the language of his heart, and so he cried out:

'Show pity, Lord, O Lord forgive;
Let a repenting sinner live.'

The six verses of that hymn-prayer decided his destiny. He became a minister and is now the old man you see before you."

The daughter of a wealthy infidel, during his absence, stole away to a revival meeting. As the loving heart of Jesus was unfolded in the sermon, she wept aloud. On reaching home she told her mother where she had been and how she felt. Her mother became very angry and said, "Your father will banish you if you persist." The next evening found her at the same place of prayer in spite of her mother's threats. At the close of the sermon she cried for mercy and poured out her heart in sobs and fervent prayers. Hymn after hymn was sung, and many prayers offered on her behalf. The last hymn was being sung. It was the one beginning:

"Show pity Lord, O Lord, forgive";

The last verse was reached.

"Yet save a trembling sinner, Lord,
Whose hope, still hovering round Thy word,
Would light on some sweet promise there,
Some sure support against despair."

As the last strain sounded in the ear of the penitent, she gently threw back her head and opened her calm, blue eyes, yet sparkling with tears, but they were tears that told of sins forgiven. Word reached her father, and as he reached home the daughter ran to the gate to meet him with a kiss, but he seized her rudely by the arm, and with his horsewhip whipped her out of the gate, telling her to begone, and with many curses forbade her return. Sadly she went weeping down the lane. A poor widow took her into her house. There she spent the night in prayer. Her father in great anguish did the same, for he could not sleep. He, too, sought and found mercy and sent for his daughter, whom he met and embraced at the same gate, saying, "I give you my heart and hand to go with you to heaven." The mother followed, and all became united in Christ.

I was seated at the table of a boarding house, at which were some fifteen guests. One of these was a gentleman full of animation, and whose vivacity created the impression that whoever else might be affected by the solemnities of the time he was not. On a Sunday morning, Rev. Dr. Perrine preached an effective sermon on the consequences of a life of sin. Full of unction and tenderness, its vivid pictures of the torments of hell produced a most solemn effect. As we were sitting at the dinner table, and remarks were freely passing in regard to the morning sermon, the young man above-mentioned expressed in strong terms his disapprobation of the sermon, and added, "Such preaching only hardens me and makes me worse."

I replied, "It is possible you think it makes you worse, when it only makes you conscious of sin that was before slumbering in your heart."

"No," said he, "it hardens me. I am at this moment less susceptible to anything like conviction for hearing that discourse. I feel more inclined to resist everything like good impressions than usual."

"Yet," I rejoined, "good impressions are those which are best adapted to secure the desired end; and I am greatly mistaken if an increase of the effect which you feel would not be greatly useful to you. If, for instance, you should read now the fifty-first Psalm, 'Show pity, Lord, O Lord, forgive,' it would take a deep hold on your heart." "Not the least," said he, "I wish I had the book, I would read it to you."

"We have one," said our landlady, who was fully aware of the excitement under which he was laboring; and the book was handed him, opened at the place. He commenced to read, with compressed lips, and firm voice:

"Show pity, Lord, O Lord forgive;
Let a repenting rebel live:
Are not Thy mercies large and free,
May not a sinner trust in Thee?"

Toward the last part of the stanza a little tremulousness of voice was plainly discernible. He rallied again, however, and commenced the third verse with more firmness:

"O wash my soul from every sin,
And make my guilty conscience clean;
Here on my heart the burden lies,
And past offenses pain my eyes."

At the last part of this stanza his voice faltered more manifestly. He commenced the next verse with great energy, and read in a loud sonorous voice, the whole company looking on in breathless silence:

"My lips with shame my sins confess."

As he read the second line:

"Against Thy law, against Thy grace,"

his lips quivered, and his utterance became difficult. He paused a little, and entered upon the third line with an apparently new determination:

"Lord, should Thy judgments grow severe,"

Yet before he came to the end his voice was almost totally choked; and when he began upon the fourth line:

"I am condemned, but Thou art clear;"

an aspect of utter discouragement marked his countenance, and he could only bring out, in broken sobs, "I am condemned," when his utterance changed to a heart-broken cry of grief, and he, rising at the same time, rushed from the room, as a deeply convicted sinner.

DR. BELCHER.

No. 133.

"STAND UP! STAND UP FOR JESUS!"—1858.

REV. GEORGE DUFFIELD, 1818—1888.

During meetings in Pennsylvania, during the year 1858, when this hymn was written, it was often sung and referred to. One morning the parents of a little girl were awakened by the repeated call of their little girl from her crib, whose pleading voice kept saying, "Papa! Mama! Papa! Mama! Mis-ser Long say, 'Tan up—tan up for Jesus.'" This little stammering voice went so deep down into the hearts of the parents, that in the same evening they did "stand up for Jesus" and became earnest and decided soldiers of the cross.

No. 134.

"COME, SACRED SPIRIT FROM ABOVE!"

REV. PHILIP DODDRIDGE, 1702—1751.

A prayer meeting of a country village was attended by but few during a season of coldness. The pastor was absent, his place being supplied by one of his deacons, who, for months had been deeply mourning in secret the sad decline. The hymn he selected with which to commence the service was the one commencing, in the most recent collections, with the line above given. As first written, however, this is the first line of the second verse, and the first verse began:

"Hear, gracious Sovereign, from Thy Throne,
And send Thy various blessings down,"

and it was with this verse that the deacon began. The last verse of the hymn reads:

"In answer to our fervent cries,
Give us to see Thy Church arise;
Or if that blessing seem too great,
Give us to mourn its low estate."

While reading this verse, the good man paused: it did not accord with the feelings of his heart: it was not the expression of his prayer. He indulged a moment's thought—swift and excellent; an alteration suggested itself—his eye sparkled with joy, and out it came:

"In answer to our fervent cries,
Give us to see Thy Church arise;
That blessing, Lord, is not too great
Though now we mourn its low estate."

Every heart was arrested, and sudden emotion so overpowered all in the little assembly that they could scarcely sing the words; but each in silence gave to the sentiment his own earnest amen. They happily proved it to be true. From that evening a revival began; the church arose from its slumber to new faith and works; and very soon the windows of Heaven were opened, and plentiful blessing came.

No. 135.

"JESUS I MY CROSS HAVE TAKEN."

REV. HENRY F. LYTE, 1793—1847.

In the "Holland Purchase" a log church was built by Methodist pioneers. It flourished well for years, but eventually some of the members died, and others moved away, till only one was left, when preaching also ceased. This mother in Israel sighed over the desolations in Zion. She loved the old forsaken sanctuary, and still kept going there on the Sabbath to worship God and plead the promises. At length it was noised abroad that she was a witch, that the old church was haunted with evil spirits, and that she went there to commune with them. Two young men, to satisfy their curiosity, secreted themselves in the loft to watch her. On her arrival she took her seat by the altar. After reading the Bible, she announced the hymn:

> "Jesus, I my cross have taken,
> All to leave, and follow Thee."

and sang it with a sweet but trembling voice, then kneeled down and poured out her heart in fervent prayer. Her pleadings broke the hearts of the young men. They began to weep and cry for mercy. She invited them down from their hiding place. They obeyed, and there at the altar, where in other days she had seen many conversions, they too knelt, and sought and found the Savior. From that hour the meetings were resumed, and a flourishing church grew up, and the old meeting house was again made to resound with the songs of God's people.

DR. STRICKLAND.

No. 136.

"SWEET IS THE WORK, MY GOD, MY KING."

Rev. Isaac Watts, 1674—1748.

During the war between the United States and Great Britain, in 1812, there lived in the Northern Neck, Virginia, a man named Deacon Epa Norris. Being captured and taken to a British vessel, they sought in vain to obtain from him the position and numbers of the American army. The commandant of the ship gave a dinner to the officers of the fleet, and did Mr. Norris the honor to select him from the American prisoners of war to be a guest. The deacon, in his homespun attire, took his seat at the table with the aristocracy of the British navy. The company sat long at the feast; they drank toasts, told stories, laughed, and sang songs. At length Mr. Norris was called on for a song. He desired to excuse himself, but in vain: he must sing. He possessed a fine, strong musical voice. In an appropriate and beautiful air, he commenced singing:

"Sweet is the work, my God, my King,
To praise Thy Name, give thanks, and sing:
To show Thy love by morning light
And talk of all Thy truth by night."

Thoughts of home, and of lost religious privileges, and of his captivity, gave an unusual pathos and power to his singing. When he had done, a solemn silence ensued. At length the commandant broke it by saying: "Mr. Norris, you are a good man, and shall return at once to your family." The commandant kept his word; for in a few days Mr. Norris was sent ashore with a handsome present of salt—then more valuable in the country than gold.

Dr. Belcher.

No. 137.

"BLEST BE THE TIE THAT BINDS."

REV. JOHN FAWCETT, 1739—1817.

After many years of separation, the Old and the New School divisions of the Presbyterian Church met in convention in separate churches at Pittsburgh, Pennsylvania, in 1869. The act of reunion is thus described:

"The two bodies having met in two churches, afterward formed on opposite sides of the street, and then moved along one block, when a halt was made. The two moderators, who headed their respective columns, then approached and grasped each other's hands, which example was followed by the two opposite ranks, until amidst welcomes, thanksgivings, and tears, they locked arms, and thus marched as one united host, to the temple of God, where they sang, 'All hail the power of Jesus' Name,' and then blended their voices in the grand old doxology, 'Praise God, from Whom all blessings flow.' The tide of feeling gradually rose till it reached its culmination, when Dr. Fowler, the moderator of the New School body, turned to Dr. Jacobus, the moderator of the Old School body, saying, 'My dear brother moderator, may we not, before I take my seat, perform a single act, symbolical of the union which has taken place between the two branches of the church. Let us clasp hands.' This challenge was immediately responded to, amid prolonged and deafening applause. After which the thousands present, amid flowing tears and swelling hearts, joined in singing:

'Blest be the tie that binds
Our hearts in Christian love;
The fellowship of kindred minds
Is like to that above.'"

No. 138.

"HOW TEDIOUS AND TASTELESS THE HOURS."

REV. JOHN NEWTON, 1725—1807.

During the Crimean war, a soldier was placed on guard as a picket several nights in succession, and became so forlorn by being night after night exposed to the mud, fog, and rain, in the darkness of the night, that he resolved to end his misery by committing suicide. While retiring to a secluded spot to execute his purpose, he heard some one in the dark tramping through the mud and rain cheerfully singing a hymn. As he listened he found it came from a Christian whose faith enabled him to sing even amid surrounding gloom. The soldier was singing:

"Content with beholding His Face,
My all to His pleasure resigned,
No changes of season or place,
Would make any change in my mind."

The despondent soldier went back to his beat resolved to make the best of his circumstances.

No. 139.

"FROM THE CROSS, UPLIFTED HIGH."

REV. THOMAS HAWEIS, 1732—1820.

Recently, says Mr. Ralph Wells, we admitted six mission children from our school into the Church. When the session came to examine the candidates, one of the elders asked a little girl of twelve years, "Maggie, what first interested your heart in the Savior?"

"It was one of those large hymns, sir, one of the printed

hymns they use in the school." The hymn was that beautiful one:

"From the cross uplifted high,
Where the Savior deigns to die,
What melodious sounds I hear
Bursting on my ravished ear!
Love's redeeming work is done,
Come and welcome, sinner, come!"

"Oh, sir!" said this child, fresh from her tenement home, "it was those kind words: 'Come and welcome, sinner, come.' I said to myself that means *ME;* for, if it means 'sinner' it is for poor Maggie."

No. 140.

"PRAISE GOD FROM WHOM ALL BLESSINGS FLOW."

Bishop Thomas Ken, 1637—1710.

In the great cotton famine in England, which desolated Lancashire for long and weary months, the conduct of the operatives was the admiration of the world. There were no riots and no excess of crimes. The people, men and women, went into the Sunday-school houses and prayed. They had been taught to do so, and they were upheld in the time of trial by the truths they had learned. When the first wagonload of cotton arrived, the people unhooked the horses and drew it themselves, and, surrounding it, began to sing. What do you think they sang? They sang the grand old doxology, while the tears came flowing down their cheeks:

"Praise God from Whom all blessings flow,
Praise Him, all creatures here below;
Praise Him above, ye heavenly host;
Praise Father, Son, and Holy Ghost."

Rev. Wm. M. Taylor.

Chaplain McCabe says that while the prisoners of the Union army were incarcerated in Libby Prison, day after day they saw comrades passing away, and their number increased by fresh, living recruits for the grave. One night, about ten o'clock, through the stillness and the darkness, they heard the tramp of coming feet, that soon stopped before the prison door, until arrangements could be made inside. In the company was a young Baptist minister, whose heart almost fainted as he looked on those cold walls and thought of the suffering inside. Tired and weary, he sat down, put his face in his hands and wept. Just then a lone voice sung out from an upper window:

"Praise God from Whom all blessings flow;"

and a dozen manly voices joined in the second line:

"Praise Him all creatures here below";

and then by the time the third line was reached, more than a score of hearts were full, and these joined to send the words on high:

"Praise Him above, ye heavenly host";

and by this time, the prison was all alive, and seemed to quiver with the sacred song, as from every room and cell those brave men sang:

"Praise Father, Son, and Holy Ghost."

As the song died out on the still night that enveloped in darkness the city, the young man arose and happily said:

"Prisons would palaces prove
If Jesus would dwell with him there."

In company with her father and some friends, a little girl of ten years, rode on horseback one summer day, to the top of Mount Washington. On that rugged summit nothing grew but some pale green moss; but the view all around was vast and impressive. Below, stretching outwards in all directions, lay a deep, silver sea of clouds, amid which lightnings were seen to part, and writhe like gilded serpents, whilst the roar of the thunder came pealing up to the mountain top. The rain was pouring in torrents below, but above the sun shone in cloudless splendor. The eye wandered like Noah's dove, but there was no resting place in that wide space. "Well, Lucy," said her father, "there is nothing to be seen here, is there?"

The child paused, clasped her hands, and then said reverently,—"O papa! I see the doxology; all around seems to say:

'Praise God from Whom all blessings flow,
Praise Him all creatures here below.'"

Pleased with his child's observation, the father himself caught a fresh inspiration.

G. J. Stevenson.

No. 141.

"GENTLE JESUS, MEEK AND MILD."

Rev. Charles Wesley, 1708—1788.

John B. Gough relates the following in one of his lectures: "I went one day with a friend away up to a small garret room. A feeble voice said, 'Come in,' and we went in. There was no light, but as soon as our eyes were dilated to the gloom, we saw, lying on a heap of chips and shavings, a boy about ten years of age, pale, but with a singularly sweet face. We asked the boy, 'What are you doing there?' 'Hush, hush! I am hiding.'

"'Hiding? What for?'

"The child showed his white delicate arms, covered with bruises and swollen. 'Who was it beat you like that?'

"'Hush! don't tell him; my father did it.'

"'What for?'

"'Poor father got drunk, and beat me because I wouldn't steal.'

"'Did you ever steal?'

"'Yes, sir, I was a thief once.'

"'Then, why don't you steal now?'

"'Because I went to ragged school, and they taught me "Thou shalt *not* steal," and told me about God in heaven. I will not steal, sir, if my father kills me.'

"'My friend said, 'I don't know what to do with you. Here is a shilling. I will see what I can do for you.'

"The boy looked at it a moment, and then said, 'But, please, sir, wouldn't you like to hear my little hymn?' We thought it strange that lying there, without fire, without food, bruised and beaten, he could sing a hymn. How could he sing the Lord's song in a strange land? But we said, 'Yes, we will hear you.' And then in a low sweet voice, the child sang:

'Gentle Jesus, meek and mild,
Look upon a little child;
Pity my simplicity,
Suffer me to come to Thee.

'Fain I would to Thee be brought;
Dearest God, forbid it not:
Give me, dearest God, a place,
In the kingdom of Thy grace.'

"'That's my little hymn; goodbye.'

"We went again in the morning, mounted the stairs, knocked at the door—no answer; opened it and went in. The shilling lay on the floor, and there, too, lay the boy, with a brave smile on his face, as if to make the best of it; and so he had, for he was dead. In the night he had gone home."

In an institution for feeble-minded children was placed a little girl from Virginia, who had been speechless from her birth. She was familiarly known as "Becca." Dr. Parish, the superintendent, describes her as one afraid of every living thing. Blocks and sticks she would nurse, but if a nicely dressed doll were presented, she would scream with fear. She loved nobody, and seemed fond of hurting little children and destroying their playthings. Little by little her antipathies and coldness of disposition gave way, and she began to show affection for her matron. She soon began to love to sit in the school room with children and listen to their little songs and hymns. In her eighth year she would steal away and make sounds when alone in some hiding place. One summer evening her nurse had put her to bed early. The birds were singing in the tree by her window; the sun had just gone away and left its golden shadows on the western sky; and in this sweet hour of twilight the imprisoned soul of the little child broke its bands, her tongue was loosed, and she lifted her voice and sang. The nurse, hearing the sound, hastened up the stairway, and, listening outside the bedroom door, was rejoiced to hear "Becca" commingling her voice with that of the birds without, and as her first utterance the appropriate language of the hymn she had heard the other children sing:

"Gentle Jesus, meek and mild,
Look upon a little child!
Pity my simplicity;
Suffer me to come to Thee."

No. 142.

"MY FAITH LOOKS UP TO THEE."

REV. RAY PALMER, 1808—1887.

Dr. Palmer, the author of this hymn, states that while a pastor at Albany, New York, a young man who had been accustomed to attend upon his ministry came one Sunday morning to his church some time before the time of service; and to pass away the time he opened a hymn book that lay in the pew. His eyes fell at once upon the words:

"My faith looks up to Thee,
Thou Lamb of Calvary,
Savior divine!"

It was just the language suited to his sin-burdened heart. While reading the hymn, the Spirit applied the truth with divine power, so that he looked at once to Jesus and lived. Calling afterward at the residence of Dr. Palmer to tell him how he had found the Savior, he learned to his great joy, for the first time, that the one to whom he was telling the story of his conversion had written the hymn.

No. 143.

"ALL HAIL THE POWER OF JESUS' NAME."

REV. EDWARD PERRONET, 1726—1792.

Rev. E. P. Scott, while laboring as a missionary in India, saw on the street one of the strangest looking heathen his eyes had ever rested on. On inquiry, he found that he was one of the inland tribes that lived away in the mountain districts, and which came down once a year to trade. Upon further investigation he found that the Gospel had never been preached to them, and that it was very hazardous to venture among them because of their murderous propensities. He was stirred with earnest desire to break unto them the bread of life. He went to his lodging place, fell on his knees, and pleaded for divine direction. Arising from his knees, he packed his valise, took his violin, with which he was accustomed to sing, and his pilgrim staff, and started in the direction of their mountain home. As he bade his fellow missionaries farewell, they said: "We shall never see you again. It is madness for you to go."

"But," said he, "I must carry Jesus to them." For two days he traveled, meeting scarcely a human being, until at last he found himself in the mountains, and suddenly surrounded by a crowd of savages. Every spear was pointed instantly at his heart. He expected that every moment would be his last. Not knowing of any other resource, he tried the power of singing the name of Jesus to them. Drawing forth his violin, he began with closed eyes to sing and play:

"All hail the power of Jesus' name,
Let angels prostrate fall:
Bring forth the royal diadem,
And crown Him Lord of all."

Being afraid to open his eyes, he sang on till the third verse, and while singing the stanza:

"Let every tribe and every tongue,
That bound creation's call,
Now shout in universal song,
The crownéd Lord of all,"

he opened his eyes to see what they were going to do, when lo! the spears had dropped from their hands, and the big tears were dropping from their eyes. They afterward invited him to their homes. He spent two and a half years among them. His labors were so richly rewarded that when he was compelled to leave them by reason of impaired health, and return to this country, they followed him between thirty and forty miles. "Oh! missionary," said they when parting, "come back to us again. There are tribes beyond us which never heard the glad tidings of salvation." He could not resist their entreaties. After visiting America he went back again to his labors and died among them.

About forty years ago, William Dawson, a Methodist local preacher, a farmer, but an original genius, and a striking and popular preacher, was speaking in London on the Divine offices of Christ. After setting Him forth as the great Teacher and Priest, he showed Him in His glory as the King of Saints. He proclaimed Him as King in His own right, and then proceeded to the coronation. His ideas were borrowed from scenes familiar to his hearers. The immense procession was marshalled. Then it moved toward the great temple to place the insignia of royalty upon the King of the universe. So vividly was all this depicted that those who listened thought they were gazing upon the long line of patriarchs, kings, prophets, apostles, martyrs, and confessors of every age and clime. They saw the great temple filled; and the grand and solemn act of coronation was about to be performed. By this time the congregation was wrought up to the highest pitch of excitement, and while expecting to hear the pealing anthem rise from the vast assembly upon which they seemed to gaze, the preacher lifted up his voice and sang:

> "All hail the power of Jesus' name!
> Let angels prostrate fall;
> Bring forth the royal diadem,
> And crown Him Lord of all!"

The effect was overwhelming. The crowd sprang to their feet, and sang the hymn with a feeling and a power which seemed to swell higher and higher at every verse. It was a jubilant multitude paying harmonious homage to their Sovereign Lord and Savior.

REV. S. W. CHRISTOPHERS.

A faithful Christian, who was dying, turned to his daughter who was bending over his bed and said, "Bring—" then his strength failed him.

"What shall I bring, father?" said the girl.

"Bring—" said he, and paused again for lack of strength.

The daughter, in an agony of desire to know her father's last request, said, "Dear father, do try to tell me what you want; I will do anything for you."

The dying man rallied all his strength, and said, "Bring—forth—the—royal—diadem—And—crown—Him—Lord—of—all," and then, as the last word passed from his lips, he ceased to breathe.

No. 144.

"COME TO JESUS, COME TO JESUS."

One Saturday night, during a Sunday school teacher's meeting, a sudden rap was heard at the lecture-room door of a church in St. Louis. The pastor, Rev. Dr. McCook, was sent for in haste to see a little dying boy. He found it was at the home of a noted gambler. This man was on bended knees beside his child. Said he, "Pray for him. Do anything you can." After prayer, the boy's lips were observed to move. They found he was trying to say, "Sing! sing!" So Dr. McCook sang the words:

"Come to Jesus, come to Jesus,
Come to Jesus, just now,
Just now, come to Jesus,
Come to Jesus, just now."

As the words "just now" were being repeated, the boy would fix his dying eyes on his father and try to emphasize by saying as loudly as he could, *"now, now, now,"* whenever the word occurred in the hymn. Next morning, as the father stood on one side of the corpse and Dr. McCook on the other, the latter re-echoed in the ears of the father, that emphatic "now" that so earnestly escaped from the pale lips that lay silent between them. That gambler opened his heart to the sound and became a devoted Christian.

E. M. Long.

No. 145.

"O DO NOT BE DISCOURAGED."

"One morning I had occasion to be in a Christian family at Norristown, Pennsylvania, which had keenly felt the pressure of hard times. They had gotten down to the scrapings of the barrel. They had nothing left for breakfast but the crumbs of other days. These were all gathered on one plate and placed in the centre of the table. All the family gathered around the scanty meal except two little boys, who were absorbed with their playthings in one corner of the room. After the father had given thanks, tears rolled down the cheeks as their eyes gazed upon the empty plates. During the sad silence that followed, the two boys dropped their toys, arose to their feet, and as if led by angel hands, marched forward to the table and sang:

'O do not be discouraged
For Jesus is your friend;
He will give you grace to conquer,
And keep you to the end.'

Tears fled as dewdrops before the rising sun. An unexpected Providence brought relief, and never since have tear drops fallen on empty dishes."

Rev. E. M. Long.

No. 146.

"FROM EVERY STORMY WIND THAT BLOWS."

Rev. Hugh Stowell, 1799—1865.

When the flames seized the house of worship of the First Baptist Church, in the Great Chicago fire, brethren who had labored hard to save it, said one to another, "Our house must go, but let us have one more prayer within its walls." And they bowed before God in the face of the coming flames, while one who had been wont to lead in the fire and thunder of battle led the cry of these faithful heroes before the mercy seat. Then, rising to their feet, they sang as they retreated:

"From every stormy wind that blows,
From every swelling tide of woes,
There is a calm, a sure retreat;
'Tis found beneath the mercy seat."

No. 147.

"DAUGHTER OF ZION! FROM THE DUST."

James Montgomery, 1771—1854.

The pastor of the New England Congregational Church of Chicago relates that at the time after the fire, when they were most afflicted by the loss of their edifice, a singular circumstance became known, which greatly cheered and encouraged them to put forth the most strenuous efforts to rebuild. It seems that among the ruins of their church were found two bits of paper, one of which proved to be the only remaining fragment of a Bible, and the only legible portion was this verse, from II Corinthians 5:1—"For we know that if our earthly house of this tabernacle were dissolved, we have a building of God, an house not made with hands eternal in the heavens." The other was a scrap from the hymn book, upon which were these words of the hymn:

"Daughter of Zion! from the dust
Exalt thy fallen head;
Again in thy Redeemer trust;
He calls thee from the dead.

"Awake, awake, put on thy strength,
Thy beautiful array;
The day of freedom dawns at length,
The Lord's appointed day.

"Rebuild thy wells, thy bounds enlarge,
And send thy heralds forth:"

No. 148.

"COME, HUMBLE SINNER, IN WHOSE BREAST."

REV. EDMUND JONES, 1772—1765.

Rev. Henry Ward Beecher says, "I remember once hearing a sermon preached by Mr. Nettleton, under which I shivered and quivered like an aspen leaf; I remember going away and trying to pray, and waiting for a change to come which should translate me; and I remember taking this hymn, and singing, and singing, and singing it, and finding it a great comfort, though it did not bring me through. It may seem very little to you; but I tell you that hymn was like the day of judgment to me, so full of anguish was I."

No. 149.

"O'ER THOSE GLOOMY HILLS OF DARKNESS."

REV. WILLIAM WILLIAMS, 1717—1791.

A negro woman in Jamaica was very fond of singing this hymn at missionary meetings, and sang it with great fervor. But whenever the plates went around for contributions she always sang with her eyes on the ceiling. On one occasion, however, the plate reached her just as she was singing with great earnestness, and with eyes as usual on the ceiling:

"Fly abroad, eternal gospel,
Win and conquer, never cease";

The colored brother who carried the plate, had apparently had experience with this sort of singing, and so he touched the good sister with the plate and said, "Sissy, it's no use for to sing 'Fly abroad' with your eyes on the ceiling; it's no use for you to sing 'fly' at all, unless you give something to make it fly."

No. 150.

"WHEN I SURVEY THE WONDROUS CROSS."

REV. ISAAC WATTS, 1674—1748.

In a church in London, this hymn was sung after a collection had been taken. When it ended, the preacher slowly repeated the verse:

"Were the whole realm of nature mine,
That were a present far too small;
Love so amazing, so divine,
Demands my soul, my life, my all."

And then added, "Well, I am surprised to hear you sing that, for do you know that altogether you have only put fifteen shillings into the plate this morning?"

No. 151.

"COME HOLY SPIRIT, HEAVENLY DOVE."

REV. ISAAC WATTS, 1674—1748.

Rev. R. V. Lawrence relates the following incident as occurring in New Jersey: "A minister was called to take charge of a congregation that his predecessor had left in a state of revival, with hearts all aglow with the heavenly fire. At the first prayer meeting service he began to read the hymn:

'Come Holy Spirit, heavenly Dove,
With all Thy quickening powers;
Kindle a flame of sacred love
In these cold hearts of ours.'

As he read the last two lines, a brother called out, 'Dear pastor, that hymn does not suit us. Our hearts are not "cold."

As the preacher still proceeded to read the next verse:

'Look how we grovel here below
Fond of these earthly toys;
Our souls can neither fly nor go,
To reach eternal joys.'

another brother responded, 'We *can* "fly" and "go" and "reach eternal joys." The confused pastor, however, persisted in reading the third verse:

'In vain we tune our formal songs,
In vain we strive to rise;
Hosannas languish on our tongues,
And our devotion dies.'

When being told again that their songs were not 'formal,' that their 'hosannas' did not 'languish,' he closed by saying, 'Well, that's my condition, if it is not yours.' And asked the prayers of the warm-hearted brethren on his behalf."

A young man, who had been the leader in gaiety among the middle ranks of the place in which he dwelt, went to a Scripture reading at the persuasion of a friend; and the Word of God went like an arrow to his heart. To stifle his convictions, he went to a neighboring public house, where several young men spent their evenings in revelry. His talent for singing made him doubly welcome amongst them. In the midst of singing a song, the words vanished from his mind; he tried in vain to recall them; the only lines he could remember were these:

"Come, Holy Spirit, heavenly Dove,
With all Thy quickening powers;
Come, shed abroad a Savior's love,
And that shall kindle ours."

He left the house deeply wounded in spirit, his pride humbled; and, seeking earnestly for pardon till he found it, he spent the rest of his life in the service of God.

No. 152.

"JESUS! THE NAME HIGH OVER ALL."

REV. CHARLES WESLEY, 1708—1788.

In a narrow alley in Boston, noted for its poverty and haunts of vice, a young gas-fitter was sent one winter evening in 1873, to repair a gas pipe. Near by was the North End Mission Chapel, surrounded by dance halls and tippling shops. The alley was very foggy and still, and the music of harps and fiddles seemed to echo in strange contrast with the inspiring strains of "Coronation" and other familiar tunes that issued from the house of God. The young gas-fitter was weary and paused at times in this extra work to listen to the commingling of musical sounds. At last there was a loud outburst of song in the chapel. Through the crisp evening air echoed the words of Wesley's hymn:

"Jesus; the name high over all,
In hell, or earth, or sky;
Angels and men before it fall,
And devils fear and fly."

He listened to the singing of three stanzas heartily sung, but could not distinguish the words. The music affected him strangely. There was something in the tinkling sound, coming out of the beer rooms that told him of the emptiness of earth's follies. "I wish I was a true Christian," said the young man, as he resumed his work in the basement. As the bell was striking nine he again paused and went to the basement window and listened. The chapel seemed silent, but there was a mingling of people, and a murmuring of voices out on the street, and the tinkling of instruments in the dance halls still went on. He stood thinking, and the old thoughts returned with greater force, that there was no hope or promise in any pursuits or pleasures which were destitute of God. The music and the sounds of laughter seemed a mockery. He again said, as he was about to resume his work, "I would like to be a Christian." Something detained him a moment more at the window. A low bent form flitted through the misty ring of light at the head of the alley, and approached with a pattering step in the deep shadows. It was an old woman returning from the chapel. She was singing. It was the hymn which he had imperfectly heard. He waited for the refrain:

"Jesus, the Name high over all,
In hell, or earth, or sky;
Angels and men before it fall,
And devils fear and fly.
O how I love Jesus,
O how I love Jesus,
O how I love Jesus,
Because He first loved me."

The old woman passed on and disappeared through one of the dark doors at the foot of the alley. She knew not the sermon her song had preached. Then and there the young man saw what he wanted to make him happy—what the world wants to make it happy—the love of Jesus. On the following day he arose in the Young Men's Christian

Association rooms, related the above story, and asked their prayers.

No. 153.

"HOW HAPPY EVERY CHILD OF GRACE."

REV. CHARLES WESLEY, 1708—1788.

About the year 1854, the unusual scene of a court room in tears was witnessed in Exeter Castle, England. A good woman had been set upon by a villain on her way from the Sunday school and was left for dead by the roadside. On being discovered, she was restored to consciousness so far as to identify the perpetrator of the crime; and then she died, singing this triumphant anthem of hope:

"How happy every child of grace,
Who knows his sins forgiven!
'This earth,' he cries, 'is not my place;
I seek my place in heaven;

" 'A country far from mortal sight;
Yet O, by faith I see
The land of rest, the saints' delight,
The heaven prepared for me.

" 'To that Jerusalem above
With singing I repair;
While in the flesh, my hope and love,
My heart and soul are there.' "

The counsel for the prosecution at the murderer's trial, in his appeal to the jury, described the death scene and rehearsed the hymn, a part of which the dying girl sang on her upward flight. The jury, all but the prisoner, wept. Who could help it? To hear in that solemn court, the youthful martyr's song of glory! And such a song!

No. 154.

"JESUS, KEEP ME NEAR THE CROSS."

MRS. FANNY JANE VAN ALSTYNE.

A small boy was run over by a car on the Third Avenue line in New York, and taken to a hosptial. A few moments before his death he said, "May I sing?" After clasping his little hands and saying the Lord's prayer, he broke out in singing the hymn:

"Jesus, keep me near the cross,
There a precious fountain,
Free to all—a healing stream,
Flows from Cavalry's mountain."

His voice gradually grew weaker as he sang:

"Near the cross I'll watch and wait,
Hoping, trusting ever,
Till I reach the golden strand,
Just beyond the river."

And with these words he crossed the river.

No. 155.

"SAFE IN THE ARMS OF JESUS."

MRS. FANNY JANE VAN ALYSTYNE.

One summer evening the author of this hymn was present at a meeting in the Water Street Mission in New York when a number of sailors were present. One of their number arose and said that for many years he had lived far from God a reckless life, until strolling along the streets the first Sunday after his vessel had come into port, he happened to hear music proceeding from that building. He stopped and listened and was induced to enter while they were singing:

"Safe in the arms of Jesus."

It so stirred his soul that he rested not till he was "safe in the arms of Jesus" himself.

No. 156.

"DEAR CHRISTIAN PEOPLE, NOW REJOICE."

REV. MARTIN LUTHER.

Martin Luther knew the power of song. Hymns could go where neither he nor his brother preachers could go, and so he began at the very outset of his work to embody his doctrines in song. This is the second hymn he wrote—his version of the forty-sixth Psalm being the first—and this is almost a complete epitome of his doctrine of salvation through faith in Christ. It flew all over Germany as if the very winds carried it, and with it went the great doctrine of the Reformation. "The whole people," wrote a Romish priest, "is singing itself into this Lutheran doctrine." A number of princes who had adopted the Lutheran faith were together at Frankfort soon after this hymn was written, and wished to have an evangelical service in one of the churches. A large congregation assembled, but the pulpit was occupied by a Roman Catholic priest, who proceeded to preach according to his own views. After listening for some time in indignant silence, the whole congregation arose and began singing this hymn, till they fairly sang the priest out of the church.

MISS CATHERINE WINKWORTH.

No. 157.

"AS I GLAD BID ADIEU TO THE WORLD'S FANCIED PLEASURE."

A young gentleman, tenderly attached to a young lady, was obliged to take a journey. During his absence she became a follower of Christ. He heard of the change and wrote her a letter full of invectives against religion and its gloomy professions. Having a good voice and playing well on the piano, she had been accustomed to entertain him with her music, especially in performing one song, of which he was very fond, the refrain of which was, "Ah, never! ah, no." At their first interview after his return, he tauntingly said, "I suppose you cannot sing me a song now?" "Oh, yes," was her response, "and I will;" and, proceeding to her piano, she sang a hymn she had composed to his favorite tune:

"As I glad bid adieu to the World's fancied pleasure,
You pity my weakness; alas! did you know
The joys of religion, that best hidden treasure,
Would you bid me resign them? Ah, never! Ah, no!

"You will surely rejoice when I say I've received
The only true pleasure attained here below.
I know by experience in whom I've believed:
Shall I give up this treasure? Ah, never! Ah, no!

"In the gay scenes of life I was happiness wooing;
But ah! in her stead I encountered a woe,
And found I was only a phantom pursuing;
Never once did I find her. Ah, never! Ah, no!

"But in these bright paths which you call melancholy,
I've found those delights which the world does not know.
Oh, did you partake them, you'd then see your folly,
Nor again bid me fly them. Ah, never! Ah, no!

By hearing these lines, his prejudices gave way, his feet entered the narrow path, and they became a truly happy pair.

DR. BELCHER.

No. 158.

"LORD OF HEAVEN! LONE AND SAD."

On a cold dark night, when the wind was blowing hard, Conrad, a worthy citizen of a little town in Germany, sat playing with his flute, while Ursula, his wife, was preparing supper. They heard a sweet voice singing outside:

"Foxes to their holes have gone,
Every bird into its nest;
But I wander here alone,
And for me there is no rest."

Tears filled the good man's eyes as he said, "What a pity it should be spoiled by being tried in such weather. I think it is the voice of a child."

"Let us open the door and see," said his wife, who had lost a little boy not long before, and whose heart was opened to take pity on the little wanderer.

Conrad opened the door and saw a ragged child who said: "Charity, good sir, for Christ's sake."

"Come in, my little one," said he, "you shall rest with me for the night."

The boy said, "Thank God," and entered. The heat of the room made him faint, but Ursula's kind care soon restored him. They gave him some supper, and then he told them that he was the son of a poor miner and wanted to be a priest. He wandered about and sang and lived on the money people gave him. His kind friends would not let him talk much, but sent him to bed. When he was asleep they looked in upon him, and were so pleased with his pleasant countenance that they determined to keep him if he was willing. In the morning they found that he was only too glad to remain. They sent him to school, and afterward he entered the monastery. There he found the Bible, which he read and from which he learned the way of life. The little voice of the little singer became the strong echo of the good news, "Justified by faith, we have peace with God through our Lord Jesus Christ." Conrad and Ursula, when they took that little singer into their house, little thought that they were nourishing the great champion of the Reformation. The poor child was Martin Luther! The following is the whole of the song which Luther sang on that memorable night:

"Lord of heaven, lone and sad,
  I would lift my soul to Thee;
Pilgrim in a foreign land,
  Gracious Father, look on me.
I shall neither faint nor die
While I walk beneath Thine Eye.

"I will stay my faith on Thee,
  And will never fear to tread
Where the Saviour-Master leads;
  He will give me daily bread.
Christ was hungry, Christ was poor,
He will feed me from His store.

"Foxes to their holes have gone,
  Every bird into its nest;
But I wander here alone,
  And for me there is no rest;
Yet I neither faint nor fear,
For the Saviour-Christ is near.

"If I live He'll be near me,
  If I die to Him I go;

He'll not leave me, I will trust Him,
And my heart no fear shall know.
Sin and sorrow I defy,
For on Jesus I rely."

Home Words.

No. 159.

"MUST JESUS BEAR THE CROSS ALONE?"

In one of the Armenian schools (for there are some schools among the Armenians; and they have had more since the missionary work began among them than before) it became noised among them that there were some Protestants. Protes, as they are called, in the school; but the teacher did not want any such element there; and he said, "If there are any boys here who are Protes, let them come upon the floor."

He did not suppose any one would arise; but four or five boys from ten to twelve years of age marched out upon the floor, declaring themselves Protes. He was a good deal confused. Hardly knowing what to say, he turned to the boys and said, "Do you believe in the Church?"

"Yes," they replied, "but we believe in the Bible more."

Then he turned to the school and said, "What shall we do to these boys for refusing to obey the Church?"

For a moment there was a pause. At last, one said, "Let us spit in their faces." So the teacher, thinking that a fine suggestion, called on the school to pass before the boys and each one to spit in their faces. They filed by, each one spitting as they passed along. Then feeling that they had triumphed over the boys, the teacher turned to the school and said, "Let us sing." And they sang a patriotic song! The boys stood silent, and did not sing; and the teacher turned to them and said, "Why do you not sing?"

They said, "We will, if you will sing a spiritual song."

Said he, "You may sing anything you wish to." And they sang these words:

"Must Jesus bear the cross alone,
And all the world go free?
No, there's a cross for every one,
And there's a cross for me.

"The consecrated cross I'll bear,
Till death shall set me free;
And then go home my crown to wear,
For there's a crown for me."

This incident was related at Plymouth Church, Brooklyn, New York, by Rev. Mr. Parmelee, missionary among the Armenians.

No. 160.

"GLORY AND HONOUR AND PRAISE. ALL GLORY, LAUD, AND HONOR."

THEODULPH.

It was on a Palm Sunday, about seven hundred and fifty years after the midnight song of Paul and Silas at Philippi, that the Emperor Louis, "the debonnaire" and his court, were on their way to the cathedral at Metz, in full procession, when, passing a dungeon, there issued from the prison bars a hymn, which as translated by Dr. Neale began:

"All glory, laud and honor
To Thee, Redeemer, King!
To Whom the lips of children
Made sweet hosannas ring."

The author was a prisoner behind those bars, and was singing the hymn he had written. The Emperor was so touched by the hymn, that he ordered the captive Bishop to be at once liberated, and directed that the hymn should be made the processional hymn for Palm Sunday. And so the hymn of praise, written behind prison bars, became a hymn of deliverance to the one who wrote it.

No. 161.

"COME, LET US ANEW OUR JOURNEY PURSUE."

REV. CHARLES WESLEY, 1708—1788.

A little girl, belonging to the Scotch Church, was permitted by her father to go to the watch night service of the Methodists in Aberdeen, on condition that she remember the text, and repeat it on her return home. At the end of the service the accustomed hymn was sung:

"Come, let us anew our journey pursue,
Roll round with the year," etc.

This was to her a novelty, and so fixed in the child's mind a love towards Methodism, that she ultimately became a member of that Society, and the wife of one of their ministers. The text failed to influence her mind seriously, but the last hymn did so effectually.

G. J. STEVENSON.

No. 162.

"BLEST BE THE DEAR UNITING LOVE."

REV. CHARLES WESLEY, 1708—1788.

John B. Gough records an incident of the use of the hymn of which this is the first line. He says: "I was twelve years of age, and my father being unable to furnish the premium necessary to my learning a trade, and having no prospect for me other than to be a gentleman's servant, made an agreement with a family of our village, who were about to emigrate to America, that they, in consideration of ten guineas paid by him, should take me with them, teach me a trade, and provide for me until I was twenty-one years of age. After much hesitation, my mother, from a sense of duty, yielded to this arrangement. I, boy-like, felt in high glee at the prospect before me. My little arrangements having been completed, on the fourth of June, 1829, I took, as I then supposed, a last view of my native village. The evening I was about to depart, a neighbor invited me to take tea at her house, which I accepted. My mother remarked to me afterwards, 'I wish you had taken tea with your mother, John'; and this little circumstance was a source of much pain to me in after years. The parting from my beloved parents was bitter. My poor mother folded me to her bosom; then she would hold me off at arm's length, and gaze fondly on my face, through her tearful eyes, reading, as only a mother could, the book of futurity to me. She hung up, on the accustomed peg, my old cap and jacket, and my school bag, and there they remained until years after she quitted the house. At length the parting words were spoken, and I left the home of my childhood, perhaps forever. A touching scene it was, as I went through the village toward the coach office that evening. As I passed through the streets, many a kind hand waved a farewell, and not a few familiar voices sounded out a hearty 'God bless you.' On the tenth of June, everything being arranged, we sailed from the Thames in the ship *Helen.* Passing Dover, we arrived off Sandgate, when it fell a dead calm, and the ship's anchors were dropped. I afforded some amusement to those around me by the eagerness with which I seized a telescope, and the positiveness with which I averred that I saw my old home. During that day, boat after boat came off to us from the shore, and friends of the family I was with, paid them visits; but I was unnoticed; my relatives did not come. After long and weary watching,

I saw a man standing up in a boat, with a white band round his hat. 'That's he! That's my father!' I shouted. He soon got on deck and almost smothered me with his kisses—from which I somewhat shrank, as his beard made very decided impressions on my smooth skin. I heard that my mother and sister had gone to a place of worship, at some distance from Sandgate, which I regretted much. When evening came on, our visitors from the shore repaired to their boats, which, when a few yards from the ship, formed in a half circle. Our friends stood up in them, and o'er the calm waters floated our blended voices, as we sang:

'Blest be the dear uniting love,
That will not let us part:
Our bodies may far off remove,
We still are one in heart.'

Boat after boat then vanished in the gloomy distance, and I went to bed. About midnight I heard my name called, and going on deck I there found my beloved mother and sister, who hearing on their return that I was in the offing, had paid half a guinea (money hard earned and with difficulty procured, yet cheerfully expended on a boatman to row them to the ship. They spent an hour with me and oh, how short it seemed!) then departed with many tears."

No. 163.

"COME, LET US JOIN OUR CHEERFUL SONGS."

REV. ISAAC WATTS, 1674—1748.

A sailor, at the approach of death, was aroused at the prospect before him. He was ill, had no Bible, nor even the power to read one. In his mental darkness, he remembered two verses of Watts's hymn commencing as above. Even his recollection was imperfect, but as he repeated to himself the line:

"'Worthy the Lamb That died,' they cry,
To be exalted thus.'"

the next ones flashed upon his memory,

"'Worthy the Lamb!' our hearts reply,
'For He was slain for us.'"

This phrase, "slain for us," gave him a glimpse of the way of salvation, revived old lessons received in the Sunday school, and brought him at last to pardon and peace.

It is related of Rev. Paxton Hood, that once when he had engaged to preach at a strange chapel, as he entered the pulpit, the deacon who announced the hymn was just giving out the lines:

"My thoughts on awful subjects roll,
Damnation and the dead."

when Mr. Hood started up and in his shrillest tones exclaimed: "Stop! Stop! My thoughts do not roll on any such subject.

"'Come, let us join our cheerful songs,
With angels round the throne,
Ten thousand, thousand, are their tongues,
But all their joys are one.'"

No. 164.

"GOD MOVES IN A MYSTERIOUS WAY."

William Cowper.

A business man entered the Fulton Street Prayer Meeting one day, heavily burdened and sadly cast down. He had hardly taken his seat, when the leader called for two verses of the hymn commencing as above. The meeting sang the verses:

"God moves in a mysterious way,
His wonders to perform;
He plants His footsteps in the sea,
And rides upon the storm.

"Judge not the Lord by feeble sense,
But trust Him for His grace;
Behind a frowning providence
He hides a smiling face."

The man felt that he was certainly walking beneath a frowning providence, but he had not felt assured of the smiling face beyond. The song cheered his heart, however, and strengthened his faith. He went away determined to look for the smiling face and soon it appeared to him, from out of the cloud; God helped him.

DR. PRIME.

The late Rev. Hugh Stowell, of Manchester, England, relates an incident concerning this hymn: "One of the Lancashire mill-owners, who had struggled hard and long to keep his hands employed during the cotton famine arising from the American war, in 1865, at last found it impossible to proceed; and calling his work people together, told them that he should be compelled, after the usual notice to close his mills. The news was received with sadness and sympathy; to them it meant privation and suffering, to him it might be ruin. None cared to speak in reply; when suddenly arose the voice of song from one of the girls, who was a Sunday-school teacher; she, feeling it to be an occasion requiring Divine help and guidance, gave out the verse of Cowper's hymn:

'Ye fearful saints fresh courage take;
The clouds ye so much dread
Are big with mercy, and shall break
In blessings on your head.'

All the mill-hands joined in singing the verse amidst deep emotion, sympathy and tears."

No. 165.

"LORD I HEAR OF SHOWERS OF BLESSING."

MRS. ELIZABETH CODNER.

The singing leader in an American Sunday school, was a man of skeptical tendencies—moral and upright, though far from being a Christian. One Sunday, this hymn was commenced as usual, but when the leader came to the passage:

"Pass me not, O gracious Saviour,
Let me live and cling to Thee";

his voice quivered, his frame shook, and in anguish he cried out, "Pray for me!" It was a scene of thrilling interest, and earnest prayers then went up from teachers and scholars, that he who had so long sung the sweet songs of Zion without feeling their power, might now sing with the spirit and the understanding also. He was happily converted and is now a faithful Christian.

No. 166.

"O WHERE SHALL REST BE FOUND?"

JAMES MONTGOMERY, 1771—1854.

In the Fulton Street, New York, Prayer Meeting, a young man said that he had gone the downward road until he was sick of sin, and of himself. He resolved to do away with himself, and stood at the edge of the wharf, pistol in hand, ready to shoot himself, and then to tumble over into the water. Just then, there flashed across his mind the words:

> " 'Tis not the whole of life to live,
> Nor all of death to die."

The words served to stay him in his mad purpose, and from that hour he began to seek a better way, and soon found the way of life.

Sabbath Reading, January, 1886.

No. 167.

"HOW CAN I SINK WITH SUCH A PROP?"

Rev. Isaac Watts, 1674—1748.

The leader of the Fulton Street, New York, Prayer Meeting, one noon said that he was present for the last time. He was about to seek a permanent home in Kansas. He had often been in the meeting before, but upon one occasion his attendance was fraught with eternal results. He came in a helpless, hopeless, lost man. He had been a sad slave to dissipation. Friends had long since ceased to indulge the hope of his improvement, and he just felt that he was sinking into ruin, here and hereafter. He sat near the leader's desk, despondent—aye, despairing. Who could help him? He could not sink much lower on earth, but with no one to pity and no one to save, he must soon sink into the hell, that seemed greedily gaping to receive him. Never more miserable, just then his ear was arrested by the words of a verse of a hymn, called for by the friend in the chair:

> "How can I sink with such a prop
> As my eternal God?"

These were all the words he caught, but they set him to thinking—thinking that possibly the Lord had led him to the meeting, and that there was yet hope for him. Next day he presented his request for prayer, and ere long was rejoicing in Christ as his Savior.

No. 168.

"VAIN, DELUSIVE WORLD ADIEU."

REV. CHARLES WESLEY, 1708—1788.

In the year 1783, it was announced at Rood, a little country village in England, that "the boy preacher" was to preach, and all the young men and women resolved to hear him. They crowded the preaching room, and listened to the sermon with profound attention; the place was still as death. At the close of the sermon the preacher gave out the hymn:

"Vain, delusive world adieu,
With all of creature good!
Only Jesus I pursue,
Who bought me with His Blood:

"All the pleasures I forego;
I trample on thy wealth and pride;
Only Jesus will I know,
And Jesus crucified."

The fine voices of the young people produced a solemn effect; the last two lines were repeated at every verse, and at the end all those present were deeply moved. The young preacher paused, spoke of the delightful effect of the singing, but arrested their attention by an earnest appeal to follow out the teaching of the hymn by taking up their baptismal vows and yielding their hearts to God that day. The appeal was so earnest, so affectionate, that thirteen young persons that night and at the prayer meeting early next morning gave their hearts to God. The preacher was Dr. Adam Clarke, and fifty years after, one of those young persons called on him, and reminded him of the hymn sung and preached that day at Rood.

No. 169.

"COMMIT THOU ALL THY GRIEFS."

REV. PAUL GERHARDT, 1606—1676.

In a little village near Warsaw there used to stand a house, and over the door an iron tablet on which was carved a raven with a ring in its beak and underneath one stanza of this hymn:

"Thou everywhere hast sway
And all things serve Thy might!
Thy every act pure blessing is,
Thy path unsullied light."

How came it there? There lived in that village a pious German peasant whose name was Dobry. He had fallen far in arrears with his rent and the landlord threatened to evict him. It was winter. All his entreaties for longer time had been in vain and next day his family would be turned out into the snow. The church bell called to evening prayer and Dobry kneeled among the rest. They sang this hymn:

"Commit thou all thy griefs
And ways into his hands,"

and as they sang something made a noise upon the window close by where Dobry knelt. Opening the window he found a raven which his grandfather had tamed and set at liberty. In its bill was a finger ring set with precious stones. Dobry took it from the bird and it was found to have been one lost by the King. It was taken to him and he rewarded Dobry so that he had no need and built for him a house of his own and to commemorate the wonderful occurrence of that wintry night this iron plate was put over its door with its raven and its ring and its song engraved upon it.

No. 170.

"O HAPPY DAY THAT FIXED MY CHOICE."

Rev. Philip Doddridge, 1702—1751.

The late Duncan Mathieson has related that on one of his evangelistic visits to Dundee, at the fair held there, he was preaching in the street, when two young women stopped to hear the singing, which began with:

"O happy day that fixed my choice
On Thee, my Saviour and my God!
Well may this glowing heart rejoice,
And tell its raptures all abroad."

Said one of the girls to the other, "Come away, we shall be too late for the fair."

The Spirit of God had already arrested the attention of the other girl, with the words "happy day" and she replied, "I dare not gang." The flighty one fled in haste and was not saved; the other remained, and that day gave her heart to God.

No. 171.

"COME WE WHO LOVE THE LORD."

Rev. Isaac Watts, 1674—1748.

Rev. Andrew Kinsman met a young clergyman with Rev. George Whitefield, at the Tabernacle house, just before

Whitefield's departure for America. There was after dinner a tremendous storm of thunder and lightning. Mr. Kinsman, supposing the clergyman "to be a serious person," put his hand on his shoulder, and quoted a stanza of this hymn, which is not in our later collections:

"The God that reigns on high,
And thunders when He please,
That rides upon the stormy sky
And manages the seas."

ending with the next stanza

"This awful God is ours,
Our Father and our Love."

It resulted in the conversion of his companion.

No. 172.

"MIGHTY GOD! WHILE ANGELS BLESS THEE."

REV. ROBERT ROBINSON, 1735—1790.

Robert Robinson was a poor boy, too poor to get the education for the Church that his mother wanted him to have; so at fourteen years of age he was apprenticed to a barber in London, who often had to find fault with him for paying more attention to his book than to his work. When seventeen, he went with some companions one Sunday for a holiday. They found an old fortune teller and made her drink to hear her maudlin talk. She predicted for Robinson that he would see his children and his children's children. This struck his quick mind and he determined to store his memory with things that might interest his family in later years. To make a beginning he went to hear George Whitefield preach that night. Whitefield was preaching on Matthew 3:7, and his words produced such an impression on young Robinson that he found little comfort until nearly three years later he became a Christian. Three years later he began to preach, and afterward became a Baptist. He was quite eccentric and was by turn a Wesleyan, Independent and Baptist, and at last a Unitarian. One day a little boy was sitting on Mr. Robinson's knee, and while sitting there, Mr. Robinson wrote a hymn for the little boy, and after reading it to him placed it in his hand for him to call his own. It began:

"Mighty God, while angels bless Thee,
May an infant lisp Thy Name."

It was set to music by Dr. Randall.

No. 173.

"COME, THOU FOUNT OF EVERY BLESSING."

Rev. Robert Robinson, 1735—1790.

In the latter part of the author's life he seemed to have lost much of his piety and often indulged in a levity not befitting his profession. He was once traveling in a stage coach with a lady, who soon perceived that he was familiar with religious subjects, although she had no suspicion as to who he was. She had just been reading this hymn, and she asked his opinion of it. He tried to waive the question and to turn the conversation into other channels, but she told how much and how often she had been helped by the hymn, and pressed him for his opinion of it, until at last he burst into tears and exclaimed, "Madam, I am the poor unhappy man who composed that hymn many years ago, and I would give a thousand worlds, if I had them, to enjoy the feelings I then had."

No. 174.

"AWAKE, MY SOUL, TO MEET THE DAY."

REV. PHILIP DODDRIDGE, 1702—1751.

The author gave to this hymn the title "A Morning Hymn to be Used at Awaking and Arising," and this was the purpose for which he himself used it. It was his habit to arise at five o'clock in the morning winter and summer, and his first act was to sing this hymn. Indeed tradition says that he began the singing while still in bed, and that when he reached the line "As, rising now I seal my vows," which was in the sixth stanza, he sprang out of bed.

No. 175.

"THINE EARTHLY SABBATH, LORD, WE LOVE."—1736.

REV. PHILIP DODDRIDGE, 1702—1751.

(See No. 34 for custom of writing hymns for sermons.)

This hymn was written to be used at the end of a sermon preached January 2, 1736, from the text, "There remaineth therefore a rest to the people of God." Hebrews, 4:9.

Dr. Gardiner Spring, of New York, wrote in his diary under date of May 25, 1851. He had been under some affliction and says that until that day he had not opened his piano to sing, since it occurred. Then he wrote, "I felt that while all God's works praise Him, my voice also should be vocal with His praise. How beautiful is this green earth on a Sabbath day! I could only give utterance to the words:

"'Thine earthly Sabbaths, Lord, we love,
But there's a nobler rest above.'"

I remember one delightful Sabbath in the home of Dr. C. L. Goodell. We gathered in the morning and sang the hymn:

"Thine earthly Sabbaths, Lord, we love,
But there's a nobler rest above."

The doctor said, "We have sung this hymn every Sabbath morning for eighteen years. On the sea, in foreign lands, at home; we have never omitted it when together." The sentiment of the hymn pervaded the home life that day. It went with us to the house of God, where it seemed to give power to prayer and praise, and to wing with love the spoken truth. It was present in the little group of friends at the evening meal: and when the day closed, which had been filled with loving ministries, its memory remained in the household like a benediction."

Rev. A. E. Duning, D.D., in *Congregationalist*, January 3, 189—.

No. 176.

"JERUSALEM, THE GLORIOUS."

Bernard of Cluny, Twelfth Century.

A small part of a Latin poem of three thousand lines, written by Bernard, a monk of Cluny in France. Five or six hymns in common use among us are taken from this poem. It is curious that about the time when St. Bernard was abbot of the Monastery of Cluny, monks from that place were sent over to England to occupy a priory just built at Castleacre, in Norfolk. So that the hymns of their leader, which within the last thirty years we are just learning to sing again, were no doubt sung in a few English churches seven hundred years ago. Would you like to know something of this old Catholic monk who lived in the forest of France eight hundred years ago? Here is a glimpse of him. He would be walking with his brother monks in the cloisters or the garden, when sometimes he would stop and say, "My brothers, I must go! there is some one waiting for me in my cell." That some one was Jesus, and he would leave his companions among the flowers while he went to meet Him and talk with Him in his cell.

No. 177.

"MY DAYS ARE GLIDING SWIFTLY BY."

REV. DAVID NELSON, 1793—1844.

The author of this hymn owned and operated a plantation in Missouri, on which negro slaves were employed. After listening to an address on slavery he declared, "I will live on roast potatoes and salt before I will hold slaves." He became an ardent advocate of the plan of colonizing the slaves in Africa, and called a meeting to discuss the subject at the close of a camp-meeting service. By this he incurred the displeasure of the slave-holders, and was driven from his home by a band of armed men. After three days and nights of wandering, he at last reached the Mississippi River opposite Quincy, Illinois, and was able to make known his condition to friends in that city. Hiding there in the bushes, with enemies behind and the river gliding swiftly by before, and on its other shore the soil of a free state where were friends and safety, he wrote on the backs of old letters he had in his pockets, the words of this hymn:

"My days are gliding swiftly by,
And I, a pilgrim stranger
Would not detain them as they fly,
These hours of toil and danger.

"For, oh, we stand on Jordan's strand,
Our friends are passing over;
And just before, the shining shore,
We may almost discover."

You will not be satisfied to have the author left where he wrote the hymn, and so I will add that in the dusk of an evening, a boat paddled across the river, and a fisherman cast his line in the water, while the boat floated along with the current, until the almost starved poet was discovered, when having caught the fish he was after, the boat was paddled back to the Illinois side.

So much for the song and its writer; now for the tune. George F. Root the composer, the same who wrote, "Tramp, tramp, tramp, the boys are marching," and "The Battle Cry of Freedom," used to spend his summers on a place called Willow Farm, near North Reading, Massachusetts, preparing work for the singing classes which he used to teach in winter. One summer day in 1854 he was working away at this sort of work, when his mother came into the room and handed him a clipping she had cut from a newspaper, saying, "George, I think that would be good for music."

He looked at it, and as he read it a melody sang itself into his mind and he jotted it down, and went on with his work. Later, when he took it up again to harmonize it, it seemed so simple and commonplace that he thought at first it was hardly worth spending time on. But thinking it might be of use to some one, it was completed, and some months later printed. He says that in later years, when he knew the song was being sung in all the churches and Sunday schools, and in mission fields, he wondered why it should be so.

No. 178.

"SO FADES THE LOVELY BLOOMING FLOWER."

Miss Anne Steele, 1717—1778.

In 1831, a young man in Salem, Massachusetts, sat down to read a story by Theodore Hook, entitled, "Passion and Principle." It was a sad story and ended sadly. When through it he laid down the book and sat thinking of what he had read, and as he thought there came into his mind a stanza of this hymn:

> "Then gentle patience smiles on pain
> And dying hope revives again!
> Hope wipes the tear from sorrow's eye
> And faith points upward to the sky."

And with the words there came an unbidden melody, and stepping to a piano in the room, he harmonized the melody, and put it upon paper and threw it into a drawer of his desk. Two years after, Lowell Mason came to Salem and opened a singing school. Toward the close of the course he asked if any of the class had ever attempted to compose any music. The tune in the desk drawer came into mind, and it was gotten and handed to Dr. Mason, who liked it so well that he asked leave to use it in a collection he was publishing. A name had to be given it, and the composer wished to use the name of his wife, Sally Cook, but all his efforts failed to poetize the words, and so he took the name of the street on which she lived when he wooed and married her.

The Peace Jubilee held in Boston in 1872, under the direction of Patrick S. Gilmore, was one of the greatest musical festivals ever known in this country. A grand coliseum was erected for its meetings capable of holding an audience of forty thousand people, and ten thousand picked singers and players from the choirs and musical societies of the country rendered the music. It was Gilmore's custom to close each day's program with a hymn tune. One day during the festival was named "President's Day," because on that day General Grant, then President of the nation, honored it with his presence. The tune for the day was "Federal Street." Every available spot in the building was occupied and more than ten thousand people were in the orchestra and choir. When the time came for the closing hymn, the leader beckoned to an old gentleman who sat among the singers, and when he came forward, he handed to him his baton, and Henry K. Oliver led that enormous choir, perhaps the largest that ever joined in the rendering of a musical composition, in singing the piece he had composed and named for this girl more than forty years before.

No. 179.

"TO THY TEMPLE WE REPAIR."

James Montgomery, 1771—1854.

A Moravian minister living in a little town in Ayrshire, Scotland, had a little boy whom his parents intended should be a minister like his father. But he began to write poetry as early as ten years of age, and showed such a love for it, that the intention to make a minister of him was abandoned. When sixteen he went to work in a retail store, but soon tiring of this, he set out with only a few shillings in his pocket, to try his fortune in the world. When twenty-one his wanderings brought him to Sheffield, and this was ever after his home. He went to work for a printer, and later became the owner and editor of a paper. He wrote and published a political song which was distasteful to the party in power, and was imprisoned for it. He was the friend of every good enterprise; of missions, of churches, of Sunday schools, and wrote hymns for them all, so that he won for himself the title of "The Poet of the Sanctuary." He never married, and died while asleep.

No. 180.

"LET PARTY NAMES NO MORE"—1769.

Rev. Benjamin Beddome, 1717—1795.

The story is told that Rev. John Wesley was at one time much troubled over the final disposition of the different sects and the probability as to the future home of each. While giving to this question much thought, he had a dream one night in which he was carried to the gates of hell. "Are there any Roman Catholics here?" asked he. "Yes, sir," was the reply. "Any Episcopalians?" "A great many." "Any Presbyterians?" "Yes." "Any Congregationalists?" "Yes." "Any Baptists?" "Yes." "Any Methodists?" and this he thought would be a clincher; but still the reply came back as before, "Yes," and away went the great founder of Methodism in high dudgeon. And then his dream transferred him to the gate of heaven, and again he put the same questions: "Are there any Roman Catholics here?" "Not one," was the reply. "Any Episcopalians?" "None." "Any Presbyterians?" "Not any." "Any Congregationalists?" "None." "Any Baptists?" "No." "Any Methodists?" "None." "Well, then," exclaimed the great Methodist, "who are they inside?" "All Christians!" came out the jubilant reply.

No. 181.

"THOUGH TROUBLES ASSAIL, AND DANGERS AFFRIGHT."

REV. JOHN NEWTON, 1725—1807.

Written in February, 1775, and first appeared in the *Gospel Magazine*, January, 1777. John Newton had a remarkable experience. He was born in London, and mingling with idle and wicked boys, he soon became as idle and bad as his companions. While a young man he became an infidel in his opinions and a profligate in his conduct. He became a sailor, deserted his ship, was brought home in irons and publicly whipped. Then he went to the coast of Africa and entered the service of a slave trader and suffered great hardships, and became as wicked and depraved as a human being could well become. In his epitaph written by himself he described himself as "once an infidel and libertine and a servant of slaves." At length he escaped and on his homeward voyage he read a religious book, and the thought struck him, "What if these things should be true?" A review of his life followed, and he became a Christian.

No. 182.

"WHEN MARSHALLED ON THE NIGHTLY PLAIN"

HENRY KIRKE WHITE, 1785—1806.

A Mr. James Miller and a Mr. Clarke were talking of Scotch melodies, and Miller expressed an ardent ambition to be able to compose a Scottish air. Mr. Clarke partly by way of a joke told him to keep his fingers on the black keys of the instrument and preserve some sort of rhythm, and what he played would be a Scottish air. Whether Miller followed the directions or not I do not know, but at any rate within a few days he had composed the air we know as "Bonnie Doon."

In the town of Nottingham, England, there was a little boy who helped his father at his work which was that of a butcher. When fourteen he was set at work at a stocking loom, with the hope that he might later on get employment in a hosiery store. A year later he entered a lawyer's office, to run his errands and pick up at odd moments the rudiments of law. When a butcher's boy, and while at the loom he had not been idle, but had won at fifteen years of age a silver medal and a pair of globes for a translation from Horace, and at seventeen he was writing for papers and magazines, and was urged to publish a volume of poems. He was at first a skeptic in religion, but gradually changed his views and became a Christian. He then left the lawyer's office, and began to study for the ministry. He won a high place at Cambridge University, but his excessive study ended his life, and he died at twenty-one, of consumption. He wrote ten hymns. This one describes his own condition as a skeptic, and his progress to Christian faith. We always sing it to the tune of "Bonnie Doon."

No. 183.

"ALWAYS WITH US, ALWAYS WITH US."

REV. EDWIN HENRY NEVIN, 1814.

Many of our hymns have been written with no thought that they would be used in the public worship of Christians, and so they were written using the singular pronoun instead of the plural. This is one of them, and if we should sing it in this way I am not sure but it would be to each of us more expressive than as it is here written. It is based on the words of Christ, "Lo, I am with you alway." (Matthew, 28:20) and if we look upon that sentence as addressed to each one of us singly it may assume a new place as a message of encouragement. Let us sing it so.

No. 184.

"FATHER BY THY LOVE AND POWER"—1836.

PROF. JOSEPH ANSTICE, 1808—1836.

This hymn will have an added interest when we know that its author dictated it to his wife at the very "evening hour" it describes; and that it expressed the thought of a feeble, dying man. Prof. Anstice, although only twenty-eight years old, had almost reached the end of life, and yet he devoted nearly the whole of each day to the students of the college in which he had been a teacher. Then when the evening hours came on, weary with the work, and suffering intensely from his disease, he sat down with his wife and composed a hymn. In this way he wrote fifty-two pieces, most of which are to be found in the hymn collections of today.

No. 185.

"I AM SO GLAD THAT OUR FATHER IN HEAVEN."

PHILIP BLISS, 1838—1876.

A ragged son of a drunkard, who had been drawn into a Sunday school and found Christ there, was so charmed with his new love and joy that unconsciously he kept humming over, "I am so glad that Jesus loves me!"

"Stop that!" roared his father; and the child stopped, but soon forgot himself, and was at it again. This time he was ordered to bed. But the words kept ringing in the father's ears, and in the middle of the night the boy heard, "Willie, Willie, wake up and sing that again!" Half awake he found that it was his father burdened with his sins, and begging the child to sing and pray for him. He was soon an earnest believer himself.

No. 186.

"NEARER MY GOD TO THEE."

MRS. SARAH FLOWER ADAMS, 1805—1849.

Sarah Flower Adams was a Unitarian, and it is objected by some to this hymn that no mention is made in it of Christ, and that the cross of which it sings is her own cross, and this is in keeping with the last stanza in which it is her own woes that are to lift her nearer to God; and to remedy this alleged defect in the hymn, Rev. Arthur Tozer Russell, a clergyman of the Church of England, has written another stanza as follows:

"Christ alone beareth me,
Where Thou dost shine:
Joint-heir He maketh me
Of the Divine:
In Christ my soul shall be
Nearer, my God, to Thee
Nearer to Thee."

Still the hymn as originally written finds a response in Christian hearts and is accepted, while the added stanza is usually rejected as not in keeping with the other verses and not needed to complete the writer's thought.

No. 187.

"WITH TEARFUL EYES I LOOK AROUND."

MISS CHARLOTTE ELLIOTT, 1789—1871.

One needs but to be reminded of it, to notice how closely this hymn and the more celebrated hymn by the same author beginning, "Just as I am, without one plea," are related to each other. In this one, each stanza ends with an invitation from Christ, "Come to Me!" while in that, each stanza ends with the response, "O Lamb of God, I come! I come!" As the hymns are both of the same meter, they can be sung antiphonally:

"With tearful eyes I look around.
Just as I am, without one plea."

"It tells me of a place of rest.
Just as I am, though tossed about."

"When against sin I strive in vain.
Just as I am and waiting not."

"When nature shudders, loath to part.
Just as I am, poor, wretched, blind."

"Come, for all else must fail and die.
Just as I am—Thy love unknown."

No. 188

"JUST AS I AM, WITHOUT ONE PLEA."

MISS CHARLOTTE ELLIOTT, 1789—1871.

A minister (Dr. Cæsar Malan) was once visiting (1822) at the house of a friend in Brighton, England. One evening he said to the daughter of his host, "I wish you were a Christian woman." She resented his speaking to her on this subject, and it was dropped; but what he had said, disturbed her, until she at last returned to him, and referring to what he had said before, said she would like to be a Christian, but she didn't know how. He talked with her a little and at last said, "You must give yourself to God just as you are."

"What! just as I am? You surely don't mean that God will accept me just as I am?"

"I mean just that," was the reply.

Nothing more was said then and soon the visitor left for his home in Switzerland. She became a Christian, and to describe how it was done she wrote a hymn, "Just as I am."

A counterpart or reply to this hymn was written by Rev. Russell Sturges Cook and sent by him to Miss Elliott. It was published in the *American Messenger*, March, 1850. The relation between the reply and the hymn is made all the closer from the fact that the wife of Mr. Cook was the daughter of Rev. Cæsar Malan. It begins, "Just as thou art, without one trace." Miss Elliott herself also wrote a hymn which bears the relation to this hymn of invitation to acceptance. The hymn begins, "With tearful eyes I look around": and each stanza ends with the invitation, "Come to Me!" (See No. 187.)

No. 189.

"JESUS, THY BLOOD AND RIGHTEOUSNESS."

For authorship see No. 63.

Sunday schools on the continent of Europe have been known but comparatively a few years. The first German Sunday-school superintendent died in 1865, at Carlsruhe. At his funeral the first four lines of this hymn were read, as containing the creed of the man who had gone. In these later days, when the creeds of the churches are the subject of so much debate, private Christians can, I think, feel safe if they can adopt as their own the simple creed of this German Sunday-school superintendent.

No. 190.

"HOW HAPPY IS THE PILGRIM'S LOT."

Rev. John Wesley, 1703—1791.

In the western part of England, many years ago, there lived a fellow not much more than half witted, whom everyone called "Foolish Dick." One morning Dick was on his way to a well for water, when an old Christian man who was leaning over his garden gate accosted him, "So you are going to the well for water, Dick?"

"Yes, sir!"

"Well, Dick, the woman of Samaria found Jesus Christ at the well."

"Did she, sir?"

"Yes, Dick!"

Dick passed on his way; but a new thought had entered his dull mind and thrilled it with new life; and when he came to the well he said to himself, "Why shouldn't I find Jesus at the well? Oh, that I could find Him!" Such a prayer never goes unanswered, and when Dick left the well his heart was as full as his pitcher, for he had found the Lord. From that time on he gave up all other occupation and spent all his time in telling to neighbors and friends the story of his conversion. His mind developed, and from talking to a few he came to preaching to the many. His memory showed a wonderful power, for a chapter in the Bible or a hymn once repeated in his hearing was his forever after, and he could quote from it at will. He went about the country as an itinerant evangelist, without money or means of support, but he always found shelter and food and clothing. He not only preached, but he sang, and this hymn was his favorite song. And when he sat by the fireside of some humble home where he had been received for the night, he would sit and wave to and fro, and sing:

"No foot of land do I possess,
No cottage in this wilderness,
A poor wayfaring man,
I lodge awhile in tents below,
Or gladly wander to and fro,
Till I my Canaan gain."

No. 191.

"COME ALL YE CHOSEN SAINTS OF GOD"—1757.

REV. JOSEPH HART, 1712—1768.

Of this hymn the author says, "The week before Easter, 1757, I had such an amazing view of the agony of Christ in the garden as I know not how well to describe. I was lost in wonder and adoration, and the impression was too deep, I believe, ever to be obliterated. I shall say no more of this, but only remark that, notwithstanding all that is talked about the sufferings of Jesus, none can know anything of them but by the Holy Ghost: and I believe that he that knows most knows but very little. It was then I made the first part of my hymn on the Passion:

"Come all ye chosen saints of God."

No. 192.

"COME, YE SINNERS, POOR AND WRETCHED."

REV. JOSEPH HART, 1712—1768.

About the year 1775, a young girl by the name of Abigail Binnell lived in the village of Shawbury, England. Her parents were strongly opposed to evangelical religion, but on one occasion she overheard some of the children of the village singing the hymn commencing:

"Come, ye sinners poor and wretched,
Weak and wounded, sick and sore:
Jesus ready stands to save you,
Filled with pity, love and power.'

By the Holy Spirit these words were applied to the young girl's soul as a call to a new and spiritual life. Her memory caught hold of them, and her mind was awakened to their import, and following the light they gave her, she became a follower of Christ. At home she was persecuted, and for a time even driven from her father's house. She was afterward, however, earnestly invited to return, and later became the wife of Rev. Thomas Harris, a well known Methodist preacher.

No. 193.

"COME, HOLY SPIRIT, COME! LET THY——"

REV. JOSEPH HART, 1712—1768.

The author of this hymn had a somewhat remarkable experience. He was the son of Christian parents, and well educated. Shortly after his conversion he fell into the delusion that he now had perfect liberty to do anything he wanted to. Nothing that he could do would be sin. This period in his life he himself describes very graphically: "In this abominable state I continued a loose backslider, an audacious apostate, a boldfaced rebel, for nine or ten years, not only sinning myself, but infecting others with the poison of my delusions." But then came a change in his life and he became an earnest Christian, a faithful preacher, and a good hymn writer.

No. 194.

"GRANDER THAN OCEAN'S STORY."

W. F. SHERWIN, 1826.

Written during a vacation rest on one of the beaches near New York City, while the author was lying under the shade of a tree watching the ocean.

No. 195.

"LORD WHEN WE BEND BEFORE THY THRONE."

REV. JOHN DACRE CARLYLE, 1759—1804.

The inspiration for this hymn was found in Asia. In 1799, the author, Rev. John Dacre Carlyle, accompanied the English ambassador to Turkey, the object of his visit being to see what literary treasures there might be in the public library of Constantinople. He extended his journey into Asia Minor. What he saw in his travels inspired his muse, and on his return he published a small book of "Poems Suggested Chiefly by Scenes in Asia Minor," etc. (1805.) This hymn is contained in that book.

No. 196.

"SAVIOR BREATHE AN EVENING BLESSING."

James Edmeston, 1791—1867.

It is to me a constant source of wonder how trivial things lead to important results. The author of this hymn was a surveyor and architect. One day he was reading a book of travels in Abyssinia, and came to a description of the pitching of the travelers' tent in the evening after the march of the day was over, and in it occurred these words: "At night their short evening hymn, 'Jesus forgive us,' stole through the camp." And so the thought of an evening hymn which should be a prayer alike for pardon and protection came into his mind, and he amplified it into this hymn, which has become one of our most popular and valued evening hymns.

No. 197.

"I LOVE THY KINGDOM, LORD."

Rev. Timothy Dwight, 1752—1817.

Here is a beautiful hymn by a busy man. He had made headway enough in his studies to enter Yale at fourteen years of age, and from that right on he was hard at work at his books at early morning hours, and by light of a candle late at night. He soon injured his eyes, so that they troubled him all his life, and for years he could only use them a few minutes at a time in any writing or reading; but he went right on as if nothing had happened; became a chaplain in the army, wrote patriotic songs and religious hymns, was elected President of Yale College, and pushed its work with such vigor that it advanced in prosperity more rapidly than ever before; wrote works of theology and volumes of sermons; and in his devotion and zeal and untiring activity in all church affairs fully exemplified the words of this hymn.

No. 198.

"COME GRACIOUS SPIRIT, HEAVENLY DOVE."

REV. SIMON BROWNE, 1680—1732.

Simon Browne began to preach before he was twenty years of age. When about forty years old, he was attacked by a highway-robber, and in the struggle which ensued Browne killed the robber. This event caused him great distress of mind and brought on a curious hallucination. He believed that God had annihilated in him the thinking substance and divested him of all consciousness, that he really had no soul. And yet, while in this condition he did some of the best work of his life. He was the author of a dictionary of the English language and wrote a commentary on First Corinthians which was a continuation of the work left unfinished by Matthew Henry when he died; and all this while he stoutly maintained that he had no power to think. One of his contemporaries, however, said of him that instead of having no soul, he wrote and acted as if he had two.

No. 199.

"BLEST BE THE TIE THAT BINDS."

REV. JOHN FAWCETT, 1739—1817.

John Fawcett was settled as pastor of a Baptist church at Wainsgate, England, in 1765, and after seven years of labor there was invited to the pastorate of a prosperous church in London and decided to accept the call. His farewell sermon had been preached, his household goods stood upon wagons at the door, and his people gathered about to bid him farewell, mingling with their parting words entreaties to remain. At last, as the story goes, the minister and his wife sat down and wept, and Mrs. Fawcett said, "O John, John, I cannot bear this! I know not how to go!"

"Nor I either," replied he, "nor will we go. Unload the wagons and put everything in the place where it was before." A letter was sent to London explaining the circumstances. Dr. Fawcett settled down to work again on his salary of less than two hundred dollars a year, and this hymn commemorates the event.

No. 200.

"AWAKE AND SING THE SONG."

WILLIAM HAMMOND, 1719—1783.

We who think three or four stanzas of a hymn quite enough to sing in our religious services, would not have enjoyed the practice of Christians of a century or two ago, I fear. Here is a hymn which, as its author wrote it, contained fourteen stanzas, and its title was, "Before Singing of Hymns, by way of Introduction:" and we may imagine perhaps how much time they devoted to the "Singing of Hymns," if they sang fourteen stanzas "by way of Introduction."

No. 201.

"JESUS MY ALL TO HEAVEN IS GONE."

REV. JOHN CENNICK, 1717—1755.

A gay boy, who attended dances and theatres, while walking along Cheapside, London, was convicted of sin. He became greatly depressed and reformed so far as to give up his gay practices; but he turned downward instead of upward—skeptical and weary of life, and prayed for death. He tried austerity and says, "I even ate acorns, leaves of trees, crabs, and grass, and wished often heartily that I could bring myself to live only upon roots and herbs." One day while thus trying to earn salvation for himself, he came upon the words, "I am thy Salvation." The words came to him like a revelation and led to his accepting Christ as his Savior. Soon after he began telling his experience to others, and soon took up the regular work of a minister of the gospel. This experience of seeking to climb up some other way, and then of accepting Jesus as "the way, the truth and the life," and then of "telling to all around what a dear Savior he had found," he commemorates in this hymn.

No. 202.

"WHEN HE COMETH, WHEN HE COMETH."

GEORGE F. ROOT, 1820.

"WHAT A FRIEND WE HAVE IN JESUS."

REV. HORATIUS BONAR, 1808.

A minister in the steerage of an English steamer asked, "What shall we sing? It must be something that we all know, and there are people here from nearly every country in Europe."

"Then it will have to be an American hymn-tune," said the master of the steerage. "Try 'His Jewels,'"

So they started up, "When He cometh, when He cometh to make up His jewels." It was written by George F. Root, the same who wrote "The Battle Cry of Freedom," "Tramp, Tramp, Tramp, the Boys are Marching," "Rosalie the Prairie Flower," etc.

"What next?" said the minister.

"What a friend we have in Jesus," was the answer; and people speaking three or four languages joined in singing this song, the tune also written by an American, Mr. C. C. Converse. The words are by Horatius Bonar, of Scotland. It was the tune that had given to the words a language that all could sing.

No. 203.

"THE LORD'S MY SHEPHERD, I'LL NOT WANT."

FRANCIS ROUSE.

This piece, out of the old "Rouse's Version," well illustrates the power of early impressions. A child only three years old used to be put to bed with his grandfather, and never until he died forgot the fervor with which he prayed, nor the feeling with which he used to repeat this paraphrase of the Twenty-third Psalm; and he particularly remembered the last stanza:

"Goodness and mercy all my life
Shall surely follow me;
And in God's house for evermore
My dwelling-place shall be."

This is the testimony of Dr. John Wilson, who for fifty years was a philanthropist and scholar residing in the East.

No. 204.

"TIME IS WINGING US AWAY"—1812.

JOHN BURTON, 1773—1822.

John Burton was a Baptist Sunday school teacher in Nottingham, England, and was greatly interested in the general welfare of Sunday schools. He wrote many hymns for their use, and compiled a hymn book for the same purpose. When about thirty years of age, he prepared a careful plan for checking disorder in Sunday schools, which suggests a possible difference between the Sunday schools of that day and of this; and another difference between the work done in Sunday schools then and now is suggested by the fact that he prepared a Sunday school spelling-book which had a very large sale. This is one of his hymns written for Sunday schools.

No. 205.

"LEAVE GOD TO ORDER ALL THY WAYS."

GEORG NEUMARK, 1621—1681.

In the year 1641, a young man of twenty years was traveling with a party of merchants from Leipzig to Lubeck. He was trying to work his way to a German University where he hoped to be able to study. After passing through the town of Magdeburg, the party was plundered by a band of highway robbers who took everything the young man had except his prayer book and a little money that he had sewed up in his clothes. He went back to Magdeburg but could get no employment there; then to Luneburg and could get nothing there; and so from town to town hunting for work and finding none, until in the middle of winter he reached the town of

Keil and fell in with one of the pastors of that town who befriended him; but still day after day passed on, and he could get no work, and he was living on the kindness of his new-found friend; but after nearly a month of this, a tutor in the family of a judge in the city fell suddenly into disgrace and ran away, and by the help of the minister the young man secured the position, "which good fortune" as he himself wrote concerning it, "coming suddenly and as if fallen from heaven, greatly rejoiced me, and on that very day I composed to the honor of my beloved Lord, this here and there well-known hymn, and had certainly cause enough to thank the Divine compassion for such unlooked-for grace shown me."

No. 206.

"COME, SAVIOR, JESUS, FROM ABOVE."

MADAME ANTOINETTE BOURIGNON, 1616—1680.

Tr. by Rev. John Wesley or J. Byrom.

The author of this hymn was a French woman. Her father had urged her to accept in marriage some one of the many suitors who had offered themselves; but she refused, and to escape her father's anger she left her home —a wanderer, and wrote this hymn, expressive of her determination to live for Christ. There are many allusions in it to the circumstances that called it forth.

No. 207.

"FROM ALL THAT DWELL BELOW THE SKIES."

REV. ISAAC WATTS, 1674—1748.

By decree of the British Government, the slaves of the West India Islands were emancipated on the first of August,

1834. Many predicted that the emancipation would be attended with pillage and blood; but these predictions were not verified, as no law was broken, no violence or insult offered to any one. "On the evening of the thirty-first of July" the negroes crowded into the chapels and remained there, engaged in exercises of devotion, until the day of their freedom dawned.

"I waited last night," wrote Mr. William Wedlock, a Methodist missionary, "for the clock to strike twelve, with deep emotion. Peace prevails throughout the whole of these western parishes, and, I believe, throughout the island. Joy is depicted on every countenance. I preached three times today to free persons. This is the first time a preacher could, with entire freedom, explain the fourth commandment to them. Thousands who have been prevented for years from keeping the Sabbath have now an opportunity of doing so."

A few days after, he wrote: "Could the friends of freedom at home have seen the thousands of clean, well-dressed, and well-behaved Negroes who poured into the town, they would have heartily rejoiced. Our large chapel was literally crammed, and many stood in the yard exposed to the rays of a scorching sun; so anxious were the newly liberated people to express their thankfulness to God for the great deliverance He has wrought. On Friday afternoon I preached from I Samuel 12:22; afterward I read to them the Governor's excellent letter of advice; then I announced the noble intention of the Bible Society to present every freed Negro with a Testament. Upon every face a smile gleamed, and tears of joy trickled down not a few swarthy cheeks. The multitude then arose in a mass, and shouted, rather than sang:

> 'Eternal are Thy mercies, Lord;
> Eternal truth attends Thy word;
> Thy praise shall sound from shore to shore,
> Till suns shall rise and set no more.' "

Thus peacefully and delightfully did the memorable first of August pass away at Montego Bay and throughout the West Indies.

Wesleyan Methodist Magazine, October, 1867.

No. 208.

"LORD IN THE MORNING THOU SHALT HEAR."

REV. ISAAC WATTS, 1674—1748.

Our Service of Song owes a double debt to Isaac Watts. He was the first to overcome by the beauty and the grace of his poetic hymns the authority of the Established Church and the prejudice of the people against the use of anything but paraphrases of the Psalms in the public service of the Church; and he was also the first to render these same Psalms in language adapted to the Christian era. He himself explains that it is his view that the Psalms "ought to be translated in such manner as we have reason to believe David would have composed them if he had lived in our day." Comparing this new plan with the literal paraphrases of those who had worked before him he says, "What need is there that I should wrap up the shining honors of my Redeemer in the dark and shadowy language of a religion that is now forever abolished." So this hymn, which is his imitation of the Fifth Psalm, makes direct reference to Christ.

No. 209.

"BEHOLD THE GLORIES OF THE LAMB."

REV. ISAAC WATTS, 1674—1748.

When about twenty years old Watts, who had been studying in London, returned to his father's house at Southampton to continue his studies there. He attended church with his parents and complained to his father of the poor quality of the hymns they used. His father was a deacon of the church, a man of taste himself, and knew something of young Isaac's poetic skill, for he had tried and failed to whip it out of him when a child. So the father suggested that he try his hand at making better ones. Before the next Sunday this hymn was written ready for their use; and so was begun the hymn writing of the man who has for now almost two hundred years stood at the head of the Poets of the Church. This is the tradition as to the origin of this hymn, and the language of the first stanza supports it.

No. 210.

"WHY SHOULD THE CHILDREN OF A KING?"

REV. ISAAC WATTS, 1674—1748.

Over a hundred years ago, on one of Mr. Wesley's visits to Chesterfield, he had commenced an out-door service in the market place. During the first prayer the constable came and demanded his presence before a magistrate. The prayer ended, the man of authority marched off with the preacher; but before doing so the man of prayer showed his faith by saying to his hearers, "Friends, sing a hymn while I am gone. I shall soon be back;" and he gave out the couplet:

"Why should the children of a King
Go mourning all their days?"

Mr. Wesley returned, and preached, before the hymn had been sung through a second time.

(See No. 34.) This hymn was written to be sung at the close of a sermon from Romans 8:14-16, and Ephesians 1:13-14.

No. 211.

"COME WE WHO LOVE THE LORD."

REV. ISAAC WATTS, 1674—1748.

As written by Watts this hymn contains ten stanzas and two of the ones usually admitted in recent collections have some incidents connected with them. They are as follows:

"The God that rules on high
And thunders when He please,
That rides upon the stormy sky
And manages the seas:

"This awful God is ours;
Our Father and our love.
He will send down His heavenly powers
To carry us above."

In 1831, a Mr. James Martin, of Liverpool, was a passenger on board the ship *Rothsay Castle* when she was wrecked between Liverpool and Beaumavis, and most of the passengers were lost. He, with a few others, caught a plank and floated with it, until one after another he saw the others swept away by the dashing waves. He was a Christian man, and there alone amid the roaring seas, he thought of this hymn and repeated these stanzas. He was afterward rescued, and little wonder that he renewed his vows to consecrate to the service of God the life that God had saved.

No. 212.

"DIVINE AND MORAL SONGS."

REV. ISAAC WATTS, 1674—1748.

When Dr. Watts was nearly forty years old, he was so often sick as to be practically an invalid, and a gentleman who knew him well, after one of his attacks, invited him to his home to recuperate. Of this invitation Watts afterward said, "This day thirty years I came hither to the house of my good friend, Sir Thomas Abney, intending to spend but one single week under his friendly roof, and I have extended my visit to the length of exactly thirty years." He stayed six years after that and then died. While on this visit, the friend at whose house he was staying suggested to him that he write some hymns for children, and this led him to the preparing of one of the most remarkable books which at that time had ever been published: "Divine and Moral Songs for the use of Children." (1715.) Millions upon millions of copies of this little book have been sold both in England and America, and it has been translated into many other languages. It contained that good old cradle song with which many even of us were sung to sleep by mothers who now sing in heaven:

"Hush, my dear, lie still and slumber,
Holy angels guard thy bed."

and it contained that wonderful apostrophe to industry:

"How doth the little busy bee
Improve each shining hour,
And gather honey all the day
From every shining flower."

and that equally wonderful exhortation to good behavior:

"Let dogs delight to bark and bite
For God hath made them so;
Let bears and lions growl and fight
For 'tis their nature to.

"But children you should never let
Your angry passions rise;
Your little hands were never made
To tear each others' eyes."

And it contained besides some beautiful hymns that have outlived a great many later born ones, and are still found in our hymnals. The following hymns are some of these:

"Great God, to Thee my voice I raise."
"Blest be the wisdom and the power."
"Great God, with wonder and with praise."
"Happy the child whose tender years."
"When we devote our youth to God."
"Youth when devoted to the Lord."
"How glorious is our heavenly King."
"Let love through all your actions run."
"Lord how delightful 'tis to see."
"O, write upon my memory Lord."
"Lord, I ascribe it to Thy grace."
"My God Who makes the sun to know."
"O 'tis a lovely thing for youth."
"Our tongues were made to bless the Lord."
"The praises of my tongue."
"There is a God Who reigns above."
"This is the day when Christ arose."
"We sing the almighty power of God."
"What blest examples do I find."

No. 213.

"JESUS, MY STRENGTH, MY HOPE"—1742.

REV. CHARLES WESLEY, 1708—1788.

There are seven stanzas in the original hymn as Wesley wrote it, and the last five of them begin with the words, "I want." The last stanza is never used because of its last four lines, which are, to say the least, peculiar. They read as follows:

"I want, I know not what!
I want, my wants to see;
I want, alas! what want I not,
When Thou art not in me."

No. 214.

"SEE HOW GREAT A FLAME ASPIRES."

REV. CHARLES WESLEY, 1708—1788.

"The colliers at Newcastle thronged to hear Charles Wesley, felt the power of truth and were converted. Upon one occasion, when he was preaching there, nine or ten thousand attentive people listened to his word. He became himself so earnest that he preached two hours. 'Many years of suffering,' he said, 'were compensated by that one service.' The country was lighted up with blazing fires, which gleamed on the faces of the preacher and people from every quarter. This gave rise to this exquisite hymn which alludes to the rapid spread of religion from small beginnings by means of revival."

No. 215.

"O JOYFUL SOUND OF GOSPEL GRACE!"

REV. CHARLES WESLEY, 1708—1788.

In a letter by Rev. Richard Reece on the subject of his late visit to America, published in the *Wesleyan Methodist Magazine* for January, 1825, occurs the following: "It is customary in New York and elsewhere, immediately after the sermon, while the stewards are making the usual collection, for the choir to sing a few verses. The last time I preached in that city, I was much charmed and affected. My subject had been the glorious privilege of true believers to have Christ living in them by His Spirit. A spirit of prayer was poured upon the congregation, and a special influence of God accompanied the word of His grace, and much affected us all. At this moment the singers, joined by most of the people, in sounds as much resembling the melody of heaven as I expect to hear on earth, began:

'O joyful sound of Gospel grace,
Christ shall in me appear;
I, even I, shall see His Face,
I shall be holy here.'

The impression made, I shall never forget. The words so well chosen, so aptly turned, so accordant with the feelings of the congregation: the voices, male and female, so melodious and yet so impassioned: and the tune so soft and devotional that the blessing of perfect love seemed to be within the reach, or rather in the possession of every worshipper. Seasons like these ought to be recorded. They are to me times of refreshing from the presence of the Lord. If our singers were everywhere pious and had judgment to adapt the words to the subject and to the state of feeling in the congregation, such a custom would greatly heighten the effect produced by the sermon."

No. 216.

"ARM OF THE LORD, AWAKE, AWAKE!"

Rev. Charles Wesley, 1708—1788.

The first chapel built by the Methodists was at Bristol, the first stone being laid on May 12, 1739, and the first meeting being held in it June 3, only three weeks later. John Wesley was present and expounded the passage, "Marvel not if the world hate you:" and they sang:

"Arm of the Lord, awake, awake!
Thine own immortal strength put on."

"And God," Mr. Wesley wrote, "even our own God, gave us His blessing."

No. 217.

"JESUS, LOVER OF MY SOUL."

REV. CHARLES WESLEY, 1708—1788.

A big Philadelphia policeman noticed a little boy crying piteously on the streets one day just after noon, and rightly surmised that the child was lost.

"Hello, Johnny, what's the matter?" he asked, kindly.

The boy looked scared to death at the sight of the big policeman but managed to sob out, "I want my mamma!"

The queer little waif was taken to the Nineteenth District Police Station. He was well dressed, wore a smart cap, and looked unusually intelligent. A volley of questions could not extract from him where he lived, and all he cared to say was, "My name is Joseph Edwards Reason, and I am five years old."

He had a clear voice and spoke with unusual distinctness. In a few minutes he had forgotten his troubles and was making friends with the station-house cat. Then he walked up to a big sergeant and said, "I can sing. Can you?"

The sergeant was so astonished at his little questioner that he only stared in reply, but none of the officers laughed. They were too astonished.

"I can sing you one of my Sunday-school songs," said the small boy. Then without waiting for an invitation, his clear voice, full of sweetness, rang out the words of

"Jesus, Lover of my soul."

The effect was startling, and every one listened respectfully. Men off duty came tiptoeing down stairs, and soon the little singer had a group of officers about him. Lumps came up in their throats, pipes were laid down, and eyes became suspiciously moist.

The prisoners who were waiting for the patrol wagon to take them to jail stopped their wrangling and listened.

The little warbler could do nothing but sing; and, to provide him with an all-night lodging, he was taken to the Central Police Station. His eyes danced as he saw the brilliantly lighted apartment, and he let go the patrol sergeant's hand cautiously to inspect the cells. In the first cell was a surly-looking man who was awaiting a hearing before Magistrate Clement for burglary. In the other cells were two "hard" characters.

"Hello, sonny! What are ye in fur?" said one of the prisoners, making a desperate attempt at a joke.

The boy looked curiously at the uninviting face through the iron bars, and said, "Mister, I can sing."

The burglar drew back abashed. Then the boy sang. His voice swelled like a bird's, and the big reserves who were waiting for the magistrate were spellbound.

To the astonishment of everybody, the prisoners joined; and the burglar supplied the harmony with his deep basso. Then the boy sang other hymns, and at last ran and gave the prisoners a drink of water at their request. As the prisoners walked to face the magistrate, the little singer went to sleep like a tired wanderer.

Golden Days.

No. 218.

"EQUIP ME FOR THE WAR"—1741.

REV. CHARLES WESLEY, 1708—1788.

One of his "Hymns on God's Everlasting Love." For the circumstances that occasioned these hymns see No. 38.

The intense aversion felt by Mr. Wesley for the Calvinistic doctrines, as well as the methods used by him and his opponents as well, in the theological contests of the times, are well illustrated in some stanzas of this hymn which are quite properly omitted in our collections. Here is one of them:

"Increase, (if that can be)
The perfect hate I feel
To Satan's horrible decree,
That genuine child of hell:
Which feigns Thee to pass by
The most of Adam's race
And leave them in their blood to die,
Shut out from saving grace."

No. 219.

"YE SIMPLE SOULS THAT STRAY."

REV. CHARLES WESLEY, 1708—1788.

John Wesley was never more calm and fearless than in the hour of danger. He was preaching at a certain time when the mob, maddened with fury, tore up the floor, while others on the outside pulled out the windows and doors of the house. Mr. Wesley walked out, looked them full in the face, and fixed his piercing eye upon them, when the mass of the people parted asunder, so that a broad way was made for him, and he passed through his enemies unharmed. Then he wrote the hymn commencing:

"Ye simple souls that stray."

and containing the stanza:

"Angels our servants are,
And keep us in our ways;
And in their watchful hands they bear
The sacred sons of grace."

"Anecdotes of Wesley," page 134.

No. 220.

"COME, O THOU ALL VICTORIOUS LORD"—1746.

REV. CHARLES WESLEY, 1708—1788.

At Portland, in Dorsetshire, England, are extensive quarries of stone, from which large quantities have been taken for many years for building purposes. St. Paul's Cathedral at London is built of stone from Portland. Many laboring men find employment here, and as the place is isolated, they are uncultured and rough, and often degraded. Just such communities as this Charles Wesley loved to seek, and so it is not strange that late one night—it was the fourth of June, 1748—after a weary journey he and his horse drew up at a house in Portland. Two days later he preached as he records it, "to a housefull of staring, loving people. Some wept, but most looked quite unawakened. At noon and night I preached on a hill in the midst of the Island. Most of the inhabitants came to hear, but few as yet feel the burden of sin or the want of a Savior." That was on Friday, and on Sunday he preached again, and as he writes it, "after evening service we had all the islanders that were able to come. I asked, 'Is it nothing to you, all ye that pass by?' About half a dozen answered, 'It is nothing to us!' by turning their backs, but the rest hearkened with greater signs of emotion than I had before observed." And then he made his prayer to God, amid the quarries and the stony hearted quarrymen, with the din of their hammers in his ears:

"Come, O Thou all victorious Lord,
Thy power to us make known!
Strike with the hammer of Thy Word
And break these hearts of stone!"

And the Lord answered that prayer and made known His power; for the next day Wesley wrote again: "Now the power and blessing came; my mouth and their hearts were opened. The rocks were broken in pieces and melted into tears on every side."

No. 221.

"ALL THANKS BE TO GOD."

REV. CHARLES WESLEY, 1708—1788.

On one of his wandering trips in search of people needing the Gospel, Charles Wesley found his way into Cornwall in the south-western part of England, among the tin mines. He was somewhat uproariously received by the roughs of the neighborhood who serenaded him with the couplet:

"Charles Wesley is come to town
To try to pull the churches down."

There is in this place a very curious pit, resembling not a little an old Roman circus, with circular seats or terraces rising all around it one above the other. This was an audience room quite to the liking of Mr. Wesley, and here he began to preach. He wrote of it that "On Sunday the tenth of August, 1746, at Gwennap, nine or ten thousand by computation listened with all eagerness, while I commended them to God and to the word of His Grace. For near two hours I was enabled to preach repentance toward God and faith in Jesus Christ. I broke out again and again in prayer and exhortation. I believed not one word would return empty. Seventy years sufferings were overpaid by one such opportunity. I expressed the gratitude of my heart in the following thanksgiving:" And then he gives this hymn, written there, as his song of thanks for so great an opportunity to preach the Gospel.

No. 222.

"CHRIST WHOSE GLORY FILLS THE SKIES."

REV. CHARLES WESLEY, 1708—1788.

There was once a poor old man, poor in this world's goods, but whose manners and appearance gave every evidence that he had learned the secret of a happy life. A person called on him once and supposed that he should touch the secret by a single question. "I suppose, sir," said he, " that the first thing you do in the morning is to pray?" "No." "No! what is it then?" "Praise," said he. "Praise is my first act, and when the day begins with praise, you soon learn the happy art of turning the bright side of things toward yourself, of looking at God's goodness until it cheers you, of marking the blessings of each hour as it passes, and of communing with a happy future until you find it possible to 'rejoice evermore, to pray without ceasing and in everything to give thanks!' and so the day passes, and from hour to hour the heart keeps up its music like a sweet peal of bells."

"Thank you, thank you, for your lesson on morning music. You must have some favorite morning hymns."

"Oh, yes, sir, many a one; and they bring their own tunes with them, for no sooner does a hymn come into my mind, than some suitable tune for it flows from my tongue. Scarcely a morning passes, sir, but these verses come up from my heart and out from my lips:

'Christ Whose glory fills the skies.'"

No. 223.

"O, FOR A THOUSAND TONGUES TO SING."

REV. CHARLES WESLEY, 1708—1788.

Tradition, probably truthful, says that Charles Wesley wrote this hymn in May, 1729, a year after his own conversion and that of his brother John, and that it was written to celebrate the anniversary of that event. Its title was "For the anniversary of one's conversion." It had eighteen stanzas beginning "Glory to God, and Praise and Love." and this begins with the seventh stanza. Peter Bohler was a Moravian minister often consulted by the Wesleys, and Charles had asked his opinion of offering praise to Christ. Bohler replied, "Had I a thousand tongues, I would praise Him with them all." This memorable utterance Charles Wesley has enshrined in the opening of this hymn. It is placed first in all Methodist Church hymnals.

In 1757, Mr. Alexander Mather, one of Wesley's itinerants, was at Nottingham and learned of a prisoner who was to be executed the following day and who was filling the air with curses and threatenings against all who had given evidence against him. Mr. Mather obtained leave to visit him, but was repulsed with the reply, "Give yourself no trouble about me. By this time tomorrow, I shall be a devil, and then I will come and tear that villain in pieces." By means of the prayers and earnest appeals of Mr. Mather he was apparently converted, asked for forgiveness of the jailor and others for his terrible threats, and acknowledged the justice of his sentence. Next day he asked and obtained permission to walk with Mr. Mather to the place of execution, instead of being carried there in the cart. While on the way, in company with Mr. Mather, he sang this hymn. He especially thought that the fourth stanza was intended for him:

"He breaks the power of cancelled sin,
He sets the prisoner free!
His Blood can make the foulest clean
His Blood availed for me."

Armenian Magazine, March, 1780.

The whole hymn, as Wesley wrote it, contains eighteen stanzas, one of which, not given here, reads as follows:

"See all your sins on Jesus laid,
The Lamb of God was slain:
His Soul was once an offering made
For every soul of man."

One of the most celebrated preachers of his time was "Billy Dawson," an eccentric layman, possessed of a vivid imagination and splendid oratorical powers. He delighted in imagery of terrible vividness and in startling sentences. Once while preaching a sermon entitled "Death on the White Horse," he gave out to be sung, this hymn. In reading it, when he reached this stanza, he cried out, "See! What? Come and see! what? I do not ask you to come and see the preacher or to hear the voice of thunder, but to come and see yourselves your sins, and your Savior:

"See all your sins on Jesus laid!
The Lamb of God was slain:
His soul was once an offering made
For every soul of man."

The effect upon the audience was instantaneous.

No. 224.

"GOD MOVES IN A MYSTERIOUS WAY."

William Cowper, 1731—1800.

Cowper's title to this hymn was "Light Shining Out of Darkness." What that darkness was, the life of the author reveals. Cowper had at one time been placed in an asylum as a lunatic. Later he so far recovered as to be taken from the asylum and allowed his freedom, but even then he was subject to fits of deep depression. In one such attack he became possessed of the delusion that it was

God's will that he should drown himself at a particular spot in the River Thames at London. In pursuance of this delusion he one evening called a carriage and ordered the driver to take him to the Tower wharf, intending as he records, "to throw myself into the river from the custom house quay. I left the coach upon the Tower wharf intending never to return to it. But I found the water low, and a porter seated on some goods as if on purpose to prevent me. This passage to the bottomless pit being mercifully shut against me, I returned to the coach and ordered the man to drive me back to my home." Then, it is said, he sat down and wrote this hymn.

Dr. R. R. Meredith relates that when his mother lay on her death bed and the forces of life were ebbing away in a current of almost unendurable pain, a son, bending over her, said, "Mother, I cannot understand why God should let you suffer so." Calmly came the reply:

"Blind unbelief is sure to err,
And scan His work in vain;
God is His own Interpreter,
And he will make it plain."

No. 225.

"I THINK, WHEN I READ THAT SWEET STORY OF OLD."

Mrs. Jemima Luke, 1813.

Our hymns have been composed in curious places. Charles Wesley wrote as he jogged along the roads of old England on the back of his steady old horse. John Henry Newman wrote on an orange-laden ship in the Mediterranean Sea.

"Christ for the world we sing,
The world to Christ we bring,"

was composed while its author was walking along the streets of Cleveland on his way home from a meeting. Neander wrote hymns in a cave, and here is a hymn written in a stage coach, to be sung by a village school in England.

No. 226.

"HEAR MY PRAYER, O HEAVENLY FATHER."

MISS HARRIET PARR, 1828.

Here is a hymn by an author who never wrote another and had no intention of furnishing this one for the use that is being made of it. Charles Dickens was at one time editor of a periodical called *Household Words*. Every year at the holiday season, an extra Christmas number was published, and in this issue of *Household Words* for 1856 there appeared a story entitled "The Wreck of the *Golden Mary*." The story relates how the *Golden Mary*, on her voyage to California, struck an iceberg, and the passengers and crew were obliged to take to the boats, in which they suffered great privations for many days. To beguile the time away, they told stories. One of the crew, Dick Tarrant by name, had been disappointed in love and had become a wild youth and had at last been shipped off to California by his friends on the *Golden Mary* to get him out of the way. After telling in a touching way some of his experiences, he goes on: "What can it be that brings all these old things over my mind? There's a child's hymn I and Tom used to say at my mother's knee, when we were little ones, keeps running through my thoughts. It's the stars, maybe! there was a little window by my bed that I used to watch them at—a window in my room at home in Cheshire! and if I was ever afraid as boys will be after reading a good ghost story, I would keep on saying it till I fell asleep."

"That was a good mother of yours, Dick! could you say

that hymn now, do you think? Some of us might like to hear it."

"It's as clear in my mind this minute as if my mother was here listening to me," said Dick. And then he repeated this hymn. Both story and hymn were entirely the creation of the author of the tale.

No. 227.

"BENEATH MORIAH'S ROCKY SIDE."

REV. ROBERT MURRAY McCHEYNE, 1813—1843.

The author of this hymn only lived thirty years, but in this time he endeared himself to a very large circle of friends by his preaching and pastoral work. In 1839, when he was twenty-six years old, he had already so overworked as to break down in health, and he joined a party of travelers to Palestine. While there he wrote a letter to a friend at home dated at Mount Carmel, June 26, 1839, and in it he writes, "Another favorite spot was the Fountain of Siloam, farther down the Valley of Jehoshaphat. It flows so softly from under the Temple, that you cannot hear the ripple of its waters. You descend a great many steps in the rock, and drink its delightful waters. I send you a small hymn on the other side, which will imprint it on your memory" And this is the hymn.

No. 228.

"O HOLY FATHER JUST AND TRUE"—1837.

JOHN GREENLEAF WHITTIER, 1808—1892.

Our Quaker poet Whittier was greatly interested in the abolition of slavery in the United States, and did much to mold the public sentiment that at last brought it about. He was apparently never more delighted than when asked to write for some occasion connected with this reform. The emancipation of the slaves in its colonies by the English Government which went into effect on the first of August, 1834, gave a new impulse to the anti-slavery movement in this country, and for many years this day was celebrated. The third anniversary, August 1, 1837, was celebrated by a great assembly at Broadway Tabernacle, New York, and Whittier wrote this hymn for that occasion, and it was first used then.

No. 229.

"WE SPEAK OF THE REALMS OF THE BLEST."

MRS. ELIZABETH MILLS, 1805—1829.

The forty-fourth verse of the one hundred and nineteenth Psalm reads as follows: "So shall I keep Thy law continually forever and ever." An English writer on the Psalms (Bridges) commenting on this verse, uses the exclamation, "We speak of heaven, but oh! to be there." Mrs. Mills, the young wife of a member of the English Parliament, had been reading this book, and this sentence fixed itself in her mind: "We speak of heaven, but oh! to be there," and the thought of the writer she wove into this hymn. New interest is added to its use when we know that in a few weeks after she wrote it, she herself, only twenty-four years old, had passed into the "realms of the blest" of which she sang.

No. 230.

"OUR FATHER, GOD, WHO ART IN HEAVEN."

REV. ADONIRAM JUDSON, 1788—1850.

The first missionaries sent out by the American Board of Commissioners for Foreign Missions sailed from Salem,

Massachusetts, February 19, 1812, for Calcutta, India. Adoniram Judson and his wife were in the party. The story of his life and adventures in India aroused such an interest in America that twenty-five thousand copies of his memoirs were sold in the first sixty days after their publication. In 1824 war was raging between Burmah and the British Government, and Judson was thrown into the prison at Ava in which those were confined who were condemned to die. For nine months in this prison he was shackled with three pairs of fetters, and then for two months more with five pairs. During this time he was only kept from starving by his wife who daily came and fed him through the prison bars. And here in this prison, like Paul and Silas, he sang songs, and this hymn was written there and bears the date, "Prison Ava, March, 1825." It is a verification of The Lord's Prayer. It contains fewer words than the original Greek, and only two more than the common English translation.

No. 231.

"FOR WHAT SHALL I PRAISE THEE?"

Miss Caroline Fry, 1787—1846.

(Afterward Mrs. Caroline Wilson.)

Caroline Fry was a farmer's daughter. The extent and character of her reading when a child, may be gathered from the fact that when fourteen years old, she had written a "History of England in Verse." This hymn of hers has this peculiarity of origin that it was written to please a pious sister, before the author herself had embraced the Christian faith. So that it is in no sense a hymn of her own experience, although we can make use of it in expressing ours.

No. 232.

"O THOU TO WHOM IN ANCIENT TIME"—1824.

Rev. John Pierpont, 1785—1866.

I wonder whether any of you remember the reading books you used when children at school. If you happened to be born in New England, long enough ago, it is not unlikely that you read from "The American First Class Reader"; and perhaps a little later from "The National Reader." I remember them both very well, and could even now recite some of the pieces they contained. They were prepared by the author of this hymn. It was printed for the dedication of a Unitarian Church, in Salem, Massachusetts, December 7, 1824. When the war of the Rebellion in the United States broke out, Mr. Pierpont was seventy-five years old, but he could not content himself to remain at home and the Governor of Massachusetts appointed him Chaplain of a regiment. His failing strength, however, was not equal to the hardships of the camp and he soon resigned.

No. 233.

"FATHER OF LIFE AND LIGHT."

"LORD AS A FAMILY WE MEET."

Samuel Fletcher, 1785—1863.

The author of these hymns was a wealthy merchant, living near Manchester, England. He was inclined toward poetry, and on one occasion when sickness prevented his attending to business, he occupied the leisure by making a collection of hymns for use in his family, and inserted in the collection a few of his own composition, these being two of that number. What sort of man he was may be inferred from the fact that for many years he gave away from thirty to forty per cent of his income, and from this little extract from his diary: "This day I removed with my family to Chatham Hill, and took possession of a house more spacious and costly than I ever expected. I pray to God that my heart may not be lifted up on this account, and that I may not be permitted to indulge proud and vain thoughts of my own sufficiency and stability, and disposed to be less earnest in seeking 'a building of God; a house not made with hands, eternal in the heavens.'"

No. 234.

"FATHER OF MERCIES! CONDESCEND."

"GO AND THE SAVIOR'S LOVE PROCLAIM"—1818.

REV. THOMAS MORELL, 1781—1840.

At the opening of this century the sending out of missionaries to heathen lands was an event more noticeable than it is today. The voyages were longer and more perilous; the dangers to be encountered among the people to whom they went were greater; the means of communication with home less frequent and regular; and a greater sacrifice of self was requisite on the part of those who went.

A young man who was a member of Mr. Morell's church had devoted himself to this work, and in 1818 a service was held in his pastor's church at which he was ordained to the ministry and set apart for the work of a missionary in India. It is not strange that his pastor deemed it an occasion worthy of special note, and he wrote these two hymns to be first sung at this solemn service.

No. 235.

"WHEN ABRAHAM'S SERVANT TO PROCURE"—1773.

REV. JOHN RYLAND, 1753—1825.

Dr. Ryland lived in Northampton, and once upon a time when a brother minister was passing through the town, he detained him quite against his will, to preach for him. The preacher, possibly as a sort of revenge for being pressed to stop and preach when he desired to go on, took for his text the words of Abraham's servant recorded in Genesis, 24:56, "Hinder me not:" and while he preached, Dr. Ryland wrote this hymn, each stanza except the first containing the words of the preacher's text. The hymn usually begins, "In all my Lord's appointed ways."

No. 236.

"LORD, TEACH A LITTLE CHILD TO PRAY."

REV. JOHN RYLAND, 1753—1825.

This hymn was written for a little girl of six years, who was dying. Her father, himself a minister (Rev Andrew Fuller) asked Dr. Ryland to write a hymn for the sick little girl, and this was written in response to that request. It was often repeated to her, and she told her father that she used often to pray over it.

No. 237.

"MY TIMES OF SORROW AND OF JOY"—1778.

REV. BENJAMIN BEDDOME, 1717—1795.

This hymn was written to be sung at the close of a sermon on the text, "My times are in Thy Hand," (Psalm, 31:15) and it is rather remarkable that the resignation to the will of God that it expresses was so well timed, for the author's son died of a fever in Edinburgh, on the very day he preached this sermon, and read for the first time this hymn.

No. 238.

"COME, OH COME! IN PIOUS LAYS."

George Wither, 1588—1667.

Here is a hymn writer who sang himself into prison and sang himself out again, and whose reputation as a poet, either good or bad, once saved his life. He wrote a political poem entitled, "Abuses stript and whipt:" and made King James I so angry by it that he threw him into prison. While here in prison he kept right on writing poetry of one sort or another, and by and by he wrote what he called a "Satire to the King;" and signed the preface, "His Majesty's most loyal subject, and yet prisoner in the Marshalsea." This procured him his release. Later he was a captain of cavalry and fought against the Covenanters in Scotland, and later while still a soldier he was made prisoner by the enemy and was about to be hung, when Sir John Denham, who was also a poet and hymn writer, requested that his life be spared, "because," as he put it, "so long as George Wither lives, Denham will not be accounted the worst poet in England.

No. 239.

"MY HOPE IS BUILT ON NOTHING LESS."

Edward Mote, 1797—1874.

Of the origin of this hymn the author says: "One morning it came into my mind as I went to labor, to write an hymn on the 'Gracious Experience of a Christian.' As I went up Holborn I had the chorus:

'On Christ the solid Rock I stand,
All other ground is sinking sand.'

In the day I had the four first verses complete, and wrote them off. On the Sabbath following I met brother King as I came out of Lisle Street Meeting, who informed me that his wife was very ill, and asked me to call and see her. I had an early tea and called afterward. He said that it was his usual custom to sing a hymn, read a portion, and engage in prayer, before he went to meeting. He looked for his hymn book but could find it nowhere. I said, 'I have some verses in my pocket,' and if he liked we would sing them. We did; and his wife enjoyed them so much, that after service he asked me, as a favor, to leave a copy of them for his wife. I went home, and by the fireside composed the last two verses, wrote the whole off, and took them to sister King. As these verses so met the dying woman's case, my attention to them was the more arrested, and I had a thousand printed for distribution."

No. 240.

"GOD WHO MADEST HEAVEN AND EARTH"—1644.

HENRY ALBERTI, 1604—1668.

The author of this hymn, although he wrote some hymns, is better known as a musician and composer than as a writer of hymns.

A tailor was once (1685) at work in the house of a Jew in Hamburg, and as he sewed he sang the stanzas of this hymn. The Jew's daughter heard the song, and the words of the third stanza attracted her attention:

"Let the night of sin depart
As this earthly night hath fled:
Jesus take me to Thy Heart;
In the Blood that Thou hast shed
Is my help and hope alone,
For the evil I have done."

She was led to make inquiry as to the Jesus of Whom the tailor sang, and at last to accept Him as her Savior.

No. 241.

"HIGH LET US SWELL OUR TUNEFUL NOTES." "MY GOD AND IS THY TABLE SPREAD."

REV. PHILIP DODDRIDGE, 1702—1751.

These hymns have had a rather singular history. They have been interlopers within the covers of the Church of England Prayer Book for three quarters of a century. It happened about the year 1820 that the printer of the Prayer Book was a dissenter. There were a few blank leaves at the end of the Prayer Book, and he took the liberty of filling these up with a few hymns which he thought would be acceptable. Among others he used these two by Dr. Doddridge. The hymns having thus gotten in, even though uninvited and unauthorized, have stayed in ever since, because although not cordially welcomed by the Churchmen, their bishops could scarcely find a good reason for putting them out.

No. 242.

"O ZION, AFFLICTED WITH WAVE UPON WAVE."

JAMES GRANT.

The author of this hymn was a Scotchman in the iron business. He was very fond of the Scotch melodies, but ashamed of the disreputable words usually sung to them, and his object in writing hymns was to provide Christian words for these melodies. This hymn was written in this way to provide religious words for the air of the "Yellow-haired Laddie."

No. 243

"I ONCE WAS A STRANGER TO GRACE AND TO GOD."

REV. ROBERT MURRAY McCHEYNE, 1813—1843.

A youth of eighteen years records of himself that on July 8, 1831, "I lost my beloved and loving brother, and began to seek a Brother Who cannot die." Four years later he began to preach, and eight years after this he died, at thirty years of age; and yet in this short time he had attained an eminent position as a preacher, popularity as a writer, and had endeared himself to a large circle of friends by his pastoral labor, and his untiring devotion. He wrote this hymn in 1834, three years after he had begun to seek for the Brother Who could not die, and it reveals what through that short acquaintance of only three years this Brother had become to him.

No. 244.

"COMMIT THOU ALL THY GRIEFS." "GIVE TO THE WINDS THY FEARS."

REV. PAUL GERHARDT, 1606—1676.

Translated by Rev. John Wesley, 1703—1791.

These are different parts of the same hymn. A German Lutheran pastor in Berlin was deposed from his office and ordered to quit the country because of his adherence to Luther's faith. He was in poverty and started with his wife on foot. One night they came to a village inn. His wife was weary with the journey, and disheartened at their friendless situation, and sat down and began to weep. Her husband tried to comfort her, and reminded her of the words of the Bible: "Commit thy way unto the Lord; trust also in Him and He will bring it to pass." "God will provide," said he, "commit our trouble to Him." He left his wife and went into the inn garden, and sitting down under an arbor, the Bible words he had just repeated to his wife formed themselves into verse:

"Commit thou all thy griefs
And ways into His Hands.
To His sure trust and tender care
Who earth and heaven commands."

Candor compels me to add that after having been given for many years as the origin of this hymn, a recent matter of fact historian with a penchant for dates, spoils it all by averring that the dates do not agree. The first word or two of each stanza in the German, is from the Bible text, and I have seen an English translation which followed the German, so that by reading the first word or two of each stanza, down the page, the text as it is in the Bible is given.

William Dawson, of Barnbow near Leeds, better known as "Billy Dawson, the farmer preacher," was at one time much troubled about his farm and other anxieties. One day he was at work on a hill top, and to divert his mind from his anxieties he took from his pocket a lot of papers that had accumulated there, and after reading them he tore them up into little pieces and threw them into the air, and blown by the wind they fluttered about like so many butterflies. Instantly there came into his mind, and he repeated it aloud and with it cheered his troubled mind:

"Give to the winds thy fears,
Hope and be undismayed!
God hears thy sighs and counts thy tears!
God shall lift up thy head."

No. 245.

"HOW ARE THY SERVANTS BLEST, O LORD."

JOSEPH ADDISON, 1672—1719.

For account of Addison and *The Spectator*, see No. 49.

This hymn appeared Saturday, September 20, 1712, at the end of an article on "The Sea." The hymn is entitled, "The Traveler's Hymn," and purports to have been written "by a gentleman upon the conclusion of his travels." Addison had embarked at Marseilles in 1700 for a foreign tour. While sailing near the shores of Italy a great storm arose. And at this time, while others gave up all for lost and the captain in despair was confessing his sins to a Capuchin friar, the Christian poet was comforting himself by writing this hymn of trust in the God who rules the waves.

No. 246.

"CREATOR, SPIRIT, BY WHOSE AID."

JOHN DRYDEN, Translator, 1632—1700.

Veni Creator Spiritus, RABANUS MAURUS.

Here is one of the most celebrated of the Latin hymns, whose author is not certainly known. If it was Rabanus Maurus, as is now generally believed, he lived in the eighth century and was an archbishop of the Roman Church in Germany. As was the custom in those days he provided an epitaph to be used when he died, which reads as follows: "Quick was my mind, but slow my body, through weakness. That which I could I have done, and what the Lord gave me." As an evidence that he did what he could, as he claims, it is related that when, in 850, a terrible famine desolated Germany, during which starving people were driven to the commission of many terrible deeds, he fed three hundred people daily at his own door. So high was this hymn held in the esteem of the people, that almost miraculous powers were ascribed to it. Speaking of it one writer said, "Whoever repeats this hymn by day or by night, him shall no enemy visible or invisible assail." In those olden times the day was divided into eight parts of three hours each, and a service was held in the churches at the end of each of these periods. At nine o'clock in the morning, the time at which, according to the Bible, the Holy Spirit descended on the Day of Pentecost, they used to sing this hymn. This might be called the world's royal hymn, for it has for hundreds of years been used in Europe at the Coronation of Emperors and Kings, and it is also used at the creation of Popes, the consecration of Bishops, and the ordaining of Priests.

No. 247.

Philip Bliss, 1838—1876.

At Christmas time, in 1876, a father left his work to spend the holidays with his children in a little town in Pennsylvania. When the holidays were over, he with his wife started on their way back to their home in Chicago. On the way he busied himself in composing a new piece of music. Suddenly there came a crash and eleven cars were tumbled down an embankment through snow and ice into a river below. The cars took fire and some were killed by the fall, some were drowned, and others unable to extricate themselves from the ruins of the wreck were burned to death. The man who had been composing the music escaped through a window, then tried to extricate his wife, but she was fastened in the wreck and could not be rescued, so he quietly stayed by her side and together they were burned to death, and not so much as a shred ever found by which to identify their remains. This was Philip Bliss the composer, hymn writer, and Gospel singer.

No. 248.

LUDWIG VON BEETHOVEN, 1770—1827.

Handel loved music when a child, and was forbidden by his father to play, but stole up into the attic when his father was absent and learned to play by himself, on an old harpsichord he found there. Beethoven was compelled to learn music against his will. He hated it because his friends tried to force it upon him, and he was sometimes beaten by his father before he would sit down to the piano. But when he was left alone to play as a recreation, he became absorbed in music, and began to compose while only a boy. When a young man he began to be deaf, so that after a while he could hear but imperfectly, and at last not at all, the music he was making; but it did not stop his composing, nor his playing, for his mental ears were not deaf, and he knew the sounds he was making and realized their harmony. He was always poor, but always generous. A concert was once given in aid of soldiers who had been wounded in battle. He supplied the music and conducted the orchestra. When he was offered pay for the service, he replied, "Say that Beethoven never accepts anything when humanity is concerned."

No. 249.

FRANCIS JOSEPH HAYDN, 1732—1809.

This tune was written by the musical composer whose greatest musical achievement perhaps was the setting of the first chapter of the Bible to music in the Oratorio we know as "The Creation." Many are the incidents that are related of him. He lived for many years in Hungary where his duty was to write music for a prince and his court. One day he was at a fair in a little village not far from where he lived, and there he saw a great many musical toys for sale. The children were trying them and the air was full of the mingled sounds of whistles and little drums and tin trumpets and a dozen other of the toys. A sudden idea seemed to strike the great composer, and when he went home from the fair he took with him one of each of the instruments he had found for sale; drums, tin trumpets, whistles, fiddles, bells, rattles, seventeen in all. For the next few days his friends must have thought him mad, for he spent his time in his room, and when any one went near they heard him playing, one after another, on these toy instruments. So the days went on, until by and by one day Haydn came out from his seclusion with a symphony, into which he had introduced in solo, or duet, or some other form, the music of each of the seventeen toys he had found at the fair. It was played at the court of the prince, and is often heard in this country, especially at children's festivals.

No. 250.

Johann C. W. A. Mozart, 1756—1791.

Mozart was a musical prodigy, perhaps the most wonderful that ever lived. He played the harpsichord when three years old; at four he played minuets to the delight of friends; at five he began to compose music; when six he astonished the Emperor Francis I at Munich by his masterly rendering of concertos on the harpsichord; and at seven his genius was the theme of conversation among musical people all over Europe. He was very sensitive; wanted to be loved by those whom he loved himself. He was greatly attached to his father. "Next to God, is papa!" he said. He was deeply religious. "Friends who have no religion cannot long be my friends," he said. His last days were sorrowful ones. The servant of an Austrian nobleman came to him one day dressed in black and asked him to write a requiem for which he promised a large price, but refused to tell who it was for. Mozart was in ill health and he imagined that the man in black was a messenger from the spirit world and that the requiem was for himself. "I am writing it for myself," he said, and he spoke of it when it was done as his own requiem, and almost as soon as it was completed he died.

No. 251.

"THE MESSIAH."

GEORGE FREDERICK HANDEL, 1685—1759.

In Great Britain, as you know, people were formerly imprisoned for debt. A century and a half ago, a great composer was in England who had been born in Halle more than fifty years before. A messenger came to him from Dublin: "Our prisons are filled with prisoners for debt. Give us a concert and let the proceeds go for the opening of the prison doors." The composer's heart was touched by the appeal from the Irish people, and in England he composed a great piece of music for the occasion. In speaking afterward of his feelings while he wrote it, he said, "I did think I saw all heaven before me, and the great God Himself. On the thirteenth day of April, 1742, at noon, in Dublin, the concert was given. Its success surpassed that of any composition that had preceded it. The hall could not contain the people who flocked day after day to hear it, and the Dublin ladies who were then wearing great crinolines in their dresses agreed to leave their hoops at home to make more room in the hall. Later, when it was given in England before King George the Second, he forgot himself and leaped to his feet, all the audience following his example. And so it has been ever since the custom for audiences to rise and stand with bowed heads while certain parts of the Messiah are being rendered. When it was first rendered in London, a nobleman who felt disposed to patronize Handel its composer, said to him, "You have given the audience an excellent entertainment."

"My Lord," answered Handel, "I should be sorry if I had only entertained them. I wish to make them better." This was the man, and this the spirit of the man who composed this tune.

No. 252.

"ELIJAH—THE ORATORIO."

FELIX MENDELSSOHN BARTHOLDY, 1809—1847.

"There was one thing in music that Mendelssohn never could do," said an old German musician.

"What was that?"

"Play a congregation out of church." And they say that was literally true. Crowds thronged the churches when he was announced to play, and the music which was intended to play the audience out, only held it more firmly in. Once the attendants at St. Paul's Cathedral, when he was playing, were impatient for the audience to be gone that they might get their suppers. But Mendelssohn kept on playing and the audience made no move to go. "There is only one way," said one of the attendants to the other.

"What is that?"

"To stop the bellows:" and they did.

There was to be a great National Festival in Birmingham, England, and Mendelssohn was invited to compose for it a new Oratorio. He accepted the task and threw all his energy into the work. It was a grand occasion when it was first produced. It was in the summer of 1846. People of all ranks, from far and near, flocked to Birmingham to hear the great work. And when at its completion Mendelssohn moved away from the stage, the eyes of the audience followed him until he disappeared, and cheer upon cheer of praise greeted his ears. This was the "Oratorio of Elijah," now so celebrated. But the production of this masterpiece shattered his nerves and consumed his life. He played and worked but little more, and in a year he was dead.

No. 253.

"BEHOLD A STRANGER AT THE DOOR."

REV. JOSEPH GRIGG, 1728—1768.

Of many men who lived as long ago as Joseph Grigg and who did far less of good we know far more. I can give you in a few words all that is known of him. His parents were poor. He wrote the hymn beginning, "Jesus and shall it ever be," when ten years old. He was a laboring mechanic; he gave this up to become the assistant pastor of a Presbyterian Church; he retired from this and married a rich wife. In an elegy written upon his death, he is called "The friend of the poor, the charm of the social circle, and the attractive and useful preacher." In 1756, when England was trembling in fear of the invasion of her coast, he preached a sermon on that subject, closing with a hymn ending with a stanza which will give a good idea of his poetic power:

"Britons shall feel, and feeling own
God is her shield, and God alone:
And heart and voice and life shall sing
To God the Universal King."

No. 254.

"MT. BLANC" (Tune.)

"The melody in part, of Mt. Blanc, was sung to me by Mrs. George Little, (now singing in Paradise) a sister of

Hon. Hugh McCulloch. She was the sweetest singer I ever heard, and this melody she had heard among the Second Adventists in Maine. It had the repetition in the last line. I added a little to the melody and harmonized it, and wrote the words at Ft. Wayne, Indiana. When I was in Geneva, a lady took me out to ride and sang this hymn in full view of Mt. Blanc, of which she seemed very fond; my sister, Mrs. Stowe, sang with me. Hence the name."

Letter from Rev. Charles Beecher.

No. 255.

"OLMUTZ."

"HAMBURG."

Gregory the Great, 540—604.

Almost fifteen hundred years ago a rich young Roman gave away his fortune to establish monasteries, and then entered one himself as a monk. Later he was elected Pope. One day he was passing through the market in Rome, where slaves were sold, and he saw among the slaves some boys who were white of body with fair forms and handsome faces, and he asked the merchant from what country he had brought them, and was told that they came from the Island of Britain, and that all the inhabitants of that country had the same beauty of face. Then the Pope asked, "Are those Islanders Christians?" and was told that they were still Idolaters. "Alas!" said the Pope, "that the Prince of Darkness should own those splendid faces! what is the name of their tribe?" he asked; and the merchant replied, "They are called Angli," and the Pope exclaimed, "They are well called Angli, for if they were but Christians they would be angels." These were our ancestors he was talking about, and they were being sold as slaves on the streets of Rome.

Gregory, for this was his name, wrote some hymns, and introduced a new method of singing into the church, which was called after him, "The Gregorian Chant." He established a singing school in Rome to teach his new method, and taught in it himself. Among the curiosities of the Astor Library in New York is a copy of a facsimile volume of manuscript music of Gregory's which was discovered some years ago in an old monastery. This is one of his chants, altered to adapt it to our present mode of singing. We owe a great deal to Gregory and ought, I think, to sing the music written by his hand with a feeling that he is something nearer to us than most of the men who lived so long ago. For he it was who sent out from Rome a missionary band of nearly forty monks to Christianize the Pagans of Britain, that is to say, our ancestors.

No. 256.

"TE DEUM LAUDAMUS."

Here is a story that dates back to the third century after Christ. It was Easter Sunday in Milan, April 25, 387. At sunrise throngs of people were hurrying through the streets to the cathedral to celebrate the Festival of the Resurrection. There was to be a baptism in the church that day, and of those to whom the rite was to be administered one was a convert from heathenism. He had been a dissipated boy and his mother had prayed for his conversion for many years. The church was famous for its music, and was known as the "Singing Church of Milan." Its Bishop was himself a musician, and he had composed an anthem for this baptismal service which was to be first sung on this Easter day. It has come down to us as his work. St. Ambrose was his name, and the boy convert at whose baptism it was first sung was St. Augustine. We call the anthem the "Te Deum." The story may be true, but it can scarcely be called veritable history. It comes down to us that it was sung in alternate parts by St. Ambrose, its composer, and St. Augustine, while Augustine was being baptized.

There is a story that Rev. Robert Hall had composed a sermon on a text that had impressed itself upon him by its grandeur and power. When the sermon was completed he took up his concordance to find the text, but it was not to be found. It was not in the Bible. It was a sentence from the "Te Deum." "All the earth doth worship Thee, the Father everlasting."

No. 257.

"AND NOW ANOTHER DAY IS GONE."

Rev. Isaac Watts, 1674—1748.

A good man in his old age once said that the first book in which, as a child, he took an interest, was a small edition of Watts's "Divine and Moral Songs" for children. Each hymn was headed by a woodcut, and one especially was his favorite. It represented a little boy, something like himself, as he thought, leaning at an open window, looking with a calm, happy face at the setting sun, which was throwing its parting light upon a quiet country scene. Many of the hymns, and that one in particular, had been read often, until they lived in his soul. But as he grew up, the impressions were worn off by more exciting and less pure thoughts and pursuits. He fell into a course of dissipation and vice, and seemed for a time to be given up to sin, and devoted to ruin. Worn down at last, and threatened with consumption, he was ordered into the country for change of air; and after some time spent in quietness and retirement, far away from the scenes of old temptations, he wandered out one evening about sunset, and hanging pensively over a gate, he watched the sun as it sank behind the tree, and was throwing its last beams upon the silent and peaceful hillside. There was a hush upon his spirit, and suddenly, as if sketched by an unseen hand before his inward eye, the little picture which used to interest his boyish mind lived again, and the hymn which it illustrated seemed to be spoken sweetly to his heart:

"And now another day is gone,
I'll sing my Maker's praise."

The tears started. He had seen many of his days gone, but as yet his Maker had never heard an evensong from his lips or from his heart. What an ungrateful life his had been! The "remembrance was grievous. But his heart was broken, and there and then the softened man made his vows of return to God, and offered the prayer which was answered in blessings which filled both the mornings and evenings of his mature life with hymns and songs of thanksgiving and praise."

No. 258.

"HOW VAIN ARE ALL THINGS HERE BELOW."

Rev. Isaac Watts, 1674—1748.

Like most young men, Watts fell in love, and with a poet like himself. Watts was a little man, and the story is told that once in company, a stranger was introduced to him, who could not keep back the not altogether courteous exclamation, "What! is this the great Watts!" To which Watts, accustomed from his childhood to the making of rhymes, improvised this reply:

"Had I an arm to reach the pole,
Or grasp old ocean with a span,
I must be measured by my soul,
The mind's the standard of the man."

Well, Watts fell in love, and the young lady measured him by his soul, but she measured him by his little body too, and replied to his suit, that "while she loved the jewel she could not admire the casket." The doctor rebelled at her decision and sent back to her the message that "flesh and blood could not bear the denial," to which the lady replied that if flesh and blood couldn't bear it "skin and bones must," for she would not marry him. Now did Watts go off and drown himself, or pine away because of his disappointment? Not he; but if the tradition is to be trusted he went straight away and wrote a hymn:

"How vain are all things here below,
How false and yet how fair!
Each pleasure hath its poison too,
And every sweet a snare."

And gave to it the title, "Love to the Creatures is Dangerous."

So he turned away from all the loves of earth, and by the last stanza of the hymn devoted himself to the cultivation of a love for Christ, and for the beauty to be found in Him.

No. 259.

"LO! ROUND THE THRONE, A GLORIOUS BAND."

REV. ROWLAND HILL, 1744—1833.

John Berridge, when in his old age, wrote a letter to a young friend who was just beginning to preach:

"My dear Rowley:

"When I began to itinerate, a multitude of dangers seemed to engulph me. My friends were up in arms, my college was provoked, my bishop incensed, the clergy on fire, and the Church canons were pointing their ghastly mouths at me; my first diocesan told me that I should soon be either in Bedlam or in jail. But, through the blessing of my God, I am yet in possession of my senses, my tithes, and my liberty; and He Who has hitherto delivered, I trust will yet deliver me from ecclesiastical fires, and the paw of the worldly bears. I have suffered from nothing except from lapidations and pillory treats, which yet have proved more frightful than hurtful. If you are invited to go out, and feel yourself inclined to do so, take a lover's leap, neck or nothing, and commend yourself to Jesus. Ask no man's leave to preach Christ; that is unevangelical and shameful. Seek not much advice about it; that is dangerous. Such advice, I find, generally comes the wrong way—heels uppermost. Most preachers love a snug church and a whole skin, and what they love they will prescribe. If you are determined to be evangelically regular, that is, secularly irregular, then expect, wherever you go, a storm will follow you, which may fright you, but will bring no real harm. Make the Lord your whole trust, and all will be well."

"Rowley" was the Rev. Rowland Hill, the author of most of this hymn. He followed the advice of his friend, and no man more than he ever had the courage of his convictions. Like Berridge, he was a member of the Church of England, but like Berridge, he would not be bound by ecclesiastical rules or limited by parish bounds. He was once complained of by other clergymen of the Church for this course, and entered as his defense this reply: "My field is the world, and I stick to my parish," and that ended the matter.

No. 260.

"JERUSALEM DIVINE! WHEN SHALL I."

REV. BENJAMIN RHODES, 1743—1815.

An old Englishman tells the story how there used to come into his neighborhood a man to preach. Of him he says:

"He was a good man and a good preacher; but I can mind his singing much better than his sermons. He used to preach not far from where I lived; and when I saw the people flocking to the chapel, I used to go to hear the famous singer. Ah, he was a singer! And I believe one great secret of his music was, that his heart was in it. His voice was like an angel's, as they say, though I never heard an angel sing; but I can scarcely think that an angel, or any other singer, could beat that happy looking preacher. He was a man with a long face, and a high, bald head. And his eyes used to sparkle as he sang, as if the hymns were coming up from his soul; and so they did. There was one hymn I always liked to hear him sing; he would sing it after the sermon; it was one of his own composing, and the tune was his too. I learned to sing it myself, and I taught my boy to sing it; and sometimes, long after that singing preacher was gone to his own 'Jerusalem divine,' my boy and I, and three or four more, used to get together of an evening, and sing it in full harmony. Oh, it was so rich; and it seemed to lift one toward heaven while we sang. This was the hymn."

No. 261.

"GOD OF MY LIFE, TO THEE."

Rev. Charles Wesley, 1708—1788.

Charles Wesley nearly always celebrated his birthdays by writing a hymn. This is one of his birthday hymns, recounting the goodness of the Lord, and it contains one very curious allusion. If you will turn to the thirty-fourth chapter of the book of Deuteronomy, the fifth verse, you will read: "So Moses the servant of the Lord died there in the land of Moab, according to the word of the Lord:" or translated literally, "at the mouth of Jehovah;" and based on this Biblical statement that Moses died "at the mouth of Jehovah," there is a very beautiful old Jewish tradition, that God drew the soul of Moses out of his body with a kiss. Wesley evidently knew of this tradition, and so he writes in one verse of this hymn:

"Then when the work is done,
The work of faith with power,
Receive Thy favorite son
In death's triumphant hour.
Like Moses to Thyself convey,
And kiss my raptured soul away."

Dr. Watts had already given poetic form to the same idea in a poem on the death of Moses in which he writes:

"Softly his fainting head he lay
Upon his Maker's breast;
His Maker kissed his soul away
And laid his flesh to rest."

No. 262.

"DAILY, DAILY SING THE PRAISES."

REV. SABINE BARING-GOULD, 1834.

Written in 1865 and printed on a card for the use of St. John's Mission, Hosbury Bridge, Yorkshire.

The young man who succeeds Mtesa, as King of Uganda, has shed the blood of three young converts of the Church Missionary Society. Like his predecessor, he is easily swayed. The captain of the royal body guard, Mugasi, was the ringleader in the persecution which fortunately did not last long. It was he who directed the execution of the three Christian lads. Their arms were first cut off; then they were bound to a scaffolding, under which a fire was made, and they were slowly burned to death. Mugasi and his men mocked them and bade them pray now, if Isa Masiya (Jesus Christ) would rescue them from his hands. The lads clung to their faith, and in the fire they sang the hymn:

"Daily, daily, sing the praises."

New York Independent, December 10, 1885.

No. 263.

"FAR FROM THE WORLD, O LORD I FLEE."

WILLIAM COWPER, 1731—1800.

When William Wilberforce, the statesman, was quite advanced in life, and had sat in Parliament for twenty-eight years, his friends induced him to contest the election for York. The poll was open, according to English custom, for fifteen days. None of the candidates had less than ten thousand votes. Daily, Mr. Wilberforce addressed meetings, and entertained friends at his house. But it was noticed that, in the midst of the excitement about him, he was singularly calm, and one of his agents relates that, as he met him, day after day, on his return to his home, he would hear him repeating something to himself. As this seemed to be in the same words always, the agent finally contrived to catch what he said, and found it to be a stanza from this hymn:

"The calm retreat, the silent shade,
With prayer and praise agree,
And seem by Thy sweet bounty made,
For those who follow Thee."

No. 264.

"WHEN MARSHALLED ON THE NIGHTLY PLAIN."

HENRY KIRKE WHITE, 1785—1806.

During one of his tours, which were so blessed to the conversion of men, Rev. Dr. Nettleton stopped at a house in the region of the Catskill Mountains. While conversing with the older members of the family, he heard two young, sweet and clear voices in a room above warbling the exquisitely beautiful air of "Bonnie Doon." "Ask them," said he to their parents, "to come down and sing it to me; for I am ardently devoted to music." The request was complied with, and he listened with delighted attention till the close of the song, when, kindly turning to the young ladies, he said, "I think I can teach you some far better words to that tune," and then sang to them that almost matchless hymn:

"When marshalled on the nightly plain,
The glittering host bestud the sky,
One star alone of all the train,
Can fix the sinner's wandering eye."

and proceeded so touchingly and tenderly to call their attention to the beauty of its sentiments, that tears soon flowed from their eyes; and these two young girls were among the first fruits of a revival which resulted from his labors.

The late Rev. Alfred Cookman, who perished in the steamship *President,* is said to have been a most excellent singer. A writer says: "There was no place for a choir where Cookman sang. His voice was melody itself. The session of Congress was about to close upon the administration of President Van Buren. Mr. Cookman had all his arrangements made to visit England, on the steamer *President*. The next Sabbath he was to take leave of the members of Congress in his farewell sermon. The day came. An hour before the usual time, the crowd was seen filling the pavements of the avenue, and pressing up the hill to Representative Hall, which was soon filled to overflowing. Unable to get seats, many went away disappointed. The whole space on the rostrum and steps was filled with Senators and Representatives. The moment had come, Mr. Cookman, evidently much affected, kneeled in a thrilling prayer, and arose with his eyes blinded with tears. His voice faltered with suppressed emotion as he gave out the hymn:

"When marshalled on the nightly plain,
The glittering host bestud the sky,
One star alone of all the train,
Can fix the sinner's wandering eye."

It was sung by Mr. Cookman alone. I can yet, in imagination, hear his voice as it filled the large hall, and as the last sounds, with their echoes, died away in the dome.

No. 265.

"AND LET THIS FEEBLE BODY DIE."

Rev. Charles Wesley, 1708—1788.

Many years ago, a pious young lady in ill health was resting on her couch, and by her side sat a beloved brother, himself scarcely well, and utterly without a feeling of love to God. His sister, as descriptive of the emotions of her soul, repeated to him, with remarkable emphasis, the lines:

"O what hath Jesus bought for me!
Before my ravished eyes
Rivers of life divine I see,
And trees of paradise:

"I see a world of spirits bright,
Who taste the pleasures there;
They all are robed in spotless white,
And conquering palms they bear."

Scarcely had she uttered these words before he began to think seriously of the state of his soul, and asked himself, "Has He bought nothing for me?" His sister soon had the happiness of having him as a companion on the Christian course; and both brother and sister, with another brother, not long after, departed for missionary fields in the island of Ceylon.

No. 266.

"MY THOUGHTS ON AWFUL SUBJECTS ROLL."

REV. ISAAC WATTS, 1674—1748.

When the late Rev. Sylvester Hutchinson was stationed on Salem Circuit, New Jersey, his first station, and while he was yet a boy, he was sitting in his temporary boarding house waiting for the hour of preaching, when two young women came in to have some sport with the boy preacher. They began to ridicule his size and his insignificant appearance, when, suddenly lifting up his head from a reclining posture, he repeated, in slow and solemn tones:

"My thoughts on solemn subjects roll,
Damnation and the dead,
What horrors seize the guilty soul,
Upon a dying bed!"

His voice, his countenance, his manner, were all adapted to make them feel that

"Tis not the whole of life to live,
Nor all of death to die."

The words of the preacher were "like nails fastened in a sure place by the Master of assemblies." Tears rolled down their cheeks; they left the room, and rested not till they found a refuge in the Son of God.

No. 267.

"I THINK WHEN I READ THAT SWEET STORY OF OLD."

Mrs. Jemima Luke, 1813.

A newsboy in New York was one day heard crying, "*Bank-Note Reporter*, sir? Three more banks down!" The little fellow had not known half a score of years, but his eyes were bright, his tongue fluent, and his manners attractive. Stepping into a counting house, with his bundle of papers under his arm, he saw two gentlemen sitting in front of a fire, engaged in trifling conversation, and proposed to one of them his inquiry, "*Bank-Note Reporter,* sir?"

"No," replied one of the gentlemen; "we don't want any. But stop! If you will sing us a song we will buy one of your *Reporters.*"

The boy agreed to the terms, and the gentlemen, with an air which showed that they anticipated sport, placed the little fellow on a high stool and told him to proceed to sing. They evidently expected to hear some jovial song, when to their astonishment he began the beautiful hymn:

"I think when I read that sweet story of old,
When Jesus was here among men,
How He called little children as lambs to His fold,
I should like to have been with Him then."

The effect upon his listeners was at once perceptible, and before he had sung through the four verses they were both in tears. When he had finished, one of the gentlemen inquired, "Where did you learn that hymn?"

"At Sabbath school," replied the boy. The reader will, of course, expect to hear that the gentlemen bought the *Reporter*, and will not be sorry to learn that, in addition to this, they presented him with a sum of money, and after they had obtained his name and residence they allowed him to go on his way.

No. 268.

"I'M A POOR SINNER AND NOTHING AT ALL."

In a parish in England, there was an old sailor who went by the name of Jack. In going along the street one day he heard a number of women singing:

"I'm a poor sinner and nothing at all;
But Jesus Christ is my all in all."

The man gave up his drunkenness, and very soon gave up his wickedness. At last he went to the minister and asked to be admitted to church membership. The minister asked, "What is your experience?"

"I have none," said Jack.

"Well then, John, I cannot admit you."

"Well," said Jack, "I have no experience but that:

'I'm a poor sinner, and nothing at all,
But Jesus Christ is my all in all.' "

"Well," said the minister, "I will ask the deacons about your admission; but you will be expected to state your experience."

The deacons were assembled, and Jack was called on to answer their questions, to which he always replied:

"I'm a poor sinner, and nothing at all,
But Jesus Christ is my all in all."

Says the old deacon, "That is not enough; tell us your doubts and fears, and why you seek admission."

"Nay," says Jack, "I have no doubt at all that

'I'm a poor sinner, and nothing at all,
But Jesus Christ is my all in all.'

and I don't fear anything either, but

'I'm a poor sinner, and nothing at all,
But Jesus Christ is my all in all.' "

Jack was admitted and to the end led a Christian life.

No. 269.

"IN THINE OWN WAY, O GOD OF LOVE."

Rev. Isaac Watts, 1674—1748.

A beautiful fact in connection with singing is told of the excellent George Whitefield. During the delivery of a sermon in Boston on the wonders of creation, providence, and redemption, a violent tempest of thunder and lightning came on, which so alarmed the congregation that they sat in breathless awe. The preacher closed his notebook, and stepping into one of the wings of the desk, fell on his knees, and with much feeling, and fine taste, repeated from Dr. Watts:

"Hark, the Eternal rends the sky,
A mighty voice before Him goes,
A voice of music to His friends,
But threatening thunder to His foes.

"Come, children, to your Father's arms,
Hide in the chambers of My grace,
Till the fierce storms be overblown,
And my revenging fury cease!"

"Let us devoutly sing to the praise and glory of God this hymn, Old Hundred." The whole congregation immediately arose and poured forth the sacred song. By the time the hymn was finished, the storm was hushed, and the sun, bursting forth, showed the magnificent arch of peace. Resuming the desk, the preacher quoted, with admirable tact, "Look upon the rainbow: praise Him That made it. Very beautiful is it in the brightness thereof! It compasseth the heaven about with a glorious circle; and the Hands of the Most High have bended it." The episode added intense interest to the service.

No. 270.

"JESUS! THE NAME HIGH OVER ALL."

REV. CHARLES WESLEY, 1708—1788.

There was a little girl, a Sunday-school scholar, severely scalded. She was taken to the hospital, and only survived a short time. There lay the little sufferer, all her last night on earth, in the doleful sick ward of that hospital; nothing was heard to break the stillness of the hour, but the ticking of the great clock. By and by there rose from her bed a low, but sweet and beautiful melody:

"Jesus! the Name to sinners dear,
The Name to sinners given;
It scatters all their guilty fears;
It turns their hell to heaven."

All was still again; nothing was heard but the ticking of the great clock in the ward. At length the voice broke out again, and even more sweet than before:

"Happy, if with my latest breath,
I may but gasp His Name;
Preach Him to all, and cry in death,
Behold, behold the Lamb!"

The nurse hastened to the bedside, but she was too late; angels had been there before, and the happy spirit of the child had gone from singing "Behold the Lamb!" on earth, to see Him in His glory above.

"Biblical Treasury."

No. 271.

"GOD IS THE REFUGE OF HIS SAINTS."

Rev. Isaac Watts, 1674—1748.

An impressive scene took place in Tremont Temple, Boston, a few days after the great fire in that city. The meeting was in the main an assemblage of the city government, the merchants, and the solid men of Boston. It was opened by religious exercises, one of which was the singing of a hymn. The selection was an impressive one, and it was sung alike by cultivated voices and by voices unused to singing, by men whose merchant palaces were still smoking only a few steps from where they were uplifting their voices in reverential awe to God. The hymn opened as follows:

"God is the Refuge of His saints,
When storms of dark distress invade;
Ere we can offer our complaints,
Behold Him present with His aid.

"Let mountains from their seats be hurled
Down to the deep and buried there,
Convulsions shake the solid world,
Our faith shall never yield to fear."

Thus far the hymn had rolled out fully and grandly, with a majesty suited to the gravity of the occasion. But lower, sweeter notes followed, and there was moisture in strong men's eyes. The stanza, so soothing, so tender, so refreshing, yet full of feeling, began:

"There is a stream whose gentle flow,
Supplies the city of our God,
Life, love and joy, still gliding through,
And watering our divine abode."

A little way from that place the hot streets, guarded by soldiers, lay smoking in the noontide sun. The scorching ashes, fanned anon by the complaining autumn wind filled all the broad area from the foot of Beacon Hill to the harbor. Marble columns lay broken and blackened, and granite walls lay crumbling in the dust. Yet, weary with watching the parched ground, the still consuming desolation of fire, the merchants whose millions had vanished could unite in a common bond of sympathy, and sing this verse of confidence and faith.

No. 272.

"WE'RE TRAVELING HOME TO HEAVEN ABOVE."

Rev. Charles Wesley, 1708—1788.

At the close of a prayer meeting at Charleston, in a public hall, the pastor urged all who were present to join their Christian band and march with them to the home of the faithful and blest, and requested the congregation to sing this hymn. It was sung with earnestness and power, and as it rose and filled the hall, it reached the ears of a husband and wife who were sleeping in a room above, and after listening to several verses, the woman sat up in bed and said, "Yes, I will go."

No. 273.

"COME WE WHO LOVE THE LORD."

Rev. Isaac Watts, 1674—1748.

A young boy of twelve, named Arthur, had been converted, and had lived a Christian life several months, when, one day, he yielded to passion, and threw a stone which nearly killed a little playmate. His sufferings from remorse and penitence for that harm that he had done and the dishonor he had cast upon his Savior were intense, and at the class meeting several days after, his sorrow was still so deep that he could not speak when called upon, and his father spoke for him. During the meeting the hymn had been sung, in which occurs the verse:

"The hill of Zion yields
A thousand sacred sweets,"

Just before the meeting closed, Arthur said, earnestly, through his tears, "I'm trying to climb up that Zion's hill." This incident was the basis of the familiar Sunday-school hymn:

"I'm trying to climb up Zion's hill,
For the Savior whispers 'Love me.'"

The Rev. Joseph Slattarie, of Chatham, England, was once walking in that town, when his attention was arrested by a youthful voice singing:

"The sorrows of the mind
Be banished from the place!
Religion never was designed
To make our pleasures less."

Pleased alike with the sweetness of the voice and the cheerful tones in which the verse was sung, he looked around to see whence the singing proceeded; but for some time he looked in vain. At length he saw a little sweep with his head popping out of a chimney and waving with a sort of triumph his brush over his head. "Oh," said the venerable minister, in relating the incident, "It made me weep in gratitude to think how singing the praises of God contributes to make even a poor chimney-sweep happy."

"Some impressions," says a young man, who went out as a missionary to the heathen, "of the importance and necessity of true religion, were made upon my mind, at a very early period. The first particular one that I recollect was, I think, when I was about five years of age. There happened one day a very vivid storm of thunder and lightning in our neighborhood; on which occasion a few Christian friends, who lived near us, terrified by its violence, came into my father's house. When under his roof, in a moment there came a most vivid flash, followed by a dreadful peal of thunder, which much alarmed the whole company, except my father, who, turning toward my mother and our friends, with the greatest composure, repeated those words of Dr. Watts:

"The God That rules on high,
And thunders when He please,
That rides upon the stormy sky,
And manages the seas.

"This awful God is ours,
Our Father and our Love,
He shall send down His heavenly powers
To carry us above."

These words, accompanied by such circumstances, sunk deep into my heart. I thought how safe and happy are those who have the great God for their Father and Friend; but being conscious that I had sinned against Him, I was afraid He was not my Father, and that instead of loving me, He was angry with me. And this for some time after continued to disturb and grieve my mind. He then proceeds to say that those early impressions were succeeded by others which terminated in his conversion."

"Arvine's Cyclopedia."

No. 274.

"THE GOD OF ABRAM PRAISE."

REV. THOMAS OLIVERS, 1725—1799.

The late Rev. T. M. Eddy, D. D., passing through the streets of Baltimore, saw an aged and feeble colored man sawing some hard wood by the side of the road. Feeling that the colored man's lot was a hard one, as he contrasted his age and feebleness with the hardness of the work to be done, he approached him to speak a few kind and encouraging words. But drawing near he heard the old man singing softly and sweetly the words:

"The God of Abram praise,
Whose all-sufficient grace
Shall guide me all my happy days
In all His ways:
He calls a worm His friend,
He calls Himself my God!
And He shall save me to the end,
Through Jesus' Blood."

The Doctor passed on, saying, "He is rich; he has a better friend than I could be, and he is safe."

No. 275.

"HOW HAPPY EVERY CHILD OF GRACE."

REV. CHARLES WESLEY, 1708—1788.

A little girl, sobbing as though her heart would break, while the warm gushing tears rolled down her cheeks, went forward to, and knelt down at, an altar, saying,

"I'm so wicked, I want you to pray for me." Soon after she arose, her face shining with a heavenly radiance, and sang:

"How happy every child of grace
Who knows his sins forgiven!"

People said, "She is only a child, she will soon get over it." But she did not. She kept on singing. And some time afterward, when her mother had company, she came into the room as happy as a lark, singing this same hymn. Her mother said, "You ought not to sing in company." But she replied, "I can't help it; it sings itself."

No. 276.

"NOW THAT THE SUN IS GLEAMING BRIGHT."

REV. JOHN HENRY NEWMAN, 1801.

It adds interest to the translation of this hymn to know that the original was sung by the death-bed of William the Conqueror, in the year 1087. His closing hours formed a night of half sleep, half stupor, the struggling expiring body taking a dull, painful, broken rest before its long earthly repose; but as the sun was just rising above the horizon, shedding brightness on the walls of the apartment, William was aroused by the tolling of the great cathedral bell, and inquired what the sound meant. "It is the hour of praise," was the answer of his attendants. Then were the priesthood in full choir welcoming with voices of gladness the renewed gift of another day, in the words of the hymn which Cardinal Newman translates as above, but before the close of the hymn William the Conqueror was dead.

No. 277.

"LATE, LATE, SO LATE! AND DARK THE NIGHT AND CHILL."

Alfred Tennyson, 1809—1892.

This hymn with its refrain, "Too late! Ye cannot enter now," was sung in a certain church and deeply impressed a lady who heard it. The next night in coming to the meeting, she was late, and the crowd was so great that she could not get in. The Spirit seemed to whisper to her, "What if this was the door of heaven, and you—too late?" She went home deeply thoughtful, and that night gave her heart to God and became a happy Christian.

No. 278.

"JESUS LOVES ME THIS I KNOW."

Miss Anna Warner, 1822.

One Sunday a man came into a Sunday school at the Boston North End Mission, drawn by the sweetness of the children's singing. He remained until the close, and came again that evening to the prayer meeting. When the customary invitation to seek the Savior was given, he came forward and found peace in believing. To a few of the workers who remained to pray with the penitent seekers, he said, "My friends, I feel that I'm a saved man, and I owe it to your children's singing, 'Jesus loves me,' this afternoon. I couldn't realize it, I've been such a miserable sinner: but after I went away I thought it over, 'Jesus loves me;' and then I thought of the next line, 'For the Bible tells me so,' and I tried to believe it, and I came here this evening to get you to pray for me." He became a regular attendant at the Mission, and while there gave the clearest evidence of a genuine change of heart. He afterward felt called to enter the ministry, and after preparation, did so and became an active pastor of a Massachusetts church.

DR. E. TOURJEE.

No. 279.

"MY LATEST SUN IS SINKING FAST."

REV. JEFFERSON HASCALL, 1807.

"Once I was detained after prayer-meeting with a few others, to converse and pray with a young woman who was under deep conviction, and who refused to go away from the place of prayer until she had found Jesus. It seemed to be all in vain that I talked with her, explaining the atonement, quoting the simplest and strongest promises of the Gospel, and urging her to an immediate and simple faith; it was all in vain that I prayed with and for her. At last, because, as it seemed, I could do nothing else, I began to sing that little hymn, the last verse of which goes:

"O bear my longing heart to Him
Who bled and died for me;
Whose Blood now cleanses from all sin,
And gives me victory."

We had sung the whole hymn through and were hushed into silence by the Spirit. During the singing of the last stanza, our friend had lifted her weeping face toward mine, and was looking intently and eagerly at me, as though she would fain drink in the words and power of the song. And now, in the hush that was upon us, reaching out both her hands to me, she said, in a plaintive kind of whisper, "Please sing that last verse again." And again we sang softly and tenderly:

"O, bear my longing heart to Him
Who bled and died for me;
Whose Blood now cleanses from all sin,
And gives me victory."

As the words and melody died away, the expression of her face changed; the darkness was overpast, and the light and gladness of His peace had come in the place of it; and with a cry of joy she turned and flung herself into the arms of her sister, who was standing near, exclaiming, "I am saved! I am saved ! Oh blessed Jesus."

REV. G. F. PENTECOST.

No. 280.

"JESUS, LOVER OF MY SOUL."

REV. CHARLES WESLEY, 1708—1788.

A poor woman, who had no hope in Christ, was dying in the attic of one of the tenement houses of New York. A minister was sent for, but his words and prayers failed to give her hope. She said again and again as he talked to her, "It's no use; I'm too wicked, and it's too late."

At length he began to sing, "Jesus, Lover of my soul," and sang two verses. Noticing her deep interest, he turned to her and said, "Can't you trust Him now?"

With a smile of joy she replied, "Other refuge have I none." Her happy face showed her acceptance of Jesus.

Several years ago a ship was burned near the English Channel. Among the passengers were a father, mother, and their little child, a daughter not many months old. When the discovery was made that the ship was on fire, and the alarm was given, there was great confusion, and the family became separated. The father was rescued and taken to Liverpool; but the mother and infant were carried overboard by the crowd, and, unnoticed by those who were doing all in their power to save the sufferers still on the ship, they drifted out of the Channel with the tide, the mother clinging to a fragment of the wreck with her little one clasped to her breast. Late in the afternoon of that day, a vessel bound from Newport, Wales, to America, was moving slowly along in her course. There was only a slight breeze, and the captain was impatiently walking the deck when his attention was called to an object some distance off, which looked like a person in the water. The officers and crew watched it for a time, and as no vessel was near from which anyone could have fallen overboard, they thought it impossible to be a human being. The captain sent a boat, which was watched with deepest interest from the ship. As the boat approached the object floating, suddenly the sound of a gentle voice was heard so softly singing, and the sailors listened to the words of the first verse:

"Jesus, Lover of my soul,
  Let me to Thy bosom fly,
While the nearer waters roll,
  While the tempest still is high!
Hide me, O my Savior, hide,
  Till the storm of life is past;
Safe into the haven guide,
  O receive my soul at last!"

Soon the rescued mother and child were safe on board the ship, and ultimately reached America. The father joined them four months afterward.

In the winter of 1872, Mr. Charles Trumbull White, being engaged in hospital work of a religious character, visited Bellevue Hospital, New York City. He was specially urged by the attendant to see an English sailor in one of the wards, who was near death. The man was found to be fast going, and unable to articulate. Mr. White, therefore, leaned down and repeated, so that he might hear them, the words of this hymn. To all appearance they were uttered to the "dull cold ear of death," and he departed, feeling as though he had failed to secure the least response. About midnight, however, of the same night, this unknown sailor seemed to arouse. He sat up in his cot, and with a clearly audible voice he spoke the words:

"Jesus, Lover of my soul,
Let me to Thy bosom fly,"

and continued until he had repeated the entire hymn. He then added other verses of hymns for several minutes, but ceased suddenly, fell back, and was dead. Who can tell how great a bridge had been thrown by those familiar words across the gulf of memory, and how great a comfort they may have brought to his dying hour?

REV. S. W. DUFFIELD, IN *English Hymns.*

Rev. Mr. Spurgeon relates that an ungodly stranger once stepping into one of his services at Exeter Hall was brought to the Cross by the words of Wesley's hymn:

"Jesus, Lover of my soul."

"Does Jesus love me?" said he. "Then why should I live in enmity to Him?" And he became a Christian.

A party of Northern tourists formed part of a large company gathered on the deck of an excursion steamer that was moving slowly down the historic Potomac one beautiful evening in the summer of 1881. A gentleman, who has since gained a national reputation as an evangelist of song, had been delighting the party with the happy rendering of many favorite hymns, the last being the sweet petition so dear to every Christian heart, "Jesus, Lover of my soul." The singer gave the first two verses with much feeling, and a peculiar emphasis upon the concluding lines that thrilled every heart. A hush had fallen upon the listeners that was not broken for some seconds after the musical notes had died away. Then a gentleman made his way from the outskirts of the crowd to the side of the singer and accosted him with, "Beg your pardon, stranger, but were you actively engaged in the late war?"

"Yes, sir," the man of song answered courteously; "I fought under General Grant."

"Well," the first speaker continued with something like a sigh, "I did my fighting on the other side, and think, indeed, am quite sure, I was very near you one bright night eighteen years ago this very month. It was such a night as this. If I am not mistaken, you were on guard duty. We of the South had sharp business on hand, and you were of the enemy. I crept near your post of duty, my murderous weapon in my hand; the shadow hid me. As you paced back and forth you were humming the tune of the hymn you have just sung. I raised my gun and aimed at your heart, and I had been selected by our commander for the work because I was a sure shot. Then out upon the night rang the words:

'Cover my defenceless head
With the shadow of Thy wing.'

Your prayer was answered. I couldn't fire after that, and there was no attack made upon your camp that night. I felt sure when I heard you sing this evening that you were the man whose life I was spared from taking."

The singer grasped the hand of the Southerner and said with much emotion: "I remember the night very well, and distinctly the feeling of depression and loneliness with which I went forth to my duty. I knew my post was one of great danger, and I was more dejected than I remember to have been at any other time during the service. I paced my lonely beat, thinking of home and friends and all that life holds dear. Then the thought of God's care for all that He has created came to me with peculiar force. If He so cares for the sparrow, how much more for man created in His own image; and I sang the prayer of my heart and ceased to feel alone. How the prayer was answered I never knew until this evening. 'Jesus, Lover of my soul' has always been a favorite hymn with me; now it will be inexpressibly dear."

This incident is related by a lady who was one of the party on the steamer.

London Freeman.

No. 281.

"LORD, I HEAR OF SHOWERS OF BLESSING."

Mrs. Elizabeth Codner.

Mrs. Codner is the wife of an English clergyman. In the year 1860 some of her young friends had been greatly interested in an account of revival work to which they had listened. She was anxious that they themselves might receive a blessing from it and wrote for them this hymn. She says, "I longed to press upon them an earnest individual appeal. Without effort, the words seemed to be given me, and they took the form of a hymn. I had no thought of sending it beyond the limit of my own circle, but passing it on to one and another, it became a word of power, and I then published it as a leaflet.

No. 282.

"O MASTER IT IS GOOD TO BE."

Rev. Arthur Penryhn Stanley, 1815—1881.

That is a very pretty and a very helpful story that is told in "Tom Brown's School Days," of the new boy who was made Tom's chum, and whose name was Arthur. He was a home-loving boy and nearly cried when Tom told him he mustn't talk about his home or his mother before the other boys, because they would call him names if he did. And then Arthur drew upon himself the attention of the whole room full of boys by washing his face before he went to bed. And then when he had washed and undressed and put his night gown on, right there in the room with its twelve beds and its twelve boys, all laughing and talking, with the light burning brightly, Arthur kneeled down beside his own bed and said his prayers. Tom's back was turned, and so at first he didn't see what Arthur was doing, but he heard the sneers and the laughs from the other beds, and he saw a slipper come flying over from the middle of the room, and then he saw it all; and in an instant the boot he had just taken off went flying straight for the head of the bully who had thrown the slipper. And then the lights went out, and Tom lay thinking, and a great panorama passed before his eyes. He saw his old home, and his mother, and he heard her voice and his own, as he promised her that he would never go to bed until he had knelt and asked God to keep him; and he remembered how that promise had been broken; and the next night he knelt too, and then other boys did; and so by the courage of the little newcomer Arthur, the whole school was changed. Arthur grew up, and when he had become a clergyman of the Church of England, he wrote this hymn.

No. 283.

"CAST THY BREAD UPON THE WATERS."

Rev. Phoebe A. Hanaford, 1829.

The author of this hymn is a married lady and yet the pastor of a Universalist church. She has a record quite unique as a breaker down of traditional customs. She was the first woman who ever offered an ordaining prayer; the first woman to exchange pulpits with her own son; the first woman to officiate at the marriage of her own daughter; the first woman regularly ordained to the ministry in Massachusetts or in New England; the first woman to serve as chaplain of the Connecticut Legislature; the first woman to attend a Masonic festival and to respond by invitation to a toast. I have no doubt she can truthfully add that she is the first "woman minister," as she calls herself, to write a hymn. She wrote an autobiography and never mentioned in it her husband's name.

No. 284.

"I HEAR THE SAVIOR SAY."

Mrs. Elvina Mabel Hall, 1818.

I am afraid that the circumstances under which this hymn was written will not increase your respect for its author, even if it does not lessen your love for the hymn. John Ryland composed a hymn while sitting in the pulpit listening to a sermon by a brother minister whom he had invited to preach for him, and it never seemed to me quite courteous to the preacher, if it was respectful of the occasion. But what shall we say of the author of this hymn, who, in the spring of 1865, sat in the choir of a Methodist church in Baltimore, and while the minister was praying, scribbled the words on the fly leaf of a copy of the "New Lute of Zion."

No. 285.

"JESUS, THE NAME HIGH OVER ALL."

Rev. Charles Wesley, 1708—1788.

Charles Wesley was once preaching in a little church in Cornwall, England, among the miners, and was condemning in no uncertain words the drunken revels of the people, when a man arose in the congregation, and with some profanity disputed the preacher's words. Mr. Wesley exclaimed, "Who is this that pleads for the devil!" and the man stepped out boldly before the congregation. Mr. Wesley immediately addressed his words to this man himself, exposing and rebuking his wickedness in such withering words as drove the man clear out of the room. This hymn is said to have been written to commemorate this victory.

No. 286.

"WESLEY'S HYMNS FOR CHILDREN."

In No. 212 will be found a note on Watts' "Divine and Moral Songs." The Wesleys, who came a little later in the century, bestowed rather faint praise on the children's hymns of Watts, by saying, "There are two ways of writing or speaking to children; the one is to let ourselves down to them, the other to lift them up to us." Dr. Watts has written in the former way, and has succeeded admirably well, speaking to children as children, and leaving them as he found them. And then they go on to describe a little book of hymns they themselves have published with an easy self-adulation that is quite refreshing. "The following hymns," they say, "are written on the other plan; they contain strong and manly sense: yet expressed in such plain and easy language as even children may understand. But when they do understand them, they will be children no longer, only in years and stature." But the "Children's Hymn Book" of the Wesleys, even with their great name and fame to help it, fell quite flat, and is now among the very rare books only to be found in library collections, while the "Divine and Moral Songs" of Watts, who "let himself down to the children," can be bought today, a century and a half after they were written, at almost any book store. And yet some of Mr. Wesley's hymns for children are good, and to be found in many of the hymnals now in use. Here is a list of them all written by Rev. Charles Wesley:

"And am I born to die?"
"And am I only born to die?"
"And must I be to judgment brought?"
"Captain of our salvation, take."
"Come Father, Son, and Holy Ghost."
"Glorious God, accept a heart."
"Hail Father, Son, and Holy Ghost."
"Loving Jesus! Gentle Lamb!"
"Maker, Savior of mankind."
"O all-creating God."
"O Thou That would'st not have."
"Thou the great eternal God."
"Thou my God art good and wise."
"Where shall true believers go?"
"Young men and maidens raise."
"Teacher, Guide of young beginners."
"God is goodness, wisdom, power."
"Holy Child of heavenly birth."
"Let children proclaim their Savior and King."
"O Father of all, the great and the small."
"Gentle Jesus, meek and mild."
"Come let us join the hosts above."
"Happy beyond description he."
"Come let us join with one accord."
"Happy man whom God doth aid."
"But who is sufficient to lead?"
"Let all that breathe Jehovah's praise."
"Good Thou art and good Thou dost."

A great many years ago an English father, whose daughter was away from home at school, wrote in a letter to her, "Buy of Mr. Evans, Mr. Wesley's 'Hymns for Children' and get them by heart. I will pay for the book and give you a penny for each hymn you learn, which I believe will amount to nearly four shillings. These hymns afforded much comfort to your sister Peggy, who is now in heaven."

No. 287.

"WHERE SHALL MY WONDERING SOUL BEGIN?"

"AND CAN IT BE THAT I SHOULD GAIN?"—1738.

REV. CHARLES WESLEY, 1708—1788.

The conversion of Charles Wesley marks an epoch in the religious history of the world as remarkable as that which dates from the conversion of "Saul of Tarsus." It occurred on May 21, 1728, and two days later he wrote in his journal, "At nine I began a hymn on my conversion but was persuaded to break off for fear of pride . . . I prayed Christ to stand by me, and finished the hymn." Thus the spiritual life that became one of the mightiest influences for good in Great Britain, and which in the great denomination of which he was one of the founders, has become a tremendous religious power the world over, exerted its first activity in composing a hymn; and this hymn writing did not stop until the author had given to the world nearly seven thousand more.

Both the hymns of which the first lines are named were written at that time, and it is not known to which Wesley referred in his journal.

No. 288.

"'O, WHERE SHALL REST BE FOUND?"

"PEOPLE OF THE LIVING GOD."

JAMES MONTGOMERY, 1771—1854.

I place these two hymns together because each is the expression of an actual experience of the author, and because one answers a question which the other asks. When Montgomery was about thirty-six years of age (in 1807) he was in great distress of mind—dissatisfied with himself—at peace neither with God nor with his own conscience. At this time and in the midst of this experience he wrote the hymn:

"O where shall rest be found
Rest for the weary soul?"

After seven years of doubt and uncertainty, he turned at last back to the Savior of whom his pious parents had taught him, and whom he himself had in his youth accepted, and was readmitted into the church, of which he first became a member while a boy. And then under the influence of this new experience he wrote the words which answer the question of his earlier hymn:

"People of the Living God,
I have sought the world around,
Paths of sin and sorrow trod,
Peace and comfort nowhere found.
Now to you my spirit turns—
Turns a fugitive unblest;
Brethren when your altar burns,
O receive me into rest."

No. 289.

"GRACIOUS SPIRIT, DOVE DIVINE!"

John Stocker.

During the latter half of the last century there was published at London a monthly called the *Gospel Magazine.* Each number contained the portrait of some well-known minister, articles of interest to the religious public, quite often a hymn tune composed for it, and at the end of each number there were several pages of religious poetry. In one of the numbers of the year 1776 (the year this nation was born) there appeared this hymn, signed J. Stocker. The writer lived at Honiton, in Devonshire, and this is all we know of him. Not quite all, though, for during that year and the next he sent to this magazine eight other pieces, all good Gospel hymns, and two of them have found frequent place in the hymn collections of the present day. From these hymns we can gain some idea of their author's talent, his education, and his spirit. Draw for yourselves the picture of John Stocker's face while I read to you one of his quaint old hymns that, for my part, I should very much like to see restored to its place in our hymnals:

1. "Thy mercy, my God, is the theme of my song,
The joy of my heart, and the boast of my tongue;
Thy free grace alone, from the first to the last,
Hath won my affections, and bound my soul fast.

2. "Without Thy sweet mercy, I could not live here,
Sin soon would reduce me to utter despair;
But, through Thy free goodness, my spirits revive,
And He That first made me, still keeps me alive.

3. "Thy mercy is more than a match for my heart,
Which wonders to feel its own hardness depart;
Dissolv'd by Thy goodness, I fall to the ground,
And weep to the praise of the mercy I found.

4. "The door of Thy mercy stands open all day
To the poor and the needy, who knock by the way;
No sinner shall ever be empty sent back,
Who comes seeking mercy for Jesus' sake.

5. "Thy mercy in Jesus exempts me from hell;
Its glories I'll sing, and its wonders I'll tell:
'Twas Jesus, my friend, when he hung on the tree,
Who opened the channel of mercy for me.

6. "Great Father of mercies! Thy goodness I own,
And the covenant love of Thy crucified Son:
All praise to the Spirit, Whose whisper divine,
Seals mercy and pardon and righteousness mine!"

No. 290.

"WHEN ISRAEL FREED FROM PHARAOH'S HAND"—1712.

REV. ISAAC WATTS, 1674—1748.

Every Saturday in the *Spectator* (for account of which see No. 49), Joseph Addison published some religious article usually ending with a hymn. These fell under the eye of Dr. Watts, who wrote a letter to the editor in which he said, "Upon reading the hymns that you have published in some late dates, I had a mind to try yesterday whether I could write one. The One Hundred and Fourteenth Psalm appears to me an admirable ode, and I began to turn it into our language. If the following essay be not too incorrigible, bestow upon it a few brightenings from your genius, that I may learn how to write better or write no more." Then follows this rendering of that Psalm.

No. 291.

"THERE IS A FOUNTAIN FILLED WITH BLOOD."

WILLIAM COWPER, 1731—1800.

A poor Sabbath scholar has fallen down a hatchway and broken his hip. The doctor says he is internally injured, and that he cannot help him. The boy's teacher is sent for, and is surprised at the greeting he receives. "Teacher, you are just in time to hear my great joy; I am going home to Jesus."

"I did not know you ever thought of such things, John; how long have you felt so?"

"Dear teacher, you never asked me; I have been longing to have you for six months. Now sing my favorite hymn with me, dear teacher." And while they sang the words:

"And sinners plunged beneath that flood,
Lose all their guilty stains."

the messenger came to call the lad home.

"Full sweetly on the evening air,
Rang out the well-known strains,
'There is a fountain filled with blood
Drawn from Immanuel's veins,
And sinners, plunged beneath that flood,
Lose all their guilty stains.'

"Thus sang a little company,
Whose hearts by grace renewed,
Had gathered in an upper room
To tell their gratitude
To Him, by Whose atoning love,
Their sins had been subdued.

"A weary man who passed that way,
Bowed down with weight of sin,
Who long had asked how such as he
Relief and rest might win,
Heard the glad sound, so sweet, so clear
Amid the city's din.

"A wand'rer on that city's streets,
And bound he knew not where,
He turned aside to seek the place,
Entered, and climbed the stair,
Intently list'ning as he rose,
To words, to him so rare.

"The dying thief rejoiced to see
That fountain in his day,
And there may I, . . . 'O what is this!
A thief, a thief, they say;'
'And there may I, though vile as he,
Wash all my sins away.'

"As thus he speaks, the room he finds,
And, e'er in prayer they bow,
He cries, 'Oh, friends, for me so lost,
Plead you for mercy now.'
They bid him pray; 'Alas,' he says,
'To pray, I know not how.'

"But taught by loving lips the way,
He learns to pray at last,
And on the Saviour of the lost
His weight of guilt to cast;
As from his contrite heart goes up
The prayer of ages past—

" 'O God, be merciful to me,
A sinner, Lord, am I;

In my despair and helplessness,
To Thee, O Lord, I cry.
Lost, helpless, ruined, hear my prayer,
Lord, save me, or I die.'

"The God Who heard the publican,
Heard this heart's honest prayer,
And he who came a child of wrath,
In sorrow and despair,
Went forth a free and happy man,
And God's own child and heir.

"O ye who have the art of song,
The talent ye possess,
Ye well may consecrate to God;
How would you dare do less?
If used for Him, O who can say
How greatly He may bless?"

R. M. OFFORD, in *New York Observer.*

Dr. Dashiell, in his "Pastor's Recollections," tells an affecting story of the power of this hymn upon the heart of a skeptic. He had been called to visit a family where the little child had just died. He found the father a man of violent prejudices against religion, especially against clergymen, owing to the unworthy conduct of a former ministerial friend. Persevering in his efforts to secure an influence with this very unpromising person, Dr. Dashiell relates that the first point of contact was this hymn. His early associations had endeared it to him, and he had never ceased to admire and love it in spite of his infidel opinions. After a considerable length of time, the skeptic met with a severe injury—his arm being drawn into machinery and crushed so that amputation was necessary. It was at first very doubtful if the patient would rally, but finally he was heard to murmur something, and as Dr. Dashiell bent over him to catch the words, he distinctly caught the language of the stanza:

"The dying thief rejoiced to see,
That fountain in his day,
And there may I, though vile as he,
Wash all my sins away."

It was a confession of faith on what seemed—though providentially it was not—the very edge of death."

"English Hymns."

Rev. H. M. Gallaher, a Baptist minister, relates the following incident. "During the War of the Rebellion in America—and I know something about it—I stood and looked at a dying soldier—not wounded, but perishing of pneumonia. I asked him if I could do anything for him.

"He said, 'I want you to read to me.'

"I did so, and asked him what next. 'Will you pray for me?'

"I prayed. Looking again, I saw his lips move, and had to get very close to hear his answer. 'Can I do anything else for you?'

" 'Yes, sir. Can you sing?' So I sang for him:

'There is a land of pure delight,
Where saints immortal reign.'

and then stopped. He was looking upward, and asked me to continue. Then I sang:

'There is a fountain filled with blood,
Drawn from Immanuel's veins.'

He asked me: 'Will you sing that over again?'

"Supposing he meant the first one, I said, 'Which? About that "land of pure delight?" '

" 'No, sir; sing that about the "fountain filled with blood.' "

At a meeting in City Road Chapel, London, to consider the wants of the neglected poor of the great city, John Boynton, a minister, related how a blaspheming scoffer took his stand by the statue of Lord Bute in Cardiff, and began an infidel harangue to a crowd of working men who gathered about him. When he had finished, a railway porter stepped up in front and said: "Aren't you going to sing before you go away?"

"Oh, no," was the reply, "we don't sing."

"Well, I do," said the porter, and he struck up at once a verse of Cowper's familiar hymn:

"The dying thief rejoiced to see
That fountain in his day;
And there have I, though vile as he,
Washed all my sins away."

On the next night he met the same speaker and the same assembly at the same place with a powerful accordion under his arm. By the attractive and spiritual singing, with its musical accompaniment, he entirely drew away the audience from the infidel speaker and sang to them the gospel of Jesus Christ, to their delight and profit."

St. Louis Christian Advocate, November 11, 1885.

Miranda N——, says a Christian pastor, was about eighteen years of age, much distinguished for personal beauty, but more for uncommon sweetness of disposition and great amiableness of deportment. There was not probably among all the people of my charge, one whose case would have been more promptly cited, and perhaps none so effectively, to disprove the doctrine of the entire sinfulness of the unregenerate heart. She was deservedly a general favorite. She seemed to entertain the kindest affection toward all, and every one who knew her, loved her. One evening at an inquiry meeting, held at my house, I noticed in a full room, a female in great apparent distress. The disturbance she made by her loud sobs, and frequent and painful interruption of the silence of the room, induced me to pass by others, and go to her at once. On coming to her seat, I was not a little surprised to find myself by the side of Miranda. The first inquiry I put to her was this: "What has brought you here, Miranda?"

With emphasis she replied, "My sins, sir."

With a view to testing the reality and depth of her convictions, I then said, "But what have *you* done, which makes either your heart or your life appear so heinously sinful?"

At the second question she broke out in a voice that reached the extreme part of the room and thrilled through every heart, for she was known and loved by every person there: *"I hate God, and I know it. I hate Christians, and I know it. I hate my own being; oh that I had never been born!"* As she uttered this acknowledgment, she arose and left the room in irrepressible agony. Deeply as I was interested in her case, I could not follow her and leave the many with whom I had yet to converse: but conducted her across the hall into the opposite room, where Mrs. S—— was employed in attendance upon a sick child. The remainder of the narrative I received from Mrs. S——. After a little conversation, as I was informed, between Mrs. S—— and Miranda, who was walking the room in great distress, her eye lighted upon a copy of "Village Hymns," which lay upon the sideboard. She eagerly caught it up and read at the first page to which she opened, these words:

"There is a fountain filled with blood,
Drawn from Immanuel's veins;
And sinners plunged beneath that flood,
Lose all their guilty stains."

As she finished this verse she dropped the book and exclaimed, "I have found my Savior! This is the Savior I need. O precious Savior." And many other expressions of the same kind. Her enmity to God was gone. Her burden was removed. Christ was all in all to her."

Arvine's "Cyclopedia."

"During the move on Atlanta, I was coming back from the front, when I learned that there was no chaplain in either of the two hospitals. I therefore determined to forego business at Chattanooga and stop over. There were many low cases, and among them an Indiana soldier sent for me in the night. He was dying,—a fair-haired youth of eighteen years. His leg had been cut off by a shell, and amputation had prostrated him beyond recovery. He was a Sunday-school boy. He wanted me to take his last words home to his mother and sister. He gave me his memorandum and pocketbook and a number of keepsakes; asked me to pull the two rings from his hand and send to his sister, and tell her that they were taken off after his hand was getting cold. After prayer, we sang the hymn commencing:

'There is a fountain filled with blood.'

He joined in, breaking the tune now and then with, 'Yes, yes, if he could trust Him, I can.' 'Yes, when I die.' 'That will be sweeter.' 'Power to save; power to save; I used to sing that hymn at home, but it was never so good as this; "power to save."' I gave him my hand for goodbye. He drew me down for a kiss. And then we left him."

"Annals of the U. S. Christian Commission."

No. 292.

"MY HEAVENLY HOME IS BRIGHT AND FAIR."

Rev. William Hunter, 1811—1877.

On January 10, 1860, the Pemberton Mill, a large cotton factory at Lawrence, Massachusetts, suddenly fell in ruins, burying the operatives in the debris. Some were rescued alive, the others would have been, but a broken lantern set the buildings on fire, and the rescuers were driven from their work. In one room there were three Mission Sunday school children imprisoned. The neighbors and friends had been working hard to get these children out and had got so near to them that their voices could be heard when the fire drove them back. Superhuman were the efforts made to rescue the children; the men bravely fought back the flames; but the fire gained fresh strength and returned to claim its victims. Then piercing shrieks rose from the spectators when they saw that the efforts of the firemen were hopeless. The children saw their fate. They then knelt down and commenced to sing this hymn:

"My heavenly home is bright and fair,
Nor pain nor death can enter there;
Its glittering towers the sun outshine;
That heavenly mansion shall be mine."

One verse of this hymn is as follows:

"Let others seek a home below,
Which flames devour, or waves o'erflow,
Be mine a happier lot to own,
A heavenly mansion, near the throne."

No. 293.

"NEARER, MY GOD, TO THEE."

Mrs. Sarah Flower Adams, 1805—1848.

"A child's song in a New York hospital startled the nurses and patients on Thursday last. On the night before, an ambulance was called from Gouverneur Hospital to a house in Hester Street for a burned child. She had been sent by her parents to the cellar for firewood, and in descending the steps she stumbled and dropped the lamp, which exploded and set her clothing on fire. The surgeon wrapped the poor, crisped, writhing form of the child in what is known as a 'prepared sheet,' and told the driver to get to the hospital quickly. There all was done for her that science could do, but it was impossible to save her life. A narcotic was given her, and she fell asleep. Waking after some hours, she asked for water. The nurse immediately called the doctor. In a minute he was beside the cot. He felt the pulse, ominously shook his head, gave some more instructions, and turned to go away. As he did so, the little creature turned half around. The dim light of a candle shone on the blackened face. The swollen lips pursed out, and, in a clear, sweet voice, the dying child began to sing the hymn:

'Nearer my God to Thee, nearer to Thee.'

The doctor and nurse stood transfixed. The other patients in the silent, darkened ward leaned on their elbows and drank in the sweet melody. The first verse completed, her strength began to fail, and with it her voice, and only the humming-like distant music of the air of the hymn could be heard. That ceased, she heaved a sigh, and all was over. Her tuneful aspiration was granted to her."

The Christian Herald, October 7, 1886.

A colporteur in Missouri, describing the labor of a single day, relates that after traveling ten miles through an unbroken prairie, he at last reached the door of a humble cabin containing a poor, old, blind man and his son and daughter. "Like many others they had sought for wealth and found only poverty in the West. The only book their house contained was an old torn United States History. They had no money to buy any books, as I saw at a glance, so I gave them two volumes of the Tract Society's publications. The old man inquired if I could sing. I answered in the affirmative and proceeded to sing that divine song so precious to every child of God, 'Nearer my God to Thee.' He accompanied me on the accordion, on which he was a skilful player. When I sang the third verse:

'There let the way appear,
Steps unto heaven;
All that Thou sendest me,
In mercy given;
Angels to beckon me
Nearer, my God, to Thee,
Nearer to Thee!'

he stopped me with his sobs, and after a few moments said, his tearful eyes telling his sincerity, 'Oh, sir, my blindness is a heavy cross, but if it will only bring me nearer to Jesus, I am no loser.' We then prayed together and spoke of our heavenly home, and remembered with pleasure, 'that there is no night there.' Though ten years in Missouri, that family had not been to a religious service in the state."

The Christian Weekly, March 16, 1872.

No. 294.

"OH SAY! CAN YOU SEE BY THE DAWN'S EARLY LIGHT."

FRANCIS SCOTT KEY, 1779—1843.

"It was my privilege to go into Richmond with General Grant's army. There I saw the captives who were in Libby prison. Many a time I wept for hours to hear what they endured. Sometimes they got letters or messages that loved ones were dying, and, of course, they could not go home to see them in their dying hour. There they were in prison one beautiful day in spring; the news had been kept from them; they had not heard what was going on around Richmond. One says while they were listening, 'I heard a band of music; they were playing the old battle tune of the Republic; I think I hear the "Star Spangled Banner." I say, boys, I believe Richmond is taken.' By-and-by they all listen and say, 'It is so.' Soon the Northern army unlocked the gates, and three thousand men were set free."

D. L. MOODY.

During the War of the Rebellion, a young lady was heard to say, "I wish I could do something for my country; I would willingly become a nurse in a hospital, but I have not physical strength. What can I do?"

A friend replied, "You can sing."

"Yes, I can sing, but what of that?"

"Go to one of the hospitals and sing for the soldiers."

The idea pleased her. She accompanied a friend who was long used to such visits, and who introduced her by saying to the patients, "Here is a young lady who has come to sing for you." At the mere announcement every face was aglow with animation, every eye was riveted upon her with expectant pleasure. She sang a few songs, commencing with the glorious "Star Spangled Banner." As the thrilling notes of that song ran through the apartment, one poor man, who had been given up by the physician as an almost hopeless case, raised himself in his cot, leaned his head upon his hand, and drank in every note like so much nectar. The effect was electrical. From that moment he began to mend, and finally recovered."

HACKETT'S "Christian Memorials of the War."

No. 295.

"WHAT MEANS THIS EAGER, ANXIOUS THRONG?"

MISS ETTA CAMPBELL.

During the Moody and Sankey meetings in Great Britain, a young man arose in one of the meetings, and said, "It was a few evenings ago, when Mr. Sankey was singing, 'Jesus of Nazareth passeth by,' that I was made to feel the need of a Savior; and when he came to the words, 'Too late, too late,' I said to myself, 'It must not be too late for me,' and I took Him to my heart then and there."

No. 296.

"WHEN HE COMETH, WHEN HE COMETH."

REV. WM. O. CUSHING, 1823.

In a Highland parish, in Scotland, a young man who had lived far from God and seemed to his minister inaccessible to the truth, was found one day deeply awakened. When asked to what this was owing, he said it was the consequence of hearing his little sister sing:

"When He cometh, when He cometh,
To make up His jewels."

No. 297.

"SAFE IN THE ARMS OF JESUS."

MISS FANNY J. VAN ALSTYNE, 1823.

During the Moody and Sankey meetings at Liverpool, England, a young man said, "I went into that hall only to scoff at all I heard. I believed only in God and the devil; the latter I thought I served well, and I sat laughing at the fools about me. Mr. Sankey sang the hymn:

'Safe in the arms of Jesus,
Safe on His gentle breast.'

A sudden thrill passed through my whole frame, and then like a dart ran through my very heart. My feelings were awful, but I listened to the second verse, and felt, 'There *is* a Saviour. Who is He? Where is He?' Instantly I realized the truth. Jesus is the Saviour. I threw myself into His loving arms, and here I am now, rejoicing in Him."

No. 298.

"SOWING THE SEED BY THE DAYLIGHT FAIR."

PHILIP BLISS, 1838—1876.

One night during the Moody and Sankey meetings in Philadelphia, the hymn, "Sowing the Seed," was announced. Mr. Sankey said, "Before we sing this song I will tell you one reason why we should sing these hymns, and that is that God is blessing them to many a poor wanderer who comes into these meetings night after night. Last week, a man who had once occupied a high position in life came into this hall and sat down. While I was singing this hymn, he took out his passbook and wrote down these words:

'Sowing the seed of a lingering pain,
Sowing the seed of a maddened brain,
Sowing the seed of a tarnished name,
Sowing the seed of eternal shame,
O what shall the harvest be?'

Last night in the inquiry room that man went down on his knees and asked God to break the chain that had dragged him down from such a high position to the lowest of the low."

No. 299.

"YET THERE IS ROOM."

REV. HORATIUS BONAR, 1808.

A young man who had been deeply impressed at one of the Moody and Sankey meetings in Great Britain, but was yet unwilling to stay to the inquirer's meeting and was about to leave the church, was arrested at the door by hearing the choir sing:

"Yet there is room! The Lamb's bright hall of song,
With its fair glory, beckons thee along;
Room, room, still room! Oh, enter, enter now!"

He felt there was room for him, went back to the pew, and after having had the truth clearly laid before him, received Christ.

No. 300.

"FOREVER WITH THE LORD."

JAMES MONTGOMERY, 1771—1854.

A little girl named Maggie, was very ill of a fever, and the van had come to take her away to the infirmary. Maggie was dressed and ready. "Maggie, it's time for you to go," said her mother.

"Ye know, mother," said Maggie, "I'll maybe no come back: will the man wait till I sing my hymn?" Even a hard heart could not have refused, and so the man waited while the little feeble voice sang:

"Here in the body pent,
Absent from Him I roam,
Yet nightly pitch my moving tent
A day's march nearer home."

And then they carried the dying child, with joyous thoughts like these filling her young heart, to the infirmary, to make from there the last stage of the journey from this to the eternal world.

No. 301.

"THE LORD'S MY LIGHT AND SAVING HEALTH."

PSALM 27.

A boy was brought to Christ when at a public school. It became known among his school-fellows, and one day, when he entered the playground, he found them drawn up in a body to meet him; and as soon as they had him in their midst, they assailed him with laughter and cries of contempt. He was taken completely by surprise; his face burned with shame and anger, and the ground seemed to be reeling under his feet. It was a Monday morning, and the first exercise, after they had entered the school, was to repeat some verses of a Psalm. A pupil was called up to repeat them, and as the poor young Christian sat bewildered among his persecutors, the first words which fell on his ears were:

"And now even at this present time,
Mine head shall lifted be,
Above all those that are my foes,
And round encompass me."

They seemed sent straight from heaven to him. They completely drove away his agitation, and made him calm and happy. He knew it was his Father saying to him, "Be strong, and of good courage"; and sorely did he need this encouragement in his hour of confession.

No. 302.

"MID PLEASURES AND PALACES THOUGH WE MAY ROAM."

JOHN HOWARD PAYNE.

One night on the banks of the Potomac, during the War of the Rebellion, as the Confederate and the Union armies lay opposite each other, the Union bands played "The Star-spangled Banner," "Hail, Columbia," and other Union songs; and the Confederates in contest played "Dixie," and other pieces of their side. It seemed that each would play the other down. By and by a band struck up "Home, Sweet Home!" The conflict ceased. The bands on the other side struck up "Home, Sweet Home," and voices from opposite sides of the river joined the chorus, "There is no place like home."

No. 303.

"NOW ISRAEL MAY SAY AND THAT TRULY."

PSALM 124.

This is known in Scotland, in its second version, as "Durie's Psalm." James Melville, in his diary—date 1582—gives an account of the incident which gave rise to the name. John Durie had been banished from his pulpit and from Edinburgh, for his boldness of speech in criticizing some of the acts of James Sixth, but the feeling in his favor was so strong that his sentence had to be reversed. He says: "Within a few days after the petition of the nobility. John Durie gat leave to gae hame to his ain flock in Edinburgh: at whase returning there was a great concours of the haill toun, wha met him at the Nether Bow; and going up the street, with bare heads and loud voices, sang to the praise of God, and testifying of great joy and consolation, the one hundred and twenty-fourth Psalm—'Now Israel may say and that trewly' till heaven and earth resound it. This noise, when the Duc (of Lennox) being in the toun heard, and ludging in the Hiegate looked out and saw, he rave his beard for anger, and hasted him off the toun."

No. 304.

"OH GIVE YE PRAISE UNTO THE LORD."

PSALM 117.

The battle of Dunbar, between the English and the Scottish armies, took place on the morning of September 3, 1650. The Scotch Army was commanded by Lesley, and that of England by Cromwell. The battle is thus described by the historian Guizot: "Cromwell had just left a prayer meeting, and mounted his horse, accompanied by Lambert, his major-general. Surveying with his glass the positions of the Scottish army, he was struck by the movement which was going on among the enemy. Lesley was preparing to throw himself across the way with all his troops. Cromwell asked nothing better than to fight. 'The Lord delivers them into our hands; they come!' he exclaimed, and he proposed to his officers to forestall the Scots and to march toward them. Monk vigorously supported the general's opinion, and solicited the command of the infantry of the advanced guard. The English spent the whole night in preparing for the struggle. A dense fog prevailed at daybreak. The first engagements were not fortunate for Cromwell and his troops. The men fought almost without seeing each other, to the cry of 'Covenant!' among the Scots, and 'The Lord of Hosts!' among the English. The Scottish lancers had thrown the English advance guard into some disorder; toward seven o'clock the regiment of Cromwell charged sharply. At the same time the sun, dispersing the mists, lit up the sea and mountains. 'Let God arise!' exclaimed Cromwell, 'and let His enemies be scattered!' Inspired by his enthusiasm, his soldiers redoubled their efforts; the Scottish cavalry wavered; an infantry corps, which yet resisted, was broken by the Ironsides. 'They run! they run!' cried the English; a rout began. 'They were now but stubble to our swords,' wrote Cromwell. At nine o'clock the battle was over; three thousand dead bodies and ten thousand prisoners testified to the victory of the English general." And on the battlefield after the victory, the army of Cromwell sang as their thanksgiving hymn, the one hundred and seventeenth Psalm.

"O give ye praise unto the Lord,
All nations that be:
Likewise ye people all, accord
His name to magnify.
For great to us-ward ever are
His loving kindnesses;
His truth endures for evermore,
The Lord I do ye bless."

No. 304a

"I AM WEARY OF MY SIN."

In the *Christian Work*, Henry F. Thompson gives the following incident: "I never could understand it. She was one of the brightest sweetest, and most amiable young ladies I ever knew; and yet she and her mother, who was a widow, lived with her grandparents, who, with the mother and an only uncle and an only brother, were the roughest people I ever knew. And it was not only the exterior that was rough. They would swear, and blackguard, and quarrel with each other in public or in private. At a certain time, when calling at the house, the young lady, at my request, sat at the instrument and played and sang. Presently she turned to a particular tune, and said: 'I think this is so beautiful,' and, as she played, sang the accompanying words:

'I am weary of my sin;
O, I long for full release;
Saviour, come and take me in,
With Thyself to dwell in peace.

'I am weary of the earth,
Where the wicked spurn Thy love;
With Thy sons of heavenly birth,
Let me worship Thee above.'

Pointing to the words, 'I am weary of my sin; O, I long for full release'; I said, 'Is that true of you, Mary?' and while the quick tear trembled on the lid, she sweetly answered, 'Yes, I want to follow Jesus.' I said, 'for such He waits, and will receive and bless them.' At the next communion season she united with the church, and for four years adorned her profession; till at the close of a Sabbath evening, she was called to join the church above."

No. 305.

"COME YE DISCONSOLATE, WHERE'ER YE LANGUISH."

Thomas Moore, 1779—1852.

At one time Mr. T. E. Perkins was sitting in the room of the Howard Mission, New York, conversing with Rev. Mr. Van Meter, when they were interrupted by the entrance of a wild-looking man, who exclaimed: "Is Awful Gardner here?"

"No," replied Mr. Van Meter.

"Then I am lost," said the man in accents of despair. "If Awful Gardner was here, he could save me; he would know how, because he's been the same road; but now I am lost"; and drawing a bowie-knife from under his vest, he was about to plunge it into his bosom, when Mr. Van Meter sprang forward and caught his arm. Seeing that it would be useless to attempt to wrest the knife from his grasp, Mr. Van Meter sought to distract the man's attention from his suicidal purpose, but the unfortunate creature was seized with a fit of delirium tremens, and became unmanageable. Mr. Perkins, not knowing what else to do, sat down at the melodion, and began to play and sing:

"Come, ye disconsolate, where'er ye languish.
Come, at God's altar fervently kneel;
Here bring your wounded hearts, here tell your anguish;
Earth has no sorrow that heaven cannot heal."

The effect was magical. The man became sufficiently calm for Mr. Van Meter to march him up and down the room, while Mr. Perkins continued to play and sing. After finishing the hymn he sang another:

"Jesus, to Thy dear arms I flee,
I have no other hope but Thee."

The effect was still more marked. After singing that hymn through Mr. Perkins commenced:

"Flee as a bird to your mountain."

As the strains of this exquisite composition filled the room, the maniac paused, sat down, covered his face with his hands, and sobbed like a child, or rather like a broken-hearted remorseful man. By this time Mrs. Van Meter, who was present when the man first burst into the room, came in with a bowl of strong coffee, which she had thoughtfully made, and as soon as the weeping stranger became sufficiently composed she gave it to him. That quieted his nerves and renewed his strength, and in a little while he became completely restored to the possession of his faculties. "Who is this man?" was the question which rose spontaneously to the lips of his deliverer, but all efforts to ascertain seemed to prove fruitless. He persistently refused to give his name, or to furnish any clue to his residence or identity. Mr. Perkins accompanied him to the St. Nicholas Hotel, where he took a room under an assumed name. As in his conversation he had chanced to mention a clergyman in Newport, Rhode Island, whom Mr. Van Meter knew, the latter immediately wrote to the clergyman, stating the case. The clergyman came by the first boat, and at once recognizing the unfortunate man, took him back again to his home in Hartford, where, before the period of his dissipation, he had been a man of wealth and responsibility. He threw off the thralldom of rum, and is now a respected Christian man.

No. 306.

"ALL PEOPLE THAT ON EARTH DO DWELL."

WILLIAM KETHE.

A remarkable incident connected with this hymn, is that of a Scottish youth, who learned from a pious mother to sing the old psalms that were as household words to them in the kirk and by the fireside. When he grew up, he wandered away from his native country, was taken captive by the Turks, and made a slave in one of the Barbary States. But he never forgot the songs of Zion, although he sang them in a strange land and to heathen ears. One night he was solacing himself in this manner, when the attention of some sailors on board of an English man-of war was directed to the familiar tune of "Old Hundred" as it came floating over the moonlit waves. At once they surmised the truth that one of their countrymen was languishing away his life as a captive. Quickly arming themselves they manned a boat, and lost no time in effecting his release.

A celebrated Scotch doctor of divinity was invited to preach where no singing was heard but by the choir. He gave out to be sung the Hundredth Psalm:

"All people that on earth do dwell,
Sing to the Lord with cheerful voice,
Him serve with mirth, His praise forth tell,
Come ye before Him and rejoice."

To the doctor's surprise, nobody but the choir opened their lips, and when they had concluded the performance, he arose and good-humoredly said: "The choir has done very well; let the congregation and me try it next." And so saying, he raised in fine style, the solemn tune of "Old Hundred." The result was that before the first stanza was ended, the whole congregation had caught the enthusiasm of their leader, and sent up a very shout of praise to Heaven in the appropriate words of the psalm; and they found it to be so heart-stirring an experience, when compared with their previous habit of being mere listeners, that they never afterward abstained so generally from joining in the psalmody.

JOHN B. GOUGH, in *Sunlight and Shadow*.

No. 307.

"THERE IS A HAPPY LAND."

ANDREW YOUNG, 1807—1889.

A clergyman relates the following incident: "One day as I was busily engaged in my study, a man about half drunk very unceremoniously entered and handed me a note from the teacher of the infant class of our Sabbath school, informing me that the bearer was the father of one of her scholars, that the child had met with an accident, and that they lived in such a place she could not visit them, and she wished me to see to it. I looked at the man: he was Irish, very repulsive in his appearance, and he answered my questions with a rough brogue. 'What is your name, sir, and where do you live?'

" 'My name is Pater M——; I live on an ould canal boat at the fut of Harrison Street. I wint there whin I was burnt out; and nobody at all at all has driv me out of it.'

" 'And what is the matter with your child?'

" 'Och! and is it Kitty, my own little darling Kitty, the only child I've lift of the six that has been born til me? Och! Kitty! she was playing about on a ship where I was til wark, and she fell down the hatchway and broke her leg (saving your prisence) and poor Kitty's leg is not set right, your riverence, for I've no money til pay the doctor, Och! poor Kitty! and I've nothing to give her to ate, your riverence.

" 'Well, Peter, I will come down and see your Kitty, and see what can be done for you.'

"I did so, and found a wretched state of things. The poor little suffering child was overjoyed to see me. I remembered her countenance—a sweet, mild little girl, not yet five years of age. She lay upon the locker or side-seat of an old canal boat which had been laid up for the winter. There was no fire, though it was a bitter cold day, no chair, no bed, no food, scarcely an article of furniture or any comfort whatever. I did what I could to relieve the wants of the little sufferer. Nothing could be done for the parents: they were both confirmed inebriates; and I found they had both been drunk the night previous, and in a quarrel had unintentionally knocked the child off the seat and broken the limb after it had been set. I obtained the services of a surgeon and had the limb set again, and then sat down on the locker to talk to little Kitty, and fed her with some nourishing food which I had brought. I asked her if she could read. No, she could not read a word; 'but I can sing,' said she.

" 'What can you sing?'

" 'Something I learned at Sabbath school.'

" 'Well, what is it you can sing, Kitty?' In a moment her sweet little voice broke out:

'There is a happy land,
Far, far away.
Where saints in glory stand,
Bright, bright as day.'

"'Well, Kitty, that is sweet. Where do you think the land of Canaan is, Kitty?'

"'Oh, I suppose it is up in the sky, where God lives and where the angels live.'

"'Do you think you will ever go there, Kitty?'

"'If I'm good, and love God I shall.'

"'Now, Kitty, is there anything else you can sing for me before I go?'

"'Oh, yes, sir: I can sing a little piece of another.'

"'Well, what is that?'

"'All who love the Lord below,
When they die; to heaven will go,
And sing with saints above,
Oh! that will be joyful!
Joyful! joyful!
Oh! that will be joyful,
When we meet to part no more!'

"Poor Kitty could not read, nor could either of her parents read. She knew nothing of heaven and divine things except what she had been taught at the Sabbath school, and most of what she remembered was associated with the words of the hymns she had learned to sing there."

No. 308.

"PEACE, TROUBLED SOUL, THOU NEED'ST NOT FEAR."

Rev. Samuel Ecking, 1757—1785.

The late Rev. James Haxley, about the year 1806, was sent by a Methodist Conference to itinerate as a missionary in Louisiana, then chiefly inhabited by French Catholics. Jimmy, as he was familiarly called, had small expectations of comfort without payment; and he seldom possessed any money. He was one evening reduced to the very verge of starvation: he had spent the preceding night in a swamp, and had taken no food for thirty-six hours, when he reached a plantation. He entered the house and asked for food and lodging. The mistress of the house, a widow, with several daughters, and several negro children playing about, recognized his calling and insultingly refused his request. He obtained, however, permission to warm himself for a few minutes before the fire. As he sat thus, he felt the demands of hunger and sleep, and looked forward to another night in the swamp. Feeling this might prove his last night on earth, he thought sweetly of the celestial city to which he felt he was traveling; his heart swelled with gladness, and he cheerfully sang one of his favorite hymns:

"Peace, troubled soul, thou need'st not fear:
Thy Great Provider still is near.
Who fed thee last will feed thee still;
Be calm, and sink into His will."

He sang the whole hymn; and when he looked around him the mother, daughters, and negroes were all in tears. "Here, Sally," said the mother, "get the preacher a good supper. Peter, put up his horse: he shall stay a week, if he pleases."

No. 309.

"THE MESSIAH."

George Frederick Handel, 1685—1759.

In the last century, a Hungarian nobleman had lost, under the most distressing circumstances, his only child, a beautiful girl, who was on the eve of marriage. Although two years had elapsed since this bereavement, the unhappy father remained in the most melancholy condition. From the hour when he had taken the last look at the dead body of his child, he had remained in the same room, shedding no tears and uttering no complaints, but remaining in a speechless state of despair. The most celebrated physicians had been consulted, and every means which could be thought of used to rouse the Count from his lethargy of grief; but all in vain, and his physician became hopeless of his recovery. Under these circumstances, a member of the family remembered to have heard the distinguished Elizabeth Mara, for ten years the first singer at the Prussian court, sing some exquisitely beautiful sacred pieces, and became impressed with the thought that, if any sound on earth could reach the heart which was already buried in his daughter's grave, her voice, which seemed to be that of an angel rather than that of a human being, would have that power. Arrangements were at length made for the trial; and, to give every possible effect to the powers of the singer, an anteroom, opening into that where the Count sat, was prepared. Mara stood alone in the foreground, yet in such a position that she could not be seen in the next room, which was hung with black, and only a faint shadowy twilight admitted, except a few golden rays from a small lamp which burned in a niche before a beautiful Madonna. Suddenly upon the solitude and silence of that sick room there broke a wonderful harmony. Elizabeth had chosen Handel's "Messiah," and took her place, deeply moved by the singular circumstances under which she was called to exert her talents. At first the music and that heavenly voice all seemed to be unheeded; but by degrees the desolate parent raised himself on his couch and glanced with earnest longing toward the spot whence those soul-moving sounds proceeded. At length when Mara sang the words, "Look and see if there be any sorrow like to my sorrow," she appeared to be inspired by the sympathy she felt; and the relatives of the Count, who listened with beating hearts, could not restrain their tears. Nor did these alone bear witness to the singer's power; happy sighs escaped from the sufferer; large tears stood in those eyes which the very extremity of grief itself had long forbidden to weep. Crossing the room with feeble steps, he prostrated himself before the image of that Heavenly One Who bore all our griefs; and, when the full choir joined in the Hallelujah Chorus, his voice of praise and thanksgiving mingled with those strains. The recovery was complete and lasting, and was the marvel of all Germany.

A lady had been in deep despondency for many months. Her sins appeared so numerous and aggravated that she dared not trust in the promises of the Gospel. These promises seemed very precious for others, but could not avail for her. Conversations with her minister and with Christian friends added to her gloom, instead of dissipating it. She attended with great eagerness the means of grace, read her Bible almost incessantly at home, and withdrew from all gay companions, and even from the most innocent social enjoyments. Her health began to suffer from extreme depression of spirits, and her friends were apprehensive of an early death. When she heard that Jenny Lind was to visit the city near which she resided, her curiosity was excited to hear her. She consulted her minister, and he advised her to go on the evening when "The Messiah" was to be sung. The rendering of those sublime passages, "I know that my Redeemer liveth," and "Come unto Me, all ye that labor and are heavy laden," by the Swedish songstress, quite overwhelmed her. She was spellbound. The words seemed clothed with a fulness of meaning she had never before discovered. The fitness of Jesus to save sinners, and his infinite condescension and pity, melted her heart. She wondered that she had ever distrusted Him, and with a childlike faith threw herself on the promises, knowing that in her case they would not fail of fulfilment. From that hour her gloom vanished, and she went forward in the path of Christian duty with a joyous and obedient heart.

No. 310.

"THERE IS A GOD THAT REIGNS ABOVE."

Rev. Isaac Watts, 1674—1748.

A poor wretched mother, religiously educated, but afterward abandoned to sin and misery, was struck with horror at hearing her own child repeat, as soon as she could well speak, some of the profane language which she had learned from herself. She trembled at the thought that she was not only herself traveling to eternal perdition, but was also leading her child there. She instantly resolved that with the first sixpence she could procure, she would obtain a copy of Dr. Watts' "Divine Songs for Children," of which she had some recollection from the days when she visited the Sunday school and would teach them to her infant daughter. She soon bought them; and on opening the book her eye caught the striking verse:

"Just as a tree cut down that fell
To north, or southward, there it lies,
So man departs to heaven or hell,
Fix'd in the state wherein he dies."

She read on. The Spirit of God impressed the words on her heart; the event led to her entire conversion, and she lived and died, a consistent professor of the religion of Christ.

No. 311.

"TO THEE I LIFT MY SOUL."

King James Second was a Papist, and endeavored to compel his subjects to become Roman Catholics. Under his reign, the "Covenanters" of Scotland were persecuted and in many cases driven from their homes to the moors and mountain gorges, where alone they could worship the God of their fathers in safety. And even in these retreats they were not safe, for the spies of the king followed them, and if any were caught attending meetings or conventicles, they were arrested and punished. Margaret Wilson of Wigton, a girl of eighteen years, with her sister Agnes, a child of thirteen, was in the habit of attending these meetings. Being informed on by a young man whom they took to be a friend, they were thrown into prison. The terror-stricken father, alarmed for the safety of his children, hastened to Edinburgh, and by paying a heavy sum, obtained the liberation of the younger daughter, but Margaret they would not release. With an older woman named Margaret Lachlan, she was condemned to be drowned for attending field and house meetings, and on the morning of May 11, 1665, the sentence was executed. They were tied to stakes between high and low water, so that when the tide should come in they would be drowned. The old woman was placed farthest out, so that the tide should reach her first, and that the sight of her struggles might perhaps terrify the other and lead her to recant, but she was faithful unto death. As the waters rose about her, she sang this psalm:

"To Thee I lift my soul,
O Lord I trust in Thee;
My God let me not be ashamed,
Nor foes triumph o'er me."

No. 312.

"GO ON, GO ON, GO ON, GO ON."

Dr. Stephen Fish gives the following account of a hymn of one word. He says: "Many Bedouin Arabs have embraced the Christian religion. Mr. M. Roysce, of Jerusalem, gave me a very interesting account of the conversion of an Arab whom he knew to be a poet. Soon after he was converted, Mr. Roysce was anxious to see if he would write religious poetry. He requested him to court the Muses, and compose for him a poem on the duties of a Christian Missionary. He did so and wrote the following:

'Taiyib, taiyib, taiyib, taiyib,
Taiyib, taiyib, taiyib,
Taiyib, taiyib, taiyib, taiyib,
Taiyib, taiyib, taiyib.'

Any trivial sentiment would not have borne repeating so many times, but the translation of 'Taiyib' is 'Go on,' and the Arab, zealous in his new life, could think of nothing but going ahead in it and growing better and better."

Christian Standard.

No. 313.

"IN EVIL LONG I TOOK DELIGHT."

REV. JOHN NEWTON, 1725—1807.

Many of Newton's hymns are autobiographic, and this is one of that class. He seemed to delight in calling attention to his own early profligacy and wickedness, but it was only for the purpose of giving greater emphasis to some following declaration of the mercy and grace which could stoop to save so vile a wretch. This purpose is exhibited in the last stanza of this hymn:

"Thus while His death my sin displays
In all its blackest hue,
Such is the mystery of grace
It seals my pardon too."

Newton prepared an epitaph which he requested should be used for himself after his death. It read as follows:

"John Newton, Clerk; once an Infidel and Libertine; A servant of slaves in Africa was by the rich mercy of our Lord and Saviour Jesus Christ, preserved, restored, pardoned, and appointed to preach the faith he had long labored to destroy," etc.

Here again in his epitaph as in so many of his hymns, this contrast is shown of God's "rich mercy" over against his own great sinfulness.

No. 314.

"AND THEY SANG A NEW SONG." Revelation 5:9.

One of the ministers of Leicester, England, in relating some pleasing incidents in connection with his pastoral work, gives the following: "On visiting one of the courts of the town, I was requested by one of the poor people to call on an old woman who had been bedridden for some years, and who lived in the neighborhood. On reaching the cottage, and finding no response to my knocking at the door, I walked in and went to the foot of the stairs, when I soon heard a faint voice requesting whoever it was to come up. In a small room at the top there lay an aged but cheerful invalid. I told her that I had been requested to call, and that I was a minister of the gospel. She replied, 'Well, then, you are just the visitor I want, and you are come at the right time; and taking up her hymn book, which lay upon the bed, said: 'Now, I have been searching for a long time to see if I can find a hymn that will do to sing in Heaven and I cannot. Now, can you?'

"I took the book and found, 'There is a land of pure delight.' 'Surely that will do?'

" 'Well, go on,' she said; 'read the hymn through.'

"Presently I came to 'Death like a narrow sea divides.' 'Ah,' she said, 'that won't do.'

"I then mentioned, 'There is a fountain filled with blood.'

" 'Go on,' she said. I then read the last verse:

'Then in a nobler, sweeter song,
I'll sing Thy power to save,
When this poor lisping, stammering tongue
Lies silent in the grave.'

" 'That won't do,' she said, smilingly: 'mine shan't be a poor lisping, stammering tongue there.' I found others, but all to no purpose.

" 'No, no dear sir, shut the book; there will have to be a new one made.' 'And they sang a new song.' "

No. 315.

"PILGRIM, BURDENED WITH THY SIN"—1785.

Rev. George Crabbe, 1754—1832.

It is quite curious to note from what surroundings some of our hymns have been transferred to our song collections. In the year 1785, there appeared in England a volume of poems by the Reverend George Crabbe, a clergyman of the Church of England. The pieces were all of a secular character. Among them was a poem entitled, "Sir Eustace Grey." It tells the story of a man, Sir Eustace Grey, who passes through the experiences of a prosperous, worldly man, loses his wealth and his family, and lands in a mad house. Here he tells to a physician and a visitor the story of his life, his prosperous days, the loss of property and the death of dear ones, the wanderings in ways of vice, the sorrows of heart and the troubles of mind, until at last, as the poem relates, he "heard an heavenly Father speak and felt the Sun of Mercy shine." "I hailed the Light," he says, "the Birth Divine! and then was sealed among the few!"

"Now hark! the holy strains begin,
And thus the sainted Preacher cries,
'Pilgrim burthened with thy sin,' " etc.

The hymn is a literary curiosity. The fourth line of each stanza contains four words, with one of which each of the four following lines begins.

No. 316.

"ONLY WAITING TILL THE SHADOWS."

MISS FRANCES LAUGHTON, 1836.

An old pauper in an almshouse was asked, "What are you doing now?" "Only waiting!" was his reply. A school girl in a little town in Maine heard the story of the old pauper's reply, and made it the title of a little poem, which she sent to the local paper of the town near by. The words were copied from paper to paper, and soon found their way into the hymn books. One stanza is usually omitted. Here it is:

"Only waiting till the angels
Open wide the mystic gate
At whose feet I long have lingered
Weary, poor, and desolate.
Even now I hear their footsteps,
And their voices far away.
If they call me I am waiting,
Only waiting to obey."

No. 317.

"BEFORE JEHOVAH'S AWFUL THRONE."

REV. ISAAC WATTS, 1674—1748

The singing of this hymn at the Music Hall in Surrey Garden, London, is thus described: "An audience of eight to ten thousand people were worshiping under the guidance of Rev. Charles H. Spurgeon. The prayer concluded, Mr. Spurgeon announced the well-known hymn beginning:

'Before Jehovah's awful throne.'

He read it through, having first announced that the tune would be the 'Old Hundredth,' and then read each verse separately before it was sung. It is scarcely possible to give any idea of the sublime effect produced by those ten thousand voices, as they swelled the massive harmonies of that grand tune with a fulness of sound rarely heard. After singing the second verse, Mr. Spurgeon said: 'I will read the third verse, and you will sing the fourth; and let the uplifting of your voices be as the sound of many waters.' His audience responded to his wish. The words were:

'We'll crowd Thy gates with thankful songs,
High as the heavens our voices raise;
And earth, with her ten thousand tongues,
Shall fill Thy courts with sounding praise.

'Wide as the world is Thy command;
Vast as eternity Thy love;
Firm as a rock Thy truth shall stand,
When rolling years shall cease to move.'

Most magnificent was the shout of praise that now went up. Not a voice was mute, save where occasionally someone's nerves were overpowered by the massive rolling chorus that rose on every side. Never did we before realize what congregational singing might become. It was an uplifting of voice and heart such as one can hope to hear only a few times in a lifetime. Much of this grand effect was no doubt owing to the majesty of the tune itself; much to the fact that all the congregation knew it; and perhaps not a little to the practice of reading each verse before it was sung."

No. 318.

"HERE O'ER THE EARTH A STRANGER I ROAM."

A collier in Staffordshire had one dear little girl, the last of four or five. This child was the light of his eyes; and as he came from the pit at night, she used to meet him at the door of his cot to welcome him home. One day when he came in to his dinner, he missed his little darling, and going into the house with his heavy coal-pit clogs, his wife called him upstairs. The stillness of the place and her quiet voice made his heart sick, and a foreboding of evil came upon him. His wife told him they were going to lose their little lamb; she had had a convulsive fit and the doctor said she could not live. As the tears made furrows down his black face, and he leaned over his darling, she said: "Daddy, sing 'Here is no rest.'"

"No, my child, I cannot sing; I'm choking; I can't sing."

"Oh! do, daddy, sing 'Here is no rest.'"

The poor fellow tried to sing:

> "Here o'er the earth as a stranger I roam,
> Here is no rest, here is no rest!"

But his voice could make no way against his trouble. Then he tried again, for he wanted to please his sweet little girl.

> "Here are afflictions and trials severe,
> Here is no rest, here is no rest!
> Here I must part with the friends I hold dear,
> Yet I am blest, yet I am blest!"

Again his voice was choked with weeping; but the little one whispered, "Come, daddy, sing, 'Sweet is the promise'"; and the poor father went on again:

"Sweet is the promise I read in His Word;
Blessed are those who have died in the Lord,
They have been called to receive their reward,
There, there is rest! there, there is rest."

"That's it, daddy!" cried the child; "that's it"; and with her arms around the collier's neck, she died happy in the Lord.

No. 319.

JESUS, I MY CROSS HAVE TAKEN."

Rev. Henry F. Lyte, 1793—1847.

Rev. George F. Pentecost gives the following from his own experience: "A year or two after I entered the ministry, I passed through an experience that on the dark side of it culminated in leading me to believe not only that I had been mistaken in supposing that God had called me to the work of the ministry, but also that I was even mistaken in supposing that I was a Christian at all. Oh! the blackness and darkness of those hours! I cannot portray the dense gloom that gathered about my soul, and was fairly pressing me down to hell. In this fearful state of mind, having almost yielded up to despair, I was returning to my home from a neighboring town where I had been assisting a ministerial brother in a protracted meeting. I got aboard the train, flung myself into a seat next a window of the car, and made another desperate effort to recover myself, my faith, my hope, my confidence in God. I prayed in spirit, I even called aloud on God, unmindful of the people around me; I went over the promises, and searched my memory through for some word of the Lord that could bring me help. But God's Word was a silent and sealed book to me, and my heart seemed to be turning into stone. In the midst of this wretchedness I was looking out of the car window up into the starlit heavens, and wondering if there was a God, if there was any Jesus, any Christ, if there was any hereafter. While thus gazing into the dimly lighted darkness without, from out of the midnight darkness within, with only a numb sense of my own wretchedness, as a man might feel who knows he is freezing to death without power to help himself, and, indeed, not caring to any longer, because it seems easier to die, I heard the low voice of singing in my heart; I say I heard the voice of singing within me, and hearkening I caught the words of it, and with my own lips in low tremulous tones began to sing:

'Jesus, I my cross have taken,
All to leave and follow Thee;
Naked, poor, despised; forsaken,
Thou from hence my all shalt be;'

I wondered at myself, and at the song; I found my heart softening; I knew that tears were in my eyes; I felt them running down my cheeks; I was away back with Jesus on the Cross; I heard His cry, 'My God! My God! why hast Thou forsaken me?' and in that same moment the Holy Ghost gave me fellowship with my Saviour, and I knew that cry from Him was not for Himself alone, but for me. I sang on through the hymn with still melting heart, with returning faith, hope, and confidence, until in a perfect ecstasy of peace I reached the lines:

'O 'tis not in grief to harm me,
While Thy love is left to me;
O 'twere not in joy to charm me,
Were that joy unmixed with Thee.'

And then like a comforted child, I fairly laid my weary heart against His dear loving heart, knowing in my soul that He loved me, that He died and rose again for me, that He lived for me and that as never before we were united to each other. Thus that precious hymn was God's hand reached out to save me when I was sinking; thus He was pleased to manifest Himself to me in a sweeter, surer, and stronger way than I had yet known Him. He had chosen to do this by, and in, a hymn, rather than by prayer, or meditation, or promise. As the cake baked on the coals and the cruse of water at his head were to Elijah, so was that hymn to me."

There is a story told of a young lady in England, who was much persecuted by her father because she had embraced the religion of Christ. Seeking to divert her mind he gave her a song to sing and play, commencing:

"Go, forget me, why should sorrow."
(See "Our Familiar Songs," p. 243.)

To his surprise and discomfiture, she sang the hymn to the tune "Ellesdie."

"Jesus, I my cross have taken,
All to leave and follow Thee."

No. 320.

"FROM DEAR NEW ENGLAND'S HAPPY SHORE."

Perhaps one of the most interesting and touching incidents connected with the history of singing occurred at the separation from each other of thirty students at the Andover Theological Seminary in 1832. A question was proposed by a single finely toned voice from the orchestra, and a response was made from the stage on which the graduating class stood—first by the Foreign Missionaries, then by the Domestic Missionaries, and finally by the Home Preachers; then followed the chorus from the whole. The whole service was as follows:

Question: "And I heard the voice of the Lord, saying, Whom shall I send, and who will go for us?" Isaiah 6:8. Those who were to go as foreign missionaries replied:

"From dear New England's happy shore,
Where all our kindred dwell,
We go,—on pagans, light to pour:
Our native land, farewell!"

Question: "And I heard the voice of the Lord, saying, Whom shall I send, and who will go for us?" Those who were to go as home missionaries then replied:

"We go where seldom on the ear
Salvation's tidings swell:
We go to dry the mourner's tear:
Our pleasant home, farewell."

Question: "And I heard the voice of the Lord, saying, Whom shall I send, and who will go for us?" Those who were to become home preachers then replied:

"Where all our earthly friendships blend,
Of Jesus' love we'll tell,
And in the work our lives will spend:
Brethren, a short farewell."

All then joined in the following chorus:

"From all these cherished scenes we go,
The home of praise and prayer,
To meet earth's gladness or earth's woe,
And many a toil to bear.

"Farewell ye friends who shared our joy,
Ye in whose hearts we dwell:
A noble work shall now employ
Our energies, farewell!

"Brethren, we press the parting hand:
Our songs of parting tell:
Then, till we reach heaven's holy land,
A sweet but brief farewell!"

The whole presented an extraordinary scene. The audience felt that it was not a mere show, not an exhibition of musical skill. The tones in which the hymn was sung were those of deep emotion; and many hearts were melted as these young servants of Christ poured forth their impassioned farewell—some of them to the scenes of their sacred studies, others to the pleasant hills and valleys and churches of New England, and others to all the endearments of their native land.

No. 321.

"PRAISE GOD FROM WHOM ALL BLESSINGS FLOW."

BISHOP THOMAS KENN, 1637—1711.

In the year 1858, a thousand gentlemen were seated at the collegiate dinner-table at Andover, Massachusetts, when the unexpected news was received of the successful laying of the Atlantic cable. The whole assembly arose from their seats spontaneously and in the majestic sounds of "Old Hundred" sang the fine words of Bishop Kenn:

"Praise God from Whom all blessings flow;
Praise Him, all creatures here below;
Praise Him above, ye heavenly host;
Praise Father, Son, and Holy Ghost!"

During the Peninsular campaign several of us (says a correspondent of one of the public journals) were sitting in our tent a few hours after sunset, on Sabbath evening, when one of the number, laying his hand on my knee, suddenly exclaimed, "Hark, what is that?" In an instant the talking ceased, and every ear was bent forward to catch the sound which had fixed the attention of our comrade. A silence ensued for a moment and then there was wafted across the air the music of that glorious anthem "Old Hundred," in which it seemed as if a thousand voices participated. All of us immediately sought the open air, and there stood until the last note died away upon the ear. Never before had we heard anything so magnificently grand as this same "Old Hundred" sung by the soldiers of the Union army on the plains of Yorktown. The air was made vocal with the music, and the woods around reverberated with the mighty strain. Beneath the canopy of heaven the soldiers gazed upward into the starlit sky, and sang, all with one voice:

"Praise God from Whom all blessings flow;
Praise Him, all creatures here below;
Praise Him above ye heavenly host;
Praise Father, Son, and Holy Ghost."

It was solemn, soul-stirring, to hear these words thus chanted that have so often stirred the holiest emotions of man's heart. It was a scene not unfitted to inspire the genius of a Christian poet or artist.

No. 322.

"HOW PLEASANT 'TIS TO SEE."

Rev. Isaac Watts, 1674—1748.

Three men became hopefully pious about the same time. They were neighbors, heads of families, and singers. For a season they lived in love and exhibited in their lives the graces of the Holy Spirit. During this period they often united in sweetly singing the praises of God. But as one of them was once passing the house of another, he heard loud words and found his friends in angry dispute. He went into the house, and began by saying, "Come, neighbors, let us sing one of our favorite hymns:

'How pleasant 'tis to see
Kindred and friends agree!'"

They became silent, looked first at him and then at each other, and then one joined the singing. The other very soon followed his example, and the three neighbors sang harmoniously together as usual, till all their angry passions were lulled to sleep. They parted in peace, and ever after lived in harmony. In this instance, at least, a hymn was better than an exhortation.

No. 323.

"O GOD, WHY HAST THOU CAST US OFF?"

PSALM 74. Scotch.

This Psalm was sung by the Covenanters before the fight at Pentland (Rullion Green), November 28, 1666. Goaded by oppression they had come from the west country in arms to present a remonstrance to the Government. They approached Edinburgh in the hope of a hearing, and of support from their friends there; but a strong force had been collected to overawe them. A minute and interesting account is given by Veitch, in his memoir, of the retreat of the weary, discouraged, and half-armed remnant by Colinton, along the east side of the Pentlands. They were intercepted by General Dalziel, through a pass in the hills near Glencorse, and sang this psalm before the action. They made a brave resistance, successful at first, but were at last broken. The fugitives were slaughtered with great barbarity, the captured shut up in Greyfriars churchyard, without food or shelter, numbers executed and banished to the Plantations. The graves of some of the slain may be seen on the hillside where they fell, and a monument which has faith and truth in its lines if rude in rhyme.

"A cloud of witnesses lie here,
Who for Christ's interests did appear;
And to restore true liberty,
O'erturned then by tyranny,
These heroes fought with great renown,
By falling got the martyr's crown."

No. 324.

"A MIGHTY FORTRESS IS OUR GOD."

Rev. Martin Luther, 1483—1546.

In 1720, a remarkable revival began in Moravia, in a town where David Nitschmann lived. The Jesuits opposed it, and the meetings were prohibited. Those who still assembled were seized and imprisoned in stables and cellars and foul outhouses. At Nitschmann's house a hundred and fifty persons were once gathered when the police broke in and seized all the books within reach. Nothing dismayed, the congregation struck up the stanza of Luther's hymn:

"And though this world, with devils filled,
Should threaten to undo us;
We will not fear, for God hath willed
His truth to triumph through us.
"The Prince of darkness grim—
We tremble not for him;
His rage we can endure,
For lo! his doom is sure,
One little word shall fell him."

Twenty heads of families, including David Nitschmann, were apprehended for this and sent to jail, Nitschmann being treated with special severity. He finally escaped; fled to the Moravians at Herrnhut; became a bishop, and afterward joined the Wesleys, in 1735, in their expedition to Savannah, Georgia.

REV. S. W. DUFFIELD.

No. 325.

"TO US SALVATION NOW HAS COME."

"ES IST DAS HEIL UNS KOMMEN HER."

REV. PAUL SPERATUS, 1484—1551.

At Heidelberg the Reformation made its way by singing. Fearing the Emperor, the Elector Frederick did not suppress the saying of the mass as soon as the people desired; and so on one occasion, just as the priest was about to begin the service standing at the high altar, a single voice led off in the singing of Paul Speratus' famous hymn:

"To us salvation now has come,
God's wondrous grace revealing;
Works never can avert our doom—
They have no power of healing.
Faith looks to God's beloved Son,
Who has for us deliverance won,
He is our great Redeemer!"

The vast congregation immediately joined, and the Elector taking the hint, mass was said no more.

No. 326.

"O GOD, LOOK DOWN FROM HEAVEN WE PRAY."

"ACH GOTT, VON HIMMEL SIEH DAREIN."

REV. MARTIN LUTHER, 1483—1546.

In the year 1529, a Romish priest was preaching at Lübeck, and just as he ended his homily, two boys commenced singing Luther's hymn:

"O God look down from heaven, we pray,
Thy tenderness awaken!
Thy saints so few, fade fast away—
Hast Thou Thy poor forsaken?
Thy word no more is taught aright,
And faith from earth hath vanished quite—
O Lord, our God, revive us!"

when the whole assembly joined as with one voice, drowning the voice of the priest with the song of Luther.

In 1527, the Council at Brunswick requested a priest at Magdeburg, who was regarded as a very learned and eloquent man, to resist the new doctrine of Luther, which was rushing as a flood over the country. He took for his subject the merit of good work in securing salvation. One of the hearers arose, and said he had learned quite a different doctrine from Holy Scriptures, and briefly stated his views as to salvation by grace. When he had finished, the priest was commencing to reply, and to reaffirm the doctrine of merits, when another of the audience began singing:

"O God, look down from heaven, we pray,
Thy tenderness awaken!"

The whole congregation immediately joined, and the priest was compelled to retire.

No. 327.

"ARISE, MY SOUL, ARISE."

REV. CHARLES WESLEY, 1708—1788.

One of the best incidents connected with this hymn is that of the missionaries who went to Patagonia. When Richard Williams and Captain Allen Gardiner attempted, in December, 1850, to carry the Gospel to Patagonia, they encountered a series of disasters which were simply heart-rending, and which culminated in the death of the whole party. They had nets but found no fish; they lost their anchor and both their small boats at Picton Island; of the larger boats, one was wrecked and became unseaworthy; the natives were hostile, and were always crying, "Yammer schooner!"—"Give me!" The company consisted of Captain Allen Gardiner and Dr. Richard Williams; and of John Maidment and Joseph Irwin, a carpenter, together with three Cornish fishermen, Pearce, Badcock, and Bryant. All were devoted Christians, and in spite of the fact that their ammunition had been forgotten and left on board the ship that brought them, they hoped to establish their mission. But disease set in. Williams and Badcock were attacked by scurvy. Provisions grew scarce. They changed their camp several times without improving their prospects. They had great difficulty in forming friendly relations with the Fuegians. And at last they were reduced to the dire necessity of waiting for help to come from England or the Falkland Islands. As a matter of judgment, it would have been much better if they had attempted to make the voyage to the Islands in their solitary boat, than to wait on hopelessly; but they preferred to remain where they were. Both Captain Gardiner and Dr. Williams kept diaries, which were afterward found. From these we learned the short sad story of their terrible privations and suffering, and that Maidment and Gardiner were probably the last survivors. The fatal entry is on September 6, and is in Captain Gardiner's hand: "I neither hunger nor thirst, though five days without food! Marvellous loving kindness to me a sinner!"

This hymn was the parting song of John Badcock, the first who died. Lying by Richard Williams' side, in the narrow and leaky cabin of the *Speedwell,* he asked his companion to sing this hymn with him, and in a few minutes he passed away. Her Majesty's ship, *Dido,* commanded by Captain Moreshead, reached Banner Cove, January 19, 1852, and found the bodies of Captain Gardiner and Mr. Maidment in the cabin which had served as their shelter. The outcome of this self-sacrifice has been the establishment, in 1872, of a permanent mission station at Ushuwia, Tierra del Fuego, with mission operations in Patagonia and among the Araucanian Indians. Professor Christlieb, in his *"Foreign Missions,"* 1880, tells us that some Pesherehs of Fuegia had declared to the missionary, Mr. Whaits, that they now understood why Captain Gardiner had taken such trouble with them, and they deeply regretted their indifference to him.

REV. S. W. DUFFIELD.

No. 328.

"BEFORE JEHOVAH'S AWFUL THRONE."

REV. ISAAC WATTS, 1674—1748.

A notable incident in connection with this hymn was its use at the time when Commodore Perry's fleet was anchored off Japan in 1853-1854. Divine Service was held on the flagship, and the chaplain, in full sight of thousands upon the shore, gave out this hymn to be sung. The marine band struck up the notes of "Old Hundred," and the natives of the empire where Christian civilization was to have such power beheld the religious worship of the nation which was knocking at their gates.

DUFFIELD'S *English Hymns.*

No. 329.

"BLEST BE THE TIE THAT BINDS."

REV. JOHN FAWCETT.

D. L. Moody relates the following: "In 1860, I had in my Sunday school a pale, delicate young man as one of the teachers. I knew his burning piety, and assigned him to the worst class in the school. They were all girls, and it was an awful class. They kept gadding around in the school-room and were laughing and carrying on all the time. And this young man had better success than any one else. One Sunday he was absent, and I tried myself to teach the class, but couldn't do anything with them; they seemed farther off than ever from any concern about their souls. Well, the day after his absence, early Monday morning, the young man came into the store where I worked, and, tottering and bloodless, threw himself down on some boxes.

" 'What's the matter?' I asked.

" 'I have been bleeding at the lungs, and they have given me up to die,' he said.

" 'But you are not afraid to die?' I questioned.

" 'No,' said he, 'I am not afraid to die, but I have got to stand before God and give an account of my stewardship, and not one of my Sunday school scholars has been brought to Jesus. I have failed to bring one, and haven't any strength to do it now.'

"He was so weighed down that I got a carriage and took that dying man in it, and we called at the home of every one of his scholars, and to each one he said, as best his faint voice would let him, 'I have come to just ask you to come to the Savior,' and then he prayed as I never heard before. And for ten days he labored in that way, sometimes walking to the nearest houses, and at the end of that ten days every one of that large class had yielded to the

Savior. Full well do I remember the night before he went away (for the doctors said he must hurry to the South) how we held a true love feast. It was the very gate of heaven, that meeting. He prayed, and they prayed; he didn't ask them, he didn't think they could pray; and then we sang:

'Blest be the tie that binds
Our hearts in Christian love,
The fellowship of Christian minds,
Is like to that above.'

"It was a beautiful night in June that he left on the Michigan Southern, and I was down to the train to help him off. And those girls gathered there again, every one, all unknown to each other, and the depot seemed a second gate to heaven, in the joyful, yet tearful communion and farewells between those newly redeemed souls and him whose crown of rejoicing it will be that he led them to Jesus. At last the gong sounded, and, supported on the platform, the dying man shook hands with every one, and whispered, 'I will meet you yonder.'"

In the life of Rev. Charles Hodge, D. D., it is related by his son, Rev. A. A. Hodge, that "From about 1868 to the year of his death (1878), each graduating class, at the very last, took a special personal farewell of Dr. Hodge. After receiving their diplomas, and the valedictory charge, and benediction of the representative of the Board of Trustees, the class formed in a circle with Dr. Hodge in the center, in the middle of the front campus. They sang (at least in April, 1869) several verses of the hymn, 'All hail the power of Jesus' name,' and the verse of the missionary hymn beginning, 'Shall we whose souls are lighted.' Then making a close ring each one crossing his arms, they held hand by hand, and sang, 'Blest be the tie that binds,' and then the long meter Doxology. After that Dr. Hodge pronounced the benediction. He then shook hands with each student, and each student shook hands with all the others, and they separated."

No. 330.

"O LORD, THOU HAST REJECTED US."

Psalm 60, Scotch.

Rev. Ebenezer Erskine was Moderator of the Synod of Perth and Stirling, and one of the leaders of those who protested against the action of the Scotch Presbyterian Church Synod, which at last ended in the "Secession" of a part of that body and the organization of the "Secession Church." When in 1740, he was driven from his church, he took his place with an immense multitude below the battlements of Stirling Castle and sang the first five verses of this psalm:

"O Lord, Thou hast rejected us,
And scattered us abroad;
Thou justly hast displeased been;
Return to us, O God.

"The earth to tremble, Thou hast made:
Therein did'st breaches make:
Do Thou thereof the breaches heal,
Because the land doth shake.

"Unto Thy people Thou hard things
Hast shew'd and on them sent;
And Thou hast caused us to drink
Wine of astonishment.

"And yet a banner Thou hast giv'n
To them who Thee do fear;
That it by them because of truth,
Displayed may appear.

"That Thy beloved people may
Delivered be from thrall;
Save with the pow'r of Thy right hand,
And hear me when I call."

No. 331.

"COME THOU ALMIGHTY KING."

REV. CHARLES WESLEY, 1708—1788.

During the Revolutionary War, and while the British had possession of Long Island, a body of troops invaded a place of worship one Sunday morning and insisted that the congregation should sing "God save the King." In reply the people did sing, but it was another set of words to the same tune:

"Come, Thou Almighty King,
Help us Thy name to sing,
Help us to praise;
Father all-glorious,
O'er all victorious,
Come and reign over us,
Ancient of days."

No. 332.

"HOW CONDESCENDING AND HOW KIND."

REV. ISAAC WATTS, 1674—1748.

The Rev. J. Leifchild tells how he was once invited to preach in Berkshire, in a straggling village where there was very little of the gospel ever heard. The rough element of the place was greatly against the service. Shouts and disturbance attended the opening of the meeting, and a large haystack, the property of his host, was set on fire. But Leifchild persevered and opened the service with a somewhat motley crowd of hearers by reading the Scripture in a solemn and earnest manner. Then he offered prayer, and felt as though he had secured somewhat of the sympathy of his audience. He next read the hymn commencing as above, and especially emphasized certain words in one of the stanzas as follows:

"Here we receive repeated seals
Of Jesus' dying love:
Hard is the heart that never feels
One soft affection move."

As he read he heard a dull noise near the door like that of a heavy weight falling. At the close of the meeting, he asked about it—when a man was pointed out who came forward and acknowledged that it was caused by a great stone which he had brought in his hand in order to hurl it at the preacher when he announced his text. "But," he said, "the prayer of the minister, and particularly the hymn that was read, touched my heart, and no sooner, sir, had you uttered the words:

'*Hard* is the heart that never feels
One soft affection move,'

than down dropped the stone." With tears in his eyes he then stayed to converse with the clergyman, and at length became a truly devout person, and was even a religious teacher in later years.

No. 333.

"HOW SAD OUR STATE BY NATURE IS."

REV. ISAAC WATTS, 1674—1748.

In Dr. Spencer's "Pastor's Sketches" occurs this incident connected with this hymn. He had given out the hymn to be sung, forgetting the possible effect it might have upon the mind of a young woman among his congregation then under deep anxiety of mind. The account proceeds: "The next day she came to tell me that she had made a new discovery.

"Well," said I, "what is that you have discovered?"

"Why, sir," said she, "the way of salvation all seems to me now perfectly plain. My darkness is all gone. I see now what I never saw before."

"Do you see that you have given up sin and the world, and given your whole heart to Christ?"

"I do not think that I am a Christian; but I have never been so happy before. All is light to me now. I see the way clear; and I am not burdened and troubled as I was."

"And how is this? What has brought you to this state of mind?"

"I do not know how it is, or what has brought me to it. But when you were reading that hymn last night, I saw the whole way of salvation for sinners perfectly plain, and wondered that I had never seen it before. I saw that I had nothing to do but trust in Christ.

'A guilty, weak and helpless worm,
On Thy kind arms I fall.'

I sat all the evening just looking at that hymn. I did not hear your prayer. I did not hear a word of your sermon. I do not know your text. I thought of nothing but that hymn; and I have been thinking of it ever since. It is so light and makes me so contented. Why, sir," said she, in the perfect simplicity of her heart, never thinking that she was repeating what had been told her a thousand times, "don't you think that the reason that we do not get out of darkness sooner is that we don't believe?"

No. 334.

"I'M NOT ASHAMED TO OWN MY LORD."

REV. ISAAC WATTS, 1674—1748.

In relating the account of a visit paid to a minister much broken in health, Dr. Leifchild says: "I found but the wreck and remnant only of what I had formerly known him to be. . . . He seemed wholly taken up with trifles and was muttering a request for sweetmeats, as though he were in reality again a child. I was confounded and appalled at what I saw and exclaimed: 'What, my old friend, do you not know me?'

"He gave no response, but simply repeated his former request. One of his daughters then said to me: 'Ask him something about the Scriptures or the Savior, and you will soon see a difference.'

"Upon this, I said to him as if complainingly: 'Well, I see you do not know me; do you know Jesus, Whom I serve in the Gospel?'

"He started and looked as if just aroused from sleep; when, lifting up his eyes, he exclaimed:

'Jesus, my God, I know His name;
His name is all my trust;
Nor will He put my soul to shame,
Nor let my hope be lost!' "

The Rev. Dr. Marks, after one of the battles on the Peninsula, in which some of the Union men were captured, gave himself up as a prisoner to the rebels that he might not be separated from those over whom he watched as a religious guide. On one occasion, he went on to the Brackett House, on the battlefield, where were four hundred and fifty of our wounded men. The flag of the country was printed on one of the publications which he was distributing; and he mentions that he often saw those mutilated men lift it to their lips and kiss the emblem of our nationality, undeterred by the presence and taunts of the enemy. There was one remarkable man in that group of sufferers, whose story, as recounted by this gentleman, deserves to be told from one age to another. His name was Nolan. His right leg had been cut off by a cannon shot, and he was lying in the midst of fifty or sixty men in one of the rooms. As I came up to him, I saw that his face was beaming with smiles, and, from his appearance, I could not have supposed for a moment that there was a single pang of pain in that body. I asked him how he had endured his suffering. He said, "I was three days and three nights out on the battlefield, and all that time heard the whisperings of angels, and I only could look up to the stars and think every one of them sang to me. The question of my own personal safety, as a believer in Christ, was settled six years ago; and now I want that all my friends should feel as I do." And then there would burst forth from his lips that sweet song:

"Jesus, my God! I know His name;
His name is all my trust;
Nor will He put my soul to shame
Nor let my hope be lost."

And this man, even in the midnight hour, would be singing and comforting those poor men around him. Subsequently, he was carried to Richmond, a prisoner. I followed my charge to that city. And as I was one day passing through the great hall of the prison, where some four hundred men were lying, with their wounds in agony, covering every inch of the floor, as I stepped over one lacerated limb and another, and looked down into their burning eyes, I heard that song again, sweeter and sweeter, and more and more distinct. At length I found my way to the singer, and it was the same man, still singing:

"Jesus, my God! I know His name,
His name is all my trust."

And so he comforted the hundreds of men about him, to whom he could not go, and silenced their murmurs and stilled their groans by this hymn. Afterward it was thought that he must die, and it was told to Nolan.

I said to him, "It is very probable that today you will be called to appear before God, and stand with the great throng before the divine throne."

"Blessed be God!" he said. "I shall be detailed from the battlefield to go up and be with Jesus forever; detailed to dwell in the world of light and glory; detailed to be wounded and to bleed and to die no more. But," he continued, "doctor, I am not going to die today. I feel that I shall live to go away from this place." And through that hour of great danger the man did live by the joy of his soul, and afterward was carried to Fortress Monroe. I heard from a soldier afterward that there he was still singing as before, and that subsequently he was removed thence to Washington, and there died and went up into the bosom of his Savior.

Christian Memorials of the War, Hackett.

No. 335.

"JESUS, LOVER OF MY SOUL."

Rev. Charles Wesley, 1708—1788.

A Mrs. Lewis, of Norwich, England, many years ago went to hear Mr. Hook preach at the Tabernacle, being under great distress of mind. She had determined to attend divine service once more, and if she obtained no peace she intended then to drown herself. The first hymn which the preacher announced was:

"Jesus, Lover of my soul."

which so startled her and suited her condition that she supposed that he "had made this hymn for her sake," for she had no doubt that some one had informed him of her state of mind. As a result of this experience, she was hopefully converted.

English Hymns.

No. 336.

"JERUSALEM THE GOLDEN."

Bernard of Cluny.

REV. JOHN MASON NEALE, Translator, 1818—1866.

There is a touching little story told with some just pride by Dr. Neale, the translator of this hymn, of a child who was ill and in great suffering. The medical attendants could do but little to ease its agonies of pain. But the child would lie without a murmur and almost without motion while the whole of the four hundred lines of the hymn on the better country, of which the hymn commencing as above is a part, were being read to it.

No. 337.

"NOW I HAVE FOUND A FRIEND."

HENRY J. M. HOPE, 1809.

Rev. Denham Smith relates the following: "A little boy, about four years old, came one day where a group of young converts were singing this hymn. Immediately the little fellow stood still, with closed lips, a very unusual thing for him, and when asked why he did not sing, he said he could not sing, for Jesus was not his: but he said, 'Will you pray for me, for I want to know Jesus as mine.' When he went home his mother said to his sisters, 'Let us sing two or three other hymns, and then "Jesus is mine?" and then perhaps he will sing it too; so they sang several others, and the little fellow caroled away at the top of his voice, until they commenced:

'Now I have found a Friend,
Jesus is mine."

His lips again closed, and in a voice of craving sorrow, turning to his mother, he said, 'Ah, mamma, why do you ask me to sing that? For Jesus is not mine.'

When his father came home in the evening and heard it, he said: 'Oh, it must be fancy in the child; a good night's sleep will wear it away; he is too young to know much of the reality of such things.' So he went to bed, and next morning when the father opened the door, what do you think he saw? There was the little one standing in his night-clothes, looking like a perfect picture of anxiety and inquiry.

"He said, 'Dear papa, is not the day after tomorrow Friday?'

"'Yes, my child.'

"'And, papa, will there not be a prayer meeting on Friday?'

"'Yes, my child.'

"'Then, will you not ask them to pray for me, that I may be able to sing, "Jesus is mine," for I have been looking for Jesus, but I cannot find Him; Jesus is not mine.'

"His papa promised that he would have him prayed for. Wednesday came, and Thursday, and at last Friday; but he could not say, 'Jesus is mine'; and amid the engagements of the day, the father actually forgot his own child. Toward the end of the meeting, the congregation arose and sang:

'Now I have found a Friend,
Jesus is mine.'

It happened that the father was in one part of the church and his little boy in another; and as they sang, the little fellow wended his way through the crowded aisles and groups of young converts till he reached the father, and resting his hands upon his knees, he burst into tears, saying, 'Dear papa, I have found Jesus! Jesus is mine!'"

No. 338.

"SOVEREIGN RULER OF THE SKIES."

Rev. John Ryland, 1753—1825.

Robert Flockhart was a field and street preacher well known in the last century. He was a soldier against the French, and when in the battle of the Isle of France, he was suddenly moved to sing. A battlefield, in the midst of flying shot and all the uproar and turmoil is a curious place for a song, but he sang a part of the hymn beginning as above:

"Plagues and death around me fly,
Till He bids I cannot die;
Not a single shaft can hit,
Till the love of God thinks fit."

And he followed this hymn with another quite as appropriate to the circumstances:

"When I tread the verge of Jordan,
Bid my anxious fears subside."

No. 339.

"O WHERE ARE KINGS AND EMPIRES NOW?"

Bishop Cleveland Coxe, 1818.

Rev. S. W. Duffield, in his "English Hymns," quotes one occasion when this hymn was very effectively used. "It was when the General Conference of the Evangelical Alliance was convened in New York City, in 1873. It was at the time when so much had been said about the 'prayer test,' and when we scarcely knew whether the faith of the Church might not have been shaken for the moment by the universal storm of skepticism. President Woolsey was giving the opening address. After referring to the prevalent scepticism, he looked up with that peculiar twinkle of the eye which we all recollect—at once expressive of denial and satisfaction—and repeated the first stanza of Bishop Coxe's hymn:

'Oh, where are kings and empires now,
Of old that went and came?
But Lord! Thy Church is praying yet,
A thousand years the same!'

For a moment there was silence. In another moment the full significance of the reference had flashed on every mind, and the response was instantaneous and universal. Shouts, waving of handkerchiefs from the ladies, clapping of hands, stamping of feet—I never knew anything like it. Round after round continued, until the storm of applause ended in a burst of grateful tears. No one doubted that the Church still believed in prayer and that the tempest had passed without the loss of a sail!"

No. 340.

"THE GOD OF ABRAM PRAISE."

REV. THOMAS OLIVERS, 1725—1799.

A young Jewess had but lately given her heart to the Savior. Her baptism enraged her father, who was the chief of his synagogue, and he vowed to kill her. She found refuge in the house of the minister who had baptized her, "and there," says an eyewitness, who was brought to Christ by the scene, "I saw her, in the hour of bitterness, when the reality of her abandonment by the house of her fathers first came upon her. It did not dampen her joy in Jesus Christ, and I shall never forget the scene when she stood, with clasped hands, her black, lustrous eyes upturned to heaven, and her dark but expressive face lighted up, and lifting up her voice sang snatches of what she had already learned to call her own hymn:

'The God of Abram praise,
Who reigns enthroned above,
Ancient of everlasting days,
And God of love:
Jehovah, great I Am,
By earth and heaven confessed,
I bow and bless the sacred name,
Forever blest."

No. 341.

"ROCK OF AGES, CLEFT FOR ME."

REV. AUGUSTUS MONTAGUE TOPLADY, 1740—1778.

Mrs. Lucy Seaman Bainbridge, who, with her husband, Dr. Bainbridge, made the tour of the world in order to study Christian missions, tells a most beautiful incident in connection with this hymn: "The Chinese women, it seems, are so anxious to 'make merit' for themselves that they will perform any labor to escape the painful transmigrations of the next life. They dread to be born again as dogs or cats, and the highest hope possessed by them is to be reborn as men. In order to secure this, they do any and every meritorious act." One whom Mrs. Bainbridge saw had with incredible labor dug a well twenty-five feet deep and some ten or fifteen feet across. With her poor, weak hands she had excavated every foot of it, and it was only after this achievement that she learned of Christ and of the free Gospel of salvation. When Mrs. Bainbridge met her she was an old woman of eighty, and stretching out her crippled and aged fingers, she and her visitor sang together:

"Nothing in my hands I bring,
Simply to Thy cross I cling."

The ship *London*, lost in the Bay of Biscay, January 11, 1866, had on board the Rev. J. D. Draper and his wife, who were bound for Australia. The last man that left the ship was asked what the passengers were doing, and he replied that the last sounds he heard were the voices of as many as could sing, singing:

"Rock of Ages, cleft for me.
Let me hide myself in Thee!"

Patrick Donnellan was an Irish boy living in County Clare, Ireland. In this county the Irish tongue being mostly spoken, the most dense ignorance and darkness prevailed. When Donnellan was fifteen, a school was opened in the neighborhood, at which he learned to read and where he received some Scriptural instruction. When about twenty years of age he became a Christian. At that time there was much persecution of those that read the Bible, by the

Romish priests, their names being read aloud by the priest at mass and the ignorant people sometimes resorting to violence in their persecution of them. It was no light matter in such a region for young Donnellan to take a stand as a disciple of Christ, but he took the stand boldly, knowing fully the possibilities before him. When asked by a Christian friend if he did not expect to suffer persecution for the name of Christ, he replied that such was his prospect, and he was aware of it. Soon after, on the sixteenth of February, 1831, he accompanied a gentleman to the house of a poor woman, who had suffered persecution because she desired to educate an only child in a knowledge of the Scriptures. Being well acquainted with the Irish language, he had been employed as an interpreter in this visit. As they returned home after this visit, they were both fired at from behind the hedge of the road and wounded; Donnellan receiving two wounds, one being in the side. From the moment the wound was examined, it was apparent that it would result in his death, and he was so informed. When relief was procured and a cart provided, the sufferer was laid on it and conveyed to the house where many awaited his arrival. This meeting was fitted to excite strong emotions. Donnellan himself, however, was calm, and having been carried into the kitchen and seated, he began to recite the hymn:

"Rock of Ages, cleft for me,
Let me hide myself in Thee;
Let the water and the blood
From Thy riven side which flowed,
Be of sin the double cure,
Cleanse me from its guilt and power."

He lived about two days after the wound, and when nearly exhausted and dying, he repeated to his sister and other members of the family the following hymn, as if he would pour into these bleeding hearts the balm of comfort:

"Rejoice for a brother deceased,
Our loss is his infinite gain;
A soul out of prison released,
And freed from its bodily chain;
With songs let us follow his flight,
And mount with his spirit above;
Escape to the mansions of light,
And lodge in the Eden of love.

"Our brother the haven hath gained,
Outflying the tempest and wind,
His rest he hath sooner obtained,
And left his companions behind;
Still tossed on a sea of distress,
Hard toiling to make the blest shore,
Where all is assurance and peace,
And sorrow and sin are no more."

When he reached the middle of the last verse he could not refrain from weeping, and this was the only occasion during his sufferings on which he gave way to tears.

Christian's Penny Magazine, May 6, 1837.

On board the ill-fated steamer *Sewanakha* was one of the Fisk Jubilee Singers. Before leaving the burning steamer and committing himself to the merciless waves, he carefully fastened upon himself and wife life preservers. Some one cruelly dragged away that of his wife, leaving her without hope, except as she could cling to her husband. This she did, placing her hands firmly on his shoulders and resting there till her strength became exhausted, she said, "I can hold on no longer."

"Try a little longer," was the response of the wearied and agonized husband. "Let us sing 'Rock of Ages.'" And as the sweet strains floated over those troubled waters, reaching the ears of the sinking and dying, little did they know, those sweet singers of Israel, whom they comforted. But lo! as they sang, one after another of those exhausted ones were seen raising their hands above the overwhelming waves, joining with a last effort in this sweet dying pleading prayer.

> "Rock of Ages, cleft for me,
> Let me hide myself in Thee."

With the song seemed to come strength; another and yet another was encouraged to renewed effort. Soon in the distance a boat was seen approaching. Singing still, they tried, and soon with superhuman strength laid hold of the lifeboat, upon which they were borne in safety to land. This incident is related by the singer himself, who said he believed Toplady's "Rock of Ages" saved many another besides himself and wife.

A Quaker lady, who for three years had visited camps and hospitals to help and cheer the sick, wounded and dying during the war of the Rebellion in America, relates the case of a little drummer boy, who had recognized no one since his fall and had given little evidence of consciousness; he was very near his end; and she whispered in his ear:

> "Rock of Ages, cleft for me,
> Let me hide myself in Thee!"

when the countenance of the brave youth brightened up, and he followed with the second stanza of the hymn, saying that his mother had taught him that hymn, and he had often sung it in Sunday school, and after a few minutes conversation he expressed a hope in the Savior, and fell asleep to wake no more to earthly scenes.

A chaplain of the Hartford Retreat for the Insane, Rev. Dr. Thompson, relates the following incident in his experience there: In passing through the halls he met an educated man whom he had long known and respected. His incoherent talk and dejected countenance arrested his attention, and he saw that a malady had remorseless sway over the body and mind of the man. The physicians had little hope of his recovery. Finding him one day in the deepest despondency, the chaplain repeated the stanza "Rock of Ages, cleft for me." Afterward when the man came to himself and was better, he reminded the faithful chaplain that the hymn was indissolubly linked with the beginning of his convalescence.

Christian Secretary, September 9, 1885.

No. 342.

"O THOU FROM WHOM ALL GOODNESS FLOWS."

REV. THOMAS HAWEIS, 1732—1820.

Mr. John B. Gough writes thus about his father: "During a retreat of the English army, when closely pursued by Marshal Soult, about the year 1809, my father, then about thirty years of age, was a soldier in the Fifty-second Light Infantry. He had been slightly wounded in the chest, and though his wound was not considered fatal, it was painful and irritating. The army had suffered fearfully from exposure, famine, and the heavy fatigues of an active campaign. I well remember my father saying to me: 'John, you will never know what hunger is till you feel the two sides of your stomach grinding together.' In that campaign, men, mad with hunger, fought like wolves over the half-decayed hoof of a bullock; and often when one of these poor animals, overcome with weakness and starvation, was staggering as if about to fall, the ready knife was applied to its throat, and the fainting soldiers, eagerly catching the blood in their hands, and hardly waiting for it to congeal, made it take the place of food. In this retreat the Fifty-second Regiment—to use an American term—was demoralized; and, while they staggered on, my father threw himself out of the ranks, under the shadow of a large rock, to die; he could go no farther. Lying there he took from his inner pocket a hymnbook (which I have today with all the marks of its seventy years upon it), and began to read the hymn in which is the verse:

'The hour is near, consign'd to death,
I own the just decree;
Savior, with my last parting breath,
I'll cry, "Remember me." '

He must die—it seemed inevitable—though far from home, in a strange land. He was a Christian, and endeavored to prepare himself for the change. Suddenly a large bird of prey, with a red neck growing out of a ruffle of feathers, came swooping along, almost brushing my father's body with its wings; and then circling up, it alighted on the point of rock and turned its blood-red eye on its intended victim. As my father saw that horrible thing watching and waiting to tear him in pieces even before life was extinct, it so filled him with horror and disgust that he cried: 'I cannot endure this; it is too terrible. When I am unable to drive that fearful thing away, it will be tearing my flesh. I cannot endure it!' He arose to his feet and fell, then crawled and struggled away, till at length he crept into a poor hut, found safety, and soon after joined his regiment. Though he was very, very ill after that frightful episode, he recovered, and died in 1871, at the remarkable age of ninety-four years."

No. 343.

"SAFE IN THE ARMS OF JESUS."

MISS FANNY VAN ALSTYNE, 1823.

Bishop Hannington, a missionary of the English Church in Central Africa, fell a martyr to his zeal in the cause of missions in October, 1885. During the last few days of his life, he kept a diary, from which the following story of his sufferings and heroism is gleaned: He was on his way to Uganda, and the king, Mwanga, was displeased because white men were coming to his capital on the eastward side; and had caused his detention by one of his chiefs, Lubwa. This took place on the twenty-first of October. While detained at Lubwa's, which is near the northeastern arm of Lake Nyanza, a soldier was placed to guard the Bishop's tent, yet he was allowed to climb a hill from which he could see the Nile. While upon the hill he was set upon by about twenty ruffians. He says, "Brahim (his head man) they bound instantly; me they threw violently to the ground, and proceeded to strip me of all valuables. Thinking they were robbers, I shouted for help, when they forced me up and hurried me away, as I thought, to throw me down a precipice close at hand. I shouted again, in spite of one threatening to kill me with a club. Twice I nearly broke away from them, and then grew faint with struggling and was dragged by the legs over the ground. I said: 'Lord, I put myself into Thy Hands. I look to Thee alone.' Then another struggle, and I got to my feet and was thus dashed along. More than once I was violently brought into contact with banana trees, some trying in their haste to force me one way, others the other, and the exertion of struggling directly after dinner gave me an agonizing pain in the stomach. In spite of all, feeling I was being dragged away to be murdered at a distance, I sang:

'Safe in the arms of Jesus.'

and

'My God I am Thine,'

and then laughed at the very agony of my situation."

And so the diary goes on relating his sufferings at the hands of these savages to whose land he had gone to tell them of the love of Christ for them, until at last his reason almost left him and he spoke of himself as very low and crying to God to release him. But through it all he found comfort and help in God's word and spoke of the Psalms he read and of the help he found in them. And at last he was taken out and murdered by those whom he had gone to help.

During a great flood of the Missouri River some years ago, the following incident occurred: A woman living near the river bank with her two children, little girls of four and ten years of age, was called away to a neighboring town for the day and left the two children in charge of the home, especially placing the younger one in charge of the older sister. At this time, although there had been heavy rains for many days, the river was still inside its banks, and no flood was expected. After the mother left, however, the rain set in again with great violence, frightening the children greatly with the incessant lightning and thunder. Sometime after night-fall the youngest fell asleep, but the elder, true to the charge committed to her, remained awake soothing the child when the noise of the tempest roused it. During the night she was startled by a dull heavy sound at the door. Springing up to open it, what was her astonishment and fright, to be met by the waters of the river, which had overflowed their banks and were beating against the house. As the door opened, the water rushed in over the child's feet and ankles; she quickly closed the door again and, going to the window, saw that the rain had ceased and that the moon was shining, but as far as she could see, it was only water, yellow water everywhere, and rising rapidly. It was almost up to the window panes already, and it was only a question how long the frail wooden door and window could bar the stream before the house would be flooded and they swept away. She almost screamed with terror, but the thought of her little sister, sleeping now, and committed to her special care, nerved her to thoughts and acts above her years. Suddenly she thought of the stairs, and gathering the sleeping child in her arms, she went softly up the steps. She laid her on the bed and kept her awful vigil alone. Oh, for one kiss from mamma's lips before the terrible waters swallowed her; the tears flowed silently, and she knelt and prayed as she had never prayed before. So the long night wore away, and the candle flickered, flared, and then died in its socket. Suddenly a sound broke on the silence which she knew too well was the breaking up of the furniture below, that awakened "Dot," the little sister, and she cried plaintively: "Will mamma never come for us, sister?"

What a pang those words sent to the sister's heart as she asked herself the question inwardly; but steadfastly she replied, "If mamma doesn't, darling, Jesus will."

"Then," said the child dreamily, "I wish He would come quick," and she dropped asleep again. Nellie held Dot closely in her arms, hoping she would wake no more, but she did, and this time it was with a loud cry: "I want mamma; oh, where's my mamma?"

It was more than Nellie could stand; she sobbed aloud and shook with nervous terror. Then, with a mighty effort, she controlled herself and said: "Don't cry, baby, sister will sing to you." Tremblingly she began:

"Safe in the arms of Jesus,
Safe on His gentle breast."

The words calmed her, and her voice found strength as she sang on to the end of the verse. With the first gleam of the morning, a boat with two oarsmen might have been seen rowing up and down the river searching for the sufferers of that awful night. "That's a deserted house, no use going there," said one; "it rocks now, and in five minutes it will be down."

"Hush," said the other, resting on his oars, as a sweet childish voice, clear and distinct, rang out across the waters:

"There shall my soul find rest."

"Father in heaven," said the man reverently, as he thought of his own babies asleep in their cradles at home. "There's a child over there." A few strong strokes brought the boat with its eager rowers up to the little window sill. He called loudly: "Who's there?" Nellie rushed to the window.

"Come, my little maid, no time to talk," and he reached out his arms to her. But she drew back. "No, Dot first," and, catching up the child, she wrapped her up in a comfort and gave her charge to the strong arms that waited without. The boat with the two saved children had hardly moved away before the old house tottered and fell into the waters, leaving no trace behind, but the children, saved by a song, were soon placed in their mother's arms.

SARAH LEIGH, in *Journal and Messenger*, January 18, 1884.

No. 344.

"THE DAY IS PAST AND GONE."

REV. JOHN LELAND, 1754—1841.

In the *Century Magazine* for September, 1885, in an article entitled "A Woman's Diary of the Siege of Vicksburg," occurs the following: "It is our custom in the evening to sit in the front room a little while in the dark, with matches and candle held ready in hand, and watch the shells, whose course at night is shown by the fuse. H—— was at the window and suddenly sprang up, crying, 'Run!'

" 'Where?'

" 'Back!'

"I started through the back room, H—— after me. I was just within the door when the crash came that threw me to the floor. It was the most appalling sensation I had ever known. Worse than earthquake, which I have also experienced. Shaken and deafened, I picked myself up; H—— struck a light to find me. I lighted mine, and the smoke guided us to the parlor I had fixed for Uncle J——. The candles were useless in the dense smoke, and it was many minutes before we could see. Then we found the entire side of the room torn out. The soldiers who had rushed in said, 'This is an eighty-pound Parrott.' It had entered through the front, burst on the pallet bed, which was in tatters; the toilet service and everything else in the room smashed. The soldiers assisted H—— to board up the break with planks to keep out prowlers, and we went to bed in the cellar as usual. This morning the yard is partially plowed by a couple that fell there in the night. I think this house, so large and prominent from the river, is perhaps taken for headquarters and specially shelled. As we descend at night to the lower regions, I think of the evening hymn that grandmother taught me when a child:

'Lord, keep us safe this night,
  Secure from all our fears;
May angels guard us while we sleep,
  Till morning light appears.'

Surely if there are heavenly guardians, we need them now."

No. 345.

"GOD IS OUR REFUGE AND OUR STRENGTH."

Psalm 46. Scotch.

There are times in the history of religious communities when the power of Christian sentiment is seen under circumstances of peculiar interest and sublimity. Such, for example, was the occasion when the representatives of the Presbyterian Church of Scotland met at Edinburgh to sever their connection with the State. A long procession of clergymen, headed by the white-haired Chalmers, issued forth from the old church of St. Giles, and proclaimed to the people by their coming that they had renounced their livings, and all State aid, and that the churches that they represented were henceforth to be free. The streets were lined, and the housetops were covered with people. Suddenly all Edinburgh seemed to burst into song:

"God is our refuge and our strength
In straits a present aid.
Therefore, although the earth remove,
We will not be afraid."

From street to street, from house-top to house-top, the grand old psalm rose, with a meaning never realized before. Children shouted for joy, and strong men wept.

No. 346.

"BEHOLD THE SAVIOR OF MANKIND."

Samuel Wesley.

"Good Friday; O how I love the return of Good Friday!" said a silver-haired saintly woman, as she sat with a friend at the door of her cottage in the evening light of that Christian memorial day. Her eyes looked as if they were reflecting holy light from the mysterious cross; and her voice was tremulous with sacred feeling as she spoke. "It was on a Good Friday evening that my heart, while yet young, was first broken, as I listened to the story of the cross; and then healed, as the music of this hymn seemed to come direct with life from heaven in those words:

'O Lamb of God! was ever pain,
Was ever love like Thine!'

O how precious that hymn has been to me ever since! It is, indeed, my Good Friday hymn. This day's return is always sweet. And that hymn is my heart's music throughout the day, and will be till I go to see Him!"

No. 347.

"HOW HAPPY IS THE PILGRIM'S LOT."

REV. JOHN WESLEY.

No doubt Mr. Wesley was sincere in all that he said in this hymn at the time it was written, but he changed his mind afterward. There are some stanzas in the hymn as he wrote it that are usually omitted, and two of them read:

"I have no sharer of my heart
To rob my Savior of a part,
And desecrate the whole:
Only betrothed to Christ am I,
And wait His coming from the sky
To wed my happy soul.

"I have no babes to hold me here,
But children more securely dear,
For mine I humbly claim:
Better than daughters or than sons,
Temples divine of Heavenly stones
Inscribed with Jesus' name."

Four years after he made this rash declaration, he had to take it all back, for he married a widow with four children. It would have been better for him, however, if he had stood by the determination of the hymn, for the match did not prove a happy one, and after leaving him several times and returning again, his wife left him not to return.

No. 348.

"O FOR A HEART TO PRAISE MY GOD."

Rev. Charles Wesley, 1708—1788.

"An aged Congregational minister and his wife, who resided in a retired North Devon village, used occasionally to visit a Methodist home in which the services of the Society were held. While they were sitting in the parlor one day, the old man took up a book from the table, and, looking at the title, threw it down, saying, 'There is no such thing in the world.' It was John Wesley's 'Plain Account of Christian Perfection.' The old lady took up the rejected volume, and opening about the middle, her eyes fell upon a passage which arrested her. 'Why,' she said, 'is this perfection? Why, John,' she cried to her husband, 'is this perfection? Listen to this. I have enjoyed this for many years. Is this perfection, as the Methodists call it? Then I have got it! Is it possible in this world, John? It is to be enjoyed even here. This blessing God gives me from day to day. Listen to this'; and she read from one of Wesley's pages.

Her husband was silent, until the Methodist mother of the house opened an old hymnbook, and asked whether they could not both join her in singing a hymn of Charles Wesley's, which expressed the same spiritual experience as John Wesley described, in a manner more tuneful, but not with less precision. 'Cannot you sing this from your hearts?' said she, repeating verse after verse.

" 'Yes,' they said.

" 'Well, then, we will sing together.' And the good Methodist woman, and the old veteran theologue, and his venerable, warm-hearted wife, sang:

'O for a heart to praise my God,
A heart from sin set free,
A heart that always feels Thy blood,
So freely spilt for me!' "

No. 349.

"MY SOUL THROUGH MY REDEEMER'S CARE."

REV. CHARLES WESLEY, 1708—1788.

Sometimes a hymn seems to remain in the memory when all things else are forgotten, and to express one's thoughts when all other forms of words fail to do so. Twenty years ago (1872) in Plymouth, England, a Christian man was dying. His power to speak was well-nigh gone, but now and then he was heard to say, as if trying to recall some half-forgotten words: "Soul—my soul." His wife, standing by his bedside, repeated various verses of Scripture and parts of hymns in which occurred something about the soul, without obtaining from the sick man any token of recognition, and at last repeated this line, when at once her husband's hand pressed hers, and as she repeated to him the words of the hymn, he showed by every means within his power, the satisfaction it gave him to hear the words.

No. 350.

"AND CAN WE FORGET IN TASTING OUR MEAT?"

Rev. Charles Wesley, 1708—1788.

The Wesleys were firm believers in giving religion a prominent part in social life, and lost no opportunity of impressing this duty upon their followers. They provided their people with metrical graces to be used before and after their meals, and while partaking of them, and introduced what was probably before unknown, the practice of singing these graces. When eighty-six years old, Mr. John Wesley met a large party of friends at dinner at Sligo. While the meal was in progress, Mr. Wesley suddenly stopped, clasping his hands and looking up as if in the attitude of prayer. Instantly all conversation ceased, and every eye was fixed upon the face of Mr. Wesley. And then he began to sing these lines:

"And can we forget
In tasting our meat
The angelical food which erelong we shall eat?
When enrolled with the blest
In glory we rest,
And forever sit down at the heavenly feast."

When he had sung this stanza, he resumed his meal, but a peculiar solemnity rested upon all who were present, and they never forgot the occasion.

No. 351.

"SALVATION! O THE JOYFUL SOUND!"

Rev. Isaac Watts, 1674—1748.

Miss Harding, the teacher of the Ladies' Society at Jerusalem, mentions the following incident of a little Jewish girl in that city, one of her scholars: "On all occasions this child is fond of quietly talking with me alone; and one evening, while seated beside me on a stone on the Jaffa Plain, while her sister and another child were playing at a little distance, she repeated to me, in a clear, sweet voice, her favorite hymn:

'Salvation! O the joyful sound!
What pleasure to our ears!
A sovereign balm to every wound,
A cordial for our fears.

Chorus:

'Glory, honor, praise and power,
Be unto the Lamb forever!
Jesus Christ is our Redeemer!
Hallelujah! praise the Lord!'

On coming to the chorus:

'Jesus Christ is our Redeemer!'

she said very earnestly, and with deep feeling, 'Oh! Ma'am, that's sweet. Jesus Christ is *our* Redeemer, *our* Redeemer! No man can redeem his brother; no money! no money! nothing but only the precious Blood of Christ!' In the mouth of a little Jewish girl, these words had great force and deep interest. The child had only been with me eight months, so I had hardly known how far she could follow the English lessons I had given. I was much affected by the circumstances."

Youth's Dayspring, June, 1850.

No. 352.

"PRAISE YE THE LORD! 'TIS GOOD TO RAISE."

REV. ISAAC WATTS, 1674—1748.

The Wesleys more than almost any other men of their times brought the power of religion into the daily lives of their followers, and taught them to live, and act, and talk, and think, as if God were a present reality to them. On one occasion Mr. John Wesley was taken with a party of friends to the top of a hill behind the town of Chatham, where a very fine view was to be had. All were impressed with the beauty of the landscape spread out beneath their feet, and many were the admiring remarks that fell from their lips. After a few minutes Mr. Wesley took off his hat and began to sing this hymn of praise to God, appropriate to the place and the occasion because of its reference to the works of God in nature. One of the friends present when that hymn was sung said that he never forgot the lesson it taught him, and that often afterward, when looking at a fine bit of scenery, he would recall the incident and say to himself or to those who were with him: "Why should we give the landscape all the praise and its Maker none?"

No. 353.

"HAPPY THE HEART WHERE GRACES REIGN."

REV. ISAAC WATTS, 1674—1748.

One of the most effective uses ever made of a hymn, by a preacher, was made of this hymn by Rev. Dr. Hannah who preached before a Methodist Conference at Sheffield, England, in 1835. The house was crowded, and the heat oppressive. The discourse was a masterly one, from the text, "And now abideth faith, hope, charity; these three; but the greatest of these is charity." The sermon was long and held the closest attention of the audience much beyond the usual time for closing, and so when the preacher reached the end of the first two divisions of his subject—"faith and hope"—he said that time would fail him to consider the third and greatest of the Christian graces, and he must leave it to eternity to reveal the full meaning of the word, and then he read this hymn. Powerful as had been the preacher's description of the graces of faith and hope, it was felt by the audience that no words of his could so clearly and effectively have stated the character and power of Christian charity, and one person present in that audience, speaking of the occasion after a lapse of over thirty years, said that the hallowed impression of the reading and singing of that hymn was still fresh upon his mind.

No. 354.

"BE PRESENT AT OUR TABLE, LORD."

REV. JOHN CENNICK.

The propriety of "asking a blessing" or "saying Grace" as it is called, before our meals, is sanctioned by the fact that Jesus Christ did it. The custom is older, however, than the Christian era, and Jesus only gave His sanction to a practice common before in Jewish families. Metrical Graces began with the Reformation, Philip Melancthon, Luther's companion and helper, having composed some in Latin. And at almost the same time (1545) they appeared in English in Great Britain. They were used both before and after the meal. The Wesleys taught their followers to use them, and Charles Wesley composed and published a small pamphlet of them, containing eleven Graces to be used "before meat," and fifteen to be used "at or after meat."

They taught their people to sing them, and this practice became very popular among the Methodists, and is continued to this day by them in many parts of England. Perhaps the most beautiful as well as the most widely used of all these Metrical Graces, is the one written by John Cennick:

"Be present at our table, Lord!
Be here and everywhere adored!
Thy creatures bless and grant that we
May feast in Paradise with Thee."

John Wesley had this stanza engraved on the family teapot.

No. 355.

"HOW MANY PASS THE GUILTY NIGHT."

"HEARKEN TO THE SOLEMN VOICE."

Rev. Charles Wesley, 1708—1788.

The coal miners of Kingswood, near Bristol, England, had the habit of spending every Saturday night at the ale houses, in drunken carousals. Mr. Wesley preached there and a great revival took place. Many miners were converted and the whole character of the place was altered. Among other changes the miners spent every Saturday night in meetings for prayer and the singing of hymns. When Mr. Wesley heard of this he determined to make such meetings general among Methodists everywhere, and appointed watchnight meetings to be held once a month at the full of the moon.

"We commonly chose," says Mr. Wesley, "the Friday night nearest the full of the moon so that those of the people who lived at a distance might have light to their homes." These watchnight meetings, especially when conducted as they often were by one of the Wesleys themselves, were meetings of great solemnity and power, and they have been from that day to this a power for good. As soon as these watchnight meetings became an established feature of the Methodist movement, Charles Wesley issued a little twelve-page pamphlet, containing eleven hymns for special use on these occasions, and the first two hymns composed by him for these watchnight meetings were these. The first one, as will be seen, refers to the origin of the watchnight service in the Saturday night drunken revels of the Kingswood colliers, and the reference is all the plainer in the form in which Wesley first wrote it, beginning, "Oft have we passed the guilty night."

No. 356.

"FLUNG TO THE HEEDLESS WINDS."

Rev. Martin Luther, 1483—1546.

It was but a few years after the Pope issued his Bull against Martin Luther and his errors, that he lighted the fires of martyrdom against Luther's followers. The first victims were two young monks who had learned the way of salvation by faith as Luther taught it and said they would rather die than recant. They died singing *Te Deum Laudamus*, and their death opened Luther's mouth in this song of victory over their heroic death, and of defiance of their murderers. It was his first hymn, and it flew all over the land as if angels carried it, and spread in every direction an enthusiasm for the faith which had inspired the heroes of whom it sang. The translation is by John Alexander Messenger and appeared in a translation of D'Aubigne's "History of the Reformation," published at Philadelphia in 1843.

No. 357.

"WHEN DOOMED TO DEATH, THE APOSTLE LAY."

WILLIAM CULLEN BRYANT.

When the Methodists were compiling the hymnal now (1892) in authorized use in their churches, they asked Mr. Bryant to write for them a hymn on the subject of temperance. He complied with their request and sent them this hymn, which was one of the last of his compositions, as he died in less than a year after it was written. When he sent the hymn, he wrote a letter in which he said: "Thinking of the subject of which you spoke in your letter, it occurred to me that the deliverance of Peter from prison might furnish matter on which to hang a temperance hymn. I have produced what is written above and it is at your service."

No. 358.

"ON THIS STONE, NOW LAID WITH PRAYER."

JOHN PIERPONT.

It makes a great difference when and where we use capital letters. Now here is a hymn written by a Unitarian, for use at the laying of the corner stone of a Unitarian chapel in Boston (May 23, 1839,) and the writer intended it to voice his own theology and that of the church for whose use it was composed; and so in writing it he began the words "Corner Stone," at the end of each stanza with capital letters, while he began the words "child" in the second stanza, and "spirit" in the third, with small letters. The change by which the hymn is made suitable for Trinitarian hymnals is hardly a fair one, for it puts into the author's mouth sentiments in which he did not believe.

No. 359.

"LORD OF THE SABBATH, HEAR OUR VOWS"—1736.

REV. PHILIP DODDRIDGE, 1702—1751.

I have heard the complaint that the Bible gives us very indefinite descriptions of heaven, and of the employments of its inhabitants. I think there is in this hymn a sufficient reply to such complaints. On the second of January, 1736, Dr. Doddridge undertook to do this in a sermon to his people, from the text, "There remaineth therefore a rest to the people of God:" and this hymn was written to be sung at the close of this sermon to illustrate his theme. A missionary who had spent thirty years in Jamaica, said of this hymn, "One who knows what it is to be exposed to the sun of the torrid zone, shudders to read the dreadful lines in which Dr. Doddridge describes Heaven as a place where there is

'No midnight shade, no clouded sun,
But sacred, high eternal noon.'

The idea is intolerable. It terrifies one to think of it. The man who wrote that hymn must have lived far North, where a glimpse of the sun was a rare favor, and his highest enjoyment to bask in its rays a livelong summer day. I met once in Jamaica," said he, "with a black boy, under the shade of some cocoanut trees, where we both had taken shelter from the glare of the noonday sun. I said, 'Well, my boy, did you ever hear of heaven?'

" 'Me hear, massa.'

" 'And what sort of a place do you think it is?'

" 'Massa, it must be a very cool place.'

This agrees with the incident related of a missionary who spoke to the Greenlanders of the fires of hell, and only aroused in them by so doing a desire to go there. However, this is a good hymn, only when we sing it, it is well to omit the stanza containing the lines referred to.

No. 360.

"PRAISE THE LORD, HIS GLORIES SHOW."

REV. HENRY FRANCIS LYTE, 1793—1847.

The fourth stanza of this hymn reads:

"Strings and wires, hands and hearts,
In the concert bear your parts!
All that breathe, your Lord adore,
Praise Him, praise Him, evermore!"

This stanza would have shut the doors of our Methodist hymnals to this fine hymn a century ago. The early Methodists held music in high esteem and made it one of their most effective means of evangelization. Indeed Charles Wesley caught up the songs and ballads which were sung on the streets and in the theaters, and wrote for them sacred words. He wrote the words:

"Listed into the cause of sin,
Why should a good be evil?
Music, alas! too long hath been
Pressed to obey the devil."

And yet they would have no instrumental music in their service of praise, and especially abhorred instruments with "strings." John Wesley said, "I have no objection to instruments of music in our chapels, provided they are neither heard nor seen." And Dr. Adam Clarke, the great Methodist commentator, wrote: "Music as a science, I admire; but instruments of music in the house of God, I abominate and abhor." And yet this hymn is now in the hymnals of our Methodist brethren, and they praise God with instruments of a good many more than ten strings.

No. 361.

"O HAPPY SAINTS WHO DWELL IN LIGHT."

REV. JOHN BERRIDGE, 1716—1793.

I am very glad there is a hymn in this book written by John Berridge, because it gives me an opportunity to tell you something of one of the quaintest old fellows (pardon the irreverence) who ever preached a sermon or gave out a hymn. His very looks were enough, it seems to me, to set a congregation off into a roar, and I wish I had his picture here for you to see. He was a clergyman of the Church of England, but no parish bounds or bishops' threats could keep him from going off on an occasional itinerant trip to preach the Gospel to those who were neglected, whether he found them in Church or field. On one of these occasions he had come, as the story goes, on a Saturday night to a little village in the north of England, and he must needs stay over Sunday there. So he requested the landlord of the inn to go to the parson of the parish and tell him that a clergyman was stopping over Sunday at the inn who would be glad to assist at the service if wanted. The vicar was cautious. "We must be careful," said he, "for you know there are many of these wandering Methodist preachers about. What sort of a man is he?"

"Oh, he is all right, sir," was the response. "You just see his nose, sir, and you will know he is no Methodist."

"Well, ask him to call on me in the morning and I will judge for myself." The call was made and Berridge's peaked red nose, and mouth suggestive of jokes and puns, and all sorts of fun, at once convinced the suspicious vicar, and he was invited to preach. But if ever a man made a mistake that vicar did, for Berridge was as earnest in his piety as he was in his fun, and when he preached he went straight for the consciences and heart of his audience, and before he had gotten half through his discourse that morning the hot, sharp sentences came in such rapid succession, that not only the people in the pews but the vicar in the pulpit found themselves arraigned as sinners in the sight of God.

John Berridge lived at about the same time as Toplady did—Toplady, who wrote "Rock of Ages, cleft for me"—and yet who engaged in such fierce controversy with the Wesleys as would drive him out of any pulpit or church in these days; but Berridge had different ideas about a preacher's duty, and he advised a young man, "Look simply to Jesus for preaching food, and what is wanted will be given, and what is given will be blessed. When your heart is right, meek and simple, Jesus will make an orator of you: When you grow lofty and pleased with your prattle, Jesus will make a fool of you. Avoid all controversy in preaching, talking, or writing: preach nothing down but the devil and nothing up but Jesus Christ."

No. 362.

"ASLEEP IN JESUS! BLESSED SLEEP."

Mrs. Margaret Mackay, 1801.

The author of this hymn, a Scotch lady, was one day walking in a churchyard in Devonshire, and she came to a tombstone bearing the simple inscription, "Sleeping in Jesus," and this inscription suggested to her the writing of this hymn, which has the words "Asleep in Jesus" as the beginning of each stanza.

No. 363.

"BRING IN THE LAMBS, THE TENDER LAMBS."

Twenty years ago there lived in a Michigan city a professional gambler who was also given to intemperance. He was raising a family of boys. His wife was a Christian, and seeing the effect of the father's habits in the boys, though frail in health she proposed to leave the city and go with her family far back in the wilderness beyond the reach of these associations, that she might save her boys and possibly reclaim her husband. The husband loved his family and consented to make the experiment, so they went over a hundred miles from their home and settled on a homestead in the wilderness. The next summer a Sunday school was organized within three miles of them. The children attended the Sunday school, but the mother was not able to walk the distance through the woods, so the father and mother remained at home. But during the summer the school had a picnic, when the children prevailed upon the father to go with them to the picnic. He led the two younger children, and not accustomed to attend such a gathering, he took a seat on a log outside the gathering with a child either side of him. He was greatly pleased with the exercises and did well his part toward furnishing dinner. The Sunday-school missionary was there, and brought his pastor with him, who was a good talker and a good singer. After the speeches and dinner, all joined in singing that stirring old piece, "Bring in the lambs, the tender lambs—O bring them into Jesus' fold." (Bradbury Trio, "New Golden Censor," page 338.)

Tears rolled down the gambler's cheeks as he looked first at one and then at the other of his lambs, and when the song was finished he came forward and asked the missionary if he had those books to sell. "I want three of them. I don't care what they cost." Then he said, "I am a dreadful wicked man and I don't know who will 'bring in my lambs.' " He urged the minister and missionary to go home with him and stay all night and "We'll have a prayer meeting," he said.

They went, and they did have a "prayer meeting." Three prayers were offered, the happy wife joining as none but a wife can pray for a husband. Then he prayed for himself and broke all the rest down by his cries and confessions. The Lord heard and answered. Then all joined in the song, "Bring in the lambs," after which he had an "experience meeting." But he was not brought into the full light till the next morning, when he was ready to "publish abroad what great things the Lord had done for him and had compassion on him." His little lambs "led him to the lamb of God."

HENRY DENSMORE.

No. 364.

"COME, O THOU TRAVELER UNKNOWN."

REV. CHARLES WESLEY, 1708—1788.

The two brothers, John and Charles Wesley, were more than usually intimate. They roomed together at Oxford, formed and led the "Young Company of Students" there which first obtained the name of "Methodists"; worked side by side in harmony in the great religious movement of their day which established the Methodist Church. Charles, the "Poet of Methodism," died first. A short time after his death, John Wesley then eighty-five years old, visited the town of Bolton, England, to preach. He began the service in his usual way, with song and prayer, and then gave out this for the second hymn, but when he came to the lines:

"My company before is gone,
And I am left alone with Thee,"

his emotion became uncontrollable, and he burst out into a flood of tears, and sat down in the pulpit, covering his face with both hands. The effect upon the congregation was such as might be expected—the people ceased to sing, and in many parts of the chapel, sat down weeping and sobbing aloud. The congregation was very large, Saturday night though it was; and the place was like a Bochim. After a while Mr. Wesley recovered himself, arose, and gave out the lines again; "and then there was such singing," said the narrator, "as I never heard before; it seemed as if the sound would lift the roof off the building." A sermon followed, remarkable for the holy influence attending the delivery, and the deep impression it seemed to make on the multitude of people.

No. 365.

"ON JORDAN'S STORMY BANKS I STAND."

Rev. Samuel Stennett, 1727—1795.

Hon. Moses F. Odell, a prominent Methodist, was among the first, after the terrible battles of the Virginia Peninsula, to hasten from Washington to minister to the wounded and dying. He relates that the Government employed large steamboats to bring away from the field the severely wounded, and that while he was ministering to the suffering and dying on one of these steamboats, whose berths and cabins were filled with them, a soldier began singing to a familiar tune the words:

"On Jordan's stormy banks I stand,
And cast a wistful eye,
On Canaan's fair and happy land,
Where my possessions lie."

Almost instantly the strain was caught up by a score or more of the sufferers, who found in this way an alleviation of their pain and an expression of their trust.

No. 366.

"JUST AS I AM WITHOUT ONE PLEA."

MISS CHARLOTTE ELLIOTT, 1789—1871.

The following fact is related by the Editor of the *Ladies' Repository,* for December, 1867: "On rising one morning, the text 'The blood of Jesus Christ his Son, cleanseth us from all sin,' was impressed upon my mind so powerfully that I felt convinced the Lord was speaking to me, and for some special purpose. On going as usual into my district that day, I was met by a poor woman, who informed me that there was a person dying close by, who would be thankful to see any one, but so weak as to preclude all excitement or fatigue. I went immediately, and found a young woman almost in the last stage of consumption, scarcely able to speak; indeed she was in a dying state. I was afraid to say much lest I should agitate the feeble life, but just whispered in her ears the words, 'The blood of Jesus Christ, his Son, cleanseth us from all sin'; also the first verse of the hymn:

'Just as I am, without one plea,
But that Thy blood was shed for me;
And that Thou bidst me come to Thee,
O Lamb of God, I come! I come!"

The dying one looked at me with great earnestness, as if drinking in the precious message, but spoke not then. I continued my visits after this during the short time she lived—about a month. On one occasion she called to her husband to 'come and hear about Jesus.' The last time I went she was waiting for me with great anxiety; and when I entered the room, and approached her dying bed, she sweetly whispered, 'The blood of Jesus Christ, his Son, cleanseth us from all sin.'

"'Just as I am, without one plea,
But that Thy blood was shed for me;
And that Thou bidst me come to Thee,
O Lamb of God, I come! I come!'"

Looking at her infant child, whose spirit had just fled to glory, she said: 'Baby, mother is coming to thee,' and in a few moments she fell asleep in Jesus."

A young man was dying, but he knew he was lost, and was in a terrible state of anxiety. The clergyman was sent for. He came, and read and administered the Sacrament to the young man, and told him he had nothing to fear. As soon as he had left, a friend said to the youth, "I hope you are happy, and can die peacefully now?"

"No!" replied the young man; "I'm not happy. I have not peace, and I cannot die without that. What shall I do?"

Shortly after another friend went to see him, and began to read him that beautiful hymn:

"Just as I am, without one plea,
But that Thy blood was shed for me,
And that Thou bidst me come to Thee,
O Lamb of God, I come! I come!"

No sooner was the first verse read, than the dying youth looked up, and with deep earnestness said, "Read that again." It was read over again, and he drank in every word, listening as for his life. As soon as the verse was finished he said, "There, that will do; I can die with that." The dear fellow there and then came to Jesus, "just as he was, without one plea," without one solitary spark of goodness—he came with all his deep need, and the Lord saved him.

"W. E.," in *Episcopal Recorder*, October 15, 1885.

No. 367.

"GREAT GOD! WHAT DO I SEE AND HEAR."

Rev. Wm. Benj. Collyer, 1781—1854.

After the World's Fair of 1851, at London, was over, the Crystal Palace was carefully taken down, and the material removed to Sydenham, where it was rebuilt, and became one of the fixed institutions of London. Rev. Samuel M. Dickson describes a musical service he once listened to there as follows: "Hark! is that thunder? It has the sound of thunder, and surely the clouds threatened it; but the truth is, a man has climbed away up to the key-board of the grand organ, and touched it! O, the witchery of glass walls! They imprison the sounds, but give the illusion of unconfined space. The music rolls around the arches of the sky, wave upon wave of sound repeating and echoing in the distance. Now there is a short, sharp piercing note—now a long swell rolling and widening till aisles and corridors are filled; then it gradually lingers into silence, or melts into a soft flute-like strain. Now there is a crash, a leap, a succession of booming discharges, and rattling, galloping reverberations, ending in a prolonged swell and a sudden stop. Fitting prelude to what is to follow. By hundreds and thousands the singers are gathering into the orchestra around the base of the organ. Soon five thousand voices wait to accompany the monster instrument, and they are children's; for the school houses of London are empty today, and this is the annual jubilee concert. No wonder is it that, as you stand upon your seat and survey the audience, the crowd of heads may be measured by acres; no wonder that they crowd the galleries, and perch upon cornices, and climb into every available nook and crevice. And now, just at three o'clock, a little man with a long baton springs upon a stand in front, telegraphs to the organist and the concert begins. The opening hymn is this beginning:

'Great God! What do I see and hear!
The end of things created!
The Judge of mankind doth appear,
On clouds of glory seated:
The trumpet sounds! the graves restore
The dead which they contained before!
Prepare, my soul, to meet Him.'

Imagine the effect, when at the end of the fourth line there was a short pause, after which an invisible trumpet pealed a long and sweeping blast, followed by the words:

'The trumpet sounds! the graves restore.'" etc.

No. 368.

"O THOU MY SOUL, BLESS GOD THE LORD."

PSALM 103, Scotch.

A clergyman who had been engaged as Seaman's Chaplain, at a Southern port, was, in the course of duty, called to the sick bed of a sailor, apparently at the gates of death from the effects of his licentiousness. He addressed him affectionately on the state of his soul. With a curse the sick man bade him begone and not harass his dying bed. The chaplain, however, told him plainly he would speak, and he must hear, for his soul was in jeopardy of eternal death. The man, however, remained silent, and even pretended to sleep during his faithful address and prayer. Again and again the visit was repeated with similar success. One day, however, the sick man made use of an expression, by which the chaplain suspected he was a Scotchman. To make sure of the fact, the chaplain repeated a verse of that version of the one hundred and third Psalm, still in use among the Churches of Scotland:

"Such pity as a father hath
Unto his children dear;
Like pity shows the Lord to such
As worship Him in fear."

The chords of the sick man's heart vibrated to the well-known language. His eyes glistened with unknown moisture. The chaplain prosecuted his advantage. Knowing the universality of religious instruction among the Scotch, he ventured an allusion to his mother. The poor prodigal burst into tears. He admitted himself to be the child of a praying mother, who had often commended him to God. He had left her long before to become a wanderer on the face of the great deep. No longer did he repel the kind attentions of the chaplain, and his monitor had the satisfaction of seeing him recover from his sickness, and arise from his bed, he verily believes, a child of God.

No. 369.

"GOD MOVES IN A MYSTERIOUS WAY."

William Cowper, 1731—1800.

In Whittle's life of Philip P. Bliss, the following incident is related: On a Sunday afternoon when a Gospel meeting was being held at the skating rink in St. Louis, by Messrs. Whittle and Bliss, there came up a fearful storm of wind and rain. The old timbers quivered ominously. Whittle was speaking, but the noise was so great as to cause him to stop. The storm continuing, plain symptoms of alarm were becoming visible in the audience. Mr. Bliss, noticing this, by an inspiration from God, struck up a verse of the grand old hymn:

"God moves in a mysterious way
His wonders to perform;
He plants His footsteps in the sea,
And rides upon the storm."

The storm was at its fiercest. Just as he sang the words, "And rides upon the storm," there was an instantaneous cessation of the storm; a little break occurred in the cloud, and a bright ray of brilliant light flashed directly and fully for a moment upon his face. His wife had been uneasy, and asked of the one who sat by her side if there was any danger. She was reassured, and when the incident occurred, she smiled and nodded saying by both look and manner "all is safe for He Who rides upon the storm, has sent the brightness of His sunshine upon us at this moment, as He sent the rainbow."

No. 370.

"MY FAITH LOOKS UP TO THEE."

Rev. Ray Palmer, 1808—1887.

During the Civil War in America, and on the evening preceding one of the most terrible battles of the war, some six or eight Christian young men, who were looking forward to the deadly strife, met together in one of their tents for prayer. After spending some time in committing themselves to God, and in Christian conversation, and freely speaking together of the probability that they would not all of them survive the morrow, it was suggested by one of the number that they should draw up a paper expressive of the feelings with which they went to stand face to face with death, and all sign it; and that this should be left as a testimony to the friends of such of them as might fall. This was unanimously agreed to; and, after consultation, it was decided that a copy of this hymn should be written out, and that each should subscribe his name to it, so that father, mother, brother, or sister, might know in what spirit they had laid down their lives. Of course they did not all meet again. The incident was related afterward by one who survived the battle.

Ray Palmer, in appendix to his "Poetical Works."

An active business man, residing in the interior of the state, was accustomed to visit the City of New York from time to time for business purposes. Before coming on a certain occasion, he had observed a swelling slowly forming on his person, which, though not troublesome as yet, occasioned him some anxiety; and, after attending to the matters for which he came, he went to submit the case to the judgment of an eminent surgeon. He was frankly told that it would prove a malignant tumor, and would probably terminate his life by the end of six months. This was, of course, a stunning blow. He was an intellectual believer in Christianity, and a man of upright life, but was without a Christian hope. Before leaving the City, he called on a Christian lady—a sister, we believe—and told her what the surgeon had said. On parting from her, she placed in his hand a printed leaflet, which he put in his pocket. Then he took the cars on the Hudson River Road, and, when seated, sank into profound thought on his position. He recalled his past life, so filled with the divine goodness, his sinful neglect to return this with love and obedience, and his failure to receive the Savior of the world into his heart. Some hours, perhaps, had passed in this way, and his heart had become full of tender feeling, when he remembered the leaflet and took it from his pocket. At once his eye rested on the words:

"My faith looks up to Thee,
Thou Lamb of Calvary!"

He read the hymn through slowly, and many times over. His heart adopted the language, a new-born faith found full and delightful expression in it, and from that time he had a tranquil rest in God. The prediction of the surgeon was fulfilled; and he died joyfully, having this song sung to him to the last.

The author of this hymn makes public the following incident concerning it. It is quoted from a letter, from a young lady who had long been a sufferer from a chronic disease: "One morning, long ago, I woke with more than the usual exhaustion, and a sense of discouragement amounting to oppression. Do you know that kind of despair so like suffocation? Bitter repinings rose in my heart; hard thoughts of God and sinful questionings. Why must it be? What shall I do? I heard the rain beating against the windows. I knew the day must be dreary, and I sighed aloud, 'What will there be to cheer me today?' And then I hastily glanced about the room, gladly discovering that I was alone, and turning again to my pillow wearily. Hark! the chords of a piano! The family must be at morning worship. Up through the register, as distinctly as if breathed at my bedside, came the strain:

> 'My faith looks up to Thee,
> Thou Lamb of Calvary,
> Savior Divine!'

I enjoyed it and listened eagerly.

> 'Now hear me while I pray,
> Take all my guilt away,
> O let me from this day
> Be wholly Thine.'

I felt calmed. I would look up for cheer. I could not say that dismal morning, 'Thou O Christ, art all I want'; but I could say, 'My faith looks up to Thee.' Afterward for several days and nights, I repeated the hymn constantly, especially the stanza, 'While life's dark maze I tread.' Maze was just the word for me. You know what a tangled wild my path of late has been."

No. 371.

"FROM GREENLAND'S ICY MOUNTAINS."

Rev. Reginald Heber, 1783—1826.

In 1852, two missionaries were sent out by Bishop James Osgood Andrews, of the Methodist Episcopal Church, to represent the South Carolina Conference on the Pacific Coast, where there was a grand rally of adventurers, a polyglottal gathering of people of every realm and of every tongue. It was a fine opportunity for American Methodism to plant itself where such a wide and effectual door was opened. One of those missionaries wrote home to report progress, and said how great was his joy one Sunday afternoon in 1853, in the Santa Clara Valley, to hear a man and his wife from South Carolina sing in front of a tent:

"Waft, waft, ye winds, His story,
And you, ye waters roll,
Till like a sea of glory,
It spreads from pole to pole:
Till o'er our ransomed nature,
The Lamb for sinners slain,
Redeemer, King, Creator,
In bliss returns to reign."

There was melody in that song. It came so unexpectedly; the missionaries had seen the hills and valleys in all their natural luxuriance of flowers and foliage for several months, but that song echoing on the air was like new life to cheer the preachers in their toil.

No. 372.

"WHEN THE HARVEST IS PAST AND THE SUMMER IS GONE."

REV. SAMUEL F. SMITH, 1808.

"In Clerkenwell a preacher and his helpers sang the hymn:

'When the harvest is past and the summer is gone.'

At one of the windows sat a poor man in an arm chair, looking very pale, who, before the meeting closed, sent for the preacher. 'Please, sir, sing that again to me, that part:

"When the holy have gone to the regions of peace."

That's where I want to go. Do you think that I can get there?' The preacher said he could.

" 'But you don't know the life I've led. You see, sir, I've been in prison thirty times, so I think I must be too bad for Christ.' So the preacher read to him the story of the crucifixion.

" 'That's what I want the Lord to do for me,' exclaimed the dying man, as the prayer of the dying thief was read. 'Thank you for coming out to preach and sing,' he said, as the preacher departed. 'The chaplain of the prison used to tell me of a Savior's love, but I did not care for it then. But I want it now, for I do want to be saved.' At the next meeting the poor man was not at the window. So the preacher went into the house, and saw that he was fast sinking. Faintly he said: 'Sir, the mist is rolling away now. I can see Jesus. Do sing it to me.' So the visitor sang:

'When the mists have rolled away.'

Then the dying man said: 'I could hear you all singing so plain tonight, "Crown Him Lord of all." Will you please pray?' The preacher prayed. Then the man said: 'Please raise my head'; and with one hand under his head, and the other in his he passed away."

Christian Herald, December 16, 1886.

No. 373.

"CHRIST, THOU THE CHAMPION OF THE BAND WHO OWN."

MATTHAUS APELLES VON LOWENSTERN, 1594—1648.

This was a favorite hymn of Niebuhr who was often heard refreshing his own soul amidst his intense labor and researches by murmuring it as a prayer:

"And give us peace: peace in the church and school,
Peace to the powers who o'er our country rule,
Peace to the conscience, peace within the heart,
Do Thou impart.

"So shall Thy goodness here be still adored,
Thou Guardian of Thy little flock, dear Lord;
And heaven and earth through all eternity
Shall worship Thee."

No. 374.

"COMMIT THOU ALL THY GRIEFS."

REV. PAUL GERHARDT, 1607—1676.

Rev. S. W. Christophers, in "The Epworth Singers" relates that "A venerable minister once said, 'The first year after my marriage was spent in the South of England, and then I was called to take a pastoral charge in South Wales. My income had been small, and my expenses somewhat large, so that when the time of starting came, I had not money enough to pay my way to our journey's end. We had done our best with the means we had, and were happily one in our repose on God's fatherly goodness. I believed that He would supply our need day by day as He had always done, and in that full trust we went off on the top of the coach. Those were old coaching days. We had got about half way towards our destination, and when I had given the coachman and guard their fees, I had but twenty pence left in my pocket. We were to go into the inn while the horses were changed, and had to be booked for the rest of the journey. Where the amount of the fare was to come from, I did not know; but still, I rested on the promise of Divine help. As I got off the coach, that verse came freshly to my mind:

"No profit canst thou gain
By self-consuming care;
To Him commend thy cause, His ear
Attends the softest prayer."

And I lifted up my heart to God in the language of the next verse:

"Thy everlasting truth,
Father, Thy ceaseless love,
Sees all Thy children's wants, and knows,
What best for each will prove."

As we walked through the lobby, I saw a paper on the floor, picked it up, and opened it. It was a ten-pound note. "The help has come in time," said I to myself. But putting the note in my pocket, I called the landlord, told him that I had found a note which I supposed somebody in the house had lost. If he could tell me the amount and the number of the note, I would let the owner have it. There was at once a hue and cry throughout the house, "Who has lost a bank note?" Nobody claimed it; nobody could describe it. The horn blew; the coach was to start; we could not stay; and hurriedly giving the landlord my address in Wales, and assuring him that I would remit the amount lost as soon as the owner of the note was identified, we took our seats, and, by and by, safely arrived at our new residence. No news of the person who had lost the note ever came, nor has any claim ever been made on me from that day to this. However, some people may account for the fact, there it is; one of many instances in my life in which God has shown Himself near to help me in the time of need.' "

No. 375.

"JESU, THOU ART MY RIGHTEOUSNESS."

Rev. Charles Wesley, 1708—1788.

"It was nearly sunset," said a traveling preacher, "and a mellow light was upon the valley up which I was footing it toward a village chapel. The light seemed to hallow the balmy quietness around me. I came at length within sight of a group of tin-washers. They were mostly young women in their picturesque sun-bonnets and working dress. They were gracefully using their long-handled instruments in regulating the action of the water on the pounded tin ore, as it was carried over a succession of sloping boards, so as to allow the cleanly washed tin to form a deposit beneath. They were singing in concert as they worked, and on passing the nearest point of the road to them, I caught some of the words of their evening song. The words came swelling up the valley:

'Wash me, and make me thus Thine own,
Wash me, and mine Thou art:'

It filled me with sacred feelings as I passed, and the softening music followed. It was an agreeable preparation for the evening worship. The time of service arrived, and the same singers came with their parents, friends and neighbors, all decently dressed for God's house, and true to the hour of prayer. I chose the same favorite hymn. New inspiration seemed to come upon them, and they made the sanctuary ring with their spirited, glowing harmony, as they sang:

'Jesu, Thou art my Righteousness,
For all my sins were Thine;
Thy death hath bought of God my peace,
Thy life hath made Him mine.'

And so they sang the whole hymn through. It was a joy to hear from the lips of so many happy young people who had known the washing of regeneration, the words of this hymn, expressing their own experience, and the joy became deeper as their faces brightened or their eyes sparkled through their tears, as they listened to their preacher's address on the words of Jesus, 'If I wash thee not, thou hast no part with me.' Every feature of the eager, upturned countenances seemed to respond, 'Lord, not my feet only, but also my hands and my head.' Nor will that parting music ever be forgotten; for as they went off in groups from the service, I could hear them singing along the hillside lane:

'Wash me, and make me thus Thine own;
Wash me and mine Thou art;
Wash me, but not my feet alone,
My hands, my head, my heart.' "

No. 376.

"THE NIGHT WAS DARK; BEHOLD, THE SHADE WAS DEEPER."

This hymn is to be found in a book entitled "The Changed Cross," published by A. D. F. Randolph. The title given to the hymn is "The Call," and no author's name is given. In Long's "Illustrated History of Hymns and Their Authors," is to be found the following incident: "An elderly gentleman came into our store one day and asked for a book entitled 'The Changed Cross.' He said it contained a hymn which led him to the Savior. Upon a little inquiry, he gave the following account: 'Twelve years ago, I was in a very agitated state of mind about my soul's welfare. I was working in a store on Federal Street one day, when I felt unusually distressed. I went up to the third story. The window was slightly lowered—about a pane's length. While there, and in this state of mind, there came suddenly a little slip of paper floating in at the window. I picked it up and found thereon these stanzas (drawing a worn slip from his pocket):

"In meek obedience to the heavenly Teacher,
Thy weary soul can find its only peace;
Seeking no aid from any human creature,
Looking to God alone for his release.

"And He will come, in His own time and power
To set His earnest-hearted children free:
Watch only through this dark and painful hour,
And the bright morning yet will break for thee."

I cried, "God be praised!" and I have been praising God ever since.' On being asked how that piece of paper came there, and why, he said, 'An angel sent it.'" The whole hymn consists of seventeen stanzas, and the two quoted above are the last two.

No. 377.

"OUT ON AN OCEAN ALL BOUNDLESS WE RIDE."

Rev. William Fairfield Warson, 1833 (Methodist).

In "Letters from Eden," published by the American Tract Society, the following incident is related: A little boy named Simon Manoogian, living in Harpoot, became a Christian when nearly nine years old, and soon after he was bitten by one of the half-wild dogs which infest that city. A few months after the bite he said one day to his teacher, "I am sick; my head aches," and the teacher sent him home to his mother. The next day he asked to have his pastor sent for, and on his arrival said to him, "I called you to say how grateful I am to you for teaching me of Jesus." The pastor read and prayed with him, and talked to him of the Savior and left him. Hydrophobia had now set in with all its attendant suffering and horror. The writer says, "I first saw him a few hours before his death, when I went expecting to see him 'not in his right mind,' as the people said he was. But this was because they had never seen such a death. Before we reached the house, he had requested them to call his teacher and schoolmates and, as I entered, was earnestly exhorting the latter to prepare to follow him. Said he to them, 'When I reach heaven, I will pray for you, that you may come there too, and not go, like the rich man, where you cannot get even a drop of water.' He asked each one to pardon everything which he had done to grieve him, and then said, 'Can we sing a hymn?' When asked what hymn, he replied:

'Out on an ocean all boundless we ride,
We're homeward bound, homeward bound;'

Till then the paroxysms of the terrible disease had regularly interrupted him, but, when we began to sing, they ceased.

The soul's power seemed to overcome and control that of the disease, and he sang in a clear, strong voice with us. When we reached the last stanza:

> 'Into the harbor of heaven we glide—
> We're home at last;
> Softly we drift on its bright silver tide—
> We're home at last.
> Glory to God! all our dangers are o'er,
> We stand secure on the glorified shore;
> "Glory to God!" we will shout evermore;
> We're home at last.'

None of us could sing that with him. And do you wonder that I was obliged to stop and weep as I gazed on the scene so new in this dark land? And do you wonder that the people, who had crowded in to witness the strange scene, thought him 'out of his head?' Not one impatient word escaped his lips. 'In a short time,' said he, 'you will put my body into the grave. Do not do it weeping, but sing the hymn:

> "Joyfully, joyfully, onward I move,
> Bound to the land of bright spirits above."

And I in heaven will take my harp and join you in your song.'"

No. 378.

"I HEAR THE SAVIOR SAY."

MRS. ALVINA M. HALL, 1818.

Mrs. S. K. Brandagee in *The Sailor's Magazine* for June, 1880, says: "A few weeks ago, in our little country Sunday school, we were singing the hymn quoted, and as the chorus rose loud and clear, 'Jesus paid it all, yes, all the debt I owe,' my eyes unconsciously turned to a young man, singing so earnestly, tears filling his eyes. After school, joining me, he said, 'I can never sing that hymn without tears; it was the means of my conversion two years ago.' A lawyer by profession, with a clear legal head, yet that simple hymn had, under the Spirit, conquered intellect, worldly tastes, and youthful follies, and led to an entire consecration to Him Whose precious Blood paid it all, long, long ago.

"A lady, listening to the conversation, said, 'Some years ago I was visiting a gay watering place, and on Sabbath evening, after some singing, not especially well suited to the Sabbath, I took my seat at the piano, with a prayer that the dear Lord would enable me, by my singing, to help some weary soul. I sang "Jesus paid it all." Two or three years afterward, visiting the same place again, a colored woman came to me saying, "Yes, you are de lady; I knows you are."

" 'What lady?' I asked.

" 'De very one who sang, "Jesus paid it all." Last night one of the waiters comes to me and says, " 'Tis de very one, I's sure I 'members her. Don't you know how sweetly she sang 'Jesus paid it all, all de debt I owes?' Yes, I neber forgets it "Jesus paid it all," and I neber forgets de dear lady who sang it so sweetly.' "

"Thus these sweet hymns, which reach the heart of learned and unlearned alike, seem to be only the beginning of that chorus, which will louder and louder grow, until the 'Lamb That was slain gathers His elect together from the four quarters of the globe to join in the grander chorus, "Now unto Him That loved us, and washed us from our sins in His own blood, and hath made us kings and priests unto God and His Father, unto Him be glory and dominion for ever and ever." ' "

No. 379.

"TODAY THE SAVIOR CALLS."

REV. S. F. SMITH, 1808.

Mr. Moody relates: "The last time I preached upon the matter of decision in religion was in old Farwell Hall. I had been for five nights preaching upon the life of Christ. I took Him from the cradle and followed Him up to the judgment hall, and on that occasion I consider I made as great a blunder as ever I made in my life. If I could recall my act I would give this right hand. It was upon that memorable night in October, and the Court House bell was sounding an alarm of fire, but I paid no attention to it. We were accustomed to hear the fire bell often, and it didn't disturb us much when it sounded. I finished the sermon upon 'What shall I do with Jesus?' And I said to the audience, 'Now, I want you to take this question with you and think over it, and next Sunday I want you to come back and tell me what you are going to do with it.' What a mistake! It seems now as if Satan was in my mind when I said this. Since then I have never dared to give an audience a week to think of their salvaton. If they were lost, they might rise up in judgment against me. 'Now is the accepted time.' We went downstairs to the other meeting, and I remember when Mr. Sankey was singing, and how his voice rang when he came to that pleading verse:

'Today the Savior calls;
For refuge fly.
The storm of justice falls
And death is nigh.'

After meeting we went home. I remember going down La Salle Street with a young man, and saw the glare of flames. I said to the young man, 'This means ruin to Chicago.' About one o'clock, Farwell Hall went, soon the church in which I had preached went down, and everything was scattered. I never saw that audience again. My friends, we don't know what may happen tomorrow, but there is one thing I do know, and that is, if you take the gift you are saved. If you have eternal life you need not fear fire, death or sickness. Let disease or death come, you can shout triumphantly over the grave if you have Christ."

No. 380.

"PASS ME NOT, O GENTLE SAVIOR."

MISS FANNY VAN ALSTYNE, 1823.

Mr. G. W. Smart, a sailor missionary, writes in the *Sailor's Magazine* for August, 1885, as follows: "Two American men-of-war have been here (Funchal, Madeira Islands) lately—the *Kearsage* and the *Pensacola.* The former came from the Congo River, and the latter from the States. The men of the *Kearsage* had forty-eight hours here. They came on shore in two parties, eighty-five in the first, and seventy-eight in the second. The "Sailors' Rest" was quite full for four nights. In addition to the beds, the cane sofas were occupied, and one man actually slept on the table in the reading room. Many of the men dined, supped and breakfasted at the 'Rest.' All were pleased that they had such a place to come to. An interesting incident occurred on one of the days. A man from the ship came in and asked leave to play the harmonium. He played several well-known tunes very nicely and then asked me for a Sankey tune book. I gave him one, and he commenced to play 'Pass me not, O gentle Savior.' Another man came in and sang it. A man who was in the dormitory came in with the tears streaming down his face, and coming up to me put a coin into my waistcoat pocket, saying as he did so: 'Look here! that hymn has knocked me over. I can't stand it. Take that for the Home.' On looking at the coin, I was surprised to find that it was a sovereign. He requested those who were singing to sing the hymn again, which they did, and he became very much affected. He afterward told me his history. He and his brother had some money left them; he squandered his and went to the bad, while his brother continued in good circumstances. He has sat, on several occasions, in bygone days, at his brother's table when the present Bishop of London, Dr. Temple, has been a guest. Now he is an able seaman in the American Navy. And this had been brought about by drink. He would not join his companions in drinking any more just then, but, of course, I have now lost sight of him."

No. 381.

"I AM SO GLAD THAT OUR FATHER IN HEAVEN."

PHILIP BLISS, 1838—1876.

"At a recent meeting in New York City, General Clinton B. Fisk spoke of his early associations with Jerry McAuley in the work, and of its extended influence. In Liverpool one night he heard a rough-looking sailor speak in a seaman's mission meeting. Though the man was rough, his face shone. 'I found Jesus over there in America,' he said, and all who heard him listened in wonder. This man was known as 'Swearing Johnny.' 'When we were paid off, I took my money to the saloons, and pretty soon I was drunk again. Then I went out into the streets, and the snow was beating against my face. As I passed along, I heard singing, and stopped to listen,' he said. 'I heard them singing "Jesus loves even me."—"I'll go in and see about it," I said to myself.' He went in and there he saw 'that wonderful man, Jerry McAuley,' and he led him to Christ.

" 'Yes,' said his wife, 'and its been nothing but Jerry McAuley and "Jesus loves me" ever since Johnny's ship came home.' "

Sailor's Magazine, April, 1885.

No. 382.

"ONE SWEETLY SOLEMN THOUGHT."

Miss Phoebe Carey.

Were the incident I want to relate to you about this hymn found floating among the newspapers without author, I should not dare tell it, but it has for its authority Rev. H. D. Ganse, the well-known Dutch Reformed pastor, who furnished it to the *Sailor's Magazine*. He relates that in the summer of 1881 he spent a few weeks at Geneva Lake, Wisconsin, and there became acquainted with a family in which there was a baby about a year old. Of this baby he says: "He was of beautiful, fair complexion and hair, with large blue eyes and ample forehead—a grave, manly, reasonable-looking baby, with as sweet an expression as I ever saw. I took to him at once and he allowed it, and I was seldom with him without having him a little while in my arms. After returning to St. Louis, since he was not in my congregation, I saw but little of him; but I never went through his neighborhood without scanning the baby carriages in hope of again meeting his sweet face. Once I was rewarded, about a year ago, and found him the picture of health and beauty. Having learned very lately that Captain Wade's family had been very sick and that a child had died, I called upon the relatives in my own congregation to be informed of the facts, and was told, to my great sorrow, that the lost child was my little friend. But the narrative then given of the circumstances preceding and attending his death, while it greatly affected me, more than relieved my grief; for even the child's death seemed to be 'swallowed up in victory.' The reader will remember that at the time of his death he was but three years and nine months old. Some weeks before, and while his health was still perfect, his attention had been attracted to Phoebe Cary's well-known hymn, in the form in which it has been set to music and is commonly sung:

'One sweetly solemn thought
Comes to me o'er and o'er,
I am nearer home today,
Than I've ever been before.

'Nearer my Father's house,
Where the many mansions be,
Nearer the great white throne,
Nearer the crystal sea.' etc.

These were singular words to fascinate such a child; but they did. Every night, after his prayer was said, and his mother had tucked him up in his bed and kissed him 'good night,' he would call out to his father with his clear ringing voice, 'Nearer to home, papa'; when his papa would be required to come from another floor and sing him the whole song. The singing, however, was subject to such interruptions as these: 'What's "great white throne," papa? What's "crystal sea," papa?'

"Whether or not he came thus to understand the words and to have interest in their meaning will appear by what follows. Certainly he had mind and character enough for understanding them. One night, after his fatal sickness had been for several days upon him, his mother, exhausted by watching, had thrown herself down across the foot of his bed, committing him for the first time to the care of a competent nurse who had been a few days with him. When the nurse attempted, at the proper hour, to give him his medicine, he called out like any baby, 'Mama, give it to baby!' His mother, rising at once to meet his wish, the nurse explained by saying, 'Baby, mama so tired.' Immediately he answered, 'Baby take it from the lady,' and he did so regularly for the rest of the night; during the whole of which he made no call for his mother again, though he lay for a good part of the time wide-awake looking at her. With the same kind of thoughtfulness, when once informed why he should not, in his sickness, kiss his parents upon their lips, he steadily said thereafter, 'Baby kiss you on the neck.'

"Such incidents will help us to judge how much intelligence there was in the sayings and acts that remain to be described. Let it be observed that he was as far as possible from fretfulness or complaining. When asked, 'How does baby feel?' his common answer was, 'Better,' or 'Pretty better.' Still his knowledge that he had done with this life, and was to have another, was perfectly distinct. Early in his sickness, as his mother came to touch his throat, he turned sadly toward her and said, 'Don't touch baby's throat any more, mamma; baby's going to die.'

"Later on, when the truth of his prophecy grew more apparent, his mother asked him, 'Don't baby want to stay with papa and mamma?' He nodded his head. 'Then pray to God to let you stay.'

"He answered very faintly, 'You pray to God.'

" 'O darling!' she said, 'I have prayed so many, many times.'

"His answer was very striking: 'Baby tired of praying to God.'

"On the morning of the day on which he died, his voice had grown very weak. He was seen to be trying to speak. His mother, bending close to him, heard him say, 'Baby going to home.' Scarcely believing what she heard, she asked him, 'Where, my darling? where are you going?' and he answered, 'Baby going to God.' "

A worker in Christ's vineyard, who has done much for our sick and wounded soldiers at Washington, writes to a friend as follows: "The hundred hymn books you sent me will be very useful, and, I think, will do much good. There is one hymn in the book that I can never forget if I live a thousand years. It is the sixty-third, beginning:

'One sweetly solemn thought,'

I had held by the bedside of a dying soldier several prayer meetings; it was at the Patent Office Hospital, and the soldiers would gather round the bedside of this interesting Christian, and we would pray with him and them, read to them, talk a little, and sing several pieces out of the hymn book. This sixty-third hymn was his favorite, and he always wanted it sung. We used to sing it to the sweet tune of Dennis. One evening, just as the sun was setting, we went in, and he wanted us to have the prayer meeting. In the course of the service, I leaned over and asked him what we should sing. He said, 'My hymn.' We knew very well what it was, and sung it as far as the conclusion of the third verse, and there we had to stop. He actually went to 'wear his starry crown,' just as we were singing at his request, those very words."

HACKETT'S "Christian Memorials of the War."

No. 383.

"IF YOU CANNOT ON THE OCEAN."

MRS. ELLEN HUNTINGTON GATES.

The ever-memorable fourth and closing anniversary of the Christian Commission was held in the Hall of the House of Representatives, Washington, D. C., on Sabbath evening, February 11, 1866. A great crowd filled the hall, overflowing the lobbies outside, and turning thousands away in a disappointed stream. The hall was draped in memory of the beloved dead, who by his presence graced the anniversary of the Commission, and by his tearful sympathy has made that occasion ever fragrant in the history and record of the institution. The Hon. Schuyler Colfax, Speaker of the House, presided. Precisely at seven o'clock the exercises began, by the singing of the noble hymn of praise:

"Jesus shall reign where'er the sun
Does his successive journeys run,
His kingdom stretch from shore to shore,
Till moons shall wax and wane no more."

The audience, rising and joining in the praise, was led by Philip Phillips, of Cincinnati. Prayer was then offered by the Rev. Dr. Boynton, Chaplain of the House, and the Scriptures were read, in the Forty-sixth Psalm, by the Rev. Dr. Taylor, Secretary of the American Bible Society. Speaker Colfax said, "I regret to inform you that the Hon. James Harlan (Secretary of the Interior) is detained by indisposition at home, and will not be able to be here as announced. Before singing the beautiful and impressive hymn, 'Your Mission,' next in order in the programme, let me read a brief note from the paper I hold in my hand. On the twenty-ninth of January, 1865, at the last anniversary meeting of this Commission, when hostile armies were contending together in deadly strife, this poem was sung as a part of the exercises of the evening. Abraham Lincoln, with his tall form, his care-furrowed face, and his nobly throbbing heart, was here, and after listening in tears, he sent up, written upon the back of this programme (holding up the precious sheet) in that plain familiar handwriting, by that hand that now lies cold in the grave, this request: 'Near the close, let us have "Your Mission" repeated by Mr. Phillips. Don't say I called for it.'" It was this incident that gave to this hymn its special interest and made it so widely known and sung all over the land. In this connection it is an interesting fact that President Lincoln gave to two hymns such notice as to establish their popularity, the other one being the one beginning:

"Oh why should the spirit of mortal be proud?"

No. 384.

"SAY, BROTHERS, WILL YOU MEET US?"

Rev. George A. Hall relates that during the last year of the war, while engaged in the work of the Christian Commission in the Union Army near Petersburgh, nightly crowded meetings were held in a little chapel by the soldiers of the Sixth Army Corps, at which were "witnessed such scenes as have never been known outside of army lines." The night before a fight on the left, the question was put to a most solemn assembly, "How many of you that are seeking Christ are ready to surrender to Him now?" In answer some twelve or fifteen came forward and knelt by the front seat, among them was an interesting youth. An old man, seeing him, darted from his seat and, pressing through the crowded aisle, threw his arms about the young soldier, sobbing, "My son, my son. He was lost and is found." Just then an Adjutant from Division headquarters, apologizing for his intrusion, called out, "All men belonging to —— Division, fall in." They were to march in the darkness of the night, to secure a position for the attack at daybreak. The men at the front seat arose, fell on each other's necks and wept. Some of them were to go. The father was not in the Division ordered out. His boy was. The parting was tender and cheerful. He kissed him and said, "Go now, my boy, since the Lord is going with you." There were hurried pledges to be faithful, and then they all took hold of hands around the altar and sang:

"Say, brothers, will you meet us,
Say, brothers, will you meet us,
Say, brothers, will you meet us,
On Canaan's happy shore?"

and hurried to their quarters to make ready to fall in. Some did not return from that fight. Two were brought into City Point Hospital badly wounded. They told us of the meeting, of their consecration, of their fearlessness in the fight, and their readiness to meet death, if it was God's will.

"Incidents of the Christian Commission."

No. 385.

"SHRINKING FROM THE COLD HAND OF DEATH."

Rev. Charles Wesley, 1708—1788.

During the last days of Rev. John Wesley, he was accustomed to preach as usual in different places in London and its vicinity, generally meeting the society after the preaching in each place, and exhorting them to love as brethren, to fear God, and honor the King, which he wished them to consider as his last advice. He then usually, if not invariably, concluded with giving out that verse:

"O that without a lingering groan,
I may the welcome word receive;
My body with my charge lay down,
And cease at once to work and live!"

No. 386.

"ALAS! AND DID MY SAVIOR BLEED."

REV. ISAAC WATTS, 1674—1748.

"Before me lies a letter written from a distant Western city in which the young man says, 'Do you remember a hymn of Watts which you made us boys learn once, beginning:

"Alas! and did my Savior bleed?"

I thought it rubbish at the time, and had nearly forgotten it, but this winter some of its lines have followed me like a detective. We have been having revival meetings, and I couldn't shake off the question:

"Was it for crimes that I have done,
He groaned upon the tree?"'

Here follows the story of the revival, and of his own surrender to Christ in the words of the last stanza of the hymn, which, doubtless have been the language of many another heart in similar circumstances:

'Here, Lord, I give myself away,—
'Tis all that I can do.'"

FRANCIS J. DYER, in *Congregationalist,* March 24, 1887.

No. 387.

"ALMOST PERSUADED NOW TO BELIEVE."

PHILIP BLISS, 1838—1876.

"In a mission of this great city (New York) a few evenings ago, there sat among the motley and changing audience a young man whose face had a kindly look. All unnoticed he sat, till in a pause he rose, saying, 'Please sing seventy-five,' and took his seat. The first stanza of 'Almost persuaded' was sung when the leader said, 'I want to ask that young man if he is a Christian.' Calmly rising, a young man of perhaps twenty years, fairly clothed, not a vicious but an undecided face, he replied, 'No, I am not a Christian, but I learned that piece in the Sunday school. I was brought up in a quiet little country village in the southern part of the United States. There I went to church and Sunday school, where I learned this hymn. I always went to church till I came to New York, then I began to run around, but I never hear that piece sung but I am almost persuaded to become a Christian.' I wish that I might record that he did then and there give his heart to Christ, but like too many others we fear he put it off to a more convenient season. The incident shows, however, the lasting influence of a hymn and how impossible it is to shake off the impressions they produce."

W. J. W. in *Christian Secretary*, September 2, 1885.

No. 388.

"I WOULD NOT LIVE ALWAY. I ASK NOT TO STAY."

REV. WM. AUGUSTUS MUHLENBERG, 1796—1877.

A correspondent of the *Religious Herald*, of Hartford, writing of a revival in that city in connection with the noonday meetings of the Y. M. C. A., in 1885, says: "A few days ago, the proprietor of one of the drinking and gambling hells of this city and also of a house of prostitution in New York, was passing the above-mentioned prayer meeting. The windows were open, and the hymn, 'I would not live alway,' reached his ear. 'Stop,' said he to his companion, 'listen to those words; they were sung at my brother's funeral. Come,' said he, 'let us go in and hear the singing.' They went in, and before the meeting closed he gave his heart to God. One week ago, he united with the church, and is now, so far as he is able, destroying the work of darkness he once builded."

No. 389.

"DEPTH OF MERCY! CAN THERE BE."

REV. CHARLES WESLEY, 1708—1788.

In the Fulton Street, New York, Prayer Meeting, a gentleman related his own experience, saying that he was some years ago sent from New York to Nashville, Tennessee, so that he might be away from his wicked companions. But he took with him his sinful appetites, and was there as here still bound by the slavery of the cup. He realized his degradation, but could not break his chains. He passed a rude place one day from which issued the sound of song. This was the song:

"Depth of mercy! can there be
Mercy still reserved for me?"

As he leaned against the door, it gave way, and entering, he found a little congregation of colored people. Among them was a colored auntie who had long been praying for the poor man's salvation. "Ah," said she, "I know you would come."

"Oh, auntie," he asked, "is there any hope for me?"

"Oh, yes, for you," and the colored saints sang on:

"God is love! I know, I feel;
Jesus weeps, and loves me still."

Weekly Witness, April 13, 1887.

No. 390.

"I WILL SING FOR JESUS."

PHILIP PHILLIPS.

One evening a great throng had gathered in the Effingham Theatre, London, in connection with William Booth's mission, to hear Mr. Phillips sing. He sang the song beginning "I will sing for Jesus." The song was wafted to the ears of a despairing man, while on his way to the London docks to commit suicide. It arrested his attention. As he listened, the verse was sung:

"Can there overtake me
Any dark disaster,
While I sing for Jesus,
My blessed, blessed Master?"

His purpose was thwarted. It brought home to his heart the memory of a mother's prayers and praises in his early days, and brought him broken-hearted to the feet of his Savior.

History of Hymns by E. M. LONG.

No. 391.

"TAKE THE NAME OF JESUS WITH YOU."

LYDIA BAXTER, 1809—1874.

I had been sitting alone in the little chapel for some time, busy at the organ in preparation for a meeting, and was about to leave the room, when an old man, who had been in the reading room adjoining, came slowly toward me, and, lifting his face toward mine, said: "I like music.

Won't you go back and play a little more for me?" He was eighty-four years old, as he told me afterward. His body was bent under the burden of the years, and as I seated myself again at the organ, he came and stood beside me, fully ripe, as it seemed for heaven. He was alive to only one great thought—Jesus the Savior and Master. He had been turning the leaves of the "Gospel Hymns," while my fingers ran over the keyboard, and presently he laid the book before me, saying: "Play that slowly, and I'll try and sing it for you." Softly and very slowly, I followed him as with a broken voice, often scarcely audible, he tried to sing:

"Take the Name of Jesus with you
Child of sorrow and of woe;
It will joy and comfort give you,
Take it then where'er you go."

It was little more than a whisper song; but as he took up the words of the chorus, a glad smile spread over his face, and his voice seemed to gather strength from his heart as he looked rather than sang:

"Precious Name! O, how sweet!
Hope of earth and joy of heaven."

It was true worship, the simple, glad expression of a loving, loyal heart. Verily, I sat alone with a saint that day, for as the other verses were sung, their wondrous meaning was interpreted by the face of the singer, and the veil seemed almost to fall away, revealing to me the things unseen. I had never seen the old man before; it is not probable that I shall ever see him again in the flesh; but his life touched mine with blessing that day, for he had unconsciously brought the Master very near. There was no music in the old man's voice; indeed, it could truthfully be said that he almost had no voice; but he drew a soul a little nearer to its Savior with what he had.

W. N. Burr, in *Illustrated Christian Weekly.*

No. 392.

"LORD I HEAR OF SHOWERS OF BLESSING."

Mrs. Elizabeth Codner.

In the year 1868 or 1869, the following note was read at one of the large union prayer meetings in the First Presbyterian Church, Rochester, at one of the E. P. Hammond meetings:

"Mr. H.: Thank you for singing that hymn "Even Me" for it was the singing of that hymn that has saved me. I was a lost woman, a wicked mother. I have stolen, and lied, and been so bad to my poor little innocent children. I have no friend. I have attended your inquiry meetings, but no one came to me on account of the crowd, so I went away always wretched, lost. But Saturday afternoon, at the First Presbyterian Church, when they all sung those beautiful words, 'Let some droppings drop on me, in blessing others, O bless me, even me,' it seemed to reach my very soul. I thought Jesus can accept me, 'even *me*,' a bad, wicked, passionate mother; and it brought me to His feet, and I feel my burden of sins removed. Jesus has accepted *me; even me.* Can you wonder that I love those words, or love to hear them sung? Ah! may I too sing them when He shall take me before His throne at the last and accept EVEN ME. God bless you.

Yours truly.

A Convert."

No. 393.

"O GOD OF LIGHT AND LOVE."

Rev. R. C. Watterson, 1812.

This hymn was written for the Annual Meeting of the Unitarian clergy and laity, Boston, May, 1845. The Hon. John Quincy Adams presided, and made the introductory address. The interest was very great, and it was throughout a most memorable occasion, by no one present ever to be forgotten. The following was sung as the fifth verse, in allusion to the venerable and illustrious presiding officer:

"Bless thou the Patriot Sire,
Who, warm with Freedom's fire,
  Spreads light around;
He like a rock has stood
'Mid strife and fire and flood,
True to his country's good,
  True to his God."

The Rev. Dr. Pierce, with his snow-white locks, at President Adams' right-hand, led in the singing; and, when this verse was commenced, he lifted up his arm and pointed to Mr. Adams, at the same time raising his voice to its utmost power, the vast multitude heartily uniting. The enthusiasm was literally beyond description."

"Singers and Songs of the Liberal Faith."

No. 394.

"I AM SO GLAD THAT OUR FATHER IN HEAVEN."

Philip Bliss, 1838—1876.

A New York City missionary one day came in his rounds to a small room in a tenement house, the home of a beautiful girl and her mother. The thought of the poor young thing and her hard lot had burdened him as he climbed up the dark stairs, the heavy sewing machine at which she sat day after day wearing out her life. He wondered that even religion could keep pure and white one lovely blossom amid such trial and such temptation, and wondered more that she did not despair. No; as he neared the landing he heard a sweet voice singing. Opening the door, and meeting the violet eyes through a thick cloud of steam with which washtubs filled the place to suffocation, he could not help exclaiming: "My poor child, how do you stand it?"

She sobered a moment; then catching up again the refrain just leaving her lips, sang on, smiling at him:

"Oh, I am so glad that Jesus loves me,
Jesus loves me, Jesus loves me;
I am so glad that Jesus loves me,
Jesus loves even me!"

No. 395.

"WHAT A FRIEND WE HAVE IN JESUS."

REV. HORATIUS BONAR, 1808.

A woman who, with her husband, had long been addicted to strong drink was at last reformed and converted through the influence of the meetings held at the Medical Mission, 81 Roosevelt Street, New York. After some time, the woman received a severe injury to her leg, necessitating her removal to the hospital.

"It was, indeed, a touching scene to witness, as the mother had to part with her two little children; but she commended them to her Heavenly Father's care, and, with a word of kindly warning to her husband to cheer up and look to the

Lord and mind not to take the drink, she left them. For some days the fever raged high, and part of the time the poor woman was quite delirious. One morning a stretcher was brought to her bedside to remove her to the operating room. She knew what it meant, and a shudder passed through her frame at the thought of what she would have to undergo, but she said: 'I'm ready to go, bless the Lord, for He will be with me.' Just then, though, a thought crossed her mind, causing a temporary feeling of depression. What was it? Why, she had heard that persons under the influence of ether uttered strange things at times, and the thought crossed her mind that perhaps she might say some bad words such as she had been wont to use in days gone by. But so changed had she become now that the very thought of her giving utterance to these things was horrible. Just then she remembered the verse sung at the mission:

'Have we trials and temptations,
Is there trouble anywhere?
We should never be discouraged,
Take it to the Lord in prayer.'

And so she lifted her heart to the Lord as the nurse lifted her body upon the operating table; 'O Lord, keep the door of my lips'; and He did so. The operation was a very tedious one, needing the removal of a large piece of bone, and it was three hours before she came to herself. On doing so, her first question was not as to her leg being on or off, but, turning to the nurse, she asked, eagerly: 'Did I say anything wrong?' On being assured that she did not, but had only whispered, 'Safe in the arms of Jesus,' she exclaimed, 'Thank God!' "

Medical Missionary Record, May, 1887.

In one of the South Sea Islands recently visited by a missionary, he found that a couple of boys who had attended the mission school at another island had unconsciously effected the conversion of some of the natives by singing the Sabbath school hymns, "Hold the Fort," and "What a Friend we have in Jesus." At the first service held by the missionary, two men who had been bitter enemies came forward and openly made known their reconciliation.

Foreign Missionary, March, 1884.

No. 396.

"NO MORE MY GOD, I BOAST NO MORE."

REV. ISAAC WATTS, 1674—1748.

This hymn has for its title in Watts' collection, "The value of Christ, and His Righteousness." Mr. Cooper, a missionary to the East Indies, had been on one occasion preaching on justification, at a military station on the Malabar coast, and on giving out the hymn at the end of the service, which was the one hundred and ninth, of the first Book of Watts, he paused and remarked, that if anyone who did not come to Christ for the bestowment of this righteousness joined in the singing of this hymn, he was insulting God. One of the soldiers who was hearing him said he was thunderstruck. "What a wretch I must be, that I am prohibited from joining in the praise of God." He went to the barracks under this impression, and found that without an interest in Christ he was a wretch indeed: and now, to all human appearances, he has fled for refuge to that atonement he had formerly neglected.

Arvine's Cyclopedia.

No. 397.

"COME HUMBLE SINNER IN WHOSE BREAST."

REV. EDMUND JONES, 1722—1765.

In his "Revival Lectures," President Finney says, "There is a hymn that has done great mischief. It begins:

'Come humble sinner in whose breast,
A thousand thoughts revolve.'

This hymn was once given by a minister to an awakened sinner, as one applicable to his case. He began to read, 'Come humble sinner.' He stopped. '"Humble sinner," that is not applicable to me. I am not humble.' Ah, how well it was for him that the Holy Ghost had taught him better than the hymn. If the hymn had said, 'Come, anxious sinner,' or 'guilty sinner,' or 'trembling sinner,' it would have been well enough, but to call him a humble sinner would not do. There are many hymns of the same character. It is very common to find sinners quoting the false sentiments of some hymn, to excuse themselves in rebellion against God."

"One glorious day in June, accompanied by an officer of the Eighth Missouri, I set out for the rifle pits. When I reached them, I found the heat stifling; and as I bent to avoid the whizzing Minié balls and the falling branches of the trees, cut off by an occasional shell, I felt that war was a terrible reality. The intense excitement of the scene, the manly, cheerful bearing of the veterans, the booming of the cannon from the battlements and the heavy mortars that were ever and anon throwing their huge iron balls into Vicksburg, and the picturesque panorama of the army encamped below, obliterated all sense of personal danger or fatigue. After a friendly talk with the men in the extreme front, and a peep again and again through the loopholes, watched and fired upon continually by the wary foe, I descended to the second ledge, where the sound of music reached us. We followed it quietly, and in a few moments stood behind a rude litter of boughs, on which lay a gray-headed soldier, face downward, with a comrade on either side. They did not perceive us but sang on the closing lines of the verse:

'Come, humble sinner, in whose breast,
A thousand thoughts revolve,
Come, with your guilt and fear oppressed,
And make this last resolve.'

I joined in the second verse:

'I'll go to Jesus, though my sin
Hath like a mountain rose;
I know His courts, I'll enter in,
Whatever may oppose.'

"In an instant each man turned and would have stopped, but I sang on with moistened eyes, and they continued. At the close of the hymn, one burst out, 'Why, ma'am, where did you come from? Did you drop from heaven into these rifle-pits? You are the first lady we have seen here,' and then the voice was choked with tears.

"I said, 'I have come from your friends at home to see you, and bring their messages of love, and the comforts that they want you to have.'

" 'Do you think so much of us as that? Why, boys, we can fight another year on that, can't we?'

" 'Yes! Yes!' they cried, and almost every hand was raised to wipe away the tears."

"Woman's Work in the Civil War."

No. 398.

"NOTHING EITHER GREAT OR SMALL."

REV. PROCTOR.

In his book, "Bringing in Sheaves," Mr. Earle relates the following: "A citizen, about thirty years ago, had such a clear view of himself as a sinner in the sight of God, and felt so deeply that he must have help or perish, that he came to my room, after midnight, to know what he should do to be saved. Oh, the agony of that soul! He walked the floor crying, 'I shall perish! What shall I do? What shall I do?' He kneeled down by a chair, and literally laid his face on the carpet. But he soon rose, saying, 'I must be lost!' His groans and cries were heartrending. I saw plainly that he needed to get a clear view of Jesus and His work, and asked him not to groan, but to be calm, and listen to me for a moment. After getting his attention, I told him that his tears and overwhelming anguish would not help him, but he must let go of all reliance upon anything but Jesus, and simply believe. I then repeated a portion of an old Scotch hymn (God be thanked for that good Scotch brother who wrote it.)

'Nothing either great or small,
Nothing sinner no;
Jesus died and paid it all,
Jesus paid it all,
Long, long ago.
All the debt I owe,
And nothing either great or small,
Remains for me to do.'

"Looking up through his tears, he asked, 'Is that it, Mr. Earle? Is that the way?'

"I replied, 'That is exactly the way.' But the light was not yet clear enough for him to fully embrace Jesus by a simple faith. He commenced groaning and pleading again, saying, 'Oh, what shall I do?'

"I said to him, 'Don't groan; let me have your attention a little longer.' I then repeated the last stanza of that beautiful hymn:

'Cast your deadly doing down,
Down at Jesus' feet;
Stand in Him, in Him, alone,
All glorious and complete.'

As the Spirit shed light upon his dark mind, he smiled through his tears, and said, 'I believe that it is; yes, that is it. Jesus died and paid it all. I thought I must do something, and could not see what I could do. How glad I am that I came here tonight. I can trust Jesus now; yes, I can trust Him.' I then asked him to kneel down and tell Jesus he could trust Him. After doing this, he left me, saying, 'Oh, I am so happy now!' "

No. 399.

"O JESUS, MY HOPE, FOR ME OFFERED UP."

REV. CHARLES WESLEY, 1708—1788.

Those who are familiar with the "History of Methodism," by Dr. George Smith, will not have forgotten the story he tells of a girl in Cornwall, who had been for some time a very great opponent of the revivals. She had been accustomed to ridicule the cries and groans of those who were in distress about their souls; but there was one defect in her mimicry. She had never really attended any of those prayer meetings. She was persuaded to go on one of these occasions, and the Spirit of God sent an arrow of conviction to her heart, and she who went to mock "remained to pray." That night she was kneeling with the penitents; that night she was privileged to find peace with God, and rejoiced in conscious pardon, and the next morning when she met her companions they found a strange change had passed over her. They looked to her for mimicry, but they found nothing but serious earnestness. So, by and by, they began to persecute her as she had persecuted others. She happened o wear earrings and it was at that time thought to be an offense against good taste and Christian propriety that anyone who was converted should wear earrings. It was pointed out to Mary that she ought not to wear them if she was truly converted to God. She retained them for awhile, but at last her heart gave way, and as she was beating the ore to pieces with a hammer, she took the earrings, put them among the ore, and hammered and smashed them until they were a mass of shining metal, and as she struck them she sang the words of the hymn she had heard the night before:

"Neither passion nor pride Thy cross can abide,
But melt in the fountain that streams from Thy side:
Let Thy life-giving Blood remove all my load,
And purge my foul conscience, and bring me to God."

No. 400.

"O LORD OF HOSTS! ALMIGHTY KING!"

Oliver Wendell Holmes, 1809.

This was called the "Army Hymn." In compliance with a request of Congress, President Lincoln appointed the last Thursday in September, 1861, as a day of fasting and prayer. Nowhere was this fast day better observed than in the Union Army. A correspondent of the *Traveller* thus describes its observance in General Banks' Division, then stationed on the Upper Potomac:

"Yesterday, the fast day appointed by the President, was observed in this Division in a marked method. All drill was omitted, of course. Public services were held in a rare manner. In accordance with a general order, all the regiments in the immediate locality assembled in a beautiful field at the entrance to Darnestown village, with full bands, and the artillery and cavalry. The Major General, Brigadiers, and other high officers, attended in full uniforms. A march, varying from a short distance to a mile and a half, brought all together, when the infantry formed in mass, flanked by artillery and cavalry. Six chaplains officiated.

Assistant Adjutant-General Drake read the General's order. Chaplain Gaylord, of the Twelfth Massachusetts, read the President's Proclamation in a most impressive manner. Chaplain Reed, of the Thirteenth Pennsylvania, read selections of Scripture, and the hymn:

'My country, 'tis of thee.'

Chaplain Phillips, of the Ninth New York, offered prayer. Chaplain Quint, of the Second Massachusetts, read the army hymn, and also made the address of the day; and Chaplain Lasher, of the Fifth Connecticut, offered the concluding prayer, and after the 'Doxology,' pronounced the Benediction. The grand mass of soldiery, as brigade after brigade took their places in perfect order; the great number of State and National banners floating in the breeze; the respect of the men, with the devoutness of many, and especially the majestic music of the united bands pouring out 'America' and 'Old Hundred,' in which blended a multitude of voices, made it a scene long to be remembered. The author of the 'Army Hymn' has never yet heard his own poem sung in all its majesty. He never will till he hears it from thousands upon thousands of men in active service, waiting impatiently for the order to advance to victory, with the sunlight playing upon sabers of dragoons, on the pieces of artillery caps, and a forest of bayonets:

'O Lord of Hosts! Almighty King!
Behold the sacrifice we bring!
To every arm Thy strength impart,
Thy Spirit shed through every heart!

'Wake in our breasts the living fires,
The holy faith that warmed our sires;
Thy Hand hath made our Nation free;
To die for her is serving Thee.

'Be Thou a pillared flame to show
The midnight snare, the silent foe;
And when the battle thunders loud,
Still guide us in its moving cloud.

'God of all nations! Sovereign Lord!
In Thy dread name we draw the sword,
We lift the starry flag on high
That fills with light our stormy sky.

'No more its flaming emblems wave,
To bar from hope the trembling slave;
No more its radiant glories shine
To blast with woe one child of Thine.

'From treason's rent, from murder's stain,
Guard Thou its folds till Peace shall reign,
Till fort and field, till shore and sea,
Join our loud anthem, *Praise to Thee!*'"

No. 401.

"JESUS AND SHALL IT EVER BE."

Joseph Grigg, 1728—1768.

In Rev. Rufus W. Clark's life of John E. Emerson, it is related that while he was a boy an inquiry meeting was held in the church where he attended, at the close of which all who desired to converse with the minister on the subject of their personal salvation were requested to remain. John accepted the invitation and tarried. While sitting in his seat, he observed some boys in the gallery pointing at him and laughing. The blood rushed to his cheeks, and feeling keenly their ridicule, he took his hat in his hand to leave the house, but just as he was rising to go these lines flashed into his mind:

"Ashamed of Jesus, that dear Friend,
On Whom my hopes of heaven depend!"

In an instant he was ready to reply:

"No! when I blush be this my shame,
That I no more revere His name."

Immediately he resumed his seat, laid aside his hat, and resolved that, God helping him, he would strive, in spite of every obstacle, to obtain salvation.

No. 402.

"CHEER UP, MY SOUL, THERE IS A MERCY SEAT."

REV. JOHN NEWTON, 1725—1807.

In "New England Revivals," by Dr. Bennett Tyler, he gives an account of a youth converted in a revival at Canton, Connecticut, who after struggling for salvation for some time says of himself: "I remained in this sorrowful situation for several days, seeking relief, but refusing the precious balm of Gilead. A certain Monday in this month was a most trying day to me. It seemed as if the whole universe gazed, with an eye of contempt, on its sinful, wretched inhabitants. But, Oh! the following Wednesday! May that precious day never be erased from my memory; the day, as I hope, in which God met my poor, perishing soul. Having taken up the 'Hartford Collection of Hymns' I began to read the two hundred and seventy-fourth:

'Cheer up, my soul, there is a mercy seat,
Sprinkled with blood, where Jesus answers prayer;
There humbly cast thyself, beneath His feet,
For never needy sinner perished there.'

And truly, I said to myself, who can wish for a higher seat, than at the feet of Sovereign mercy? And my heart was now ready to thank God that I was in His hands."

No. 403.

"HARK! THE VOICE OF LOVE AND MERCY."

Jonathan Evans, 1748—1809.

At the beginning of the nineteenth century the religion of the Shetland Islands was a degenerated form of the Presbyterian Church of Scotland, that contained very little indeed of the life and power of Godliness. A mission of the Independent Church had been established and was beginning to infuse a more spiritual religion into the lives of the people.

Sinclair Thomson, a young man of twenty-five, was a member of the established church of the island, not only in good and regular standing, but by reason of considerable musical skill, holding the office of precentor of the parish, the duty of that office being to conduct the singing on all occasions of public worship. And yet young Thomson was a smuggler, and the keeper of a gin house, a great stickler for the orthodoxy of his church, but a stranger to anything like vital religion. One Sunday morning in 1809, he, with two other young men, were on their way to the parish church. There was to be no service there, but it was the law that, whenever a wedding was to take place, it should be proclaimed from the kirk pulpit three Sabbaths in succession. This was the duty of the precentor, and though no service should be held, still the proclamation must be made, and the two other men were taken along as witnesses. On the way the men became warm and stopped at a wayside cottage for rest and water. A woman was within, engaged in reading a little book. Thomson, finding out that the woman was not a member of the kirk, but of the mission church of the Independents, told her that she was doing wrong and that on his way back from the kirk he would stop and have a talk with her about it. This he did, but his words were such as might be expected from such a one as he; more decided than winning. The woman sat in silence. Stung a little that she gave him no reply, and half conscious that she was "answering a fool according to his folly," he became bitter and irritable in his language. Perceiving finally that he had plunged into a controversy where the contention was all on his own side, and somewhat at a loss how to close the interview, he finally asked, "Will you lend me that little book which you are reading?"

She held it out to him at once, with the words, "You are welcome to it as your own." He was surprised and pleased. The book proved to be on "The Propriety of Observing the Communion Every Sabbath," and the reading of it led him to looking up the passages of Scripture to which it referred, and this again to still further investigation, until at last he came to a point where he concluded that his own religion was only a cold formal thing devoid of life or reality. His first resort for comfort was in a reformation of his life, and of increased zeal in outward religious duties. He established family worship, admonished his neighbors of their sins, abandoned his smuggling, studied the Bible daily, and in all these ways went about to establish his own righteousness. All this gave him comfort, but why it failed he did not understand. He longed for some good minister, in whom he could confide, to guide him in the right way, but no such one was at his hand. The "missionary preachers" were twenty-four miles away, and to them he could not go. At last light broke in from a quarter quite unexpected.

He had by some means gained possession of one of the hymn books used by the Independents, and had learned some of their tunes. One day, while engaged in his house at some handiwork, he was singing some of those hymns to himself, almost unconsciously. It was the hymn commencing:

"Hark! the voice of love and mercy
Sounds aloud from Calvary;
See! it rends the rocks asunder,
Shakes the earth and veils the sky.
'It is finished:'
Hear the dying Savior cry."

Nothing in the hymn particularly drew his attention until he came to the last verse:

"Now redemption is completed,
Sin atoned, the curse removed;
Satan, death, and hell defeated,
As the rising fully proved.
All is finished:
There our hopes do rest unmoved."

The last line especially impressed him:

"There our hopes do rest unmoved."

He paused in his work, exclaiming, "Where, where?" He went back over the verses of the hymn to ascertain *where* the sinner's "hopes do rest unmoved." The Gospel provision shone in upon his mind, the full, blessed beam of the Sun of Righteousness. Sinclair Thomson soon began preaching and became a great power for good all over Shetland, preaching for nearly fifty years.

SINCLAIR THOMSON, or the "Shetland Apostle."

No. 404.

"HEAR, O SINNER! MERCY HAILS YOU."

REV. ANDREW REED, 1787—1862.

In his "Revival Lectures," President Finney says: "I once heard a celebrated organist produce a remarkable effect in a protracted meeting. The organ was a powerful one, and the double bass pipes were like thunder. The hymn was given out that has these lines:

'See the storm of vengeance gathering
  O'er the path you dare to tread!
Hark the awful thunder rolling
  Loud and louder o'er your head!
    Turn, O sinner!
Lest the lightning strike you dead.'

"When he came to these words, we first heard the distant roar of thunder, then it grew nearer and louder, till at the word 'louder,' there was a crash that seemed almost to overpower the whole congregation. Such things in their proper place do good. But common singing dissipates feeling. It should always be such as not to take away feeling, but to deepen it."

No. 405.

"FROM DEEP DISTRESS TO THEE I PRAY."

MILLS, Translator.

This is a translation of a hymn by Martin Luther, who based it on the one hundred and thirtieth Psalm, which he greatly loved. This hymn took a great hold upon the German people when it was first written, and was very soon being sung all over the country. On the sixth of May, of the year in which it was written, a poor old weaver sang it through the streets of Magdeburg and offered it for sale at a price that suited the poorest. He was cast into prison by the burgomaster, but two hundred citizens marched to the Town Hall, and would not leave till he was freed. This prayer psalm had also its comforting power on the one who wrote it. When Luther, during the Augsburg Diet, was at the castle of Coburg, and had to suffer much from inward and outward trials, he fell into a swoon. When he awoke from it, he said: "Come, and in defiance of the devil, let us sing the Psalm, 'From deep distress to Thee I pray'; let us sing it in full chorus, and extol and praise God." This hymn was also sung at the funeral of the great friend and protector of Luther, Frederick the Wise, in 1525. And when the body of Luther, himself, was on its way from Eisleben, where he died, to Wittenberg, where he lies buried, it rested for a night, February 20, 1546, in the church in Halle of which Justus Jonas, the bosom friend of Luther, was pastor. This hymn was given out by Jonas, and sung by the thousands who thronged and wept around Luther's coffin.

No. 406.

"I SAW ONE HANGING ON A TREE."

REV. JOHN NEWTON, 1725—1807.

A little Sunday school boy was badly wounded at a spinning mill in Dundee, Scotland. After being taken home, he lingered for a few days and then died. His mother came to the mill to see the boy's teacher, and tell him about his death. The teacher asked her how he died.

"He was singing all the time," said she.

"Tell me what he was singing?" said the teacher.

"He was singing:

'O, the Lamb, the loving Lamb,
The Lamb upon Calvary;
The Lamb that was slain, and liveth again,
To intercede for me.'"

NEWTON'S "Life of Christ."

No. 407.

"THE LORD'S MY SHEPHERD, I'LL NOT WANT."

Rev. William Whittingham.

Mr. Robert Pollock, author of "The Course of Time," also wrote "The Persecuted Family," a narrative of the sufferings of the Covenanters in the reign of Charles Second. It is the biography of the family of Rev. James Bruce, one of the clergymen who refused compliance with the orders of the king, and were therefore ejected from their pulpits and churches. After Mr. Bruce had been in this way turned out of both his church and his home, he retired to a little farm house four miles away from the village where he had preached, and continued preaching to such of his flock as he could gather together, in the fields and houses of the peasants. But soon the persecution became still more severe, and the ejected clergy were forbidden to preach even in the fields, and the people were forbidden under the severest penalties from giving them shelter or food. Mr. Bruce was now compelled to betake himself, with his family, to a wandering life, now sheltered in some barn; now in some shepherd's hut; and now exposed without cover to all sorts of weather. A cave on the banks of the Ayr became a place of their frequent resort. It had been formed in the precipitous banks by the hands of men, as a hiding-place in the former troublous times of Scotland, and was roomy enough to admit five or six persons. The entrance to this retreat was by rude and difficult steps, cut out of the stone; and over its mouth, concealing it from view, hung the straggling branches of the birch and hazel, that had struck their roots into the seams of the rock. Two or three rude seats, some straw and blankets, made up the furniture of the cave. And to this place, in the darkness of the night, did the peasants of the surrounding country come with food for their pastor and his family, and to receive in return instruction, advice, and comfort.

For nearly four years this cave was their home, and during this time many of his flock had been thrown into prison, and sent into banishment, had endured the cruelties of torture, or died on the scaffold, and although they had had many hair-breadth escapes, yet none of them had fallen into the hands of their enemies.

On a Sabbath evening in the month of September, Mr. Bruce, with his wife and children, left the cave, to meet some of his flock, in a wild glen in the neighborhood, where he was to deliver a sermon. When they arrived at the appointed place, there was about a score assembled—some of them stood, some seated themselves on the cold turf, while Mr. Bruce took his station by a large stone, on which he rested the Bible, and read, or rather repeated, for the night was dark, the following verses from the twenty-third Psalm:

"The Lord's my shepherd, I'll not want;
He makes me down to lie
In pastures green: He leadeth me
The quiet waters by.

"My soul he doth restore again;
And me to walk doth make
Within the paths of righteousness,
Ev'n for his own name's sake.

"Yea, though I walk in death's dark vale,
Yet will I fear none ill;
For thou art with me; and thy rod
And staff me comfort still."

And then the people sang the words their minister had read, joined him in prayer, and listened to a sermon from his lips, and were just receiving from his hands the benediction, when the services were interrupted by a company of soldiers, who had stolen upon them unperceived. They fled into a morass too soft to permit the pursuit of the soldiers who were on horseback, and so escaped except Mrs. Bruce, who was shot and almost instantly killed.

No. 408.

"WE ARE JOYOUSLY VOYAGING OVER THE MAIN."

Rev. William Hunter, 1811—1877.

Among the band of young converts, at Mr. Moody's Sunday school at Chicago, which all the time increased around him, was a little girl whose father owned a small vessel, in which he freighted lumber. Having given her own heart to the Savior, she tried to persuade her father to do the same. But he was a man having no taste for religion, though he was very fond of the child, whom he took with him on a certain voyage, during which she tried in vain to establish a prayer meeting in the little cabin, and to convert some of the crew.

On arriving at the lumber camp, this little missionary commenced a Sunday school, as nearly as possible like the North Market Mission. Not content with this, and hearing of another encampment of woodcutters similar to their own, she opened a second school among them also. During the severe northern winter she presided personally over these institutions, riding on horseback through the woods every Sunday, after the manner of the early Methodist pioneers. It may be supposed that these two schools in the woods were of a very simple character, since the little girl herself was the entire force of officers and teachers; and all the library and literature in use among them was her own little copy of the New Testament. The result of her labor cannot now be given; but it is easy to imagine the tender interest with which these rough woodsmen sat at the feet of their child missionary, charmed by her Christian courage, and cheered by her simple faith.

The lumber season being over, the little vessel started for Chicago. During the voyage a terrible storm arose, disabling the craft, and driving her rapidly toward a lee shore. The crew being completely exhausted, and expecting in a few minutes to be drowned, begged the little girl to pray for them, which she did, with the greatest composure. When she had told the good Lord all about them, and asked Him to take them out of their danger, if He thought best, and, above all things, to forgive their sins and make them ready for heaven, she began, in a clear sweet voice, to sing that little Sunday school hymn:

"We are joyously voyaging over the main,
Bound for the evergreen shore,
Whose inhabitants never of sickness complain,
And never see death any more;
Then let the hurricane roar,
It will the sooner be o'er;
We will weather the blast, and will land at last,
Safe on the evergreen shore."

With the song new strength and hope seemed to come to the arms and hearts of the crew; and renewing their efforts to weather the point which threatened their destruction, and aided perhaps by some slight change in the wind, or abatement of the storm, the little craft weathered the rocks of the headland close enough to toss a biscuit ashore, and then swung out safely on the open course for home.

"D. L. Moody, and His Work," by DANIELS.

In the Life of "Uncle John Vassar" by his nephew, Rev. T. E. Vassar, occurs the following incident: "I shall not soon forget the delight with which I first heard him singing a song, whose lively notes and cheerful, rejoicing confidence accorded admirably with his own spirit. It was toward the close of a crowded meeting in a long chapel. He rose after a prayer, and turned round in the aisle so as to face the congregation. His right hand held the left by two fingers, and kept it out of the way behind his back. Standing in his humble but easy manner, he began in a low voice:

'We are joyously voyaging over the main,
Bound for the evergreen shore,
Whose inhabitants never of sickness complain,
And never see death any more.'

Warming as he went on, he kept looking over the audience to observe their feeling; and before he had finished he was clapping his hands quietly in time to the tune, and leading us all in the chorus, like an enthusiastic singing teacher. The hymn, though familiar now, was then new to most of us, but we could not help joining with Uncle John, to the best of our ability, in the chorus. Few, perhaps none, went away from the meeting that night without resolving to secure transportation in that good ship, for which, according to his wont, Uncle John was looking up passengers."

No. 409.

"ALAS! AND DID MY SAVIOR BLEED."

REV. ISAAC WATTS, 1674—1748.

In the same book, in connection with the last anecdote, the following incident is given: "There is one tune he used to sing which we call 'Vassar' still. The words he used to put to it were,

'Alas, and did my Savior bleed';

"There was a Catholic woman who would not listen to him or take a tract from his hand, but she finally did suffer him to sing. And to this tune, whose proper name I do not know, he sang the verse:

'But drops of grief can ne'er repay
The debt of love I owe
Here, Lord, I give myself away—
'Tis all that I can do.'

and at its close she was utterly subdued and ultimately became a true Christian. Her experience she used to sum up in the words, 'Ah, those drops of grief, those drops of grief—I couldn't get over them.' "

No. 410.

"THE VOICE OF FREE GRACE CRIES, 'ESCAPE TO THE MOUNTAIN.' "

Rev. Richard Burdsall, 1735—1824.

In the autobiography of Dr. Lyman Beecher, it is related that: "One Sabbath evening, when there was a meeting of such persons as desired personal conversation on the subject of religion, many persons being present, and while quite a number of those who used to come to his aid on such occasions were engaged in conversation with such persons as had come up for religious instruction and guidance, he came to me and said, 'I want you to sing now. We'll sing:

"The voice of free grace cries, 'escape to the mountain'."

He then called for the attention of all to the hymn which was sung by all who were disposed to take part. At its close, he made a few remarks, and the conversations were resumed. The next day, or soon after, I met him, when he said to me, 'Well, one person gave up his heart during the singing of the hymn, as he told me afterward, and probably there were others of whom I had not heard.'"

No. 411.

"WELCOME, HAPPY MORNING! AGE TO AGE SHALL SAY."

This hymn was written toward the close of the sixth century, by Venantius Honorius Clementianus Fortunatus, Bishop of Poictiers.

"Evangelical Hymnal," No. 596.

Jerome of Prague, the celebrated lay reformer, after once recanting and acknowledging the errors of his companions, Wickliffe and Huss, and assenting to the condemnation of the latter, was troubled over what he had done and demanded a new trial. At this trial he manifested great courage and replied to the charges of heresy with eloquence and power. He was, however, condemned to martyrdom, and burned at the stake. After he had been tied to the stake, he observed the executioner about to set fire to the fagots behind his back, and cried out to him, "Bring thy torch hither; perform thy office before my face. Had I feared death, I might have avoided it." As the wood began to blaze he sang this hymn, which the violence of the flames about him did not interrupt.

No. 412.

"COME SAINTS AND SINNERS HEAR ME TELL."

In an address delivered at the Baptist Church, Hyde Park, Massachusetts, by Hon. Elijah A. Morse, in 1887, he relates the following incident: "Some time ago an old man came to me in Canton and said, 'I am going to such a place, won't you let me stay all night; I haven't any money, and I can't get there tonight; won't you give me a place to sleep?'

"I have known the old man for several years, and I said, 'Come in, old man, and you'll be welcome.'

"Well, he spent the night with me, and in the morning he said, 'Mr. Morse, you have been very kind to me; I haven't any money, and I know you don't want any money, but I'll tell you what I'll do to pay you. I'll sing you a song my mother used to sing eighty years ago.'

"I called my little sons around me, and said, 'Old man, let us have the song.' It was about union with God. It went something like this:

'Come saints and sinners hear me tell
  The wonders of Immanuel,
Who saved me from a burning hell,
And brought my soul with Him to dwell;
  And gave me heavenly union.

'When Jesus saw me from on high—
  Beheld my soul in ruin lie,
He looked on me with pitying eye
And said to me as He passed by,
  "With God you have no union."

'Then I began to weep and pray;
  I looked this way and that to fly;
But still I found no refuge nigh;
Then sought salvation for to buy;
  But still I found no union.

'But when I hated all my sin,
  My dear Redeemer took me in,
And with his blood He washed me clean,
And O what seasons I have seen,
  E'er since I felt this union.

'I praised the Lord both night and day,
I went from house to house to pray,
And if I met one on the way
Always I found something to say,
About this heavenly union.

'Come heaven and earth unite your lays,
And give to Jesus endless praise;
And O! my soul look up and gaze!
He bleeds, He dies, your debt He pays,
And gives you heavenly union.

'O, could I like an angel sound
Salvation through the world around;
Old Satan's kingdom to confound,
And triumph on Immanuel's ground,
And cause a general union!

'And when we reach those blessed plains
Where love divine triumphant reigns,
We'll bid adieu to all our pains,
And join the sweet angelic strains,
To one eternal union.

'There we shall see as we are seen,
Without a veil of flesh between;
And not a cloud to intervene,
For all is pleasant and serene,
In climes of heavenly union.

'Almighty God, teach every tongue,
To shout and sing the Union Song;
All praises to Thy Name belong;
Let Zion sing, "Thy kingdom come,"
And fill this world with union.' "

No. 413.

"COME YE SINNERS POOR AND NEEDY."

JOSEPH HART.

"When the richest American of his day was in his last fatal sickness, a Christian friend proposed to sing for him, and the hymn he named was, 'Come ye sinners poor and needy.'

" 'Yes, yes,' replied the dying millionaire, 'sing that for me; I feel poor and needy.' Yet at that moment the stock markets of the globe were watching and waiting for the demise of the man who could shake them with a nod of his head! 'Poor and needy!' How the sand sweeps from under a man's soul in such an hour as that!"

THEODORE CUYLER.

No. 414.

"GIVE TO THE WINDS THY FEARS."

REV. PAUL GERHARDT, 1607—1676.

Translated by REV. JOHN WESLEY, 1703—1791.

When the "Women's Crusade" against the liquor saloons was commenced in Ohio, this hymn was used before they started out on their first effort. The account is thus given in the Centennial Temperance Volume:

"Mrs. Cowden, our Methodist minister's wife, was then requested to sing a familiar air:

'Give to the winds thy fears,
Hope and be undismayed:
God hears thy sighs and counts thy tears;
God shall lift up thy head.'

And while thus engaged the women, seventy-five in number, fell in line, two and two, and proceeded first to the drug stores, and then to the hotels and saloons. Thus the first brave consecrated company went out for duty for God and humanity in the Women's Crusade. Till the middle of the following June, they visited the saloons almost daily."

No. 415.

"ES WOLL UNS GOTT GENADIG SEYN."

REV. MARTIN LUTHER, 1483—1546.

"MAY GOD UNTO US GRACIOUS BE."

Translated by ARTHUR TOZER RUSSEL, 1806—

Spangenburg relates a story about this hymn. The Chief Councillor and Captain Commandant of the Duke of Regenstein, Hans de Lunderstedt, was a zealous advocate of the new doctrine, to which his master, the old Duke, was bitterly opposed. The old man had never read or understood a word of Luther's teaching, and would have nothing to do with anything new. The priests had told him that it was execrable heresy that was now abroad; and filled his ears with all manner of evil reports. A preacher one Sunday allowed the people to sing for the first tme *"Es woll uns Gott genadig seyn,"* and also *"Ein feste Burg ist unser Gott."* This was told to the Duke, and represented as a most disgraceful infraction of all Church order, and a most imprudent and outrageous attack on her doctrines.

The Duke was furious. He went instantly for Hans de Lunderstedt, and ordered him to drag the rebellious preacher by the hair of his head to Halberstadt, to be examined as to these heretical hymns, and to suffer the punishment due to his wicked presumption. The wise commandant humbly besought the Duke to be cautious; for, after all, the hymns might not have been so bad as the priests had represented. He said that he was well acquainted with the offending preacher, and knew him to be a good citizen and a loyal subject, who would never allow anything improper to be sung in his church.

The Duke, still angry, replied: "The hymns may be what they please; it is enough for me that they are Luther's and therefore must be heretical. I will allow nothing of that sort in my duchy."

The captain inquired whether his grace really knew what the hymns were? The Duke answered, "Yes, one begins, '*Ein feste Burg ist unser Gott,*' and the other, '*Es woll uns Gott genadig seyn.*' I will not allow any such stuff to be sung in my churches. Go and bring the insolent heretic before me instantly."

The captain quietly rejoined; "Most gracious master! you know my fidelity to your interests. I beseech you to consider well what you are saying, and wishing to do. Does not your grace want God to be still your stronghold? Are you not willing that men in your duchy should praise and glorify Him? Do you not also wish that God may be gracious to us now, as the hymn expresses it; and that men should call upon Him? Who else but God would be gracious to us? Is it the favor of the devil that we should seek?"

The old Duke was struck by this representation of the matter, and the wise and good councillor went on to say that the hymns were not made by Luther, but that they were psalms of David, and words of Holy Scripture which Luther had only translated into German, so as to be understood by the people, and turned into verse, that they might be sung. The spirit of these hymns is only the spirit of prayer to God, bringing peace and consolation to poor troubled men. The Duke being now thoroughly interested, Hans read to him the whole of the hymns. The Duke was more than satisfied; his anger was turned away, and a desire was excited in him to read Luther's other writings. That he did so, and that he profited by the advice of his faithful and pious councillor, we have good reason to believe, for shortly after he opened the door for the introduction of the new teaching into his duchy, and was a warm friend and patron of the preachers of the Gospel.

LUTHER'S *Table-Talk.*

No. 416.

"NUN BITTEN WIR DEN HEILIGEN GEIST."

"NOW PRAY WE ALL GOD, THE COMFORTER."

Translated by ARTHUR TOZER RUSSEL, 1806.

One of the converted students of Wittenberg was the son of the Burgermeister of Zullichau. The young graduate and divine preached the first Gospel sermon ever heard in the church of his native town. He began by singing the hymn, *"Nun bitten wir den Heiligen Geist."* If the people had ever heard *"Veni Creator Spiritus,"* the Latin invocation had fallen on ears unintelligent and unmoved, compared with the effect produced by the plain words heard in their own tongue from the earnest preacher. The Burgermeister was so enraged that he rose up and hastened from the church, exclaiming, "Now we invoke the devil!" But this interruption only riveted the attention of the audience upon the son of the graceless father.

LUTHER'S *Table-Talk.*

A learned doctor in Frankfort was at one time earnestly refuting the new heresy of Luther. The people listened patiently for a time, but at length as with one voice, raised the tune to the hymn, *"Nun bitten wir den Heiligen Geist."* The preacher recommenced after they had sung, but the people again interrupted him with the hymn, *"Nun freut euch, liebe Christen, gemein";* (Dear Christian saints lift up your hearts in joy). The preacher was obliged to leave the ground in possession of his psalm-singing opponents.

LUTHER'S *Table-Talk.*

No. 417.

"SWEET HOUR OF PRAYER, SWEET HOUR OF PRAYER."

W. W. WALFORD.

"NEARER MY GOD TO THEE."

MRS. SARAH FLOWER ADAMS, 1805—1848.

Mrs. Merriam Grant, one of the ladies injured in the terrible railroad accident at Chatsworth, Illinois, in 1887, tells the following pathetic incident of the disaster. She was in the rear car with her husband. In the car was a company of six people. In order that they might sit together, Mr. and Mrs. Grant changed seats with a young man and his bride. Their courtesy saved their lives, for the young people were both killed. Mrs. Grant thought this party were theatrical people, or concert singers, they were so jolly and sang so well. They could sing, and they laughed and told stories and anticipated the pleasure of the trip until late at night. Then Mrs. Grant composed herself to sleep in her chair, covering her face with her handkerchief. Nearly everybody in the car was quiet but the jolly party of six. About this time the young bride was requested to sing "Sweet Hour of Prayer." Something in the desire to sleep and rest recalled the sweet old song. The young woman sang; all listened; while the train sped on.

"Sweet hour of prayer, sweet hour of prayer,
That calls me from a world of care,
And bids me at my Father's throne
Make all my wants and wishes known."

There was a pause, and the clear voice went on again:

"And since He bids me seek His face,
Believe His word, and trust His grace,
I'll cast on Him my every care
And wait for thee, sweet hour of prayer."

Oh, how little did the singer and her audience think that, to most of them, the morning would never come for another "Sweet hour of prayer!" And then what was it? Did they sing it as the last and most fitting song before closing their eyes to sleep; or did the angel of death bring the thought to their minds? Whatever it was, all raised their voices in that grandest of prayers, "Nearer, my God, to Thee," and all, singing it, went to their death.

"Though like a wanderer, the sun gone down,
Darkness be over me, my rest a stone"

went the melody above the roar of the doomed train. Their sun had gone down, but they did not know it. Darkness would soon be over them, but they knew it not. And as the little gleam of fire appeared, far down the track, their voices swelled in,

"Yet in my dreams I'd be,
Nearer, my God, to Thee."

The speed of the train increased down the grade. Again the song swelled:

"There let the way appear,
Steps unto heaven."

The way was already in sight:

"All that Thou sendest me,
In mercy given."

And then, with but a moment of life left for each—even when poor Edward McClintock's hand was giving its last desperate wrench to the throttle of his engine—the singers sang:

"Angels to beckon me,
Nearer my God to Thee."

Enough. It was finished. The engines struck the frail bridge and it sank. The car containing the singers crashed like a thunderbolt through the two cars in front of it, killing and grinding as a foot kills a worm. In the same instant another car crashed through it and the singers were dead.

Peoria Transcript.

No. 418.

"HOW BRIGHT THESE GLORIOUS SPIRITS SHINE."

W. Cameron, 1751—1811.

An evangelist, who did much for the temporal and spiritual welfare of the soldiers of the Crimean War, and by his cheerful manner won many of them to Christ, was returning one night from before Sebastopol to his comfortless lodgings at Balaklava, and wading almost ankle-deep in mud; he lifted up his eyes and viewed the bright, calm stars that shone overhead, and his soul soaring beyond them, he cheered his toilsome way by singing to a well-known tune the inspiring hymn beginning:

"How bright these glorious spirits shine!
Whence all their bright array?
How came they to the blissful seats
Of everlasting day?

"Lo, these are they from sufferings great,
Who came to realms of light,
And in the blood of Christ have washed
Those robes that shine so bright."

Next day, as he was on his way to the trenches, he fell in with a poor soldier in miserable circumstances; his clothing was meager, tattered, and muddy, and his toes were sticking out at the side of his wornout shoes. The evangelist, Mr. Matheson, asked, in his frank way, how he was getting on, and seeing his wretched condition, gave him half a sovereign to buy a pair of shoes. The soldier replied, that, although he was far from being well or comfortable in mind, he was much better than he was yesterday. This excited Mr. Matheson's curiosity, and he pressed him to tell why he was so excessively wretched yesterday, which he did with some hesitancy and reluctance.

"As I thought," said the soldier, "of all we had passed through since we came out here, that we had been before this ugly place so long, and that we appeared as far from taking it as the first day we sat down before it, I was perfectly miserable, and could hardly have been worse; death seemed preferable to life, and I resolved I would kill myself and be done with it. I took up my musket and went down there about eleven o'clock last night, and was making all ready to dispatch myself, when a person I could not distinguish in the darkness passed down near me, wading through the mud, but apparently in a happy mood of mind; for he was singing:

'How bright these glorious spirits shine'

in a tune with which I was familiar, and I said to myself, 'Well, now, this is very cowardly, for that man's circumstances are, no doubt, as bad as mine, and yet he seems to be happy'; but on listening to the words he was singing, I thought he must be in possession of a source of happiness and have a something to support him to which I was a stranger. I wished I only knew how to be as happy as he was, and with that I put my musket under my arm and returned, and I feel better today, and more resolved to bear the worst."

How great was his surprise to be told that the singer who had charmed away his evil spirit was now before him.

"Was it you? Then I won't keep your half sovereign. I won't keep it now, for your singing last night has given me much more than I can express." Mr. Matheson told him of his own source of happiness, and pointed him to the Cross and the Savior, and the unhappy soldier of the Crimea became a joyous soldier of Christ.

E. P. HAMMOND.

No. 419.

"THERE IS A GATE THAT STANDS AJAR."

LYDIA BAXTER, 1809—1874.

At a meeting of the Wesleyan Missionary Society in Exeter Hall, London, in 1887, Dr. Wenyon, Medical Missionary from South China, said: "A man came to me for an operation. As I found that the action of the heart was very weak, I asked if he could do without chloroform. He was a timid man. He was afraid, he said; but after considering a moment, he said: 'I will stand it if you will let me sing.' I said, 'Sing away as much as you like, my friend.' I began to operate, and he began to sing, in the Chinese version:

'There is a gate that stands ajar,
And through its portals gleaming,
A radiance from the cross afar,
A Savior's love revealing.
Oh, depth of mercy, can it be
That gate was left ajar for me,
Was left ajar for me?'

I performed the operation, and still he was singing, and he never flinched."

Medical Missionary Record, February, 1888.

A pretty commentary on the word "ajar" as used in this

hymn comes from a little boy, and is related in the "Golden Rule."

"Ray," I said, "set the door ajar for mamma."

"Yes, ma'am." And the eager little feet rushed across the floor and opened the door wide.

"Why, my dear child," I said, "don't you know what 'ajar' means? It means that you should open the door just a little bit."

"The boy stopped in the middle of the floor, and gave me an astonished look out of his blue eyes, as he said, 'Why, mamma! don't you know the verse, "There is a gate that stands ajar?" And do you think that Jesus would open the heaven door just a little bit? I tell you "ajar" means very, very wide open.' "

No. 420.

"BRIGHT SPARKLES IN THE CHURCH-YARD."

This is one of the old-time slave songs of the South, sung by the Fisk Jubilee Singers.

"There were two young girls, and both were inmates of a gilded palace of sin in the city. One was hardened in her sin—the other had only waded ankle deep into the black moat which circles the walls of perdition. The other night they went to hear the Jubilee Singers, and sat unnoticed in the gallery. The sweet, tender music, so touching and true to nature, entered like a limpid stream into the soul of the younger girl, and filled her whole heart. She leaned forward and caught every word, with her eyes shining and her lips trembling. People turned round and wondered at the fair face, and watched her soul shining through her great eyes, but they never suspected who she was or whence she had come. There she sat still and immobile, with her small, gloved hands tightly clenched, and every nerve in her little body strung to an almost painful tension. All was still in the pavilion. The very gas lights held themselves motionless, as if afraid to make a sound. The great audience was hushed. And then a note sweet and tender, but full and rich as moonlight, swelled and rose like a sea, and then, like a shower of pearls falling through the sounding waters, a woman's voice sang:

'Bright sparkles in the church-yard,
Give light unto the tomb;
Bright summer-spring's over—
Sweet flowers in their bloom.'

The girl in the gallery gave a great, shuddering sob. The singer looked up and went on:

'My mother once—
My mother twice—
In the heaven she'll rejoice,
In the heaven once—
In the heaven twice—
In the heaven she'll rejoice.'

"Again the girl in the gallery gave a long, shuddering sob, and hid her white stricken face in her trembling hands. But still the music fluttered about her like the rustling of an angel's wings:

"Oh mother, don't you love your darling child?
Oh, rock me in the cradle all the day.'

She sat still and heard till the last cadence of the music had wandered out into the moonlight, where the angels, who wished to learn it by heart, caught it up, and bore it in triumph into Heaven. 'I must go from here,' said the girl hoarsely, 'Let me go, don't follow me—I will be better soon.' Her comrade reasoned with her, but she kept saying hoarsely, 'Let me go—I will be better soon.' She hurried out and fled like a frightened deer. She was mad! Her eyes were hot and dry, her brain was bursting, and all the while a wondrous choir was singing in her ears:

> 'Bright sparkles in the church-yard,
> Give light unto the tomb;
> Bright summer-spring's over—
> Sweet flowers in their bloom.'

"She fled like a hunted thing till the lights of the city were far behind and she was alone on a country road. She stopped to rest a moment, but the chorus went onward through the sky and she could not stop, for the words were beckoning to her:

> 'My mother once—
> My mother twice—
> In the heaven she'll rejoice.'

"Tireless she followed on, on, on, the long, long night. The moon went down and she grew blind and staggered and groped her way, but still she said hoarsely, 'I must go on. I'll be better soon.' In the morning a farmer threw open his door and saw lying on his steps the soiled figure of a girl. He picked her up and laid her on his own bed, and his wife laid the wild, pleading face against her warm bosom. A stream of music reached the ears of the dying girl:

> 'Oh, mother, don't you love your darling child?
> Oh rock me in the cradle all the day.'

She sank back with a weak, pleased smile. 'Rock me, mother, that's it—oh! how nice—how nice it is. Oh, rock me, mother, rock me, mother. I am too tired to say my prayers tonight, mother. Let me sleep, mother, and kiss me, but let me sleep—sleep!' And she closed her eyes and slept, and the choir in Paradise, lest they might wake her, sang softly:

'My mother once—
My mother twice—
In the heaven she'll rejoice,
In the heaven once—
In the heaven twice—
In the heaven she'll rejoice.'"
Toronto Evening News, October 10, 1881.

No. 421.

"O, SING OF JESUS, LAMB OF GOD."

T. C. Kane, 1830.

"In the year 1874, the Fisk Jubilee Singers visited this country. (England.) At this time a gentleman in London heard them singing the hymn, 'O sing of Jesus, Lamb of God.' He listened with manifest pleasure to the beautiful hymn, and so pleased was he that he offered the singers a sum of money if they would sing that particular hymn wherever they went. They promised, and one night, when singing it at a meeting at Dublin, a lady came forward to the president at the close, and told him that she had been wandering in darkness for thirty years, but that night she got her eyes opened while they were singing the chorus, 'I'm redeemed, I'm redeemed through the blood of the Lamb that was slain.' The thrilling words had gone right to her heart, and revealed Jesus to her for the first time."
Christian Herald, January 27, 1887.

No. 422.

"PATRIOTIC SINGING."

I remember of passing, one hot day in the summer of 1862, the mansion of a wealthy Virginian whose sympathies were strongly with the other side. Colonel Webster was riding some little distance in advance of the column, and as he arrived opposite the house, the blinds were suddenly closed with a loud slam, indicating that the lordly descendant of the Cavaliers was not over and above pleased with the approach of the Yankees. This act greatly amused the Colonel, and he laughed until he grew red in the face. Then, evidently having hit upon a pleasant expedient by which the recreant Southerner could be reminded of his abandoned loyalty, he allowed the regiment to pass on until the colors came opposite the house. The order to halt was then given, and the men were brought to the front.

While they were wondering "what was up," the band came down from the head of the column and formed in front of the house. "Now, Mr. Martland," said the Colonel, addressing the bandmaster, "I want you to see if you can't warm this old fellow up a little. He's probably a proud descendant of England—most of these high-toned Virginians are—so suppose you give him 'America,' to start with; that's partly English, you know." And the concert began with the soothing strains of 'My Country, 'tis of thee,' the regiment lustily singing the last verse, but only a slight tremor was noticeable in the blinds—none of them was opened. "Now try 'Yankee Doodle,' " said the Colonel. "Perhaps that will remind him of the way his forefathers and ours fought together in the War of the Revolution." So "Yankee Doodle" was played, but still there was no evidence of life within the mansion.

"I think he must be a hard customer," said the Colonel. "It may be that the 'Star Spangled Banner' will fetch him. Try that." And the beautiful strains of that grand old song were sent out with a sweetness that should have moved the old man's heart if it had been as hard even as stone, but still the blinds were unyielding. Then the "Red, White, and Blue," "Hail Columbia," and other patriotic airs were in turn tried, but still the old Virginian remained obstinate. Even "Carry me back to old Virginia" had not the slightest effect. Just as we were beginning to think that we would be obliged to give it up as a bad job, Martland struck up "Home, Sweet Home," and the piece was rendered with a degree of beauty and feeling that would be hard to excel. As the last notes died away, the blinds flew open, and the door, too, and the old Virginian stepped out upon the piazza with a broad smile upon his face. He had surrendered, apparently only because he felt obliged to, but now that the ice was broken, he became genial and even hospitable. The officers of the regiment were invited in, and such refreshments as the house afforded were offered them, while the wish of the men, quite loudly expressed, that the old flag be put out, was complied with; and with the "Stars and Stripes" floating from an upper window, and the old man standing at the gate laughing, we moved on.

Newspaper clipping. 1888.

No. 423.

"YES, MY NATIVE LAND, I LOVE THEE."

REV. S. F. SMITH, 1808.

Some fifty years ago there took place in a rural town in New York a simple service that touched the hearts of all who witnessed it. It had reference to the departure of a missionary for Oregon. The missionary was a young lady, greatly beloved in the town. She was a member of the choir or body of singers. A hymn, then familiar, was given out by the minister, beginning:

"Yes, my native land, I love thee."

As it was being sung, many of the singers were deeply affected, and one by one ceased to sustain the simple melody. The young missionary found herself at last singing nearly or quite alone:

"Scenes of sacred peace and pleasure,
Holy days and Sabbath bell
Richest, brightest, sweetest treasure,
Can I say a last farewell?
Can I leave you,
Far in heathen lands to dwell?

"Yes, I hasten from you gladly—
From the scenes I loved so well:
Far away, ye billows bear me
Lovely, native land, farewell:
Pleased I leave thee,
Far in heathen lands to dwell.

"In the deserts let me labor;
On the mountains let me tell
How He died—the blessed Savior—
To redeem a world from hell;
Let me hasten,
Far in heathen lands to dwell."

Years afterward, this incident was distinctly remembered when it was announced that this woman's influence as the wife of a pioneer missionary had contributed much to bringing to the United States a territory larger in extent than Great Britain and Ireland, and nearly four times as large as New England. This vast region is now known as the State of Oregon, and the Territories of Washington and Idaho. In the spring of 1836, two newly married missionaries and their wives began a bridal tour from New York to Walla Walla, a distance of thirty-five hundred miles. The expedition is now famous in history as "Whitman and Spaulding's," the names of the two clergymen who, with their wives, then started on horseback for the Rocky Mountains and the regions beyond.

In this sublime journey into the regions of nature's most stupendous monuments, the health of Mrs. Spaulding failed. "Do not put me on the horse again," she said one morning. "Leave me here, and save yourselves for the great work. Tell mother I am glad I came." But her strength revived, and she went on. Twenty-five hundred miles from home, the party looked down from the Pacific slope, and beheld a new empire. It was a July day, under a blazing sun. The crowns of mountains filled the air around them. Before them lay the vast and mysterious rivers of the Platte, Yellowstone, and Columbia, with their luxuriant valleys.

The missionaries rested. "Let us have a season of devotion," said their leader. They lifted the American flag in the clear air. They then laid a Bible beneath it on the ground and opened it. Then they knelt under the flag and around the open Bible, and took formal possession of the western side of the continent for the Christian Church. Our history has few pictures that are more poetic. It was like Balboa at Panama or La Salle on the Mississippi.

Youth's Companion, March 19, 1885.

No. 424.

"I'M A PILGRIM BOUND FOR GLORY."

In "The Salvation War" for 1884, it is related: "In connection with the prosecution of eleven of our officers and soldiers in the university city of New Haven for singing in the streets, one of the most interesting episodes in the Army's history took place. Against the attack made upon us at the instance of Christian authority, we were defended by a Jewish solicitor, who called upon the court to allow him to prove that the singing of our soldiers was neither irreverent, blasphemous, nor disorderly, but quite unobjectionable. So the eleven soldiers sang in court:

'I'm a pilgrim bound for glory,
I'm a pilgrim going home;
Come and hear me tell my story—
All that love the Savior come.'

"It seems that they sang in the dock with their usual happiness, clapping their hands for joy. The female captain explained that the object of the army in singing in the street was to beseech sinners to make their peace with God and to become good citizens. Judge Deming, to his honor, decided that we had not broken the law nor intended to do so."

No. 425.

"O TELL ME NO MORE OF THIS WORLD'S VAIN STORE."

JOHN GAMBOLD, 1711—1771.

In the life of Rev. Rowland Hill, by the Rev. Edwin Sidney, it is said that during the last eighteen months, or thereabouts, of Mr. Hill's life, he engaged in almost every cause, with the impression that it would probably be the last effort he should make for it. His friend, Mr. George Clayton, in a letter to me, thus strikingly depicted his manner and feelings on one of these occasions:

"The last time he occupied my pulpit at Walworth, when he preached excellently for an hour on behalf of a charitable institution (it was in the winter, twelve months before his death), he retired to the vestry after service, under feelings of great and manifest exhaustion. There he remained, till every individual save the pew-openers, his servant, and myself, had left the place. At length, he seemed, with some reluctance, to have summoned energy enough to take his departure, intimating that it was in all probability the last time he should preach in Walworth. Charles (Mr. Hill's servant) went before to open the carriage door—the pew-openers remained in the vestry. I offered my arm, which he declined, and then followed him as he passed down the aisle of the chapel. The lights were nearly extinguished, the silence was profound, nothing indeed was heard, but the slow majestic tread of his own footsteps, when in an undertone he thus soliloquized:

'And when I'm to die, "Receive me," I'll cry,
For Jesus hath loved me, I cannot tell why:
But this I do find, we two are so joined,
He'll not live in glory and leave me behind.'

To my heart this was a scene of unequalled solemnity, nor can I ever recur to it without a revival of that hallowed, sacred, shuddering sympathy, which it originally awakened."

No. 426.

"I HEARD THE VOICE OF JESUS SAY."

REV. HORATIUS BONAR, 1808.

A poor English girl in Miss Leigh's home in Paris, ill in body and hopeless in spirit, was greatly affected by hearing some children singing:

"I heard the voice of Jesus say."

When they came to the words "Weary and worn and sad," she moaned, "That's me! That's me! What did He do? Fill it up, fill it up!"

She never rested until she had heard the whole of the hymn which tells how Jesus gives rest to such. By and by she asked, "Is that true?" On being answered, "Yes," she asked, "Have you come to Jesus? Has He given you rest?" "He has." Raising herself she asked, "Do you mind my coming very close to you? May be it would be easier to go to Jesus with one who has been before than to go to Him alone." So saying she nestled her head on the shoulder of her who watched, and clutching her as one in the agony of death, she murmured, "Now, try and take me with you to Jesus."

The Sunday at Home.

No. 427.

"THOU GOD OF TRUTH AND LOVE."

REV. CHARLES WESLEY, 1708—1788.

Here is a love story in a hymn. The author remained single until forty years old. Then he began to doubt whether this was the proper thing to do. "How know I whether it is best to marry or no?" said he, and soon after he met a fine young lady in Wales, and she so impressed him that he concluded to ask his brother John about it; but John was a cautious adviser on such a delicate matter as this, although bold enough on ordinary occasions, and he "neither opposed, nor much encouraged," the courtship. Then the lover went to another clerical friend. He also was cautious and advised him "to pray and wait for a Providential opening." This he did. He prayed, and he waited, and the more he prayed and the more he waited, the more he concluded that he wanted that girl. And as he thought, and prayed, and waited, he writes that he "expressed the various searchings of his heart, in many hymns on the important occasion." He has not told us in so many words which of his hymns these are, but in the same year when he was married, he issued a volume of hymns containing quite a number of pieces entitled "Hymns for Christian Friends," and there is good reason to believe that they are the hymns referred to and that they were first addressed to one Christian friend in particular. These hymns have required some alteration, as can easily be imagined, to fit them for our public service of song.

Possibly some of you have thought of wedding days, and it may do you no harm to hear Charles Wesley's description of his. Here it is, taken from his diary:

Saturday, April 8, 1749.

'Sweet day! so cool, so calm, so bright,
The bridal of the earth and sky.'

Not a cloud was to be seen from morning till night. I rose at four; spent three hours and a half in prayer or singing, with my brother, with Sally, with Beck. At eight I led my Sally to church. Her father, sisters, Lady Rice (?), Grace Bowers, Betty Williams and, I think, Billy Tucker and Mr. James were all the persons present. At the church door, I thought of the prophecy of a jealous friend, that if 'we were even at the church door to be married, she was sure, by revelation, that we could get no farther.' We both smiled at the remembrance. We got farther. Mr. Gwynne gave her to me (under God). My brother joined our hands. It was a most solemn season of love. Never had I more of the Divine presence in the sacrament. My brother gave out the following hymn:

'Come, thou Everlasting Lord.'

He then prayed over us in strong faith. We walked back to the house and joined again in prayer. Prayer and thanksgiving was our whole employment. We were cheerful without mirth; serious without sadness."

No. 428.

"WORSHIP AND THANKS AND BLESSING."

REV. CHARLES WESLEY, 1708—1788.

The title of this hymn given to it by its author suggests the circumstances under which it was written; it was "written after a deliverance in a Tumult." It is scarcely conceivable to us that in England, a professedly Christian country, no longer ago than the time of the Wesleys, ministers of the Gospel traveling from place to place, were in danger of being set upon by mobs, and their very lives put in jeopardy, for no other cause but the fact that they preached the Gospel outside the pale of the Established Church. But it is strictly true, nevertheless, and history records many instances. Here is one recorded by Mr. Wesley himself. It occurred in 1747 in a place called Devizes.

"After riding two or three hundred yards," says Mr. Wesley, "I looked back and saw Mr. Merton on the ground, in the midst of the mob, and two bull dogs upon him. One was first let loose, which leaped at the horse's nose; but the horse with his foot beat him down. The other fastened on his nose, and hung there, till Mr. Merton, with the butt end of his whip, felled him to the ground. Then the first dog, recovering, flew at the horse's breast and fastened there. The beast reared up and Mr. Merton slid gently off. The dog kept his hold till the flesh tore off. Then some of the men took off the dogs, and others cried, 'Let them alone.' I stopped the horse and delivered him to my friend, who remounted with great composure, and we rode on leisurely as before till out of sight."

It was fresh from such a scene as this, that Mr. Wesley wrote this hymn and gave it this descriptive title.

No. 429.

"GOD OF MY LIFE, WHAT JUST RETURN."

Rev. Charles Wesley, 1708—1788.

A few months after the conversion of Mr. Wesley, he was taken so seriously ill that he did not expect to recover. When restored to health, he wrote this hymn as a song of gratitude for his recovery. Some of the omitted stanzas refer to this personal experience. Like these:

"Jesus to my deliverance flew,
When sunk in mortal pangs I lay;
Pale death his ancient Conqueror knew,
And trembled and ungrasped his prey.

"The fever turned its backward course,
Arrested by Almighty power;
Sudden expired its fiery force,
And anguish gnawed my side no more."

No. 430.

"GLORY TO GOD WHOSE SOVEREIGN GRACE."

Rev. Charles Wesley, 1708—1788.

George Whitefield, the celebrated evangelist, was once in Bristol, England, and spoke of visiting America to endeavor to convert the savages of the great Western continent. The friends to whom he spoke exclaimed, "What need of going to America to convert savage Indians? Have we not savages enough at home? If you want to convert Indians, there are colliers enough at Kingswood." Kingswood was a wood near Bristol which had once belonged to the king, but coal had been discovered there, and in the time of Whitefield and of Wesley it was inhabited by a horde of lawless men, ignorant, depraved, and brutal. Whitefield and Wesley both preached and worked at Kingswood, and with such success as to change and renovate the entire neighborhood. This hymn is Mr. Wesley's song of triumph over the success of the Gospel in working such a wonderful change. The reference to "senseless stones" and "reprobates" and "outcasts" is indicative of the characer of the people of whom the hymn was written, and an omitted stanza is plainer still:

"Suffice that for the season past,
Hell's horrid language filled our tongues;
We all Thy words behind us cast,
And loudly sang the drunkard's songs."

No. 431.

"O LOVE DIVINE, HOW SWEET THOU ART!"

REV. CHARLES WESLEY, 1708—1788.

At one time Rev. William Dawson, the eccentric but very eloquent preacher, had given a very impressive sermon, and at its close had given out this hymn to be sung. The choir was singing the hymn beginning:

"God only knows the love of God."

when Mr. Dawson shouted, "Stop, friends! If angels, the first-born sons of light, cannot understand the height, the breadth, the depth, the length of the love of God, how can we expect to fathom it while here below?" and then he repeated with a feeling and emphasis that thrilled the whole audience and gave to the hymn and the sentiment it conveyed a meaning they never possessed before. "God only knows the love of God."

No. 432.

"EARTHQUAKE HYMNS"—1750.

REV. CHARLES WESLEY, 1708—1788.

On February 8, 1750, there was an earthquake in London which greatly terrified the people, many of whom ran in hot haste to the churches and chapels as if they thought that these would afford them shelter. Just a month later there came a second and much severer shock. Charles Wesley was preaching at "The Foundry," as his chapel was called, and had just repeated his text, when the walls of the building were shaken and the people cried out with fear. Mr. Wesley, always intrepid in the midst of danger, immediately changed his text and shouted, "Therefore will we not fear, though the earth be removed and the hills be carried into the midst of the sea. The God of Jacob is our Refuge." And then he preached from this new text a sermon suited to the terrified condition of his audience. Many of the people thought the Judgment Day was at hand. Both the Government and the Church took steps to allay the alarm. Forms of prayer were composed to be read in the churches "by His Majesty's special command," and the highest dignitary of the church sent out a letter to the clergy and people on the same subject. Mr. Wesley thought this a good opportunity to direct the attention of the people to God, and the things of eternity, and so he issued a pamphlet containing nineteen hymns which were, as he said, "Occasioned by the Earthquake." These hymns did much to allay the alarm of the people, and to turn their thoughts to religious matters. Six years later (in 1756) occurred the great earthquake at Lisbon, Spain, by which it has been estimated that sixty thousand people lost their lives in a few moments. This event again startled the people not only of England but of all Europe, and these "Earthquake Hymns" were republished with three additional hymns, and again exerted great influence in quieting the people and in turning them to God.

No. 433.

"RIGHTEOUS GOD WHOSE VENGEFUL VIALS"—1756.

REV. CHARLES WESLEY, 1708—1788.

The circumstances of the British Nation at the beginning of the year 1756 were such as to excite alarm in almost every way. A terrible disease had in some parts of the country swept away nearly all the cattle. An earthquake in Spain had swallowed up a large part of the city of Lisbon and destroyed sixty thousand people almost in a moment, and a dread of terrible coming events had pervaded all of Europe. The quarrel had commenced which ended in the old French War in this country. There were threats of an invasion of the land from France, and a great conflict between Catholics and Protestants seemed imminent. In view of all these gathering clouds, the King of England appointed a day of national fasting and prayer. The two Wesleys were patriots as well as preachers, and keenly alive to all that affected the welfare of the nation. John Wesley published addresses intended to warn the people of the impending dangers, and his brother Charles rendered a different but no less effective service by publishing a pamphlet containing seventeen hymns, appropriate to the circumstances of the times. This is one of these hymns.

No. 434.

"TO HEAVEN I LIFT MY WAITING EYES."

REV ISAAC WATTS, 1674—1748.

The first vaccination for smallpox was in 1796. Previous to that time its ravages had been terrible, and its appearance as greatly to be dreaded as that of the plague. A young lady friend of Rev. John Newton, to whom we are indebted for so many good hymns, was away from home and desired to return, but hesitated because of the presence of the smallpox in the neighborhood, and so through a mutual friend she applied to Mr. Newton for advice. He replied, "Give my love to your friend. I dare not advise! but if she can quietly return at the usual time, and neither run intentionally into the way of the smallpox, nor run out of the way, but leave it simply with the Lord, I shall not blame her. My prescription is to read Dr. Watts's Psalm 121 every morning before breakfast, and pray over it till the cure is effected—*Probatum est.*" And then he quotes a stanza from this Psalm, written in another meter from the one we have here, as follows:

"Hast Thou not given Thy word,
  To save my soul from death?
And I can trust my Lord
  To keep my mortal breath.
I'll go and come
  Nor fear to die,
Till from on high,
  Thou call me home."

No. 435.

"WHEN ISRAEL OF THE LORD BELOVED."

Sir Walter Scott, 1771—1832.

One would scarcely look for a hymn writer among novelists nor for a hymn in a novel. But here is a hymn by one of the most successful novelists, Sir Walter Scott, and it is taken from one of his most successful romances, "Ivanhoe" (1820). You remember how Rebecca, the beautiful Jewish maiden, is charged with witchcraft and sorcery, and tried before a tribunal of Knights Templars, and how when, after hearing the evidence against her, sentence of death is about to be pronounced, she appeals to the last tribunal. "There is yet one chance of life left to me," she says, "even by your own fierce laws. I challenge the privilege of trial by combat and will appear by my champion"; and taking off her glove she flings it down before the Grand Master, who has conducted the farce of a trial. And then in the prison awaiting the day of combat, but knowing of no one on whom she can call to appear and defend her with sword and lance, but with full faith in the God of Israel, she sings her evening hymn of prayer and faith, in these words.

No. 436.

"THE GATHERING CLOUDS WITH ASPECT DARK."

REV. JOHN NEWTON, 1725—1807.

Here is a hymn which should be of interest to Americans, for although written in England, it was directly connected with the battle of Lexington, which began the Revolutionary War. That battle occurred on April 19, 1775, and the news reached England the latter part of May. On the last day of that month Mr. Newton recorded in his diary: "The paper this evening brought an account of the commencement of hostilities in New England, and many killed on both sides. These things, I fear, are the beginning of sorrows. O that I could be suitably affected by what I see and hear."

Mr. Newton at once called upon his people to hold extraordinary meetings for prayer on account of the times, and he records that although the first meeting was held at five o'clock in the morning, more people were present than usually came in the evening. On Sunday, June 11, he preached a sermon on the times, giving a sketch of the state of the English nation, to arouse his people to more earnest prayer by "apprising them," as he says, " of the importance of the present crisis." And this hymn was written to be sung on that occasion. It was also published the next month (July) in the *Gospel Magazine*. This incident throws a little side light on the history of the Revolutionary struggle in this country by showing how it affected the Christian people of England.

No. 437.

"AS THY DAYS, THY STRENGTH SHALL BE."

MISS FRANCES RIDLEY HAVERGAL.

The author of this hymn has herself told how it came to be written: "The New Year's Bells were ringing in St. Nicholas' Church, close to our home. I was sleeping with my sister; she roused me to hear them, and quoted the text: 'As thy days thy strength shall be,' as a New Year's motto. I did not answer, but presently returned it to her in rhyme (the two first stanzas). She was pleased, so I finished it next day and gave it to her.

No. 438.

"ALL YE THAT PASS BY, TO JESUS DRAW NIGH."

REV. CHARLES WESLEY, 1708—1788.

Rev. George Whitefield, the celebrated evangelist, was once announced to preach in the market place at Nottingham, England. People came from far and near to listen, for his reputation was great. Among them came a man from a neighboring town, and just as he rode up to the outskirts of the great crowd, Mr. Whitefield gave out this hymn, and the first words that caught the newcomer's ears from the great preacher's lips were these:

"All ye that pass by, to Jesus draw nigh
To you is it nothing that Jesus should die?"

The words seemed addressed directly to him, and the inquiry of the last line never was out of his mind, until he had answered it, that to him it was everything that Jesus had died.

No. 439.

"FIFTY-FIRST PSALM."

One of the earliest recollections of the New England children of a generation ago was the verses and pictures of the "New England Primer," "which for a century and a half was in those parts the first book in religion and morals as well as in learning and in literature." It contained that wonderful poetic alphabet which began:

"In Adam's fall
We sinned all."

and ended with,

"Zaccheus he
Did climb the tree
His Lord to see."

and it contained that beautiful cradle song beginning:

"Hush my dear lie still and slumber,
Holy angels guard thy bed."

It was embellished with cuts, and one of these was entitled "The burning of Mr. John Rogers"; and with the picture was the story of his martyrdom. He was a faithful minister of the Gospel, too faithful for his times. He incurred the displeasure of Queen Mary, "Bloody Mary" she was called, who confined him first in his own home and then in Newgate prison and then condemned him to be burned. The Primer tells the story how at Smithfield on February 14, 1554, his wife and children tried to bid him farewell as he was on his way from the prison to the stake, but the cruel officers would not permit them to speak to him, and so the Primer says, "His wife with nine small children and one at her breast, followed him to the stake: with which sorrowful sight he was not in the least daunted, but with wonderful patience died courageously for the Gospel of Jesus Christ." John Rogers was the first martyr in Queen Mary's reign, and on his way from Newgate to Smithfield, he sang this fifty-first Psalm.

No. 440.

"HOLY GHOST, WITH LIGHT DIVINE."

REV. ANDREW REED, 1788—1862.

We hear it said sometimes nowadays that a minister can tell a congregation all he knows in about ten years, and that about that time he had better go to a new place where he can preach his old sermons to a new audience. That is an unjust thing to say, usually, but now and then it is true; and pastorates are shorter in these days than they were a generation ago. The author of this hymn, as soon as he had completed his education, became pastor of the church of which he was already a member and of which his father before him had been a member too, and he stayed right there, an acceptable and able preacher for over half a century, until he died. In addition to his duties as a pastor and preacher, he became a great leader in philanthropic effort, and himself founded no less than six asylums for the sick and helpless at London, where he lived. He was also an author, and in this direction had at one time a curious experience. In early life he had been familiar with a very peculiar and sad history, which so affected him that when he supposed the chief actor in it to be dead, he published the story under the name of "No Fiction, A Narrative Founded on Fact." The book attracted great attention and many editions of it were published, but the man whom he had supposed to be dead turned out to be alive and lively too; for although a fictitious name had beeen given him in the story, he recognized himself, and published an indignant denial of much of the narrative. Dr. Reed had a boy, who proposed to write his father's life, if he would furnish him the material. Dr. Reed wrote it himself, in condensed form, by replying as follows: "To my saucy boy, who said he would write my life and asked for materials.

A. R.

"I was born yesterday:
I shall die tomorrow:
I must not spend today,
In telling what I have done;
But in doing what I may for Him
Who has done all for me.
I sprang from the people;
I have lived for the people;
The most, for the most unhappy.
And the people when they know it,
Will not allow me to die out of
loving remembrance."

No. 441.

"AMAZING GRACE! HOW SWEET THE SOUND."

REV. JOHN NEWTON, 1725—1807.

I would like to give you two pen pictures. The date is 1735. An English sea captain takes his eleven-year-old boy with him to sea. Seven years of a sailor's life, and then a vacation on shore, where he meets a girl of fourteen years, whose charms delay him till his ship sails leaving him behind. Three years more of life on the sea, and he is home again, a deserter, in irons, degraded and flogged. He is an infidel now, a profligate, profane, licentious wretch. Off to the sea again, and as the ship passes a small palm-covered island off the African coast he leaves her, and enters the service of an English slave-dealer. Here he gives himself up to every form of wickedness with perfect abandon. He has scarcely clothes to cover him, and he is content to keep himself from starving with bits of food given him by the slaves. "Had you seen me then," he writes, "go pensive and solitary in the dead of night, to wash my own shirt, upon the rocks, and afterward put it on wet, that it might dry upon my back while I slept: had you seen me so poor a figure that, when a boat's crew came to the island, shame often constrained me to hide myself in the woods, from the sight of strangers; especially had you known that my conduct, principles, and heart were still darker than my outward condition:" and so he writes on, of himself.

One day a ship goes sailing by, and he signals her, hoping to trade such things as he can offer for supplies. At first the captain declines to stop, but at last rounds to, and our vagabond goes aboard. Now leave this picture as it is, and let me tell you that in far away England, the father has heard of his boy's whereabouts and condition and has commissioned the captain of a ship to try to find and bring him back. And the girl for whose sake he let his ship go away and leave him, sends messages of friendship. The captain has searched faithfully but without success for the wanderer, and has started onward on his voyage, and this is the very ship, and the man he has sought in vain stands on her deck. The captain tells him that his father has sent for him to come home, but he declines to go; and then he lies to him and tells him he has fallen heir to a fortune, and he wavers, and then he tells him that Mary Catlett wants him to come back, and he consents to go. And this finishes the first of the pictures I am trying to draw. And now for the second picture I must take you to a little English village called Olney, where a curate of the Church of England is endearing himself to the people of his flock by his faithful preaching, as he gathers them together on the Sabbath, and by the hearty sympathy with which he enters into all the affairs of their lives. He writes for them to read the story of his life, and tells them of his wanderings from home, and country, and God, and how he was at last brought back to God, and country, and home. And he writes hymns for them to sing in their church, and their prayer meetings, and their homes. And in his sermons, and his books, and his hymns, he never tires of telling how God has lifted him up out of the horrible pit and the miry clay. And these two pictures are of the same person. The first, as he was transformed by the spirit of evil until nearly all likeness of humanity was lost, and the second, as he was transformed again by the Spirit of God into some likeness to Christ.

No. 442.

"JESUS SHOW US THY SALVATION."

REV. CHARLES WESLEY, 1708—1788.

Christians of the Episcopal Church should prize this hymn, for although written by the great Methodist poet

Wesley, it is based on a passage from the "Litany" in the "Book of Common Prayer". "By the mystery of the holy incarnation! by the holy nativity and circumcision! by thy baptism, fasting and temptation! by thine agony and bloody sweat! by thy cross and passion! by thy precious death and burial! by the glorious resurrection and ascension! and by the coming of the Holy Ghost! Good Lord, deliver us!" Now compare this from the Litany with the hymn; many lines are exact copies, and the whole hymn is a paraphrase of it.

No. 443.

"STAY, THOU INSULTED SPIRIT, STAY."

REV. CHARLES WESLEY, 1708—1788.

This hymn may be called the half-way post in the author's career. He died in his eighty-first year, and this was published when he was forty-two. The last line of the second stanza, which now reads, "For many long, rebellious years," Wesley wrote, "For forty long, rebellious years." There is one other hymn of his of the same sort, the one beginning:

"God is in this and every place,"

in one stanza of which he writes:

"And have I measured half my days,
And half my journey run," etc.

This also was written when he was about forty years old, and seems to indicate that he expected to live to be eighty.

No. 444.

"JESUS, THOU ALL-REDEEMING LORD."

REV. CHARLES WESLEY, 1708—1788.

The title of this hymn tells the circumstances of its origin, "Before Preaching to the Colliers in Leicestershire." If Mr. Wesley was as plain in his preaching as in his hymns, he certainly made himself understood by his hearers. This hymn, written to be sung to an assemblage of degraded, reckless men, has some stanzas which later compilers deem it wise to omit; one of these omitted stanzas will serve to show you the style of several more:

"Ye liars and blasphemers too,
Who speak the phrase of hell,
Ye murderers all, He died for you
He loved your souls so well."

Another hymn beginning, "Lovers of pleasure more than God," is taken from this piece.

No. 445.

"THE PRAYING SPIRIT BREATHE."

REV. CHARLES WESLEY, 1708—1788.

There are but few hymns that have been written especially for business men. The one by Dr. Horatius Bonar beginning, "Calm me, O God, and keep me calm," is, I think, well suited to their needs, but it was not written with this in view; indeed I do not remember any hymns so written, but this and one other by the same author. This has for its title, "For Believers, in an Hurry of Business." We are accustomed to look upon this as the age of hurry, but it would seem from this title that there was a "hurry of business" a century and a half ago, and that it attracted the notice of at least one of the preachers of that day, and led him to provide for it this prayerful hymn. The other hymn referred to above is the one beginning, "Lo! I come with joy to do," and has for its title, "For a Believer in Worldly Business."

No. 446.

"AH! LOVELY APPEARANCE OF DEATH."

Rev. Charles Wesley, 1708—1788.

Mr. Wesley's views of death were peculiar. He can scarcely be said to have invested it with any thought of mourning. He composed quite a number of funeral hymns for the use of his followers, but the one beginning,

"Rejoice for a brother deceased,"

sets the pattern for nearly all of them. He once wrote of the body of a friend who died, "No sight upon earth in my eyes, is half so lovely," and of a young miss whose remains he had just seen he wrote, "A more beautiful corpse I never saw." These glimpses of his views about death, will amply account for a hymn beginning with such words as the above.

No. 447.

"AWAY MY UNBELIEVING FEAR."

Rev. Charles Wesley, 1708—1788.

The Methodist Love-feasts have always been characterized by the relation of personal experiences by those who share in them. At one such meeting an aged man who had been rich, but by a succession of adversities had been brought down to extreme poverty, arose and said, "I have known what it is to be well off in the world, and I loved Jesus then! and I have known what it is to be in want, but I love Him still. I have been like the apostle 'Instructed both to be full and to be hungry; both to abound and to suffer need'; but I am content. 'Although the fig tree shall not blossom, neither shall fruit be in the vines; the labor of the olive shall fail, and the fields shall yield no meat! the flocks shall be cut off from the fold, and there shall be no herd in the stalls! yet I will rejoice in the Lord, I will joy in the God of my salvation.' And then the old man struck up a song. It was the second stanza of this hymn:

'Although the vine its fruit deny,
Although the olive yield no oil,
The withering fig tree droop and die;
The fields elude the tiller's toil,
The empty stall no herd afford,
And perish all the bleating race,
Yet will I triumph in the Lord,
The God of my salvation praise.' "

No. 448.

"HYMNS OF INTERCESSION."

REV. CHARLES WESLEY, 1708—1788.

In the year 1758, England, as well as nearly all the nations of Europe, was engaged in war. The Wesleys found time enough always to keep themselves and their people in full sympathy with the nation and with the world about them, and during these troublous times the principal Methodist Societies throughout England held special meetings at noon of every Friday to pray for the nation, the church, and the world. In these circumstances Charles Wesley wrote and published a tract of forty hymns, entitled, "Hymns of Intercession for all Mankind:" containing hymns of prayer, for the King, the Church, the Fleet, the Army, for Prisoners, Our Enemies, and other subjects appropriate for use at these meetings.

No. 449.

"HYMNS ON THE EXPECTED INVASION."

REV. CHARLES WESLEY, 1708—1788.

In the year 1758, England, as well as most of the nations of Europe, was at war. During the next year, 1759, the French made several unsuccessful attempts to invade England, and as he had done amid the turmoil of the previous year, so now Mr. Wesley wrote hymns for the people suited to the times they were living in. A tract was published entitled, "Hymns on the Expected Invasion," containing eight pieces.

No. 450.

"HYMNS FOR THE USE OF FAMILIES," etc.

REV. CHARLES WESLEY, 1708—1788.

The Wesley brothers, John and Charles, published over forty books, large and small, of Sacred Poetry. Among all of these, the book whose title is given above is probably entitled to preeminence. Of the pieces in this book, it is said that probably not a single hymn in it was written with reference to an imaginary case which might occur, but that all were written under the excitement of actual experience in his own family, or the family of some friend, so that a personal history is connected with them all.

No. 451.

"HYMNS FOR CONDEMNED MALEFACTORS."

REV. CHARLES WESLEY, 1708—1788.

Although Charles Wesley preached almost daily, wrote seven thousand hymns, and performed much other work of a public character, he still found time to do a great deal of work with individuals. He became greatly interested in criminals, and visited many in the prisons, and especially such as were condemned to death. The very last work he published was a tract entitled, "Prayers for Condemned Malefactors." These prayers were hymns, suited to the circumstances of these poor men: hymns of penitence and confession, hymns of prayer for pardon, and hymns of trust in God. In a note which Mr. Wesley himself wrote at the end of one of these hymns, he says, "These prayers were answered Thursday, April 28, 1785, on nineteen malefactors who all died penitent."

No. 452.

"GREAT GOD OF WONDERS! ALL THY WAYS."

REV. SAMUEL DAVIES, 1723—1761.

England used to send her convicts to a penal settlement in the South Sea, and if by any means a convict escaped and was recaptured he was sent to "Macquarie's Harbour, Van Diemen's Land." Here, with no companions but other convicts like themselves, they grew to be almost fiends. Sometimes they escaped and formed themselves into gangs of robbers and murderers. A gentleman who used often to visit them in their cells, relates that he has seen them brought in, with the flesh of murdered victims in their pockets, which they had intended to use as food. One such man said of himself, that he thought no more of killing men and women than of killing dogs, and added that the only occasion when he was at all disturbed in his mind by what he had done, was when he had dashed out the brains of a baby before the eyes of its mother. Yet even these men were reached by the mercy of God, and some of them converted. This hymn seemed specially adapted to their wants and they repeated it and sang it, sometimes at the gallows where they were hung. To what remote places a hymn may wander or what hearts it may reach, finds illustration in this hymn, written by a President of Princeton College, and sung under the gallows in Van Diemen's Land.

No. 453.

"HOW SWEET THE NAME OF JESUS SOUNDS."

Rev. John Newton, 1725—1807.

John and Charles Wesley left to their followers a collection of hymns which continued in use as the authorized hymnal of the Methodist Church for a great many years after its compilers had left the earth. When at last it was revised, the new hymn book was a great subject of discussion among the Methodist people. Among the new hymns inserted in the book was this one. And one Methodist said to another, as they chatted about the new book, "I wonder if Newton, when he wrote that hymn, divined that he was ministering comfort to so many poor Methodists. I used often to go," he said, "to the house of a music master, who was also singer, preacher, and saint, all in one, when I was jaded with travel and study. Oh, what a heaven used to steal in upon my soul, while he sat at the piano and with tender voice sang:

'How sweet the name of Jesus sounds
In a believer's ear!

It soothes his sorrows, heals his wounds
And drives away his fear.'

And the hymn became all the more hallowed to me when this same singer told me how his mother used to sing it too."

No. 454.

"GIVE ME THE WINGS OF FAITH TO RISE."

REV. ISAAC WATTS, 1708—1788.

Philip Doddridge was in the habit of composing hymns to enforce the teachings of his sermons. Such hymns were read at the close of the service and sung by the congregation. But Doddridge and Watts were good friends, and Doddridge often used the hymns his friend had written. He once wrote a letter to Watts in which he told him what an effect upon his audience the use of this hymn had produced. "On Wednesday last," he wrote, "I was preaching in a barn to a pretty large assembly of plain country people, in a village a few miles off. After a sermon from Hebrews 6:12, we sung one of your hymns,

'Give me the wings of faith to rise,'

and in that part of the worship, I had the satisfaction to observe tears in the eyes of several of the auditory: and after the service was over, some of them told me that they were not able to sing, so deeply were their minds affected by it: and the clerk in particular told me he could hardly utter the words of it. These were most of them poor people who work for their living."

No. 455.

"PLUNGED IN A GULF OF DARK DESPAIR."

REV. ISAAC WATTS, 1708—1788.

A minister in England was once preaching to a large congregation before dawn on Christmas morning. His theme was appropriate to the day, "The love of God in the gift of His Son." At the close of his sermon he asked, "Where is there love among men like the love of life? and yet is there a father who would give the life of his son to save his own? History tells of a soldier who received into his own heart the blade intended to kill his King, but is there a father here who would give his son's life to save another though that one were his best friend? But if there were such an one, is there one who would give the life of his son to save a foe? But God has so loved us, enemies and rebels against Him, that He gave His only begotton Son, that we might not perish but have everlasting life." And then he repeated a stanza of this hymn:

"O! for such love let rocks and hills
Their lasting silence break,
And all harmonious human tongues
The Savior's praises speak!"

And as he ended, a voice in the audience shouted, "Hallelujah!" and then another and another repeated the cry, and then catching the inspiration of the lines the minister had used, the whole congregation arose and sang the next stanza of the hymn:

"Angels! assist our mighty joys,
Strike all your harps of gold!
But when you raise your highest notes,
His love can ne'er be told."

No. 456.

Rev. Isaac Watts, 1708—1788.

In the latter part of the seventeenth century the deacon of an Independent church at Southampton, England, was imprisoned because of his nonconformity to the Church of England. His wife used to come and sit on the stone steps of the prison door, with a baby in her arms. A few years later, when the baby had grown to be a boy of seven, his mother kept a boarding school, and she had a custom of offering a farthing for the best poetic composition from her scholars. One day there was handed in a couplet running as follows:

"I write not for your farthing, but to try,
How I, your farthing writers can outvie."

This couplet won the prize and the teacher was rejoiced to find that her own seven-year-old boy was the writer. He kept on rhyming until the habit made him a sort of nuisance in the family, and his father, now released from prison, threatened that if he did not stop verse-making he would whip him. It wasn't many days, either, until he had an opportunity to carry his threat into execution, and while he was applying the rod, the culprit tearfully exclaimed:

"Dear father do some pity take,
And I will no more verses make."

This settled the matter, for the father wisely concluded that so incorrigible a rhymster couldn't be cured by whipping, and he was allowed to rhyme on without further molestation, and while still a young man he had substituted many of his Psalms and Hymns for the uncouth forms till then in use. It was Isaac Watts.

No. 457.

"JESUS, LORD, THY SERVANTS SEE."

Rev. Benjamin Schmolke.

Translated by Frances Elizabeth Cox.

On September 12, 1716, a fire broke out at the town of Schweidnitz, in Silesia, which destroyed half the town. The author of this hymn, who was a pastor in the town, suffered much from this fire, as also did many of his people. He wrote this hymn to commemorate the event, and for many years it was sung at an annual religious service held in the town on the anniversary of the fire.

No. 458.

"LORD, IT BELONGS NOT TO MY CARE."

Rev. Richard Baxter.

In the days of Oliver Cromwell, there lived a man, who, though a constant sufferer from disease, did a prodigious amount of work. He wrote books to the number of a hundred and sixty-eight. He was driven from place to place. He was in prison once for preaching, was kept out of his own pulpit by a guard of soldiers, was fined for preaching again, and at last at seventy years of age, he stood before a judge, accused of writing a paraphrase of the New Testament.

"Richard! Richard!" cried the judge, as he pointed his finger at him. "Thou art an old fellow, an old knave! thou hast written books enough to fill a cart, every one of them as full of sedition as an egg is full of meat. Hadst thou been whipped out of thy writing trade forty years ago, it had been happy." And so he sent the old man to jail again. When, at last, at seventy-six years of age, worn out with hardship and disease, he lay sick and dying, he was asked, "How are you now?"

"Almost well," was the reply, and this is the spirit of his hymn:

"Lord, it belongs not to my care,
Whether I live or die."

No. 459.

"NOW HUSH YOUR CRIES AND SHED NO TEAR."

Nicholas Herman.

Three centuries and a half ago, there lived in a little mountain village between Saxony and Bohemia, a man who did the duties of head master in the schools, and of precentor and organist in the church. His interest in the children of the village led him to write hymns for them which he intended should drive out the songs they often heard of vicious sort, and his love of music led him to write tunes for the words, so that the children sang both his words and his music. This hymn, written by him, was a great favorite with Prince Albert of England, husband of Queen Victoria, often called "the Good Prince," and it was sung at his funeral. Its author had some curious notions, and one of them was about the way musicians like himself would spend their time in heaven. "Every organist or Lutanist," said he, "in that life too, will take some holy text, and strike upon his organ or his lute; and every one will be able to sing at sight, and by himself four or five different parts. There will be no more confusion and mistakes, which now often put many a good musician out of heart, especially when he has to begin again several times over."

No. 460.

"ALL PRAISE TO THEE MY GOD THIS NIGHT."

BISHOP KEN, 1637—1711.

"HARK! THE HERALD ANGELS SING."

REV. CHARLES WESLEY, 1708—1788.

"LO! HE COMES WITH CLOUDS DESCENDING."

REV. C. WESLEY AND REV. M. MADAN.

"ROCK OF AGES, CLEFT FOR ME."

REV. A. M. TOPLADY, 1740—1778.

Some years ago, an English clergyman, interested in hymns, took the trouble to examine fifty-two of the hymnals then in use by the various branches of the Anglican Church in Great Britain and America, and to make up a list of the hymns which seemed to be most highly prized as indicated by the number of books containing them. Not a single hymn was to be found in the fifty-two books, and but four were found in fifty-one of them. These were the four hymns whose first lines are given above. Of course the estimate of the value placed upon the hymns would be greater if the books had been taken from different denominations, but it is worth something as it is.

No. 461.

"MUCH IN SORROW, OFT IN WOE."

"OFT IN DANGER, OFT IN WOE."

"OFT IN SORROW, OFT IN WOE."

HENRY KIRKE WHITE, 1785—1806.

These are merely different beginnings of the same hymn. In 1805, a young man's name was on the records of St. John's College in England, as a "Sizar." That was a student who worked his way. He had certain work to do in connection with the school, and for this work his expenses were smaller than those of other students. At the next examinations this youth of twenty years stood highest in his class. And a year later he did the same, but he did it at the cost of his life, for the long hours of work and study brought on consumption and he died that same year. After his death, this hymn was found, scribbled on the back of a mathematical paper, and evidently written while he was pursuing his study of mathematics by the light of the midnight lamp. It stopped abruptly at the end of the second line of the third stanza:

"Shrink not, Christians! will ye yield?
Will ye quit the painful field?"

Here sleep or sickness had overtaken him, and his last hymn was left unfinished. But twenty years later an English lady (Miss Frances Fuller Maitland) took up the lines as he had left them and finished the hymn.

No. 462.

"THOU SOFT FLOWING KEDRON, BY THY SILVER STREAM."

MADAM DE FLEURY.

It is well to base poetic fervor on historic fact, otherwise ludicrous blunders are liable to occur. As a matter of fact, the Kedron is a very muddy little stream which only flows about three months in the year, during the season of heavy rains, and during the remainder of the year is entirely dry.

No. 463.

"IN GRIEF AND FEAR TO THEE, O LORD."

REV. WILLIAM BULLOCK.

A lady came to England, some years ago, with her invalid husband, who was an officer in military service in India. She was a native of Tasmania and had been converted through the work of a missionary who had lived in her country when she was a child. In telling the story of her life, she told how she had gone with her husband to India, and had there shared with him a great many perils. "But the worst of all," said she, "was in the time of pestilence. The cholera was in the camp and that was awful. My earlier religious impressions were revived, and amidst my fears for my husband and myself, I used to pray in the words of a hymn entitled, 'The Church in Plague or Pestilence.'

'In grief and fear to Thee, O Lord,
We now for succor fly;
Thine awful judgments are abroad,
O, shield us lest we die.' "

"Oh, how I prayed," she said:

"'Oh, look with pity on the scene
Of sadness and of dread,
And let Thine angel stand between
The living and the dead!'

And the Lord answered me, and we were saved, my husband and I."

The hymn she used as her prayer was written by an English missionary, who had himself been a witness to just such scenes as she was passing through, and who wrote the hymn, as his own prayer, and for the help of others.

No. 464.

"THE LOST CHORD."

"Seated One Day at the Organ."

MISS ADELAIDE ANN PROCTOR, 1835—1864.

About sixty years ago, a little girl in London, whose father was a poet, began to show a love for poetry herself. She made for herself a little album, as she called it, of note paper, just as many of us did when we were children, and before she could write plainly herself, her mother copied for her into this little book, the poems she liked best. Later, she sent a little poem of her own composing to Charles Dickens, who was the editor of *Household Words,* under an assumed name, and he was so much pleased with it that he asked for more, and so she kept on until she died. Charles Dickens, in writing about the earnestness of her life, said: "Now it was the visitation of the sick that had possession of her; now it was the sheltering of the homeless; now it was the teaching of the densely ignorant; now it was the raising up of those who had wandered and got trodden under foot; now it was the wider employment of her own sex in the general business of life; and now it was all these things at once." And with such work, it is not strange that she wore herself out and died at twenty-nine. The music was written by Sir Arthur Sullivan, well known as the author of "Pinafore" and other light music, but who has written some good sacred music as well. The tune to which we sing the favorite hymn,

> 'Onward Christian soldiers,
> Marching as to war,
> With the cross of Jesus
> Going on before"

is a good specimen. He was one of the first composers to depart from the old-time method of setting all the stanzas of a hymn to the same music.

No. 465.

"NICÆA."

Have you ever wondered how our tunes came by their names? Upon these names there often hangs a history, and there is one hanging upon this. It takes us back into the latter part of the second century and into the neighborhood of Palestine, where a priest by the name of Arius began to preach the doctrine that Christ was not the equal of the Father. This was the beginning of that doctrine which in different form is now known as Unitarianism. A great dispute arose, and early in the third century the Emperor Constantine called together the Bishops of the whole Christian Church, to discuss and decide what should be done with Arius and his doctrine. The Emperor himself presided at the meetings, and the result of the discussion was the issuance of a creed, which declared in formal words the doctrine of the Trinity. This creed has come down to this day as "The Nicene Creed" and the Council which proclaimed it was assembled in Nicæa, a city of Asia Minor, about fifty miles away from Constantinople. When Heber's hymn beginning, "Holy! Holy! Holy; Lord God Almighty," became popular, a tune was written expressly for it by Dr. J. B. Dykes, one of the most successful composers of church music in England. The hymn was written for Trinity Sunday, and is a hymn of praise to the Triune God, so what more appropriate name could be found for the tune to which it was to be sung than that of the city, in which centuries before, the doctrine was proclaimed which both hymn and tune were intended to honor.

No. 466.

"AWAKE, MY SOUL TO MEET THE DAY."

Rev. Philip Doddridge, 1702—1751.

Dr. Doddridge arose at five o'clock in the morning at all seasons of the year. He wrote this hymn for his own use, and by it he made the very act of arising an exercise of devotion. His title for it was, "A Morning Hymn, to be Sung at Awakening and Arising." It is said that when in using it he reached words, "as rising now," etc., he sprang out of bed. The thought almost has an element of ludicrousness in it, and yet a day so well begun, would likely feel the influence of its beginning through all its hours.

No. 467.

"DEPTH OF MERCY! CAN THERE BE."

Rev. Charles Wesley, 1708—1788.

An actress was passing along the street of a little English town, when she heard singing in a cottage by the roadside.

Curiosity led her to look in at the open door, and there she saw a few poor people gathered together and heard the lines,

> "Depth of mercy can there be,
> Mercy still reserved for me?"

The tune was sweet but she heeded not the music. It was the words that had caught her attention. She remained long enough to hear a prayer, uncouth in language but sincere and fervid, and then she left; but those words followed her, and she resolved to find them again, so she obtained the hymn book containing them and read and reread them, and they led to her conversion. For a time she excused herself from attending on the stage, until at last the manager of the theater called upon her and asked her to take the principal part in a new play. Then she told him of the change in her life. At first he ridiculed and then he pled the loss it would be to him for her to refuse, and at last she consented to appear once more. The character she was to assume required of her that she should sing a song when she came upon the stage. The night came and the curtain rose, and the orchestra began playing an accompaniment to her song, but she stood silent. The music soon ceased, and then with clasped hands and eyes suffused with tears, she sang, not the song of the play, but:

> "Depth of mercy can there be,
> Mercy still reserved for me?
> Can my God His wrath forbear,
> Me the chief of sinners spare?

No. 468.

"JESUS AND SHALL IT EVER BE."

JOSEPH GRIGG.

Quite a number of the hymns in common use among us have been written by persons not yet out of their teens.

This one was written by a boy of ten years, and although some few words in it have been altered by compilers who have used it in their books, the hymn remains essentially as the boy wrote it, and it is doubtful whether even the altered words are improvements over the original form.

No. 469.

"THE GREAT ARCHANGEL'S TRUMP SHALL SOUND."

Rev. Charles Wesley, 1708—1788.

On one of his visits to the town of Leeds, Mr. Wesley preached in the upper room of an old building which was densely packed and many stood without unable to gain admission. Suddenly the timbers gave way and the floor fell, taking over a hundred people with it into the room below. None were killed but several were severely hurt. Mr. Wesley himself was stunned for a moment, but almost immediately recovered and quieted the panic-stricken people by singing, "Praise God from Whom all blessings flow." This is part of a hymn written to commemorate this remarkable escape from death.

No. 470.

"THOU HIDDEN LOVE OF GOD WHOSE HEIGHT."

Gerhard Tersteegen, (German).

Translated by Rev. John Wesley, 1703—1791.

If tradition is to be relied upon, this hymn, so far as relates to its translation by John Wesley, is due to an unfortunate love affair in which he became involved while in America, an incident in his life that cost him much of reputation. Mr. Wesley, himself, declares the hymn to have been written in Savannah, and says of one of its stanzas, that it gives his religious sentiments at that time. This stanza is:

"Is there a thing beneath the sun
That strives with Thee my heart to share?
Ah! tear it thence and reign alone,
The Lord of every motion there!"

Dr. Southey, one of Mr. Wesley's biographers, connects the love affair with the writing of this hymn, and a certain "Miss Sophia" as the one who was referred to.

No. 471.

"PEACE, DOUBTING HEART! MY GOD'S I AM."

REV. CHARLES WESLEY, 1708—1788.

The author himself once made good use of his own hymn, perhaps saving his life and the lives of a boat's crew. He had engaged a boat to take him from St. Ives to the Scilly Isles. A storm arose and the crew began to be afraid, when Mr. Wesley began to sing:

"When passing through the watery deep,
I ask in faith His promised aid;
The waves an awful distance keep
And shrink from my devoted head.
Fearless, their violence I dare,
They cannot harm, for God is there."

The song gave new courage to the men and they brought the boat in safety to the shore.

No. 472.

"O THAT THE LORD WOULD GRACIOUS BE."

Rev. Martin Luther, 1483—1546.

Luther's hymns and Luther's music flew through Germany as if supernaturally winged. Not only did professed Protestants sing them, but they were the songs of the street and the workshop and the field. Everywhere, people were singing his hymns and unconsciously spreading his doctrines. They even crept into Romish churches. It is told of this hymn that it, with several others, was introduced into the chapel service of the Duke Henry of Wolfenbüttel, and that a priest made complaint. When the Duke asked what hymns they were of which he complained, the priest replied, "May it please your Highness they are such as this:

"O! that the Lord would gracious be"!

"Hold! Hold!" replied the Duke, "must the Devil then be gracious? Whose grace are we to seek if not that of God only?" And so the Lutheran hymns kept their place even in the Romish chapel.

No. 473.

"THE LAST HOPE." (Music by Gottschalk.)

Gottschalk, the pianist and composer, was at one time in the Island of Cuba, and while there was the guest of an invalid lady. Her disease was incurable and greatly aggravated by anxiety about a son who was absent. The greatest relief she found was from Gottschalk's music. One evening she was suffering more than usual, and exclaimed to the musician, "Oh, for Heaven's sake, play me something." So he sat down to the piano and began to improvise the melody of this piece. As he brought out in music one thought after another, the idea took possession of him that he was playing for her for the last time. The next day he went to another part of the Island, and at the end of a week returned. As he reached the top of a hill that overlooked the town in which she lived, he heard the bell of the little church tolling for a burial and soon he met a funeral train winding up the hill. It was the body of his friend to whom he had played, that they were bearing away to burial. Then he recalled the melody he had played, arranged the different parts, and in memory of the occasion when it was improvised, he named it "The Last Hope." Whenever afterward he played at private assemblies or for friends, he always finished his performance with this piece. A very beautiful hymn tune has been taken out of this composition, which sometimes goes by the original name and is sometimes called "Mercy."

No. 474.

"HAIL COLUMBIA, HAPPY LAND."

Joseph Hopkinson.

The music which we now call "Hail Columbia" was written by a German by the name of Feyles whose home was in Philadelphia. He composed it in 1789 and it was first played in that year at Trenton, New Jersey, when Washington was on his way to New York to be inaugurated as first President of the United States. It is thus associated with the very birth of the nation, and has that claim at least to be considered our national air. Its composer gave to it the name of "President's March" because of the event in honor of which it was composed. The words we now sing to it were written nine years later, in 1798, by Joseph Hopkinson, a young Philadelphia lawyer. A young singer by the name of Fox, connected with the theater in that city, was to have a benefit on a certain Monday night, but on Saturday afternoon not a ticket had been sold, and his benefit seemed likely to result in a loss. Political feeling was running very high, there seemed every prospect of a war with France, and Congress was then in session in the city deliberating on that question. The thought struck the singer that if he could get a new patriotic song written to the tune of "President's March," then a very popular tune, it would save him from the failure that otherwise seemed inevitable. Hopkinson, the lawyer, was an old schoolmate of his, and to him he went late Saturday afternoon and told him the situation he was in, and what he wanted. Hopkinson promised to try what he could do, and the next afternoon gave him the words now so familiar. Monday morning the newspapers and flaming posters announced the new patriotic song to be sung that night to the tune of "President's March." The theater was filled to overflowing. The song was sung. There was not a word in it to offend either political party, not a word of France or England, but a reference to Washington, the great leader beloved by all, and an appeal to the patriotism of the people. And the appeal was not in vain; nine times the audience recalled the singer to the stage to repeat the song, and then all arising, amid tremendous enthusiasm, they joined in the final chorus. It was repeated night after night, and was sung all over the city, on the streets, and in assemblies of citizens. It quelled the strife of parties, and almost in a day bound the whole nation together and saved it from the impending danger.

No. 475.

"TRUE LOVE CAN NE'ER FORGET."

SAMUEL LOVER.

In ancient times there were professional bards who gained their livelihood by their art. They sang the praises and the loves of kings and the bravery of heroes. Their songs were never written, but handed down from generation to generation by word of mouth. The last of the Irish bards, as well as one of the greatest was Turlogh O'Carolan, who died no longer ago than 1738. The songs he composed and sang became very celebrated. He became blind while young and passed the remainder of his life in darkness. The story runs that when a youth he fell in love with Bridget Cruise, but the course of true love as usual did not run smooth and they never married. Twenty years later, as the blind bard was playing the harp by the waterside, a boat drew to the shore, and the blind man, stretching his hand to assist a lady to alight, recognized by the touch of her hand his ladylove of long years agone. This story, half mythical perhaps, is told in verse in the song beginning, "True love can ne'er forget."

No. 476.

"YANKEE DOODLE."

The name now given to this tune had its origin here in America. It is a corruption of the word English, or *Anglais*, as it is in French, as imperfectly pronounced by the Indians, and its meaning would be "English simpleton." Where the tune originated no one knows. It bears a close resemblance to an old song sung in the vineyards of France. The Spaniards recognize it as much like an ancient ballad of theirs. Louis Kossuth, when he heard it in this country, said it was an old Hungarian dance, and the Dutch claim it as one of their own low-country songs. Its first appearance in this country was in June, 1755. The British army was on the shores of the Hudson river, and recruits for the provincial army came pouring in from all the country round. They came in all sorts of dress, as a writer has described it, "some with long coats, some with short coats, and some with no coats at all." The arms and accoutrements they brought were as various as their coats, and the music to which they marched was more ridiculous than either, for it was the uncouth music of two centuries before. Their whole appearance excited the mirth of their opponents, as well it might, and a certain Dr. Shackburg, Surgeon in the English Army, told them he would give them a tune to march by; so he wrote out "Yankee Doodle," and presented it to the simple country soldiers as one of the celebrated martial airs of Europe. They liked it. It was easy to play and soon in all the camps of the American Army the soldiers were drilling to the music of "Yankee Doodle." And as in this way it may be said to have been the music with which the American Revolution began, so it was literally the music with which it ended, for when Lord Cornwallis surrendered his army to General Washington at Yorktown, his troops marched into the American lines to the music of this same "Yankee Doodle."

The War of 1812, as it is called, between this country and Great Britain, was terminated by a treaty made at the city of Ghent in Belgium. When the Ministers of the two countries had concluded their labors, the burghers of the old Dutch city where they met, resolved to give an entertainment in their honor, and desired to use in it the national airs of the two nations now happily at peace again. So their musical director called on the American Ministers for the national air of the United States. None of them knew exactly what tune to name, and as to that neither you nor I could do any better now that three-quarters of a century more of national life has passed away. But they finally decided to give "Yankee Doodle." Then the director asked if any of them had the music, but no one had it, and then he suggested to Henry Clay that perhaps he might sing or whistle it. "Never whistled or sung a tune in my life," said Clay, "but perhaps Mr. Bayard can." But Mr. Bayard couldn't, and so the question went through the five distinguished Americans and not one of them could sing or whistle. What to do they hardly knew, until Mr. Clay exclaimed, "I have it," and called his negro servant, whom he had brought with him from Kentucky, and he whistled while the Dutch musician took down the notes, and at the grand entertainment the finest band of Ghent played "Yankee Doodle" with variations as the national air of the United States.

No. 477.

"THE DAY OF RESURRECTION."

JOHN DAMASCENE, (in Greek).

Translated by REV. JOHN MASON NEALE, 1818—1866.

Dean Stanley has described the singing of this hymn in the Greek Church at Athens on Easter Morning. "As midnight approached, the Archbishop with his priests, accompanied by the King and Queen, left the church and stationed themselves on the platform, which was raised considerably from the ground, so that they were distinctly seen by the people. Everyone now remained in breathless expectation, holding their unlighted tapers in readiness when the glad moment should arrive, while the priests still continued murmuring their melancholy chant in a low half whisper. Suddenly a single report of a cannon announced that twelve o'clock had struck, and that Easter day had begun; then the old Archbishop, elevating the cross, exclaimed in a loud, exulting tone, '*Christos anesti!*' and instantly every single individual of all that host took up the cry, and the vast multitude broke through and dispelled forever the intense and mournful silence which they had maintained so long, with one spontaneous shout of indescribable joy and triumph, 'Christ is risen, Christ is risen.' At the same moment the oppressive darkness was succeeded by a blaze of light from thousands of tapers which, communicating one with another, seemed to send streams of fire in all directions, rendering the minutest objects distinctly visible, and casting the most vivid glow on the expressive faces, full of exultation, of the rejoicing crowd; bands of music struck up the gayest strains; the roll of the drum through the town, and further on the pealing of the cannon announced, far and near, these 'glad tidings of great joy'; while from hill and plain, from the sea shore and the far olive grove, rocket after rocket ascending to the clear blue sky, answered back with their mute eloquence that Christ is risen indeed, and told of other tongues that were repeating those blessed words, and other hearts that leap for joy; everywhere men clasped each other's hands and congratulated one another, and embraced with countenances beaming with delight, as though to each one separately some wonderful happiness had been proclaimed; and so in truth it was; and all the while, rising above the mingling of many sounds, each one of which was a sound of gladness, the aged priests were distinctly heard chanting forth a glorious old 'hymn of victory' in tones so loud and clear that they seemed to have regained their youth and strength to tell the world that Christ is risen from the dead, having trampled death beneath His feet, and henceforth they that are in the tombs have everlasting life."

No. 478.

"WHY THOSE FEARS? BEHOLD, 'TIS JESUS."

REV. THOMAS KELLY, 1769—1854.

Mr. Christopher gives the following story of a sea voyager: "I was once on my way to the Antipodes. The vessel was a transport; but a number of troops were also on board. All went on safely, however, till one night, the horrors of which I can never forget. I was fast asleep in my berth, when about the middle of the night I was startled by a shock, then alarmed by a strange hubbub of creaking timbers, shuffling feet, and hoarse voices, striving with the whistling, roaring wind. Then came a thundering crash; down went the vessel on her beam ends; and down came the rushing sea, all but filling the cabins, and putting out the lights. There was an awful hush for a moment, but soon broken by an officer, who, leaping from an adjoining berth, cried, 'This is like hell when the fire is put out!' But just then some gentle spirit seemed to touch my tremulous heart; and a sweet calm came over my soul. Then I felt as if voices from the better land were singing to me that beautiful hymn:

> 'Why those fears? Behold, 'tis Jesus
> Holds the helm and guides the ship,' etc.

We lived to outride the storm, but as long as I live, I shall feel that the experience of that night ever hallowed to me the memory of Thomas Kelly. His long life was not spent in vain, if that hymn alone had been all its fruit."

No. 479.

"SPEAK GENTLY, IT IS BETTER FAR."

DAVID BATES.

The author of this song was a Philadelphia broker and was nicknamed by his fellow brokers "Old Mortality." One day he sat writing at his desk at home, while his wife was sewing near him, and two little children were having a pretty lively romp. Their noise disturbed the mother, who asked them to be quieter. But they were soon making as much noise as ever, and then came another reproof, the effect of which only lasted a few minutes, when the nervous mother sprang to her feet and exclaimed, "I'll teach you to be quiet." The boys avoided a box on the ears by a quick escape from the room.

"Speak gently, wife, speak gently," said Mr. Bates, and turning to his desk he took a fresh sheet of paper and wrote these words. At the supper table he handed it to his wife. She saw the title and, thinking it a second reproof, said she didn't want to see it and handed it back unread.

The next day at his office a literary friend came in, and Mr. Bates showed it to him. "This is a good thing, Bates," said his friend, "you should have it published." And acting upon the suggestion, he sent it with a note to L. A. Godey, editor of *Godey's Magazine,* published in Philadelphia. Within a few days he received a check from Mr. Godey for one hundred dollars, with a note complimenting the poem. Mr. Bates looked at the check in amazement, and exclaimed, "Well, this is the biggest one hundred dollars I ever saw!" He kept it locked up in his desk for a long time, and would occasionally take it out and look at it.

The poem has been translated into many languages and is greatly admired by foreigners, especially by the cultured Brazilian Emperor. When Rev. J. C. Fletcher, the celebrated American missionary, was in Brazil, he visited Dom Pedro. During the call of the Reverend gentleman, the Emperor said, "I have something to show you, and shall be very glad if you can tell me the name of the author." He at once led the way into his private library, where one of the most prominent objects in the room was a large tablet reaching from the floor to the ceiling, on which appeared the familiar poem "Speak Gently," in both the English and the Portuguese languages.

"Do you know who wrote this?" asked Dom Pedro.

"Yes," replied Mr. Fletcher, "the writer was formerly a fellow townsman of mine, Mr. David Bates."

"I consider it," said the Emperor, "the most beautiful poem of any language that I have ever read. I require all the members of my household to memorize it, and as far as possible, to follow its teachings." Upon Mr. Fletcher's return home, the Emperor sent by him a complimentary letter to the author, expressing his appreciation of the lines and his gratification at learning their authorship.

No. 480.

"THE MOONLIGHT SONATA."

Ludwig von Beethoven, 1770—1827.

The *Wide-Awake Magazine* tells a pretty story of the way that Beethoven composed this beautiful piece of music. He was going by a small house one evening and heard someone playing his "Symphony in F" on the piano. He stopped to listen, and heard a voice say, "What would I not give to hear that piece played by some one who could do it justice."

The composer opened the door and entered. "Pardon me," said Beethoven, somewhat embarrassed; "pardon me, but I heard music, and was tempted to enter. I am a musician!" The girl blushed, and the young man assumed a grave, almost severe manner. "I heard also some of your words," continued Beethoven. "You wish to hear, that is, you would like—in short, would you like me to play to you?"

There was something so strange, so comical in the whole affair, and something so agreeable and eccentric in Beethoven's manner, that we all involuntarily smiled. "Thank you," said the young shoemaker, "but our piano is bad, and then we have no music."

"No music!" repeated Beethoven. "How then did mademoiselle—?" He stopped and colored, for the young girl had just turned toward him, and by her sad, veiled eyes he saw that she was blind. "I entreat you to pardon me," stammered he, "but I did not remark at first. You play, then, from memory."

"Entirely!"

"And where have you heard this music before?"

"Never, excepting the music in the street." She seemed frightened, so Beethoven did not add another word, but seated himself at the instrument and began to play.

"He had not touched many notes when I guessed," says the narrator, who accompanied him, "what would follow, and how sublime he would be that evening. I was not deceived. Never, during the many years I knew him, did I hear him play as on this occasion for the blind girl and her brother on that old dilapidated piano. At last the shoemaker rose, and approached him, and said in a low voice: 'Wonderful man, who are you then?' Beethoven raised his head, as if he had not comprehended. The young man repeated the question. The composer smiled as only he could smile. 'Listen,' said he; and he played the first movement in the "F Symphony." A cry of joy escaped from the lips of the brother and sister. They recognized the player and cried: 'You are, then, Beethoven!' He rose to go, but they detained him. 'Play for us once more, just once more,' they said. He allowed himself to be led back to the instrument. The brilliant rays of the moon entered the curtainless windows and lighted up his broad, earnest, and expressive forehead. 'I am going to improvise a sonata to the moonlight,' he said, playfully. He contemplated for some moments the sky sparkling with stars; then his fingers rested on the piano, and he began to play in a low, sad, but wonderfully sweet strain. The harmony issued from the instrument as sweet and even as the bright rays of the beautiful moonlight spread over the shadows on the ground."

No. 481.

"IL TROVATORE."

"The Anvil Chorus."

When Verdi was putting the finishing touches upon "Il Trovatore," he was visited in his study by a privileged friend, who was one of the ablest musicians and critics. The latter was permitted to glance over the score and try the "Anvil Chorus" on the pianoforte. "What do you think of that?" asked the master.

"Trash!" said the connoisseur.

Verdi rubbed his hands and chuckled. "Now look at this—and this—and this," he said.

"Rubbish!"

The composer arose and embraced his friend with a burst of joy.

"What do you mean by such strange conduct?" asked the critical one.

"My dear friend," responded the master, "I have been composing a 'popular' opera; in it I resolved to please everybody except the great judges and classicists like you. Had I pleased you I would have pleased no one else; what you say assures me of success. In three months 'Il Trovatore' will be sung, and roared, and whistled, and barrel-organed all over Italy." And so it was!

No. 482.

"CHILD OF THE REGIMENT."

"Ask me not why my heart with fond emotion."

Charles Jefferys, Author.

During the occupation of the Tyrol by the French, and after a skirmish between the hostile ranks, an infant child was found alone in their camp by the Eleventh Regiment of the Grand Army of Napoleon; by that regiment she was fostered and beloved, and all were proud of the charming *vivandière*. Maria, the name given to the child, upon the attainment of her eighteenth year, was discovered to be the daughter of the Marchioness de Berkenfield, and by her removed to a sphere more consonant with the dignity of her birth. Still the affectionate girl found it impossible to shake off the attachment of her childhood, and being reproached by her mother with want of pride, defended herself in the words of this song, which was so exquisitely sung by the renowned cantatrice, Jenny Lind, in the "Child of the Regiment," as to entitle it to be called with propriety the gem of that favorite opera.

No. 482a.

"BLEST BE THE TIE THAT BINDS."

REV. JOHN FAWCETT.

A great international convention of Young Men's Christian Associations was held in Stockholm, Sweden, in August, 1888. Delegates were present from every civilized land on the globe, speaking many languages, but all devoted to the cause of Christ. The convention ended by a grand Mass Meeting on Sunday evening, August 19. At the close of this meeting, just before they were to separate for their homes in the four quarters of the earth, never to meet again alive, the delegates joined hands and closed the meeting by the singing of this hymn.

No. 483.

"HOLY GHOST, DISPEL OUR SADNESS."

This hymn has been a sort of football among hymn writers and hymn menders for two hundred and fifty years. Paul Gerhardt wrote it in German in 1648. Awhile later it was translated into English by John Christian Jacobi. In 1776, Augustus Montague Toplady, who wrote "Rock of Ages," made it over, condensing it from ten stanzas into six. In 1849, the editors of the "Methodist Episcopal

Hymnal" wanted to use it, but not badly enough to take it as it was. So they transposed parts of it and altered others. And in 1876, when the same book was revised, the editors changed it still further. What the future has in store for it remains to be seen, but it started with ten eight-line stanzas and now has but four four-line stanzas.

No. 484.

"O COME AND MOURN WITH ME AWHILE"—1849.

Rev. Frederick William Faber, 1814—1863.

Notice that refrain, repeated at the end of each stanza, "Jesus, my Love, is crucified." This hymn was written in 1849. And yet it embalms in sacred verse words that were spoken by one who was ordained to his ministry by "the disciple whom Jesus loved," and that were spoken within a few years after that disciple's death, if not while he was yet alive. St. Ignatius, of Antioch, after faithfully ministering to the people of his flock at Antioch, while fierce fires of persecution raged about them, was at last condemned by Trajan to be thrown to the wild beasts in the Amphitheatre. And while on his way thither December 20, in the year 107 or 115, frequently exclaimed, as if he were being honored to follow in the footsteps of Christ, "My Love was crucified."

No. 485.

"SPIRIT, LEAVE THY HOUSE OF CLAY."

James Montgomery, 1771—1854.

When Montgomery was a young man and editing a paper in Sheffield, England, his editorials attracted the notice and roused the opposition of the Government party, which twice caused his arrest for alleged sedition. The second arrest resulted in his imprisonment, and while in prison he had for a fellow convict a Quaker by the name of Joseph Browne, who was also imprisoned on account of his opinions. Mr. Browne died not long after, and Mr. Montgomery wrote this hymn in his memory, giving to it this dedication: "Verses to the memory of the late Joseph Browne of Lothersdale, one of the people called Quakers, who had suffered a long confinement in the Castle of York, and loss of all his worldly goods, for conscience sake."

No. 486.

"THE LORD IS OUR REFUGE, THE LORD IS OUR GUIDE"—(Psalm Forty-six).

Rev. Henry F. Lyte, 1793—1847.

The author of this hymn was the minister of a seaside town in South Devon, England. There were many fishermen's families among his flock, and sometimes when by chance the men were ashore, the congregation would be largely made up of fishermen and their families. One summer Sunday morning in 1838 when he entered his church, he found it filled with such an audience. He began by telling them of his pleasure at seeing them there, and then said that he should speak almost entirely to them. He took for his text the words of the Master to the fishermen of Galilee, "Cast the net on the right side of the ship and ye shall find," and then there followed a loving and faithful appeal to those who see "God's wonders in the deep," and then he closed with this version he had himself composed of the Forty-sixth Psalm.

No. 487.

"MET AGAIN IN JESUS' NAME."

REV. JOHN PYER, 1790—1859.

The history of this hymn is the history of a tent. The tent was built in 1814 for religious services at Bristol, England. A wild young man, whose waywardness had caused grief to his widowed mother, had been converted and had often spoken as a lay preacher in this tent. At last he gave up his business, and then he and the tent moved about over England, from Bristol to London, and from London to Manchester, until the man, by years of unremitting toil, was compelled to abandon his tent and settle down to less laborious work; but even then he took no rest, and was found one day sitting in his study chair —dead with the harness on. He wrote a few good hymns and this one among the rest.

No. 488.

"KATHLEEN MAVOURNEEN."

"Kathleen Mavourneen, the Gray Dawn Is Breaking."

Thomas W. Higginson relates that he was once at a little musical party in New York where several accomplished amateur singers were present, and with them the eminent professional, Adelaide Phillips. The amateurs were first called. Each chose some difficult operatic passage and sang her best. When it came to the great singer's turn, instead of exhibiting her ability to eclipse the other singers, she simply seated herself at the piano, and sang "Kathleen Mavourneen" with such thrilling sweetness, that a young Irish girl who was setting the supper table in the next room, forgot her work, threw herself into a chair, put her apron over her face, and cried as if her heart would break.

No. 489.

"O GOD OF BETHEL BY WHOSE HAND."

REV. PHILIP DODDRIDGE, 1702—1751.

I am often astonished to note into what far-off places and by what circuitous paths our hymns have traveled in their mission of comfort to human hearts. Here is a hymn written in England and first read and sung at the close of a sermon one winter Sunday in 1736 (January 16), finding its way by and by into the Scotch Paraphrases, and so into the church and family worship of the Presbyterians of Scotland and fixing itself in their memories and their hearts; and then a hundred years after it was written, turning up again in the heart of Africa, to comfort and encourage a Scotchman who had wandered thither. David Livingston was a Scotch boy and had become familiar with the hymn book his parents used, in the days of his boyhood. And when in manhood he had become the famous explorer of the African Continent, he carried with him in his travels a little pocket copy of the old home hymn book; and when, in the depths of African forests, dangers seemed thick about him, and food seemed likely to fail, he records that often he would take out the old hymn book, and seated under some sheltering tree, would read aloud the words of this hymn, and arise encouraged and comforted.

No. 490.

"VAIN, DELUSIVE WORLD ADIEU."

REV. CHARLES WESLEY, 1708—1788.

Rev. Adam Clarke was the great Methodist commentator. His comments on the Bible fill six great volumes, and they were for many years among the most popular, at least among Methodists. When Adam Clarke was a young man of twenty-three, he was one of Wesley's itinerant preachers and was sent by him to preach on one occasion in a little country village in England. At the close of one of their services in a crowded room, they were singing this hymn, when Mr. Clarke stopped them and made an earnest appeal to the young people present to follow out the teaching of the hymn and give themselves to God. Thirteen took his advice and there between the stanzas of this hymn began the Christian life. To me a hymn which a century and a half ago was used and sung under such conditions becomes almost a sacred thing.

No. 491.

"JESUS, THESE EYES HAVE NEVER SEEN."

Rev. Ray Palmer, 1808—1887.

It is a constant wonder what apparently trivial things are always leading us toward things of high importance. Now here is a hymn that has become known and loved the world around, and it had its origin in an occurrence of trifling moment. Its author was sitting in his study at Albany, New York, preparing a sermon which had Christ for its special theme. Needing a volume from his bookcase, which had doors to it, he arose and opened the bookcase door, when the book he wanted appeared right before his eyes. It occurred to him that in some such way, as the opening of a door, the face of Christ, near us all the time, but unseen, would be revealed to us, and the thought filled his heart so that he turned to his desk and wrote this hymn. Although the author is best known by the hymn, "My faith looks up to Thee," he himself preferred this to any other he had written. And when he was dying and had become so feeble that his words were scarcely audible, he was heard to whisper one of its stanzas:

"When death these mortal eyes shall seal,
And still this throbbing heart,
The rending veil shall Thee reveal,
All glorious as Thou art."

No. 492.

"MY FAITH LOOKS UP TO THEE."

Rev. Ray Palmer, 1808—1887.

This hymn affords an illustration of the peculiar craze called "Anglomania." It was published in a hymn book in 1832, and although the book became quite well known, this hymn attracted little attention beyond being reprinted in a few newspapers. An English minister (Dr. Andrew Reed), himself a hymn writer, while on a visit to America, found it floating about in a newspaper, cut it out and carried it to England with him and inserted it without any author's name in a hymn book he compiled. It had several years of English life before it was much known here, and then some American compiler, going as so many Americans do to England for his goods, found this and imported it again to the country of its birth.

No. 493.

"YET THERE IS ROOM! THE LAMB'S BRIGHT HALL."

Rev. Horatius Bonar, 1808—1889.

When Moody and Sankey visited Scotland, no one entered more heartily into their work than Rev. Horatius Bonar. At that time, although the hymns he had written were used in the worship of song in churches all over the world, they had never been heard in his own church, which still retained the old version of the Psalms honored by the use of several generations of worshippers. Mr. Bonar wrote several hymns especially for the use of Mr. Sankey in these evangelistic services and this one among the rest.

While Moody and Sankey were in Scotland, a gay young woman was one day invited by a friend to go with her to their meeting. At first she declined, saying she did not care to hear them, but at last consented and went. Neither Mr. Sankey's singing, nor Mr. Moody's preaching made any impression upon her, and she wondered why people were making such a stir about such a commonplace sort of service. At last came the time to close, and Mr. Sankey ended the meeting by singing alone, this hymn, which had been written for him by Mr. Bonar. He had reached the last stanza:

"Ere night that gate may close, and seal thy doom,
Then the last, low, long cry, 'No room, no room!
No room, no room! Oh, woeful cry, no room!' "

These closing words startled her like a sudden peal of thunder. She went away, but the words followed her and kept repeating themselves over and over in her ears, "No room! No room! No room!" And they brought her at last to a committal of herself to Christ.

No. 494.

"FEAR NOT, O LITTLE FLOCK, THE FOE."

Gustavus Adolphus, King of Sweden, in prose.
Dr. Jacob Fabricius, in poetry, 1593—1654.
Miss Catherine Winkworth, 1829—1873.

This hymn was born in one of the most terrible times that ever troubled Europe—the Thirty Years' War—which began soon after the death of Luther, and was the effort of the Roman Church to crush out the Reformation he had started. Count Tilly, a German soldier, had been placed at the head of the armies of the Catholic League, and for twenty years he devastated the Protestant cities and provinces, overcoming every army that appeared against him, and never being defeated in a single battle.

On the tenth of May, 1631, he captured the City of Madgeburg and permitted his soldiers to burn the town and massacre in cold blood twenty-five thousand of its inhabitants. But this was his last victory. A new soldier had come upon the scene. Gustavus Adolphus, King of Sweden, had become the champion of the Protestant Union, had landed the year before with an army, small but determined, on the northern coast, and was sweeping southward with a record of victories, almost as uniform as that of the Catholic Commander. They met on the seventh of September, 1631, near Leipsic, and Gustavus was victorious over the general, and the army, which had never before been vanquished, and then while his army rested, he wrote down roughly in prose, a hymn for them to sing, and his chaplain changed it into verse, and here it is translated for us by an English lady, Miss Winkworth.

His army often sang it after that as they kneeled upon the battle field before the fight began, and they sang it on the morning of the day its author fell, while leading them against the army of the Catholics.

Tilly had been again defeated, and slain, on the battle field, by Gustavus; and Wallenstein, another celebrated general, now commanded his army. It was at Lutzen, November 6, 1632, Gustavus had spent the night in preparing for the contest, and after a foggy morning, at about ten o'clock the mist had risen, disclosing the opposing armies. The army of Gustavus, as was their custom, knelt down for a moment of prayer, then sang the old battle hymn of Luther—"A Mighty Fortress is our God, A

Bulwark never failing," and then the hymn of their own commander,

"Fear not, O little flock, the foe."

And then they charged upon the enemy.

The battle was hot and seemed at one time likely to go against the Protestants. Just then Gustavus was wounded and fell to the ground, and his horse galloped riderless back. His soldiers saw and recognized the horse of the King, and this roused them to such a fury that they swept over against the Catholic Army with a force that nothing could resist, and gained the day, but Gustavus, the King, was dead.

As we sing this hymn, let us remember amid what terrible scenes it had its birth, and what a part it has had in the great contest that gave to Germany religious liberty.

No. 495.

"JUST AS I AM WITHOUT ONE PLEA."

Miss Charlotte Elliott, 1789—1871.

An English sea captain, notorious for his wickedness, once attempted to commit suicide but was brought back to life.

Thinking of himself as alive, and yet if he could have had his own way, as dead, he was impressed with the thought that an overruling Providence had stepped in to thwart his purpose, and that some better life awaited him. With this impression he went into a little seaside church and listened to a sermon, at the end of which the preacher invited any one who wished to be saved to come the next evening and talk with him. He went, and soon had told all the story of his life to the minister, who made him no reply, but took a hymn book, turned down a leaf at a particular hymn, handed it to the man, and told him to take it home and read that hymn carefully as if in the presence of God, and to "mean it when he read it."

The captain turned away somewhat indignant at the way he had been treated. "Have I come all this way," he thought, "merely to be sent away with a hymn book?" On his way out of the church he thought he would see right then what the hymn was which he had been told to read, "and to mean it when he read." So he sat down in a pew and read the words of this hymn, "Just as I am without one plea."

The words startled him when he thought of the minister's direction, but he read on, every line and word seeming to have been written for him. He caught the minister's thought, and made the words his own then and there, and went away a saved man.

No. 496.

"JESUS! THE NAME HIGH OVER ALL."

REV. CHARLES WESLEY, 1708—1788.

How the hymns we heard our mothers sing when we were children come back to us in after years, and sometimes mould and fashion our lives.

There is a story of a mother with whom this hymn was a favorite so that she used to sing it while engaged in her daily duties. One stanza attracted the attention of her little daughter, and fixed itself in her memory:

"Oh that the world might taste and see
The riches of His grace;
His arms of grace that compass me,
Would all mankind embrace."

From this verse, sung by the mother during her childhood, there came to her the thought of devoting her life to the work of foreign missions, and she is now (1890) at work among the women of India, telling them "the riches of His grace."

No. 497.

"WHAT MEANS THIS EAGER ANXIOUS THRONG."

MISS ETTA CAMPBELL.

During the year 1864, there was a great revival of religion in Newark, New Jersey. At one of the meetings, Mr. R. G. Pardee made an address based on the answer given to blind Bartimeus when he asked the meaning of the multitude whose tramping feet he heard as they passed the place where he sat begging. "And they told him that Jesus of Nazareth passeth by." (Luke, 18:37.)

Miss Campbell was present, and it seemed to her a fitting subject for a poem descriptive of the throngs that were then pressing along the streets of Newark drawn by the manifest presence of Christ. It soon found its way into a collection of revival hymns first set to the tune of "Sweet hour of prayer" and later to a tune of its own, composed by Mr. Theodore Perkins.

The Rev. E. P. Hammond relates that a gambler once came into a revival meeting at Lockport, New York, where this song was being sung. He was converted, and a few days later, in telling his experience, he said that this hymn had been the means of awakening him, and added that when he went out of the church that day, as he was passing over the canal, he took from his pocket his pack of cards, the implements of his profession, which he called "The Devil's Testament with its fifty-two leaves," and threw them into the water below.

No. 498.

"THERE IS A FOUNTAIN FILLED WITH BLOOD."

WILLIAM COWPER, 1721—1800.

This hymn is as cordially hated by some as it is cordially loved by others. It has been called "The Slaughter House Hymn," and those especially who look to Christ as an example to be followed, rather than as the One whose blood cleanseth from all sin, protest against its use . Even James Montgomery, earnest Christian that he was, disliked it, but his criticism was mostly against the first couplet.

He thought it incorrect to speak of "a fountain filled with blood," and he tried to mend the fault by a stanza of his own.

"From Calvary's cross a fountain flows,
Of water and of blood:
More healing than Bethesda's pool,
Or famed Siloam's flood."

But this stanza, more correct in phraseology possibly, fell flat, and Cowper's is still sung, and will be, perhaps, as long as the old Bible verse is remembered which says that, "In that day there shall be a fountain opened in the house of David, and to the inhabitants of Jerusalem, for sin and for uncleanness."

No. 499.

"ALONE, YET NOT ALONE AM I."

During the old French War in this country, a party of Indians, then allies of the French, made a descent upon the town of Carlisle, Pennsylvania, killing the father and son of a poor German family, and carrying two little girls away captive; the mother was absent from home.

Many years after, one of these little girls, with many other captives, was released and taken back to the place from which she had been taken. Relatives and friends of those who had been captured so many years before came to see if they could recognize their lost ones, and among them came this mother seeking her two lost children. The girl had grown beyond recognition, and she failed to find her.

At last the officer having them in charge inquired if she could not remember something with which her children were familiar at home, and which might help them to recognize her if they were present. She replied that there was a hymn that she used to sing to them often, and she began to sing it over again:

"Alone, yet not alone am I,
Though in this solitude so drear!
I feel my Savior always nigh."

She had only gotten so far when a young woman came rushing from the crowd of released captives, and threw herself into her arms, and together, the mother and daughter sang the remaining lines:

"He comes the weary hours to cheer,
I am with Him and He with me,
Even here, alone I cannot be."

No. 500.

"THE SON OF GOD! THE LORD OF LIFE."

George Mogridge, 1787—1854.

In England sixty or seventy years ago, there lived a man who had been in the Japan-ware business, but had failed and turned his attention to the writing of books for children. At this he proved more successful, and his books became the standard stories for the children of that day. They were full of adventure and fun, and at the same time always contained a good moral that made them safe for any child to read.

He wrote under the name of "Old Humphrey," and that name became as familiar to the children of old England as that of "Peter Parley" to the children of New England.

His name was George Mogridge, and he wrote poetry as well as prose. This hymn is one of his.

No. 501.

"THAT DAY OF WRATH, THAT DREADFUL DAY."

Sir Walter Scott, 1771—1832.

A little more than a century ago (in 1786) a Scotch boy of fifteen years, of delicate constitution, might have been seen limping about, for he was lame, listening to the tellers of old stories, and reading as his fancy or his whim directed, in history, or poetry, or story.

Ten years later he ventured to publish a book himself, and then, year after year, he sent out book after book, always of poetry. "Marion," "The Lady of the Lake," "The Lay of the Last Minstrel," and so on, and then suddenly he changed his course and wrote no more poetry but sent out one after another romances in prose, until twenty-seven of the Waverly Novels had appeared, and the author was rich and lived in a beautiful home. Then his publishers failed, and left him with an expensive home and a great burden of debt. But he determined to ask no favors, but to pay every debt by the fruit of his pen. This his books eventually did, but it was at the expense of the author's life. Worn out by the task he had set himself to do, he gave up his work and his books, and called a son-in-law to read to him from that book which, he said, was the only one a dying man cared to hear, and so he died.

This hymn is a translation of an old Latin hymn of the thirteenth century by Thomas of Celano; introduced by Sir Walter Scott into the "Lay of the Last Minstrel."

It is in the sixth canto of the poem, the one beginning with the words familiar to most of the school boys:

"Breathes there a man with soul so dead,
Who never to himself hath said,
'This is my own, my native land!'"

The marriage feast of Lady Margaret has been described, the minstrels have one after another sung their songs, and the sudden gloom, the single flash of lightning, and the single thunder peal have terrified the guests, and they had gone on pilgrimage to Melrose Abbey. And then the poem goes on:

"And slow up the dim aisle afar,
With sable cowl and scapular,
And snow white stoles in order due,
The holy Fathers two and two
In long procession came:
Taper and host and book they bear,
And holy banner flourished fair
With the Redeemer's name.
Above the prostrate pilgrim band,
The Mitred Abbot stretched his hand,
And blessed them as they kneeled.
With holy cross he signed them all,
And prayed they might be sage in hall
And fortunate in field.
Then Mass was sung and prayers were said
And solemn requiem for the dead:
And bells toll'd out their mighty peal
For the departed spirit's weal;

And ever in the office close
The hymn of Intercession rose:
And far the echoing aisles prolong,
The awful burthen of the song,
'That day of wrath, that awful day.'"

No. 502.

"ARISE, MY SOUL, ARISE."

REV. CHARLES WESLEY, 1708—1788.

Rev. Mr. Cranswick, for many years a missionary to the West Indies, refers to this hymn as one of the most useful he has ever met. He says he has a record of over two hundred persons who were apparently converted during the singing of it. He made great use of it in revival services and would frequently ask inquirers to join in the singing of it as far as they could do so heartily, making its sentiments their own. Sometimes they would hesitate at one of the stanzas, and then he would have the whole audience begin the hymn again. Usually they faltered at the last stanza.

"My God is reconciled:
His pardoning voice I hear:
He owns me for his child:
I can no longer fear:
With confidence I now draw nigh:
And 'Father, Abba, Father,' cry."

And then they would all begin again and sing along through the experiences of which the different stanzas sing, until at last, with bright faces and joyous hearts, the whole hymn could be sung.

No. 503.

"O DAY OF REST AND GLADNESS, O DAY OF JOY AND LIGHT."

CHRISTOPHER WORDSWORTH, *Bishop.*

One Sunday morning there was a visitor at the house of the author of this hymn who was to officiate in the pulpit that day. He was with Wordsworth in the library when the latter put his arm in his and said, "Come upstairs with me, the ladies are going to sing a hymn to encourage you in your labor for the day." So they went and sang from slips of paper on which had been written, this hymn. Several days later the visitor found out that Wordsworth himself had written it.

No. 504.

"LORD DISMISS US WITH THY BLESSING, BID US NOW DEPART IN PEACE."

REV. ROBERT HAWKER, 1753—1828.

There is a funny story connected with this hymn, which, however, does not spoil the hymn by being told. The author published a little collection of hymns such as were sung by the children of the Sunday school connected with his church, and this one was included in the collection, but with no author's name attached. It was the custom to sing it at the close of the evening service, so that it became quite well known to his people.

One day a young grandson of Dr. Hawker, who afterward became a very eccentric clergyman, but who was then young, came to the Doctor's study with a paper in his hand and said, "Grandfather, I don't altogether like that hymn, 'Lord dismiss us with thy blessing.' I think it might be improved in meter and language, and would be better if somewhat longer."

"Oh indeed," said Dr. Hawker, getting a little red in the face, "and what emendations commend themselves to your precocious wisdom?"

"This is my improved version," said the youngster, and then he read four stanzas of his own writing. When he had finished reading his own, he read the short hymn as it was in the book and added, "Now this is crude and flat, don't you think so, Grandfather?"

"Crude and flat, sir! Why, you young puppy, it is mine! I wrote that hymn."

"Oh! I beg your pardon, Grandfather, I did not know that. It is a very nice hymn, indeed, but—but," as he went through the door, "mine is better."

However, we still sing the Grandfather's hymn.

No. 505.

"O SACRED HEAD, ONCE WOUNDED."

This is one of seven "passion hymns" written in Latin by St. Bernard of Clairvaux, a monk of the Roman Church. They are addressed respectively to the feet, the knees, the hands, the side, the breast, the heart, and the face of the Savior on the cross. This is the last of the seven, addressed to the face. It was and still is one of the best of the Latin hymns. The German translation was equally popular, and the English words have found a place in nearly all our hymnals.

Just see what a combination this hymn presents. Three learned men of three different races, living in three different centuries, belonging to three different churches, and speaking three different languages, have united their work to prepare it for our use.

No. 506.

"LIFE IS WEARY, SAVIOR, TAKE ME."

"LEAVE GOD TO ORDER ALL THY WAYS."

GEORGE NEUMARK, 1621.

A poor young man gained his living, in Hamburg by his skill upon the violin, but by and by he fell sick so that he could no longer play, and so could no longer earn his food.

One night he stole off to a Jew and pawned his violin for a little money to buy bread. As he was putting the instrument into the hands of the money lender, he looked at it as if it were his child and asked if he might play just one more tune upon it.

"Of all sad hearts that have left your door," said he, "mine is the saddest." The tears came to his eyes, and his voice choked, and then he took the instrument and began to play a tune exquisitely soft, and then began to sing a hymn which he himself had written:

"Life is weary, Savior, take me."

He played and sang, and then laid down the violin and rushed out of the door, but as he went he stumbled against some one in the darkness. Some one who had been listening to his song.

"Could you tell me where I could get a copy of that song?" The inquirer was the servant of a wealthy man, who learned the story of the violin and its owner, and took him into his employ. He soon reclaimed his old violin, and with it went to see his old landlady, who had always been his friend in trouble. As soon as it was known that he had come, her room filled up with neighbors and friends, eager to hear him play and sing, and to them he sang another hymn which he also wrote himself:

"Leave God to order all thy ways.
And hope in Him, whate'er betide."

This was George Neumark. When asked if he wrote the hymn he replied, "Well, yes; I am the instrument, but God swept the strings. All I knew was that these words, 'Who trusts in God's unchanging love,' lay like a soft burden on my heart. I went over them again and again, and so they shaped themselves into a song."

No. 507.

"ONWARD, CHRISTIAN SOLDIERS, MARCHING AS TO WAR."

REV. SABINE BARING-GOULD.

A Mission School in England, at its festivals, was in the habit of marching from the schoolroom to the Parish church with a banner at the head of the procession with the cross inscribed upon it, and the author wrote this hymn to be sung on the way. This explains the language of the stanza:

"Onward, Christian soldiers,
Marching as to war,
With the cross of Jesus,
Going on before."

It has been the occasion of a story just a little bit laughable, but not too much so to spoil the usefulness of the hymn, which, with the excellent tune written for it by Sir Arthur Sullivan has become very popular.

The Bishop of Ripon was on one occasion about to join in a church processional, when he noticed a banner before him with a cross on it and requested that it be removed, as he disliked the idea of this use of the cross. The rector said, "My Lord, we are about to sing as a processional, 'Onward, Christian soldiers;' shall we alter the last lines to read, 'With the cross of Jesus left behind the door?' " "Substitute another hymn," said the Bishop, and they did so.

No. 508.

"LORD DISMISS US WITH THY BLESSING,
FILL OUR HEARTS WITH JOY AND PEACE,
LET US EACH THY LOVE POSSESSING,
TRIUMPH IN REDEEMING GRACE."

HON. AND REV. EALTER SHIRLEY, 1725—1786.

The author of this hymn was a devoted preacher of the gospel, and when he had passed his three-score years, and was so great a sufferer as not to be able to appear in the pulpit or even to lie down in bed, he was often to be found sitting in a chair in his own house preaching to an audience that filled the rooms and stairways of a spacious dwelling, as far as his voice could be heard.

For those who gathered thus to listen to his words, he composed a hymn to be sung as they parted from him, and from each other, which has been used as a closing hymn for a century and more.

The authorship of the hymn as given above is not certain. By some it is claimed for John Fawcett, who wrote "Blest be the tie that binds," but Fawcett did not claim it for himself.

No. 509.

JOHN SEBASTIAN BACH.

In 1685 (March 21) there was born a little German boy, who soon began to show a love for music. He was an orphan and lived with a brother who was a church organist, but the little boy went ahead so rapidly with his musical studies, that he outstripped his older brother, who was jealous of his progress, forbade his doing anything but his daily allotted task, and kept him from getting the books he coveted.

In an old cupboard in the house they lived in, the boy knew there was, away on the upper shelf, a rare old book of manuscript music, and he never passed the old cupboard, without a thought how he might get this book.

The upper part of the cupboard door was of lattice work, and he thought he might possibly squeeze his little hand through this, and contrive to pull the soft parchment through, so he watched his opportunity when no one was about, and got the book safely into his possession. Now if he could only copy it before it should be missed, but how,—for his brother refused him candles or lights, but he could not refuse him moonlight. So waiting for moonlight nights, and working at the window of his little room, he at last copied the whole book; but no sooner had he begun to use the music it contained than his brother found him out and burned the book before his very eyes.

Somehow it seems to me that when I see written above a tune we sing the name of this boy, John Sebastian Bach, I take a little greater interest in the music for knowing of these struggles of his boyhood.

No. 510.

"GREENVILLE" (Tune).

Jean Jacques Rousseau, 1712—1778.

Something of the sacredness of this tune may be lost to us if we learn its origin and its composer.

An adventurer roaming about France and Switzerland, a profligate with a mistress in each new city he made his home, an infidel or sceptic in religion, a brilliant writer and a good musician, such and worse was Rousseau.

In 1752 he published an opera in French entitled "Le Devin de Village."

In one of the scenes there is a melody, without words, headed "Pantomime" and arranged for stringed instruments. About forty years later this appeared in England with the words of a love song attached. A quarter of a century later it was again published under the name of "Rousseau's Dream," and under this title with the words of the love song, it is still to be found in song collections, in just the form in which we sing it to sacred words, under the name of "Greenville."

No. 511.

"O THOU WHO CAMEST FROM ABOVE."

REV. CHARLES WESLEY.

When the Methodist preachers met in conference with Mr. Wesley, he kept them busy telling their experiences, and so at one such conference a number of them agreed among themselves that they would turn the tables on him by asking him his, so when the hour arrived one of them addressed him: "Mr. Wesley, you often ask us about our experiences and now we should like to be favored with yours."

"Very well," was the reply, "you shall have it." And then he repeated this hymn. "That is my experience," said he, "can any Christian give a better?"

No. 512.

"TELL ME THE OLD, OLD STORY."

"I LOVE TO TELL THE STORY."

MISS KATE HANKEY.

These two hymns are the two parts of a "Life of Jesus in Verse," written by an English lady in 1866. The first part is entitled, "The Story Wanted," and the second, "The Story Told."

A few months after they were published in England, there was a Y. M. C. A. convention at Montreal. Among those present was Major General Russell, who was then in command of the English forces detailed to protect the Canadian frontier from the much talked of Fenian raid. He arose in the meeting and read the first part, beginning with the words, "Tell me the old, old story," from a manuscript copy he held in his hand; as he read it the tears rolled down his cheeks, and the sight of an old soldier, reading a simple song like that, and weeping as he read, attracted much attention in the meeting.

Mr. M. H. Doane of Cincinnati heard him read it, obtained of him a copy, and on the stagecoach, riding from the Glenn Falls House to the Crawford, in the White Mountains, he wrote the music for it, and sang it in the hotel parlor that evening.

It is somewhat curious that these two hymns led to the writing of a third a few months later by Mrs. Emily Huntingdon Miller in the same meter, and intended as a sequel to the others, and beginning,

"I love to hear the story."

No. 513.

"NORTHFIELD" (Tune).

JEREMIAH INGALLS, 1764—1838.

Mr. Ingalls was one of the early tune writers of America, following soon after William Billings.

The tradition is, that traveling in Massachusetts, on one occasion he became very hungry, and stopping at a wayside inn, he ordered dinner, which was long delayed.

The delay gave him time to think of his spiritual hunger, and to compose this tune.

It is often used for the hymn beginning:

"Lo! what a glorious sight appears."

No. 514.

"WELLESLEY" (Tune).

MISS LIZZIE S. TOURGEE.

This tune was written by a school girl, daughter of the eminent composer and singer, Dr. Eben Tourgee. She was a member of the High School at Newton, Massachusetts.

A hymn for the graduating class had been written, and she had been asked to write the music for it. She took it to her father, telling him that she did not know how to compose a tune appropriate to the words.

"Sit down to the piano," replied her father, "put the words before you and try."

She did as directed, and this tune came floating into her mind. Her father, in publishing it later, gave it the name of the college near by, "Wellesley."

No. 515.

"PEACE MY HEART, BE CALM, BE STILL."

REV. CHARLES WESLEY, 1708—1788.

The wife of Charles Wesley was at one time attacked by smallpox, and before she had entirely recovered, their first born child died of the same disease.

The father wrote this hymn for his own, but more especially for his wife's comfort, entitling it, "A Mother's Act of Resignation on the Death of a Child."

A city pastor once found his way into a cellar, in one of the poverty-stricken parts of Manchester, England.

The father was dying of consumption, and the mother was bending over the body of her dead child.

The minister tried first to console the mother in her sorrow, and then turned to the father, and told him of the bright hope there was for those who died in childhood.

The man replied that he knew of no such hope, and pointing to a shelf, on which were a few infidel books, he said, those books contained his opinions.

"Yes," said the minister, "but these books give you no comfort now. I'm not going to dispute with you, but I have a wife, and we, too, have lost a child. My wife was reconciled to her loss, by thinking what her child had gained, and there is a hymn written by a man in just such circumstances as you are in now, that helped us, and it may help you." And then he read this hymn.

When he finished, the mother's face was calm, and there was a tear in the father's eye. Then he prayed, and when he had ended, it was the mother's voice that first spoke. "I will follow my child to Jesus," said she; "And so will I," the father responded.

No. 516.

"WHEN THOU MY RIGHTEOUS JUDGE SHALT COME."

SELINA SHIRLEY, COUNTESS OF HUNTINGDON.

A titled lady spoke offensively of Lady Huntingdon, in the presence of King George the Third, and he replied, "Pray, madam, are you acquainted with Lady Huntingdon?"

"I am not," was the reply.

"Have you ever been in her company?" again the King asked.

"Never," said the somewhat astonished lady.

"Never form your opinion of any one," said the King, "from the ill-natured remarks and censures of others. Judge for yourself, and you have my leave to tell everybody how highly I think of Lady Huntingdon."

Lady Huntingdon, and her husband too, were earnest Christian people. She employed preachers, and built chapels for them to preach in, and gathered about her so many zealous evangelists, that they formed almost a denomination by themselves, and were known as, "The Lady Huntingdon Connexion." They annoyed some of the less-zealous clergy of the established church, and a Bishop once complained to that same King George the Third, that these zealous preachers of Lady Huntingdon disturbed his diocese.

"Make Bishops of them, make Bishops of them," the King replied.

"That might be done," the Bishop rejoined, "but please your Majesty, we cannot make a Bishop of Lady Huntingdon."

" 'Tis true," chimed in the Queen, "but it would be a lucky circumstance if you could, for she puts you all to shame."

This was the sort of woman who though no great poet, yet wrote one or two hymns which have survived their author, and come down to us.

No. 517.

"SISTER, THOU WAST MILD AND LOVELY."

REV. SAMUEL F. SMITH.

This hymn, written by the author of, "My Country, 'tis of Thee," was once made very apt use of by Dr. Lowell Mason, in connection with the composition of one of his own tunes.

He was, in 1833, teaching music in the public schools of Boston. In July of that year, a girl of sixteen died, who had been a member of the Mt. Vernon School, much beloved by her companions, and who had taken much interest in Dr. Mason's singing lessons.

When the hour for the next lesson after her death arrived, Dr. Mason entered the room, and at once commenced writing upon the blackboard a series of exercises for the pupils to sing. He said but little, and nothing about the girl who had died, but these blackboard exercises were all of a plaintive sort, in harmony with the feeling of solemnity which pervaded the school.

When the music hour was nearly done, he rapidly combined the short passages they had been practising into a tune, and had them sing it several times, until they had become a little familiar with it, and then he quickly wrote on the board beneath the music, the words of this hymn:

"Sister, thou wast mild and lovely."

And the whole school sang it to the tune just written for it, when Dr. Mason closed the lesson, and left the room.

The impression left on the minds of the pupils, by this delicate tribute to their companion who had died, was deep and lasting.

In memory of the occasion, he gave to the tune the name of the school, "Mt. Vernon."

No. 518.

"ALL HAIL THE POWER OF JESUS' NAME."

REV. EDWARD PERRONET.

One evening John Wesley was preaching in his chapel in London, when he chanced to see, sitting among the audience, a brother minister, with whom he had had some acquaintance, but whom he had never heard preach.

This seemed to him like a long-sought opportunity, and so, without so much as saying, "By your leave, Sir," he announced that the man would preach in that pulpit on the following morning at five o'clock.

The preacher so unceremoniously announced did not wish to disturb the meeting by a refusal, especially as that would seem to oppose Mr. Wesley, and yet he didn't altogether like that method of arranging matters.

Next morning at five o'clock he was in the pulpit. After the opening service was over, he said that he had been announced to preach, without consultation, and should do so only at the expense of his own feelings, out of respect for Mr. Wesley. But that although weak, and unprepared, he should give them the best sermon they had ever heard, and then he read the Sermon on the Mount, and without a word of comment, closed the service with song and prayer.

This was Edward Perronet, who wrote one splendid hymn:

"All hail the power of Jesus' name."

It is needless to suggest, that if the good brothers had lived in these times, neither one of them would have done so discourteous a thing.

No. 519.

"WHOSOEVER HEARETH, SHOUT, SHOUT THE SOUND."

PHILIP BLISS.

In the winter of 1869, a young evangelist from England, named Henry Moorhouse, came to this country to preach.

He was quite small in stature, and boyish in appearance, and scarcely more than a boy in years.

Some one tells the story of going to hear him one evening, when he took for his text the words recorded in John, 3:16, "God so loved the world," etc., and thinking that he never heard so much brought out of that wonderful text before. So he went next night, to see what he would have to say on some other verse, and was surprised to hear the same text announced, and another sermon, different entirely from the first, and throwing still more light upon the words.

And so for six successive evenings, this boy preacher, as he was called, preached from the same text, unfolding each evening more and more of its meaning and power.

This hymn, with the tune to which it is sung, was written by Mr. Bliss, after listening to these six sermons, to embody the new views he had received, of the freeness and fulness of the gospel invitation, as given in this text.

No. 520.

"I LOVE TO STEAL AWHILE AWAY"—1818.

MRS. PHOEBE HINSDALE BROWN, 1783—1861.

Phoebe Hinsdale was an orphan girl at Canaan, New York.

A few months of school in each year, forgetting between times nearly all she had been taught before, found her at eighteen years of age, still unable to read.

She married a house painter by the name of Brown, who took her to Ellington, Connecticut; but marriage did not improve her fortune. She was poor, and pressed by the hard, unending cares of the house, and of children, and sometimes in the early evening, just to have a bit of quiet, she would leave her kitchen, and her children, and walk back and forth, under a row of elms, that grew along the roadside, between her home and the nearest neighbor.

One day she was visiting at the house of her pastor, Rev. Dr. Hyde, and his neighbor, with others, was present. Just as Mrs. Brown was rising to go home, this lady turned to her, and somewhat curtly said, "Mrs. Brown, why do you come up at evening so near our house, and then go back without coming in? If you want anything, why don't you come in and ask for it? I could not think who it was, and sent my girl down the garden to see; and she said it was you, that you came to the fence, but seeing her turned quickly away, muttering something to yourself."

Mrs. Brown made no reply, but that evening, after the children were all in bed, except the baby, she sat down in the kitchen with the baby in her arms, and burst into a flood of tears, and then she wrote what she called, "An Apology for her Twilight Rambles," addressing them to this lady.

"I love to steal awhile away,
From little ones and care."

This was strictly true. "I had," she says, "four little children, a small unfurnished house, a sick sister in the only furnished room, and there was not a place above or below, where I could retire for devotion without a liability to be interrupted."

But after the unkind words spoken to her that day, she never took that walk again.

No. 521.

"LISTED INTO THE CAUSE OF SIN."

Rev. Charles Wesley.

Charles Wesley stood in the open air, one day, in a seaport town of England, and began to sing. This was the way in which he often gathered an audience, and it was his purpose now, when his singing had drawn a crowd together, to preach a sermon to them.

But there came along a party of jolly sailors, "half seas over" with grog, and hearing the singing, they stopped and began to sing themselves. But their song was one of their own, and not that which Mr. Wesley sang.

He could not compete against their greater numbers, and so he made one of those quick turns, at which he was such an adept, and having caught the music of the song they sang, he challenged them to come back again later in the day, and he would be there and sing them a new song to their own tune.

They came at the appointed time, and so did he, and this was the song he sang. The tars were generous fellows, and owning themselves beaten, they enjoyed the song, and stayed to hear the sermon that came after it.

The tune was, "Nancy Dawson."

No. 522.

Miss Anne Steele.

In the town of Broughton, England, there was a Baptist preacher who had been born there, and yet was an exception to the proverb, about the honor a prophet has in his own country, for he was so popular a preacher that he drew away the flock of the curate of the Established Church, who complained to his Bishop of the depletion of his parish, and asked how he might best oppose him.

"Go home," said the Bishop, "and preach better sermons than Henry Steele, and your people will return."

It may seem a little far-fetched as an introduction to this hymn, to relate an incident about her father's uncle, as I have done, but when the Rev. Henry Steele laid down the pastorate of that church, his nephew took it up, and carried it on for sixty years, and the incident will give you the surroundings amid which Anne Steele was nurtured.

This father wrote in his diary one day—it was November 29, 1757—"This day Nannie sent a part of her composition to London to be printed. I entreat a gracious God, who enabled and stirred her up to such a work, to direct it, and bless it, for the good and comfort of many."

And later, three times at least, the father records in his diary, his prayer that the book his daughter has written may be made useful in the world.

Is it any wonder that hymns, so tended by a father's care, and followed as they started out, by a father's prayers, have come down to us through a century and a quarter, and are still singing their way along among the churches?

No. 523.

Bernard of Clairvaux, 1091—1153.

One of the most wonderful, as well as one of the best of men, was Bernard the Monk of Clairvaux.

The story of his life reads like a romance. An evening might be spent in talking about it, and the talk would be stimulating to every noble virtue and pure thought.

When twenty-five years old, he was chosen leader of a band of twelve monks, who started out to found a new monastery.

The spot was a valley, in the midst of pathless forests, and haunted by robber bands. It was called the "Valley of

Wormwood," but he, with the band which gathered about him, transformed it into a place of beauty, and changed its name to "Clairvaux," the bright valley.

He was an eloquent preacher, and he preached the crusade, until his appeal stirred not only France, but Europe, to wrest from the hands of the Turk the Holy Land and Sepulcher. But he preached a crusade against sin in the heart, and in the life, as well as a crusade against the Turks.

He was one of the most active men of his age, shared in all its contests, and worked with unceasing diligence to reform the religion of the church, and the lives of the people.

His personal life and influence was as lovely as it was commanding. His eyes were described as "dove like," his face as "angelic," his smile as "benevolent," his letters as "the bread of consolation," and men who had come under his influence, flocked to him at Clairvaux, to be near him for counsel, and sympathy, and help, and as they stood weeping about his bed, when at sixty-two he was dying, his last whispered words were: "I am in a strait betwixt two, having a desire to depart and be with Christ, which is far better; nevertheless the love of my children urgeth me to remain here below."

No. 524.

"A DEEP AND HOLY AWE."

JOACHIM NEANDER.

One day a wild and careless German boy, with a couple of boon companions, went into a church in Bremen to ridicule the service. But the sermon they heard touched the leader's conscience, and set him thinking, and then led him to reform his wild life.

He was fond of hunting, and one day he followed his game so far, that night came on, and he lost his way among the mountains, where climbing even by daylight was perilous.

After wandering about a while, he suddenly found himself on the edge of a cliff, where another forward step would throw him down a precipice. He was almost overcome with terror, and prayed to God for rescue, and promised if it were given to devote his life to His service.

All at once, as if by miracle, he felt his strength and courage return, and he imagined a hand was leading him. He followed it, and it brought him safely to his home.

He kept his vow. By and by he became head master of a school at Düsseldorf, and he taught religion to his scholars as well as mathematics, and outside of school he preached, and held other religious services.

These gave offense, and he was commanded not to preach, was deposed from his school, and banished from the town. It was in the summer when this occurred, and he wandered away into a glen on the River Rhine, and here he lived for several months in a cave in the rocks, still known as "Neander's Cave," and here he wrote hymns, which remembering his promise to God, he called "Songs of the Covenant," and this was one of these songs written in "Neander's Cave."

No. 525.

"O LORD THY HEAVENLY GRACE IMPART."

Rev. John Frederick Oberlin, 1740—1826.

In the year 1767, a young man of twenty-seven years became the pastor of a little mountain village, in the north-eastern part of France between Alsace and Lorraine.

He found his people few in numbers, poor, ignorant, and for the most part irreligious.

He entered at once into the life of the people, taught them better modes of cultivation than they had known before, helped them to build roads and to improve their homes, sent their boys away to learn trades, and founded a school for those who remained at home, and while caring for their souls, so interested himself in their temporal welfare too, that the population increased fivefold, and the place was everywhere spoken of for the piety, and prosperity of its people.

One Sunday in 1820, he preached a sermon to his people from the text, "He shall see of the travail of His soul, and shall be satisfied," and at the close of the sermon he read this hymn, and then said, "My dear friends, may these be the feelings of our hearts, and as such let us sing them," and then the whole congregation joined in singing the words their pastor had written.

No. 526.

"I WANT TO BE AN ANGEL."

Mrs. Sydney P. Gill.

For many years this was a very popular Sunday school song, and perhaps at that time it was useful, but there are better hymns for that use now, containing sentiments more natural and helpful.

Its author had been teaching the infant class, in a Philadelphia Sunday school, and angels had been the subject of the lesson.

At the close a little child spoke up, "I want to be an angel." The child died a few days after, and the hymn was written to be sung in her memory, in the school to which she belonged.

No. 527.

"JUST AS I AM WITHOUT ONE PLEA."

Miss Charlotte Elliott.

John B. Gough tells a curious story, the point of which is associated with the singing of this hymn.

Sitting in a city church, one morning, he was annoyed by the actions of a man whom the usher showed into the same pew.

The man's face was repulsive, "mottled," as Mr. Gough described it, "like castile soap." His lips twitched, and every now and then his mouth would make a singular sound.

Mr. Gough moved away from him as far as he could, to the other end of the pew. By and by the audience arose to sing this hymn:

> "Just as I am, without one plea,
> But that Thy blood was shed for me."

The man knew the hymn, and sang without any book. And Mr. Gough said to himself, "He can't be such a very disagreeable man after all," and he moved along a little nearer to him. But such work as he made of the singing, "It was awful, positively awful. I never heard anything like it," said Mr. Gough, "and every now and then in the midst of the singing his mouth would twitch out that strange sound, and then he would sing faster to catch up with the music."

At the end of one stanza, while the organist was playing the interlude, he leaned over toward Mr. Gough and whispered, "would you be kind enough to give me the first line of the next verse?" Mr. Gough repeated it to him:

> "Just as I am, poor, wretched, blind."

"That's it!" said he, "that's it, and I am blind, God help me!" And the tears ran down his face, "And I am wretched, and I am a paralytic." And then he tried to sing,

> "Just as I am, poor, wretched, blind,
> Sight, riches, healing of the mind,
> Yea all I need, in Thee to find,
> O Lamb of God I come! I come!"

"And at that moment," says Mr. Gough, "with the new revelation he had made of himself to me, it seemed to me I had never heard in my life a Beethoven Symphony with as much music in it as the blundering singing of that poor, blind paralytic."

No. 528.

"CHRISTIANS, AWAKE, SALUTE THE HAPPY MORN."

JOHN BYRON.

A century and a half ago, in England, it was a rare streak of good fortune for a man to keep out of jail his whole life through, provided he had any opinions. Party feeling ran very high, and a new party coming into power not only appointed its adherents to the offices, but put its opponents behind prison bars, where it was supposed their opinions would do less harm than in the open air.

And then there was always a possibility that the king of today might be the refugee or the pretender of tomorrow.

John Byron, who lived from 1700 to 1763, and taught shorthand for a living much of the time, was as quaint as he was pious, and fully alive to the danger of having too pronounced political opinions.

He favored the House of Stuart, but on one occasion he was present when toasts were in order, and he was called on for a toast to the King. With quick wit he improvised a stanza which extricated him from his dilemma, and gave him some celebrity as well:

"God bless the King,
I mean the Faith's defender:
God bless, no harm in blessing, the Pretender:
But who Pretender is, or who is King,
God bless us all, that's quite another thing."

No. 529.

"HE IS GONE, A CLOUD OF LIGHT."

REV. ARTHUR PENRHYN STANLEY.

It is a never-ending wonder, when one traces things back to their causes, to see how prominent a factor in the world's history have been occurrences, in themselves trivial.

Some children had been reading the story of the Ascension of Christ, "While they beheld, He was taken up, and a cloud received Him, out of their sight, and while they looked steadfastly toward heaven as He went up," etc., and they asked their father how the disciples felt after that, and complained that there was no hymn that spoke of it.

The father told Dean Stanley of this, and asked if he could not write a hymn to supply the vacancy the children had noticed.

It was done, and soon after published in a magazine, with no thought that it would have other fate than that befalling other bits of poetry so published.

But the children had told a want of many another disciple, and the piece soon found its way into the hymnals, and has made for itself a permanent place in the song service of Christians, especially those who love to recognize with suitable worship each year as the anniversary days come round, the chief events in the life of Christ.

Sir Arthur Sullivan composed for it the tune of "St. Patrick," to which it is usually sung.

No. 530.

"I AM SO GLAD THAT OUR FATHER IN HEAVEN."

PHILIP BLISS.

Soon after Mr. Bliss began his work as a singing evangelist, there came into use a revival song, the chorus of which began, "O how I love Jesus," and Mr. Bliss heard and sang this song a great many times, until he said to himself, "I have sung long enough of my poor love for Christ, and now I will sing of His love for me." So he wrote the hymn:

> "I am so glad that our Father in Heaven,
> Tells of His love in the book he has given,
> Wonderful things in the Bible I see,
> This is the dearest that Jesus loves me."

This is a much more appropriate subject for a hymn than the other, and more in accord with the teaching of the Bible, which says, "Herein is love, not that we loved God, but that He loved us."

No. 531.

GRANVILLE MAXIM.

In the early part of the present century, there lived in the town of Buckfield, Maine, a man of marked ability, but of eccentric habits.

He was a great lover of music, and many of the melodies, used in revival services of that day, were of his composition.

Tradition tells the story, that in early life he was disappointed in a love affair, and one morning took a rope, and wandered away into the forest, intending to commit suicide.

He sat down to rest and think, at a deserted logging camp, and as he sat he heard a bird singing her lament, over some robber of her nest. By and by he thought he would leave some memento which might chance to come to the eye of the lady he loved, and that would tell her of his grief.

So he cut a piece of birch bark, and wrote on it a stanza:

> "As on some lonely building top,
> The sparrow tells her moan,
> Far from the tents of joy and hope,
> I'll sit and grieve alone."

And then he began to write a melody to suit the words, and becoming more and more interested in the song, he added other parts until he had completed a beautiful piece of music, and then he pictured to himself how the song would sound, if a skilful choir should perform it, and with it all his thought of suicide vanished away.

He found a purpose for which to live, and he returned to the town, and to useful pursuits.

The hymn, "Come Holy Spirit, Heavenly Dove," was formerly sung to the tune of "Turner," composed by Mr. Maxim, and other tunes by him, once popular, but now fallen into disuse were, "Buckfield" and "Portland."

No. 532.

Francis Joseph Haydn, 1732—1809.

One day two elderly gentlemen were dining together in Hamburg. They were both masters of music, one living at Hamburg and the other at Vienna.

They were talking of music, and musicians, when suddenly the one who was at home declared to the other that he had right then in his house a boy, who was, he thought, a musical prodigy.

He had found him at his father's house in the country, singing and keeping time with a couple of sticks, while his father played the harp and his mother sang. He had brought him to his home, and was teaching him music.

So the boy was brought in from the kitchen, where he was eating his dinner with the cook, and although bashful at first, as soon as he was told to sing, forgot it all, and throwing his head back, burst out into melody like a bird.

The visitor was delighted, and exclaimed, "He shall come to Vienna with me, and sing in my choir." And so he carried the boy away from Hamburg to Vienna, and there his fine sweet voice delighted all the town.

One day the roguish boy cut off the tail of one of the singer's wigs, and his master turned him out, right then and there, of choir and home.

It was a winter's night, and the poor boy was friendless and homeless. At last as he wandered along the street he thought of a poor barber who had once spoken kindly to him, and to this house he went.

The barber took him in and gave him a home, and by and by, when the poor homeless boy had become the famous composer, Francis Joseph Haydn, he married the barber's daughter.

Haydn gathered about him a circle of musical young fellows like himself, and their chief recreation was going about Vienna on moonlight nights serenading famous musicians.

One night they played one of Haydn's compositions under the window of Herr Curtz, the leader of the opera in the city. Suddenly a window opened and Herr Curtz himself shouted to know who was playing the violin. "Joseph Haydn," came back the answer.

"Whose music is it?"

"My own," and almost before the young player knew what was going on, Curtz was down to the ground, had him by the collar, and was marching him upstairs into the master's music room. Then he told him that he wanted him to compose some music for him, and gave him his subject.

Haydn went to the piano, and soon caught the thought Herr Curtz wished to express, and got a hundred florins for his work. Soon after he got an appointment in the household of Prince Esterhazy, when his curious duty was to have a piece of music ready to lay at the Prince's plate at breakfast every morning.

No. 533.

"THE HARMONIOUS BLACKSMITH."

George Frederick Handel.

Handel was one day going to the palace of the Duke of Chandos, near London, when he was overtaken by a shower of rain, and took shelter in a blacksmith shop.

The blacksmith kept on with his work, and sang a song as he worked.

Handel was attracted by the song, but more by the curious fact that the blacksmith's hammer kept time with the song, and drew from the anvil two harmonious sounds according with the melody of the song, and making a sort of continuous bass. He remembered the air with its queer accompaniment, and when he returned home composed this piece of music.

No. 534.

"JORDAN" (Tune).

William Billings, 1746—1800.

This tune was composed by the first American musical composer of whom there is any record.

He was a Boston tanner without education but with much natural genius. He is described as somewhat deformed, blind of one eye, one leg shorter than the other, one arm somewhat withered, and continually taking snuff. He published half a dozen books of music, in each of which he sifted out the inferior work of the book which had preceded it, or improved them by his increased experience.

His music was much ridiculed by some, as may be inferred from the fact that some one hung a couple of cats over his tanner's sign as an intimation that their harmonies were much like his.

However, his tunes were very popular, and were indeed

almost the only music known in New England during the last quarter of the last century.

The American Army also used them in camp, and march, through the years of the Revolution, and they did much to encourage and cheer the soldier's hearts.

One of the tunes was named "Chester," and he wrote the words as well as the music. It was a patriotic hymn appropriate to those stirring times, beginning:

> "Let tyrants shake their iron rod,
> And slavery clank her galling chains:
> We'll fear them not—we trust in God;
> New England's God forever reigns."

But although he was a patriot in full sympathy with the political independence of the colonies, still in Christian worship he saw no reason why the independent colonies should not be in unison with the mother country, and so he wrote a stanza, which if we give to it the pronunciation of the olden time, makes very good rhyme:

> "Oh, praise the Lord with one consent,
> And in this grand design,
> Let Britain and the colonies
> Unanimously join."

Mr. Billings died in 1800, and lies buried in the old "Granary Burial Ground" in Boston, with no stone to mark his grave.

Some of his tunes are, "Chester," "Majesty," "Rock of Ages," "Christ the Lord is Risen Indeed," "Jordan," etc.

No. 535.

Rev. Samuel Medley, 1738.

Nearly a hundred and fifty years ago, in 1758, an English boy, not yet twenty years of age, entered the English navy, and was soon after wounded in a battle.

His wound proved very serious, and the surgeon told him he was afraid that amputation was the only thing that would save his life. "But," said he, "I can tell tomorrow morning."

The boy had been religiously trained by a pious father, but while in the navy he had led a profligate life. But now the surgeon's words brought rushing back to him the prayers he had heard his father offer, and he began to pray himself, spending much of the night in that way.

When the surgeon examined the wounds next morning, he lifted his hands in surprise, and exclaimed, "This is little short of a miracle." So favorable a change had taken place that no amputation was needed, and the wounds speedily healed.

The boy resolved to reform his life, but like many another who makes that resolution in his own strength, he failed. Returning to his home he lived with his grandfather, and one Sunday evening he asked the servant if his grandfather was going out to church. "No," was the reply, "he is coming to read a sermon to you."

And the young man was compelled to listen to one of Dr. Watts' sermons. He was indifferent at first, but soon the words of the sermon began to touch his heart, and as soon as it was ended, and his grandfather had left the room, he fell on his knees in prayer, and was soon after converted, and later he became a preacher of the gospel.

I think it adds interest to a hymn, sometimes, to know something of the experiences through which its author passed.

No. 536.

"CREATION," Oratorio—1799.

FRANCIS JOSEPH HAYDN, 1732—1809.

The idea of setting to music, to be sung, the Bible story of the creation of the world, must have come from a man of daring as well as of genius.

Haydn's "Oratorio" was first produced in Vienna in 1799. The words for it, except those taken from the Book of Genesis, were arranged from Milton's "Paradise Lost."

The Oratorio was at once a great success, and is still among the grandest of the Oratorios.

No. 537.

" 'TIS RELIGION THAT CAN GIVE."

MARY MASTERS.

There are hymns written by men and women of the highest literary culture, and hymns of high poetic merit, which have made no history for themselves; while there are others of no literary value, and written by illiterate authors, which have yet become powers for good.

A century and a half ago, in 1733, a poor English woman published a little volume of poems, and in the preface it is stated that she was "never taught her English grammar. Her education rose no higher than the spelling book or the writing master; her genius to poetry was always browbeat and discountenanced by her parents," and more of like import.

Twenty years later, in 1755, she published still another book, and in it appeared what she called a "Short Ejaculation" containing but six lines, as follows:

" 'Tis religion that can give
Sweetest pleasures while we live;
'Tis religion must supply
Solid comfort when we die,
After death its joys will be
Lasting as Eternity."

I do not know what the history of these six lines has been, as they have sung their way along the years for this century and a half, but somewhere along the road, some one, probably a singing evangelist, interlined it with a refrain, and lengthened it with a chorus so that it read:

" 'Tis religion that can give,
In the light, in the light,
Sweetest pleasure while we live,
In the light of God.

"Let us walk in the light,
In the light, in the light,
Let us walk in the light,
In the light of God."

In this form, as it was sung during a revival time, a young man heard it in a congregation, as he says, of "common people, by voices many of them cracked and discordant," and yet he says: "I think it was the singing of that simple old hymn and chorus that awakened in me the desire to be a Christian by setting before me its promise of 'sweetest pleasure' and 'solid comfort' in strong contrast with the unsatisfactory portions I was getting from worldly pleasures, and the fear of death that was constantly before me." And then he adds, "Eternity only will reveal the power that hymn had over me, both in bringing me to God, and in strengthening and encouraging me in the first days of trial and temptation, that came to me as a young Christian."

You will agree that there is still another thing, that Eternity alone will reveal, of the results growing out of the singing of this hymn, when I tell you that the young man who thus describes the effect it had upon him, was Rev. George F. Pentecost.

No. 538.

"COME LET US JOIN OUR FRIENDS ABOVE."

Rev. Charles Wesley.

The author of this hymn died three years before his brother John. They had been roommates in college days, and from that time on through sixty years of preaching, and writing, and working, had been companions and co-workers in founding the great denomination of Methodists.

One Sunday morning, after the death of Charles, the surviving brother John, himself an aged man, arose in the pulpit of the City Road Chapel, London, to announce the opening hymn, but instead of doing so, he stood silent with eyes closed for nearly ten full minutes. Then with a feeling that told of the emotion of his heart, he began to read this hymn:

"Come let us join our friends above,
That have obtained the prize,
And on the eagle wings of love,
To joys celestial rise."

It seemed to those who were present as if they were about to witness the meeting again of the brother who had "obtained the prize" with the one who was still striving for it. And when they sang the hymn it seemed almost as if the host that had "crossed the flood" were joining voices with those on the hither side.

No. 539.

"IN THE CHRISTIAN'S HOME IN GLORY."

REV. SAMUEL YOUNG HARMAR, 1809.

The influence, upon after life, of hymns learned in childhood, can hardly be measured. They come into the mind when least expected, and sometimes when least desired, but always on some good errand.

An English actor was one evening in the midst of a play on the stage, when this hymn which he had learned in his childhood came rushing into his mind, and so unmanned him that he was obliged to go to the manager and tell him that he could not go on.

In an effort to stifle the thoughts which the hymn brought to his mind, he went to the bar of the theater, and drank.

He shortly after attended one of the Moody and Sankey meetings, and was converted, and then related this incident.

No. 540.

"COME, O THOU TRAVELER UNKNOWN."

REV. CHARLES WESLEY.

This is a very celebrated hymn, which has received the admiring notice of poets and critics ever since it was written. The hymn is entitled, "Wrestling Jacob," and this was a famous subject with Mr. Wesley not only in poetry but in prose.

His journal records not less than eight different occasions when he preached upon that theme, and he records also that in most cases the preaching was effective upon the audience.

No. 541.

"WATCHMAN, TELL US OF THE NIGHT."

SIR JOHN BOWRING.

An old writer says that, "Whenever the Holy Ghost inspireth a new hymn, it is His wont to inspire someone with a good tune to fit it."

This seems to me to be eminently true of this hymn, and the tune to which we sing it.

The hymn was written and published in England, in 1825, and the tune was written for it, and the two were published together in this country in 1831.

The hymn is a dialogue, and Lowell Mason's tune for it was entitled a "Dialogue and Chorus." The dialogue being rendered by a soprano voice singing the first two lines, a tenor the second two, and so on alternately, and the full chorus repeating the last two lines of the stanza to different music. The music is practically the same, however, as we use it now.

No. 542.

"THREE FISHERS WENT SAILING OUT INTO THE WEST."

REV. CHARLES KINGSLEY.

The author of this song, well known as a preacher, poet, and novelist, who died but a few years ago, spent his boyhood in a little fishing town on the English coast, where his father was rector of the parish. He often saw the fleet of herring fishers put out to sea, and witnessed the little religious service it was the custom to hold on the wharf before they started, in which the fishermen and their wives, and sweethearts, and children, joined.

Later in life, after a weary day, he recalled this scene of his youth, and wrote this song.

No. 543.

"'MID PLEASURES AND PALACES."

"HOME, SWEET HOME."

JOHN HOWARD PAYNE.

A hundred years ago, in 1792, a little boy was born in New York City, who was destined to supply the world with one of its sweetest, most valued songs.

From the place of his birth to East Hampton, the most easterly town of Long Island, then to Boston, back to New

York, to Schenectady to college, then as an actor to New York, Baltimore, and Boston, thence to London and Paris, and Berlin, and back again to America, and then to Tunis in Africa, where he died, the author of "Home, Sweet Home" was himself a homeless wanderer his whole life long. His song was written when he was nearly starving, with an attic for his home in Paris, and when the words he had written were known all over the world, he himself said that he had often heard them sung in London, Paris, and Berlin, "when he had not a shilling to buy his next meal with, nor a place to lay his head."

He had written quite a number of plays which were successful in every way save in bringing money to their author, and in 1823 Charles Kemble, who was manager of Covent Garden in London, bought a quantity of these dramatic productions.

Among them was a play entitled, "Clavi, the Maid of Milan." This play Kemble asked the author to alter into an opera, and in doing so he introduced into it the words of "Home, Sweet Home."

A sister of Mrs. Charles Kean was the chief singer at Covent Garden then, and she first sang the song as a part of this opera. So that the words were first heard in a celebrated theater, under the management of a celebrated man, and sung by a celebrated singer.

The music was written for the words, though not for that occasion. Sir Henry Rowley Bishop, an English composer, then a young man, had been engaged to edit a collection of the national melodies of all countries.

While engaged in this work, he discovered that he had no melody from Sicily, and so he invented this, and it was published in the collection as a Sicilian air, when as a fact it was the invention of a London musician.

The song, with the words of Payne, became at once immensely popular. A hundred thousand copies were sold within a year, the publisher was greatly enriched, even the lady who first rendered it was, by the singing of it, brought to the notice of a wealthy gentleman who became her husband, and Payne, who wrote it, received not so much as the price of a night's lodging.

No. 544.

"GUIDE ME O THOU GREAT JEHOVAH."

Rev. William Williams, 1717—1791.

Almost two hundred years ago, there lived in a village of Wales, a good deacon of an Independent church. He lived in the times that were troublous for the churches, and for Christians who wished to worship in any other than the way established by the state; and the church of which he was a deacon had to meet for a time in a cave during the hours of twilight, to avoid being swooped down upon, and scattered or imprisoned by the King's soldiers.

This good deacon had a boy who was intended for a physician, and went away to college to prepare for this profession.

On his way home from college, he was passing through a little Welsh village one Sunday morning, when he heard the ringing of a parish church bell, and turned in to rest and listen.

The service was formal and cold, and made no impression on the young fellow's mind, but as he passed out of the church, he noticed that the people instead of scattering to their homes, remained in the churchyard as if expecting someone, and in a few minutes a man took his stand upon one of the flat tombstones and began to talk.

There was nothing cold or formal now, but hot, fiery torrents of speech, and like the preaching of John the Baptist, it was a call to "repent for the Kingdom of Heaven is at hand."

The young man went into the churchyard intending to be a doctor, but he came out with his face set another way, and soon after he became a preacher. All over Wales, for the next half century, that man went traveling on foot and with horse three thousand miles a year, preaching the Gospel of Christ. He was a poet as well as a preacher, and oftentimes improvised poetry in his extemporaneous sermons.

He was absent-minded sometimes, and thereby hangs a tale. He was away from home and family one Sunday holding a service by the seashore.

A friend was conducting the opening service, and while he was praying a cuckoo began to sing close by the open window.

When the prayer was ended, our poet preacher arose to give out the hymn, but instead of a hymn it was a poetic appeal to the cuckoo to fly away to the preacher's home, and tell Molly, his wife, that he was alive, and then to go to another town and tell Jack, his son, to keep his place, and added a wish, that should they fail to meet again on earth, they might not fail to meet in heaven.

Just then his friend touched him, and reminded him that while what he was giving to the people might be a very good sentiment, it was hardly a hymn. And the poet, suddenly coming to himself, thought of the great sea whose waves were breaking just outside the door, and without a moment's hesitation gave out another stanza:

"Salvation like a boundless sea
Keeps swelling on the shore:
Here shall the weak and helpless find
Enough for ever more."

Perhaps this little glimpse of the life of William Williams will give new interest to the hymns he wrote. Only two of them have found their way into the English hymnals.

"Guide me O Thou great Jehovah,"

and

"O'er those gloomy hills of darkness."

No. 545.

"MY FAITH LOOKS UP TO THEE."

REV. RAY PALMER.

Mr. Palmer was a young man just out of college, and not yet entered upon his theological studies. He was in poor health, and teaching a ladies' school in New York City.

It was then that this hymn was written, and the stanzas, the author says, simply gave form to what he felt.

"I recollect," he says, "that I wrote them with very tender emotion, and ended the last line with tears."

Once written, the lines went into his pocketbook, until one day Dr. Lowell Mason met him on a street in Boston, and asked him if he had not some hymn that he would contribute to a new book that he was compiling. The pocketbook was produced, and the little hymn was handed out.

On reaching home, Dr. Mason was so much interested in the words, that he composed for it the tune, "Olivet," to which it is even now almost always sung.

A few days later he met the author again and said, "Mr. Palmer, you may live many years, and do many good things, but I think you will be best known to posterity as the author of,

"My faith looks up to thee."

No. 546.

"IN THE WAVES AND MIGHTY WATERS."

DAVID WILLIAMS, 1718—1784.

David Williams was a Welsh schoolmaster who had a turbulent wife. He preached as well as taught, and the story is, that one night on reaching home his wife assailed him with a bitter scolding. Outside a storm was raging, but he preferred that to the storm that was raging in his home. So out he went again into the darkness, and stood on the bank of a river near, and its rushing torrent, and the wailing of the winds brought to his mind the time when his feet should stand on the brink of another river, and what hand would help him then, so he wrote:

"In the waves and mighty waters,
No one will support my head,
But my Savior, my Beloved
Who was stricken in my stead:
In the cold and mortal river,
He will hold my head above,
I shall through the waves go singing,
For one look of Him I love."

This short hymn has become known wherever the Welsh language is spoken. An incident connected with it has given to it the title of "The Miner's Hymn."

In the month of April, 1877, a colliery in Wales was flooded, and fourteen miners found themselves imprisoned waiting helplessly for death. The whole nation seemed to turn its thought toward that coal pit, and as the rescue party toiled on by day and night, every hour seemed to make the suspense more painful.

So seven days passed, with no signs of the imprisoned miners, and hope was nearly lost, but on the eighth day nine of the miners were found, and found alive though nearly dead for want of food and air. And as they told their story, it came out that despair would have driven them mad, had they not cheered themselves by singing over and over the words of this hymn.

No. 547.

Miss Ann Griffiths, 1776.

In the year of our Independence as a Nation, a farmer's daughter was born in Wales. When she had grown to be a young woman, she was as gay as the gayest, and fond of dance and song.

On the way to one such merrymaking gathering, an old servant of her father induced her to go aside into a chapel meeting.

A word spoken by the preacher proved to be a message for her, and she went to her home instead of to the dance, and soon became as widely known for her earnest piety as she had been for her gaiety.

Soon, as she went about her work as a farmer's girl, or as she walked through the woods, and fields, and country roads, she began to think in poetry, and her piety expressed itself in hymns. But she never wrote them down, and but for a servant girl in her father's house the world would not have known them.

To this servant girl she used to recite her hymns as they were composed, and then the two girls would sing them to some Welsh tune, over and over again.

When the composer had died, the servant girl, who by this time had married, repeated them over to her husband, who wrote them down, and so they were preserved.

No. 548.

"LAND AHEAD! ITS FRUITS ARE WAVING."

Rev. E. Adams.

This hymn is a memento of a very curious bit of history:

In the latter part of the eighteenth century (1789) a British ship left one of the Sandwich Islands with a cargo of bread fruit plants, which were to be transplanted into the soil of one of the West India Islands.

A few days later a part of the crew mutinied, put the captain and those who were loyal to him adrift in a boat, and for twenty years nothing was heard of ship or men.

Then a Nantucket whaler stopped at what had always been supposed to be an uninhabited island in the Pacific, called Pitcairns Island, and was greatly surprised to find it the home of the long lost and almost forgotten mutineers of the old ship *Bounty*.

One of the mutineers, who had assumed the name of John Adams, had drawn up a little code of laws, by which the little band was governed. He had been their teacher and stranger than all, their religious leader too, for he had organized religious worship after the form of the Church of England, and then and even down to the present day they are a Christian people.

When, after presiding over his little kingdom wisely and beneficently for many years, until it had come to be called "The Paradise of the Pacific," John Adams, the mutineer, lay dying, he exclaimed, as if his eyes saw beyond the veil, "Land in sight!"

"Are you happy?" asked one standing by.

"Rounding the cape into the harbor," was the jubilant reply, and then at last, as he grew weaker, "Let go the anchor," he exclaimed, and he was dead.

These words were woven into a song not many years ago, and, with the music to which they are attached, have become quite popular.

No. 549.

"LO! THE DAY OF REST DECLINETH."

REV. CHANDLER ROBBINS, 1810—1882.

The daughter of the author of this hymn was returning from Europe on a Cunard steamer.

An aged Scotch Presbyterian minister and his wife were among the passengers. The party were singing hymns on the deck one Sabbath evening, when the minister went to his stateroom and brought back a book of hymns and tunes, to show to the party what, he said, was the sweetest hymn he knew, set to the sweetest tune.

What was the surprise of the author's daughter, who, by the way, was married, and only known to the Scotchman by her husband's name, to hear him repeat the first line of the hymn her own father had written, and to hear him sing it to the tune, "Bedford Street," which had been composed for the hymn by Mr. L. B. Barnes, President of the Handel and Haydn Society of Boston, and named for the street upon which stood her father's church.

No. 550.

"FINDING NO PLACE OF REST."

Mr. John Brooke Greenwood, 1828.

This hymn has had the experience of getting into company where it was not wanted, and of not being able to withdraw.

Its author was a merchant of Manchester, England, and a member of a Congregational church of that city.

The verses fell into the hands of a relative of the author, who was a Roman Catholic, and through her into the hands of her priest, and he passed it along into the columns of a Roman Catholic newspaper.

Somewhere on the way they lost the signature.

Awhile after, Rev. Orby Shipley, a Roman Catholic priest, and one of the strictest of that church, conceived the idea that members of that church ought not to use, in their devotions, hymns written by any not members of their own particular branch of the household of faith.

So he published a collection called, "Annus Sanctus," purporting to contain not a single piece not written by a faithful adherent of the Romish Church.

Finding this hymn to be good poetry, and correct in sentiment, and withal in the columns of a Roman Catholic paper, he included it in his book.

And so in this immaculate selection by monks, and priests, and cardinals, there stands this hymn by a plain Congregational cotton merchant.

No. 551.

"THE KING OF GLORY WE PROCLAIM."

JAMES MONTGOMERY.

At the annual meeting of the Church Missionary Society of England, which has under its charge the foreign mission work of the Church of England, held in the spring of 1848, it was arranged to hold that autumn, a jubilee service, which all its mission stations throughout the world should join in.

James Montgomery was invited to prepare a hymn for the occasion, which should be translated into all the languages spoken by the people among whom they had missions, and which should be sung in all those places on that day as a jubilee hymn.

He wrote this hymn, and when the autumn came, at the central meeting in London, he was able, although in his seventy-seventh year, to join in the first singing of the hymn, which that day literally followed the sun in its course, until it had belted the earth with song.

No. 552.

"GREAT GOD, THE NATIONS OF THE EARTH."

Rev. William Ward, 1769—1821.

Just before William Carey, the celebrated Baptist missionary, left England for his field of work in India, he met on a street of Hull, a boy who had been converted, and who was working in a printing office in that town.

"We shall want some one by and by," said Carey to the boy, "to print the Bible for us in the languages of India. Hold yourself in readiness when you are needed."

The boy never forgot the words, and a few years later he went to India to do for Dr. Carey and his associates the very work which he had been told he would be needed for, and while on the voyage he wrote this hymn.

No. 553.

"TELL IT OUT AMONG THE NATIONS."

Miss Frances Ridley Havergal, 1836—1879.

This hymn was written one Sunday when the author was prevented by sickness from attending church. She was following the order of service of the Episcopal Church, and had read the words, "Tell it out among the heathen, that the Lord is King," when the thought came to her that the words would make a good beginning for a hymn. With the thought the words for the hymn came to her faster than she could write them, and with them the music, and in a few minutes the hymn was written and the tune for it composed. The tune was named "Epenetus."

No. 554.

"JUST AS I AM, WITHOUT ONE PLEA."

Miss Charlotte Elliott, 1789—1871.

An English magazine, in 1887, invited its readers to send in lists of what they regarded as the best hundred hymns. About thirty-five hundred lists were received, and this hymn was found to be one of the chief favorites of the people, but three hymns having a higher number of votes. These were, "Rock of Ages," "Abide with Me," and "Jesus Lover of my Soul."

No. 555.

"HOW SWEET THE NAME OF JESUS SOUNDS."

Rev. John Newton, 1725—1807.

An English magazine, in 1887, invited its readers to send in lists of what they regarded as the best hundred hymns. About thirty-five hundred such lists were sent in, and this hymn was found to be one of the chief favorites, but four hymns having a higher number of votes. These were, "Rock of Ages," "Abide with Me," "Jesus Lover of my Soul," and "Just as I Am."

No. 556.

"GOLDEN HARPS ARE SOUNDING."

Miss Frances Ridley Havergal, 1836—1879.

The author of this hymn was visiting some friends, and while with them went to a boys' school. Being very tired, she leaned against the playground wall, while a friend who accompanied her went into the school. Returning in a few minutes, he found her scribbling on an old envelope the words of this hymn, the thought of which had just suggested itself to her.

No. 557.

"JERUSALEM, THE GOLDEN."

BERNARD OF CLUNY.

Some years ago there was published in England, the biography of a little boy under the title, "A Little Child Shall Lead Them." In this book it is related that when this child was suffering agonies which the physicians declared were almost unparalleled, he would lie without a motion or a murmur while the whole of this long poem of four hundred lines was read to him.

No. 558.

"MY GOD, MY FATHER, WHILE I STRAY."

MISS CHARLOTTE ELLIOTT, 1789—1871.

An English magazine, in 1887, invited its readers to send in lists of what they considered the best hundred hymns. About thirty-five hundred such lists were sent in, and this hymn was found to be among the chief favorites, but five hymns standing higher on the list. These were, "Rock of Ages," "Abide with Me," "Jesus Lover of My Soul," "Just as I Am," and, "How Sweet the Name of Jesus Sounds."

No. 559.

"JESUS LOVER OF MY SOUL."

REV. CHARLES WESLEY, 1708—1788.

An English magazine, in 1887, asked its readers to send in lists of what they considered the best hundred hymns. About thirty-five hundred such lists were received, and this hymn was found to stand third in favor among the readers of that periodical, the two better liked being "Rock of Ages," and "Abide with Me."

No. 560.

"I LAY MY SINS ON JESUS."

REV. HORATIUS BONAR, 1808—1889.

Unlike many writers of hymns, Dr. Bonar kept no record of where, or when, or why his hymns were written. It is known that a few of them were written for the use of Mr. Sankey when he and Mr. Moody were holding evangelistic meetings in Scotland. It is also known that he was in the habit of writing them while traveling on railroad trains. This one was written when the author was a young man, not yet the pastor of a church, but serving as assistant to a minister in Leith, Scotland. It was written for the children of the Sunday school connected with this church.

No. 561.

"I GAVE MY LIFE FOR THEE."

MISS FRANCES RIDLEY HAVERGAL, 1836—1879.

This idea of a hymn, to be sung by a mixed congregation of people, in which the words supposed to be spoken by the Savior are sung back to Him by the audience, is a very near approach to profanity. This hymn had great currency in the earlier days of the Moody and Sankey "Gospel Hymn Books," but is now quite properly almost entirely discarded. The author was but a young lady of twenty-two and was in Germany. She came in one day quite tired and sat down where a picture with the words of this first line for a motto hung directly before her. The lines of the hymn came into her mind almost at once, and she wrote them down with a pencil on a scrap of paper. Reading them over, they did not satisfy her, and she threw them into the fire, but they fell out unburned, and she picked them up and saved them. Later she showed them to her father, Rev. W. H. Havergal, who thought them worthy of use and wrote for them the tune "Baca." Later the impropriety of singing such words was noticed, and the hymn changed in all its stanzas so as to make it a song addressed to Christ, beginning:

"Thy life was given for me."

No. 562.

"ART THOU WEARY, ART THOU LANGUID."

St. Stephen, 725—794.

It is a long way from the lonely monastery in the valley of the Kedron to the sands of Cape Cod, and a long time from the middle of the eighth century when this hymn was written, to the middle of the nineteenth. And as widely different as these places and times, is one use recently made of this hymn, written by the distinguished old hermit monk of Mar Saba. It occurs in the novel, "Cape Cod Folks," written some years ago by Miss Sally Pratt McLean. Two of the prominent characters in that novel are George Olver and Ben Cradlebow. Near the end of the story Ben is drowned in a fierce storm while trying with Olver to save a boat's crew from the same fate.

Just before the storm the two have been at work mending an old craft, and after the storm is over, and Ben Cradlebow is dead, with the neighbors gathered in one of the cottages on the shore, the Captain tells the story, "By and by him and George Olver struck up a song. I've heern 'em sing it before, them two. As nigh as I calk'late, it's about findin' rest in Jesus, and one a askin' questions, all fa'r and squar', to know the way and whether it's a goin' to lead thar straight or not, and the other answerin'. And he—he was a tinkerin', way up on the foremast, George Olver and the rest on us was astern—and I'll hear to my dyin' day how his voice came a floatin' down to us thar—chantin'-like it was, cl'ar and fearless and low. So he asks, for findin' Jesus, if thar's any marks to foller by; and George Olver, he answers about them bleedin' nail prints, and the great one in His side. So then that voice comes down agin, askin' if thar's any crown, like other kings, to tell Him by; and George Olver, he answers straight about that crown o' thorns. Then says that other voice, floatin' so strong and cl'ar, and if he gin up all and follered, what should he have? What now? So George Olver, he sings deep o' the trials and the sorrowin'. But that other voice never shook, a askin' and what if he helt to Him to the end, what then should it be, what then? George Olver answers: 'Forevermore, the sorrowin' ended—Death gone over.' Then he sings out, like his mind was all made up, 'And if he undertook it, would he likely be turned away?' 'And it's likelier,' George Olver answers him, 'That heaven and earth shall pass.' So I'll hear it to my dyin' day—his voice a floatin' down to me from up above thar, somewhar, askin' them questions that nobody could ever answer like, so soon, he answered 'em for himself."

No. 563.

"FROM GREENLAND'S ICY MOUNTAINS."

To the tune of

" 'TWAS WHEN THE SEAS WERE ROARING."

The first singing of Heber's missionary hymn affords a striking illustration of the scarcity of good hymn tunes at that time and of the readiness with which music entirely secular was used with sacred words. A poet by the name of John Gay—the same, by the way, who wrote the song of "Black-eyed Susan"—about the year 1720 brought out in London a new play, new, not only in words, but in style, for the action in it was intended to be tragic while the language was absurd. The title was "What D'ye Call It?" and when it was played, some of the audience, seeing the acting but catching but few of the words, were ready to shed tears at the pathetic scene, while others who sat nearer and not only saw the play but heard the words, were splitting their sides with laughter at the absurdity of the combination. The author of the play introduced into it a song, the music of which was furnished by a no less renowned composer than George Frederick Handel. The song began, " 'Twas when the seas were roaring." The play soon became obsolete, but the song retained its popularity, and is sung even now. When Heber handed the copy of this hymn to Dean Shipley to be used at the church service on the following morning he asked, "To what tune will it go?" and then suddenly added, "Oh! it will go to ' 'Twas when the seas were roaring.' " And to that music first heard as part of an uproarious comedy on the stage was our great missionary hymn first sung.

No. 564.

"NOW BEGIN THE HEAVENLY THEME."

Rev. Martin Madan, 1726—1790.

A young lawyer in London, who cared neither for religion nor its ministers, was spending the evening with companions as gay as himself, when they commissioned him to go out and hear John Wesley, who was preaching that evening in the neighborhood, and to come back to them and report for their sport how he looked, acted and spoke. Just as he entered the room where the service was held, Mr. Wesley was announcing his text, "Prepare to meet thy God." The gay lawyer was deeply impressed at once and more so as the sermon proceeded.

When it was finished, he returned to his companions, who shouted, "Well, have you taken off the old Methodist?"

"No, gentlemen," was the reply, "but he has taken me off."

He forsook them at once, became a Christian, and turned from the practice of the law to the preaching of the gospel. He was passionately fond of music and made a collection of hymns, which had a remarkable influence on the hymn service of his day. This hymn is often attributed to him, although it is not certainly known that he wrote it, or any other; but many hymns that he used in his collection were amended and improved by him, and have been in use ever since in his amended form rather than in the shape their authors wrote them.

No. 565.

"ART THOU WEARY, ART THOU LANGUID."

St. Stephen in Green, 725—794.

Rev. John Mason Neale, Translator.

The valley of the Kedron from Jerusalem to the Dead Sea is a ravine between cliffs that rise on either side so abruptly as to be almost inaccessible. These hillsides are full of caves hewn into the face of the rock and used as burial places centuries before the time of Christ.

A few centuries after His coming there arose a passion among religionists for a hermit life, and these caves, which had before been only the resting places of the dead, became the homes of the living. Gradually these hermits associated themselves together, and passages were often cut from cave to cave, and walls of masonry along the face of the cliff were added, to give support to buildings connected with these caves. Not far from the Dead Sea, in the Kedron Valley, there is still standing a monastery which had such a beginning. Several times during the fourteen hundred years since it was founded, it has been plundered and its monks murdered by Bedouin Arabs and Turks, and for safety's sake, it has been surrounded by massive walls, partly the natural rock of the cliff and partly masonry. Inside these walls there is a curious maze of cells and chambers perched one above another mostly cut out of the solid rock, and reached by steps and narrow paths. Travelers still visit it, and are hospitably fed and lodged by the monks who make it their home.

Almost twelve hundred years ago, a boy of ten years was placed in this monastery under the care of his uncle, who was one of its hermit monks, and for sixty years, until he died, one of these cells cut in the rock in which some patriarch of Old Testament times had been entombed, was his sleeping room by night, and his place of meditation and prayer by day. And here he wrote this hymn, which is so popular with us today. His name was Stephen, and this gives name to the tune "Stephanos," written for the hymn by Mr. Monk.

No. 566.

"GRACIOUS SPIRIT, DWELL WITH ME."

REV. THOMAS TOKE LYNCH, 1818—1871.

When a young man, Mr. Lynch was a school teacher in England, and at the same time he was in the habit of gathering poor people together and preaching to them. His personal appearance was peculiar, so peculiar that when at college he arose for the first time to speak, his fellow students greeted him with laughter. He published a volume of poetry entitled "The Rivulet," and in this all his hymns appeared. The book was no sooner published than the London *Morning Advertiser*, which was not only the organ of certain London clergymen, but of the London brewers as well, pounced upon both book and author. The hymns, it was said, "might have been written by a Deist, and many of them might be sung by Freethinkers." They were said to be "Christless" and "contradicting the Word of God" and also such as "might have been written by a man who had never seen a Bible." The attack became so fierce and unrelenting, both against book and author, that at last a company including some of the foremost ministers of England published a protest against so wanton and unjust an accusation. Lynch himself published a reply in poetry, the title page of which contained a few lines, which will illustrate the bitterness with which he had been fought.

"Quote him to death! Quote him to death!
Hit him and hear not a word that he saith.
Shout and cry out, for this is the man
Out of whose Spirit the 'Rivulet' ran.
What is his book but a cauldron that brims
Over and over with poisonous hymns?"

This is one of the hymns which was so hunted and hooted at when first it was written.

No. 567.

"MINE EYES HAVE SEEN THE GLORY OF THE COMING OF THE LORD."

Mrs. Julia Ward Howe (See No. 109).

In the Autumn of 1861, Mrs. Howe visited Washington, and while there drove out one day to witness a review of troops that was to take place a little way out of the city. While on the way out, a sudden movement of Southern troops near the city cut off a small party of Union soldiers and broke up the expected review. Riding back along the road, the way was filled with soldiers, so that she could drive but slowly, and her party began to sing some of the well-known war songs, and among them "John Brown's body lies a mouldering in the grave." This song pleased the soldiers very much and they joined in the singing of it. Rev. James Freeman Clarke, who was one of the party, said to Mrs. Howe, "You ought to write some new words to that tune." The next morning, when Mrs. Howe awoke, she was astonished to find words arranging themselves in her mind to fit the "John Brown" tune. And soon the whole hymn was thought out, and she arose, and in the uncertain light scrawled it down upon paper, and then went back to bed for another nap. It was published soon after but was first brought into prominence by Chaplain McCabe in a lecture in Washington, just after he had been released from Libby Prison, telling how he had obtained a copy of it and sung it after a Union victory.

No. 568.

Giovanni Pierluigi da Palestrina, 1524—1594.

In 1564, the Council of Trent, considered the question of church music. The old plain chant had gradually been built upon by the musicians, until it was thought the music of the churches had become extravagant, and elaborate, and detrimental to the spirit of worship. A large party in the Church favored sweeping all these more recent innovations away by edict of the Church and returning to the simple uninspiring chanting of former times. There was an organist just then in Trent who was very anxious as to the result. He admitted the excesses into which the musical composers had fallen, but thought a style of music might be found befitting the sacred uses of the Church and yet appealing to the musical taste of the best musicians. He pleaded with the members of the council so eloquently that at last they consented that a committee of their number might listen to three masses he would present. The first of these was to be sung in the Sistine Chapel at Rome, June 19, 1565. It was a day of great importance to the interests of music, for on the decision of the committee rested the future of ecclesiastical music, and much of the future of musical composers as well. The night before the eventful day, the organist spent alone, in prayer and final preparation for the morrow.

The Chapel was filled with the most famous people in Rome, and the Pope himself was in the audience. No decision from the committee was needed other than a formal one, for the Pope himself declared that "A triumphant host of angels in the New Jerusalem might have sung to the apostle of the Apocalypse some such inspiring strains." And so it was decided that music of the style of this by Palestrina might be composed and used by the Church in its worship. Palestrina lived thirty years after this and composed masses and hymns for all occasions of the Church, many of which have come down to our own times and are used in our churches now.

No. 569.

"I WOULD NOT LIVE ALWAY, I ASK NOT TO STAY."

REV. WILLIAM AUGUSTUS MUHLENBERG, 1796—1877.

I consider this hymn among the curiosities of literature. The love of life is something that has been implanted in our very natures. Animals have it. And the possession of reasoning powers only makes the love of it more intense. The Bible commends it, and promises it as the reward of righteousness. We condemn in unmeasured terms any one who so lives as to endanger or shorten it. The noblest monument of the man who wrote the hymn is that he projected and for years presided over St. Luke's Hospital in New York, the mission of which was to prolong and save it. Although you will join heartily in the singing of it, it does not express your sentiments unless by disease or misfortune you have become morbid in your thoughts. It was only by a chance that the hymn got into a hymn book. It had been published in a religious newspaper and was offered by Dr. Onderdonk to a committee of the Protestant Episcopal Church which was revising its church hymnal. When this committee came to vote upon the hymns one by one, Dr. Onderdonk was absent, but the author of the hymn himself was present. The hymn was pronounced very good but rather sentimental and so was rejected, Dr. Muhlenberg, who, by the way, was not suspected of being the author, voting against it. Next morning when Dr. Onderdonk found it had been thrown out, he went about among the members of the committee and prevailed upon them to restore it. So into the hymnal it went, and once in, it has stayed in. That was in 1826, and now in 1893, after almost seventy years have passed, out of the thirty principal hymnals in use by the Evangelical denominations of America but five omit it.

No. 570.

"AWAKED BY SINAI'S AWFUL SOUND."

REV. SAMSON OCCUM.

When George Whitefield, the English evangelist, visited America in the middle of the last century, one of his converts was an Indian boy of the Mohegan tribe, whose fading glories were later related by Cooper in his novel, "The Last of the Mohicans." This Indian boy was instructed in a school in Lebanon, Connecticut, and later became a preacher of the gospel, sometime among the Montauk Indians on Long Island and again among the Oneidas in New York. Later he went to England to solicit money for the school at which he had been taught, and attracted much attention there, as the first Indian preacher they had ever heard. He succeeded in raising about ten thousand pounds, and this money raised by the Indian preacher was the financial foundation of Dartmouth College. He has the unique distinction of being the only American Indian who has contributed to our store of sacred song.

No. 571.

"A MIGHTY FORTRESS IS OUR GOD"—1527.

REV. MARTIN LUTHER, 1483—1546.

This is a paraphrase of the forty-sixth Psalm. It has been called the battle hymn of Protestantism, for it was written in the very year when the Evangelical Princes delivered their protest at the Diet of Spires, from which the name of Protestant is derived, and it became almost at once the song of the Protestant Churches and people all over Germany. Their armies sang it as they went into battle, and their martyrs when they stood amid the flames. It is characteristic of its author and has been called "Luther in Song." It is as rugged as he and is full of his faith and courage. When he was a Romish monk, he was an earnest, honest one, and he afterward said that "if ever a monk got to heaven by monkery he was determined to get there." Yet here he is singing:

"Did we in our own strength confide
Our striving would be losing."

The hymn was a great favorite with Luther himself, and he often sang it for cheer and comfort. When fatigued with the contest in which he was engaged or dismayed by its dangers, he would say to Melancthon, his companion and helper, "Come, Philip, let us sing the forty-sixth Psalm."

No. 572.

"O MOTHER DEAR JERUSALEM."

REV. DAVID DICKSON, 1583—1663.

Without doubt the most remarkable hymn in all our collections is the one known by the general name of "The New Jerusalem." At least two books have been written about it, devoted to the task of tracing it back to its source. It first took definite form in the hands of Bernard, the Monk of Cluny, in the twelfth century, who embodied it in a Latin poem of twelve thousand lines. But a century earlier, Hildebert, another monk of France, had written a poem from which Bernard drew some of his. And a century earlier still, Peter Damian, an Italian cardinal, had written on the same subject, and farther back than all, Gregory, the Pope, five hundred years before had given the leading thought of the hymn to them all. But even he did not originate it. To the Bible itself in the fragmentary sayings of Paul and the Apocalypse of John must we go for the idea and the imagery of the hymn. The hymn in its oldest English form, has about it a cloud of mystery. It is in the form of an old manuscript in the British Museum, undated, but known to belong to the end of the sixteenth century. It is entitled, "A Song made by F. B. P. to the tune of Diana." Many have been the conjectures as to whom these initials stand for, and the most probable is that they belong to one Francis Baker, Priest, and that he was a prisoner in the tower of London when Romish priests in England were suffering persecution. A few years later a Scotch Presbyterian minister, Rev. David Dickson, gave to the hymn essentially the form in which it has come down to us.

No. 573.

"JUST AS I AM, WITHOUT ONE PLEA."

MISS CHARLOTTE ELLIOTT, 1789—1871.

Raratonga is one of the Islands of the Pacific and has a hymn book in its own language. There are two translations of this hymn in it; one by Rev. W. Wyatt Gill and the other by Rev. Aaron Buzacott, both missionaries on the Island. Mr. Gill had just lost two little boys by death, and on the last Sabbath before they died, he and the boys had sung this hymn together, it being one of their favorities. One of the first thoughts of the bereaved father was to translate the words now so endeared to him into the language of the people among whom he was laboring. When his companion in the mission, Mr. Buzacott, read the hymn, it interested him so much that he made an independent translation of it himself and both were included in the Island Hymnal.

No. 574.

"AT EVEN ERE THE SUN WAS SET."

REV. HENRY TWELLS, 1823.

A great many years ago a great physician came to a little town lying on the shore of a lake, and performed a wonderful cure upon a woman who had been sick of a fever. It was in the house of a fisherman where this occurred, and the woman who had been sick was the mother of the fisherman's wife. They were well known in the place, and the news of the cure spread through the town. As soon as the glare and heat of the day were past, at the evening time, when the sun was setting, the people brought their sick to the fisherman's house, from all over the town, and the story relates that many of them were healed. This incident, simple though it seems, an English minister thought worthy of enshrining in a hymn. It had been already better done, however, by an American lady, Mrs. Lydia Huntley Sigourney, in a hymn beginning:

"Judea's Summer day went down
And lo! from vale and plain,
Around the heavenly Healer thronged
A sick and sorrowing train."

No. 575.

"GOD IS THE REFUGE OF HIS SAINTS"—1719.

REV. ISAAC WATTS, 1674—1748.

Some years ago an English lady while out walking one evening on the bank of a river, saw a man approaching the stream whose strange actions convinced her that he intended suicide. What to do she hardly knew, but she wanted to prevent the crime if possible, and inspired by a sudden thought, she approached him and repeated the words from the forty-sixth Psalm. "There is a river, the streams whereof shall make glad the city of God," and immediately walked away. Who the man was she did not know, nor did she know the result of what she had done, but some time after, as she was walking on a street in London, she heard footsteps close behind her, and a voice whispered over her shoulder. "'There is a river the streams whereof shall make glad the city of God,' and I have found that river." She turned quickly about, but the man had turned also and was walking rapidly away. She never knew who it was, but she knew by this curious meeting that her use of the words of old David's Psalm had not only saved a man from suicide but had led him into the life of the Christian. This hymn is Dr. Watts' version of this Psalm.

(This incident was related by the lady herself to Dr. Paxton, Professor at Princeton, New Jersey, and by him related to me.)

No. 576.

"JESUS! JESUS! COME AND SAVE US."

HENRY BATEMAN.

The author of this hymn was a business man of London, diligent enough in business to acquire a fortune, fervent enough in spirit to write many a hymn, and "serving the Lord" in many an enterprise of philanthropy and religion. One day he went into a noonday prayer meeting (Wednesday, September 7, 1862) held in Crosby Hall in London, and while there he heard a prayer in which the words were frequently repeated, "O Jesus! Jesus! come and help and bless." This prayer suggested to him this hymn.

No. 577.

"THERE CAME TO THE BEACH A POOR EXILE OF ERIN."

"THE EXILE OF ERIN."

THOMAS CAMPBELL, 1777—1844.

Thomas Campbell began writing poetry at an early age. His "Pleasure of Hope," which is even now almost a classic, was written before he was twenty-two years old, and brought its author at once into prominence. He used his first earnings to visit Germany, and while there he met Anthony McCann and a number of other Irish refugees who had been engaged in the Irish Rebellion of 1798, and had become exiles from their homes. The forlorn condition of these men aroused Campbell's sympathy and led him to write this song, which soon found its way to Ireland and, set to the air of an old Irish Melody, "Savourneen Deelish," has become known and loved by almost every native of the Green Isle. This visit of the poet, although it lasted only a year, gave rise to four songs which have become well known the world over. While going from Munich to Luiz, he witnessed from the walls of a convent, the bloody battle of Hohenlinden, and saw the victorious French Cavalry enter the nearest town wiping their bloody swords on their horses' manes. This battle he described in the piece familiar to every school boy, beginning "On Linden when the sun was low." Awhile after he visited the battle-field at Ratisbon, and an incident that occurred there led to his writing "The Soldier's Dream," beginning "Our bugles sang truce, for the night cloud had lowered."

Before leaving England, Campbell was a frequent visitor at a home where the evenings were spent in singing. A favorite song with him at these musical gatherings was "Ye Gentlemen of England," and he determined to write words for it himself. Little by little he jotted down the lines of a patriotic song, and while in Germany he gave to it its finishing touches and named it "Ye mariners of England." His song of sympathy for the Irish Rebels who were exiled from home, had already been published in England, and when he returned there he was arrested for treason, on suspicion that he had not only sympathized with the rebels in their exile but in their rebellion. His trunk was searched for treasonable letters, but instead of them the manuscript of this song, "Ye Mariners of England," was discovered, and its patriotic sentiments proved its author's loyalty and he was set at liberty.

No. 578.

"ALONG THE BANKS WHERE BABEL'S CURRENT FLOWS"—(Psalm 127).

JOEL BARLOW.

This hymn brings us into contact with one of the most versatile geniuses of a century ago. He was a soldier in the war of the Revolution, a writer of patriotic songs, a preacher, a lawyer, an editor, a bookseller, American Consul at Algiers where he concluded a treaty which led to the release of many captives, and at last American Minister to France. During the Revolutionary War and at its close the most popular hymn book in this country was "Watts' Psalms and Hymns" but when the colonies separated from the Mother Country, many of these hymns, which had been written by Watts with special reference to Great Britain, needed to be changed to adapt them to the use of an independent people. For example, there is a hymn in many of our books beginning:

"Eternal Wisdom! Thee we praise,
Thee the creation sings."

As written by Watts, this piece refers to the "British Isles," "Albion," the "Thames" and the "Severn" and has other local allusions. In view of this, the Congregational churches of Connecticut, in 1785, engaged Mr. Barlow to make such alterations in the hymns of Watts as should adapt them to use in Christian churches without regard to their locality. This work Mr. Barlow did. This paraphrase of the one hundred and twenty-seventh Psalm is not an alteration of Watts but the sole work of Mr. Barlow.

No. 579.

"OH! MEAN MAY SEEM THIS HOUSE OF CLAY."

REV. THOMAS HORNBLOWER GILL, 1819.

The alteration of hymns has been practiced to such an extent as to be not only grossly unjust to the authors, but an outrage upon common honesty. I have seen hymns addressed to Christ, altered by Unitarians so as to be addressed to God the Father; and by Romanists, to the Virgin Mary; and by Mormons, to Brigham Young. The author of this hymn was brought up a strict Unitarian, but was a great admirer of Watts' hymns. He read them as Watts wrote them, and many of them again as they had been altered to suit the doctrines of the Unitarian Church, and was first led to doubt the truth of Unitarianism by noticing "the contrast between their native power and beauty, and their shrunken and dwindled plight when shorn of their inspiring theology by Unitarian mutilations." He therefore began to study for himself and gradually the fact that Christ is divine became clear to him. When he had become fully convinced of this, he celebrated his new-found faith in this hymn. This fact will give greater significance to the allusions to "the Lord" in every stanza and almost every line of it.

No. 580.

"STAND UP, STAND UP FOR JESUS."

REV. GEORGE DUFFIELD, 1818.

In the year 1858 a great revival occurred in Philadelphia, so remarkable that distinguished from others it is usually spoken of as "The Work of God in Philadelphia." Its acknowledged leader was Rev. Dudley A. Tyng. During this revival he preached one Sunday in Jayne's Hall, to an audience of five thousand people, from the text (Exodus 10:11), "Go now, ye that are men, and serve the Lord." It was one of the most successful sermons of modern times, for it was thought that at least a thousand persons decided at that time to follow the command of the text. That was on the sixteenth of April, 1858. The Wednesday following, he went into his barn where a mule was at work on a horsepower shelling corn. He patted the animal on the neck, his sleeve was caught in the machinery, and his arm literally torn out by the roots. He died in a few hours, and just before his death sent a message to the men who had been his associates in the revival work. "Tell them," said he, "to stand up for Jesus."

On the following Sunday Rev. George Duffield preached a memorial sermon, taking for his text (Ephesians 6:14), "Stand therefore having your loins girt about with truth and having on the breastplate of righteousness," and wrote this hymn, not to be sung but as a poetic embodiment of the last words of his dead friend. It soon found its way into the newspapers and then into the hymn books where it has won for itself, wedded to the stirring tune of "Webb," a permanent place.

No. 581.

"O LORD OUR GOD, WITH EARNEST CARE."

This hymn is a literary curiosity. Its five stanzas are made up of translations of as many stanzas clipped out of four different Latin hymns, written by three different authors, in three different centuries and in at least two different countries. The originals of the first and fourth stanzas are by Gregory the Great, Pope of Rome in the sixth century. The second and third by Hilary, who lived in Gaul in the fourth century, and the fifth by some unknown author who lived in the seventh century. The translations are also by different hands, the first four stanzas being the work of Rev. John Mason Neale, and the fifth that of some unknown translator.

No. 582.

"JESUS AT THY COMMAND"—1774.

"O'ER THOSE GLOOMY HILLS OF DARKNESS"—1772.

Rev. William Williams, 1717—1791.

The history of missions contains no more wonderful story than that of work in the Islands of the Pacific. It was the first mission undertaken by the London Missionary Society, a society whose relation to missionary effort in Great Britain is about the same as that of the American Board in this country. Its first band of missionaries sailed from London August 10, 1796. Early in the morning of that day their vessel swung out into the river Thames, bearing at the masthead a flag the like of which had never before floated on the breeze. It was purple, with three white doves bearing olive branches in their bills.

The shore was crowded with friends who waved to them tearful farewells, for they expected never to see them again until they should meet them in heaven. As the ship moved slowly down the river the company gathered on her deck sang the hymn:

"Jesus at thy command
We launch into the deep."

After a voyage of more than half a year the same company gathered on the ship's deck saw a long low range of hills outlined dimly along the horizon. It was the Island of Tahiti, to whose inhabitants they had come to tell the gospel message. Soon the canoes of the Islanders were dancing in the waves about the ship, and the natives heard for the first time the music of Christian song as the mission band sang the hymn:

O'er those gloomy hills of darkness
Look my soul, be still and gaze,
All the promises do travel
On a glorious day of grace.
Blessed Jubilee
Let thy glorious morning dawn."

These two hymns thus mark the beginning of a mission enterprise which has spread over all the Islands of the South Pacific Ocean, with a history unparalleled in the annals of mission work.

No. 583.

"LEOMINSTER" (Tune).

GEORGE WILLIAM MARTIN, 1828—1881.

This tune, associated with Dr. Bonar's hymn, "A few more years shall roll," is usually credited to Sir Arthur

S. Sullivan, who harmonized it, but the melody was composed by George William Martin, of whom this incident is told: Prince Albert, husband of Queen Victoria, had composed a piece of music, and sent a request to Sir George S. Smart, a noted chorister, to come to Buckingham Palace with a few choir boys to perform it. Young Martin was one of the boys who went. When they reached the presence of His Royal Highness, he handed a copy of his music to Martin with the question, "Can you sing that at sight?"

"Yes, sir," came the quick reply, and he did it quite to the Prince's satisfaction.

There seems nothing in this incident to us in democratic America worth relating, but things are different in England, and the musical party had no sooner gotten outside the palace gate than young Martin got a tremendous whack on the ear from their leader for using so common a title as "Sir" in addressing the husband of the Queen.

No. 584.

"AUSTRIA" (Tune).

Franz Joseph Haydn, 1732—1809.

This piece was composed for the words of a national hymn, and was first performed in public on the birthday of the Emperor of Austria, February 12, 1797. Mendelsohn once made use of it in a manner which added to its popularity, as well as to the wonder with which the people regarded him. He was in London in 1842 and went one summer Sunday evening to St. Peter's Church. As he entered the congregation were singing this tune. Mendelssohn was asked to play the voluntary at the close of the service, and took this tune which the people had just sung, for his theme, and for a full half hour improvised variations of it, never repeating himself, until it seemed as if every possible use had been made of it. And yet a few evenings later at another Church, when asked to take the same theme, he played an entirely different arrangement of it, with new and wonderful changes and all improvised as he played.

No. 585.

"EVAN" (Tune).

REV. WILLIAM HENRY HAVERGAL.

DR. LOWELL MASON.

Very little is known of the circumstances under which most of our music was written. This tune, however, is an exception. Robert Burns, the Scottish poet, once visited the house of Dr. Laurie, and when he left there was found on a table in the room he had occupied a little poem of six stanzas. It was the poet's prayer for each member of the family whose hospitality he had enjoyed. Half a century later Rev. William Henry Havergal, a minister of the Church of England, composed music for this poem. A copy of his song crossed the ocean and fell into the hands of Dr. Lowell Mason, who was much pleased with it. He selected from it four strains and arranged them into a hymn tune; so that while in our books of church song the tune to which Dr. Mason gave the name "Evan" is credited to Mr. Havergal, to Dr. Mason belongs the credit of fitting it for our use in religious worship.

No. 586.

"HASTINGS" (Tune).

DR. THOMAS HASTINGS, 1784—1872.

Composed by Dr. Thomas Hastings for words of his own writing; but though he acknowledged the hymn to be his he signed the tune with a fictitious name "K.—L.—F.—F.—." The reason for this he gives as follows: "I had found that a foreigner's name went a great way, and that very ordinary tunes would be sung if Palestrina, or Pucitta, etc., were over them, while a better tune by Hastings would go unnoticed." This seems to indicate that the admiration of the present generation for imported goods comes to them naturally by inheritance.

No. 587.

"GANGES" (Tune).

This tune was composed not far from the time when Occum's hymn was written. Its author lived in or near Troy, New York, but who or what he was is quite unknown. It is not impossible that the tune was written for the words of Occum as it is found in books published early in the century under the name of "Indian Philosopher," and accompanied by Occum's hymn, "Awaked by Sinai's awful sound."

No. 588.

"PAX TECUM" (Tune.)—1878.

Rev. G. T. Caldbeck was for many years a missionary in China. While there he became greatly impressed by the beauty of the hymn written by Rev. E. H. Bickersteth beginning:

"Peace, perfect peace."

and although unskilful in music, he wrote for it a tune and sent it in manuscript to England, to the author of the hymn. It was there corrected a little and soon after published.

No. 589.

"SHIRLAND" (Tune).

SAMUEL STANLEY, 1767—1822.

About a hundred years ago a little congregation of worshippers met in what was known as Carr's Lane Meeting House, Birmingham, England. After a little the singing in that church began to attract attention, and the congregation increased. In a few years more the singing had become famous, and it was no unusual thing for members of other congregations not far distant to slip out of their own churches as soon as the sermon was over, and run to Carr's Lane Meeting House to listen to the closing hymn. Samuel Stanley, the composer of this tune, was the leader of the singing at this church, and it was his skill as a leader, as well as his ability as a musician that made the music there so famous.

No. 590.

"SELMA" (Tune).

ROBERT ARCHIBALD SMITH, 1780—1829.

A hundred years ago, a silk weaver's boy in the town of Reading, England, was the wonder of the town for his skill in playing on such a rustic whistle as all boys know how to make. When a little older the whistle gave place to the flute and this again to the violin. Musical talent was not highly appreciated by his father, who tried his best to teach him what he thought the far higher art of weaving at a loom. His success was poor, and often when he came to see what progress he was making with his weaving, he would catch him scratching musical notes with a pin on the frame work of the loom. The boy became a skilful musician, leader of a famous choir in Edinburgh, composed a great deal of church music, this tune among others, and many well-known secular songs.

No. 591.

"YORK" (Tune).

There is no land on the face of the earth in which the singing of hymns has borne so prominent a part in its history as in Scotland. They did not call them hymns but Psalms, for the words were paraphrases and usually awkward and uncouth ones, too, of the Psalms of David. The people sang them in their kirks, in their homes, as they worked in the fields, or walked on the roads. They encouraged each other with them when they went into battle, and voiced in them at its close their victory or defeat. They sang Psalms when hunted through forests and swamps, and caves, and when about to suffer martyrdom for their faith. A few of the old tunes they used have come down to us, and they should be retained in service if only to remind us of the wonderful history interwoven with them through more than three centuries. "York" is one of them, and it is supposed to have been put into its present form by John Milton, father of the poet who wrote "Paradise Lost." It has been a very popular tune in England, and it is said that within the memory of people now living it was used as a lullaby song by half the nurses of England, and the chimes of many country churches played it six or eight times over every twenty-four hours. The tune was intended to be sung fast. In the days when tunes were scarce, it has been known for "York" to be sung fifteen times in one week in the same church.

No. 592.

HENRY J. GAUNTLETT, 1806—1876.

The little church at Olney, England, is an important spot to lovers of sacred song. It was here that John Newton ministered and with William Cowper wrote the hymns which have endeared them both to Christian people all over the world. After Newton there came a minister named Gauntlett, who was a good musician, but he had a little boy who was a better one; so much better that at nine years of age he was appointed the organist of his father's church. Later he went to London and became one of the leaders if not the pioneer in a movement that has effected a complete revolution in the music of the church. Turn to the index of composers in any hymnal published within the last ten years and compare it with the similar index in earlier books, and a new set of music writers will be seen to have come to the front. Barnby, Dykes, Hopkins, Monk, and Sir Arthur Sullivan will be found furnishing more tunes than almost all others put together. And Mr. Henry J. Gauntlett, the son of the Olney minister, opened the way for them all. The church music of today owes much to him.

No. 593.

"AVON" (Tune).

HUGH WILSON, 1764—1824.

It is said that no tune book of any importance has been published in Great Britain for the last sixty years that does not contain this tune. And almost the same thing can be said of books published in this country. It was composed by a Scotch shoemaker, but it required a lawsuit to find it out. Editors were in the habit of assigning it to almost any one, apparently, whom their fancy suggested, but at last a Glasgow publisher, who actually owned the copyright, brought suit against someone who had published the tune without permission, and it was proven that Hugh Wilson, a poor shoemaker, had composed it. He employed his spare time in study, made sundials for those who wanted them, led the Psalm singing in the village Kirk, started the first Sunday school in the town where he lived, and in all ways made his life as useful as he could. He composed a great many tunes, but when he was dying he caused the manuscript copies to be destroyed, only three or four escaping. He named this tune "Fenwick" after the town where he was born, but in Great Britain it is now known as "Martyrdom."

No. 594.

"THOU HOLY SPIRIT, WE PRAY TO THEE."—COVERDALE.

"NOW PRAY WE ALL GOD THE COMFORTER."—A. T. RUSSELL.

"NOW ON THE HOLY GHOST WE CALL, FOR PERFECT—"—FRY.

"TO THEE THOU HOLY SPIRIT NOW."—FRY.

"HOLY SPIRIT! GRANT US OUR DESIRE."—J. ANDERSON.

"OH! HOLY GHOST TO THEE WE PRAY."—DR. J. HUNT.

"NOW CRAVE WE OF THE HOLY GHOST."—R. MASSIE.

"NOW PRAY WE TO THE HOLY GHOST."—GEORGE MACDONALD.

"NOW ON THE HOLY GHOST WE CALL, TO GIVE—"—J. D. BURNS.

The above are all translations of the German:

"NUN BITTEN WIR DEN HEILIGEN GEIST."

"IN PEACE AND JOY I NOW DEPART, ACCORDING—"—C. WINKWORTH.

"WITH PEACE AND JOY FROM EARTH I GO."—MISS FRY.

"GOD'S WILL BE DONE! WITH JOY OF HEART."—J. ANDERSON.

"GLADLY FROM EARTH AND TIME I CEASE."—DR. J. HUNT.

"THY WILL BE DONE! WITH JOYFUL HEART."—J. ANDERSON.

"IN PEACE AND JOY I NOW DEPART, IT IS—"—R. MASSIE.

"IN PEACE AND JOY AWAY I GO."—GEO. MACDONALD.

"IN PEACE AND JOY I NOW DEPART, AS—"—GEORGE MACDONALD.

"IN JOY AND PEACE I ONWARD FARE."—N. L. FROTHINGHAM.

The above are all translations of the German by Martin Luther:

"MIT FRIED UND FREUD ICH FAHR DAHIN."

Not long after the hymn of Martin Luther was written beginning:

"Mit Fried und Freud ich fahr dahin,"

a party of nearly a hundred fishermen were engaged in their work on the ice between Copenhagen and an Island in the Sound that runs between Denmark and Sweden, when suddenly the ice gave way and began running out with the current. They were soon separated from each other and about thirty of the party were drowned. While they were still near together, one of them who had been religiously trained called to the others, "Dear brethren, let us not fall into despair because we shall lose our lives! but let us prove by our conduct that we have been hearers of God's word." And then they all joined in singing together these hymns; the first a prayer to the Holy Spirit for faith and strength, and the second a metrical version of the Song of Simeon,

"Now lettest thou thy servant depart in peace."

No. 595.

"HOLY SPIRIT, ONCE AGAIN."—Miss C. Winkworth.

"COME, O COME, THOU QUICKENING SPIRIT, THOU—" —Charles W. Schaeffer.

"COME, THOU SPIRIT EVER LIVING."—R. Massie.

The above are all translations from the German:

"*KOMM, O KOMM, DU GEIST DES LEBENS.*"—Heinrich Held.

In some cities of this country where the German element was strong, the watchmen, as they went about the streets at night, were accustomed in early times to call the hour of the night and to add something of the condition of affairs for the information of the wakeful citizens. "Twelve o'clock and all's well;" "one o'clock and a starlight night." This custom came from the Fatherland, where the watchman often added to his hourly announcement a stanza from some hymn or song.

The story is related by Kubler that in a town in Northern Germany a very poor woman, who with her two children had had nothing to eat for four days, was driven to despair and in the night she resolved to murder her children. She was just taking up the youngest, with a knife in her hand, when the watchman, who at that moment passed under her low window, and saw through a hole in the shutter what she was intending, suddenly knocked and entered the room. He inquired about her trouble, gave her a little money, and promised to bring her help. And then he went out to his beat and as he called the hours through the streets of the city he sang a stanza of his hymn:

"And when e'er a yearning strong
Presses out the bitter cry
'Ah my God, how long, how long?'
Then O let me find Thee nigh,
And thy words of healing balm
Bring me courage, patience, calm."

No. 596.

"AGAIN THE CIRCLING SEASONS TELL."—W. J. COPELAND.

"HAIL THE JOYFUL DAY'S RETURN."—R. CAMPBELL.

"BLEST JOYS FROM MIGHTY WONDERS WROUGHT."—J. M. NEALE.

"ROUND ROLL THE WEEKS OUR HEARTS TO GREET."—W. J. BLEW.

"JOY! BECAUSE THE CIRCLING YEAR."—J. ELLERTON and F. J. A. HORT.

"AGAIN THE SLOWLY CIRCLING YEAR."—E. CASWELL.

"BLEST SEASON! WHICH WITH GLADNESS FRAUGHT."—J. D. CHAMBERS.

These are translations of the Latin hymn *"Beata nobis gaudia."* Hilary of Poitiers, 305—367.

About the year 305 there was born in France—it was not called France then, but Gaul—a boy who later became one of the greatest men of the age. His parents were idolaters and he was brought up a heathen. He was well educated and in his studies he came across a copy of the Bible which, out of curiosity, he began to read. He himself tells the story how step by step his reading brought him out of heathenism into Christian faith.

"When I found," he says, "in Exodus, how God was called 'I am that I am,' and when I read in Isaiah (40:12) of a Deity who 'held the wind in His fists,' and again (66:1) of Him who said, 'Heaven is my throne and earth is my footstool,' then this surpasssed all my heathen conceptions of grandeur and power. And when I read (Psalms, 138:7) how this great God loved and cared for His children, so that we could say, 'though I walk in the midst of trouble, Thou wilt revive me,' 'Thou shalt stretch forth thine hand against the wrath of mine enemies, and Thy right hand shall save me, then was I drawn towards this Mighty Being by a sentiment of confidence and trust."

And then he found the gospel of John—it was a new book then—and its opening sentences that told of the Word, "which was with God and which was God," made the whole system of Christian theology clear to him and he became a Christian. The Arian heresy, which dethroned the Christ for whose sake he had turned from the idolatry of his ancestors, soon spread over the land, and against it he fought with tongue and pen; and when by and by its priests outnumbered those who stood with him, he was banished from the land. He had a wife and daughter at home, and there is still to be found a letter which Abra, Hilary's daughter, wrote him while he was in exile; but more important than Abra's letter to her father, is Hilary's answer to his daughter. In it he tells her to keep her soul and her conduct pure; and after much counsel he ends by enclosing two hymns which she may use in the worship of God, one in the morning, and the other in the evening. The evening hymn is lost, but the morning hymn still exists, beginning in the Latin, *'Lucis largitor splendide'*—

"Thou Splendid Giver of the light."

This is the oldest Latin hymn, and Hilary is the oldest Latin hymn writer, and Abra, his daughter, was the first singer of these new hymns which have in later years enriched our hymnody.

No. 597.

"EWING" (Tune).

ALEXANDER EWING, 1830.

Just as some of our sweetest hymns have come from authors whose only claim to literary fame rests on a single hymn, so some of our sweetest tunes come from composers who are not professional musicians. The composer of this tune is a paymaster in the English Army, with the rank of Lieutenant-Colonel, and wears a medal gained by service in the war between England and China in 1860. It was composed for the words of Bernard's hymn beginning:

"For thee, O dear, dear Country,"

but is usually used for another part of the same hymn beginning, "Jerusalem, the Golden." Hymn tinkers alter nearly all our hymns and tune menders play all sorts of pranks with our music. While Colonel Ewing was absent in China, they got hold of his tune and, without so much as saying "by your leave, sir," they changed the time to suit themselves and published it. Speaking of this he says, "In my opinion the alteration of the rhythm has very much vulgarized my little tune. It now seems to me a good deal like a polka. I hate to hear it."

No. 598.

"O'ER THOSE GLOOMY HILLS OF DARKNESS."

Rev. William Williams, 1717—1791.

The author of this hymn spent fifty years in traveling throughout the length and breadth of his native land preaching the gospel. On one occasion he stopped over night in a little Welsh village, and next morning, arising before the sun, he saw a long low range of hills lying dark under the mists, but behind them in the eastern sky, the rays of the morning were beginning to give promise of approaching day. The imagery of this morning scene among the hills he transferred to this missionary hymn.

No. 599.

"BETHANY" (Tune).

This tune, to which the name of Dr. Lowell Mason is given as composer, brings into curious contact old times and new, things sacred and things secular. Dr. Mason set the tune to the hymn beginning, "Nearer, my God, to Thee," and its fitness for these words has kept the two together in all our hymnals. But the tune is only an adaptation of an old song. Nearly a hundred years ago, a young Irish poet, of rollicking disposition and habits, began the issue of a series of songs, set to the ancient music of Ireland. These melodies were arranged for him by Sir John Stevenson, an Irish violinist. They became immensely popular, and Tom Moore's "Irish Melodies" were heard at the theaters, concert rooms, on the streets, and in the homes of the people. Among these was one, still a favorite everywhere. It began with the words:

"Oft in the stilly night,
Ere slumber's chain has bound me,
Fond memory brings the light
Of other days around me."

The notes of the first line of this song are the same as those of the first line of "Bethany," which is based all the way through on the old Irish song.

No. 600.

"HERALD ANGELS" (Tune).

This tune is a fragment taken from a musical composition of Mendelssohn, entitled the *"Festgesang,"* written to celebrate the fourth centenary of the invention of printing and first performed at Leipzig, June 23, 1840. The German words sung to the first line were *"Gutenberg der grosse Mann."*

No. 601.

GEORGE FREDERICK HANDEL, 1685—1759.

Just two hundred years ago, a German doctor started in his carriage to visit one of the German dukes. He had a little boy who was very fond of music, but who had been forbidden by his father to play or sing, as he considered music only an amusement and not a profession. The boy, knowing that at the old castle where his father was going, there were music rooms and musical instruments, made up his mind to accompany him, if possible, on this trip, and when the carriage had gone a little way along the road, the boy was found running behind it as fast as his little legs would carry him. He was picked up, and promising good behavior was taken along. Arriving at the castle, he was left pretty much to himself, and soon found his way to the chapel and the organ. In spite of parental commands he had already learned to play by stealth, and the Sunday afternoon after the chapel service was over and he supposed everybody had left the room, he mounted the organ stool and began to play. The duke himself, however, had remained behind and heard with astonishment the playing of the six-year-old child. His influence induced the father to consent that his boy should have a musical education. This was the beginning of the musical career of George Frederick Handel, the composer of the "Oratorio of The Messiah," and who has been called the "Monarch of Composers." Most of the tunes of Handel now to be found in our hymnals are extracts from oratorios or operas he wrote. Thus the tune "Samson" comes from the oratorio of that name. It is the chorus beginning:

"Then round about the starry throne" (1742).

"Solomon" is from a solo beginning:

"What though I trace,"

in the oratorio of "Solomon" (1748).

"Theodora" is from the solo in the oratorio of that name beginning:

"Angels ever bright and fair" (1749).

"Saul" is from the "Dead March" in the oratorio of that name (1738).

"Mamre" is from the solo:

"Shall I on Mamre's fertile plain,"

in the oratorio of "Joshua" (1747).

"David" is adapted from an opera entitled "Sosarme" (1732).

"Georgia" is an adaptation of a song beginning:

"See the conquering hero."

"Saxony" is from a song in an opera entitled "Siroe" (1728).

"Goss" is from a duet beginning, "Cease thy anguish," in the Oratorio "Athalia" (1733).

There are, however, three tunes composed by Handel for as many of Charles Wesley's hymns. The celebrated comedian Rich was proprietor of Covent Garden Theater in London when Handel's oratorios were performed there. Mr. Rich's wife had been converted at a Methodist meeting and had made the acquaintance of Mr. Wesley. At her request Handel wrote a tune named "Gospel" for Mr. Wesley's hymn beginning:

"Rejoice the Lord is King;"

one entitled "Cannons" or "Chandos" for the hymn,

"Sinners obey the gospel call";

and one named "Kedron" for the words,

"O Love Divine, how sweet thou art."

No. 602.

Lowell Mason, 1792—1872.

About the year 1820, a young man from Massachusetts became clerk in a bank in Savannah, Georgia. His aptitude for music had made him the leader of the choir in his native town, and in Savannah he soon became the conductor of the choir of the leading Presbyterian church of the city. The collections of church music of the day were not satisfactory to him, and to satisfy his own desire for something better he began collecting tunes himself. When he had enough for a book, he obtained leave of absence from his work, and came north to Philadelphia to get it published. He was not working for money, and he offered the copyright of his collection to the publishers of that city, asking no compensation but a few copies of the book for his own use. But even at this price he could find no one willing to undertake its publication. He made the same proposal to Boston publishers but with no better success, and was about to return to Savannah, unsuccessful and discouraged, when a musical gentleman in Boston, whom he casually met, asked to see his collection. He was much pleased with it, showed it to the Handel and Haydn Society, then the foremost musical society in Boston, and this society published the book, giving its compiler an interest in the profits. The book became immensely popular and quickly ran through seventeen editions. The young man was Lowell Mason, and this event decided the course of his life. He gave up his position at Savannah and became the organist at Dr. Lyman Beecher's Church in Boston, and from that time until the end of his life was identified with the church music of the country. Together with Dr. Thomas Hastings, he may be said to have revolutionized the sacred music of the land. He delivered lectures, conducted conventions, taught classes, composed tunes, stimulated others to similar work, and in all possible ways sought to arouse the interest of the people in better music for their church services. And even now, after so many others have arisen both in this country and England as composers of sacred music, his name stands most prominent in nearly every hymnal of the church.

No. 603.

Felice de Giardini, 1716-1796.

In 1750, an Italian violinist made his first appearance in London, and by his superb playing created a great sensation. He remained in England more than thirty years, and although he was erratic, selfish, and unpleasant, he maintained his popularity among the people by his great skill upon the violin. While there the Countess of Huntingdon, who had become deeply interested in the Methodist Movement and was devoting her wealth to the establishing of churches and employment of preachers, used her influence upon the great violinist to get him to compose a few pieces of sacred music for use in the Methodist churches. The tune named "Athens" was one of these. Late in life he started a comic opera in London which failed. He was in no sense a religious man.

No. 604.

JEAN BAPTISTE FAURE, 1830.

Half a century ago or more, a boy was found drawing crowds about him on the streets of Paris by the marvelous voice with which he sang. Friends were found for him and he received a musical education, while his voice grew purer and finer as it became more cultivated. Everyone was prophesying a brilliant future for him, when suddenly he lost his voice, and after waiting months hoping for it to return, he turned to the study of instrumental music. Awhile after, thinking of the voice he had lost, he bethought himself of prayer, and prayed "give me back my voice and I will use it for charity and for good." His voice gradually returned and he became the great church singer of Paris, and wrote an ode to charity which has become celebrated. "Palm Branches" is the work of his genius.

No. 605.

REV. JOHN FAWCETT, 1739—1817.

When twenty-five years old, John Fawcett became the pastor of a little Baptist church among the mountains of

Yorkshire, England. His salary was twenty-five pounds a year, equivalent to about one hundred and twenty dollars of our money. Eight years later he accepted a call to a prominent London church, and made his preparations to go, but when the leave-taking came, his people gathered about him with so much sorrow at the parting, and such evident affection for him, that he put his goods, which were already loaded upon wagons, back into the house, and sent word to the London church that he could not come. It was a fortunate thing for the song service of the church, for he put the experience he had just passed through into that hymn, which has become so precious:

"Blest be the tie that binds
Our hearts in Christian love."

The sequel is that he remained pastor of that little church for more than fifty years, until a stroke of paralysis ended his ministry and his life. How he managed to support a wife and family upon so meager a salary is partly explained by a notice printed on the flyleaf of a hymn book which he compiled, and which read as follows:

"At Brearly Hall, in Midgely, near Halifax, a pleasant and healthy situation. Youths are genteely boarded and trained up in useful learning, with great tenderness, fidelity, and care, and upon reasonable terms."

No. 606.

"JESUS LOVES ME, THIS I KNOW."

MISS ANNA B. WARNER, 1822.

In 1880, Miss Warner published a novel entitled, "Say and Seal." One of the heroes of the book is a little motherless boy named Johnny Fax, who learns the story of the love of Jesus from his day school teacher, Mr. Linden, and his Sunday-school teacher, Faith Derrick. Johnny is taken sick, and these two teachers become his nurses. The little boy is never so happy as when he is nestling in Mr. Linden's arms, and forgets his suffering and falls alseep, while he tells him Bible stories or sings to him some children's hymns. The day on which the little boy died, he was very restless, and had asked Mr. Linden to "walk," and so wrapped in his teacher's arms he was being carried back and forth across the room. The motion soothed his restlessness and soon he said, "Sing," and so Mr. Linden, as he walked with the little dying boy, sang to him softly, the words of this hymn:

"Jesus loves me this I know
For the Bible tells me so.
Little ones to Him belong,
They are weak but He is strong."

The author of the hymn in writing about it says that, "for the time Johnny Fax was so intensely real, so vividly in my heart, that the hymn was written *for him,* as if he had been a living child."

No. 607.

Felix Mendelssohn-Bartholdy, 1809—1847.

One evening a friend entered a room where a young man was seated apparently buried in thought with an open Bible before him. He started up as he saw his visitor and his face was gleaming with light.

"Listen," said he, and then he read from the book before him, that passage from the First Book of Kings: "And behold, the Lord passed by, and a great and strong wind rent the mountains, and brake in pieces the rocks, before the Lord; but the Lord was not in the wind, and after the wind an earthquake; but the Lord was not in the earthquake, and after the earthquake, a fire; but the Lord was not in the fire; and after the fire a still small voice." (I Kings, 19:11, 12.) This was Felix Mendelssohn, and he read the words which had inspired him to write that wonderful Oratorio of "Elijah." Nine years of labor did the musician put into that composition, and then on August 26, 1846, he led in its first performance at the annual musical festival at Birmingham, England. A great audience gathered from all over England greeted his appearance, and remained spellbound as the musical drama proceeded, and when at the close the composer moved away from his place on the stage, cheer upon cheer greeted his ears from every side. It was for him a moment of splendid triumph, but a triumph that cost him his life, for even while he was receiving the congratulations of kings and princes, upon the great work he had composed, he became weak from exhaustion.

"Play, play," said a friend to him just afterward.

"I cannot play," was the reply, "I have no strength," and within a year he had died.

No. 608.

Rev. Samuel Dunn.

A gentleman once invited another to go with him to an outdoor religious service. He said, describing it, that when they entered the town he found himself marched in a procession with a lot of praying and singing men, to a position just in front of a booth occupied by a company of wandering actors, where he soon discovered that it would be almost impossible for him to preserve his gravity. He saw directly before him the clown of the company, grinning by the side of a huge, black dog standing on its hind legs with clerical bands around its neck and one of the tracts issued by the man, at whose invitation he had gone, dangling from his paw. But while he was finding it so hard to repress a smile, not a muscle of his leader's face was moved. He was there with an important message, which he intended to deliver. With a clear voice he gave out a hymn, and his men sang with all their voices, and they had need to, for the actors' band struck up and the clown began to caper. When the singing was ended, several men prayed, and then he himself was called upon to speak, but failed to be heard above the din from the stage. Then the leader tried, and when he failed he stood silent holding up one after another, large placards, with scripture sentences printed on them. At last the players tried throwing fireworks among the people on the preachers' stand, and a party of rough miners, who up to this point had enjoyed the fun, decided that this was not fair play, and made a grand onset on the players' band and drove them all from the scene, and then the leader secured a quiet crowd and gave to them an earnest gospel sermon. Such a man must certainly have been earnest and such a man must certainly have been brave. It was Samuel Dunn.

No. 609.

"WEBB" (Tune).

GEORGE JAMES WEBB, 1803—1887.

This tune, which is associated in all minds with the missionary hymn, beginning:

"The morning light is breaking,"

was written on the ocean in 1830, as a secular song. It was first published with the words:

" 'Tis dawn, the lark is singing."

For forty years Webb was organist of the Old South Church, Boston, and was a Swedenborgian in religion.

No. 610.

"EVENTIDE" (Tune).

This tune first appears in "Hymns Ancient and Modern." The general charge of this book was in the hands of Sir Henry Baker, while Dr. Monk had charge of the musical matter. One evening they were going out together, when they suddenly remembered that there was no tune provided for Lyte's hymn "Abide with Me," and on the spur of the moment Dr. Monk sat down and wrote it, inside of ten minutes, although one of his assistants sat at a piano within six feet of him, playing a Fantasia by Thalberg.

No. 611.

"KILMARNOCK" (Tune).

Neil Douglas, 1776—1862.

In the same year when our independence as a nation was declared, a boy was born at Greenock, a little seaport town of Scotland. The boy was fond of boats and of the sea, and so he naturally became a sailor. When eighteen years of age, he was sailing on a privateer engaged in the war between England and France, and their ship was lying at the port where he was born, when news came of Lord Howe's great victory over the French fleet. His vessel with others was ordered to fire a salute. Neil was helping to handle a cannon when, by a premature discharge, his right arm was torn off, his right cheek carried away, and his eyesight destroyed. The boy had always been a favorite, and friends gathered round him after this calamity and helped in every possible way to make his life cheerful. At their suggestion he learned to sing, and progressed so rapidly that he was soon teaching music himself, and this he kept on doing with great success until old age compelled him to give it up. He composed a hundred and fifty pieces of sacred music, and a few secular songs.

No. 612.

"ST. MATTHEW" (Tune).

Composed by William Croft, an English organist. We often hear of persons being affected to tears by the reading of some hymn which stirs their emotions. This tune affords an instance of the same result following the performance of a piece of music. At a great musical festival at York, England, in 1823, the celebrated singer Catalini heard this tune sung and was so affected by it that she could with the greatest difficulty regain her composure enough to sing the song:

"Angels ever bright and fair,"

which she was expected to do at the close of the singing of this piece.

No. 613.

"HYMNS ANCIENT AND MODERN."

REV. SIR HENRY WILLIAMS BAKER, 1821—1877.

DR. WILLIAM HENRY MONK, 1823—1889.

Without doubt the most remarkable hymnal ever compiled is the English book entitled, "Hymns Ancient and Modern." It was first published in 1861 and its immense popularity can be imagined from the fact that in the twenty-eight years following over twenty-seven millions of copies were sold. The literary work was done by a syndicate of about forty clergymen all connected with the Church of England, with Rev. Sir Henry Williams Baker as their leader. Upon him fell the larger share of the work, but it was not any superiority in the hymns selected that gave to the book its popularity, so much as the peculiar beauty and fitness of its tunes. The musical editor was Dr. William Henry Monk. Some of the music he composed himself and he was wonderfully successful in obtaining the aid of the best living composers of church music. He was an enthusiast in his profession. Tunes came to him at all sorts of times and in all sorts of places. The tune named "Aber," which he composed for the words "O perfect life of love," came to him in the night, and he got out of bed to note it down. The tune "Advent," sometimes named "Beverly," written for the words "Thou art coming, O my Savior," was composed on a railway train. "Easter Hymn" was written in competition for a prize of five guineas, which had been offered by an English Musical Society for the best music for the words:

"Jesus Christ is risen today."

and which was awarded to this tune. "Eventide," written for the words:

"Abide with me, fast falls the eventide,"

was undertaken on the spur of the moment and completed within ten minutes, while one of Thalberg's Fantasias was being played on a piano only a few feet distant from where the composer sat. But it was Monk's music and his skill in selecting music which gave to the hymn book named its phenomenal success. So that it has been pithily said concerning it that while "in a dozen years from the date of its publication not twenty of its original hymns were sung as written, in the churches, not twenty of its tunes were unsung in the same churches."

No. 614.

"THE CREATION" (Oratorio).

When Francis Joseph Haydn was old and feeble, in 1809, the people of Vienna desired to do him honor, and so arranged for a performance of this oratorio with all possible arrangement for effective performance. Haydn had to be carried to the theater. When the music reached the place where occurs the words, "Let there be light," Haydn arose, and pointing toward heaven said, "It comes from thence," and then the people remembered that Haydn had done his work under the influence and help of prayer, and knew that he felt that he had been inspired from heaven.

No. 615.

"ST. ALPHEGE" (Tune).

Dr. Henry J. Gauntlett.

While the composer was at dinner one evening, a messenger came from the church to tell him that the prayer tune for a hymn they were to sing that evening, beginning:

"The hymn of glory sing we,"

was mislaid, and asking what should be done. "Give me some paper," said Dr. Gauntlett, and in a few minutes this tune was written and sent back by the messenger.

No. 616.

Rev. John Bacchus Dykes, 1823—1876.

Many of the tunes which have become standards among us, are regular, and solid in their composition, and are applicable to the words of almost any of the old meters in which they are written. To compose a tune that in addition to suiting the meter also embodies the sentiment of a particular hymn is comparatively a recent improvement in our song worship. Rev. J. B. Dykes, who died in 1876, may almost be said to be the originator of the idea. Many of his tunes were written with the purpose of making the music the exponent of one particular hymn, and it was his desire that the words and the music might become so fitted to each other as to become inseparable companions. To these tunes he gave names which are suggestive of the theme. Examples are to be found in the tunes named *"Veni Creator,"* written for a hymn beginning:

"Come Holy Ghost, Creator, Come";

"St. Crosse," for a hymn on the Crucifixion; "Anatolius," for the hymn beginning:

"The day is past and over";

written by an old Greek hymn writer by that name. "Nicæa," written for the hymn beginning:

"Holy, Holy, Holy, Lord God Almighty,"

which is a hymn on the Trinity, Nicæa being the town in which the famous Council met which proclaimed the "Nicene Creed," in which the doctrine of the Trinity was first formulated. "Olivet," written for the Ascension hymn beginning:

"Thou art gone up on high,"

and named for the Mount of Olives from which Christ ascended; "Melita," written for the hymn for sailors, beginning:

"Eternal Father! strong to save,
Whose arm doth bind the restless wave."

the tune being named for the island where St. Paul was shipwrecked; "Requiescat," written for the hymn of rest, beginning:

"Now the laborer's task is over."

Dr. Dykes was a vicar of the Church of England, and he made the composition of a tune as much a religious service as the writing of a sermon, always offering a short prayer before commencing to compose a piece of music. He made his family his critics. It was the practice for his children to spend Sunday evenings singing hymns to the music their father had written for them, and as they sang they offered suggestions and criticisms which he not infrequently adopted.

No. 617.

"OLD HUNDRED" (Tune).

Many attempts have been made to trace this tune to its source, and at least one entire book has been devoted to the effort, but all without success. Its first appearance, so far as known, was in what is known as the "Genevan Psalter" in 1551. This book was first published in 1548 by Clement Marot and then contained thirty psalms in the French language. John Calvin, the theologian about whose doctrines people quarrel so much these days, induced him to add to this, and two years later a second edition was published containing fifty psalms. The tune of "Old Hundred" was not in either of these books, but, Marot having died, Calvin induced his friend Beza to continue the work and in 1551 he issued a new edition with thirty-four new Psalms, and in this "Old Hundred" appeared, set to the words of the one hundred and thirty-fourth Psalm. Very little church music at that time was strictly original. Many of the tunes in this Psalter are known to be but scraps of other music arranged together in a new way, and there are some evidences that this grand old tune had such an ignoble origin. The tune found its way to England very soon and was published there set to the one hundredth Psalm in 1562. It then went by the name of "The Hundredth." By and by the Psalm book of Sternhold and Hopkins, then in use, was superseded by that of Tate and Brady, and this tune, because it came out of the old book, was dubbed "Old Hundredth," which in later times was shortened to "Old Hundred."

No. 618.

"MY COUNTRY, 'TIS OF THEE."

REV. SAMUEL FRANCIS SMITH, 1808.

The author of this hymn tells the story of its origin. He says: "I was one dismal day in the month of February standing near my window and casually turning over a collection of German songs which had been presented to me by Lowell Mason, one of the most noted musicians of that time. I came to one which I liked. My attention was attracted to the words, which were of a patriotic nature, and the impulse came over me to make a patriotic hymn for my own country. I began at once and at the end of half an hour put the piece into my portfolio and went to my supper, thinking no more of the circumstance. The next time I went to Boston I took the song with me and gave it to Mr. Mason. He did not refer to it at our next meeting and it passed wholly out of my mind. On the next Fourth of July, as I was passing Park Street Church, I was attracted by the sound of music. I entered and found the building filled with boys and girls engaged in celebrating the day.

Glancing over a program held by a person in front of me, I saw that the last piece was a song entitled, 'My Country, 'tis of Thee.'" The tune to which we sing it, and which we have rechristened "America," is of disputed origin. It was probably composed by Henry Carey, an Englishman, who was born in 1685 and died in 1743. A public banquet was given in 1740 to celebrate the capture of Porto Bello, a South American city, by Admiral Vernon of the English Navy. At this feast Carey sang a song, the words and music of which were supposed to be his own. The words were the ones which altered a little are now used in Great Britain as a national hymn, beginning:

"God bless our gracious Queen,"

and the music is the same as that to which we sing,

"My Country, 'tis of Thee."

It can scarcely now be claimed as a national hymn, for Prussia, Hanover, Brunswick, Saxony, Sweden, and other European nations make use of it similar to ours. So that it has almost become an International Hymn. If Carey, the composer, needs additional honor, it may be added that he also wrote the song entitled:

"Sally in Our Alley."

He ended his life by suicide.

No. 619.

"GOD OF MY LIFE, WHOSE GRACIOUS POWER."

REV. CHARLES WESLEY, 1708—1788.

This hymn well illustrates the skill with which editors have often by pruning fitted a hymn of private experience to public worship. The whole hymn contains fifteen stanzas, and in them the author recounts particular instances of God's providential care of him. He tells of deliverances from shipwreck, fever, and other diseases, and from death itself. Out of these the editors have culled a stanza here and there fit for general use.

No. 620.

"HEAR, LORD, THE SONG OF PRAISE AND PRAYER."

WILLIAM COWPER, 1731—1800.

Mr. Cowper, one day in 1789, wrote a letter to a friend in which he said, "My friend, the vicar of the next parish (Olney), engaged me day before yesterday to furnish him next Sunday with a hymn to be sung on occasion of his preaching to the children of the Sunday school, of which hymn I have not yet produced a syllable." He got the hymn finished, however, before Sunday, and this is it.

No. 621.

"IN THE HOUR OF TRIAL, JESU, PRAY FOR ME."

JAMES MONTGOMERY, 1771—1854.

In 1834, a lady asked the author of this hymn to write something in her album. He compiled and wrote there this hymn, entitling it "Prayers for Pilgrimage," and basing it on the words of Jesus to Peter, "I have prayed for thee, that thy faith fail not."

No. 622.

"IN SLEEP'S SERENE OBLIVION LAID."

John Hawkesworth, 1715—1773.

John Hawkesworth did not have the advantages of early education, but was trained to mechanical occupation. He taught himself, however, and acquired such a reputation as a writer as to receive the degree of LL.D. One night, about a month before his death, he was unable to sleep, and so occupied the time in composing this hymn, which in the morning he dictated to his wife.

No. 623.

"STRONG SON OF GOD, IMMORTAL LOVE."

Alfred, Lord Tennyson, 1809.

The author of this hymn, while at Trinity College, Cambridge, England, about 1828, formed an intimate friendship with Arthur H. Hallam, a son of the historian. Hallam afterward became engaged to Tennyson's sister. Hallam had finished his college course and was studying law. In 1833, with his father, he visited the Continent, and while at Vienna a sudden rush of blood to the head caused his death. As Tennyson described it, "God's finger touched him and he slept." The impressions produced by this sudden death of his intimate friend led Tennyson to write what is perhaps his best poem, "In Memoriam." This is the introduction to that poem.

No. 624.

"TAKE MY LIFE AND LET IT BE."

Miss Frances Ridley Havergal, 1836—1879.

The author of this hymn went for a five-day visit to the home of some friends. It was in 1874. There were ten persons in the house, some unconverted and some Christians, but as she says "not *rejoicing* Christians." She prayed, "Lord give me all in this house," and as she writes it in her somewhat exuberant style, "And He just *did!* Before I left the house every one had got a blessing. The last night of my visit I was too happy to sleep and passed most of the night in praise and renewal of my own consecration, and these little couplets formed themselves and chimed in my heart one after another till they finished with, 'Ever, only, All for thee.' "

No. 625.

"THY WORD, O LORD, THY PRECIOUS WORD ALONE."

Alfred Midlane, 1825.

One hymn has sometimes led to the writing of another. The author of this hymn was one Sunday morning walking along the shore of an English lake thinking of Cardinal Newman's hymn, "Lead, kindly Light," the circumstances that led to its being written, and the later career of its author, whom he had just seen, arrayed in all the glory of a Cardinal at a requiem mass. His thought was that the light that Newman sought was a delusive one like the "Will o' the Wisp," and that the only safe light to follow in time of doubt and uncertainty is the word of God. With this thought he took out his memorandum book and wrote this hymn.

No. 626.

"WHAT CAN WASH AWAY MY STAIN?"

REV. ROBERT LOWRY, 1826.

A man, whose wicked life was troubling him, was traveling by night on a railway train. He stopped at a station and a workman passed along with his hammer testing the wheels, and as he went from wheel to wheel he sang softly to himself the words:

"What can wash away my stain?
Nothing but the blood of Jesus.
What can make me whole again?
Nothing but the blood of Jesus."

The words of the song brought to the troubled heart in the car above him the message of peace, and he went on his way, rejoicing in the "blood which cleanseth from all sin."

No. 627.

"HARK THE GOSPEL NEWS IS SOUNDING."

REV. HUGH BOURNE, 1772—1852.
WILLIAM SANDERS.

This has been called "The Primitive Methodist Grand March," from the fact that it is much used by them in outdoor processions. It was once being sung at the dusk of evening in a little English hamlet, and a young man who was just then anxiously thinking of his soul's greatest need, was leaning against a wall a little way off. He heard the music, and the words of the refrain were borne to him too, on the cool evening air, "none need perish." It was the message he needed just at that time, and it led him to Christ.

No. 628.

"AH, HOW SHALL FALLEN MAN."

REV. ISAAC WATTS, 1674—1748.

A good deal is said and said justly about the altering or mending of hymns. A hymn becomes perhaps a favorite with us, and we find out who its author was, and there is a sort of bond of friendship between us, for did he not write a hymn we have learned to love? Well, perhaps he did and perhaps he didn't. Here is one written by the inventor of hymns, Dr. Watts, but it has been so amended and emended, transposed and altered, that only a single line remains just as its author wrote it. That line is worthy of note; it is the third line of the first stanza:

"If he contend in righteousness."

No. 629.

"MY JESUS AS THOU WILT."

REV. BENJAMIN ACHMOLKE, 1672—1737.

There was a time in Germany, from about 1650 to 1750, when religion was at a very low ebb. Lutheranism had, as one expresses it, been petrified from living conviction into dead dogma, and most of the people while giving a formal observance to religious services, applied very little of it to their lives. It was the first part of the eighteenth century of which it was said that in Germany no satire could be witty except at the expense of the Bible, and Bible texts or sacred hymns were made the frequent subject of jest and laughter. At that time there arose in Germany a movement looking to more spiritual living, which was afterward in contempt called Pietism. The Pietists prohibited many forms of amusement, were evangelical in their doctrine, and as the name implies taught the highest piety in life and thought. Although very different from the Methodist movement which arose in England three-quarters of a century later, it still in many respects bore a striking resemblance to it. Methodism and Pietism were alike a reaction from a formal lifeless religious condition; they both obtained their names from the ridicule of their opponents, and each gave rise to what might be called a new style of religious hymns. The author of this hymn was a Pietist.

No. 630.

"SAVIOR, VISIT THY PLANTATION."

REV. JOHN NEWTON, 1725—1807.

John Newton wrote in his diary in 1775, "I usually make one hymn a week to expound at the Great House." The "Great House" was a large unoccupied residence in Olney, the use of which Newton had obtained for the weekly prayer meeting of his people. A hymn that can be "expounded" is a hymn that will live. Newton's hymns are not of high poetic merit, but they can be "expounded," and so they fit into human experience, and meet a want of Christian singers. Those weekly prayer meetings at the "Great House" in Olney must have been of unusual interest. Cowper, the poet, was a regular attendant; so bashful that he could seldom be induced to take any part, and yet gifted in prayer as much as in poetry, but Newton himself expounding to his people one of his own hymns must have given to those gatherings a peculiar charm. Imagine him reading for the first time the hymn:

"Savior, visit Thy plantation!
Grant us, Lord, a gracious rain!
All will come to desolation,
Unless Thou return again."

We can almost imagine we hear his voice. "Ah, how I remember the time when I was working on a plantation on the African coast. We were only ten degrees from the equator and the heat was almost unbearable. From November to May no rain fell and the ground became dry and parched. Nothing grew; nothing could grow. The little slips of lemon plants I had set out during the rainy season of the year before, which then looked gay and green, were drooping and likely to die. Nothing that we could do was of any help; help could only come from the sky. How we watched the clouds along the horizon, and hoped they would not keep at a distance, but would come to us with their reviving showers. Just as it is in our spiritual lives, there come times when our religious life seems dried up. There is no growth, no fruit, no beauty. Our hearts seem dry and stony. We think of the times when our spirits were nourished by God's word, and we were happy, and we compare those times with these and think what a sad decline there is. We need a rain! a rain from heaven! A shower of God's grace. Let us pray for it my people, that from this very hour while we are gathered here, God may begin to revive His work in our hearts."

And so out of his own experience he would expound to them the hymn. And then perhaps he would tell them the story how once his master on the plantation sneeringly said to him as he pointed to the little plants he had set out, " 'Who knows but by the time these grow up and bear, you may go home to England, obtain the command of a ship and come back to eat their fruit.' But just what he said to me so tauntingly actually happened, for I did go home to England, and became Captain of a ship, and I really did go back and saw those very plants I had set out grown to trees and bearing fruit."

No. 631.

"O MASTER, IT IS GOOD TO BE."

Rev. Arthur Penrhyn Stanley, 1815—1881.

It is a little remarkable that when the Bible has been versified from beginning to end and almost every scene it depicts made the subject of many hymns, so noteworthy an event as the Transfiguration should have been overlooked. Charles Wesley, with his six thousand hymns, has none of this subject, nor Watts, nor Doddridge. The fact that in all English hymnology there was no Transfiguration hymn was brought to the attention of Dean Stanley, and it led him to write this hymn.

No. 632.

Mrs. Cecil Frances Alexander, 1823.

In the house of a gentleman in County Tyrone in the North of Ireland, it was the custom for each member of the family to deposit in a box in the father's study, such compositions either in poetry or prose as they chose to write. This practice was begun with the children of the family as soon as they could write. It was understood that the writing was to be disguised so that the authors of the pieces would not be known. Every Saturday evening the box was emptied and the compositions read and talked about by the family. Soon after one of the little daughters of the family learned to write, scraps of poetry began to make their appearance in the box, and as she grew older these poetic bits became longer and better, and it was not long until the father and mother had discovered that their daughter Fannie had the true gift of poetry. She is now the wife of Rev. William Alexander, Bishop of Derry, who has himself written some very good hymns, but none so popular as those of his wife. She has written nearly four hundred, and one little book of hers entitled "Hymns for Little Children" has reached a sale of more than a quarter of a million of copies. She receives quite an income from her literary work, all of which she devotes to the support of a school for deaf mutes located near her home.

No. 633.

"HARK, THE VOICE OF JESUS CALLING."

REV. DANIEL MARCH, 1816.

The author of this hymn was to preach in Philadelphia on the eighteenth of October, 1868, to the Christian Association of that city. At the last moment almost, he learned that one of the hymns that had been selected was not suitable to his theme, which was based on the words in Isaiah, 6:8, "Here am I, send me." In "great haste," he says, he wrote this hymn to be substituted for the other, and it was sung from the manuscript. Although written so hurriedly it is scarcely ever altered in the collections containing it.

No. 634.

"LORD, WHILE FOR ALL MANKIND WE PRAY."

REV. JOHN REYNELL WREFORD.

When Queen Victoria ascended the throne of England, there was a new inspiration given to the poets of that country, and songs and hymns were brought out in great numbers on subjects connected with the new Queen or the nation. This was one of the number, and it was intended as a prayer for the nation under its new ruler.

No. 635.

"TO-DAY THE SAVIOR CALLS."

THOMAS HASTINGS.

Sometimes a hymn is sung under circumstances which make it almost prophetic. On the evening when the Chicago fire broke out, Mr. D. L. Moody spoke at Farwell Hall to an audience of three thousand persons. During the meeting this hymn was sung, and ten persons expressed their determination to begin the Christian life. As they went out into the street, the flames were seen rising high against the sky, and three of the number perished in the conflagration.

No. 636.

"DAY IS DYING IN THE WEST."

MISS MARY A. LATHBURY.

You know the story of "Ten Times One is Ten" written by Dr. Edward Everett Hale. Dr. Hale formulated a motto for one of these "Ten Times One Clubs." It was:

"Look up and not down,
Look out and not in,
Look forward and not back,
Lend a hand."

Miss Mary A. Lathbury saw these mottoes on the wall of a friend's parlor in 1874, in Orange, New Jersey, and conceived the thought of a "Look up Legion" which has grown into a membership of many thousands among the boys and girls of the Methodist Church. This same Miss Lathbury has "lent a hand" in our service of song, by writing this and other hymns. This one was written in the summer of 1880 at the request of Rev. John H. Vincent as a vesper song for meetings of the "C. L. S. C.," of which he was the head.

No. 637.

"CHRIST, FOR THE WORLD WE SING."

REV. SAMUEL WOLCOTT.

In the year 1869, the Young Men's Christian Associations of Ohio met in convention in one of the churches of Cleveland. Across the end of the audience room above the pulpit, they had hung in evergreen letters the motto, "Christ for the world, and the world for Christ." Dr. Wolcott saw the motto as he sat in the meeting; it fixed itself in his mind, and on his way home, as he walked along the street, he put it into the words of this hymn.

No. 638.

"BEYOND THE STARRY SKIES."

In most books, this hymn is credited to Rev. James Fanch alone or coupled with Dr. Daniel Turner, both English Baptists, but their version is probably an enlargement of an earlier piece composed by John Berridge, a very eccentric but very devoted minister of the Church of England, and his brother, who was a humble porter.

The story is told that the clergyman called on his

brother to take a letter for him, and received the reply that he "couldn't go as he was writing a hymn." "That's my business," said the preacher, "you take the letter and I'll finish the hymn." When the porter got back his clerical brother had not yet completed the hymn, the last stanza proving too much for him.

"O, I have that," cried the porter, and added the four last lines a little differently from our present version:

"They brought his chariot from above,
To bear him to his throne.
Clapped their triumphant wings and cried,
'The glorious work is done.'"

No. 639.

"FRIEND AFTER FRIEND DEPARTS."

James Montgomery.

When Montgomery was in middle life (forty-six) there came to Sheffield where he lived a clergyman of the Church of England to be curate of the church in that city. Although Montgomery was a Moravian he soon formed a close friendship with the curate. They compiled a hymn book together, each furnishing many of his own composition, while together they edited the hymns of other writers, altering, and clipping, and adding to them in a way which was reckless of all authority or respect; but however much they may have hurt the feelings of other poets, their own friendship was cemented very closely by the work, so that when, after six years of companionship, Dr. Cotterill died, Mr. Montgomery enshrined his grief in the words of this hymn.

No. 640.

"RETURN, O WANDERER TO THY HOME."

THOMAS HASTINGS.

Not far from the year 1830, a minister at Utica, New York, was preaching a sermon on "The Prodigal Son." Two hundred converts were present. At the close of the sermon the preacher cried with very tender emphasis, "Sinner, come home! Come home! Come home!" The author of this hymn was present. He had already returned to his Father himself, but the words so impressed him that he made them the keynote of a hymn which has been very effective in revival services ever since, and so has perpetuated the Utica sermon.

No. 641.

"FROM GREENLAND'S ICY MOUNTAINS."

REV. R. HEBER.

The second stanza of this hymn gives an example of correct description:

> "What though the spicy breezes
> Blow soft o'er Ceylon's isle."

A few years after the hymn was written its author went to India as Bishop of Calcutta and when off the Island of Ceylon he noted in his journal, "Though we were too far off Ceylon to catch the odors of the land, yet it is, we are assured, perfectly true that such odors are perceptible to a very considerable distance. In the straits of Malacca a smell like that of a hawthorn hedge is commonly experienced, and from Ceylon at thirty or forty miles, under certain circumstances a yet more agreeable scent is inhaled."

No. 642.

"JESUS, I LOVE THY CHARMING NAME."

REV. PHILLIP DODDRIDGE.

The name of Jesus often remains with the aged and feeble-minded after other names are forgotten. There is a story of an old minister who had grown quite feeble in mind from long illness, who instantly roused himself when some one in his presence spoke of Christ with doubt of his divinity and his equality with God. "Stuff! poison!" he exclaimed, "do not let it into your minds!" and then he repeated this hymn with vigor and emphasis. As soon as he had finished it he relapsed again into apparent indifference to the persons and the conversation around him.

No. 643.

"IF YOU CANNOT ON THE OCEAN."

MRS ELLEN HUNTINGDON GATES.

About this hymn the author says, "The lines were written upon my slate, one snowy afternoon, in the winter of 1860. I know, as I know now, that the poem was only a simple little thing; but somehow I had a presentiment that it had wings, and would fly into sorrowful hearts, uplifting and strengthening them."

No. 644.

JOHANN WALTHER, 1496—1570.

In a little German village there lived a man who worked at the trade of a tailor through the week and then on

Sundays played the organ at the village church. For this last service, although everyone said his music was wonderful, the Parish paid him a sum equivalent to twenty dollars a year. With a wife and half a dozen children to support, they were always poor; so poor indeed and so hopeless of better condition that the pastor of the little church urged him to go to the city and play to the prince, "for," said he, "the court organist cannot possibly play so well as you." But the modest musician refused to go.

One night there came the cry of fire, and the musician's little cottage with all that it contained was burned to ashes. Then he bethought him of his pastor's words, and decided to go to the city. His pastor gave him a letter to the prince, and a few days later he stood at the great stone steps of the palace, and was driven away by a guard who thought him a beggar. He turned to go away and stood for a moment not knowing what to do, while hot tears found their way down his cheeks. Just then a pleasant-voiced man accosted him, and finding that he wished to see the prince, took him into his own little room, for he proved to be the prince's chamberlain. To him he told his story and gave his letter, and was told to wait a while and he should see the prince, and, while he waited, to go into the chapel and amuse himself by playing on the great organ. Seating himself there he hardly dared to touch the keys of an instrument so much grander than anything he had ever seen, but he softly played the music used among the Germans then to the words:

"Commit thou all thy griefs
And ways into His hands,
To His sure trust and tender care,
Who earth and heaven commands."

Then as the sound of the music overcame his bashfulness he forgot himself and drew from the great organ such floods of melody as had never filled the place before.

Suddenly a hand was laid upon his shoulder and a pleasant voice addressed him, "Well done, my new organist! Stop playing now and talk with my chamberlain." It was the prince himself to whom the chamberlain had already told the story and who had stolen in to hear for himself what the poor musician could do. The chamberlain told him that he was to be from that time organist to the prince, with a home for his family and a salary that to him seemed princely. At first he could scarcely believe his ears, but in a moment the tears ran down his cheeks again, only this time they were tears of joy. "What will my dear wife say when I tell her this?" he cried, and then with eyes lifted to the sky he repeated the words of the Psalm, "Oh give thanks unto the Lord, for He is good, for His mercy endureth forever." He is celebrated most as a musician, but he wrote a few hymns.

No. 645.

Thomas Augustine Arne, 1710—1778.

Son of a wealthy London upholsterer, and intended by his father for a lawyer. He was forbidden to play at home, but managed to convey a spinet to his room, and to learn the use of the keys by muffling the strings with a handkerchief. One day his father called at a gentleman's house where a musical party was in full blast and was both amazed and disgusted to see his boy filling the place of first fiddler. After this, however, he was allowed to study at home and soon became skilful. "Rule Britannia" was the closing song in a piece entitled "Alfred," written jointly by David Mallet and James Thompson, author of "The Seasons." The words were set to music by Dr. Arne, to celebrate the anniversary of the accession of the House of Hanover and first sung in a temporary theatre erected at Bucks, where the Prince of Wales resided. Dr. Arne's last words were those of song. He was attempting to illustrate with his voice a musical idea, when his voice faltered, the sounds grew fainter, and song and breathing ceased together.

No. 646.

"JESUS, SHEPHERD OF THE SHEEP."

REV. HENRY COOKE.

This hymn may be more interesting to us if we know something of its author. It is not a familiar name in our hymn books, indeed so far as known this is the only hymn he ever wrote, and yet it seems pretty certain that the one who could write such a hymn as this could write others. Henry Cooke was an Irishman with the wit of his race, and their eloquence too. He was pastor of a Presbyterian Church in Ireland, at a time when the pulpits and the pews of his denomination in Ireland were poisoned through and through with the doctrines of Unitarianism. He became the champion of orthodoxy, and for half a lifetime, waged relentless war against the heresy that was in the churches. He was tireless in his work, writing, debating, preaching, planning to re-establish Christ as divine in the faith of the Irish Church. In this he was successful, and he lived to see his denomination in Ireland re-established as an orthodox Trinitarian body. If such a person should write a hymn, and but a single one, it could not well be other than this one is, full of the faith of Christ. Rev. John Hall, of New York, was the pupil and friend of its author.

No. 647.

"JESUS, IN THY DYING WOES."

REV. THOMAS B. POLLOCK.

By comparing the accounts given of the crucifixion of Christ in the different gospels, it can be found that while on the cross Jesus spoke at seven different times. He prayed for those who were crucifying Him, "Father, forgive them! for they know not what they do." He said to the thief, "To-day shalt thou be with me in paradise." And to his mother, as she stood with John, the beloved disciple, "Woman, behold thy son." At the ninth hour, he cried to God again, "Why hast thou forsaken me," and said to his friends, "I thirst," and then at the end he cried, "It is finished," and offered the prayer, "Father, into thy hands I commend my Spirit." These words, which are called sometimes "The seven words of Christ upon the cross," have been woven into a hymn, of seven parts, referring, respectively, to these seven sayings of Christ. The first part begins with the line:

"Jesus, in Thy dying woes."

No. 648.

"WHEN MY FINAL FAREWELL TO THE WORLD I HAVE SAID."

M. F. Hearn.

During the visit of Moody and Sankey to Great Britain in 1875, an infidel, a man past middle life who for years had zealously attacked the Christian religion on all possible occasions, began attending their meetings for the avowed purpose of scoffing at the service and, as he said, "exposing the humbug." One night Mr. Sankey sang this hymn, and when he came to the stanza:

"There are little ones glancing about in my path,
 In want of a friend and a guide.
There are dear little eyes looking up into mine,
 Whose tears might be easily dried.

But Jesus may beckon the children away,
In the midst of their grief and their glee;
Will any of them at the beautiful gate
Be waiting and watching for me!"

the memory of a baby face that had once looked up into his, but which had been long ago "beckoned away," came up before him so vividly, that he was melted to tears, and the truth of a living Christ, in whose presence his child was living, made of the man who came an infidel, an earnest Christian worker.

During the Moody and Sankey meetings at the Tabernacle built for their use in Chicago, a man arose and related his own experience. He said that he had been so intemperate that two years before, when his mother died, on his way to notify some neighbors that she was dying, he stopped at a saloon and got drunk. He had recently come to Chicago to put himself into a reformatory institution and had got drunk on his way to the city. One Sunday he wandered into the Tabernacle to rest, being broken down physically and mentally by drink. Mr. Sankey sang this hymn, and it set him to thinking about his mother and that word of all others, said he, "had power to touch my hardened heart." All Sunday night he had paced the streets unable to think of anything but his mother in heaven, waiting and watching for him, and on Monday he had gone back to the revival services and been converted there.

No. 649.

"THERE IS A LAND OF PURE DELIGHT."

REV. ISAAC WATTS.

Dr. Talmadge in one of his sermons says, "I do not know how we shall stand the first day in Heaven. I once gave out in church the hymn:

'There is a land of pure delight
Where saints immortal reign.
Infinite day excludes the night
And pleasures banish pain.'

"An old man standing in front of the pulpit sang heartily the first stanza, and then he sat down weeping. I said to him afterward, 'Father Linton, what made you cry over that hymn?'

"He answered, 'I could not stand it, the joys that are coming.'"

No. 650.

"COME, MY SOUL, THY SUIT PREPARE."

Rev. John Newton.

In very olden times, there lived a king who surpassed in the splendor of his court all who had lived before him. His name signified "the peaceful king." It is related of him that once upon a time he went to one of the celebrated shrines of his land to offer sacrifices to his God, and this he did in a manner befitting his wealth and rank, for he offered a thousand burnt offerings upon the altar there. The God he worshipped responded to the splendid gift by appearing to him in a dream by night and saying to him, "Ask what I shall give thee." You will find the story recorded in the First Book of Kings, 3:5. In commenting on this story, Matthew Henry, the quaint old English divine, says that, "Whatever God sends down to us in a promise, we ought to send back to Him in a prayer."

John Newton was a firm believer in the power and efficacy of prayer, and taking this response of Solomon's God, to the worship of his subject as his theme, he wrote this hymn to be sung at the little prayer meeting at Olney. Rev.

Charles Spurgeon was in the habit of having one or two stanzas from this hymn chanted softly each Sunday by his great congregation just before his prayer.

No. 651.

"CHRIST IS BORN, TELL FORTH HIS FAME."

St. Cosmas (died about 760).

This hymn takes us back twelve hundred years, and to the land where the Christ was born whose birthday it commemorates. An orphan boy was adopted by a man who had one boy of his own, and the two lived for a time together at Damascus, then went together to the Monastery of St. Saba, in the wilderness between Jerusalem and the Dead Sea, and there spent their lives together as monks. They both had poetic tastes and stimulated each other in the writing of hymns by selecting the same theme for their poems, and trying in friendly rivalry to see which should best succeed. St. Stephen, who wrote the hymn "Art thou weary, art thou languid," was the nephew of one of these boys, St. John of Damascus, and all three were monks together in St. Saba.

No. 652.

"FATHER! I OWN THY VOICE."

Rev. Samuel Wolcott.

The author of this hymn tells the story of its origin, and of all the others he has written as well, as follows:

"In the year 1868, Rev. Darius E. Jones requested me to mark for him the published hymns which I would use in a new collection. After a partial performance of this service, near the close of the year, the query arose in my mind, 'Can I not write a hymn?' I was then in my fifty-sixth year, had never put two rhymes together, and had taken it for granted that I was as incompetent to write a hymn or even a stanza as to work a miracle. However, I resolved that I would try to write a hymn of five stanzas, and proceeded to plan it precisely as I would plan a sermon. I said, the first stanza shall be a recognition of God the Father; the second, a recognition of Christ the Redeemer; the third, a prayer to God the Father; the fourth, a prayer to Christ the Redeemer, and the fifth shall blend the two in one address. All this, you understand, without any train of thought in my mind; and a perfect recipe for wooden stanzas it would be difficult to frame. I went to work to fill out my plan, and the result was the hymn as it now stands, 'Father! I own Thy voice.'

"I cannot express to you my surprise when I found that I had written what could actually be sung. I sent the hymn to Mr. Jones, who was so much pleased with it that he composed a tune to it, and inserted both in his 'Songs for the New Life' (Chicago, 1869). I have not seen the hymn in any other collection, but I retain a natural predilection for it. I soon tried my hand again. The Young Men's Christian Association of Ohio met in one of our churches, with their motto, in evergreen letters over the pulpit: 'Christ for the World, and the World for Christ.' This suggested the hymn, 'Christ for the world we sing.' "

No. 653.

"ANGELS HOLY, HIGH, AND LOWLY."

PROF. JOHN STUART BLACKIE.

If there is nothing of special interest to be said about a hymn as to its origin or use, we can often clothe it with new value in our use of it by some little glimpse of its author, as to what sort of man he was, how he looked, acted, spoke. Here is a scrap by the author of this hymn, which, I am sure, will make us feel a little better acquainted with him and make his hymn more enjoyable. He says: "I sometimes wish myself back in the Middle Ages, when the minstrel was the only teacher, and when singing was almost the only sermon. And I will tell you why; reading is a stupid, dull kind of thing, but singing stirs up the whole soul. In the best days of the world there was no reading and no books at all. Homer never saw a book, never could have seen a book. I think we see a great deal too many books. A great number of people become mere reading machines having no living functions at all. I would like some time to give you a lecture on the logic of education. It simply means that you must learn to use your legs, your arms, your ears, your tongues, and your throats—every part of your soul and your body—rather than be crammed up with all sorts of things, and then measured with red tape by a gentleman from London. Especially if you wish to be happy cultivate song. I am rather a young-old boy, and I am one of the happiest creatures under the sun at this moment; and my amusement is to sing songs. In railway coaches, and other places, I see a number smoking what they call tobacco. Well, whatever may be said about that, it is not an intellectual or a moral stimulant, and the flavor of it is not at all like the rose, or any poetic thing I know. It is essentially a vulgar sort of amusement. My amusement is to sing songs. At home I am always singing Scotch songs; and abroad, when those wretches are smoking, I hum to myself, 'Scots wha hae,' 'A man's a man for a' that,' and songs of that kind. I advise you to do the same. Your soul will become a singing bird, and then the devil won't get near it."

No. 654.

"HOW FIRM A FOUNDATION, YE SAINTS OF THE LORD."

Dr. C. S. Robinson relates that once in the old oratory at evening devotion in Princeton Seminary the elder Dr. Hodge, then venerable with years and piety, paused as he read this hymn, preparatory to the singing, and in the depth of his emotion was obliged to close his delivery of the final lines with a mere gesture of pathetic and adoring wonder at the matchless grace of God in Christ, and his hand silently beat time to the rhythm instead:

"I'll never—no never—no never—forsake!"

No. 655.

"LORD OF ALL BEING; THRONED AFAR."

OLIVER WENDELL HOLMES.

Most people have read those two delightful books, "The Autocrat of the Breakfast Table" and "The Professor at the Breakfast Table," both written by Dr. Oliver Wendell Holmes and both of which before being published as books appeared as serials in the *Atlantic Monthly.* In the number of that periodical for December, 1859, the last of the papers making up "The Professor at the Breakfast Table" appeared, and it ends as follows: "And so my year's record is finished. The Professor has talked less than his predecessor (The Autocrat of the Breakfast Table), but he has heard and seen more. Thanks to all those friends who from time to time have sent their messages of kindly recognition and fellow feeling. Peace to all such as may have been vexed in spirit by any utterance the pages have repeated. They will doubtless forget for the moment the difference in the lines of truth we look at through our human prisms, and join in singing (inwardly) this hymn to the Source of the light we all need to lead us, and the warmth which alone can make us all brothers." Then follows this beautiful lyric.

No. 656.

"O THOU FROM WHOM ALL GOODNESS FLOWS."

Rev. Thomas Haweis.

This hymn deserves a place among missionary hymns if for no other reason than that it afforded to a devoted missionary comfort and strength under persecution. No doctrine of the Christian faith is so obnoxious to Mohammedans as that of the Divinity of Christ, for it gives to Him the place they want for Mohammed. Rev. Henry Martyn, when a missionary among them, records that, "It is this doctrine which exposes me to the contempt of the learned Mohammedans, in whom it is difficult to say whether pride or ignorance predominates. Their sneers are more difficult to bear than the brickbats that the boys sometimes throw at me; however, both are an honor of which I am not worthy. How many times in the day have I occasion to repeat the words:

'If on my face, for Thy dear Name,
Shame and reproaches be;
All hail, reproach, and welcome, shame,
If Thou remember me.' "

On June 12, 1812, the scene is repeated. One of the Viziers (it is in Persia) says to him: "You had better say, 'God is God, and Mohammed is the prophet of God.'

Martyn replied: "God is God, and Jesus is the Son of God."

They were fiercely enraged, and cried out in wrath and contempt, and one said: "What will you say when your tongue is burnt out for this blasphemy?"

"Thus," continues Martyn, "I walked away alone to my tent, to pass the rest of the day in heat and dirt. 'What have I done,' thought I, 'to merit all this scorn? Nothing, I trust, but bearing testimony to Jesus.' I thought over these things in prayer, and found that peace which Christ hath promised to His disciples."

No. 657.

"THERE IS AN EYE THAT NEVER SLEEPS."

REV. J. C. WALLACE, 1793—1841.

This hymn is a fine statement of the power of prayer, and may, therefore, be called worshipful, but there is not a word in it of prayer itself. Duffield fitly appends to it the incident related by Edward Pierrepont, in his book, "From Fifth Avenue to Alaska." Mr. Pierrepont was on a hunting expedition in the mountains of Wyoming and became lost. He was alone, without food, fire, or shelter in the midst of a driving snowstorm. "The snow flakes," he says, "became thicker than ever. Round and round we wheeled. My hands became nearly too numb to guide the horse, and it seemed as if we should never reach the place of descent. We could hardly see twenty feet ahead; all sides looked perpendicular; and, although up at this great altitude, not a glimpse could I catch of the surrounding country. The bare ridge was about one mile in circumference, and my former horse tracks had long ago been obliterated. At last I recognized a curiously twisted fir, and saw that I had been merely making a circle. In despair, knowing that at this altitude without fire the morning would find me frozen, strangely there came to my mind these words of Tennyson:

> 'More things are wrought by prayer
> Than this world dreams of';

and I earnestly prayed that for one moment the storm might abate and allow me a glimpse of where I was. Hardly had I uttered the words when one of the most striking incidents of my life took place. It may have been a mere coincidence, but I was so impressed with the occurrence that I could but feel that the act, which the memory of Tennyson's lines prompted, had something to do with the phenomenon which so quickly followed. Suddenly the wind lulled; the snow ceased falling; the heavy shrouds of mist which hung over the valley and mountain tops lifted; and low in the west the declining sun, having but brief time to light, shone brightly. The huge, lone ranges, as far as the eye could reach, sparkled in their new white robes; and the winding stream near which the old camp lay seemed but a mile distant. Even the tired old horse raised his head as if encouraged with new life. I soon found the hitherto hidden descent, and quickly gained the lower ridge, the gradual slope of which I knew would bring me back to camp. For full thirty minutes the sky remained clear, with the exception of large fleecy clouds driving across its face; then, as suddenly, the wind swept through the valleys, and all became dark and threatening as before."

No. 658.

"LET US GATHER UP THE SUNBEAMS."

MRS. ALBERT SMITH.

Philip Phillips, who by his services of song held all over the world acquired the title of "the Singing Pilgrim," once held a service in the Jerry McCauley Mission in Water Street, New York. It was on a Sunday evening, and the room was crowded with the most vicious characters of the city. Just as the exercises were about to begin, Kit Burns, a notorious and desperate character, and a band of about thirty "roughs" marched up the aisle and seated themselves directly in front of Mr. Phillips. He feared they intended to make trouble, but with a prayer for help he began the service.

By and by some one called out from the door, "Kit, you're wanted."

Rising at once in his seat, Kit sent back the answer, "Tell 'em to go to h—ll."

The singing went on and soon the rowdy outside put his head in at the door again and shouted, "Kit, you're wanted outside."

This time Burns stood up again and in his hoarse voice called out, "Tell 'em this is the first Jesus meeting I've ever been at, and I shall stay till it's out." The power of song had enchained him. During the meeting this song was sung with its oft repeated refrain, "Then scatter seeds of kindness." A few days after, one of the women who had been present at the meeting was found drunk on the street near by. She was taken into the mission room where she lay for some time sleeping off her drunken stupor. When she awoke she looked around, and not recognizing the surroundings concluded she was in the "Tombs" and began to talk to herself. "Now I'll have to stay here thirty days. My business will all go to sticks! I know that policeman, d—n him! when I get out I'll fix him!" But just here she looked more carefully about the room and saw that she had mistaken the place, and then the talk went on: "Humph! I ain't in the Tombs after all. Where am I?—Oh, I see, I'm in that place where they scatter seeds of kindness." The matron overheard her, spoke to her, gave her a bath, and a cup of tea. Some friends gathered about her, and before she left the place she was converted. She died not long after, having remained steadfast to the end.

No. 659.

"I GAVE MY LIFE FOR THEE."

Miss F. R. Havergal.

On one occasion when Philip Phillips held a service of song in Philadelphia, Mr. R. Pearsall Smith, well known as the author of "The Rest of Faith," was in the audience. Shortly after he wrote to Mr. Phillips, asking him to visit his father's house and sing some of his songs there. "My father," wrote Mr. Smith, "is a good man, but although all his children are Christians, he has never made a profession. Now I have faith to believe that if you will go there and sing some of your songs, he will give his heart to Christ."

Mr. Phillips went to the old man's house, no one being present outside the family except Rev. Alfred Cookman and himself. He sang song after song, the old white-haired man listening attentively. At last Mr. Phillips sang this piece, and at its close the old man asked, "Will you please sing that over again?" So the piece was repeated. When the stanza:

"I spent long years for thee
In weariness and woe;
That one Eternity
Of joy thou mightest know!
I spent long years for thee, for thee!
Hast thou spent one for me?"

was finished he was weeping. "Let us pray," said Mr. Cookman, and at its close the old man gave himself to Christ.

No. 660.

"PRAISE GOD FROM WHOM ALL BLESSINGS FLOW."

THOMAS KEN.

One of the singular uses to which this doxology has been put was on the occasion of an important election in Ohio, October 15, 1884. On the evening of that day an immense crowd filled the street in New York City in front of the headquarters of the Republican Party, where the news as it was received over the wires was being given to them through a stereopticon. It was at two o'clock in the morning and the crowd was uproariously singing, "We won't go home 'till morning." At this hour came the last message announcing the success of the party in the distant state, and immediately following it the stereopticon flashed out the line:

"Praise God from Whom all blessings flow."
"Good Night!"

A deep-toned man in the throng pitched the tune, and a mighty volume of song swelled upward as they sang the doxology to its close. Then the lights went out and the crowd dispersed to their homes.

No. 661.

"PRAYER IS THE SOUL'S SINCERE DESIRE."

JAMES MONTGOMERY.

When the author of this hymn was eighty-three years of age, he conducted the family worship in the home where he lived, and it was noticed that he was especially fervent in prayer. Well might he have been so for it was the last time his voice was heard on earth. At the close of the prayer he retired to his room, where he was found the next day unconscious on the floor. He had had an apoplectic stroke sometime during the night, and died that afternoon. The incident is worth relating in connection with this hymn because it illustrates in the case of the poet himself the words of the stanza:

"Prayer is the Christian's vital breath,
The Christian's native air,
His watchword at the gates of death;
He enters Heaven with prayer."

No. 662.

"ROCK OF AGES, CLEFT FOR ME."

REV. AUGUSTUS TOPLADY.

An American minister entered an Armenian church in Constantinople and joined them in their worship, although he understood not a word of what was said. During the singing of a hymn he noticed many of the people in tears, and was curious to know what hymn so affected them. Upon inquiry he found it was a Turkish translation of "Rock of Ages, cleft for me."

No. 663.

"SAINTS OF GOD! THE DAWN IS BRIGHTENING."

MRS. MARY MAXWELL.

In the year 1875, Rev. Sheldon Jackson, then Superintendent of Home Missions in the West under the Presbyterian

Board wanted a "home mission hymn." Not finding what he wanted among existing hymns, he offered two prizes, one of fifty dollars for a poem and one of a hundred dollars for a hymn. The offer was published in two hundred religious newspapers, and thus became widely known. Seven hundred pieces were offered in competition, and a committee consisting of Dr. S. I. Prime of the *New York Observer*, Dr. Thomas S. Hastings, and Rev. Edwin F. Hatfield, examined them. This hymn was chosen from the entire list as best adapted to use as a Home Missionary Hymn. It is an interesting incident that its author refused to accept the prize she had earned except upon the condition that her name should not be divulged, and so the hymn was made public as written by "A Lady of Virginia." Eight or ten years later she permitted her name to be attached to it.

No. 664.

"TAKE ME, O MY FATHER, TAKE ME."

REV. RAY PALMER.

A hymn that succeeds in bringing comfort and cheer to but a single life when comfort and cheer are needed has surely done a worthy work, and the author of this hymn knew to a certainty that this hymn yielded such result. An English lady had been very ill; too weak to speak or scarcely think, and during these weary hours the words of this hymn had been her comfort. When she recovered, so great was her sense of gratitude for the good she had received from them, that she took pains to write to Dr. Palmer, and to thank him for the service he had rendered her.

No. 665.

"THE MORNING LIGHT IS BREAKING."

REV. S. F. SMITH.

It is not often given to one person to write a hymn which shall become the national hymn of a great people, and another which shall become the rallying song of a great religious enterprise. Yet the author of this hymn has done it in the hymn:

"My country, 'tis of thee."

and this one before us. It has been his privilege also, as he himself says, to hear it sung in five or six different languages in Europe and Asia. It is a favorite with the Burmans, Karens, and Telegus in Asia and among the Portuguese Protestants in their own country and in Brazil. It has also been translated into Siamese. So that it can fairly be said to be sung around the world.

No. 666.

"THERE IS A LAND IMMORTAL."

THOMAS MACKELLER.

A boy in New York City at fourteeen years of age became a compositor on a weekly paper in that city. Soon after he entered the employment of the Harpers and became proofreader. While hard at work during the day, he spent his spare time at night in writing verses of one sort or another. He was poor and had much of the support of the family to provide. Later he went to Philadelphia and became proofreader in a type foundry there. By and by he was allowed to invest his little savings in buying a small interest in the business. And at last he became the head of the firm of MacKeller, Smiths, and Jordan, the great type founders of Philadelphia. He kept up his habit of writing poetry after his day's work was over, and one evening while writing a piece for a friend, a fancy struck him of a religious nature. "I laid aside," he says, "the work in hand and pursuing the new idea, I at once produced the hymn:

"There is a land immortal."

No. 667.

"THOU ART GONE TO THE GRAVE BUT WE WILL NOT DEPLORE THEE."

Reginald Heber.

Written in December, 1818, in memory of an only child which died in that month, aged six months. Of this event Heber wrote, "I am myself more cut down than I thought I should be, but I hope not impatient. I do not forget that to have possessed her at all, and to have enjoyed the pleasure of looking at her and caressing her for six months was God's free gift, and still less do I forget that He who has taken her will at length, I hope, restore her to us."

No. 668.

"UPWARD I LIFT MINE EYES."

Rev. Isaac Watts.

In 1777 (June 3), Rev. John Newton wrote to a friend "give my love to your friend. I dare not advise; but if she can quietly return at the usual time, and neither run intentionally into the way of the smallpox, nor out of the way, but leave it simply with the Lord, I shall not blame her. My prescription is to read Dr. Watts' Psalm one hundred and twenty-one every morning before breakfast, and pray over it till the cure is effected.

'Hast thou not given thy word
To save my soul from death,
And I can trust my Lord
To keep my mortal breath?
I'll go and come,
Nor fear to die.
Till from on high
Thou call me home!' "

This is the "Psalm one hundred and twenty-one," which Dr. Newton advised the use of in case of smallpox.

No. 669.

"WE COME TO THE FOUNTAIN, WE STAND BY THE WAVE."

Rev. Geo. W. Bethune.

This hymn is unique in that it is a hymn especially for use at the rite of baptism by immersion, and yet it was written by a minister of the Dutch Reformed Church, who was thoroughly antagonistic to the peculiar doctrine of immersion. It is not a little strange, too, that it was written at the request of a Baptist clergyman, Rev. J. S. Holmes, who wanted it for the "Baptist Hymn and Tune Book" of which he was the editor. Referring to the request that had been made of him Dr. Bethune said, "I have the vanity to think that I can write a better hymn of that kind than any that I have seen in their collections." And this is the hymn he wrote.

No. 670.

"THERE IS A HAPPY LAND, FAR, FAR AWAY."

ANDREW YOUNG.

The author of this hymn tells its origin as follows: He was spending the evening at a house where the lady and her family were musical. "After tea, the lady of whom I speak, played, among other pieces of music, one which was entitled, 'The Siege of Delhi' (Clive's, not Clyde's siege). As is well known, in that selection there occurs a very sweet air—soft, pathetic, and yet with an influence that stirs while it enamours the sense. My friend played it so beautifully that I requested a repetition of it and after that begged for another repetition, and yet another, until I would for some time have nothing else played. My soul was won by its charm and rapture, and I was for the time being, like 'one beside himself,' as if carried away to another world of being by some potent and mysterious influence. Leaving the house shortly afterward, and still in an excited state of feeling, I was filled with but one strong controlling desire, *viz.*, to write words appropriate, as far as possible (for I had the rhythmic faculty), to the highly devotional suggestiveness of the music. During the entire night my heart throbbed with a strange emotion; thoughts thronged my brain; words began to take a melodious flow, and in the early morning hours my first act was to sit down and write the words of a hymn, identical almost in every particular with those now composing it.

"That was fifty years ago, and yet, even now, I feel, notwithstanding that long intervening lapse of time, with its many experiences, as if the inspiration with which Divine Providence was pleased to bless me on that memorable occasion (for I at least can never forget it) had occurred only yesterday. For if ever there was an inbreathing in a human soul of a heaven-born inspiration,

I am as certain as I live that it was when I wrote the words of 'The Happy Land.' Little remains to be told. Of the composer of the soul-captivating air, I have never been able to learn anything. Some persons in writing lately on the subject of the hymn have spoken of the air referred to as being an old Indian melody, one that possibly had been heard in the Indian 'forest primeval,' many and many a year ago. I do not think anything of the kind. The music of the 'Siege of Delhi' is probably not more than seventy or eighty years old, and very likely the work of a British composer. But whoever the writer of it was, I would gladly give something to know and to express my very great acknowledgment for its blessed inspiration."

No. 671

"I REMEMBER A VOICE WHICH ONCE GUIDED MY WAY."

"COME THIS WAY, MY FATHER."

Hon. A. W. Wildes.

The little song "Come this way, my Father," was written by me during a season of great affliction occasioned by the loss of my darling little Frank (the hero of the story). The narrative and song were first published in the *Waterville Mail* in the year 1850. The scene of the occurrence was Boothbay, a little harbor about fifteen miles east of Bath, Maine.

During a short visit to the seashore of our state, some two years since, with a party of friends, it was proposed one bright afternoon that we should make up a party and go down the harbor on a fishing excursion.

We accordingly started, and after sailing about three miles, a young lady of the company declined going further, and requested us to land her on one of the small islands in the harbor, where she proposed to stay until our return. My little boy, then about four years old, preferred remaining with her. Accordingly we left them and proceeded some six miles further. We remained out much longer than we intended, and as night approached a thick fog set in from the sea, entirely enshrouding us. Without compass, and not knowing the right way to steer, we groped our way along for some hours, until we discovered the breaking of the surf on the rocks of one of the islands, but were at a loss to know which one of them. I stood up in the stern of the boat, where I had been steering, and shouted with all my strength. I listened a moment, and heard through the thick fog and above the breaking of the surf, the sweet voice of my boy calling, "Come this way, father—steer straight for me—I'm waiting for you!" We steered by that sound, and soon my little boy leaped to my arms with joy, saying, "I knew you would hear me, father!" and nestled to sleep on my bosom. The child and the maiden are both sleeping now. They died in two short weeks after the period I refer to, with hardly an interval of time between their deaths. Now, when tossed upon the rough sea of life, without compass or guide, enveloped in fog and surrounded by rocks, I seem to hear the sound of that cherub voice calling from the bright shore, "Come this way, father!—steer straight for me!" When oppressed with sadness, I take my way to our quiet cemetery, and still, as I stand by one little mound, the same musical voice echoes from thence, "Come this way, my father! I'm waiting for thee!" With this I enclose a correct copy of the song.

Yours very truly,

A. W. Wildes.

I remember a voice
  Which once guided my way,
When lost on the sea,
  Fog-enshrouded I lay;

'Twas the voice of a child,
  As he stood on the shore—
It sounded out clear
  O'er the dark billows' roar,
"Come this way, my father!
  Steer straight for me,
Here safe on the shore
  I am waiting for thee."

I remember that voice,
  As it led our lone way,
'Midst rocks and through breakers
  And high dashing spray;
How sweet to my heart
  Did it sound from the shore,
As it echoed out clear
  O'er the dark billows' roar.
"Come this way, my father,
  Steer straight for me,
Here safe on the shore
  I am waiting for thee."

I remember my joy
  When I held to my breast
The form of that dear one,
  And soothed it to rest;
For the tones of my child
  Whispered soft to my ear,
"I called you, dear father,
  I knew you would hear
The voice of your darling,
  Far o'er the dark sea,
While safe on the shore
  I was waiting for thee."

That voice now is hushed
  Which then guided my way,

The form I then pressed
Is now mingling with clay;
But the tones of my child
Still sound in my ear,
"I am calling you, father!
O can you not hear
The voice of your darling,
As you toss on life's sea,
For on a bright shore
I am waiting for thee."

I remember that voice—
In many a lone hour
It speaks to my heart
With fresh beauty and power,
And still echoes far out
Over life's troubled wave,
And sounds from the loved lips
That lie in the grave,
"Come this way, my father!
O steer straight for me!
Here safely in heaven
I am waiting for thee!"

No. 672.

"GIVE TO THE WINDS THY FEARS."
"COMMIT THOU ALL THY GRIEFS."

PAUL GERHARDT.

Not far from the town of Warsaw in Poland, there still is standing a peasant's house, which has above its door an iron tablet upon which appears the figure of a raven with a ring in its beak and underneath it in the German language the first four lines of this hymn. To account for this iron plate, with its raven, and its ring, and its inscription a wonderful story must be told.

There lived near by at one time a German peasant named Dobry. He had not been able to pay his rent, and the landlord had threatened to eject him from his house. It was in the dead of winter, and the poor peasant had thrice appealed for mercy, but in vain. The next day he and his wife and little ones were to be turned out into the cold and the snow. But Dobry did not lose courage or hope. If man would not show mercy, God would, and gathering his family about him he kneeled and prayed for help from the God of the poor, and when the prayer was ended, they began to sing together this hymn.

At one of the pauses between the stanzas, a tapping on the window was heard. Dobry ran and opened it, and a tame raven which had been trained by Dobry's grandfather and then set at liberty, hopped in, bearing in its beak a jeweled ring. This was identified as one that had been lost by the King, who rewarded Dobry handsomely for returning it, and later built for him a house for his own, and put this iron plate above the door.

No. 673.

"JUST AS I AM, WITHOUT ONE PLEA."

MISS CHARLOTTE ELLIOTT.

A little street waif once entered the office of a New York City missionary and held up a torn and dirty piece of paper. "Please, sir," said the boy, "father sent me to get a clean paper like this." It was a copy of this hymn, and the father wanted a clean one like it, because his little girl, sister of the boy whom he had sent, liked it and used to sing it while she lived, and when she died they had found this dirty, worn copy of it in her pocket, and now in memory of the dead child he wanted a clean copy to frame and hang up in his room.

No. 674.

John Berridge, 1716—1793.

One of the most eccentric and at the same time earnest men who ever lived became a vicar of the Church of England. He would never limit himself to any parish but in spite of bishops he went far and wide over England preaching in churches if permitted, if not, in barns or fields. The formal, worldly men he met whether clergy or laity were rebuked by him without stint and they called him "The old devil."

Once when riding in a section where he was not known to preach, he was accosted by a stranger riding along the same road, and as they talked the stranger said, "Do you know Berridge? They tell me he is a troublesome, good-for-nothing fellow."

"Yes, I know him," was Berridge's reply. "And I assure you half his wickedness has not been told."

And when they reached the place where Berridge was to preach, the stranger went into a pew and was astounded in a few moments to see his traveling companion step into the pulpit. "Is it possible," he cried, at the close of the service, "Can you forgive me; will you admit me to your house?"

"Yes, and to my heart," was the bluff reply.

He never married, and he gives the reason. He prayed about it and asked God for a sign; then he opened the Bible to see what verse his eye should light on first. The first verse he saw said nothing applicable to the subject in hand, but the second time he tried it he struck the plain command, "Thou shalt not take to thee a wife," and he didn't. But these are only the eccentric characteristics of the man. He was full of courage and cheerfulness all his life long, and when he came to die and someone said to him, "The Lord has enabled you to fight a good fight."

"Blessed be His name for it," was the answer.

"He will soon call you up higher."

"Ay, Ay," was the reply, "higher! higher! higher!"

No. 675.

"BLESSING, HONOR, THANKS AND PRAISE."

Rev. Charles Wesley.

The Wesley brothers, who together founded the great Methodist Church and gave to the Church Universal a splendid legacy of song, came by their love of hymns and singing by inheritance. When John was a puny child he and a hymn were almost the only things saved from the burning parsonage. And the last words of the mother of the Wesleys were, "Children, as soon as I am released, sing a Psalm of praise to God." The children obeyed their mother's injunction by singing this hymn, and they kept on singing hymns, until they joined her in heaven.

No. 676.

"NEARER, MY GOD, TO THEE."

Mrs. S. F. Adams.

A writer in the *Sunday School Times*, tells the following incident concerning this hymn!

"You never knew our neighbor, Mrs. G—— so I must tell you of her in the first place. She was one of the most lovable women I ever knew—always cheerful and sympathetic. Although she never seemed to realize it, she was the leading spirit in all our Christian efforts, inspiring us all with her bright sunny ways. Mr. G—— was just such a husband as you would wish such a woman to have. A lovely daughter, two promising boys, and a little curly-headed tot, the pet of all, completed the happiest home circle it has been my good fortune to enter. In the spring of that year, Mrs. G—— had a severe illness. After many weeks of suffering, she rose from her sick bed, but with the loss of her reason. The woman we had so admired and honored was a complete wreck, henceforth to be a burden in the home she had before made so happy.

"I knew Mr. G—— to be a man of deepest piety. Often I had heard him, in our prayer-meetings, thank God for 'a religion that could comfort us in the darkest hours of trial.' My own religious experience was quite limited then, and I confess I was wondering whether he found grace sufficient to support him under this terrible blow—whether he could say, 'As for God, His way is perfect.'

"When the evening came for the next prayer meeting, he was at his post as usual. His face was pale, but otherwise calm, even peaceful. He had always led the congregation in singing; and when the meeting had progressed a little, our pastor, who was leading, asked him to start 'Nearer, my God, to Thee.' From the first words, the old hymn I had known from my childhood began to take on a new meaning. I had thought it a beautiful conception, and I liked the music; but tonight it was the impassioned outpouring of a soul filled with intensest longing for God, as the weary, benighted, storm-driven traveler longs for home. The song was soon a solo. Every heart in the little congregation was stirred. Tears choked our utterance and blinded our eyes. The singer seemed unconscious that he sang alone, or that he had any hearers save God. What infinite pathos he threw into the pleading,

'There let the way appear
Steps unto heaven:
All that Thou sendest me,
In mercy given:
Angels to beckon me
Nearer, my God, to Thee!
Nearer to Thee.'

"It was not a pleading that the afflicting hand might be removed, but for a faith that could pierce the gloom and recognize it as the hand of love. Even while he asked the answer came. A note of victory shook the air as he sang:

'Out of my stony griefs
Bethel I'll raise;
So by my woes to be
Nearer, my God, to Thee!
Nearer to Thee!"

"I felt certain that he had had an experience like that of Moses on Sinai, for his face shone; and we knew that the most joyous man among us that night was he over whose home there hung so dark a pall of misery."

No. 677.

"ALL HAIL THE POWER OF JESUS' NAME."

REV. E. PERRONET.

It was Sunday; we were marching to our first battle. We waded through miles of sand and numberless streams. Overcome by the heat, men dropped from the ranks, and even horses fell out by the way. To nerve the heart and quicken the step we sang the stirring army songs. At last the cannons were heard in our front, and we knew the vedettes were at work. We soon smelt powder, and thought of home. We soon were foot-weary and exhausted, and the power of song was exhausted too. Suddenly the colonel rode up to us, in company with the general, and exclaimed: "For Heaven's sake, give them something to cheer them on!" Instantly that grand old hymn, "Coronation," came to our minds:

"All hail the power of Jesus' name!
Let angels prostrate fall;
Bring forth the royal diadem,
And crown Him Lord of all."

We sent it forth, and it flew up and down that extended column until the whole army was inspired by the hymn. The boys sped onward to battle as if charged by a thousand galvanic batteries; and while the heavens were ringing with song, the God of nations seemed calling unto his angels to descend and lead us on to victory. At midnight the enemy had fled; and as I lay with my head pillowed on my gunstock, the full, round moon looked down upon the living and the dead, seeming to say to us: "The song for the church is the song for the army."

No. 678.

"THERE IS A SPOT TO ME MORE DEAR."

Rev. Wm. Hunter.

At one of the Pittsburgh Conference love feasts the eloquent and gifted James G. Sansom, for forty-two years an earnest and faithful Methodist preacher, narrated the circumstances of his conversion in such a graphic and effective manner that it electrified the entire congregation, and left a profound impression on all hearts. Dr. Hunter was present and heard the recital, and while Sansom's pathetic tones were still lingering in his memory he translated the experience into verse. The hymn thus originated became at once a great favorite, and was widely and frequently sung by the Methodists of the time. It was generally known as "Sansom's Hymn," and appeared in the "Minstrel of Zion" set to a tune called "Sansom." As both the singer and the song have now passed away, and as the hymn is not readily accessible to all, I venture to reproduce it in its entirety, and add that it is not only a fair specimen of Dr. Hunter's powers of versification, but it remains as a tribute to the memory of one of the most faithful, eloquent, and genial Christian ministers Methodism has ever given to the world. The hymn reads:

"There is a spot to me more dear
Than native vale or mountain,
A spot for which affection's tear
Springs grateful from its fountain.
'Tis not where kindred souls abound,
Though that is almost heaven,
But where I first my Savior found,
And felt my sins forgiven.

"Hard was my toil to reach the shore,
Long tossed upon the ocean;
Above me was the thunder's roar,
Beneath, the wave's commotion;
Darkly the pall of night was thrown
Around me, faint with terror;
In that dark hour how did my groan
Ascend for years of error.

"Sinking and panting, as for breath,
I knew not help was near me;
And cried, 'O save me, Lord, from death!
Immortal Jesus, hear me!'

Then quick as thought I felt Him mine,
  My Savior stood before me;
I saw His brightness round me shine,
  And shouted 'Glory! glory!'

"O sacred hour! O hallowed spot!
  Where love divine first found me;
Wherever falls my distant lot,
  My heart shall linger round thee:
And when from earth I rise to soar
  Up to my home in heaven,
Down will I cast my eyes once more
  Where I was first forgiven."

No. 679.

"SOFTLY AND TENDERLY, JESUS IS CALLING."

An accident occurred to the engine of a train running through the mountains of Tennessee and the passengers were delayed at a little village hotel, while the damage was being repaired. A lady and a gentleman among the passengers were shown into the little dismal parlor, in one corner of which stood an old-fashioned piano badly out of tune. The only other occupant of the room was an old lady, who was evidently a boarder there. Outside it was dark and rainy, but this did not seem to interfere with the comfort of a group of loafers who smoked under the parlor window. To pass away the time the young lady sat down to the piano, and after playing a waltz or two, struck into "Old Hundred." At this the old lady came over to the piano and spoke.

"I was thinking, my dear" she said hesitatingly, "that if you could sing a little mite, just some old hymn or something it would seem real good. Who knows but it would help them poor boys out there? They're most likely away from their homes and their mothers, and it ain't probable they hear much good music—The Lord's music, you know."

After some hesitation the young lady consented, and together they sang hymn after hymn, the old lady listening with evident delight. Outside the men laid down their pipes and all conversation stopped that they might the better hear. By and by the young lady sang alone:

"Softly and tenderly Jesus is calling,
Calling for you and for me!
See, on the portals He's waiting and watching,
Watching for you and for me.
Come home! Come home! ye who are weary
Come home!
Earnestly, tenderly, Jesus is calling,
Calling, O Sinner, come home!"

As the last sweet strain died away one young man on the outside, with a face better than that of most of those about him, stealthily brushed away a tear. Just then the message came that the train was ready and the singers went on their way. Several years later this same gentleman stood in a little group of men who were listening to the words of an evangelist and gospel singer, who had just been singing to an audience the words of this very song. When he had finished he turned to the group and said, "I remember well the first time I heard that hymn. It was in a little hotel in the mountains of Tennessee, where I had been squandering my substance, a real Prodigal Son. There came one afternoon a little company of people who were delayed by an accident to the train, and one or two of them began singing around the piano. The lady's voice I shall never forget. She sang one of my mother's old hymns and then this one 'Come home.' Wherever I went the next few days, I seemed to hear that voice saying, 'Come home'—and the end of it was I came."

"Not the end, sir," said the astonished gentleman. And

then he told him his part of the story and how the white-haired old lady had prompted the singing, and her thought that it might do some of the boys on the outside good.

No. 680.

"THE BEST FIFTY AMERICAN HYMNS."

In 1889 *The Observer* of New York offered a prize of fifty dollars for the list of fifty hymns by American authors most nearly conforming to the general verdict of all the competitors. Six hundred and ninety-nine lists were received, but two hundred and seventy-three of them had to be rejected because of some imperfection so that four hundred and twenty-six lists competed. The fifty hymns receiving the highest number of votes are given below with their standing in the list and the number of votes each received,

1. "My faith looks up to Thee."—RAY PALMER.... 417
2. "One sweetly, solemn thought."—PHOEBE CARY 407
3 "My country 'tis of thee."—S. F. SMITH........ 380
4. "Stand up, stand up for Jesus."—G. DUFFIELD.. 380
5. "Softly now the light of day."—G. W. DOANE.... 373
6. "I love thy kingdom Lord."—T. DWIGHT........ 373
7. "More love to Thee, O Christ."—E. PRENTISS.... 367
8. "I love to steal awhile away."—PHOEBE H. BROWN 349
9. "I would not live alway."—WM. A. MUHLENBERG. 335
10. "Gently, Lord, oh! gently lead us."—T. HASTINGS 321
11. "The morning light is breaking."—S. F. SMITH.. 302
12. "There is an hour of peaceful rest."—W. B. TAPPAN 266
13. "'Tis midnight; and on Olive's brow."—W. B. TAPPAN 262
14. "Thou art the Way, to Thee alone."—G. W.DOANE 250
15. "It came upon the midnight clear."—E. H. SEARS 238

44. "Almost persuaded now to believe."—P. P. BLISS 134
45. "The day is past and gone. The evening."— J. LELAND 134
46. "I need Thee every hour."—A. S. HAWKES...... 130
47. "Knocking, knocking, who is there?"—H. B. STOWE 127
48. "Take me, oh my Father, take me."—RAY PALMER 126
49. "Come, Jesus Redeemer, abide Thou with me."—RAY PALMER 124
50. "We may not climb the heavenly steeps."— J. G. WHITTIER 123

No. 681.

"JESUS, MY LORD, TO THEE I CRY."

ELIZA H. HAMILTON.

Right in the track of the terrible tornado that devastated a considerable part of Louisville on the night of Thursday, March 27, 1890, was one of the Mission Sunday schools conducted by students of the Southern Baptist Theological Seminary. Ten of the scholars in this school were killed in the storm, several of them at their homes. In the fated "Falls City Hall," where many children were gathered in some festivity, and where several lodges were in session and most of the loss of life occurred, two of the children of our school were caught by the falling timbers and walls, and though not seriously hurt were imprisoned, so as to see no way of escape. The little girls thought their end had come, and their minds reverted to the Sunday school songs they had learned, and they began to sing, with their weak and tremulous voices, the hymn "Take me as I am," composed by Eliza H. Hamilton, and set to music by Ira D. Sankey. Amid the roar of the tornado and the thunder and lightning that accompanied it, their little voices sounded through the ruins of the building, where some scores of others had been instantly crushed to death. They sang what seemed singularly appropriate and touching:

"Jesus, my Lord, to Thee I cry,
Unless Thou help me I must die;
Oh, bring Thy free salvation nigh,
And take me as I am.

"No preparation can I make,
My best resolves I only break,
Yet save me for Thine own name's sake,
And take me as I am.

"Behold me, Savior, at Thy feet,
Deal with me as Thou seest meet;
Thy work begin, Thy work complete,
And save me as I am."

I think I shall never sing that song again without thinking of those little girls shut in by the ruins, and finding their only consolation in the lessons and songs they had learned at the mission Sunday school.

No. 682.

"MERCY AND JUDGMENT ARE MY SONG."

REV. ISAAC WATTS.

At a Fourth of July celebration in Westfield Connecticut, 1846, the Rev. Mr. Waldo, a Revolutionary veteran, was present, and at the dinner table told the following incident:

He remarked that there was a single incident that came within his personal knowledge, which he believed was not generally known. It was that Washington, on the day that he assumed the command of the American Army at Cambridge, read and caused to be sung the one hundred and first Psalm, a portion of which is published:

"If I am raised to bear the sword,
I'll take my counsel from Thy word;
Thy justice and Thy heavenly grace
Shall be the pattern of my ways.

"No sons of slander, rage and strife,
Shall be companions of my life;
The haughty look, the heart of pride,
Within my doors shall ne'er abide.

"I'll search the land and raise the just
To posts of honor, wealth, and trust;
The men that work Thy holy will,
Shall be my friends and favorites still.

"In vain shall sinners hope to rise
By flattering or malicious lies;
Nor while the innocent I guard,
Shall bold offenders e'er be spared.

"The impious crew (that factious band),
Shall hide their heads or quit the land,
And all that break the public rest,
Where I have power, shall be suppressed."

This Psalm the reverend worthy deacon lined off to the company in true primitive style, a line at a time, which was sung to the tune of "Old Hundred" that tune being, as the old veteran said, "just the thing for it."

No. 683.

"THE LORD'S MY SHEPHERD, I'LL NOT WANT."

FRANCIS ROUSE.

One of the English ladies who went to the Crimea with Florence Nightingale to nurse the sick and wounded soldiers, found in a Scutari hospital a Highlander near death, and yet hard against God. She spoke to him, but he would make no answer. He even drew the sheet up over his head to keep her from speaking to him again. The next time she went through that ward he saw her coming toward his cot, and he covered his face again. Seating herself beside the bed, she began to repeat, in a low, kind voice, the Nursery Psalm:

"The Lord's my Shepherd, I'll not want,
He makes me down to lie
In pastures green. He leadeth me
The quiet waters by."

She noticed that before the psalm was finished, his hand went up to his eyes under the sheet. The next time she came, he was quite ready to listen to what she had to say of Jesus and His love. He gave his heart to the Lord, and five days later he died in great peace.

The Nursery Psalm was used to touch a chord that was not quite paralyzed by his bitter enmity against God. It was "mony a weary mile" from his mother's knee in the Highland cottage where, with her loving hand on his bonny, bright head, she had taught him the dear old psalm, to the Crimean hospital, where a rough, hardened soldier, he lay dying; yet the mother's love, like Christ's tenderness, reached all the way, and drew him back to God.

No. 684.

"JOHN BROWN'S BODY" (Tune).

The tune of "John Brown's Body" had its origin before the words that are now known or remembered in connection with it. It was sung before the War of the Rebellion, as long ago, at least, as 1856, to words which do not now remain in use, at certain New England camp meetings and revival services. Two members of the Boston militia company called the "Tigers," happening to be at a camp meeting in a small town in New Hampshire, heard the song sung to religious words, and remembered the air. The name of one of these men was Purington, and of the other John Brown. Not long after this the war broke out, and the "Tigers" were made a part of the Twelfth Massachusetts Regiment of Volunteers, which rendezvoused at Fort Warren, in Boston Harbor. Here the two men already named, Purington and Brown, formed, with two others, named Edgerly and Greenleaf, a quartette, and the quartette sang, among its other songs, all sorts of words of their own "getting up" to this tune.

John Brown was a good-natured Scotchman, and the members of the quartette say they sang "John Brown this and John Brown that" to the tune, until, by an almost unconscious change, the hero of them was changed from John Brown, of the "Tigers" to John Brown, of Harper's Ferry, and the grand and simple verse came into existence:

> "John Brown's body lies a-mouldering in the ground
> But his soul is marching on."

Before this time the masses of the North had not been in exact sympathy with the purposes of John Brown, but the excitement of the early days of the war called out a sentiment which these words exactly fitted. Whenever the soldier quartette were in Boston they were called upon to sing this song. The Twelfth Regiment took it up. Samuel

C. Perkins, of Brockton, a member of Maitland's Band, which was stationed with the Regiment at Fort Warren, wrote down the air while a soldier whistled it. Then the band played it every day. When Edward Everett formally presented the set of colors of the Twelfth Regiment on Boston Common, the speech of acceptance being made by Colonel Fletcher Webster of the Regiment, the tune was played, and the multitude fairly went mad over it. The band played the tune going up State Street in June, 1861, and the soldiers sang it as they marched along. The crowd along the sidewalk took up the air and joined in the chorus:

"Glory, glory, hallelujah,
His soul is marching on!"

Soon after the regiment sang it in marching through New York on the way to Baltimore, with the same effect. It spread at once through the army and throughout the country, and became the anthem of the Union. In December, 1861, Mrs. Julia Ward Howe wrote for the air the words beginning,

"Mine eyes have seen the glory of the coming of the Lord."

which was called "The Battle Hymn of the Republic," and soon became immensely popular, but never supplanted in common use the old, simple words. This is the story of the origin of "John Brown's Body," as told by the members of the band and the regiment with which it had its use as a popular song.

No. 685.

"JESUS, I MY CROSS HAVE TAKEN."

REV. H. F. LYTE.

At a large assembly, a Sunday school anniversary, it was found that the speakers expected had failed, and none was ready to take their places. After some singing the meeting became dull, and the interest seemed to be dying out. The superintendent, who had set his heart on success, was anxious, and at a loss what to do, but finally gave a general invitation to the scholars to repeat any texts or hymns they had learned. He was pleasantly answered, but only for a short time. A stranger on the platform had noticed on the front seat a boy of Jewish caste, with piercing eyes, and wondered why he was there. In the midst of deep silence he arose and repeated:

"Jesus, I my cross have taken,
All to leave and follow Thee;
Naked, poor, despised, forsaken,
Thou, from hence, my all shalt be"—

in a voice so thrilling as to move the whole audience. Many eyes were moist, for the story of the young Jew was known. The father had told him he must either leave Sunday school or quit home forever, and the hymn showed what he had given up to follow Christ. The meeting was inspired with new life. Friends gathered round him at the close, and business men united in securing him a situation by which he could earn his own living.

No. 686.

"NOTHING BUT LEAVES, THE SPIRIT GRIEVES."

Mrs. Lucy E. Akerman, 1816—1874.

This hymn was suggested by a sermon by Moncure D. Conway from the text, Mark 11:13. "And when He came to it He found nothing but leaves."

A man heard Mr. Sankey sing the melody "Nothing but leaves." The words "nothing but leaves" stuck to him, so he committed the hymn to memory and sang it to himself when he was alone, or as he walked the busy streets. And what was the result? He said that every line and every word told him undeniable truths that went straight to his heart. He overhauled his whole life—over fifty years—and he said, "I could not find a single ear of good grain; nothing but leaves, withered leaves!" And that thought led him to seek the Lord until he found peace in Him, and then bore living fruit for Jesus.

No. 687.

"THE OLD OAKEN BUCKET."

SAMUEL WOODWORTH.

Woodworth was a printer, and intemperate. He was in the habit of dropping into the liquor saloon kept by a man by the name of Mallory. One day after drinking a glass of brandy and water, he smacked his lips and declared that Mallory's brandy was superior to any drink he had ever tasted.

"No" said Mallory, "you are mistaken; there was a drink which we both once thought was far ahead of this."

"What was it?" asked Woodworth.

"The fresh water we used to drink out of the old oak bucket that hung in the well, when we came in from the field on a sultry day."

"True," cried Woodworth, and a tear stood on his cheek as he said it. Going to his printing office he seated himself at a desk, and began to write:

"How dear to my heart are the scenes of my childhood."

No. 688.

"THE SONG OF THE SHIRT."

THOMAS HOOD.

Tom Hood was prompted to write this song by the condition of thousands of working women in the city of London. It was the work of a single evening. He handed it to his wife to read.

"Now mind Tom, mind my words," said she, "this will tell wonderfully. It is one of the best things you ever did."

Awhile after Mark Lemon, Editor of London *Punch*, found a letter in his morning mail, enclosing a poem, and a letter from its author, saying that the poem enclosed had been rejected by three London journals, and asked him not to return it but to throw it into the wastebasket if he did not think it worth using, as he was sick of the sight of it. It was this same "Song of the Shirt." Mr. Lemon liked it although some of his co-editors did not, and it was published in *Punch*, December 16, 1843. It created a great sensation. It trebled the sale of the paper. People of every class were moved by it. It was sung on the streets and in palaces. And when Tom Hood died a monument was placed above his grave, paid for by a great popular subscription on which was placed an inscription he himself had desired, "He sang the Song of the Shirt."

No. 689.

"ABIDE WITH ME, FAST FALLS THE EVENTIDE."

REV. H. F. LYTE.

A young man left his home in the country and came to New York City, where he fell into temptation and ere long was far on the road to ruin. One evening as he passed along the street on his way to join his vicious companions, he heard the sound of singing and caught the words:

"Abide with me, fast falls the eventide,
The darkness deepens, Lord with me abide."

He stopped as suddenly as if arrested by the hand of God, for these were the words and this was the song his mother sang to him every night, as she put him to bed, and her image and all the sweet memories of his childhood's home came rushing into his mind. He turned back and entered the church from which the music came, found different friends and companions there and became a Christian.

No. 690.

FOR A SEASON CALLED TO PART."

REV. JOHN NEWTON.

It is doubtful if ever a more intimate friendship or close affection existed between pastor and people, than that which grew up between John Newton and his church at Olney. The Olney hymn book which has become celebrated in hymnology consisted of the hymns which week after week Newton and Cowper had prepared for use in the weekly prayer meeting of his people, and this hymn is a good illustration of the way in which they made common lot of the experiences of their lives. In the year 1776, Newton was the victim of a tumor on his thigh and in November of that year he decided to go to London to undergo a surgical operation for its removal. This was before the day of anæsthetics and the operation would be painful, and possibly fatal. So at the prayer meeting before his departure this hymn written for the occasion was read and sung together by pastor and people. The knowledge of these circumstances under which it was written will interpret to us its words. The hymn beginning "As the sun's enlivening eye," is the same hymn.

No. 691.

"COME O MY SOUL! IN SACRED LAYS."

Rev. Thomas Blacklock.

This hymn is a specimen of what can be accomplished in spite of great obstacles. A Scotch boy was stricken with smallpox when six months old, from which he recovered only with the total loss of his sight. But in spite of this he obtained a liberal education, was for a short time pastor of a church in Scotland, then the head of a school for boys, the author of several books, and the writer of good poetry. A friend said of him that he had known him to dictate thirty or forty verses of poetry as fast as they could be written down, but the moment he was at a loss for a word to his liking, he would stop and seldom resume his work until some later time. It is probable, therefore, that this hymn was composed in this way, being dictated by the blind poet as rapidly as it could be written down.

There is in the second stanza a reminder of a very remarkable characteristic of his writing, namely, that he excelled in accurate descriptions of the world of nature, although his eyes had never seen the things his words described. The author of the hymn has left for us a portrait of himself in verse:

"Straight is my person, but of little size,
Lean are my cheeks, and hollow are my eyes;
My youthful down is like my talent, rare,
Politely distant stands each single hair.
My voice too rough to charm a lady's ear,
So smooth a child may listen without fear." etc.

No. 692.

"EIN' FESTE BURG" (Tune).

MARTIN LUTHER, 1483—1546.

Composed in Coburg Castle where Luther was protected during the meeting of the diet at Augsburg. In great anxiety he here wrote the hymn, composed the tune, and sang it. Both tune and words have been often used in later works. Meyerbeer in "Les Huguenots" puts it into the mouths of an old Huguenot soldier and his companions as their death song. Mendelssohn introduces the music into his "Reformation Symphony." Bach uses it in several cantatas. Raff in an overture, and Wagner in his "Kaiser March." Mendelssohn's use of it is probably the most in keeping with the name and work of its composer. The first part of his symphony is broken and confused, but intermixed at intervals with strains from Luther's Song. This is like the beginning of Luther's work, when his doctrines were just becoming known to the people. Gradually the din grows louder and harsher, but Luther's music is heard more frequently and distinctly, and now and then a strain rises clear and loud above the noise, and at length in the climax of the symphony, all the instruments sweep together into the notes of Luther's hymn.

No. 693.

"AM I A SOLDIER OF THE CROSS?"

REV. ISAAC WATTS.

It was the custom with many ministers of the time of Watts to write a hymn nearly every week with which to close the sermon of the following Sunday, and the hymn was then sung by the congregation. A great many of the hymns of Watts, and Doddridge, and Beddome were thus written.

One winter Sunday in 1727 in a little English church, the minister gave out as his text, the words of Paul to the Christians at Corinth, "Watch ye, stand fast in the faith, quit you like men, be strong" (I Cor. 16:13). Those were the days of long sermons and many heads. The preacher first described Christian courage, and then recounted some of the occasions for it:

"Piety in the presence of unchristian people.
Courage before infidels and scoffers.
In the practice of unfashionable virtues.
In pleading the cause of the oppressed.
In reproving sin.
In works of reformation.
In the peculiar circumstances of daily life, as when a servant is forced to tell the truth.
Martyr faith, *i. e.*, passive valor in bearing affliction, and in enduring persecution."

And then at the close of the sermon, to enforce its teachings he repeated this hymn, and it was then first sung by his hearers.

No. 694.

"COME WE WHO LOVE THE LORD."

Rev. Isaac Watts.

There was once a difficulty in the choir of a New England church, presided over by a somewhat celebrated minister, named Samuel West. The choir had refused to sing, and the pastor gave out this hymn, and after reading it solemnly through, looked up at the rebellious choir and said, "Please commence with the second stanza." This reads,

"Let those refuse to sing
Who never knew our God,
But children of the heavenly King,
May speak their joys abroad."

It is needless to say that the choir chose to sing rather than by silence to apply to themselves the classification of those who refused.

No. 695.

"DEAR LORD, AND MASTER MINE."

THOMAS H. GILL.

The author of this hymn after preparatory education declined to enter Oxford, because he could not sign the "Thirty-nine Articles" required for admission, the doctrines to which he objected being those of the Trinity and the Divinity of Christ. He was the son of Unitarian parents, and had been trained in their faith. From the age of nineteen to twenty-six he devoted himself to the study of the Greek New Testament, until as he himself records, "The assiduous perusal of the Greek Testament for many years showed me clearly that Unitarianism failed to interpret the Book of Life. As truth after truth broke upon my gaze, God put a new song into my mouth." This is one of the "new songs," and its language, especially in the first stanza, is appropriate to the change that had come to him from opposition and unbelief, to faith and loyalty.

No. 696.

"HE LEADETH ME, O BLESSED THOUGHT."

REV. J. H. GILMORE.

The author of this hymn had been talking one evening at the prayer meeting of a Baptist church in Philadelphia, about the twenty-third Psalm, and had been especially impressed with the blessedness of being led by God, of the mere fact of His leadership altogether apart from the way in which He leads, or what He leads us to. At the close of the service he went to the home of one of the deacons of the church, and there in conversation the same subject was continued. As they talked, the blessedness of this leadership so grew upon him that taking out his pencil he wrote the hymn, just as it now stands, and handed it to his wife. Without his knowledge she sent it to a Baptist paper and it was published. Three years later he went to Rochester, New York, to preach and was shown into the church soon after his arrival in town. As he entered he took up a hymn book, saying to himself, "I wonder what they sing here." The book opened at his own hymn and this was the first that he knew that it had found a place among the songs of the Church. The hymn has become very popular, and has been translated into many languages for missionary use. The tune by Wm. B. Bradbury, "He leadeth me," was composed for this hymn.

No. 697.

"O THOU GOD, WHO HEAREST PRAYER."

JOSIAH CONDER, 1789—1855.

The author of this hymn fell from his horse while riding one day, and met with very severe injuries, which confined him to his bed for a while and nearly ended his life. It was while so confined and suffering from his injury that he wrote this hymn. One stanza contains a couplet, now usually omitted, referring directly to his condition:

"Listen to my feeble breath
Now I touch the gates of death:"

and the whole hymn is his prayer for recovery.

No. 698.

"WE SHALL MEET BEYOND THE RIVER."

REV. JOHN ATKINSON, 1835.

The author's mother had recently died (February, 1867) and he was alone one night in his study near midnight, and was thinking of the mother he had lost, and also of revival services in which he had just been engaged. Under the influence of these thoughts, the substance of this hymn, as he says, "seemed to sing itself into my heart. I said to myself, I had better write that down or I shall lose it, and there in the silence of my study, not far from midnight, I wrote the hymn."

No. 699.

"COMMIT THOU ALL THY GRIEFS."

PAUL GERHARDT.

Near the close of the last century, a pastor was Chaplain to the Swedish Embassy in Paris, and preached alternately in Swedish and in German. One Sunday this hymn was being sung, as a pale man entered, took his seat in the last pew, and resting his head on his hand, looked on to his neighbor's book, but did not sing. At the end of the hymn the Chaplain took for his text the words of the Psalm on which the hymn is based (Psalm 37:5), "Commit thy way unto the Lord! Trust also in Him, and He shall bring it to pass." When the sermon was over, the stranger sprang to his feet, pressed forward and took the preacher by the hand exclaiming, "You have saved my life." Then he related how he had come from Germany to Paris, and built up a prosperous business, but in consequence of the war had lost everything and with his family was plunged into poverty and distress. In his misery he had resolved to throw himself into the Seine, and was on his way thither when the sound of the singing had reminded him of brighter days, and had drawn him into the chapel to hear it through. The pastor's sermon had completed what the hymn had begun, and given him new courage. The pastor helped him to employment and he regained his old position as a merchant and remained faithful to the church, but during the reign of terror left Paris and settled in Bremen. Later on the pastor also quitted Paris and went to Bremen too, and was recognized by his former friend, who found for him an appointment there.

No. 700.

"JERUSALEM MY HAPPY HOME."

"F. B. P."

This hymn, which had its inspiration in the old Latin hymn of St. Bernard of Cluny, from which we get our "Jerusalem the Golden" and several other hymns, has a somewhat curious history.

A manuscript was discovered some years ago in the British Museum, with a notation that it had been bought at an auction sale in 1844. Upon examination it proved to be a collection of songs quite miscellaneous in character, and evidently dating from the reign of Queen Elizabeth. One of these songs was headed, "A dittie most excellent for every man to reade, that doth intend for to repent, and to amend with spede," to the tune of "A Rich Merchantman," or "John come kiss me now." Another piece was entitled, "The Parliament of Devils." Among the collection is one which is entitled, "A Song made by F. B. P. to the tune of Diana." This is the song, but who its author was has ever been subject for discussion. There was a certain Francis Baker Porter, a Roman Catholic priest and author, who was imprisoned in the Tower of London, during the reign of Queen Elizabeth, and many think that from behind the prison walls he sang this song of longing for the liberty of Heaven. Others with more earnestness than evidence construe the initials "F. B. P." to mean Francis Baker, priest. This seems less probable than the other. But whoever "F. B. P." may have been, his song was knocked about until the auctioneer at last knocked it off to the buyer for the British Museum, where it lay buried until resurrected and polished up for the song service of these later days.

No. 701.

"SAFE IN THE ARMS OF JESUS."

Fanny Crosby (Mrs. Van Alstyne).

The author of this hymn, blind from infancy, has written more than three thousand hymns. Many of them, as might be expected, of little value, but many others that have become classic in the hymnody of the Church. The facility with which she throws her ideas into verse is well illustrated by this hymn, which was written in twenty minutes, for Mr. W. H. Doane, who suggested the subject and waited while she composed it. On another occasion he called on her one afternoon and asked for a hymn to be sung at a service that evening, and while he waited she composed the hymn:

"Jesus keep me near the cross."

She had a wonderful memory, as witness this incident. Mr. Philip Phillips, the "Singing Pilgrim," called upon her at one time and gave to her eighty subjects upon which he wished her to write hymns. Forty of these he left with her. Not a word of the hymns on any of these subjects was written down, until one day she sent for Mr. Phillips, and dictated to him as he wrote, the whole forty hymns. She had written secular songs as well as sacred, that have become popular, as for instance, "Hazel Dell," "Rosalie the Prairie Flower," "There's Music in the Air," etc.

No. 702.

"OH, SWEETLY BREATHE THE LYRES ABOVE."

REV. RAY PALMER.

During the winter of 1842–1843, there was a revival of religion in the church over which Dr. Palmer presided. At one communion service quite a number of converts had been received into the church, and as part of the service "O happy day that fixed my choice" had been sung. At the next communion, several others were to be received, and as the pastor did not like to repeat the use of the same hymn, he composed this one to be used in its stead.

No. 703.

"PORTUGUESE HYMN" (Tune).

It is an ancient custom of European sovereigns to employ in their service a number of boy singers who perform the music in the chapels where their royal employers worship. These choirs are called "Children of the Chapel Royal," and they are led and taught by another servant of the sovereign, called the "Chapel Master." This person follows the sovereign from place to place wherever he may go. Marcus Portugal was Chapel Master to the King of Portugal and composed this music as an offertory piece, that is, a tune to be played in the church while the people were bringing their contributions to the plate. His royal Master visited Brazil in 1808, and Portugal went with him, remaining there until he died in 1834. When Dom Pedro, Emperor of Brazil, the same who, in 1876, in company with President Grant, started the machinery of the Centennial Exposition at Philadelphia into motion, was a little boy, this Marcus Portugal still led the music of the Chapel service where he worshipped in Rio Janeiro.

No. 704.

"OH, COME AND LET US ALL WITH ONE ACCORD."

ANON.

This is a version of the ninety-fifth Psalm, written by some unknown author, and at some unknown time, but it is evidently old. In the time of Baxter, who died in 1689, it was a common thing so to compose a hymn, that it could be sung in either of two meters. This was done by including the necessary words to lengthen the lines in brackets so that the hymn would make sense either with or without their use. Some of Baxter's hymns were written in this way, and this hymn is one of the same sort, as it can be reduced to a long meter by striking out two syllables from each line, as thus:

"O come let all with one accord,
Lift up our voice and praise the Lord,
Let us this evening bless His name,
Yea, let us magnify the same."

No. 705.

"COME THOU FOUNT OF EVERY BLESSING."

R. ROBINSON.

There is a story which concerns the Rev. Dr. Muhlenberg, author of the hymn "I would not live alway," and concerns also the fourth stanza of this hymn. The Doctor had a pupil whose self-righteousness disturbed him, and one day he handed him a slip of paper on which he had written a version of this stanza corrected to suit the occasion.

"I did seek Thee when a stranger
Looking for the fold of God!
I to save my soul from danger,
Earned redemption in Thy blood."

Its effect upon the student is not recorded.

No. 706.

"O LITTLE CHILDREN, SING."

"JESUS, YOUR LORD AND KING."

MISS ANNA B. WARNER.

In 1860 there was published a novel entitled "Say and Seal." It was the joint work of two sisters, who had years before made themselves famous by the production of "The Wide, Wide World," one of the most widely read novels ever written. One of the principal characters in "Say and Seal" is a man by the name of Linden, who makes his appearance in a little village on the shore of Long Island Sound, as teacher of the village school. He is provided with a boarding place by the school committee and this boarding place provides another important character in the story, in the person of Faith Derrick the daughter of the family. Mr. Linden becomes a favorite among the families of the poor and the sick, and the children all become his friends. One New Year's Day he and Faith start upon a round of visits, to sick and needy families, with a sleigh full of provisions, and clothing and toys. One of the last visits made is at a home where a large family of children greet them, for each of whom as well as for the common table there is a special gift. When all have been distributed one of the children, little Mary, says to her mother, "Ma, will Mr. Linden sing for us today?" "I dare say if you ask him pretty," is the reply, and then it is discovered that when Mr. Linden meets these people in their homes he is in the habit of singing to them songs and hymns. And so after some urging Mr. Linden sings for them a "Child's Christmas Hymn" of five stanzas beginning:

"O little children, sing.
Jesus, your Lord and King
For you a child became:
On that bright Christmas day
He in a manger lay,
Who hath the one Almighty name!"

Of course the story is all fiction, and as to most of it, the two sisters, who wrote it in its preface say that the public shall never know what part each wrote; but as to this little hymn as well as two others which in the story Mr. Linden sings to a little boy who is sick and is soon to die, one of the sisters Miss Anna B. Warner confesses that they are of her composing.

No. 707.

"LO! GOD IS HERE, LET US ADORE."

Gerhard Tersteegen.

Rev. John Wesley, Translator

This hymn has been in use in mission work to encourage those engaged in it when lonely in a heathen land. Rev.

Dr. Coke and Rev. Benjamin Clough, the first an old missionary and the other a new recruit in the service, were together in Hindostan, when Dr. Coke exclaimed to his young companion, "My dear brother, I am dead to all but India."

The thought of such complete consecration cheered the young man, who was tempted to homesickness, and he began to sing a stanza of this hymn, not now often included in our hymnals:

"Glad the toys of earth we leave,
Wealth, pleasure, fame, for Thee alone;
To Thee our will, soul, flesh, we give,
Oh, take, oh, seal them for Thine own."

And as he sang the aged misssionary joined him in the song, and so together, the old man nearly through, and the young man but just begun, made the hymn at once a renewal of their consecration to the work of missions, and a prayer for divine approval.

No. 708.

"O LORD, I WOULD DELIGHT IN THEE."

REV. JOHN RYLAND.

The author of this hymn when a young man was engaged to be married to a young lady who was taken with a dangerous sickness, from which it was feared, she would not recover. Filled with anxiety he called at her home to inquire about her, and was told by the servant that if he would return in half an hour he could hear the opinion of the doctors who were then holding a consultation on the case. He went away to an empty house near by, and sitting down on a large stone, wrote this hymn, expressive of his trust in God amid trouble. When he called at the house again he received a favorable report; the young lady recovered and later they were married.

The same hymn is often used in a different meter, beginning:

"Lord I delight in thee."

In the author's manuscript there is appended to this hymn the date of December 3, 1777, and this note: "I recollect deeper feelings of mind in composing this hymn than perhaps I ever felt in making any other."

No. 709.

"WOODMAN SPARE THAT TREE."

George P. Morris.

Years ago when New York City was smaller than at present, the author of this song, was one day driving with a friend near Bloomingdale. The friend suggested that they turn into a woodland road to look at an old tree, which as he said had been planted by his grandfather, near the cottage where he was born. On the way he told how the old tree whenever he saw it brought back the old times when, as a happy boy with father and mother and sisters, he had sat under its shade.

As they approached the tree, they saw an old man, with his coat off, and an ax. "What are you going to do?" inquired Mr. Morris' companion, "You are surely not going to cut down that tree?"

"Yes I am though," was the blunt reply.

Further talk brought out the fact that the old man was now the owner of the cottage and did not fancy having the great tree so near his house, and besides he wanted it for firewood. In reply to the question, how much it was worth, he said, "About ten dollars," and the result was a bargain struck on the spot, and the money paid, by which he agreed to let the tree stand, his daughter who stood by agreeing that it should stand as long as she lived. This incident led Mr. Morris to write the song:

"Woodman spare that tree."

No. 710.

"JOYFULLY, JOYFULLY ONWARD I MOVE."

REV. WM. HUNTER.

Rev. J. M. Thoburn, a Methodist missionary in India, relates that at one time, he was traveling at the foot of the Himalaya Mountains, in a section of the country, strange to him, and the shades of evening were gathering about him, as he was pressing forward in search of shelter for the night. The country was infested with wild beasts and other dangers beset him as he moved on in the silence. Suddenly a wailing sound from a distant spot broke on the air and as he listened it seemed to be coming nearer. At last it was made out to be a human voice, and a few moments later the voice of song could be distinguished. It was a native Hindoo, singing in his own language, but with the old tune familiar in America, this hymn of Dr. Hunter's:

"Joyfully, joyfully onward I move
Bound for the land of bright spirits above."

The hymn was composed while the author was riding on horseback over the mountains of West Virginia, the thought in his mind being the reward of the faithful itinerant at the end of his work, and the hymn was nearly complete before he had an opportunity to write it down. As soon as he reached a stopping place, he alighted from his horse, and like Charles Wesley, calling for pen and ink, committed the words to paper.

No. 711.

"LEAVE GOD TO ORDER ALL THY WAYS."

George Neumark.

Miss C. Winkworth, Translator.

Several of our hymns were composed as parts of novels, with no thought of their ever being used for public worship; but here is one which is unique in that a novel has been written, which weaves the facts known about its author and its origin into a very pretty love story. Its title is, "The Lutanist of St. Jacobi's." It is by Catherine Drew, and can be found in Munroe's "Seaside Library."

No. 712.

"MINE EYES HAVE SEEN THE GLORY OF THE COMING OF THE LORD."

Mrs. Julia Ward Howe.

This hymn was published in the *Atlantic Monthly*, February, 1862. A Methodist minister then in Putnam, Ohio, saw it and was so charmed with it that he committed it to memory at once. He became an army chaplain, was captured by the Confederates and sent to Libby Prison. He was an enthusiastic singer, and soon had the prisoners holding a regular service of song every evening. Here this wonderful song was first sung, and it did much to keep up the courage of those unfortunate prisoners.

Not long after, this Methodist minister, who was none other than the celebrated Chaplain McCabe, was released from Libby and came to Washington. A great meeting of the Christian Commission was held in the Hall of Representatives just at that time (winter of 1863–1864), and the hall was crowded in every part. While Geo. H. Stewart, of Philadelphia, President of the Commission, was speaking, a door opened at the side of the platform and a tall man, slightly stooped, entered. There was a glance between him and the speaker, and then he took a seat near by and the speech went on. At its conclusion, Chaplain McCabe was introduced and sang this hymn, as only he could sing it. As he neared the end of the song, the tall stooping man was seen to write on a scrap of paper, which went to Mr. Stewart. It was a request from Abraham Lincoln, for he it was, the President of the nation, that Chaplain McCabe would repeat the song. As he came forward to do so, he prefaced the singing with a message which the Union prisoners in Libby had commissioned him to bring to the President. It was that, notwithstanding the terrible suffering they were enduring there, they wanted him "not to mind them and to allow no sympathy for them to prevent his marching straight onward until the rebellion was crushed, slavery extinguished, and the Union restored." And then he sang once more the "Battle Hymn of the Republic," the audience joining in the chorus. With each succeeding stanza the enthusiasm rose higher, until at last, with an expression absolutely impossible to describe, he sang the closing couplet:

> "As He died to make men holy
> Let us die to make men free."

The audience were almost wild as they shouted rather than sang the final chorus.

No. 713.

"RESCUE THE PERISHING, CARE FOR THE DYING."

FANNY CROSBY.

The author of this hymn, though blind, often visited the Sunday schools and missions about New York. On one occasion she was visiting one of the missions, when her own hymn, "Rescue the Perishing," was sung. At its close a young man arose and said, "It was this hymn that brought me to Christ. I was passing along the street one night, ragged and hungry, my time and money having been wasted in drink. I heard some voices singing:

'Rescue the perishing
Care for the dying
Snatch them in pity
From sin and the grave.'

I followed the sound of the voices and found myself in a little mission meeting. I took a back seat just to hear the hymn through. I was just ready to perish that night, but that hymn saved me. I wish I could see the one who wrote that hymn." And in a few minutes they led the blind woman, who had written the words, up to the man who had been saved by the words of her hymn.

No. 714.

"HIS MOTHER'S SONGS."

"Beneath the hot midsummer sun
The men had marched all day;
And now beside a rippling stream
Upon the grass they lay.

"Tiring of games and idle jests,
As swept the hours along,
They called to one who mused apart,
'Come, friend, give us a song.'

" 'I fear I cannot please,' he said;
'The only songs I know
Are those my mother used to sing
For me long years ago.'

" 'Sing one of those,' a rough voice cried,
'There's none but true men here;
To every mother's son of us
A mother's songs are dear.'

"Then sweetly rose the singer's voice
Amid unwonted calm,
'Am I a soldier of the cross,
A follower of the Lamb?'

" 'And shall I fear to own His cause'—
The very stream was stilled,
And hearts that never throbbed with fear
With tender thoughts were filled.

"Ended the song; the singer said,
As to his feet he rose,
'Thanks to you all, my friends; good night
God grant us sweet repose.'

" 'Sing us one more,' the captain begged;
The soldier bent his head,
Then glancing round, with smiling lips,
'You'll join with me,' he said.

" 'We'll sing this old familiar air,
Sweet as the bugle call,

"All hail the power of Jesus' name,
Let angels prostrate fall."

"Ah! wondrous was the old tune's spell
As on the singer sang,
Man after man fell into line,
And loud the voices rang.

"The songs are done, the camp is still,
Naught but the stream is heard;
But ah! the depths of every soul
By those old hymns are stirred.

"And up from many a bearded lip,
In whispers soft and low,
Rises the prayer the mother taught
The boy long years ago."

No. 715.

"THE OLD PSALM TUNE."

MRS. H. B. STOWE.

"You asked, dear friend, the other day,
Why still my charmed ear
Rejoiceth in uncultured tone,
That old psalm tune to hear?

"I've heard full oft in foreign lands
The grand orchestral strain,
Where music's ancient masters live,
Revealed on earth again.

"And well I feel the magic power,
When skilled and cultured art

Its cunning web of sweetness weaves
Around the captured heart.

"But yet, dear friend, tho' rudely sung,
That old psalm tune hath still
A pulse of power beyond them all
My inmost soul to thrill.

"Those halting tones that sound to you,
Are not the tones I hear;
But voices of the loved and lost
Then meet my longing ear.

"I hear my angel mother's voice—
Those were the words she sung;
I hear my brother's ringing tones,
As once on earth they rung:

"And friends that walk in white above
Come round me like a cloud,
And far above those earthly notes
Their singing sounds aloud.

"There may be discord, as you say;
Those voices poorly ring;
But there's no discord in the strain
Those upper spirits sing.

"For they who sing are of the blest,
The calm and glorified,
Whose hours are one eternal rest
On Heaven's sweet flowing tide.

"Their life is music, and accord;
Their souls and hearts keep time
In one sweet concert with the Lord—
One concert vast, sublime.

"And thro' the hymns they sang on earth
Sometimes a sweetness falls,
On those they loved and left below,
And softly homeward calls.

"Bells from our own dear fatherland,
Borne trembling o'er the sea—
The narrow sea that they have crossed,
The shores where we shall be.

"Oh sing, sing on, beloved souls;
Sing cares and griefs to rest;
Sing, till entranced we arise
To join you 'mid the blest."

No. 716.

"CROWN HIM LORD OF ALL."

Miss L. M. Latimer.

In 1835, when Rev. Edward Webb, D.D., and other missionaries sailed for India, the last words they heard from their native land were:

"Crown Him Lord of all."

"They hushed their breath, that noble band,
To catch the last farewell;
The dear home shore receding fast
With every ocean swell.
Above the city's noise and din
A song rose on the air——
A song of triumph and of joy
From loved ones gathered there.

"'All hail the power of Jesus' name!'
And, clear as bugle call,
The words came floating on the air,
Oh! 'crown him Lord of all!'
They caught the spirit of the hymn,
Danger and death looked small
To those brave ones, who gave their lives
To crown Him Lord of all.

"A battle hymn, that song sped on,
The world for Christ, the call—
For every island of the sea
Shall crown Him Lord of all.
On Himalaya's sunny slope,
By Delhi's kingly wall,
They lay their lives down at His feet,
And crown Him Lord of all.

"The Southern Cross begins to bend,
The morning dawns at last
Idol and shrine, and mosque and tower
At Jesus' feet are cast.
Triumphant Zion, lift thy head,
Let every burden fall.
Come cast your trophies at His feet,
And crown Him Lord of all."

No. 717.

"RAIN ON THE ROOF."

COATES KINNEY.

Mr. Kinney gives this account of the origin of the song: "The verses were written when I was about twenty years of age, as nearly as I can remember. They were inspired close to the rafters of a little story-and-a-half frame house. The language, as first published, was not composed, it came. I had just a little more to do with it than I had with the coming of the rain. The poem, in its entirety, came and asked me to put it down, the next afternoon, in the course of a solitary and aimless squandering of a young man's time along a no-whither road through a summer wood. Every word of it is a fact, and was a tremendous heart throb."

The words were sent to Emerson Bennett, at that time editor of *The Columbia*, at Cincinnati, who threw them aside, as not being quite up to *The Columbia's* standard! A few days later, the publisher of the paper, Mr. Penrose Jones, rummaging in the drawers of rejected manuscripts, came across Mr. Kinney's, and, holding it up, wanted to know, "What the dickens do you mean, Mr. Bennett, by putting this here?" The next day it went into print in *The Columbia*, and immediately afterward, to the surprise and disgust of Mr. Bennett, it went all over the world.

No. 718.

"A LIFE ON THE OCEAN WAVE."

EPES SARGENT.

"A Life on the Ocean Wave" was written for Henry Russell. The subject of the song was suggested to me as I was walking one breezy, sun-bright morning in spring, on the Battery, New York, and looking out upon the ships and the small craft under full sail. Having completed my song and my walk together, I went to the office of *The Mirror*, wrote out the words, and showed them to my good friend, George P. Morris.

After reading the piece, he said, "My dear boy, this is not a song; it will never do for music; but it is a very nice little lyric; so let me take it and publish it in *The Mirror*."

I consented, and concluded that Morris was right. Some days after the publication of the piece, I met Russell. "Where is that song?" asked he.

"I tried my hand at one and failed," said I.

"How do you know that?"

"Morris tells me that it won't answer."

"And is Morris infallible? Hand me the piece, young man, and let us go into Hewitt's back room here, at the corner of Park Place and Broadway, and see what we can make out of your lines."

We passed through the music store. Russell seated himself at the piano; read over the lines attentively; hummed an air or two to himself; then ran his fingers over the keys, then stopped as if nonplussed. Suddenly a bright idea seemed to dawn upon him; a melody had all at once floated into his brain, and he began to hum it, and to sway himself to its movement. Then striking the keys tentatively a few times, he at last confidently launched into the air since known as "A Life on the Ocean Wave."

"I've got it!" he exclaimed. It was all the work of a few minutes. I pronounced the melody a success, and it proved so. The copyright of the song became very valuable, though I never got anything from it myself. It at once became a favorite, and soon the bands were playing it in the streets. A year or two after its publication, I received from England copies of five or six different editions that had been issued there by competing publishers.

No. 719.

"I'D BE A BUTTERFLY."

Thomas Haynes Bayly.

Thomas Haynes Bayly and his bride were visiting Lord Ashtown, when, on going to the drawing-room after dinner, one day, the gentlemen found it deserted, and Mr. Bayly went to the garden in pursuit of the ladies. Seeing him, they playfully hid themselves in the winding avenues. He followed floating laughs and laces a while, and then sat down in a tempting arbor. When the ladies joined him, he showed them the manuscript of "I'd be a Butterfly," that moment written. Mrs. Bayly composed an air, and it was sung that evening to a large party assembled in their honor.

No. 720.

"IN THY CLEFT, O ROCK OF AGES."

FANNY CROSBY.

"Not long since, I was called to see a member of my church who was very ill. His disease prostrated him, in mind and body, to the last degree; and there was a look about him which I did not like. During one of my visits I told him of a little song I knew, which I called 'my song,' because I like it so much, and am constantly singing it. I asked him if he would like to hear it, at the same time fearing he might be too sick and weak.

"He answered in a voice I could scarcely hear: 'Yes; sing it, please.' So I sang:

'Hide Thou me——'

as found in 'Gospel Hymns,' page 374. As I sang the last verse he was completely overcome, and wept so as to alarm me for a moment, for he was very weak. But he soon regained composure; and I knelt by his bed in prayer.

"As I was about to go, he said: 'Will you not sing one verse of that song, again, for me?'

"I replied: 'Yes, indeed, and gladly, the whole of it, if you choose.' Then closing his eyes, he listened very quietly.

"After this second singing, he asked: 'Is that all?' I told him, 'Yes: it has only three verses.'

" 'Oh,' he exclaimed, 'there ought to be forty thousand of them! It has done me so much good—so much good!' And, for the first time during his illness, there came a bright expression upon his face.

"I never go to see him now, but that he calls for the song. He is better; and I believe the song 'turned the scales' in his favor. Well, I thought I would try to compose a couple more verses for him; and, today, when I sang them, with the others, his delight was great. I send the hymn to you, as I now have it. You will see that my verses are inserted, and appear, alternately, with the others; the words which are not mine bearing the quotation marks."

"HIDE THOU ME."

"Thou art my hiding place"—
(Psalm 32:7).

"In Thy cleft, O Rock of Ages,
Hide Thou me.
When the fitful tempest rages,
Hide Thou me.
Where no mortal arm can sever,
From my heart, Thy love forever,
Hide me, O Thou Rock of Ages
Hide Thou me."

When cares my earth-path darken,
Guide Thou me.
May I, then, for Thy voice hearken,
Call Thou me.
Let Thy grace prevent my straying;
Keep me steadfast watching—praying;
Keep me, O Thou Rock of Ages,
Close to Thee.

"From the snare of sinful pleasure,
Hide Thou me;
Thou my heart's eternal treasure,
Hide Thou me.
When the world its power is wielding,
And my heart is almost yielding,
Hide me, O Thou Rock of Ages,
Hide Thou me."

In the time of pain and weakness,
Help Thou me;
Give me, still, of faith and meekness;
Help Thou me.
If in spirit sore and broken,
Cheer me with some dear love-token;
Help me, O Thou Rock of Ages,
Help Thou me.

"In the night of lonely sorrow,
Hide Thou me;
Till, in glory, dawns the morrow,
Hide Thou me.
In the sight of Jordan's billow,
Let Thy bosom be my pillow;
Hide me, O Thou Rock of Ages,
Hide Thou me."

No. 721.

"MAIST ONIE DAY."

The following beautiful lines were composed by Timothy Swan, the well-known author of the celebrated tunes "China" and "Poland," when in the seventy-fifth year of his age. They were sent to his son, then a resident of New York:

"Ye ken, dear bairn, that we maun part;
When death, cauld death, shall bid us start;
But when he'll send his dreadfu' dart
We canna say.
Sae we'll be ready for his dart
Maist onie day.

"We'll keep a' right an' gude wi'in.
Our walk will then be free fra' sin;
Upright we'll step thro' theck and thin,
Straight on our way;
Deal just wi' a', the prize we'll win
Maist onie day.

"Ye ken there's Ane wha's just and wise,
Has said that a' bairns should rise
An' soar aboon the lofty skies,
And there shall stay;
Being well prepared, we'll gain the prize
Maist onie day.

"When He wha made a' things just right,
Shall ca' us hence to realms of light,
Be it morn, or noon, or e'en, or night,
We will obey.
We'll be prepared to ta' our flight
Maist onie day.

"Our lamps we'll fill brimfu' o' oil,
That's gude and pure—that wulna spoil;
We'll keep them burnin' a' the while,
To light our way.
Our walk bein' done we'll quit the soil
Maist onie day."

No. 722.

"MERTON" (Tune).

Henry K. Oliver.

General Oliver was for twenty years the director of music and organist of the North Church in Salem, from 1828 to 1849. One Sunday in 1843, during the pastorate of the Rev. Dr. John Brazer, the hymns for the entire day, six in number, were sent before service to the director, that he might leisurely select appropriate tunes. These were all fixed upon, excepting the sixth, which was to close the afternoon service, it being Dr. Doddridge's beautiful hymn, "Ye golden lamps of heaven, farewell!"

All through the day the director could recall no tune which he thought well adapted to the words. The clergyman had got well on in his sermon in the afternoon, and the director had made no selection; as, however, he was conning the words over, more intent upon them than upon the words of the preacher, a melody floated into his mind, and taking paper and pencil, he secured it, adding the parts in score for his own use, and then giving to each singer his part on a slip. The singers were of rare excellence, both in voice and skill; and the new tune, given with earnestness and effect, took at once.

The next day General Oliver accidentally met Dr. Brazer, who inquired about the new tune, its author, and where it could be found, adding that he did not remember ever to have heard it before.

"I never did myself," replied its author; and then confessing that he had employed his time otherwise than in attending to the sermon, asked the good minister to forgive his neglect.

"Oh, yes," said Dr. Brazer, "but look a moment; have I not a right to complain that you, a member of my church, a teacher in my Sunday school, and the leader of my choir, should have set so bad an example as to be seen by the singers writing music, instead of listening to my preaching?"

"Yes, yes; I have done evil, in that view of the case," was the reply. "But the thought came suddenly, and had I not penciled it down it would have been lost; and now, being secured, it may possibly do some good in its way. I accept the reproof; but tell me, suppose that while we were leading the worship at our end of the church, and the people and their minister were joining therein, either in voice or in spirit, as they should do, some new thought which had not occurred to you during your work at the sermon in your study should suddenly suggest itself, would you not just quietly pencil it down on the margin of your notes, so that we, the people, might have the benefit of it?"

"Oh, yes," replied Dr. Brazer; "I have done that many times, and with good effect too."

"Yes, yes," was the retort; "so I have heard. Now don't you think it wrong for the minister of the parish, seated, as he is, in open sight of all the worshipers, to be seen of all scribbling marginal notes while the choir is endeavoring to lead the people in their songs of praise? Hey, Doctor, whose notes are the more sinful—yours of the margin or mine of the score? So, in the way of rebuke, let's call it an even thing, and if sin it be, let's sin no more."

A hearty laugh followed between the friends, and it was agreed that "sauce for a goose would be sauce for a gander."

"Olden-Time Music."

No. 723.

"O SACRED HEAD ONCE WOUNDED."

St. Bernard of Clairvaux

This hymn may fairly take its place among missionary hymns, for after being translated from Latin into German, and from German into English, it has again been translated from the English into many of the languages of heathen countries, and has been found useful there. Rev. Dr. Schwartz, a celebrated missionary to India, made this his dying song. He was thought to be already dead, and his fellow missionary, with several native Tamil converts, gathered at his bedside, began to sing this hymn in the Tamil tongue. While they sang the first stanza, no sign of recognition or consciousness came from the still form before them, but when they stopped at the close of the stanza, the voice they supposed to be hushed in death took up the second stanza of the hymn, and sang it through with clear and distinct utterance, and then was heard no more.

No. 724.

"BLOW YE THE TRUMPET, BLOW!"

Rarely was there ever witnessed a scene of more thrilling interest than that of the reunion of the Old and New School divisions of the Presbyterian Church, which took place in Pittsburgh in May, 1869. On the day appointed the two bodies met in their respective places, and then, having formed in the street in parallel columns, joined ranks, one of each assembly arm in arm with one of the other, and so marched to the place where the services were to be held. As the head of the column entered the church, already crowded, save the seats reserved for the delegates, the audience struck up the hymn, "Blow ye the trumpet, blow!" and when all were in their places, "All hail the power of Jesus' name!" After the reading of the Scriptures came the hymn of Watts, "Blest are the sons of peace."

The interest of the occasion culminated when Dr. Fowler, the moderator of the New School Assembly, at the close of his remarks, turned to Dr. Jacobus, the moderator of the Old School Assembly, and said: "My dear brother moderator, may we not, before I take my seat, perform a single act symbolical of the union which has taken place between the two branches of the church? Let us clasp hands!" This challenge was immediately responded to, when all joined in singing the grand old doxology of Bishop Ken, "Praise God from whom all blessings flow!" And at the conclusion of Dr. Jacobus' remarks, amid flowing tears and with swelling hearts, the thousands present joined in singing the precious hymn, written just about a century before, by that grand and tuneful Baptist minister, John Fawcett, himself a convert of George Whitefield, "Blest be the tie that binds." Little did those happy Presbyterians think or care that two of the hymns for this hour of their supreme gladness were furnished by Methodists, one by a Congregationalist, one by an Episcopalian bishop, and one by a Baptist, while their own denomination did not furnish a single one.

No. 725.

"CONVERTED TUNES."

John Newton was once an infidel and libertine, profane, and blasphemous, and yet when he had been converted and wrote the hymn:

> "How sweet the name of Jesus sounds,
> In a believer's ear,"

no one refused to sing the hymn because of the former life of its author. No one would refuse to worship in a church built upon the spot where once a whiskey distillery had stood, but would the rather rejoice at the new use to which the ground was put. Why should not the same reason justify the adoption into sacred music of a tune once used for secular purposes? Charles Wesley once stood in the open air in an English seaport town and began to sing. This was his way of gathering an audience, and his purpose was, when the people had been drawn together, to preach to them a gospel sermon. But as he sang, there came along a party of sailors, "half seas over" with their grog, and drowned the hymn with a rollicking song of their own. With characteristic quickness of wit he challenged them to return in the afternoon and he would sing them a new song to their own tune. They came at the appointed time and so did Mr. Wesley, and to their own carousing music of "Nancy Dawson" he sang a song he had in the meanwhile composed, beginning with the words:

" 'Listed into the cause of sin
Why should a good be evil?
Music alas! too long has been
Pressed to obey the devil."

Not a few of the tunes now in good and regular standing in our collections of sacred music began their careers in some opera love song, or other purely secular sphere.

A tune called "Opal" in "The Plymouth Collection" is a familiar old song accompanying the words:

"Fresh and strong the breeze is blowing."

Another in the same book called "Emerald" is a song composed by Thomas Haynes Bayly for the words:

"Shades of evening, close not o'er us."

Another in the same book called "Bdellium" was originally the air of a very indecent song, afterward used by Robert Burns to better words beginning:

"Saw ye my ain love?"

In the same book a tune called "All's Well" is adapted from a song of the sixteenth century called "Begone, Old

Care," which was itself altered from a piece called "The Queen's Jig." It became obsolete, but in 1792 was revived and became popular again, in a pantomime ballet called "William Tell," performed at "Sadler's Wells," the oldest theater in London. The tune called "Bruce," in the same book, is only a slightly changed form of an old Scotch air called "Hey tuttie, taittie," which an old tradition says was the marching song of Robert Bruce at the battle of Bannockburn in 1314. Robert Burns gave to it a fresh popularity by writing for it the ode beginning:

"Scots, wha ha'e wi' Wallace bled,
Scots, wham Bruce has often led," etc.

The tune of "Ellesdie," often used for the hymn beginning, "Jesus I my cross have taken," was at first a secular song beginning:

"Go, forget me! why should sorrow
O'er that brow a shadow fling?"

The words were written by Rev. Charles Wolfe, the same who wrote the piece entitled:

"The burial of Sir John Moore."

"Weber" is made up out of the opening chorus of the opera of "Oberon," where fairies come dancing upon the stage singing:

"Light as fairies, foot can fall,
Pace ye elves, your master's hall."

"Ganges" was an East Indian love song. "Cranbrook" an old song of the sea, the words beginning:

"Come all my jolly sailors all."

"Belmont," a simple song beginning, "My mother bids me bind my hair," and the tune "Diana," or "New Jerusalem," was an old English ballad beginning:

"O man in desperation."

The tune called "Smyrna" is an extract called "Batti Batti" from the opera of "Don Giovanni." "Herold" is the prayer of "Zampa," the opera by Herold for whom the tune is named. "Arcadia" was arranged by Thomas Hastings from the opera of "Orpheus," by Offenbach; and "Ariel" was taken in the same way by Lowell Mason from Mozart's "Magic Flute."

No. 726.

"COME TO JESUS JUST NOW."

There is in our "Gospel Hymns" a piece not in any way entitled to be called a hymn. It dignifies it too highly almost to call it a ditty. Each stanza is nothing but a four times repeated sentence. It originated in England, probably among the Methodists, but no one knows where or when. Rev. Newman Hall, an English Congregational minister, celebrated for his earnestness in all evangelistic movements, left a dinner party one evening at the town of Hull, to go out to preach to a throng who had gathered in the street. As he approached the spot someone was singing to the crowd:

"Come to Jesus, come to Jesus,
Come to Jesus just now."

Mr. Hall caught up the words and made them the theme of an earnest extemporaneous sermon. Soon afterward he repeated it in his own church to his own people, and a while later, when kept from his ordinary work by sickness, he wrote and condensed it into a little tract, and two thousand copies were printed. It met with a wonderful reception, and was called for in all directions, until at last accounts it had been translated into thirty languages and nearly four millions of copies had been printed, and the demand still goes on. So much for the casual singing of a song to a crowd gathered on the street.

No. 727.

"EMMELAR."

In the later hymn books compiled by Rev. C. S. Robinson, four tunes will be found either composed or arranged by "Emmelar." No such name appears in any list of musical composers either American or European. But if the three syllables of the word are separated, they will be found to stand for three letters of the alphabet, "M. L. R.," and these are the initials of Dr. Robinson's own daughter, whose maiden name was Mary L. Robinson. She is now the wife of Mr. Frank Gaylord, and resides with her husband in Paris, where he is engaged in evangelical work. She is credited with good musical taste, and assisted her father by the composition or arrangement of these pieces for his books. Here are the tunes to which her name is attached, "Clyde," "Armstrong," "LaMonte," and "Carolyn."

No. 728.

"I KNOW THAT MY REDEEMER LIVES AND—"

Rev. Charles Wesley.

Among the curiosities of literature, some of our well-known hymns deserve a place. Such a hymn as the one beginning,

"In the Cross of Christ I glory,"

when we find its author to have been a Unitarian, is surely deserving of such a position. So is the beautiful hymn for use at the rite of baptism by immersion,

"We come to the fountain, we stand by the wave,"

written by Rev. Geo. W. Bethune, a minister of the Dutch Reformed Church, and a non-believer in the Immersionists' view of baptism. And reversing the order, a hymn on denominational union by Rev. Benjamin Beddone, beginning,

"Let party names no more
The Christian world divide."

And here is a hymn by the great poet of Methodism, which sings in joyful confidence the pet doctrine of Calvinism and the abhorrence of every Methodist, the doctrine of "Divine Sovereignty."

"He wills that I should holy be!
What can withstand His will?
The counsel of His grace in me,
He surely shall fulfill."

No. 729.

"O HOLY GHOST, THOU FOUNT OF LIGHT."

ADAM OF ST. VICTOR.

REV. EDWARD CASWALL, Translator.

One is not likely to suspect how some of the hymns, which have within the last decade or two found acceptance in our service of song, carry us far back into the past, when all the singing was done by the priests in Latin or Greek, and the music was severely simple. This hymn as written in Latin by Adam of St. Victor was a "sequence," and "sequences" had a curious origin. The service of the old Roman Church provided for the reading of a lesson from the Epistles and another from one of the Gospels. Between the two, the officiating deacon had to pass from one part of the chancel to another, and while he was doing this the worshipers sang an "Alleluia" to give him time to make the change decorously and with dignity; and to lengthen out the time, they lengthened out the final note, until the last syllable came to be nearly interminable, and every one was heartily tired of it. So a sort of a "rhythmical prayer" was invented to be sung in this interval instead of the long drawn-out "Alleluia," and many of the priestly poets of those times composed such prayers to which the name of "sequences" was given.

No. 730.

"ETERNAL LIGHT! ETERNAL LIGHT!"

REV. THOMAS BINNEY.

The author of this hymn was a Congregational minister who for many years while pastor of a London church bore a conspicuous part in the religious life of England. Earlier in life he was pastor of a church on the Isle of Wight, and while there, as the story goes, he was walking one night when the whole sky seemed brilliant with stars shining like the eyes of God. Led by the stars looking down upon him, he thought of the eye of God, forever on him, by night as well as by day, and enshrined the thought in this hymn.

No. 731.

"HALLE" (Tune).

In an opera called "Le Nozze di Figaro," composed by Mozart, there is a song sung by a barber commencing with the words:

"Haply your Lordship may be for dancing,
I to such prancing,
Play the guitar."

It is not now known whether the music was composed by Mozart with the other parts of the opera, or was one of the popular airs of the day, introduced by him into his composition. Dr. Thomas Hastings arranged this barber's song, and set to it an evening hymn of his own, beginning:

"Now from labor and from care."

He gave to it the name of "Halle" and by this name it has ever since remained in popular use in America. In 1861, Dr. W. H. Monk again seized upon the old barber's song and arranged it for the words of Keble's hymn:

"Sun of my Soul, Thou Savior dear,"

and published it in "Hymns Ancient and Modern" under the name of "Hursley." The tune has traveled under several aliases, sometimes as "Keble," when associated with Keble's hymn, again as "Pascal," and still again as "'Stillorgan," and in some books it loses all identity and appears simply as a "Huguenot Air," but to Dr. Hastings belongs the credit of first introducing it to sacred music.

No. 732.

"NEAR THE CROSS WAS MARY WEEPING."

JACOBUS DE BENEDICTUS.

Here is a hymn which has needed a good deal of expurgation to make it worthy of a place in our Protestant hymnals. It was originally written as a song of worship of the Virgin Mary. Its author is not certainly known, but it is attributed to Jacobus de Benedictus, an Italian nobleman who lived in the thirteenth century. In addition to his true name given above, he had another by which he was as often called "Jacoponus," which meant "Big James" or "Silly James." In many of his actions he was a clown and a buffoon. On one occasion he covered himself with sticky grease and then rolled himself in feathers of various colors, and in this elegant attire appeared at the wedding of his niece. This is a specimen of his eccentricities which gave to him the name of "Silly James," but he had many sterling qualities, and he wrote many a hymn.

This hymn, if we study its history, brings us into contact with one of the fanatical crazes of the middle ages. In the eleventh century there rose a sect called "Flagellants," who proclaimed the doctrine of self whipping, as an atonement for their own sins and for the sins of others, too. The craze spread rapidly through nearly all the countries of Europe, and processions of men, women, and even children passed through the cities and villages whipping their naked backs and singing religious songs as they marched. This hymn was the one most frequently used, and it became known and popular in every corner of Europe, as sung by these processions of Flagellants.

No. 733.

"O JESUS, SWEET THE TEARS I SHED."

REV. RAY PALMER.

A curious circumstance revealed the origin of this hymn. It was floating about in the religious periodicals with simply the name "Palmer" attached as author, which was quite indefinite. At last a hymn book compiler was led to use it in his book, but was obliged to cut off a stanza to make it fit his page. This disfigurement brought the author to him, bewailing with grief the mutilation of his hymn. Apology was offered and accepted, and then Dr. Palmer confessed that the verses of this hymn were more than usually dear to him because they described a real experience he had once had, an outburst of actual tears in view of the thought of Jesus dying on the Cross.

No. 734.

"WELCOME HAPPY MORNING."

"FORTUNATUS," V. H. C.

REV. JOHN ELLERTON, TRANSLATOR.

Singing this hymn in these days, we should not forget one singer who sang it in other days and different circumstances. There lived in the town of Prague, almost five hundred years ago, a layman who became as active and able a reformer of the abuses which had crept into the Romish Church, as did Luther in Germany. He held disputations with the defenders of Rome, circulated the literature of the reformers, and endeavored to defend John Huss, the great reformer and martyr, when he was under arrest and in prison. At last his own turn came, and the fagots of the martyrs' fire piled about him, the blaze was kindled, and as it rose about him, he sang this song:

"Welcome happy morning,
Age to age shall say,
Hell to-day is vanquished,
Heaven is won to-day."

No. 735.

"HARK FROM THE TOMBS A DOLEFUL SOUND."

REV. ISAAC WATTS.

This can scarcely be called a missionary hymn, and yet it has had a great influence on American Missionary Work. A boy of fifteen years, gay and ambitious, was with a party of his cousins, who were playing jokes on him, when as another joke they began to sing this hymn, to the tune of "Bangor," for the sake of seeing what effect it would have upon him. As they sang it slowly and solemnly and without a smile, he sat silent. It pierced into his very soul, and for the first time he felt himself to be a sinner and in danger of being lost. His conversion took place soon after, and he became one of the five who met at the historical haystack in Williamstown, Massachusetts, and out of this grew the American Board of Commissioners for Foreign Missions. His name was Samuel J. Mills.

No. 736.

"MEAR" (Tune).

This tune is linked to a hymn, which in New England at least, in the olden time was always sung to its music, and to anyone whose childhood was spent there, the old tune must recall memories of those whose voices sang it then but who now sing "the New Song" in Heaven. A few years ago a little poem appeared in a Hartford, Connecticut, paper, which tells the story of this old tune so well that it is worth repeating:

"I heard the words of the preacher
As he read that psalm so dear,
Which mother sang at our cradle
To the ancient tune of Mear.

"And I felt her angel presence,
As sung were those blessed words;
My heart was with rapture filling,
As sweet as the song of birds.

"I longed for the land of summer,
Life's river, with waters clear,
For the calm, sweet eyes of mother,
Who sang the old tune of Mear.

"To-day that e'er-welcomed cadence
Of song floated back to me;
Over the paths of my childhood
It lovingly came, all free.

"I thanked the good All-Father
For this memory bright and clear;
The saintly smile of my mother,
And her low voice singing Mear.

"Ah, me! the father has rested
Many and many a year;
The mother who sang by our cradle
Has gone to a higher sphere.

"Brothers and sisters have parted;
Some live in the Better Land,
And some are waiting their summons,
Sojourners yet on life's strand.

"I feel when we meet up yonder,
Where cometh no sigh nor tear,
Our mother will softly sing us
That grand old tune of Mear."

No. 737.

"GREAT GOD, WHEN I APPROACH THY THRONE."

Rev. W. H. Bathurst.

"The story is told of a merchant whose life was once saved at the price of another man's in a shipwreck. He was aided, as the waves tossed him helpless and exhausted up against a cliff, by the outstretched hand of a longshoreman; but, even while he sank down upon the rock where he was saved, he had the unspeakable horror of beholding his rescuer swept off the foothold and instantly drowned before his eyes. He could never get over the shock; he was not crazed, he was as strong and bright as ever. But whenever he had finished his business errand, he would go up to the salesman of whom he bought his goods, and, taking his hand, would say gently, "A man died for me!" He never omitted this act; some thought him queer, but he always came back to remove his hat, put out his hand, and almost whisper, "A man died for me." His eyes would be moist, his tones would be tremulous, but he was not crazy—only reverent and grateful—as he said his quiet little sentence, "A man died for me."

No. 738.

"HELMSLEY" (Tune).

This tune was an old English love song sung by Mistress Anne Catley at "Sadler's Wells," the oldest theater in London, in a play called "The Golden Pippin" to the words:

"Guardian Angels now protect me
Send me back the youth I love."

It was also used as a dancing tune, and became a common street ballad. Here Thomas Olivers, the famous converted shoemaker, heard it. Like all the Methodist preachers of that day, he was on the watch for good music for the church, and hearing this song on the street, he seized upon its melody and arranged it into this tune, which was at first known by the name of "Olivers" but was afterward called "Helmsley."

No. 739.

"MONSON" (Tune).

Here is an instance of a tune composed by a son for a hymn written by his mother. Rev. S. R. Brown was one of the first American Missionaries to Japan. He was the son of Mrs. Phoebe H. Brown, who wrote the hymn beginning, "I love to steal awhile away," and this tune was composed for these words and the name given to it of the town in Massachusetts in which his mother lived. After his mother's death, he wrote of her this tribute: "To her I owe all I am, and if I have done any good in the world, to her under God it is due. She seems even now to have me in her hands, holding me up for work for Christ, and His cause, with a grasp I can feel."

No. 740.

"O LORD THY WORK REVIVE."

MRS. PHOEBE H. BROWN.

Long before there was any foreign missionary society in America, through which monies could be contributed for that cause, a poor woman in Massachusetts became interested in the heathen, and although her life was a constant struggle with poverty, she used to save small sums of money which she was in the habit of sending to English missionaries in Africa and India, through a Christian merchant in Philadelphia, who had ships sailing to those countries. It is not strange that the son of such a mother should enter the mission field, and one of the earliest missionaries to Japan was Rev. S. R. Brown, the only son of this poor Massachusetts woman. Lovers of hymns know her well as the author of the hymn beginning:

"I love to steal awhile away
From every cumbering care."

And here is another of her hymns, written for use when Christians meet to pray for an advancement of Christ's cause both at home and abroad.[1]

No. 741.

"O THOU MY SOUL FORGET NO MORE."

KRISHNU PAL.

In the year 1781 John Thomas, a young Englishman of twenty-four years listened to a sermon in an English

[1] For this son's tribute to his mother see No. 739.

church preached by Dr. Samuel Stennett, the same who wrote our hymn, "Majestic sweetness sits enthroned." The text was the words of Christ in John 6:27: "Labor not for the meat which perisheth, but for that meat which endureth unto everlasting life," etc. The result of that sermon was the young man's conversion. He had just finished his studies as a physician and had secured an appointment as a naval surgeon, and been assigned to an East Indiaman bound for Bengal. On landing in Calcutta, he longed for Christian companionship, and advertised in the *India Gazette,* November 1, 1783. No missionary had yet told the story of the Cross in India, and his advertisement brought no response. This young man was the first Englishman to study the Hindoo language for the purpose of preaching the gospel in it. Later he returned to England and was the first appointed missionary to India, the celebrated Carey going with him as his assistant. Together these men spent years in work among the natives without seeing a single convert. At the end of that time a Hindoo carpenter while at work fell and broke his arm. Dr. Thomas was called to set the broken limb, and when he had done this he told the Gospel story to the crowd that had assembled. The carpenter whom he had helped heard the story and wept as he heard it, and soon he came to the missionaries to hear more about it. He was converted, renounced his caste, and was baptized in the Ganges, becoming thus the first convert to Christianity in the mission. He became an ardent student, wrote tracts for his people, and composed several hymns. This one has been translated for our use into English by Dr. Marshmann and is the only hymn in our English collections written by a Hindoo.

No. 742.

"HAIL, TRANQUIL HOUR OF CLOSING DAY!"

REV. LEONARD BACON.

In 1845, the Congregational Churches of Connecticut appointed a committee to compile for their use a new hymnal. The author of this hymn, who was one of that committee, wanted to include in the collection the hymn of Phoebe H. Brown beginning "I love to steal awhile away," but Rev. Dr. Nettleton, in whose "Village Hymns" that hymn first appeared and who owned the copyright, refused permission for its use. So Dr. Bacon wrote this hymn to take its place, and some people have thought that he imitated Mrs. Brown's work closely enough to be entitled to the name of plagiarist.

No. 743.

SIR ARTHUR S. SULLIVAN.

It is a pleasant thing when we become familiar with the name of someone who ministers by his music or his writings to our week-day pleasure, to find that the same one is in sympathy with us in our religious moods as well. I remember with what pleasure I once learned that a western gentleman famous for the dry drollery of his stories and lectures, could make one cry as well as laugh, and that he preached as good sermons as he wrote jokes. And so I think we shall esteem all the more highly the man who composed in lighter vein, the music of "Pinafore," and "Patience," when we find him also to be the writer of some of the sweetest of our sacred songs.

No. 744.

"I LAY MY SINS ON JESUS."
"I WAS A WANDERING SHEEP."

Rev. Horatius Bonar.

The author of these hymns was in the habit of holding special Sabbath School Services for the children, and he wrote for each such service a special hymn, the singing of which was followed by a short address. The hymns above named were some of those written for these children's services.

No. 745.

"THE HEAVENS DECLARE THY GLORY LORD."

Rev. Isaac Watts.

Dr. C. S. Robinson relates the following incident:

"Once, as I entered the observatory of Harvard College, at the close of day, a friend who had led me there asked that I might be shown the new instrument that had just been introduced. The professor replied, courteously, "Yes; I think there may be time enough yet for him to see a star if you will find one."

My companion "found one" by looking in a worn little book of astronomical tables lying there on the desk, and replied quietly, "There is one at 5:20." So in a hurried instant, the covering was stripped off from the great brass tube, and prone upon his back, under the eyepiece, lay the enthusiastic professor. While my friend stood by with what seemed a tack hammer in his hand, I noticed that he kept his eyes on a tall chronometer clock near us. Suddenly two sounds broke the impressive stillness; we had been waiting for the star. One was the word "there" spoken by the professor, the other was the tap of the hammer on the stone top of the table by my companion. Both occurred at the same instant—the same particle of the instant—they were positively simultaneous. But the man who spoke the word could not see the clock; he was looking at the star that came swinging along till it touched the spiderweb line in his instrument; and the other man who struck the hammerstroke could not see the star; he was looking at the second-hand on the dial plate. When the index in its simplicity of regular duty marked twenty minutes after five there fell the click on the stone; and then, too, there came on in the heavens, millions of miles away, one of God's stars, having no speech, but rolling in on time, as he bade it ages ago. Then I was invited to look in and see the world of light and beauty as it swept the next fiber in the tube. But afterward I went curiously to the book and found that it had been published ten years before, and that its calculations ran far away into the future, and that it had been based on calculations a thousand years old. And God's fidelity to the covenant of nature, here now almost three thousand years after David had made the nineteenth Psalm, had brought the glorious creature of the sky into the field of Harvard College's instrument just as that patient clock reached the second needed for the truth of the ancient prediction. Need I say that those two professors almost wondered (so used to such things were they) at the awestruck devotion, the hushed reverence, with which I left the room.

No. 746.

"THERE IS A CITY GREAT AND STRONG."

REV. DENNIS WORTMAN. 1835.

This hymn is simply an extract from a long poem entitled "Reliques of the Christ" written by a man who did not know before that he could write poetry at all. "Suffering," he says, "from nervous prostration and unable to sleep, the beginning of this poem came to me one night in November, 1871." The first three stanzas were thought out then, or rather came to him almost involuntarily, and more came the same way the next morning, and so for seventeen years, at odd moments, when the inspiration seized him, he worked away at the idea he had conceived. When published, the book became popular and ranks among the best productions of modern times.

No. 747.

"LORD JESUS THINK OF ME."

SYNESIUS.

It was Simon, "a man of Cyrene," (Matthew 27:32) who was compelled to bear the cross upon which Christ was crucified. Among those who were scattered abroad after Stephen was killed were some who were men of Cyrene. And in the church at Antioch there was a leader named "Lucius of Cyrene." This Cyrene was the principal city of Northern Africa, and its citizens bore frequent part in the affairs of the early church. About 400 years after Christ there came into notice there a philosopher named Synesius, who bore the unique distinction of being able to trace his lineage back without a missing link through seventeen centuries. Of this Gibbon, the historian, took notice and said it was unequalled in the history of mankind. He was a pagan, but he married a Christian wife, and under her influence became a semi-Christian (if such a thing can be) himself. His ability and character were such that he was by and by made a bishop of the Church. He wrote some poetry, and from one of his odes this hymn has been translated by Rev. A. W. Chatfield, a vicar of the Church of England.

No. 748.

"TAKE MY LIFE AND LET IT BE."

MISS F. R. HAVERGAL.

This hymn was written in 1874, and four years later, in 1878, the author wrote a letter which is a fine commentary on one of its stanzas. She says, "The Lord has shown me another little step, and of course I have taken it with extreme delight. 'Take my silver and my gold,' now means shipping off all my ornaments (including a jewel cabinet which is really fit for a countess) to the Church Missionary House, where they will be accepted and disposed of for me. I retain only a brooch or two for daily wear, which are memorials of my dear parents; also a locket with the only portrait I have of my niece in heaven. But these I redeem so that the whole value goes to the Church Missionary Society. I had no idea I had such a jeweler's shop; nearly fifty articles are being packed off. I don't think I need tell you I never packed a box with such pleasure."

No. 749.

"THE SANDS OF TIME ARE SINKING."

"OH, CHRIST, HE IS THE FOUNTAIN."

MRS. ANNE ROSS COUSIN.

Samuel Rutherford was one of the heroic old Scotch Covenanters of whom the world was not worthy. Settled as the minister of a little church in a secluded valley in the South of Scotland in a village called Anwoth, he made himself known and his influence felt all over England and Scotland and across the channel on the Continent. By and by the Established Church began to persecute him. They banished him from the little town he loved, and burned the books he had written, and at last cited him to appear before Parliament on a charge of treason. He was ill when the summons came and soon was dying. He sent back word to his persecutors, "I am summoned before a higher court; that first summons I behoove to answer; and ere a few days arrive, I shall be where few kings and great folks come."

A few days later, as the sun was sinking, a friend said to him, "What think ye now of Christ?" And the answer came, "O, that all my brethren in the land may know what a Master I have served, and what peace I have this day! I shall sleep in Christ, and when I awake I shall be satisfied with His likeness. This night shall close the door, and put my anchor within the veil; and I shall go away in a sleep by five of the clock in the morning. Glory! glory to my Creator and Redeemer forever! I shall live and adore Him. Oh, for arms to embrace Him. Oh, for a well-tuned harp! Glory! glory dwelleth in Immanuel's land."

He died at the time he predicted. That was two hundred years ago and more, but within the last fifty years a Scotch lady, reading his biography, and coming upon these last words, wove them into a poem of nineteen stanzas, from which have been culled these two hymns. Some of the old Covenanter's earlier sayings, but more especially these dying words, "Glory, glory dwelleth in Immanuel's land," she enshrined in her poem.

No. 750.

"THOUGH NOW THE NATIONS SIT BENEATH."

This hymn has passed through more metamorphoses than a butterfly. About the year 1800 there was a hymn book published in England which contained it in its original form, and which assigned its authorship to Sarah Slinn. Who this lady was, when or where she was born, where she lived or when or where she died, has never been ascertained. This once she comes into public notice, and immediately retires into obscurity. Some years later Leonard Bacon, a theological student at Andover, altered the hymn, leaving out parts and adding others, and republished it. A few years later Rev. Asahel Nettleton revised it again and inserted it in a book he compiled. The compilers of a new hymn book a few years later liked it well enough to use it, but changed it again, and later still Leonard Bacon, by this time a pastor in active service, revised it once more, and included it in still another hymn book. By this time, as may well be imagined, there was not much left of Sarah Slinn, only a distant resemblance to her hymn in two lines, and it usually stands accredited in the books to Leonard Bacon, who was the first and the last "tinker" who tried to mend her verses.

No. 751.

"LOVE DIVINE ALL LOVE EXCELLING."

REV. CHARLES WESLEY.

"Come unto Me all ye that labor and are heavy-laden, and I will give you rest. Take My yoke upon you and learn of Me for I am meek and lowly in heart; and ye shall find rest to your souls" (Matthew, 11:28,29). Did you ever notice that these words of Christ describe two different kinds of rest? In one He offers to give to the heavy-laden who come to Him, in the other one that they shall find for themselves who take His yoke upon them and learn of Him. Charles Wesley had made this discovery, and he embodied it in the second stanza of this hymn, the fourth line of which he wrote, "Let us find that second rest." But some hymn tinker who had not made the discovery spoiled the force of Wesley's allusion by changing the line to read, "Let us find the promised rest."

C. S. Robinson.

No. 752.

"O, GOD OF ABRAHAM EVER SURE."

Rev. Leonard Bacon.

In 1845, the Congregational Churches of Connecticut appointed a committee to prepare for their use a new hymnal. The author of this hymn, who was one of this committee, desired to use in the collection the hymn of Mrs. A. B. Hyde, beginning "Dear Savior, if these lambs should stray." This hymn first appeared in the "Village Hymns" of Dr. Nettleton, and he owned the copyright. Dr. Bacon asked permission to copy the hymn into the new collection and was refused(so he set to work to make a subsitute, and this is the result. Some people have been ungracious enough to say that his admiration for Mrs. Hyde's hymn led him to imitate it in his own too closely to warrant any claim to originality on his part.

No. 753.

"YE SERVANTS OF GOD, YOUR MASTER PROCLAIM."

Rev. Charles Wesley.

The warrant and the encouragement for Christian Missions are found in the last words of Christ to His disciples, as they are given by Matthew and Mark. "Go ye into all the world and preach the gospel to every creature."

"All power is given unto Me in heaven and in earth,"

"Lo I am with you alway even unto the end of the world."

In the year 1744 England was at war with France, and her people were in great fear of an invasion of her shores to dethrone her reigning king, George II, and restore to the throne the House of Stuart. In the general excitement, the Methodists were accused of being secret friends of France and of working in her interest. Their meetings were broken up by mobs, their preachers were impressed into the army, and even the Wesleys were placed under arrest. In the midst of these troublous times, the great Methodist leaders published a little pamphlet of hymns for the encouragement of their followers, and to draw from the very persecutions through which they were passing strength to be faithful to the cause they had espoused. This little pamphlet was entitled "Hymns for Times of Trouble and Persecution." This hymn was one of the number it contained, and the special use for which it was intended is set forth in its heading, "To be sung in a Tumult." It embodies the words of Christ given above, and is therefore a fitting hymn with which to begin a missionary meeting.

No. 754.

"SHINE, MIGHTY GOD, ON ZION SHINE."

Rev. Isaac Watts, altered by Joel Barlow.

This is a paraphrase of the sixty-seventh Psalm. The title given to this Psalm in the Bible is "A prayer for the enlargement of God's Kingdom, to the joy of the people and the increase of God's blessings."

This designates it as an appropriate missionary hymn. Dr. Watts gave to it, however, a somewhat narrow scope and applied it to the British Nation. He wrote the first line "Shine, Mighty God! on Britain Shine," and in the third stanza he wrote the last two lines:

"While British tongues exalt His praise,
And British hearts rejoice."

In this form the hymn came to this country, and up to the time of the American Revolution it was so sung in American churches. It was this sort of a hymn book that was in use in the New Jersey church near which there was a battle between the British and the Continentals. It is said that the minister of the church was encouraging the boys who were fighting, when their stock of paper for gun wads gave out. As soon as he knew the situation, he ran into the meeting house and soon came rushing out again with his arms full of hymn books which he quickly distributed among the soldiers shouting, "Give 'em Watts, boys! give 'em Watts." At the end of the war, the churches thought these local allusions in the hymns no longer appropriate, and so they engaged the services of Joel Barlow, a Connecticut lawyer and poet, who had been an army chaplain through the war and had written many a stirring patriotic song for the soldiers' use, to revise these hymns and take the "British" out of them. His work was exceptionally happy in the case of this Psalm, for he not only restored it to the original sentiment of the Poet of Israel, but gave to us in it for these later days an excellent missionary song.

No. 755.

"NOW LET OUR SOULS ON WINGS SUBLIME."

REV. THOMAS GIBBONS, 1720—1785.

Dr. Gibbons was one of the industrious workers of his times, adding to the ordinary duties of a pastor the work of teaching logic, metaphysics, ethics and rhetoric at an academy, delivering weekly lectures, writing books on theology, and adding to all of these frequent attempts at poetry. Like many other preachers of his day he often closed his sermons with a hymn composed for that especial purpose, and this hymn was given at the end of a sermon from the text, "Then shall the dust return to the earth as it was, and the spirit shall return unto God who gave it." Ecclesiastes, 12:7.

No. 756.

"NOT ALL THE BLOOD OF BEASTS."

ISAAC WATTS

When Henry Obookiah, the Sandwich Island heathen boy, who came to this country and was educated here, asked how it could be that Jesus being only one person could make atonement by his death for everyone—so many, his teacher was at a loss for a moment how to make it plain to him; then she loosed from the fringe of her dress a handful of little beads, and placed them in one of the boy's hands, and then suddenly drew off her diamond ring, and placed it in his other hand, and asked him which was the most valuable. Heathen though he was, he caught the idea in an instant that Watts so aptly puts into the stanza:

"But Christ the heavenly Lamb
Takes all our sins away,
A sacrifice of Nobler Name,
And richer blood than they."

No. 757.

"COME, THOU SOUL TRANSFORMING SPIRIT."

REV. JONATHAN EVANS, 1748—1809.

The author of this hymn worked in a ribbon factory until he was twenty-one years of age; he had up to that time received no religious instruction, and was a companion of the degraded and profligate. When twenty-eight years of age he was converted and began at once to work for Christ. He remained a business man all his life but soon began to preach and to gather neglected children together for religious instruction. He fitted up a boathouse on the bank of a canal as a place for religious meetings, and this soon grew into a chapel, where he was soon installed as pastor. He was something of a doctor also and attended to the bodily ailments of his people as well as to their spiritual troubles.

No. 758.

"ST. ANNE" (Tune).

There is a great deal said as to the right of any editor to alter the words of a hymn from those originally used by its author, but right or wrong, it is so often done that very few hymns stand now in our collections as they were first written. It is perhaps not as generally known, or at least it is not so often referred to, that the music of our tunes has been as often tampered with as the words that are sung to them. This tune called "St. Anne," written now almost two hundred years ago (1708) by the organist of Westminster Chapel, and named in honor of the Church of St. Anne at Westminster, is an instance of this tune-tinkering proclivity. In his "Studies of Worship Music," Dr. Curwen gives seven different forms in which he has found the tune in recent English Collections, and the tune in "*Laudes Domini*" differs from them all. In the year 1872, the Prince of Wales recovered from a severe illness and a celebration was held in the Crystal Palace at London, commemorating his safe recovery. For this festival Sir Arthur Sullivan composed an elaborate Te Deum, in the course of which he introduced the music of this tune.

No. 759.

"FREE FROM THE LAW, O HAPPY CONDITION."

P. P. Bliss.

"YET THERE IS ROOM! THE LAMB'S BRIGHT HALL OF SONG."

Horatius Bonar.

Mr. W. J. Orsman is an evangelist who has earned the name of "The Apostle of the Costermongers," in one of the lowest parts of London. He uses bands of singers who sing Gospel songs on the street corners and in open spaces, where crowds can be gathered. One Sunday afternoon Mr. Orsman was sent for to visit a dying man in "Wilderness Row," who had been first led into the gospel meetings by the singing of these songs, and afterward had been converted. The sick man spoke of the help these gospel songs had been to him and said, "Oh, if I could only hear them once more before I die." Mr. Orsman's band of singers was at that moment singing on the street not far away, and they were sent for to come to the house. They stood outside on the pavement under the window where the man lay dying, like serenaders, and softly sang the pieces he had asked for, while he listened and smiled at the words which had to him such deep meaning then.

No. 760.

"MY GOD, MY FATHER, WHILE I STRAY."

Miss Charlotte Elliott.

There is a sweet little story told of an English choir boy who had been sick with scarlet fever, and when the fever had gone had not strength enough left to recover. One Sunday evening his bed had been drawn close to the open window, so that he might see the people as they gathered for vesper service. He heard the bells as they rang, and when they had stopped he heard the sound of the organ in the church where he had been used to sing, and then it stopped, and he lay with closed eyes for a while and then he heard the organ again and he knew the people were coming out of the church, and soon he heard the sound of footsteps on the gravel walk up to the house where he was.

"Lift me up, mother," he whispered. "The choir boys are coming, I can hear them. Wave my handkerchief to them, mother."

The tramping of the feet stopped under his window, and a boy's voice said, "We want to sing to Claude."

"Let them sing, mother; let me hear them just once more." And so the mother nodded permission from the window, and gathered there in the glow of the sunset the choir boys sang to their sick companion:

> "My God, my Father, while I stray
> Far from my home, in life's rough way,
> Oh, teach me from my heart to say,
> Thy will be done!"

and as they sang, the dying boy raised his voice too, and with what strength he could command, he joined them as they sang:

> "If Thou shouldst call me to resign
> What most I prize, it ne'er was mine,
> I only yield Thee what is Thine,
> Thy will be done."

When the hymn was finished the choir boys walked quietly away and Claude whispered to his mother, "Mother, write over my grave, 'Thy will be done.' " And so he died.

No. 761.

"THERE IS A HAPPY LAND."

ANDREW YOUNG.

A college student in Virginia, somewhat proud of his attainments, thought to himself that if ever he became a Christian it would be through some eloquent sermon by some distinguished pulpit orator. On one occasion he was hunting deer, when the sound of a woman's voice singing caught his ear. Following it, he soon came to a log cabin in the mountains, beside which an old negro woman was busy washing clothes, and singing as she worked. As he came nearer he noticed that she was blind as well as old, and so she did not notice that she had a listener to her song. As she bent over her tub, she would sing softly to herself the words:

"There is a happy land,
Far, far away,"

and now and then she would stop her work and straighten up, and turning her sightless eyes towards the sky, would change the tune and sing at the top of her voice until the whole woods seemed full of the song:

"There is a land of pure delight
Where saints immortal dwell,
Infinite day excludes the night
And pleasures banish pain."

After a while the young man made his presence known and said to her, "Auntie, I see you are blind."

"No, Massa, I is not blind, I can't see you, nor dese trees and rocks, nor dese yer mountains, but I can see into de kingdom, I can see de 'Happy land, far, far away.' "

The student proud of his education and attainments was taught a lesson. He went away silent and thoughtful, and afterward said that it was not any eloquent sermon that brought him to Christ but the forest song of the happy negro woman.

No. 762.

"O LOVE THAT WILL NOT LET ME GO."

REV. GEORGE MATHESON.

"Written," the author says, "in the Manse of Innellan one summer evening in 1882. It was composed with extreme rapidity, and I felt myself rather in the position of one being dictated to, than of an original artist. I was suffering from extreme mental distress, and the hymn was the fruit of pain." Innellan was the place in Argylshire, Scotland, where the author was the minister. He became blind in boyhood, but in spite of this he graduated with honors, and became a useful minister.

No. 763.

"WHEN I SURVEY THE WONDROUS CROSS."

ISAAC WATTS.

"IN THE CROSS OF CHRIST I GLORY."

J. BOWRING.

A celebrated French infidel once told the brilliant French statesman Talleyrand of his chagrin at his lack of success in devising a scheme which should supersede Christianity. He had endeavored to bring into vogue a system of benevolence and religion based on rationalism, but had not been able to produce a system that people would accept. "What shall I do?" asked he of Talleyrand.

"I hardly know," was the reply, "what you can do? Still," said he, after a moment's pause, and with a smile, "there is one plan you might try."

"What is it?" eagerly asked the other.

"I recommend to you," said Talleyrand, "that you be crucified for mankind, and rise again the third day." The reply came like a flash of lightning, and the infidel reformer stood for a moment awed by the stupendous fact suggested to him.

C. S. Robinson.

No. 764.

"JAPHET" (Tune).

This tune first appeared in Robinson's "*Laudes Domini*" in 1884. It is an arrangement of the music in Rubinstein's "Song of the Children of Japhet" in "The Tower of Babel," and takes its name from this. The arrangement is by Mr. Charles Fitzsimmons, organist of the Madison Avenue Presbyterian Church, New York.

No. 765.

"ELLERTON" (Tune).

E. J. Hopkins.

This was composed for the hymn beginning:

"Savior, again to Thy dear Name we raise."

by John Ellerton, for whom the tune is named. This tune is now usually printed with four parts, but as originally written and used, it had a common melody running through it all, but the harmonies were changed for each stanza of the hymn.

No. 766.

"O LOVE, WHO FORMEDST ME TO WEAR."

JOHANN SCHEFFLER.

C. WINKWORTH, Translator.

In 1722, a German missionary in Madras sang this hymn, and was so delighted with it, that he wished his native scholars to share it with him. He began to work upon a Malabar rendering of it the same evening, and did not rest until he had finished it, two hours after midnight. His version met with such success that he translated more than a hundred hymns from the German into the native tongue, and they are still sung in Southern India.

C. S. ROBINSON.

No. 767.

"SOMETIMES A LIGHT SURPRISES."

WILLIAM COWPER.

It is sometimes of interest to know the source from which a poet draws his inspiration. In the margin of the "Olney Hymns" where this hymn first appeared Cowper puts a reference to let us know that the phrase in the last two lines of the second stanza:

"Let the unknown to-morrow
Bring with it what it may."

was taken from Matthew 6: 34, "Take, therefore, no thought for the morrow, for the morrow shall take thought for the things of itself, sufficient unto the day is the evil thereof," and that the thought of the first lines of the last stanza, come from the prophecy of Habakuk, 3: 17-18: "Although the fig tree shall not blossom," etc.

No. 768.

"AND ARE WE YET ALIVE?"

REV. CHARLES WESLEY.

The author's title to this hymn was "At the Meeting of Friends," and Methodists have honored it, by using it almost without exception as the opening hymn at the annual meetings of their Conference.

Rev. Dr. Thomas H. Stockton of Philadelphia, when near death, had lingered on beyond what any of his friends had thought it possible for him to do. He had fallen into a sleep from which none of those near him expected he would awake on earth, when suddenly he roused himself and seeing that he was still in the flesh, he repeated the first stanza of this hymn.

No. 769.

"AND CANST THOU, SINNER, SLIGHT."

MRS. ABIGAIL B. HYDE.

It was at the house of Rev. Lavius Hyde, in Ellington, Connecticut, that Mrs. Phœbe Brown was asked by the lady who was her next-door neighbor, why she walked along the roadside in the twilight, until near her house, and then went back again. This was the discourteous question which drew the poetic answer from Mrs. Brown, which has become almost a classic among us:

"I love to steal awhile away
From little ones and care,
And spend the hours of setting day
In gratitude and prayer."

The wife of the minister was the friend of the poor painter's wife who wrote the verse and she herself wrote several hymns. This one was sent to Rev. Ashael Nettleton, and was often used by him in revival services in the New England States.

No. 770.

"A PILGRIM THROUGH THIS LONELY WORLD."

SIR EDWARD DENNY, 1796.

John Gambold, Bishop of the Moravian Church in England, and a hymn writer of some repute, wrote a poem entitled "John's Description of Jesus," in which occurs this passage:

"Cheerful He was to us!
But let me tell you, sons, He was within
A pensive man, and always had a load
upon His spirits."

These lines are placed at the head of Sir Edward Denny's hymn in the book in which it first appeared, and the hymn is evidently based upon the quotation.

No. 771.

"ACQUAINT THYSELF QUICKLY, O SINNER, WITH GOD."

WILLIAM KNOX, 1789-1825.

A farmer's son in Scotland, the tenant of fertile farms under a Scottish Duke, became dissipated, with the usual result of loss of property and place. Then he drifted to

Edinburgh, and obtained employment by writing for the newspapers of that city. Then he began to write a certain style of poetry in pensive vein, and these pieces he collected into little books and published them. This hymn is one of these, and it is based on the words of Eliphaz, the Temanite, one of Job's "Miserable Comforters" as they are found in Job, 22: 21, 27, and 28: "Acquaint now thyself with him, and be at peace. Thereby good shall come to thee. Thou shalt make thy prayer unto him, and he shall hear thee and thou shalt pay thy vows. Thou shalt also decree a thing and it shall be established unto thee, and the light shall shine upon thy ways."

No. 772.

"AWAKE, MY SOUL, AND WITH THE SUN."

"GLORY TO THEE, MY GOD, THIS NIGHT."

THOMAS KEN.

Those who are troubled with insomnia will find a fellow sufferer in the author of our splendid doxology, and will appreciate some of his verses which he called "Anodynes." They were composed during the night hours when sleep forsook him, and sometimes in hours of pain by day. One of these reads:

"Pain keeps me walking in the night;
 I longing lie for morning light;
Methinks the sluggish sun
 Forgets he this day's course must run.
O heavenly torch! Why this delay
 In giving us our wonted day?
I feel my watch, I tell my clock,
 I hear each crowing of the cock;

Even Egypt, when three days
The heavens withheld the solar rays
And all in thickest darkness dwelt,
Night more affecting never felt."

The line "I feel my watch" is explained by the fact that the sleepless bishop had a watch so constructed that he could by his fingers "discern the time to half a quarter of an hour." This watch still exists and is preserved as a precious relic. Another of his "Anodynes" is as follows:

"As in the night I restless lie,
I the watch-candle keep in eye;
The innocent I often blame
For the slow wasting of its flame.
My curtain oft I draw away,
Eager to catch the morning ray;
But when the morning gilds the skies,
The morning no relief supplies."

Ken's morning hymn beginning "Awake my soul and with the sun" was a favorite with the author himself, and it is said that he often sang it himself to the accompaniment of his lute, when he rose from his bed.

No. 773.

"PRECIOUS PROMISE GOD HATH GIVEN."

NATHANIEL NILES, 1835.

The author of this hymn was a lawyer doing business in New York City, and residing in Morristown, New Jersey. He wrote it on the margin of a newspaper in the railway car between his home and his office.

No. 774.

"FAIREST LORD JESUS! RULER OF ALL NATIONS."

Richard Storrs Willis is neither the author nor the translator, but may be called the discoverer of this hymn. It comes from Westphalia, and it with the melody attached called the "Crusaders' Hymn" was wont to be sung according to tradition by German Knights of the Crusade, in the twelfth century while marching to Jerusalem. The popularity of both words and music in Germany may be inferred from the statement made by Mr. Willis that a few years ago in a missionary meeting in Germany, three voices began the singing of it, but before they had proceeded far hundreds had joined them in the singing.

No. 775.

"SOW IN THE MORN THY SEED."

James Montgomery.

Every Whitsunday (Seventh Sunday after Easter) all the Sunday schools in the town of Sheffield, England, where Montgomery lived were accustomed to meet in one of the public squares of the city and exchange greetings and sing together. For a quarter of a century, Mr. Montgomery composed a new hymn each year for the use of these meetings. This was the hymn written for the year 1832. As many as twenty thousand children sometimes joined in these open-air services.

No. 776.

"PEACE, DOUBTING HEART! MY GOD'S I AM."

REV. CHARLES WESLEY.

In 1826 an English mail boat named the *Maria* in the West India Ocean was within sight of the Island of Antigua, with a number of missionaries with their families on board, when a terrible storm arose; the boat was wrecked, and all were lost except one lady, the wife of one of the missionaries. She tells the story that when the storm arose and consternation spread among the passengers and crew, a little boy, the son of one of the missionaries, commenced singing a stanza of this hymn:

"When passing through the watery deep,
I ask in faith His promised aid,
The waves an awful distance keep
And shrink from my devoted head;
Fearless their violence I dare,
They cannot harm for God is there!"

and did much by his singing to calm the fears of the terror-stricken people.

No. 777.

"LIGHT OF THE LONELY PILGRIM'S HEART."

EDWARD DENNY, 1796.

Sir Edward Denny was an Irish Baron, a member of the denomination known as "Brethren." He was a firm believer in the second coming of Christ and wrote this hymn as a prayer for His speedy appearance, giving to it the title, "The Heart Watching for the Morning." The sense in which we usually use the hymn is different from the one he had in mind when he wrote it.

No. 778.

"SHALL WE GATHER AT THE RIVER."

REV. ROBERT LOWRY.

This hymn was written on a sultry afternoon in July, 1864, in the author's study in Elliott Place in Brooklyn, New York, and when he had written the hymn, he sat down at his parlor organ and composed the tune for it, which has ever since been used with it.

No. 779.

"SERVANT OF GOD, WELL DONE! REST FROM . . ."

JAMES MONTGOMERY.

A Methodist minister by the name of Thomas Taylor, preaching one Sunday in an English town declared that he hoped to die an old soldier of Jesus Christ, with his sword in his hand. Although then in apparently good health, he died the next day, and James Montgomery wrote this hymn to his memory.

No. 780.

"THE CHURCH'S ONE FOUNDATION."

REV. S. J. STONE.

"When the Pan Angelican Synod some few years ago was held in St. Paul's in London, the whole body of dignitaries, belonging to the whole English Establishment, entered the cathedral in the presence of an immense congregation, which rose to receive the procession, singing:

"The Church's one Foundation is Jesus Christ the Lord."
ROBINSON.

No. 781.

"THE VOICE OF FREE GRACE CRIES, ESCAPE TO THE MOUNTAIN."

REV. RICHARD BURDSALL.

The author of this hymn was one day about the year 1796, passing a public house, or what we should in these days call a barroom, and as he passed he overheard a song, the air of which pleased his fancy so much that, though no poet and having never tried to be, he wrote these words to fit the barroom melody, and they have poetry enough in them to have floated them along to our time, and religion enough to have kept them in our church hymn books.

No. 782.

"PRAISE TO THE HOLIEST IN THE HEIGHT."

REV. JOHN H. NEWMAN.

We have several hymns that were written as parts of novels, and here is one that occurs in a drama, or to be precise a dramatic poem, by Cardinal Newman. The poem is entitled, "The Dream of Gerontius." In it Gerontius dies and holds a dialogue with an angel, hears choirs of angels sing, and this hymn he hears in his dream, sung by the "Fifth Choir of Angelicals."

No. 783.

"LORD, A LITTLE BAND AND LOWLY."

MRS. M. E. SHELLY.

"At a Sunday school meeting in Manchester, the Rev. John Curwen one evening gave a lecture on singing. He sang a very pretty and simple tune, to which he said he had no suitable words, and wished that someone would write a hymn to it. I wrote these verses and gave them to him after the close of the meeting." So says the author of the hymn. The tune which gave rise to the hymn was a German one, and has attained great popularity in English Sunday school collections under the name of "Glover."

No. 784.

"LORD, I KNOW THY GRACE IS NIGH ME."

REV. H. D. GANSE.

While living in New York, Dr. Ganse was called to visit a family in Freehold, New Jersey, which was in affliction. While there, at night as he crossed the threshold of his bedroom the first couplet of this hymn ran through his mind, unannounced. It was midwinter in a farmhouse and his room had no fire, so he composed the remainder of the hymn in bed, in the darkness, and completed it as he says "with no little feeling" before he slept.

No. 785.

"ON JORDAN'S STORMY BANKS I STAND."

REV. SAMUEL STENNETT.

"I'll tell you what, I heard singin' to-night that made me wish I was in heaven, or good enough to go there," said an old backwoodsman to his wife, as, entering their log hut, he sat down to his evening meal.

"Where did you hear it?" she asked.

"At our neighbor's up yonder. They must feel something I don't know about, or they couldn't sing so."

"When they first came here," said his wife, "I thought they were proud and stiff; but they were real good neighbors, and I heard after they were good church folks too."

"Well," said he, "I mean to go to church tomorrow, and see if I can't hear some singin' like that."

The singer knew that her neighbors were ignorant, rough, and unbelieving, nearing the decline of life, and unwilling to be approached on the subject of religion. One glorious summer evening, as the sun was going down, the lady seated herself at the window, and involuntarily tuned her voice to sing. When near the close of the hymn, she cast her eyes to the field where her neighbor was at work, and saw that he was listening intently. Instantly the thought flashed into her mind, "Oh, if I could raise that poor man to think of heaven." She closed her refrain, and then commenced:

"On Jordan's stormy banks I stand,"

singing it "with the spirit and the understanding also." And as she sang, the old man listened, almost spellbound. The singer wished to glorify God by leading one of His creatures to think of Him. "I will sing God's praises whenever he can hear me, and perhaps he may be led to praise the Lord himself," was her resolve. The next Lord's day the old man was at church. This cheered the lady, and she said, "I will sing whenever he comes." Ere another week was closed he was at work again. This time she sang:

"Just as I am, without one plea,
But that Thy blood was shed for me."

Slowly but distinctly she sang, that he might take in the full meaning of the words, and feeling their sweet pathos in her inmost soul she sang the hymn. The listener shook his head, and rubbed his hand quickly over his eyes. The next Lord's day evening he was among the people of God, earnestly inquiring the way of salvation. Being thus successful in bringing the husband in the way of life, the singer next tried to draw the wife, and so one day invited her into the parlor to hear her piano. She had never seen or heard such an instrument, and was wonderstruck. The lady called her daughters to her side and all joined in singing, "All hail the power of Jesus' Name," to the old tune, "Coronation."

"Do you like that?" asked the lady.

"Oh, it's nice. I b'l'eve I heered that tune somewhere when I was a girl, but I've forgot."

"Probably you heard it at church. It is often sung there. We cannot sing the praises of Jesus too often, for He came to save us poor sinners." Then they all sang, "Come, humble sinner, in whose breast," etc. When the woman arose to go, she was invited to "Come again."

"Oh, I'll come often if I can hear you sing."

"Mother, you take a strange way to win souls!"

"Why not, my daughter? Has not God commanded that whatsoever we do, should be done to His glory? And if He has given us voices to sing, should we not use them in His service? There are many ears that will listen to a hymn for the sake of the tune, that will not hear a word from the Bible. Our voices and our musical instruments should all be employed in winning lost souls."

No. 786.

"GOD OF ALL GRACE AND MAJESTY."

REV. CHARLES WESLEY.

Mr. Wesley was at one time with a large party of friends who had met to dine together, when the whole party was exceedingly amused at some anecdote related either by Mr. Wesley himself or one of the preachers who accompanied him. The hearty laugh was followed, as usual, by a momentary silence; and just when the conversation was about to be resumed, Mr. Wesley stood up, and all eyes were, of course, turned to him. He paused a moment, and then lifting up his hand in a manner quite his own repeated with solemn voice a stanza of this hymn:

"Still may I walk as in Thy sight,
My strict observer see;
And Thou by reverent love unite
My child-like heart to Thee;
Still let me, till my days are past
At Jesus' feet abide;
So shall He lift me up at last
And seat me at His side."

The effect may be easily imagined. It was as happy as instantaneous. The full stream of feeling was diverted into the right channel, and the pleasures of the parlor, became a preparation for the services of the sanctuary.

No. 787.

"HOSANNA BE THE CHILDREN'S SONG."

JAMES MONTGOMERY.

In the year 1829 the author of this hymn wrote as follows:

"It has occurred to me that a Sunday school Jubilee in the year 1831, fifty years from the origin of Sunday schools, might be the means of extraordinary and happy excitement to the public mind in favor of these institutions." The suggestion met with general approval and the Jubilee was arranged for September 14, 1831, the birthday of Robert Raikes. All over Great Britain immense gatherings were held, and the largest churches and public halls were inadequate to contain the throngs of friends of Sunday schools who assembled. As had been predicted by Mr. Montgomery, the Sunday school as a religious institution received a tremendous impetus from these Jubilee meetings. It was fitting that the man who had first conceived the idea of the Jubilee should furnish for it its opening song. Mr. Montgomery was asked to write a hymn for the occasion and this hymn was his response to the invitation. It was sung on that day in all the Jubilee Assemblies in Great Britain, and took at once a favorite place in the "Sunday school song collections."

No. 788.

"ON THE MOUNTAIN'S TOP APPEARING."

REV. THOMAS KELLY.

A hundred years ago there were no ocean cables or swift steamers to bear quick news of the world's doings. The London Missionary Society which had at its first meeting decided that the island of Tahiti should be its first mission field, was compelled to wait for three long years before any tidings came from the missionaries they had sent there. Each year upon the anniversary of its organization a great meeting was held in London at which were gathered the friends of missions from all the British Isles. Reports were heard, addresses listened to, sermons preached, and for each annual meeting some poet wrote a hymn. Among the most ardent of its friends was an Irish preacher celebrated alike for his scholarly learning, his deep piety, and his active interest in every work of philanthropy. Just before the fourth gathering of the Society, news had come from the little band of workers far away in the Pacific

Sea, that they had been kindly received by the natives, their message heard with attention and interest, and they entertained bright hopes of success in their work. This news soon found its way to the Irish preacher who was poet as well as preacher, and drew from him a hymn "On the good news from Tahiti" based on the words of Isaiah: "How beautiful upon the mountains are the feet of Him that bringeth good tidings that publisheth peace." The meeting in London following the reception of this "good news from Tahiti" was a very enthusiastic one, and Thomas Kelly's hymn was there first sung.

No. 789.

"DAILY, DAILY, SING THE PRAISES."

This hymn written in England by a clergyman of the Church of England, as a processional hymn, to be sung by boys as they marched into a quiet church in Yorkshire, found its way into the heart of Africa, and translated into the language of the land, became the death song of another band of boys as they passed through the gates of martyrdom into the Temple not made with hands. It happened at the Uganda Mission, where Bishop Hannington was afterwards murdered, on January, 1885, and the story is simply told in an English paper:

"Two native lads who had been kidnapped, but subsequently released, reported that they had been taken with Kakumba, and Ashe's boy as also Serwanga, a tall, fine fellow, a baptized lad, whom Majasi, the leader of the hostile party, had caught, and Duta's wife Sarah and her child, to a place outside the capital. That Serwanga, Kakumba, and Ashe's boy had been tortured by having their arms cut off, and they were then bound alive to a scaffolding under which a fire was made, and they were slowly burned to death. Majasi and his men mocked them and bade them pray now if Jesus Christ would rescue them from his hands. The dear lads clung to their faith and in the fire they sang:

"Daily, daily, sing the praises
Of the city God hath made."

No. 790.

"TO-DAY THOU LIVEST YET."

A young law student was ill in Berlin. The doctor directed his bed to be moved to a corner of the room where the light would not trouble him. On this side of the room there was but a thin partition between him and the occupants of the adjoining room, and before he had lain there long he heard these words repeated over and over again by some one on the other side of the partition:

"To-day thou livest yet,
To-day turn thou to God!
For ere to-morrow comes
Thou may'st be with the clod."

These words fixed themselves in the sick man's memory and led to his conversion. It happened that a little boy had not learned his lesson at school that day and these lines were the part he had been unable to commit to memory, and his father had put him into the corner of the room next to the place where this sick man lay, to learn the verse and he was repeating it over and over to fix it in his mind. I would like to have those who believe that events come by chance, tell me how many shakes of the dice box would probably bring about such a coincidence of time and place and circumstances as were required to bring that sick sinner into the reach of that child's voice just when he was repeating that verse. It is easier to believe that:

"Deep in unfathomable mines
Of never failing skill.
He treasures up His bright designs
And works His sovereign will."

No. 791.

"COME, LORD, THE DROOPING SINNER CHEER."

In January, 1759, a woman named Hannah Harrison was giving an exhortation at a Methodist meeting in Yorkshire, England. Five or six young men entered the room just as she was repeating the stanza:

"Come, Lord, the drooping sinner cheer,
Nor let thy chariot wheels delay!
Appear, in my poor heart, appear!
My God! My Savior, come away."

One of these young men twenty-two years of age, was struck with the words, and said, in writing of it afterwards, "I was cut to the heart. I could neither speak nor stir, I was convinced there was something in religion which I had never known. I returned home but these words, 'My God! My Savior, come away,' were continually sounding in my heart, and from that time another young man and I forsook our trifling company." This was Mr. John Atlay. He was converted and afterwards became a successful preacher of the Gospel.

No. 792.

"MY JESUS, STAY THOU BY ME."

In the year 1796 the army of France, which was then at war with Germany, was defeated by the Army of Archduke Charles. A horde of fugitives from the defeated army swept through a little town angry at their defeat and glad of an opportunity for revenge. So they plundered the town, murdering such of its inhabitants as had not fled to the forests, and set fire to the buildings. A German mother was watching at the bedside of a child too sick to be taken to the forest to which her neighbors all had fled. She bolted her cottage door, and sinking to her knees by the cradle of the sick child began to pray. Outside she heard the shouts of the soldiers and the shrieks of their hapless victims. At last her own door was broken in and a French soldier rushed in with bayonet pointed at her. She laid her hands over her child as if to protect it and raised her voice aloud:

"My Jesus, stay thou by me
And let no foe come nigh me
Safe sheltered by thy wing,
But should the foe alarm me
O! let him never harm me
But still thine angels round me sing."

The soldier stopped midway in the room, and stood while she prayed, and then stepped softly to the cradle; he laid his hand gently on the sick child's head, his lips moved, as if to speak, the tears fell down his cheeks, he gave his hand to the woman, and walked away in silence. By and by, she arose from her place and looked out of her window; she saw the soldier still standing at her door, and there he remained, protecting her and her home from the assaults of his comrades until the troop at last marched away from the village and then he joined them.

No. 793.

"JESUS, AT THY COMMAND I LAUNCH INTO THE DEEP."

AUTHOR UNKNOWN. FIRST APPEARED ABOUT 1774.

"O'er the gloomy hills of darkness."

REV. WILLIAM WILLIAMS, 1772.

Early in the morning of the tenth of August, 1796, a vessel swung out into the river Thames at London, to start upon a voyage which was to mark an epoch in the history of the world. A flag of new design floated at her masthead. White doves upon a purple ground bore in their beaks each one an olive branch of green. Upon the deck there stood a band of thirty men, who had offered their services for a new enterprise. Upon the river's bank had gathered a great crowd of those who were their friends or friends of the enterprise in which they were engaged. And there were tears and prayers and sad farewells, for neither those who went, nor those who bade them go, looked for a meeting until they should meet in heaven. This was the *Duff*, the first Foreign Mission ship, and this was the first flag of Foreign Missions, and this the first band of Foreign Missionaries starting on the first Foreign Mission of modern times. And as the ship moved slowly down the river, the friends who were waving farewells from the shore heard wafted to their ears from their friends who stood upon the deck of the ship the first song of Foreign Missions:

"Jesus, at thy command
I launch into the deep
And leave my native land
Where sin lulls all asleep
For thee I would the world resign
And sail to heaven with Thee and Thine."

Seven months later on a Sunday morning, March 5, 1797, this same mission band, which had been all this time tossed upon the waves of the deep, stood together on the deck of the *Duff* looking off at a low range of hills which stood dimly outlined against the sky. It was the Island of Tahiti, in the South Pacific, to whose inhabitants they had come to tell the Gospel story. In a few hours the canoes of the Islanders were dancing in the waves all about the ship, and many of the men had clambered up her sides, and swarmed over her deck, to trade or steal. And here in full sight of the land where they were to labor, and above whose hills hung the gloom of heathen darkness, these missionaries gathered close together on the deck of their ship and stilled the babel of unintelligible sounds about them with the music of their hymn, which marks the beginning of that wonderful missionary work, which has filled the Islands of the Pacific with the light of Christian civilization.

No. 794.

"STABAT MATER" (Music).

G. A. Rossini.

After Rossini had retired from public life, and had resolved to write no more music for publication, a celebrated Spaniard (Don Vazela) asked him to write music for the great Latin hymn, *"Stabat Mater,"* not to be made public but to be performed in his own private chapel. Rossini although very gay in his younger days was a devout Catholic, and quite in sympathy with the subject, and so in spite of his resolution, he accepted the commission and wrote the music. An accident gave it to the public. Don Vazela died, his heirs sold the manuscript, and in an incredibly short time, the music of *"Stabat Mater"* was being sung in the Catholic churches all over Europe.

No. 795.

"DAY OF JUDGMENT, DAY OF WONDERS."

REV. JOHN NEWTON.

John Newton kept a diary, and from it we get many a glimpse of his daily life and work among the people of the little town of Olney. One day in 1775 he wrote in his diary: "I usually make one hymn a week to expound at the Great House." The "Great House" was where Newton and Cowper gathered the people together for a weekly meeting. Newton's hymns have been criticised as "unpoetic," "tame," "poor," "bald," and "matter-of-fact," and yet they are hymns that live, and the reason is that they are hymns that can be "expounded." A hymn that can be expounded is a hymn that will live, because it will fit into human experience, and will touch human want. This is one of the hymns which Newton wrote "to expound." In his diary he records that on Sunday evening, June 26, 1775, he spoke from a hymn on the day of judgment, and he records that the hymn "took him the most of two days to finish." The hymn has become one of the most popular of Newton's hymns, and has been translated into several languages.

No. 796.

"CRAWFORD" (Tune).

In Haydn's Oratorio of "The Creation," in the account of the third day of Creation, after a recitative with the words taken from Genesis, "And God said let the earth bring forth grass, the herb yielding seed, and the fruit tree yielding fruit after his kind, whose seed is in itself, upon the earth; and it was so," then comes a soprano solo, beginning with the words from Milton's "Paradise Lost,"

"With verdure clad the fields appear, Delightful to the ravished sense." It is No. 9 of the Oratorio, and this solo forms the air of this tune we know as "Crawford."

No. 797.

"THE CREATION" (Tune).

The words for Haydn's Oratorio, "The Creation" with the exception of those taken verbatim from the Book of Genesis, are arranged from Milton's "Paradise Lost." Number 12 begins with the Biblical account of the fourth day of Creation. A recitative with the words, "And God said, Let there be lights in the firmament of Heaven, to divide the day from the night, and to give light upon the earth; And let them be for signs and for seasons, and for days and for years. He made the stars also." Then follows another recitative with words from Milton, "In splendor bright is rising now the sun, and darts his rays; A joyful, happy spouse. A giant proud and glad, To run his measured course. With softer beams and milder light, steps on the silver moon through silent night. The space immense of the azure sky innumerous hosts of radiant orbs adorn. And the sons of God announced the fourth day, in song divine, proclaiming thus his power." Then comes the Angel's song in perhaps the grandest chorus of the whole Oratorio, beginning with the words:

"The heavens are telling the glory of God."

The air of this chorus forms the air of this tune, to which is appropriately sung the hymn of Addison's:

"The spacious firmament on high
With all the blue ethereal sky."

No. 798.

"NOBODY KNOWS DE TROUBLE I SEE."

(Negro Slave Song.)

During and after the war of the Rebellion, the lands of many Southerners known to be actually engaged in the Rebellion, were confiscated by the United States, and in many places parcels of these lands sufficient for homes and small farms were assigned by the government to the negroes. At the close of the war an effort was made by the original owners to regain possession of their lands, and great distress was brought upon the negroes, who had in many cases put these lands under cultivation, built little cabins upon them, and were growing crops for the support of their families. As Commander of the Freedman's Bureau, Major General O. O. Howard, was often made the arbitrator in these contests for the possession of the lands. It is related that at one time shortly after the war, the negroes upon the Sea Islands had come into great trouble over an attempt to dispossess them of their homes, by the former owners. On the one hand was a lawyer from Charleston, South Carolina, urging the claim of the old slave masters, and on the other the plaint of the defenceless negroes appealing for protection. While awaiting a delay in the proceedings, the General asked the people to strike up one of their songs. There was a moment of silence and then in the midst of the assembly an old colored woman started in alone:

"Nobody knows de trouble I see."

As she advanced with the song one after another fell in until the whole assembly had joined. The melody was so affecting and the words so expressive of the condition in which the singers were placed, that the General, although sitting in the capacity of judge, as well as others who were with him, was scarcely able to refrain from tears, and the effect was more powerful than any argument could have produced.

No. 799.

"BANGOR" (Tune).

There are at least two tunes by this name. One is a Welsh tune of unknown authorship. The other was composed by William Tans'ur, an English composer, whose music was published in 1736. This tune was the innocent cause of an incident which seems ludicrous now. In the early part of the last century, sacred music in Scotland had nearly ceased to exist. The power of reading music was nearly a lost art, and the number of tunes in use was reduced to twelve. By long traditional use these tunes came to be regarded by the common people as hardly less inspired than the Psalms which were sung to them. Dr. Guthrie told a story of an old servant in his family whose reverence for the old Psalms was so great that she would not so much as let her eyes rest on the words of a hymn, and who revered the tunes as highly as the words, and who when new hymns and new tunes were spoken of as likely to come into use, vowed that she "Wad sing the Psalms o'David, to the tunes o'David, and nothing else."

The late Dr. Fletcher of London relates that one day the precentor in the church of his father at Leith, began to sing "Bangor" which was a new tune, and not one of the twelve. He had scarcely begun to sing when the minister jumped to his feet and taking the great pulpit Bible in both hands brought it down with all his force on the unsuspecting head of the poor precentor, daring him ever to start such a tune in his Kirk again.

No. 800.

"O, BLESSED SAVIOR, IN THY LOVE."

REV. JOSEPH STENNETT.

In these days when the language we speak contains fifty thousand hymns, and of the making of hymn books there is no end, it is difficult to conceive of a time not very far back when not a dozen hymns existed in the English language. Paraphrases of the Psalms were numerous enough and for the most part as unpoetic as numerous, but of hymns there was none, and none called for. Curious opinions prevailed. By many it was urged that only Christians should sing in church. Congregational singing was objected to, because, "when all speak none can hear." Singing words which others had written, it was urged opened the way for the use of prayers which others had written. Violent controversies broke out among the churches, as to who should sing, what should be sung, and even as to singing at all in church. One of the first concessions made to the singing of hymns in the regular church services, was, to permit of the singing of a hymn at the close of the Communion Service. To this objections were effectually silenced by reference to the example of Christ as given in Matthew, 26:30, "and when they had sung an hymn they went out into the Mount of Olives." Such hymns were first sung in 1673. And it was for this use that the Rev. Joseph Stennett, a Baptist preacher of some celebrity who lived in London, composed and published a little pamphlet of thirty-seven hymns and among them this one.

No. 801.

"COME, MY SOUL, THOU MUST BE WAKING."

F. R. L. F. VON, 1654—1699 (Lutheran).

A life like that of Gladstone refreshes us, by its constant reminder that a life amid the turmoil of politics is not of necessity inconsistent with a life of earnest piety. Germany as well as England has had such a man, in the author of this hymn. He died two centuries ago, after twenty years of constant and active service in various political capacities, but it has been said of him that he was not more distinguished, by genius and worldly distinction, than by Christian holiness. This hymn received a remarkable illustration in the closing moments of its author's life. It was early morning and the first rays of the dawn broke into his sick chamber. He asked that he might be taken to the window, that he might look once more at the rising sun. After looking steadily at it for some time, he cried out, "Oh! if the appearance of this earthly and created thing is so beautiful, how shall I be enraptured by the unspeakable glory of the Creator himself!" The thought and the effort to express it overpowered him and he fell back exhausted and died.

No. 802.

"JESUS, MY ALL" (Tune).

There is a very pretty romance connected with this piece of music. A young Irish surgeon practising his profession in Dublin, became involved in a scandal and was compelled to quit the country. He went to England, and soon there occurred the first of a series of incidents which by and by gave to him the title of "The Fortunate Irishman." A lady's carriage overturned and he was first to reach her and to offer assistance. She was somewhat injured, and asked him to travel with her to her home in London. There she gave him a generous gift, and a general invitation to her house, where he soon after met a young lady of noble birth, who fell in love with him at first sight. Our young surgeon had neither money nor title, and to prevent a marriage of the young lovers, all sorts of expedients were resorted to by the lady's family. One of the expedients was the sending her away on several journeys. On one of these journeys while at the town of Bath, the love sick girl wrote a song to her absent darling, which she set to an ancient Irish melody he had often sung to her:

"What's this dull town to me?
Robin's not near.
What was 't I wished to see,
What wished to hear?
Where's all the joy and mirth
Made this town a heaven on earth?
Oh, these all fled with thee,
Robin Adair."

The sequel is soon told, love conquered; the lovers were married, enjoyed a happy life, and died over a hundred years ago, leaving the story and the song of Robin Adair to find their way down to us together.

No. 803.

Franz Peter Schubert, 1797.

Schubert was a poor man's son, and gained his first knowledge of music by visits to a piano factory near his home, and by practice without a teacher on an old instrument in his father's house. When eight years old he composed his first piece of piano music. At eleven he sang in the parish choir, at thirteen he was too poor to buy and so was begging music paper from his friends and filling all he got with music of his own. At eighteen he composed the "Erl King," one of his most celebrated pieces. From this time on everything he touched turned to music. If he saw a beautiful poem, his first thought was to set it to music, and it was just the same if it was a worthless rhyme. Once when strolling through a little village, he happened to see a volume of Shakespeare, and opening it he read: "Hark hark, the lark at heaven's gate sings." At once he exclaimed "Oh, such a melody has come into my head; If only I had music paper at hand." A friend drew some lines on a bill of fare, and there amid the confusion and noise of an inn, he wrote the beautiful song that is known by this title. He was obliged to support himself by his compositions, and so he wrote almost continuously; songs and symphonies and operas came in rapid succession from his pen, yet he was always poor, and at thirty-one he died, lonely and disconsolate, leaving behind him more than five hundred unpublished songs.

No. 804.

Gioachino Antonio Rossini.

A hundred years ago almost, a family of musicians might have been seen wandering from town to town in Italy, attending fairs and other public gatherings, the father playing the French horn, and the mother singing. With them wandered their little son, who soon began to add his voice to the songs they played and sang in the Italian villages. His pure soprano voice soon attracted the attention of priests, and he began to sing in the Romish churches, and when eighteen years old to compose. His progress was rapid. The composer and his music became very popular not only in Italy, but in France and England. Rossini was indolent. He often composed in bed, during cold weather to save the expense of a fire, and on one such occasion he had just finished a duet for an opera when it slipped from the bed to the floor. He tried to reach it with his hand, but failing in this, rather than get out of his warm bed to get it, he composed another.

No. 805.

"ON THE FOUNT OF LIFE ETERNAL."

PETER DAMIANI, 998—1072.

Almost a thousand years ago an Italian mother abandoned her babe just born. A servant discovered the luckless boy and cared for him, until by and by the mother relented and received him back again. While he was yet a little boy both parents died, and an older brother took him in charge, but more as a slave than a brother. He sent him into the fields to feed swine. By and by another brother more tender-hearted took note of the amiable disposition and natural ability of the boy and had him educated. The boy's name was Peter, and the name of this brother who befriended him was Damian, and so the boy became known as "Damian's Peter" or as it would be in Latin, "Peter Damiani." The scholar soon became a teacher, and his progress was rapid. He soon became a monk, and then Superior of the Monastery, then founder of new monasteries, and soon bishop and cardinal of the Church of Rome. He was a "Dr. Parkhurst" among the corruptions of his times. His protest against the terrible wickedness of the priests as well as of the people, he put into a book, which was appropriately named "The Gomorrah Book." It made a great stir. Books were not printed then, but copied by the pen. Those whose crimes were exposed by "The Gomorrah Book" borrowed it, claiming that they wanted to have some copies made, and Peter came near never seeing his book again, but at last he got it and it has been preserved and handed down, for us to read if we wish to. Peter was the originator of a curious fanaticism. He found in the monasteries a law that any monk for violation of the monastic discipline, might be whipped with five strokes, to bring him to his senses. Starting from this Peter argued that if five strokes were beneficial, six would be more so, and if they were inflicted willingly upon oneself, the credit would be greater still. And if these strokes would be placed to one's credit on the account books of Heaven, when given for one's own sins, they certainly would if applied for the sins of others. A sort of scale of prices was soon established, by which three thousand strokes paid off for oneself or one's friends a year of purgatorial punishment. The mania which we have all read about, under the name of flagellation spread far and wide in Europe, dying away and reappearing in successive centuries, and if we congratulate ourselves that our age and country is too enlightened to indulge in such a superstition, we have only to go to the Californian coast to find it still practised by adherents of the Romish church. And Peter Damiani, the abandoned child, the swineherd, monk, cardinal and flagellant, was the author of this hymn.

INDEX